W9-AZE-510

400 BEST-EVER SOUPS

400 BEST-EVER SOUPS

A fabulous collection of delicious soups from all over the world –
every recipe shown step-by-step with over 1600 color photographs

CONSULTANT EDITOR: ANNE SHEASBY

JG PRESS

Published by World Publications Group, Inc.
140 Laurel Street
East Bridgewater, MA 02333
www.wrldpub.net

© Anness Publishing Ltd 2005, 2007

Produced by Anness Publishing Limited,
Hermes House, 88–89 Blackfriars Road, London SE1 8HA
tel. 020 7401 2077; fax 020 7633 9499
www.annesspublishing.com

If you like the images in this book and would like to investigate using them for publishing, promotions or advertising,
please visit our website www.practicalpictures.com for more information.

Publisher: Joanna Lorenz; **Editorial Director:** Judith Simons;
Project Editors: Felicity Forster and Molly Perham; **Designer:** Nigel Partridge;
Copy Editor: Molly Perham; **Editorial Reader:** Rosie Fairhead; **Production Controller:** Pedro Nelson
Recipe contributors: Catherine Atkinson, Alex Barker, Michelle Berriedale-Johnson, Angela Boggiano, Janet Brinkworth, Carla Capalbo, Kit Chan, Jacqueline Clark, Maxine Clark, Frances Cleary, Carole Clements, Andi Clevely, Trish Davies, Roz Denny, Patrizia Diemling, Matthew Drennan, Sarah Edmonds, Joanna Farrow, Rafi Fernandez, Christine France, Sarah Gates, Shirley Gill, Rosamund Grant, Rebekah Hassan, Deh-Ta Hsiung, Shehzad Husain, Judy Jackson, Sheila Kimberley, Masaki Ko, Elisabeth Lambert Ortiz, Ruby Le Bois, Gilly Love, Lesley Mackley, Norma MacMillan, Sue Maggs, Kathy Man, Sallie Morris, Annie Nichols, Maggie Pannell, Katherine Richmond, Anne Sheasby, Jenny Stacey, Liz Trigg, Hilaire Walden, Laura Washburn, Steven Wheeler, Kate Whiteman, Elizabeth Wolf-Cohen, Jeni Wright
Photographers: Karl Adamson, Edward Allwright, David Armstrong, Steve Baxter, James Duncan, John Freeman, Ian Garlick, Michelle Garrett, Amanda Heywood, Janine Hosegood, David Jordan, William Lingwood, Patrick McLeary, Michael Michaels, Thomas Odulate, Juliet Piddington, Peter Reilly.

ETHICAL TRADING POLICY
Because of our ongoing ecological investment programme, you, as our customer, can have the pleasure and reassurance of knowing that a tree is being cultivated on your behalf to naturally replace the materials used to make the book you are holding. For further information about this scheme, go to www.annesspublishing.com/trees

ISBN 10: 1 57215 154 4
ISBN 13: 9781572151543

Printed and bound in China

All rights reserved. No part of this publication may be reproduced, stored in a retrieval system, or transmitted in any way or by any means, electronic, mechanical, photocopying, recording or otherwise, without the prior written permission of the copyright holder.

A CIP catalogue record for this book is available from the British Library.

Recipes in this book previously published in *The Soup Bible* and *The New Book of Soups*

NOTES
Bracketed terms are intended for American readers.
For all recipes, quantities are given in both metric and imperial measures and, where appropriate, in standard cups and spoons. Follow one set of measures, but not a mixture, because they are not interchangeable.
Standard spoon and cup measures are level. 1 tsp = 5ml, 1 tbsp = 15ml, 1 cup = 250ml/8fl oz.
Australian standard tablespoons are 20ml. Australian readers should use 3 tsp in place of 1 tbsp for measuring small quantities.
American pints are 16fl oz/2 cups. American readers should use 20fl oz/2.5 cups in place of 1 pint when measuring liquids.
Electric oven temperatures in this book are for conventional ovens. When using a fan oven, the temperature will probably need to be reduced by about 10–20°C/20–40°F. Since ovens vary, you should check with your manufacturer's instruction book for guidance.
The nutritional analysis given for each recipe is calculated per portion (i.e. serving or item), unless otherwise stated. If the recipe gives a range, such as Serves 4–6, then the nutritional analysis will be for the smaller portion size, i.e. 6 servings. Measurements for sodium do not include salt added to taste.
Medium (US large) eggs are used unless otherwise stated.

CONTENTS

6

INTRODUCTION

Soups are very versatile and can be made using many different ingredients. One of the great things about soup is that you can put a selection of fresh, raw and sometimes cooked ingredients into a pan with some well-flavoured stock, let the mixture bubble away for a short while, and within no time at all you have created a delicious, flavourful, home-made soup with very little effort.

Many soups are quick and easy to make and simply combine a few key ingredients with added flavourings, such as herbs or spices, whereas other soups – perhaps those ideal for a special occasion or a more substantial meal – may require a little more preparation.

Below: Tom Yam Gung with Tofu is a famous Thai speciality.

Some soups make ideal appetizers to a meal, and they are always a popular choice, while others are substantial enough to be meals in themselves, served with plenty of fresh crusty bread as an accompaniment. There are light and refreshing soups that are chilled, ideal for summer dining *al fresco*, and rich and creamy soups, perfect for meals shared with family and friends. Whichever kind you choose, it is well worth the effort to create fresh and flavourful soups in your own kitchen.

An essential ingredient in most soups is a good well-flavoured stock, preferably home-made. Stock (bouillon) cubes and stock powder save time, but it is hard to beat the flavour and quality of home-made stocks, and they are relatively easy and inexpensive to make.

Above: Meatballs in Pasta Soup with Basil makes a substantial main course.

Once you have a good basic stock, whether it is vegetable, fish, meat or chicken stock, there is a huge range of soups that you can create in your kitchen. However, remember that your stock will only be as good as the quality of the ingredients used to make it – you cannot produce a good, tasty stock from old, limp, past-their-best vegetables! If you are really short of time, you could choose one of the chilled fresh stock products available from some supermarkets and delicatessens.

Very little specialist equipment is needed to make soups, although you will find that a food processor or blender is invaluable and will save time and effort when you want to purée soup mixtures before serving – although pressing the soup through a sieve (strainer) or using a hand-held blender are perfectly good alternatives. You will probably already have in your kitchen a good-quality heavy pan, a sharp knife and chopping board, and a vegetable peeler.

The addition of an attractive garnish, perhaps a sprinkling of chopped fresh herbs, some vegetables cut in julienne strips, or a swirl of cream added at the last minute, will enhance even the simplest of soups. Soups may be served on their own or topped with a few crunchy croûtons or grilled croûtes.

6

Soups feature in every cuisine around the world – whether they are called gumbos, potages, broths, chowders or consommées. Now that once-unfamiliar ingredients are readily available in specialist food stores and many supermarkets, there is absolutely no reason why you cannot make these in your own home.

In summer, choose from cold soups such as French Vichyssoise, Chilled Avocado with Cumin from Spain, or Mexican Chilled Coconut Soup. Creamy vegetable soups include Irish Parsnip Soup, Caribbean Peanut and Potato Soup, or Asparagus and Pea Soup with Parmesan Cheese. Chunky vegetable and legume soups are ideal winter warmers. You could try classic Russian Borscht with *Kvas* and Sour Cream, or Tuscan Bean Soup. Or serve a hot and spicy soup, such as North African Spiced Soup. Pasta and noodle soups range from Borlotti Bean and Pasta Soup and Avgolemono with Pasta to more exotic choices, such as Malaysian Prawn Laksa and Udon Noodles with Egg Broth and Ginger.

Soups made with chicken, meat, fish or shellfish are full of nourishment and make a complete meal served with

Below: Corn and Red Chilli Chowder is for those who enjoy hot and spicy food.

Above: Soda bread is traditionally served with this Irish Country Soup.

slices or chunks of fresh crusty bread or bread rolls, served warm or cold. Here the choice is wide and varied – from traditional Irish Country Soup and Lobster Bisque to the more unusual and exotic Smoked Haddock Chowder, Vermouth Soup with Seared Scallops, Rocket Oil and Caviar, or Scallop and Jerusalem Artichoke Soup.

Each recipe in this book has easy-to-follow step-by-step instructions and a beautiful colour photograph to show the finished dish. Few dishes give more all-round pleasure than a good home-made soup, and in this wonderful collection of recipes the world of soups is yours to explore.

VEGETABLES

Using vegetables offers the cook an infinite number of culinary possibilities, including creating a wide range of delicious and flavourful soups. The choice of vegetables is immense, and the growing demand for organic produce has led to pesticide-free vegetables becoming widely available. Vegetables are an essential component of a healthy diet and have countless nutritional benefits. They are at their most nutritious when freshly picked.

Carrots

The best carrots are not restricted to the cold winter months – summer welcomes the slender, sweet new crop, often sold with their feathery tops. Look for firm, smooth carrots – the smaller they are, the sweeter they taste. Carrots should be prepared just before use to preserve their valuable nutrients. They are delicious in Carrot and Orange Soup, as well as being an important ingredient in many other soups and in home-made stock. Raw carrots, cut into thin julienne strips, make an unusual and attractive garnish.

Right: Carrots give soup a sweet flavour, and add colour too.

Beetroot

Beetroot (beet) is the key ingredient in the classic Russian Borscht. It also combines well with other flavours, for example in Beetroot Soup with Mascarpone Brioche, which is a light and refreshing choice, or alternatively the more substantial dish Fragrant Beetroot and Vegetable Soup with Spiced Lamb Kubbeh. If you are cooking beetroot whole, wash it carefully in order not to damage the skin or the nutrients and prevent the colour leaching out. Trim the stalks to about 2.5cm (1in) above the root. Small beetroots are sweeter and more tender than the larger ones.

Below: Celeriac is bumpy with patchy brown, white and green skin.

Celeriac

Strictly speaking, celeriac is a root vegetable, as it is the root of certain kinds of celery. It has a similar but less pronounced flavour than celery, but when cooked it is more akin to potatoes. It is an ingredient in soups such as Cream of Celeriac and Spinach Soup.

Swedes

The globe-shaped swede (rutabaga) has pale orange-coloured flesh with a delicate sweet flavour. Trim off the thick peel, then treat in the same way as other root vegetables. For soups, swede is usually peeled and diced, and then cooked with other vegetables and stock until tender. It could be finely chopped and integrated in chunky vegetable soups, or maybe cooked with stock and other ingredients, and then puréed to create a smooth soup.

Left: Beetroot's deep ruby-red colour adds a vibrant hue to soups. It is a classic ingredient of the Russian soup Borscht.

Above: Parsnips are best used in the winter months and make good, hearty, warming soups.

Parsnips

These winter root vegetables have a sweet, creamy flavour and are a delicious element in many soups. Parsnips are best purchased after the first frost of the year, as the cold converts their starches into sugar, enhancing their sweetness. Scrub them well before use and peel only if the skin is tough. Avoid large roots, which can be rather woody.

Turnips

Turnips have many health-giving qualities, and small turnips with their green tops intact are especially nutritious. Their crisp, ivory flesh, which is enclosed in white, green and pink-tinged skin, has a pleasant, slightly peppery flavour, the intensity of which depends on their size and the time of harvesting. Turnips add a lovely flavour and a warming substance to any vegetable-based soups, such as the Russian Spinach and Root Vegetable Soup.

Jerusalem artichokes

This small, knobbly tuber has a sweet, nutty flavour. Peeling can be fiddly, although scrubbing and trimming is usually sufficient. Store in the refrigerator for up to one week. Use in the same way as potatoes – they make good, creamy soups.

Potatoes

There are thousands of potato varieties, and many lend themselves to particular cooking methods. Main crop potatoes, such as Estima and Maris Piper, and sweet potatoes (preferably the orange-fleshed variety which have a better flavour than the cream-fleshed type) are ideal for using in soups. Potatoes are also good (especially when mashed or puréed) as a thickener for some soups. Discard any potatoes with green patches. Vitamins and minerals are stored in, or just beneath, the skin, so it is best to use potatoes unpeeled.

Buying and storing root vegetables

Seek out bright, firm, unwrinkled root vegetables and tubers, which do not have soft patches. When possible, choose organically grown produce, and buy in small quantities to ensure freshness. Store root vegetables in a cool, dark place.

Broccoli

This nutritious vegetable should be a regular part of everyone's diet. Two types are commonly available: purple-sprouting, which has fine, leafy stems and a delicate head, and calabrese, the more substantial green variety with a tightly budded top

Above: Trim the stalks from broccoli and divide it into florets. The stems of young broccoli can be sliced and used, too.

and thick stalk. Choose broccoli that has bright, compact florets. Yellowing florets, a limp woody stalk and a pungent smell are an indication of overmaturity. Broccoli adds flavour and texture as well as a lovely colour to soups. Once cooked, it is often puréed to create an attractive green-coloured soup. It is a versatile vegetable and combines well in soups with other ingredients.

Cauliflower

The cream-coloured compact florets, or curds, should be encased in large, bright green leaves. There are also varieties with purple or green florets. Raw or cooked cauliflower has a mild flavour and is delicious when combined with other ingredients to make tasty soups such as Curried Cauliflower Soup or Cream of Cauliflower.

Cabbage

There are several different varieties of cabbage, and one of the best to use in soups is Savoy, which has substantial, crinkly leaves with a strong flavour. Firm red and white cabbages are also good for soups as they retain their texture well.

Left: Cauliflower can be used either raw or cooked.

Spinach

This dark green leaf provides an excellent source of cancer-fighting antioxidants. It contains about four times more beta carotene than broccoli. It is also rich in fibre, which can help to lower harmful levels of LDL cholesterol in the body, reducing the risk of heart disease and stroke. Spinach does contain iron but not in such a rich supply as was once thought. It also contains oxalic acid, which inhibits the absorption of iron and calcium in the body. However, eating spinach with a vitamin C-rich food will increase absorption. Spinach also contains vitamins C and B6, calcium, potassium, folate, thiamine and zinc. Spinach and other leafy green vegetables are ideal shredded and added to soups or cooked in them and then puréed to create flavourful, nutritious dishes with a lovely deep green colour, ideal for swirling cream into just before serving.

Pumpkins

These are native to America, where they are traditionally eaten at Thanksgiving. Small pumpkins have sweeter, less fibrous flesh than the larger ones. Pumpkin can be used in smooth soups such as Pumpkin Soup with Rice. Squash, such as the butternut variety, makes an alternative to pumpkin – Roasted Garlic and Butternut Squash Soup with Tomato Salsa will waken up the taste buds.

Right: Making soup is an effective way of using up an excess of courgettes in the autumn.

Below: Fresh, crisp cucumbers are excellent in chilled soups.

Above: Corn works particularly well in creamy fish-based soups.

Courgettes

The most widely available summer squash, courgettes (zucchini) have most flavour when they are small and young. Standard courgettes, as well as baby courgettes, may be used on their own or with other ingredients, such as mint and yogurt, to create delicious soups. They are a key ingredient in Greek Aubergine and Courgette Soup, served with tzatziki.

Cucumbers

The Chinese say food should be enjoyed for its texture as well as for its flavour; cucumbers have a unique texture and refreshing, cool taste. Varieties include English cucumbers, ridged cucumbers, gherkins and kirbys. Cucumbers are ideal for chilled soups such as Cucumber and Salmon Soup with Salsa, and Chilled Cucumber and Prawn Soup.

Corn

There are several varieties of corn – the kind we eat on the cob is also known as sweetcorn. Baby corn cobs are picked when they are immature and are cooked and eaten whole. Corn and baby corn, as well as canned or frozen corn kernels, are all used in creative soup recipes such as Corn and Potato Chowder, or Corn and Red Chilli Chowder.

Fennel

Florence fennel is closely related to the herb and spice of the same name. The short, fat bulbs have a similar texture to celery and are topped wtih edible feathery fronds. Fennel has a mild aniseed flavour, which is most potent when eaten raw. Cooking tempers the flavour, giving it a delicious sweetness. Fennel marries wonderfully with fish in Bourride of Red Mullet and Fennel.

Tomatoes

There are dozens of varieties to choose from, which vary in colour, shape and size. The egg-shaped plum tomato is perfect for many types of cooking, including soups, as it has a rich flavour and a high proportion of flesh to seeds – but it must be used when fully ripe. Too often, store-bought tomatoes are bland and tasteless because they have been picked too young. Vine-ripened and cherry tomatoes, together with large beefsteak tomatoes, have good flavour and are also good for soups. Sun-dried tomatoes add a rich intensity to soups. Genetically engineered tomatoes are now sold in some countries; check the label. If tomatoes are cooked with their skins on, you will find that the soup may need puréeing and straining to remove skins and seeds.

Peeling and seeding tomatoes

Tomato seeds can give soups a bitter flavour. Removing them and the tomato skins will also give a smoother result, which is preferable for many soups.

1 Immerse the tomato in boiling water and leave for about 30 seconds – the base of each tomato can be slashed to make peeling easier.

2 Lift out the tomato with a slotted spoon, rinse in cold water to cool slightly, and then peel off the skin.

3 Cut the tomato in half, then scoop out the seeds with a teaspoon and remove the hard core. Dice or coarsely chop the flesh according to the recipe.

Buying and storing tomatoes

When buying tomatoes, look for deep-red fruit that has a firm, yielding flesh. Tomatoes that are grown and sold locally will generally have the best flavour. Farmers' markets are a good place to buy vegetables, or you could grow your own. To improve the flavour of a slightly hard tomato, leave it to ripen fully at room temperature. It is best to avoid refrigeration because this stops the ripening process and adversely affects the taste and texture of the tomato.

Peppers

In spite of their name, (bell) peppers have nothing to do with the spice pepper used as a seasoning. They are actually members of the capsicum family and are called sweet peppers, bell peppers and even bull-nose peppers. The colour of the pepper tells you something about its flavour. Green peppers are the least mature of all and have a fresh "raw" flavour. Red peppers are ripened green peppers and are distinctly sweeter. Yellow/orange peppers taste more or less like red peppers, although perhaps slightly less sweet. Peppers add a lovely flavour and colour to soups such as Gazpacho or Chilled Tomato and Sweet Pepper Soup.

Right: Peppers add wonderful colours to soups – red, green, yellow and orange.

Above: Puréed avocados make soups really creamy.

Chillies

Native to America, this member of the capsicum family is extensively used in many cuisines, including Mexican, Indian, Thai, South American and African. There are more than 200 different varieties, and they add a fiery spiciness to soups.

Avocados

Strictly a fruit rather than a vegetable, the avocado has been known by many names – butter pear and alligator pear to name but two. There are four varieties: Hass, the purple-black small bumpy avocado, the Ettinger and Fuerte, which are pear-shaped and have smooth green skin, and the Nabal, which is rounder in shape. The black-coloured Hass has golden-yellow flesh, while green avocados have pale green to yellow flesh. Avocados can be used to make tempting soups such as Avocado and Lime Soup with Green Chilli Salsa.

*Right: Aubergine
is delicious in
minestrone
soups.*

Leeks

Like onions and garlic, leeks have a
long history and are versatile, having
their own distinct, subtle flavour. They
are less pungent than onions, but are
still therapeutically beneficial. Excellent
in soups, leeks add delicious flavour
and texture to many recipes. A classic
combination of leeks and potatoes
produces the popular soup
Vichyssoise, which can be
served hot or cold as a light
starter. Commercially grown
leeks are usually about
25cm (10in) long, but you
may occasionally see baby leeks,
which are very mild and tender and can
also be used in soups. Try winter soups
such as Chicken, Leek and Celery Soup
or Irish Leek and Blue Cheese Soup.

Aubergines

The dark-purple, glossy-skinned
aubergine (eggplant) is the most
familiar variety, although it is the small,
ivory-white egg-shaped variety that has
inspired its American name. There is
also the bright-green pea aubergine
that is used in Asian cooking, and a
pale-purple Chinese aubergine. Creamy
Aubergine Soup with Mozzarella and
Gremolata is a delicious soup that will
impress your dinner party guests.

Celery

Celery has a sharp and savoury flavour,
which makes it excellent for soups and
stocks. The tangy, astringent flavour
and crunchy texture of celery contrasts
well with the other ingredients. Most
supermarkets sell both green and white
celery (when celery grows naturally
the stalks are green; banking up earth
against the shoots makes it pale and
white). Look for celery with fresh-
looking leaves, and avoid any that
have outer stalks missing.

Onions

Every cuisine in the world
includes onions in one form or
another. They are an essential
flavouring, offering a range of taste
sensations, from the sweet and juicy
red onion and powerfully pungent
white onion to the light and fresh
spring onion (scallion). Pearl
onions and shallots are the babies
of the family. Shallots and leeks can
be used in place of onions in many
recipes, while spring onions may be
used as a flavouring or garnish.

Buying and storing onions

When buying, choose onions that have
dry, papery skins and are heavy for their
size. They will keep for 1–2 months in a
cool, dark place.

Garlic

An ingredient that everyone who does
any cooking at all will need, garlic is a
bulb that is available in many varieties.
Their papery skins can be white, pink
or purple. Colour makes no difference
to taste, but the attraction of the large
purple bulbs is that they make a
beautiful display in the kitchen. As a
general rule, the smaller the garlic bulb,
the stronger it is likely to be. If stored
in a cool, dry place and not in the
refrigerator, garlic will keep for up
to eight weeks.

*Above: Garlic is used in
meat and vegetable soups.*

*Above: Spring onions, shallots and
onions add essential flavour to soups.*

Above: Shiitake mushrooms are popular in Japanese soups.

Mushrooms

The most common cultivated variety of mushroom is actually one type in various stages of maturity. The button (white) mushroom is the youngest and has, as its name suggests, a tight, white, button-like cap. It has a mild flavour. Cap mushrooms are slightly more mature and larger in size, while the flat field (portabello) mushroom is the largest variety and has dark, open gills. Flat mushrooms have the most prominent flavour. Mushrooms are a useful ingredient in many soups, and add flavour and texture, as well as colour (especially the brown cap/ chestnut [cremini] or field mushrooms). Fresh and dried wild mushrooms also add a delicious taste to some soup recipes, such as Wild Mushroom with Soft Polenta.

Several varieties of wild mushroom are now available in supermarkets, for example oyster and shiitake. Oyster mushrooms are ear-shaped fungi that grow on rotting wood. Cap, gills and stem are all the same colour, which can be greyish brown, pink or yellow. They are now widely cultivated, although they are generally thought of as wild mushrooms. Delicious in both flavour and texture,

they are softer than button (white) mushrooms when cooked but seem more substantial, having more of a "bite" to them.

Shiitake mushrooms are Japanese fungi from the variety of tree mushrooms (called *take* in Japan, the *shii* being the hardwood tree from which they are harvested). They have a meaty, slightly acid flavour and a distinct slippery texture. Try them in Shiitake Mushroom Laksa.

Buying and storing mushrooms

Buy mushrooms that smell and look fresh. Avoid ones with damp, slimy patches and any that are discoloured. Store in a paper bag in the refrigerator for up to 4 days. Wipe mushrooms with damp kitchen paper before use but never wash or soak them.

Rocket

Usually thought of as a salad vegetable, rocket is actually a herb with a strong peppery taste that adds flavour and colour to soups such as Leek, Potato and Rocket Soup.

Sorrel

Another salad vegetable that is a herb, sorrel has a refreshing, sharp flavour. In soups it is good mixed with other herbs and green leaves, as in Sorrel, Spinach and Dill Soup. Salad leaves are best when they are very fresh, and do not keep well. Avoid leaves that are wilted or discoloured. Store in the refrigerator for 3–4 days.

Above: Rocket gives soups a strong, peppery flavour.

Above: Fresh sorrel mixes well with other herbs.

Cleaning leeks

Leeks need meticulous cleaning to remove any grit and earth that may hide between the layers of leaves. This method will ensure that the very last tiny piece of grit will be washed away.

1 Trim off the root, them trim the top of the green part and discard. Remove any tough or damaged outer leaves.

2 Slash the green part of the leek into quarters and rinse the entire leek well under cold running water, separating the layers to remove any hidden dirt or grit. Slice or leave whole, depending on the recipe.

LEGUMES

Pulses, lentils and peas provide the cook with a diverse range of flavours and textures, and they are a great addition to soups. They have long been a staple food in the Middle East, South America, India and the Mediterranean. Low in fat and high in complex carbohydrates, vitamins and minerals, legumes are an important source of protein for vegetarians, matching animal-based sources when eaten with cereals.

PULSES

The edible seeds from plants belonging to the legume family, pulses are packed with protein, vitamins, minerals and fibre, and are low in fat. For the cook, their ability to absorb the flavours of other foods means that pulses can be used as the base for an infinite number of dishes, and many are ideal in soups.

Red kidney beans

These are dark red-brown kidney-shaped beans that keep their shape and colour when cooked. They are excellent in soups as well as many other dishes. Raw kidney beans contain a substance that cannot be digested and which may cause food poisoning if the toxins are not extracted. It is therefore essential that you fast-boil red kidney beans for 15 minutes before use.

Above: Dried broad beans can be used when fresh ones are not in season.

Broad beans

Usually eaten in their fresh form, broad (fava) beans change in colour from green to brown when dried, making them difficult to recognize. The outer skin can be very tough and chewy, and some people prefer to remove it after cooking. Broad beans add delicious flavour to soups – try Broad Bean Minestrone or Catalan Potato and Broad Bean Soup.

Cannellini beans

These small, white, kidney-shaped beans – sometimes called white kidney beans – have a soft, creamy texture when cooked and are popular in Italian cooking. They can be used in place of haricot (navy) beans and make a tasty addition to soups such as Pasta, Bean and Vegetable Soup.

Chickpeas

Also known as garbanzo beans, robust and hearty chickpeas have a delicious nutty flavour and creamy texture. They need lengthy cooking and are much

Left: Cannellini beans give soups a velvety and creamy texture, as well as extra fibre.

Cooking kidney beans

Most types of beans, with the exception of aduki beans and mung beans, require soaking for 5–6 hours or overnight and then boiling rapidly for 10–15 minutes to remove any harmful toxins. This is particularly important for kidney beans, which can cause serious food poisoning if not treated in this way.

1 Put the beans in a sieve (strainer) or colander and wash them well under cold running water.

2 Place the washed beans in a large bowl that allows plenty of room for expansion. Cover with cold water and leave to soak overnight or for 8–12 hours, then drain and rinse.

3 Place the beans in a large pan and cover with fresh cold water. Bring to the boil and boil rapidly for 10–15 minutes, then reduce the heat and simmer for 1–1½ hours until tender.

4 Drain and use as required.

used in Middle Eastern cooking, including soups such as Moroccan Chickpea and Lentil Soup with Honey Buns and North African Spiced Soup.

Soya beans

These small, oval beans contain all the nutritional properties of animal products but are without the disadvantages. They are extremely dense and need to be soaked for up to 12 hours before cooking. They combine well with robust ingredients such as garlic, herbs and spices, and they make a healthy addition to soups. Soya beans are also used to make tofu, tempeh, textured vegetable protein (TVP), flour and the different versions of soy sauce. Tofu is widely used in Asian soups – try Thai Hot and Sweet Vegetable and Tofu Soup, which uses tofu as an ingredient.

Below: Chickpeas add heartiness to soups.

Right: Soya beans vary in colour from creamy-yellow through brown to black.

Buying and storing beans

Look for plump, shiny beans with unbroken skins. Beans toughen with age so, although they will keep for up to a year in a cool, dry place, it is best to buy them in small quantities from stores with a regular turnover. Avoid any that look dusty or dirty or smell musty, and store them in an airtight container in a cool, dark, dry place.

LENTILS AND PEAS

These are among our oldest foods. Lentils are hard even when fresh, so they are always sold dried. Unlike other pulses, they do not need soaking before being cooked.

Red lentils

Bright orange-coloured red split lentils, sometimes known as Egyptian lentils, are the most familiar variety. They cook in just 20 minutes, then disintegrating into a thick purée. They are ideal for thickening soups. Try creative recipes such as Thai-style Lentil and Coconut Soup, or Spiced Lentil Soup with Parsley Cream.

Puy lentils

These tiny, dark blue-green lentils are superior in taste and texture to other varieties and are great added to soups.

Green and brown lentils

Sometimes referred to as continental lentils, these pulses

Above, from top: Red lentils and puy lentils make excellent thickeners for soup.

retain their disc shape when cooked. They take longer to cook than split lentils – about 40–45 minutes – and are ideal for adding to warming soups.

Peas

Dried peas come from the field pea, not the garden pea, which is eaten fresh. Unlike lentils, peas are soft when young and require drying. They are available whole or split; the latter have a sweeter flavour and cook more quickly. Like split lentils, split peas do not hold their shape when cooked, making them perfect for soups. They take about 45 minutes to cook. Dried peas require soaking overnight before use.

Buying and storing lentils and peas

Although lentils and peas can be kept for up to a year, they toughen with time. Buy from stores with a fast turnover of stock and store in airtight containers in a cool, dark place.

MEAT AND POULTRY

Packed with high-quality protein, meat is an excellent food and is used in a variety of soup recipes. Careful rearing means leaner animals and hence healthier cuts of meat, making it perfectly possible to follow current dietary advice while still enjoying meat and poultry. Nowadays we are spoilt for choice with all the types and cuts of meat available. Most butchers and many supermarkets with fresh meat counters are only too happy to advise you on the best cuts of meat to use for all your recipes, including soups.

Chicken

The stock from cooking chicken makes an ideal basis for many delicious soups. If you can, choose corn-fed, free-range or organic birds for the best flavour. Cuts used in soups include breasts, legs and thighs. Boneless thighs or breasts are a good buy.

Duck

There isn't much meat on a duck, so buy big rather than small birds or choose duck breasts. Although leaner than it used to be, duck is still a fatty meat, so remove as much of the fat as possible before cooking. Duck goes well with oranges, and Duck Broth with Orange Spiced Dumplings is a delicious recipe. Lean duck can be used instead of chicken in some soups.

Below, from left: Corn-fed, free-range and organic chickens give the best flavour for chicken stocks.

Turkey

A turkey isn't just for Christmas – today's smaller birds are perfect for soups. Try recipes such as Chinese Chicken and Chilli Soup, or Chicken, Leek and Celery Soup, using turkey in place of chicken.

Bacon

Used in soups to add flavour, bacon can be bought sliced, in lardons (thin strips or dice), or in a piece. It is available smoked or unsmoked (green), and in different cuts – back (lean) or streaky (fatty). Bacon is a key ingredient in Irish Kidney and Bacon Soup, and Bacon Broth.

Pancetta

Pancetta is belly of pork that is cured with salt and spices, and it is eaten either raw in very thin slices, or cut more thickly and used in cooking. It can be substituted for bacon in soup recipes. Try it in the delicious Bacon and Chickpea Soup with Tortilla Chips.

Above: Bacon and pancetta can be used interchangeably.

Beef, lamb and pork

Some soup recipes call for the addition of beef, lamb or pork. These not only bring flavour to a dish, but also make a valuable contribution in terms of nutrition, since they are a source of high-quality protein. When making soup, the best cuts of beef, lamb and pork to choose are steak, chops or fillet, although other cuts such as pork belly, neck of lamb and minced beef, lamb or pork are also used, so be guided by the recipe or ask your butcher for advice. Meat bones are also used for making stocks.

Kidneys

Lamb, pork and ox (beef) kidney may all be used in soups. Ox kidney has the strongest flavour.

FISH

Fish is one of the quickest and easiest foods to cook, and makes an ideal ingredient for soups. As well as being delicious to eat, it is also very nutritious and a great source of easily digestible protein as well as other important nutrients such as B vitamins. White fish such as skinless cod, haddock and monkfish are naturally low in fat. Oily fish such as salmon, trout and mackerel are rich in omega-3 fats, which are beneficial to health, and we are actively encouraged to eat oily fish at least once a week. Oily fish are also a good source of all the B vitamins as well as vitamins A and D.

TYPES OF FISH

We have access to a wide range of fresh sea fish, as well as river and lake fish, some caught from our local shores and others imported from further afield. Although some fish is seasonal, many varieties are available all year round from good fishmongers, supermarkets and town markets.

Both white fish, such as haddock, cod, monkfish and mullet, and oily fish, such as mackerel and salmon, are used as an ingredient in creative soup recipes. Smoked fish such as smoked haddock or smoked cod are also used to create flavourful soups.

Whichever type of fish you are using as an ingredient in your soup, it is always best to buy firm, fresh fish.

Below: Cod blends well with cream or milk to make delicious fish chowders.

Round sea fish

This is a large group of fish that includes cod, haddock, whiting and mackerel, as well as more exotic varieties such as John Dory (or porgy), red mullet or snapper and parrot fish. These fish have a rounded body shape with eyes at each side of the head, and swim with the dorsal fin uppermost. These fish are normally sold whole or in fillets, cutlets or steaks.

Flat sea fish

Plaice, dabs, turbot, sole and skate are common examples of flat sea fish. Flat fish swim on their sides and have both eyes on top of their head. They usually have a white (blind) side and a darker upper surface, which is coloured to camouflage them within their local habitat. Flat fish are usually sold whole or filleted.

Freshwater fish

Freshwater fish may live in freshwater rivers or lakes and include varieties such as salmon, trout and pike. They are usually sold whole or in fillets, steaks or cutlets.

Above: Trout makes a tasty alternative to the more usual clam chowder.

Smoked fish

Fish is usually smoked by one of two methods: hot smoke or cold smoke. Typical examples of smoked fish include haddock, cod, salmon, mackerel, trout and kippers (smoked herrings).

Below: Smoked haddock is sold whole, as fillets (shown here) or thinly sliced.

SHELLFISH

We are fortunate to have a good selection of fresh and frozen shellfish available all year round, either shellfish caught off our local shores, or varieties caught further afield and imported. Many shellfish and crustaceans have wonderfully exotic names and almost all shellfish is considered edible, from clams to razor-shells, sea snails and small scallops. Shellfish is at its best when eaten fresh and in season. Frozen shellfish is also available and is a good substitute if fresh is not available.

SHRIMPS AND PRAWNS

There are many varieties of shrimps and prawns, which are known collectively as shrimp in the United States. The smallest are tiny pink or brown shrimp. Next in size come the pink prawns with a delicate flavour. Then there are the larger variety of prawn, which turn bright red when they are cooked. They are highly prized for their fine, strong flavour. Best, and most expensive of all, are large succulent king prawns (jumbo shrimp) which have a superb flavour and texture. Similar to these is the cicala, which resembles a small, flat lobster. Shrimp and prawns can be used in a variety of different tasty soups such as Prawn and Egg-knot Soup, and Wonton and Prawn Tail Soup.

Shrimps and prawns should have bright shells that feel firm to the touch; if they look limp or smell of ammonia, then do not buy them.

CRUSTACEANS AND MOLLUSCS

Crustaceans range from crabs and lobsters to bright orange crawfish. Squid and cuttlefish are molluscs – their shells are located inside their bodies.

Crab

There are dozens of varieties of crab, ranging from the large common crab to tiny shore crabs that are good only for making soup. All kinds of crabmeat, both fresh and canned, can be used in creative soup recipes. Try recipes such as Crab, Coconut and Coriander Soup, or Chinese Crab and Corn Soup.

Scallops

Scallops are available almost all year round, but are best in winter when the roes are full and firm. Always try to buy them with their delicious coral, although this is not always possible. You can buy them shelled, which saves the effort of cleaning them. But if you clean them yourself, the beard and all dark coloured parts must be removed before

Below: The common or brown crab contains plenty of tasty meat.

Peeling and deveining raw prawns
Raw prawns and large shrimps are often peeled before cooking. Raw prawns must have their intestinal tracts removed before cooking, a process called "deveining". It is not necessary to devein shrimps.

1 Pull off the head and legs from each prawn or shrimp, then carefully peel off the body shell. Leave on the tail "fan" if you wish.

2 To remove the intestinal vein from prawns, make a shallow incision down the centre of the curved back of the prawn using a small sharp knife, cutting all the way from the tail to the head.

3 Pick out the thin black vein that runs the length of the prawn with the tip of the knife and discard.

Cleaning and preparing squid
Before you start, rinse the squid under cold running water.

1 Holding the body firmly in one hand, grasp the tentacles at the base with the other, and gently but firmly pull the head away from the body. As you do this the soft yellowish entrails will come away.

2 Use a sharp knife to cut off the tentacles from the head of the squid. Reserve the tentacles but discard the hard beak in the middle. Remove and reserve the ink sac, then discard the head.

3 Peel the membrane away from the body. Pull out the "quill". Wash the body under cold running water. Cut the body, flaps and tentacles to the required size.

they are cooked and eaten. Frozen scallops have little or no taste. Scallops are an ingredient in exotic soups such as Seafood Chowder, Vermouth Soup with Seared Scallops, and Scallop and Jerusalem Artichoke Soup.

Lobsters

These are the ultimate luxury seafood. Their flesh has a delicious flavour and makes wonderful soups. Lobsters must be bought live or freshly boiled. Try the luxurious, velvety Lobster Bisque topped with double (heavy) cream to really appreciate this superior seafood.

Squid and cuttlefish

These molluscs are indistinguishable in taste, but cuttlefish have a larger head and a wider body with stubbier tentacles. Once the bone has been removed, cuttlefish are very tender. The shell of a squid is nothing more than a long, thin, transparent quill. Both squid and cuttlefish have ten tentacles. Squid is more commonly used in soup recipes. Small squid and cuttlefish should be cooked briefly, just until they turn opaque, or they will become rubbery and tough. Larger specimens need long, slow cooking to make them tender, making them ideal for use in some soups. Try delicious Coconut and Seafood Soup.

Mussels

These shellfish have a smooth texture and sweet flavour. Both whole and shelled mussels may be used in soups, and they also make an attractive garnish, cooked and served in their open shells. Try flavourful soups such as Saffron-flavoured Mussel Soup.

Right: Queen scallops are smaller and cheaper than the larger king scallops, but have the same flavour.

Clams

There are many different types of clam, ranging from the tiny smooth-shelled variety to long, thin razor shells and the large Venus clams with beautiful ridged shells. All have a sweet flavour and a slightly chewy texture. Because they vary so much in size, it is best to ask the fishmonger how many clams you will need for a particular soup or be guided by the recipe. Try tempting recipes such as Clam Chowder or Chilli Clam Broth.

Buying and storing shellfish

When buying fresh shellfish such as scallops, mussels, clams and oysters, look for those with tightly closed shells. They are still alive when sold fresh, and any sign of an open shell may indicate that they are far from fresh. A sharp tap on the shell may persuade the shellfish to close up, but otherwise, avoid it. When buying cooked shellfish such as crab, lobster and prawns (shrimp), make sure the shells are intact. They should feel quite heavy and have a fresh, agreeable smell.

Once purchased, keep fresh shellfish chilled, and store in the refrigerator, covered with a damp cloth, until it is ready to use. As a general rule, fresh shellfish, as well as frozen (defrosted) shellfish, is best eaten on the day you purchase it or used within 24 hours – your fishmonger will be able to advise you more on the length of time recommended for storing shellfish.

EGGS AND DAIRY PRODUCE

These foods are staples in almost every kitchen in the world and have been used in cooking for thousands of years. Eggs and dairy products such as yogurt are important as thickeners in soups, as well as adding essential flavour, texture and substance.

EGGS

Both the cooking qualities of eggs and their decorative nature make them the ideal ingredient for tempting soups. They can be used to thicken soups, such as Egg and Cheese Soup and Saffron Seafood Soup, and as an attractive garnish in soups such as Spicy Tomato and Egg Drop Soup, Portuguese Garlic Soup and Prawn and Egg-knot Soup.

CREAM

Single (light) cream is excellent for enriching soups. Unlike double (heavy) or whipping cream, single cream will separate if heated too fiercely. If you are planning to freeze a soup that is enriched with cream towards the end of the cooking time, it is advisable to freeze it without adding the cream. Reheat the dish fully, then lower the heat and add the cream. Most of the soups in the Creamy

Below: Eggs may be used to thicken soups or as a garnish.

Vegetable Soups section contain cream, for example Cream of Red Pepper Soup, Jerusalem Artichoke Soup and Simple Cream of Onion Soup.

Sour cream is a thick-textured cream that is treated with lactic acid, which gives it its typical tang. It is not the same as cream that has turned sour through age. Full-fat sour cream contains about 20 per cent fat, although low- and non-fat versions are also available. Care should be taken when cooking, as it can curdle if heated to too high a temperature or too rapidly. It can be used in the same way as cream and is ideal for enriching and garnishing soups, such as Creamy Beetroot Soup, Roasted Root Vegetable Soup, and Sweet and Sour Cabbage, Beetroot and Tomato Borscht.

Crème fraîche, a rich, cultured French cream, is similar to sour cream, but is milder tasting. Its high fat

Left: Single and double cream can be stirred into soups or used as a garnish.

content, at around 35 per cent, means that it does not curdle when cooked. It may be used to enrich soups and as a garnish. Tomato Soup with Black Olive Ciabatta Toasts, and Hungarian Cherry Soup both have a garnish of crème fraîche, and it may be substituted in soups garnished with double cream.

MILK

Often referred to as a complete food, milk can be used in both chilled and warm soups. Used in small quantities, it is very useful for adjusting the consistency of soups. It can be used as a substitute for cream if you want a soup to taste less rich, as well as to counteract the heat of chillies in a spicy soup. Soups that contain milk rather than cream include Broccoli and Almond Soup, and Cauliflower and Walnut Cream.

YOGURT

Praised for its health-giving qualities, yogurt has earned a reputation as one of the most valuable health foods. Its consistency may be thin or thick. Greek (US strained plain) and Greek-style yogurts, which are made from cow's or ewe's milk, contain about 10g of fat per 100g – just enough to prevent them from curdling during cooking. However, although these yogurts are higher in fat

Below: Mozzarella is added to soups to provide texture and absorb flavours.

Above: Stilton has a strong flavour and is a popular choice for adding to soups.

Home-made pesto
Grated Parmesan and Pecorino cheeses are sprinkled over Italian soups to add flavour. They are also an ingredient in pesto, which makes a tasty garnish.

1 Put 75g/3oz/1^1/2 cups basil, 25g/1oz/2 tbsp pine nuts, and 3 chopped garlic cloves into a mortar. Grind with a pestle until the mixture forms a chunky paste.

2 Work in 125g/4oz/1^1/3 cups mixed freshly grated Parmesan and Pecorino cheese and 120ml/4fl oz/^{1}/2 cup olive oil.

than other types of yogurt, they still contain less fat than cream and they are a healthier alternative. Cultures are added to milk to produce natural (plain) yogurt. It has a smooth, creamy texture and a fresh, slightly acidic flavour. Soya yogurt is a dairy-free yogurt that is made from soya milk and is widely available from most wholefood stores and supermarkets. Soups that are made with yogurt include Spiced Mango Soup with Yogurt, and Yogurt Soup.

CHEESE

There are several cheeses that can be enjoyed in soups, the main ones being blue cheese, mozzarella and Cheddar. The type of milk, its fat content and the method used to make the cheese all help to define its individual character.

Blue cheese gives a wonderful creamy tang to soups. Stilton has a strong and robust taste that goes well with vegetables such as broccoli, leeks and courgettes – it is a key ingredient in Pear and Watercress Soup. The pears also combine well with blue cheese – another delicious example is Pear and Roquefort Soup with Caramelized Pears. If you prefer a milder flavour, try blue cheeses such as Dolcelatte or Bleu

d'Causses, which melt in the mouth just like cream. Try Creamy Courgette and Dolcelatte Soup, which is deliciously creamy and rich.

Mozzarella, probably the most famous of Italian fresh cheeses, is a soft and springy mild white cheese and can be used in soups to add texture rather than a specific taste. The juices, oils and flavours of the other ingredients are absorbed and intensified by the mild layers of the cheese. This, and the fact that mozzarella melts to become elastic, has made it popular in soups such as Aubergine Soup with Mozzarella and Gremolata.

Cheddar cheese crumbled on top of soup creates a zingy dish quickly and elegantly. Try Cauliflower and Broccoli Soup with Cheddar Cheese Croûtes.

Above: Cheddar cheese can be grated and sprinkled on top of soups to add protein and flavour.

PASTA AND NOODLES

The wide range of fresh and dried pasta available to us today ensures that you have plenty of choice when it comes to selecting which pasta to cook. Pasta is a nutritious food and plays an important part in a healthy, well-balanced diet. It is low in fat and provides a good source of carbohydrate. Pasta, especially small shapes such as stellette or pastina, is ideal for use in soups and is an important ingredient in recipes such as Pasta, Bean and Vegetable Soup.

SOUP PASTA

These tiny shapes, of which there are hundreds of different varieties, are mostly made from plain durum wheat pasta, although you may find them made with egg and even flavoured with carrot or spinach.

Types of soup pasta

Teeny-weeny pasta shapes are called pastina in Italian, and there are literally hundreds of different ones to choose from. In Italy they are always served in broths and clear soups, and are regarded almost as nursery food because they are so often served for children's meals.

Shapes of pastina vary enormously, and seem to get more and more fanciful as the market demands. The smallest and most plain

pasta per minestre (pasta for soups) is like tiny grains. Some look like rice and are in fact called risi or risoni, while others are more like barley and are called orzi. Fregola, from Sardinia, looks like couscous, and has a similar nutty texture and flavour. Semi di melone is like melon seeds, as its name suggests, while acini de pepe or peperini is named after peppercorns, which it resembles in shape and size if not in colour. Coralline, grattini and occhi are three more very popular tiny pasta shapes.

The next size up are the ones that are most popular with children. These include alfabeti and alfabetini (alphabet shapes), stelline and stellette (stars), rotellini (tiny wagon wheels) and anellini, which can be tiny rings, sometimes with ridges that make them look very pretty, or larger hoops. Ditali are similar to anellini but slightly thicker, while tubettini are thicker still.

Another category of pasta per minestre consists of slightly larger shapes, more like miniature versions of familiar types of short pasta. Their

names end in "ine", "ette" or "etti", denoting that they are the diminutive forms. These include conchigliette (little shells), farfalline and farfallette (little bows), funghetti (little mushrooms), lumachine (little snails), quadretti and quadrettini (little squares), orecchiettini (little ears), renette (like baby penne) and tubetti (little tubes). The size of these varies: the smaller ones are for use in clear broths, while the larger ones are more often used in making thicker soups.

Buying and storing soup pasta

The quality of pasta varies tremendously – choose good-quality Italian brands made from 100 per cent durum wheat, and buy fresh pasta from an Italian delicatessen rather than pre-packed fresh pasta from the supermarket.

Dried pasta will keep almost indefinitely in the store cupboard (pantry), but if you keep it in a storage jar, it is a good idea to use it all up before adding any from a new packet.

Fresh pasta is usually sold loose and is best cooked the same day, but can be kept in the refrigerator for a day or two. Fresh pasta from a supermarket is likely to be packed in plastic packs and bags and will keep for 3–4 days in the refrigerator. Fresh pasta freezes well and should be cooked from frozen. Convenient packs of supermarket pasta have the advantage of being easy to store in the freezer.

Left: Tiny soup pasta is available in hundreds of different shapes.

NOODLES

The fast food of the East, noodles can be made from wheat flour, rice, mung bean flour or buckwheat flour. Noodles can be used in a variety of flavourful soup recipes. Try some tasty soups such as Soba Noodles in Hot Soup with Tempura, Thai Cellophane Noodle Soup, Chiang Mai Noodle Soup, or Sapporo-style Ramen Noodles in Soup.

Wheat noodles

These are available in two types: plain and egg. Plain noodles are made from strong flour and water; they can be flat or round and come in various thicknesses. Egg noodles are more common than the wheat variety, and are sold both fresh and dried. The Chinese types are available in various thicknesses. Very fine egg noodles, which resemble vermicelli, are usually sold in individual coils. More substantial wholewheat egg noodles are widely available from larger supermarkets.

Udon and ramen are types of Japanese noodles. Udon noodles are thick and can be round or flat. They are available fresh, pre-cooked or dried. Wholewheat udon noodles have a more robust flavour. Ramen egg noodles are sold in coils and in Japan are often cooked and served with an accompanying broth.

Above:
Egg noodles add flavour and texture to Chinese soups.

Rice noodles

These very fine, delicate noodles are made from rice and are opaque-white in colour. Like wheat noodles, they come in various widths, from the very thin strands known as rice vermicelli, which are popular in Thailand and southern China, to the thicker rice sticks, which are used more in Vietnam and Malaysia.

Cellophane noodles

Made from mung beans, cellophane noodles are translucent and do not need to be boiled; they are simply soaked in boiling water for 10–15 minutes. They have a fantastic texture, which they retain when cooked, never becoming soggy.

Buckwheat noodles

Soba are the best-known type of buckwheat noodles. They are a much darker colour than wheat noodles – almost brownish-grey. In Japan they are traditionally used in soups.

Left: Rice noodles form the basis of many Asian soup recipes.

Below: Cellophane noodles do not need to be boiled.

Buying and storing noodles

Dried noodles are readily available in supermarkets. Packets of fresh noodles are found in the chiller cabinets of Asian stores and some supermarkets. They must be stored in the refrigerator or freezer. Dried noodles will keep for many months in an airtight container in a cool, dry place.

HERBS AND SPICES

Herbs, the aromatic and fragrant plants that we use to add flavour and colour to our dishes, have been cultivated all over the world for centuries. The majority of herbs are familiar as culinary herbs, but many are also good for medicinal and cosmetic purposes. In cookery, herbs are chosen mainly for their flavouring and seasoning properties as well as adding colour and texture to dishes. Herbs, both fresh and dried, add delicious flavour and aroma to a whole variety of dishes, including many hot and chilled soups.

HERBS

Herbs can make a significant difference to the flavour and aroma of a soup, and they can enliven the simplest of dishes.

Basil

This delicate aromatic herb is widely used in Italian and Thai cooking. The leaves bruise easily, so they are best used whole or torn, rather than cut with a knife.

Bay

These dark-green, glossy leaves are best left to dry for a few days before use. They have a robust, spicy flavour and are an essential ingredient in home-made stocks and for a bouquet garni.

Coriander

Warm and spicy, coriander (cilantro) looks similar to flat leaf parsley but its taste is completely different.

Dill

The mild yet distinctive, aniseed flavour of dill makes a good addition to soups, for example in Sorrel, Spinach and Dill Soup.

Kaffir lime leaves

These glossy green leaves are commonly used in Asian cuisines, lending a citrus flavour to soups. They are available fresh from Asian stores, or dried from large supermarkets.

Mint

Mint, a popular herb, has deep green leaves with an unmistakable strong and tangy scent and flavour. It is used in soup recipes such as Iced Melon Soup with Sorbet.

Oregano

This is a wild variety of marjoram with a robust flavour. It goes well with tomato-based soups.

Parsley

There are two types of parsley: flat leaf and curly. Both taste relatively similar, but the flat leaf variety is preferable in cooked dishes. Parsley is an excellent source of vitamin C, iron and calcium.

Above: Tarragon goes well with chicken and shellfish.

Above: Indian-style soups use spicy coriander.

Tarragon

This small, perennial plant bears slim green leaves, and its distinctive taste is said to be a cross between aniseed and mint. It marries well with chicken and shellfish in soups.

Thyme

This robustly flavoured aromatic herb is good in tomato-based soups, as well as soups containing lentils and beans. It is also an essential ingredient in a classic bouquet garni.

Buying and storing herbs

Fresh herbs are widely available, sold loose, in packets or growing in pots. Place stems in a jar half-filled with water and cover with a plastic bag. Sealed with an elastic band, the herbs should keep for about a week.

Right: Basil is an important herb in Italian cooking.

SPICES

Highly revered for thousands of years, spices – the seeds, fruit, pods, bark and buds of plants – add flavour, colour and interest to the most unassuming of ingredients, while the evocative aroma of spices stimulates the appetite. Spices add delicious flavour to many soup recipes.

Chillies

Chillies are available fresh as well as in dried, powdered and flaked form. Dried chillies tend to be hotter than fresh, and this is certainly true of chilli flakes, which contain both the seeds and the flesh. The best pure chilli powders do not contain added ingredients, such as onion and garlic. All types of chilli may be used in a variety of soup recipes.

Coriander

Alongside cumin, ground coriander is a key ingredient in Indian curry powders and garam masala, and in northern Europe the ivory-coloured seeds are used as a pickling spice. Coriander seeds have a sweet, earthy, burnt-orange flavour that is more pronounced than the fresh leaves. The ready-ground powder rapidly loses its flavour and aroma, so it is best to buy whole seeds, which are easily ground in a mortar using a pestle, or in a coffee grinder. Before grinding, lightly dry-roast the seeds in a frying pan to enhance their flavour. Coriander adds delicious flavour and warmth to soups.

Cumin

Cumin is a familiar component of Indian, Mexican, North African and Middle Eastern cooking and is added to soups to give a delicious flavour and aroma. The seeds have a robust aroma and slightly bitter taste, which is tempered by dry-roasting. Black cumin seeds are milder and sweeter. Ground cumin can be harsh, so it is best to buy the whole seeds and grind them just before use to be sure of a fresh flavour.

Ginger

Fresh root ginger is spicy, peppery and fragrant, and adds a hot, yet refreshing, flavour to soups such as the Japanese Miso Broth with Spring Onions and Tofu. When buying ginger, look for firm, thin-skinned and unblemished roots and avoid withered, woody-looking roots as these are likely to be dry and fibrous.

Left: Lemon grass stalks are essential in many Asian soup recipes.

Left: Cumin adds taste and aroma.

Lemon grass

This long fibrous stalk has a fragrant citrus aroma and flavour when cut. It is familiar in South-east Asian cooking and may be used as an ingredient in soups from this region. To use, remove the tough, woody outer layers, trim the root, then cut off the lower 5cm (2in) and slice or pound in a mortar using a pestle. Bottled chopped lemon grass and lemon grass purée are also available.

Pepper

Undoubtedly the oldest, most widely used spice in the world, pepper is a versatile seasoning and is invaluable for soups, because it not only adds flavour of its own to a dish, but also brings out the flavour of the other ingredients.

Saffron

The world's most expensive spice is made from the dried stigmas of *Crocus salivus*. Only a tiny amount of this bright orange spice is needed to add a wonderful colour and delicate flavour to fish and shellfish soups.

Salt

It is usually best to leave the seasoning of stocks and soups until the last minute, just before serving. Add salt a little bit at a time, until you have the seasoned flavour you require.

Above: Pink, black and white peppercorns bring out the flavour of your chosen soup ingredients.

Buying and storing spices

Always buy spices in small quantities from a store with a regular turnover. Store in airtight jars in a cool place.

OTHER FLAVOURINGS

There are many other flavourings that are used to add depth to soups – for example, olive oil, flavoured oils and vinegars, alcohol, chilli sauce, pesto and soy sauce, as well as more exotic flavourings such as dashi or fish sauce. Many add that important final touch or richness to a soup, contributing an important element to the overall character. Listed below are some of the flavourings used in this book.

Oils and vinegars

Flavoured oils and vinegars are brilliant for splashing into finished soups to pack an extra punch. Consider chilli oil for a super-fiery flavour in a spicy soup, or basil or rocket oil to enliven a fish or Mediterranean-style soup. Infuse virgin olive oil with chillies, roasted whole garlic cloves, whole spices, woody herbs or citrus peel instead of buying flavoured oil. Flavour and colour oil with soft aromatic herbs such as basil. Vinegar adds bite to some soups, so look out for the many types available, including wine vinegars, balsamic vinegar, sherry vinegar and fruit-flavoured vinegars, such as raspberry.

Alcohol

Add to soups in moderation. The golden rule is to simmer the soup for a few minutes to cook off the strong alcohol, leaving the flavour. White wine, Pernod and vermouth work very well with creamy fish soups.

Flavoured creams

These provide a wonderful way to introduce contrasting flavour to a finished soup. Crème fraîche or whipped double (heavy) cream can be transformed by adding a purée of fresh herbs, grilled (bell) peppers or sun-dried tomatoes. Infused saffron and pesto can also be added.

Flavoured butters

Flavoured butters can be spread on warm bread to accompany a soup, or added to each bowl just before serving. Flavourings range from herbs and spices to shellfish.

Coconut milk

Buy this in cans or long-life cartons, or make it yourself at home. Put 225g/8oz/ 2²/₃ cups desiccated (dry unsweetened shredded) coconut into a food processor, add 450ml/³/₄ pint/ scant 2 cups boiling water and process for about 30 seconds. Leave to cool slightly, then transfer to a sieve (strainer) lined with muslin (cheesecloth) placed over a bowl and gather the ends of the cloth. Twist to extract the liquid.

Left: Balsamic vinegar is used in Italian soups.

Left: Raspberry vinegar adds colour.

Above: Chilli sauces add heat and flavour to soups.

Pesto and pistou

Pesto and pistou are closely related, the latter hailing from southern France, where it is stirred into a rich vegetable soup. Both are made by mixing crushed garlic, basil and olive oil, and pesto also contains pine nuts and Parmesan cheese. Stir into soup to add flavour and colour.

Chilli sauce

For those who like very hot food, chilli sauce can be offered at the table, or a dash can be added to flavour soups during cooking or to individual servings of soup.

Soy sauce

Made from fermented soya beans, soy sauce is one of Asia's most important contributions to the global pantry. There are three types of Chinese soy sauce on the market: light, dark and regular. As a rule, light soy sauce is used for soups. It is the initial extraction, like the first pressing of virgin olive oil. It has the most delicate flavour and is light brown in colour with a "beany" fragrance.

Left: Shoyu is a full-flavoured Japanese soy sauce.

Right: Soy sauces are available in different strengths.

There are several different types of Japanese soy sauce, too. Usukuchi soy sauce is light in colour and tastes less salty than the Chinese light soy. Tamari is dark and thick with a strong flavour, and is even less salty than the light type. Shoyu is a full-flavoured sauce that is aged for up to two years. In between, there is the very popular Kikkoman, a brand name for the equivalent of the Chinese regular soy sauce – neither too weak nor too strong.

The Indonesian kecap manis is thick and black, with a powerful aroma but a surprisingly sweet taste.

Soy sauce is used as a flavouring in Japanese soups such as Clear Soup with Seafood Sticks, and Sapporo-style Ramen Noodles in Soup.

Fish sauce

Fish sauce is an essential seasoning for Thai and Vietnamese cooking, in the same way that soy sauce is important to the Chinese and the Japanese. In Vietnam it is often made using shrimp, but in Thailand the sauce is more often made using salted, fermented fish.

All types of fish sauce have a pungent flavour and aroma and are very salty. Thai *nam pla* has a slightly stronger flavour and aroma than the Vietnamese or Chinese versions. The colour of fish sauce can vary considerably; lighter-coloured sauces are considered to be better than darker versions. Fish sauce is used to season some soup recipes such as Coconut and Seafood Soup, and Thai Pumpkin, Prawn and Coconut Soup.

Shrimp paste

Known in Malaysia as *blachan*, this is an essential ingredient in many South-east Asian dishes, including soups. It is made from tiny shrimps that have been salted, dried, pounded and then left to ferment in the hot humid conditions until the aroma is very pungent. The colour of the paste can be anything from oyster pink to purplish brown, depending upon the type of shrimp and the precise process used. It is compressed and sold in block form or packed in tiny tubs or jars. The moment you unwrap it, the smell of rotten fish is quite overpowering, but this vanishes during cooking. Shrimp paste adds depth and pungency to a soup, for example in Balinese Vegetable Soup, a popular dish served on beans.

Miso

Many Japanese start the day with a bowl of miso soup for breakfast. Miso is one of the oldest traditional ingredients. Boiled *daizu* (soya beans) are crushed, then mixed with a culture called *koji*, which is made with wheat and rice, barley or beans. The fermented mixture is allowed to mature for up to three years. Numerous kinds and brands of miso are available in supermarkets. They are categorized into three basic grades according to strength of flavour and colour: shiro-miso (white, light and made with rice). aka-miso (red, medium and made with barley), and kuro-miso (black, strong and made with soya beans). Miso is quite salty and has a strong fermented bean flavour. Try it in Miso Broth with Spring Onions and Tofu.

Mirin

This amber-coloured, heavily sweetened sake is used only in cooking. It is one of Japan's ancient sake and is made from *shochu* (distilled sake). There is a synthetically made, cheap mirin-like liquid available called mirin-fuhmi (mirin flavouring), as opposed to hon-mirin (real mirin). Hon-mirin has an alcohol content of 14 per cent, whereas mirin-fuhmi is only 1 per cent. Both are available in bottles of 300ml/^{1}/$_2$ pint/1^1/$_4$ cups or 600ml/1 pint/2^1/$_2$ cups from Asian stores and good supermarkets. Mirin has a syrupy texture and adds a mild sweetness to soups.

Left: Thai fish sauce adds a strong, salty flavour to soups.

EQUIPMENT AND TECHNIQUES

One advantage of making your own soups is that you won't need any specialist equipment to try a wide range of tasty recipes. You will need basic equipment such as good knives and a chopping board or two, as well as a good-quality heavy-based pan and utensils such as wooden spoons etc. One additional piece of equipment that is very useful in soup-making is a food processor or blender, to enable you to purée cooked soups, if you wish. However, if you don't have one of these, many of the soups that require puréeing can simply be hand-pressed to make them smooth.

Heavy-based pan

For making soups you should choose a good-quality heavy-based pan. A good pan that conducts and holds heat well allows the vegetables to cook for longer before browning, so that they can be softened without changing colour. If you are health-conscious, choose a good-quality non-stick pan, and

Right: There are many different types of vegetable peeler.

Below: Using a balloon whisk.

you may be able to slightly reduce the amount of butter or oil used to sauté the vegetables.

Vegetable peelers

The quickest way to peel vegetables is to use a swivel peeler. For example, trim off the top and end of a carrot, then hold the carrot in one hand and run the peeler away from you down its length, turning the carrot as you work. Use a julienne peeler to cut vegetables such as carrots and courgettes into thin julienne strips. Use julienne strips of vegetables in recipes or as an attractive garnish for chilled or cooked hot soups.

Wooden spoon

Use a wooden spoon to stir soups. This will not damage the base of the pan (important if the pan is non-stick). However, wood absorbs flavours, so wash and dry the spoon well after use, and do not leave the spoon in the soup while it is cooking.

Below: Using a wooden mushroom or champignon.

Chopping an onion

Use a small knife to trim the root end of the onion and remove the skin with the tough layer underneath. Cut the onion in half. Place the cut side down on a chopping board and use a large sharp knife to slice down through the onion without cutting its root. Slice horizontally through the onion. Finally, cut down across all the original cuts and the onion will fall apart into fine dice.

Whisk

A balloon whisk is useful when making some soups, for quickly incorporating ingredients such as eggs and cream, which could curdle, or flour mixtures that can form lumps. Steady the pan or bowl with one hand and, holding the whisk in the other hand, make quick flicking movements.

Wooden mushroom

A wooden mushroom (or champignon), which looks like a large, flat toadstool, is useful for pressing ingredients through a fine sieve (strainer) to give a smooth purée. The back of a large spoon or ladle can also be used.

Blender

A hand-held blender is brilliant, as it allows you to blend the soup directly in the pan. Controlling the speed is easy, to give the required consistency. Be careful when using a hand-held blender in a non-stick pan, and be sure not to let the blender touch the base or sides of the pan because it will cause damage to the surface.

Chopping fresh herbs

Rinse and thoroughly dry the herbs and remove the leaves from the stalks, if necessary (this is essential when chopping herbs such as rosemary, which has very tough, woody stalks. Place the herbs on a chopping board and, using a knife or other sharp tool, cut the herbs into small pieces (as finely or as coarsely as you wish), holding the tip of the blade against the chopping board and rocking the blade back and forth.

Alternatively, you can use a mezzaluna ("half-moon" in Italian). This is a curved crescent-shaped blade attached to two handles, which rocks back and forth over the herbs to chop them. It is good for chopping a lot of herbs at once.

Above: Aubergine Soup with Mozzarella and Gremolata, made smooth and creamy using a food processor or blender.

Mouli-legume

A more traditional method is to use a mouli-legume, a cooking instrument from France that is a cross between a sieve (strainer) and a food mill. It sits over a bowl and has a blade to press the food through two fine sieves. The blade is turned by hand to push the soup through the sieves, leaving all the fibres and solids behind. A mouli-legume can grind food quickly into a coarse or fine texture.

Electric food processor and blender

The most common items of equipment for puréeing soups are food processors and free-standing blenders. Both types of machine are quick and efficient, but the food processor does not produce as smooth a result as a conventional blender, and for some recipes the soup will need to be strained afterwards. Food processors can also be used for finely chopping and slicing vegetables for salsas and garnishes.

Below: Using a mouli-legume.

Below: Using a hand-held blender.

Below: Using a food processor.

MAKING STOCKS

Fresh stocks are indispensable for creating good home-made soups. They add a depth of flavour that plain water just cannot achieve. Although many supermarkets now sell tubs of fresh stock, these may be expensive, especially if you need large quantities. Making your own is surprisingly easy and much more economical, particularly if you can use leftovers.

Home-made stocks aren't just cheaper, they are also a lot tastier, and they are much more nutritious too, precisely because they are made with fresh, natural ingredients. You can, of course, use stock (bouillon) cubes, granules or bouillon powder, but be sure to check the seasoning as these tend to be particularly high in salt.

Use the appropriate stock for the soup you are making. Onion soup, for example, is improved with a good beef stock. Be careful to use a vegetable stock, though, if you are catering for vegetarians. Recipes are given here for vegetable stock, fish stock, chicken stock, meat stock and basic stocks for Chinese and Japanese cooking.

Freezing stock

A good idea for keen and regular soup makers is to freeze portions of concentrated home-made stock in plastic freezer bags, or ice-cube trays, so you always have a supply at your disposal whenever you need some. Frozen stock can be stored in the freezer for up to three months (fish stock for up to 2 months). Ensure that you label each stock carefully for easy identification later.

Vegetable stock

Use this versatile stock as the basis for all vegetarian soups. It may also be used for meat, poultry or fish soups.

MAKES 2.5 LITRES/4½ PINTS/10 CUPS

INGREDIENTS
2 leeks, roughly chopped
3 celery sticks, roughly chopped
1 large onion, unpeeled, roughly chopped
2 pieces fresh root ginger, chopped
1 yellow (bell) pepper, chopped
1 parsnip, chopped
mushroom stalks
tomato peelings
45ml/3 tbsp light soy sauce
3 bay leaves
a bunch of parsley stalks
3 sprigs of fresh thyme
1 sprig of fresh rosemary
10ml/2 tsp salt
freshly ground black pepper
3.5 litres/6 pints/15 cups cold water

1 Put all the ingredients into a stockpot or large pan. Bring slowly to the boil, then lower the heat and simmer for 30 minutes, stirring from time to time.

2 Allow to cool. Strain, then discard the vegetables. The stock is ready to use.

Fish stock

Fish stock is much quicker to make than poultry or meat stock. Ask your fishmonger for heads, bones and trimmings from white fish. Lobster or crab shell pieces (taken after boiling lobster or crab and scooping out the meat) can also be used in place of fish trimmings to make a tasty fish stock, together with the other flavourings listed.

MAKES 1 LITRE/1¾ PINTS/4 CUPS

INGREDIENTS
675g/1½ lb heads, bones and trimmings from white fish
1 onion, sliced
2 celery sticks with leaves, chopped
1 carrot, sliced
½ lemon, sliced (optional)
1 bay leaf
a few sprigs of fresh parsley
6 black peppercorns
1.35 litres/2¼ pints/6 cups cold water
150ml/¼ pint/⅔ cup dry white wine

1 Rinse the fish heads, bones and trimmings well under cold running water. Put in a stockpot or large pan with the vegetables and lemon, if using, the herbs, peppercorns, water and wine. Bring to the boil, skimming the surface frequently, then reduce the heat and simmer for 25 minutes.

2 Strain the stock without pressing down on the ingredients in the sieve (strainer). If not using immediately, leave to cool and then refrigerate. Use within 2 days.

Chicken stock

A good home-made poultry stock is invaluable in the kitchen. If poultry giblets are available, add them (except the livers) with the wings. Once made, chicken stock can be kept in an airtight container in the refrigerator for 3–4 days, or frozen for longer storage (up to 3 months).

MAKES ABOUT 2.5 LITRES/4½ PINTS/
10 CUPS

INGREDIENTS
    1.2–1.3kg/2½–3lb chicken or turkey
        (wings, backs and necks)
    2 onions, unpeeled, quartered
    1 tbsp olive oil
    4 litres/7 pints/16 cups
        cold water
    2 carrots, roughly chopped
    2 celery sticks, with leaves if
        possible, roughly chopped
    a small handful of parsley stalks
    a few sprigs of fresh thyme or
        5ml/1 tsp dried
    1 or 2 bay leaves
    10 black peppercorns,
        lightly crushed

1 Combine the poultry wings, backs and necks in a stockpot or large pan with the onion quarters and the oil.

2 Cook over a moderate heat, stirring occasionally, until the poultry and onions are lightly and evenly browned.

Right: Moroccan Chicken Soup with Charmoula Butter uses a good-quality home-made stock for a rich flavour.

3 Add the water and stir well to mix in the sediment on the bottom of the pan. Bring to the boil and skim off any impurities as they rise to the surface of the stock.

4 Add the chopped carrots and celery, fresh parsley, thyme, bay leaf and black peppercorns. Partly cover the stockpot and simmer the stock for 3 hours.

5 Strain the stock through a sieve (strainer) into a bowl. Discard the chicken bones and the vegetables. Leave the stock to cool, then chill in the refrigerator for an hour.

6 When cold, carefully remove the layer of fat that will have set on the surface. The stock is now ready to use in your chosen soup recipe.

Meat stock

The most delicious meat soups rely on a good home-made stock for success. A stock (bouillon) cube will do if you have no time to make your own, but fresh home-made stock will give a much better flavour and basis for soups, so it's well worth spending a little time making your own. Once it is made, meat stock can be kept in the refrigerator for up to 4 days, or frozen for up to 3 months.

MAKES ABOUT 2 LITRES/3½ PINTS/8 CUPS

INGREDIENTS
    1.8kg/4lb beef bones, such as
        shin, leg, neck and shank, or
        veal or lamb bones, cut into
        6cm/2½ in pieces
    2 onions, unpeeled, quartered
    2 carrots, roughly chopped
    2 celery sticks, with leaves if
        possible, roughly chopped
    2 tomatoes, coarsely chopped
    4.5 litres/7½ pints/18¾ cups
        cold water
    a handful of parsley stalks
    few sprigs of fresh thyme or
        5ml/1 tsp dried
    2 bay leaves
    10 black peppercorns, lightly crushed

3 Transfer the bones and roasted vegetables to a stockpot or large pan. Spoon off the fat from the roasting pan. Add a little of the water to the roasting pan or casserole and bring to the boil on top of the stove, stirring well to scrape up any browned bits. Pour this liquid into the stockpot.

4 Add the remaining water to the pot. Bring just to the boil, skimming frequently to remove all the foam from the surface. Add the parsley, thyme, bay leaves and peppercorns.

5 Partly cover the stockpot and simmer the beef stock for 4–6 hours. The bones and vegetables should always be covered with enough liquid, so top up with a little boiling water from time to time if necessary.

6 Strain the stock through a colander, then skim as much fat as possible from the surface. If possible, cool the stock and then refrigerate it; the fat will rise to the top and set in a layer that can be removed easily.

Stock for Chinese cooking

This stock is an excellent basis for soup-making, and is ideal for Asian soups. Refrigerate the stock when cool – it will keep for up to 4 days. Alternatively, it can be frozen in small containers for up to 3 months and defrosted when required.

MAKES 2.5 LITRES/4½ PINTS/11 CUPS

INGREDIENTS
    675g/1½lb chicken portions
    675g/1½lb pork spareribs
    3.75 litres/6½ pints/15 cups
        cold water
    3–4 pieces fresh root ginger,
        unpeeled, crushed
    3–4 spring onions (scallions),
        each tied into a knot
    45–60ml/3–4 tbsp Chinese rice wine
        or dry sherry

Below: Braised Cabbage Soup with Beef and Horseradish Cream.

1 Preheat the oven to 230°C/450°F/ Gas 8. Put the bones in a roasting pan or casserole dish and roast, turning occasionally, for 30 minutes, until they start to brown.

2 Add the onions, carrots, celery and tomatoes and baste with the fat in the pan. Roast for a further 20–30 minutes until the bones are well browned. Stir and baste occasionally.

Above: Kombu seaweed is used in Japanese stocks.

1 Use a sharp knife to trim off any excess fat from the chicken and spareribs, then chop them into small pieces.

3 Bring the stock to the boil and skim off the froth. Reduce the heat and simmer over a gentle heat, uncovered, for 2–3 hours.

Stock for Japanese cooking

Dashi is the stock that gives the characteristically Japanese flavour to many dishes. Known as Ichiban-dashi, it is used for delicately flavoured dishes, including soups. Of course instant stock is available in all Japanese supermarkets, either in granule form, in concentrate or even in a tea-bag style. Follow the instructions on the packet.

MAKES ABOUT 800ML/1⅓ PINTS/3½ CUPS

INGREDIENTS
  10g/¼ oz dried kombu seaweed
  10–15g/¼ –½ oz dried bonito flakes

2 Place the chicken and sparerib pieces into a stockpot or large pan with the cold water. Add the crushed fresh root ginger and the spring onions tied in knots.

4 Strain the stock, discarding the pork, chicken, ginger and spring onion knots. Add the Chinese rice wine or dry sherry and return to the boil. Simmer for 2–3 minutes.

1 Wipe the kombu seaweed with a damp cloth and cut two slits in it with scissors, so that it flavours the stock effectively.

2 Soak the kombu in 900ml/1½ pints/3¾ cups cold water for 30–60 minutes.

3 Heat the kombu in its soaking water in a pan over a moderate heat. Just before the water boils, remove the seaweed. Add the bonito flakes and bring to the boil over a high heat, then remove the pan from the heat.

4 Leave the stock until all the bonito flakes have sunk to the bottom of the pan. Line a sieve (strainer) with kitchen paper or muslin (cheesecloth) and place it over a large mixing bowl, then gently strain the stock. Use as required or cool and refrigerate for up to 2 days.

Left: A Chinese-style soup made with home-made Chinese stock.

THICKENING SOUPS

Many soups do not need any thickening ingredients added, as the puréed soup is thick enough. Vegetables such as potatoes, onions and carrots, once cooked and puréed in a soup, will often help to thicken the soup sufficiently. If your soup does need thickening, try one of the methods below.

Beurre manié

This smooth flour and butter paste is used to thicken soups at the end of the cooking time. Equal quantities of plain flour and butter are kneaded together, then a small knob of the paste is added to the soup and whisked until it is fully incorporated before adding the next. The soup is brought to the boil and simmered for about 1 minute, until thickened and to avoid a raw flour flavour. A similarly useful paste can be made using flour and cream.

Cream

Double (heavy) cream can be used to thicken a fine soup. It is added towards the end of cooking, then the soup is brought to the boil and simmered gently for a few minutes until the soup is slightly reduced and thickened.

Ground almonds

Ground almonds can be used as a thickener in soups, and they add extra flavour as well as texture to the soup. The delicate flavour of almonds blends particularly well with fish- and chicken-based soups. However, ground almonds

Below: Making beurre manié.

Above: Adding ground almonds.

do not thicken soup in the same way that ingredients such as flour and cornflour (cornstarch) do, to make a thick, smooth soup. Instead they add body, texture, flavour and richness.

Cornflour or arrowroot

These fine flours are mixed with a little cold water (about double the volume of the dry ingredient) to make a smooth, thick, but runny paste. Stir the paste into the hot soup and simmer, stirring, until thickened. Cornflour (cornstarch) takes about 3 minutes to thicken completely and lose its raw flavour. Arrowroot achieves maximum thickness on boiling and tends to become slightly thinner if it is allowed to simmer for any length of time, so this is usually

Below: Mixing cornflour with water.

Above: Adding breadcrumbs.

avoided. Cornflour gives an opaque result, but arrowroot becomes clear when it boils, so it is useful for thickening clear liquids and soups.

Breadcrumbs

The more rustic approach is to use fresh white breadcrumbs to thicken soup. They can be toasted in oil before being stirred into a simmering soup, or added directly to a finished dish.

Eggs

Beaten eggs, egg yolks, or a mixture of eggs and a little cream can be used to enrich and slightly thicken a smooth soup. Whisk into the hot soup, but do not allow it to boil once they are added or it will curdle.

Below: Whisking in beaten eggs.

GARNISHES

Garnishes should look attractive, be edible, complement the flavour of the soup and add that final finishing touch. Some typical ones include sprinkling the soup with chopped herbs or stirring them into it just before serving, or topping thick, rich soups with a fresh herb sprig or two for an attractive garnish. Croûtons, made from either plain or flavoured bread, add appeal and crunch to many soups. Below are some typical garnishes, as well as a few tips for some more unusual ones.

Swirled cream

A swirl of cream is the classic finish for many soups, such as a smooth tomato soup and Vichyssoise. This garnish gives a professional finish to your soup, although the technique is simplicity itself.

1 Transfer the cream into a jug with a good pouring lip. Pour a swirl on to the surface of each bowl of soup.

2 Draw the tip of a fine skewer quickly backwards and forwards through the cream to create a delicate pattern. Serve the soup immediately.

Above: Frying croûtes in oil.

Herbs

Adding a handful of chopped fresh herbs to a bowl of soup just before serving can make a good soup look great. A bundle of chives makes a dainty garnish. Cut 5–6 chives to about 6cm/2½in long and tie them in a bundle using another length of chive.

Fried croûtons

This classic garnish adds texture as well as flavour to soups. To make croûtons, cut bread into small cubes and fry in a little oil. Toss the bread continuously so that the cubes are golden all over, then drain on kitchen paper.

Grilled croûtes

Topped with grilled cheese, croûtes not only look good, but taste great in all sorts of soups. To make them, toast small slices of baguette on both sides. If you like, you can rub the toast with a cut clove of garlic, then top with grated Cheddar or Parmesan, a crumbled blue cheese, such as Stilton, or a slice of goat's (chèvre) cheese. Grill (broil) briefly until the cheese is beginning to melt.

Crisp-fried shallots

Finely sliced shallots make a quick garnish for smooth lentil and vegetable soups. Cut them crossways into rings, then shallow fry in hot oil until crisp.

Above: Making vegetable julienne.

Crisps

Try shop-bought thick-cut crisps (US potato chips) or tortilla chips; alternatively, make your own vegetable crisps (chips). Wafer-thin slices of fresh raw beetroot (beet), pumpkin and parsnip can all be deep-fried in hot oil for a few moments to produce delicious and unusual crisps.

Vegetable julienne

An effective way of preparing ingredients for adding a splash of colour to soup is to cut them into julienne strips. Shreds of spring onions (scallions) or red and green chillies make great garnishes.

Below: Diced tomatoes, onions and coriander make an attractive garnish.

CHILLED SOUPS

What could be a nicer way of starting a meal on a warm summer evening than a bowl of chilled soup, served al fresco *with a bottle of chilled white wine? In this section there are traditional favourites, such as French Vichyssoise and Spanish Gazpacho, as well as more unusual soups, such as Chilled Garlic and Almond Soup with Grapes, and Beetroot Soup with Mascarpone Brioche. Enjoy fresh summer herbs at their best in Melon and Basil Soup, or Sorrel, Spinach and Dill Soup.*

VICHYSSOISE

THIS CLASSIC CHILLED SUMMER SOUP WAS FIRST CREATED IN THE 1920S BY LOUIS DIAT, CHEF AT THE NEW YORK RITZ-CARLTON. HE NAMED IT AFTER VICHY, NEAR HIS HOME IN FRANCE.

3 Stir in the stock or water, 5ml/1 tsp salt and pepper to taste. Bring to the boil, then reduce the heat and partly cover the pan. Simmer for 15 minutes, or until the potatoes are soft.

4 Cool, then process the soup until smooth in a blender or food processor. Strain the soup into a bowl and stir in the cream. Taste and adjust the seasoning and add a little iced water if the consistency of the soup seems too thick.

5 Chill the soup for at least 4 hours or until very cold. Taste the chilled soup for seasoning and add a squeeze of lemon juice, if required. Pour the soup into bowls and sprinkle with chopped chives. Serve immediately.

SERVES 4–6

INGREDIENTS
  50g/2oz/¼ cup unsalted butter
  450g/1lb leeks, white parts only,
    thinly sliced
  3 large shallots, sliced
  250g/9oz floury potatoes (such as
    King Edward or Maris Piper), peeled
    and cut into chunks
  1 litre/1¾ pints/4 cups light chicken
    stock or water
  300ml/½ pint/1¼ cups double
    (heavy) cream
  iced water (optional)
  a little lemon juice (optional)
  salt and ground black pepper
  chopped fresh chives,
    to garnish

1 Melt the butter in a heavy-based pan and cook the leeks and shallots gently, covered, for 15–20 minutes, until soft but not browned.

2 Add the potatoes and cook, uncovered, for a few minutes.

VARIATIONS
• **Potage Bonne Femme** For this hot leek and potato soup, use 1 chopped onion instead of the shallots and 450g/1lb potatoes. Halve the quantity of double (heavy) cream and reheat the puréed soup, adding a little milk if the soup seems very thick. Deep-fried shredded leek may be used to garnish the soup, instead of chopped fresh chives.
• **Chilled Leek and Sorrel or Watercress Soup** Add about 50g/2oz/1 cup shredded sorrel to the soup at the end of cooking. Finish and chill as in the main recipe, then serve the soup garnished with a little pile of finely shredded sorrel. The same quantity of watercress can be used in the same way.

Energy 547kcal/2260kJ; Protein 4.6g; Carbohydrate 17.7g, of which sugars 6.8g; Fat 51.4g, of which saturates 31.7g; Cholesterol 129mg; Calcium 79mg; Fibre 3.6g; Sodium 103mg.

CUCUMBER AND SALMON SOUP WITH SALSA

CHARRED SALMON BRINGS A HINT OF HEAT TO THE REFRESHING FLAVOURS OF THIS CHILLED SOUP.
GOOD-LOOKING AND BEAUTIFULLY LIGHT, IT MAKES THE PERFECT OPENER FOR AN AL FRESCO MEAL.

SERVES 4

INGREDIENTS

 3 medium cucumbers
 300ml/½ pint/1¼ cups Greek
   (US strained plain) yogurt
 250ml/8fl oz/1 cup vegetable
   stock, chilled
 120ml/4fl oz/½ cup crème fraîche
 15ml/1 tbsp chopped fresh chervil
 15ml/1 tbsp chopped fresh chives
 15ml/1 tbsp chopped fresh
   flat leaf parsley
 1 small fresh red chilli, seeded and
   very finely chopped
 a little oil, for brushing
 225g/8oz salmon fillet, skinned and
   cut into eight thin slices
 salt and ground black pepper
 fresh chervil or chives, to garnish

4 Brush a griddle or frying pan with oil and heat until very hot. Add the salmon slices and sear them for 1–2 minutes, then turn over carefully and sear the other side until tender and charred.

5 Ladle the chilled soup into soup bowls. Top each portion with two slices of salmon, then pile a portion of salsa in the centre. Garnish with the chervil or chives and serve.

1 Peel two of the cucumbers and halve them lengthways. Scoop out and discard the seeds, then roughly chop the flesh. Purée the chopped flesh in a food processor or blender.

2 Add the yogurt, stock, crème fraîche, chervil, chives and seasoning, and process until smooth. Pour the mixture into a bowl, cover and chill.

3 Peel, halve and seed the remaining cucumber. Cut the flesh into small neat dice. Mix with the chopped parsley and chilli in a bowl. Cover the salsa and chill until required.

Energy 314kcal/1299kJ; Protein 17.8g; Carbohydrate 3.9g, of which sugars 3.7g; Fat 26.1g, of which saturates 13.1g; Cholesterol 62mg; Calcium 183mg; Fibre 1.2g; Sodium 92mg.

CHILLED COCONUT SOUP

REFRESHING, COOLING AND NOT TOO FILLING, THIS SOUP IS THE PERFECT ANTIDOTE TO HOT WEATHER. EXCELLENT FOR SERVING AFTER AN APPETIZER, IT WILL REFRESH THE PALATE.

SERVES 6

INGREDIENTS

1.2 litres/2 pints/5 cups milk
225g/8oz/2⅔ cups desiccated
   (dry unsweetened shredded)
   coconut
400ml/14fl oz/1⅔ cups
   coconut milk
400ml/14fl oz/1⅔ cups
   chicken stock
200ml/7fl oz/scant 1 cup double
   (heavy) cream
2.5ml/½ tsp salt
2.5ml/½ tsp ground white
   pepper
5ml/1 tsp caster (superfine) sugar
small bunch of fresh coriander
   (cilantro)

1 Pour the milk into a large pan. Bring it to the boil, stir in the coconut, lower the heat and allow to simmer for 30 minutes. Spoon the mixture into a food processor and process until smooth. This may take a while – up to 5 minutes – so pause frequently and scrape down the sides of the bowl.

2 Rinse the pan to remove any coconut that remains, pour in the processed mixture and add the coconut milk. Stir in the chicken stock (home-made, if possible, which gives a better flavour than a stock [bouillon] cube), cream, salt, pepper and sugar. Bring to the boil, stirring occasionally, then lower the heat and cook for 10 minutes.

3 Reserve a few coriander leaves to garnish, then chop the rest finely and stir into the soup. Pour the soup into a large bowl, let it cool, then cover and put into the refrigerator until chilled. Just before serving, taste the soup and adjust the seasoning, as chilling will alter the taste. Serve in chilled bowls, garnished with the coriander leaves.

Energy 499kcal/2068kJ; Protein 9.6g; Carbohydrate 15.6g, of which sugars 15.6g; Fat 44.8g, of which saturates 33.4g; Cholesterol 58mg; Calcium 284mg; Fibre 5.1g; Sodium 341mg.

AVOCADO AND LIME SOUP WITH A GREEN CHILLI SALSA

INSPIRED BY GUACAMOLE, THE POPULAR AVOCADO DIP, THIS CREAMY SOUP RELIES ON GOOD-QUALITY RIPE AVOCADOS FOR ITS FLAVOUR AND COLOUR.

SERVES 4

INGREDIENTS

3 ripe avocados
juice of 1½ limes
1 garlic clove, crushed
handful of ice cubes
400ml/14fl oz/1⅔ cups vegetable
  stock, chilled
400ml/14fl oz/1⅔ cups milk, chilled
150ml/¼ pint/⅔ cup soured
  cream, chilled
few drops of Tabasco sauce
salt and ground black pepper
fresh coriander (cilantro) leaves,
  to garnish
extra virgin olive oil, to serve
For the salsa
4 tomatoes, peeled, seeded and
  finely diced
2 spring onions (scallions), finely
  chopped
1 green chilli, seeded and finely
  chopped
15ml/1 tbsp chopped fresh
  coriander leaves
juice of ½ lime

1 Prepare the salsa first. Mix all the ingredients together and season well. Chill in the refrigerator until required.

2 Halve the avocados and remove the stones (pits). Scoop the flesh out of the avocado skins using a spoon or melon baller and place in a food processor or blender. Add the lime juice, garlic, ice cubes and 150ml/¼ pint/⅔ cup of the chilled vegetable stock.

3 Process the soup until smooth. Pour into a large bowl and stir in the remaining vegetable stock, chilled milk, soured cream and Tabasco sauce. Season to taste.

COOK'S TIPS
• It is easy to remove the stone (pit) from an avocado. Halve the avocado and simply tap the stone firmly with the edge of a large knife. Twist the knife gently and the stone will pop out.
• This soup may discolour if left standing for too long, but the flavour will not be spoilt. Give the soup a quick whisk just before serving.

4 Ladle the soup into bowls or glasses and spoon a little salsa on top. Add a splash of olive oil to each portion and garnish with fresh coriander leaves. Serve immediately.

Energy 353kcal/1463kJ; Protein 7.3g; Carbohydrate 11.1g, of which sugars 9.6g; Fat 31.2g, of which saturates 10.5g; Cholesterol 28mg; Calcium 175mg; Fibre 4.8g; Sodium 73mg.

CHILLED GARLIC AND ALMOND SOUP WITH GRAPES

THIS CREAMY CHILLED SUMMER SOUP IS BASED ON AN ANCIENT MOORISH RECIPE FROM ANDALUSIA IN SOUTHERN SPAIN. ALMONDS AND PINE NUTS ARE TYPICAL INGREDIENTS OF THIS REGION.

SERVES 6

INGREDIENTS
75g/3oz/¾ cup blanched almonds
50g/2oz/½ cup pine nuts
6 large garlic cloves, peeled
200g/7oz good-quality day-old bread, crusts removed
900ml–1 litre/1½–1¾ pints/3¾–4 cups still mineral water, chilled
120ml/4fl oz/½ cup extra virgin olive oil, plus extra to serve
15ml/1 tbsp sherry vinegar
30–45ml/2–3 tbsp dry sherry
250g/9oz grapes, peeled, halved and seeded
salt and ground white pepper
ice cubes and chopped fresh chives, to garnish

1 Roast the almonds and pine nuts together in a dry pan over a moderate heat until they are very lightly browned. Cool, then grind to a powder.

2 Blanch the garlic in boiling water for 3 minutes. Drain and rinse.

3 Soak the bread in 300ml/½ pint/1¼ cups of the water for 10 minutes, then squeeze dry. Process the garlic, bread, nuts and 5ml/1 tsp salt in a food processor or blender until they form a paste.

4 Gradually blend in the olive oil and sherry vinegar, followed by sufficient water to make a smooth soup with a creamy consistency.

5 Stir in 30ml/2 tbsp of the sherry. Adjust the seasoning and add more dry sherry to taste. Chill for at least 3 hours, then adjust the seasoning again and stir in a little more chilled water if the soup has thickened. Reserve a few grapes for the garnish and stir the remainder into the soup.

6 Ladle the soup into bowls (glass bowls look particularly good) and garnish with ice cubes, the reserved grapes and chopped fresh chives. Serve with additional extra virgin olive oil to drizzle over the soup to taste just before it is eaten.

COOK'S TIPS
• Toasting the nuts slightly accentuates their flavour, but you can omit this step if you prefer a paler soup.
• Blanching the garlic softens its flavour.

Energy 380kcal/1582kJ; Protein 7g; Carbohydrate 26.1g, of which sugars 8.4g; Fat 27.3g, of which saturates 3g; Cholesterol 0mg; Calcium 83mg; Fibre 2.2g; Sodium 150mg.

ROASTED PEPPER SOUP
WITH PARMESAN TOAST

THE SECRET OF THIS SOUP IS TO SERVE IT JUST COLD, NOT OVER-CHILLED, TOPPED WITH HOT PARMESAN TOAST DRIPPING WITH CHEESE AND MELTED BUTTER.

SERVES 4

INGREDIENTS

1 onion, quartered
4 garlic cloves, unpeeled
2 red (bell) peppers, seeded
  and quartered
2 yellow (bell) peppers, seeded
  and quartered
30–45ml/2–3 tbsp olive oil
grated rind and juice of 1 orange
200g/7oz can chopped tomatoes
600ml/1 pint/2½ cups cold water
salt and ground black pepper
30ml/2 tbsp chopped fresh chives,
  to garnish (optional)
For the hot Parmesan toast
1 medium baguette
50g/2oz/¼ cup butter

1 Preheat the oven to 200°C/400°F/ Gas 6. Put the onion, garlic and peppers in a roasting tin (pan). Drizzle the oil over the vegetables and mix well, then turn the pieces of pepper skin sides up. Roast for 25–30 minutes, until slightly charred, then allow to cool slightly.

2 Squeeze the garlic flesh out of the skins into a food processor or blender. Add the roasted vegetables, orange rind and juice, tomatoes and water. Process until smooth.

COOK'S TIP
If you don't have a champignon, then use the bottom of a large ladle or the back of a wooden spoon instead.

3 Press the mixture through a sieve into a bowl using a champignon. Season well and chill for 30 minutes.

4 Make the Parmesan toasts when you are ready to serve the soup. Preheat the grill (broiler) to high. Tear the baguette in half lengthways, then tear or cut it across to give four large pieces. Spread the pieces of bread with butter.

5 Pare most of the Parmesan into thin slices or shavings using a swivel-bladed vegetable knife or a small paring knife, then finely grate the remainder.

6 Arrange the sliced Parmesan on the toasts, then dredge with the grated cheese. Transfer the cheese-topped baguette pieces to a large baking sheet or grill (broiler) rack and toast under the grill for a few minutes until the topping is well browned.

7 Ladle the chilled soup into large, shallow bowls and sprinkle with chopped fresh chives, if using, and plenty of freshly ground black pepper.

8 Serve the craggy hot Parmesan toast with the chilled soup.

Energy 124kcal/516kJ; Protein 2.4g; Carbohydrate 15g, of which sugars 14.2g; Fat 6.4g, of which saturates 1g; Cholesterol 0mg; Calcium 23mg; Fibre 3.5g; Sodium 13mg.

CHILLED CUCUMBER AND PRAWN SOUP

IF YOU'VE NEVER SERVED A CHILLED SOUP BEFORE, THIS IS THE ONE TO TRY. DELICIOUS AND LIGHT, IT'S THE PERFECT WAY TO CELEBRATE SUMMER.

2 Stir in the milk, bring almost to boiling point, then lower the heat and simmer for 5 minutes. Tip the soup into a blender or food processor and purée until very smooth. Season to taste.

3 Pour the soup into a large bowl and leave to cool. When cool, stir in the prawns, chopped herbs and cream. Cover, transfer to the refrigerator and chill for at least 2 hours.

4 To serve, ladle the soup into four individual bowls, top each portion with a dollop of crème fraîche, if using, and place a prawn over the edge of each dish. Scatter over a little extra chopped dill and tuck two or three chives under the prawns on the edge of the bowls to garnish. Serve at once.

SERVES 4

INGREDIENTS
  25g/1oz/2 tbsp butter
  2 shallots, finely chopped
  2 garlic cloves, crushed
  1 cucumber, peeled, seeded
    and diced
  300ml/½ pint/1¼ cups milk
  225g/8oz cooked peeled prawns
    (shrimp)
  15ml/1 tbsp each finely chopped
    fresh mint, dill, chives and chervil
  300ml/½ pint/1¼ cups
    whipping cream
  salt and ground white pepper
For the garnish
  30ml/2 tbsp crème fraîche (optional)
  4 large, cooked prawns, peeled with
    tail intact
  fresh dill and chives

1 Melt the butter in a pan and cook the shallots and garlic over a low heat until soft but not coloured. Add the cucumber and cook gently, stirring frequently, until tender.

COOK'S TIP
If you prefer hot soup, reheat it gently until hot but not boiling. Do not boil, or the delicate flavour will be spoilt.

VARIATION
If you like, you can use other cooked shellfish in place of the peeled prawns (shrimp) – try fresh, frozen or canned crab meat or cooked, flaked salmon.

Energy 412kcal/1704kJ; Protein 14.2g; Carbohydrate 6g, of which sugars 6g; Fat 37g, of which saturates 23g; Cholesterol 206mg; Calcium 184mg; Fibre 0.2g; Sodium 197mg.

HUNGARIAN CHERRY SOUP

SOUPS MADE FROM SEASONAL FRUITS ARE A FAVOURITE CENTRAL EUROPEAN TREAT, AND CHERRY SOUP IS ONE OF THE GLORIES OF THE HUNGARIAN TABLE. IT IS OFTEN SERVED AT THE START OF A DAIRY MEAL, SUCH AS AT THE FESTIVAL OF SHAVUOT WHEN DAIRY FOODS ARE TRADITIONALLY FEASTED UPON, AND IS DELICIOUS SERVED WITH AN EXTRA SPOONFUL OR TWO OF SOUR CREAM.

SERVES 6

INGREDIENTS

1kg/2¼lb fresh, frozen or canned
  sour cherries, such as Morello or
  Montmorency, pitted
250ml/8fl oz/1 cup water
175–250g/6–9oz/about 1 cup sugar,
  to taste
1–2 cinnamon sticks, each about
  5cm/2in long
750ml/1¼ pints/3 cups dry red wine
5ml/1 tsp almond essence (extract),
  or to taste
250ml/8fl oz/1 cup single
  (light) cream
250ml/8fl oz/1 cup sour cream or
  crème fraîche

1 Put the pitted cherries, water, sugar, cinnamon and wine in a large pan. Bring to the boil, reduce the heat and simmer for 20–30 minutes, until the cherries are tender. Remove from the heat and add the almond essence.

2 In a bowl, stir a few tablespoons of single cream into the sour cream or crème fraîche to thin it down, then stir in the rest until the mixture is smooth. Stir the mixture into the cherry soup, then chill until ready to serve.

Energy 518kcal/2163kJ; Protein 4.1g; Carbohydrate 51.8g, of which sugars 51.7g; Fat 24.8g, of which saturates 16.4g; Cholesterol 70mg; Calcium 107mg; Fibre 1.5g; Sodium 34mg.

PEA SOUP WITH PROSCIUTTO

THIS QUICK AND SIMPLE SOUP IS DELICIOUSLY CREAMY, BUT LIGHT AND REFRESHING.
USING FROZEN PEAS CUTS OUT THE LABOUR INVOLVED IN SHELLING FRESH PEAS, WITHOUT
COMPROMISING THE FLAVOUR.

SERVES 6

INGREDIENTS
  25g/1oz/2 tbsp butter
  1 leek, sliced
  1 garlic clove, crushed
  450g/1lb/4 cups frozen petits pois
    (baby peas)
  1.2 litres/2 pints/5 cups
    vegetable stock
  small bunch of fresh chives,
    coarsely chopped
  300ml/½ pint/1¼ cups double
    (heavy) cream
  90ml/6 tbsp Greek (US strained
    plain) yogurt
  4 slices prosciutto, roughly chopped
  salt and ground black pepper
  fresh chives, to garnish

1 Melt the butter in a pan. Add the leek and garlic, cover and cook gently for 4–5 minutes, until softened.

2 Stir in the petits pois, vegetable stock and chives. Bring slowly to the boil, then simmer for 5 minutes. Set aside to cool slightly.

3 Process the soup in a food processor or blender until smooth. Pour into a bowl, stir in the cream and season to taste with salt and black pepper. Chill in the refrigerator for at least 2 hours.

4 When ready to serve, ladle the soup into bowls and add a spoonful of Greek yogurt to the centre of each bowl. Scatter the chopped prosciutto over the top of the soup and garnish with chives before serving.

COOK'S TIP
For a clever and attractive garnish, cut five lengths of chive to about 6cm/2½in long, then use another chive to tie them together. Lay a bundle of chives on top of each bowl of soup.

Energy 378kcal/1561kJ; Protein 9.7g; Carbohydrate 10.6g, of which sugars 3.7g; Fat 33.5g, of which saturates 20g; Cholesterol 85mg; Calcium 71mg; Fibre 4.2g; Sodium 198mg.

GAZPACHO WITH AVOCADO SALSA

*TOMATOES, CUCUMBER AND PEPPERS FORM THE BASIS OF THIS CLASSIC CHILLED SOUP. ADD A
SPOONFUL OF CHUNKY, FRESH AVOCADO SALSA AND A SCATTERING OF CROÛTONS, AND SERVE FOR
A LIGHT LUNCH OR SIMPLE SUPPER ON A WARM SUMMER DAY.*

SERVES 4

INGREDIENTS
  2 slices day-old white bread, cubed
  600ml/1 pint/2½ cups chilled water
  1kg/2¼lb fresh tomatoes
  1 cucumber
  1 red (bell) pepper, halved, seeded
    and chopped
  1 fresh green chilli, seeded
    and chopped
  2 garlic cloves, chopped
  30ml/2 tbsp extra virgin olive oil
  juice of 1 lime and 1 lemon
  a few drops of Tabasco sauce
  salt and ground black pepper
  8 ice cubes, to garnish
  a handful of basil leaves, to garnish
For the croûtons
  2 slices day-old bread,
    crusts removed
  1 garlic clove, halved
  15ml/1 tbsp olive oil
For the avocado salsa
  1 ripe avocado
  5ml/1 tsp lemon juice
  2.5cm/1in piece cucumber, diced
  ½ red chilli, seeded and
    finely chopped

1 Place the bread in a large bowl and pour over 150ml/¼pint/⅔ cup of the water. Leave to soak for 5 minutes.

2 Meanwhile, place the tomatoes in a bowl and cover with boiling water. Leave for 30 seconds, then peel off the skin, remove the seeds and finely chop the flesh.

3 Thinly peel the cucumber, cut it in half lengthways and scoop out the seeds with a teaspoon. Discard the inner part and chop the flesh.

4 Place the bread, tomatoes, cucumber, red pepper, chilli, garlic, olive oil, citrus juices and Tabasco in a food processor or blender with the remaining 450ml/¾ pint/scant 2 cups chilled water and blend until well combined but still chunky. Season to taste and chill for 2–3 hours.

5 To make the croûtons, rub the slices of bread with the garlic clove. Cut the bread into cubes and place in a plastic bag with the olive oil. Seal the bag and shake until the bread cubes are coated with the oil.

6 Heat a large non-stick frying pan and fry the croûtons over a medium heat until crisp and golden.

7 Just before serving, make the avocado salsa. Halve the avocado, remove the stone (pit), then peel and dice. Toss the avocado in the lemon juice to prevent it from browning, then place it in a serving bowl and add the cucumber and chilli. Mix well.

8 Ladle the soup into four chilled bowls and add a couple of ice cubes to each. Top each portion with a good spoonful of avocado salsa. Garnish with the basil and sprinkle the croûtons over the top of the salsa.

Energy 278kcal/1166kJ; Protein 6.4g; Carbohydrate 32.2g, of which sugars 12.1g; Fat 14.6g, of which saturates 2.6g; Cholesterol 0mg; Calcium 80mg; Fibre 5.1g; Sodium 209mg.

CHILLED AVOCADO SOUP WITH CUMIN

ANDALUSIA IS HOME TO BOTH AVOCADOS AND GAZPACHO, SO IT IS NOT SURPRISING THAT THIS
CHILLED AVOCADO SOUP, WHICH IS ALSO KNOWN AS GREEN GAZPACHO, WAS INVENTED THERE.
IN SPAIN, THIS DELICIOUSLY MILD, CREAMY SOUP IS KNOWN AS SOPA DE AGUACATE.

SERVES 4

INGREDIENTS

   3 ripe avocados
   1 bunch spring onions (scallions),
     white parts only, trimmed and
     roughly chopped
   2 garlic cloves, chopped
   juice of 1 lemon
   1.5ml/¼ tsp ground cumin
   1.5ml/¼ tsp paprika
   450ml/¾ pint/scant 2 cups fresh
     chicken stock, cooled and all
     fat skimmed off
   300ml/½ pint/1¼ cups iced water
   salt and ground black pepper
   roughly chopped fresh flat leaf
     parsley, to garnish

1 Starting half a day ahead, put the flesh of one avocado in a food processor or blender. Add the spring onions, garlic and lemon juice and purée until smooth. Add the second avocado and purée, then the third, with the spices and seasoning. Purée until smooth.

2 Gradually add the chicken stock. Pour the soup into a metal bowl and chill.

3 To serve, stir in the iced water, then season to taste with plenty of salt and black pepper. Garnish with chopped parsley and serve immediately.

Energy 242kcal/1001kJ; Protein 2.8g; Carbohydrate 3g, of which sugars 1.3g; Fat 24.2g, of which saturates 5.2g; Cholesterol 0mg; Calcium 22mg; Fibre 4.6g; Sodium 9mg.

BEETROOT SOUP WITH MASCARPONE BRIOCHE

ALTHOUGH IT SOUNDS QUITE COMPLEX, THIS SOUP IS ACTUALLY RIDICULOUSLY EASY TO MAKE. THE SWEET, EARTHY FLAVOUR OF FRESH, COOKED BEETROOT IS COMBINED WITH ZESTY ORANGE AND TART CRANBERRY JUICE.

SERVES 4

INGREDIENTS

350g/12oz cooked beetroot (beet), roughly chopped
grated rind and juice of 1 orange
600ml/1 pint/2½ cups unsweetened cranberry juice
450ml/¾ pint/scant 2 cups Greek (US strained plain) yogurt
a little Tabasco sauce
4 slices brioche
60ml/4 tbsp mascarpone
salt and ground black pepper
fresh mint sprigs and cooked cranberries, to garnish

2 Press the purée through a sieve (strainer) into a clean bowl. Stir in the remaining cranberry juice and the Tabasco sauce. Season with salt and black pepper to taste. Chill the soup in the refrigerator for at least 2 hours.

3 Preheat the grill (broiler). Using a large pastry cutter, stamp a round out of each slice of brioche.

COOK'S TIP
If the combination of cranberry and orange is a little tart, add a pinch or two of caster (superfine) sugar to the soup, according to taste.

4 Arrange the brioche rounds on a grill (broiler) rack and toast until golden. Ladle the soup into bowls and top each with brioche and mascarpone. Garnish with mint and cranberries.

1 Purée the beetroot with the orange rind and juice, half the cranberry juice and the yogurt in a food processor or blender until smooth.

Energy 404kcal/1695kJ; Protein 13.5g; Carbohydrate 53.5g, of which sugars 17.2g; Fat 16.6g, of which saturates 7.2g; Cholesterol 13mg; Calcium 237mg; Fibre 1.7g; Sodium 264mg.

SPICED MANGO SOUP WITH YOGURT

THIS DELICIOUS, LIGHT SOUP COMES FROM CHUTNEY MARY'S, AN ANGLO-INDIAN RESTAURANT IN LONDON. IT IS BEST WHEN SERVED LIGHTLY CHILLED.

SERVES 4

INGREDIENTS
  2 ripe mangoes
  15ml/1 tbsp gram flour
  120ml/4fl oz/½ cup natural (plain)
    yogurt
  900ml/1½ pints/3¾ cups cold water
  2.5ml/½ tsp grated fresh root ginger
  2 red chillies, seeded and finely
    chopped
  30ml/2 tbsp olive oil
  2.5ml/½ tsp mustard seeds
  2.5ml/½ tsp cumin seeds
  8 curry leaves
  salt and ground black pepper
  fresh mint leaves, shredded,
    to garnish
  natural yogurt, to serve

1 Peel the mangoes, remove the stones and cut the flesh into chunks. Purée in a food processor or blender until smooth.

2 Pour into a pan and stir in the gram flour, yogurt, water, ginger and chillies. Bring to the boil, stirring occasionally. Simmer for 4–5 minutes until thickened slightly, then set aside off the heat.

3 Heat the oil in a frying pan. Add the mustard seeds and cook for a few seconds until they begin to pop, then add the cumin seeds.

4 Add the curry leaves and then cook for 5 minutes. Stir the spice mixture into the soup, return it to the heat and cook for 10 minutes.

5 Press through a mouli-legume or a sieve (strainer), if you like, then season to taste. Leave the soup to cool completely, then chill for at least 1 hour.

6 Ladle the soup into bowls, and top each with a dollop of yogurt. Garnish with shredded mint leaves and serve.

Energy 121kcal/508kJ; Protein 2.8g; Carbohydrate 14.7g, of which sugars 12.7g; Fat 6.2g, of which saturates 1g; Cholesterol 0mg; Calcium 73mg; Fibre 2.4g; Sodium 28mg.

ICED MELON SOUP <u>WITH</u> SORBET

*USE DIFFERENT MELONS FOR THE COOL SOUP AND ICE SORBET TO CREATE A SUBTLE CONTRAST
IN FLAVOUR AND COLOUR. TRY A COMBINATION OF CHARENTAIS, OGEN OR CANTALOUPE.*

SERVES 6–8

INGREDIENTS
   2.25kg/5–5¼lb very ripe melon
   45ml/3 tbsp orange juice
   30ml/2 tbsp lemon juice
   mint leaves, to garnish
For the sorbet (sherbet)
   25g/1oz/2 tbsp granulated
     sugar
   120ml/4fl oz/½ cup water
   2.25kg/5–5¼lb very ripe melon
   juice of 2 limes
   30ml/2 tbsp chopped fresh mint

1 To make the melon and mint sorbet, put the sugar and water into a pan and heat gently until the sugar dissolves. Bring to the boil and simmer for 4–5 minutes, then remove from the heat and leave to cool.

2 Halve the melon. Scrape out the seeds, then scoop out the flesh. Purée in a food processor or blender with the cooled syrup and lime juice.

3 Stir in the mint and pour the melon mixture into an ice-cream maker. Churn, following the manufacturer's instructions, or until the sorbet is smooth and firm. Alternatively, pour the mixture into a suitable container and freeze until icy around the edges. Transfer to a food processor or blender and process until smooth.

4 Repeat the freezing and processing two or three times or until the mixture is smooth and holding its shape, then freeze until firm.

5 To make the chilled melon soup, prepare the melon as in step 2 and purée it in a food processor or blender. Pour the purée into a bowl and stir in the orange and lemon juice. Place the soup in the refrigerator for 30–40 minutes, but do not chill it for too long as this will dull its flavour.

6 Ladle the soup into bowls and add a large scoop of the melon and mint sorbet to each. Garnish with mint leaves and serve at once.

Energy 117kcal/494kJ; Protein 3.1g; Carbohydrate 26g, of which sugars 26g; Fat 0.8g, of which saturates 0g; Cholesterol 0mg; Calcium 101mg; Fibre 5.3g; Sodium 39mg.

MELON AND BASIL SOUP

THIS IS A DELICIOUSLY REFRESHING CHILLED FRUIT SOUP, JUST RIGHT FOR A SUMMER LUNCH PARTY. THE SHREDDED BASIL COMPLEMENTS THE TASTE OF THE MELON.

SERVES 4–6

INGREDIENTS

2 Charentais or rock melons
75g/3oz/scant ½ cup caster
(superfine) sugar
175ml/6fl oz/¾ cup water
finely grated rind and
juice of 1 lime
45ml/3 tbsp shredded fresh basil,
plus whole leaves to garnish

COOK'S TIP

Add the syrup in two stages, as the amount of sugar needed will depend on the sweetness of the melon.

1 Cut the melons in half across the middle. Scrape out the seeds and discard. Using a melon baller, scoop out 20–24 balls and set aside to use for the garnish.

2 Scoop out the remaining flesh and place in a blender or food processor.

3 Place the sugar, water and lime rind in a small pan over a low heat. Stir until dissolved, bring to the boil and simmer for 2–3 minutes. Remove from the heat and leave to cool slightly. Blend half the mixture with the melon flesh until smooth, adding the remaining syrup and lime juice to taste.

4 Pour the mixture into a bowl, stir in the shredded basil and chill. Serve garnished with whole basil leaves and the reserved melon balls.

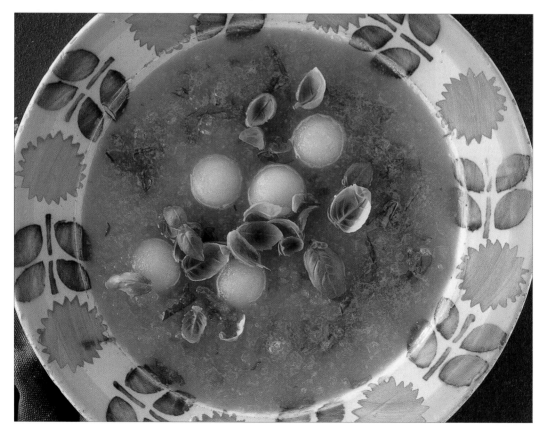

Energy 129kcal/550kJ; Protein 1.7g; Carbohydrate 31.7g, of which sugars 31.7g; Fat 0.3g, of which saturates 0g; Cholesterol 0mg; Calcium 50mg; Fibre 1.3g; Sodium 104mg.

WATERCRESS AND ORANGE SOUP

THIS IS A HEALTHY AND REFRESHING SOUP, WHICH IS GOOD SERVED CHILLED ON A SUMMER'S DAY OR HOT WHEN THERE IS A CHILL IN THE AIR.

SERVES 4

INGREDIENTS
  1 large onion, chopped
  15ml/1 tbsp olive oil
  2 bunches or bags of washed
    watercress
  grated rind and juice of 1 large
    orange
  600ml/1 pint/2½ cups vegetable
    stock
  150ml/¼ pint/⅔ cup single
    (light) cream
  10ml/2 tsp cornflour (cornstarch)
  salt and ground black pepper
  a little double (heavy) cream or
    natural (plain) yogurt, to garnish
  4 orange wedges, to serve

1 Soften the onion in the oil in a large pan. Add the watercress, unchopped, to the onion. Cover and cook for about 5 minutes until softened.

2 Add the orange rind and juice and the stock. Bring to the boil, cover the pan and simmer for 10–15 minutes.

3 Process in a blender or food processor until smooth.

4 Put through a sieve (strainer) if you want the soup even smoother.

5 Blend the cream with the cornflour until no lumps remain, then add to the soup. Season to taste.

6 Bring the soup gently back to the boil, stirring until just slightly thickened.

7 Leave to cool before chilling in the refrigerator. Serve with a swirl of cream or yogurt and a wedge of orange.

Energy 144kcal/599kJ; Protein 3.6g; Carbohydrate 9.4g, of which sugars 5.6g; Fat 10.6g, of which saturates 5.1g; Cholesterol 21mg; Calcium 136mg; Fibre 1.7g; Sodium 40mg.

MIAMI CHILLED AVOCADO SOUP

AVOCADOS ARE COMBINED WITH LEMON JUICE, DRY SHERRY AND AN OPTIONAL DASH OF HOT PEPPER SAUCE, TO MAKE THIS SUBTLE CHILLED SOUP.

3 Peel the cucumber and halve it lengthways. Scoop out and discard the seeds, then roughly chop the flesh. Add to the avocado with the sherry and most of the onions, reserving a few for the garnish. Process again until smooth.

4 In a large bowl, combine the avocado mixture with the chicken stock. Whisk until well blended. Season with the salt and a few drops of hot pepper sauce, if you like. Cover the bowl and place in the refrigerator to chill thoroughly.

SERVES 4

INGREDIENTS
  2 large or 3 medium ripe
    avocados
  15ml/1 tbsp fresh lemon juice
  1 small cucumber
  30ml/2 tbsp dry sherry
  25g/1oz/¼ cup coarsely chopped
    spring onions (scallions), with
    some of the green stems
  475ml/16fl oz/2 cups mild-
    flavoured chicken stock
  5ml/1 tsp salt
  hot pepper sauce (optional)
  natural (plain) yogurt, to garnish

1 Halve the avocados, remove the stones (pits) and peel, and chop roughly.

2 Place the flesh in a food processor or blender. Add the lemon juice and process until very smooth.

5 To serve, fill individual bowls with the soup. Place a spoonful of yogurt in the centre of each bowl and swirl with a spoon. Sprinkle the soup with the reserved chopped spring onions.

Energy 155kcal/640kJ; Protein 1.8g; Carbohydrate 2.1g, of which sugars 1g; Fat 14.5g, of which saturates 3.1g; Cholesterol 0mg; Calcium 16mg; Fibre 2.8g; Sodium 7mg.

CHILLED ASPARAGUS SOUP

THIS DELICATE, PALE GREEN SOUP, GARNISHED WITH A SWIRL OF CREAM OR YOGURT, IS AS PRETTY AS IT IS DELICIOUS AND IS THE REAL TASTE OF SUMMER.

SERVES 6

INGREDIENTS
900g/2lb fresh asparagus
60ml/4 tbsp butter or olive oil
175g/6oz/1½ cups sliced leeks or
  spring onions (scallions)
45ml/3 tbsp flour
1.5 litres/2½ pints/6¼ cups
  chicken stock or water
120ml/4fl oz/½ cup single
  (light) cream or natural
  (plain) yogurt
15ml/1 tbsp chopped fresh
  tarragon or chervil
salt and ground black pepper

3 Heat the butter or oil in a pan. Add the leeks or spring onions and cook over a low heat for 5–8 minutes until softened. Stir in the asparagus, cover and cook for 6–8 minutes until tender.

4 Add the flour and stir well to blend. Cook for 3–4 minutes, uncovered, stirring occasionally.

5 Add the stock or water. Bring to the boil, stirring frequently, then reduce the heat and simmer for 30 minutes. Season with salt and pepper.

6 Purée the soup in a food processor or food mill. If necessary, strain to remove any coarse fibres. Stir in the asparagus tips, most of the cream or yogurt, and the herbs. Chill well. Stir before serving and check the seasoning. Garnish each bowl with a swirl of cream or yogurt.

1 Cut the top 6cm/2½in off the asparagus spears and blanch in boiling water for 5–6 minutes until just tender. Drain thoroughly. Cut each tip into two or three pieces and set aside.

2 Trim the ends of the stalks, removing any brown or woody parts. Chop the stalks into 1cm/½in pieces.

Energy 157kcal/649kJ; Protein 5.7g; Carbohydrate 4.4g, of which sugars 4.2g; Fat 13.1g, of which saturates 7.8g; Cholesterol 32mg; Calcium 72mg; Fibre 3g; Sodium 70mg.

GREEN PEA AND MINT SOUP

PERFECT PARTNERS, PEAS AND MINT REALLY CAPTURE THE FLAVOURS OF SUMMER IN THIS DELICIOUS LIGHTLY CHILLED SOUP.

SERVES 4

INGREDIENTS

    50g/2oz/4 tbsp butter
    4 spring onions (scallions), chopped
    450g/1lb fresh or frozen peas
    600ml/1 pint/2½ cups vegetable
      stock
    2 large sprigs fresh mint
    600ml/1 pint/2½ cups milk
    a pinch of sugar (optional)
    salt and freshly ground black
      pepper
    small sprigs of fresh mint, to
      garnish
    single (light) cream, to serve

1 Heat the butter in a large heavy pan. Add the chopped spring onions and cook gently on a low heat for 5–6 minutes until they are softened but not browned.

2 Stir the peas into the pan, add the stock and mint, and bring to the boil. Cover and simmer gently for about 30 minutes if you are using fresh peas (15 minutes for frozen peas), until they are tender. Reserve about 45ml/3 tbsp of the peas for a garnish.

3 Pour the soup into a food processor or blender, add the milk and purée until smooth. Season to taste, adding a pinch of sugar, if you like. Leave to cool, then chill lightly in the refrigerator.

4 Pour the soup into bowls. Swirl a little cream into each, then garnish with the mint and the reserved peas.

Energy 258kcal/1072kJ; Protein 13.1g; Carbohydrate 20.1g, of which sugars 10g; Fat 14.6g, of which saturates 8.5g; Cholesterol 36mg; Calcium 210mg; Fibre 5.5g; Sodium 142mg.

SUMMER TOMATO SOUP

TOMATOES FLAVOURED WITH FRESH SUMMER HERBS FORM THE BASIS OF THIS REFRESHING AND COLOURFUL SOUP. MAKE IT WHEN THE TOMATO SEASON IS AT ITS PEAK.

SERVES 4

INGREDIENTS

  15ml/1 tbsp olive oil
  1 large onion, chopped
  1 carrot, chopped
  1kg/2¼lb ripe tomatoes,
    quartered
  2 garlic cloves, chopped
  5 sprigs of fresh thyme, or
    1.5ml/¼ tsp dried thyme
  4 or 5 sprigs of fresh marjoram,
    or 1.5ml/¼ tsp dried
  1 bay leaf
  45ml/3 tbsp crème fraîche, sour
    cream or natural (plain) yogurt,
    plus a little extra to garnish
  salt and ground black pepper

1 Heat the olive oil in a large, preferably stainless-steel pan or flameproof casserole.

2 Add the onion and carrot and cook over a medium heat for 3–4 minutes until just softened, stirring occasionally.

3 Add the quartered tomatoes, chopped garlic and herbs. Reduce the heat and simmer, covered, for 30 minutes.

4 Discard the bay leaf and press the soup through a sieve (strainer). Stir in the cream or yogurt and season to taste. Cool, then chill in the refrigerator. Serve with a garnish of cream or yogurt.

VARIATION
You could use oregano instead of marjoram, and parsley instead of thyme.

COOK'S TIP
The success of this soup depends on having ripe, full-flavoured tomatoes, such as the oval plum variety.

Energy 138kcal/576kJ; Protein 3g; Carbohydrate 13.7g, of which sugars 12.4g; Fat 8.3g, of which saturates 3.7g; Cholesterol 13mg; Calcium 61mg; Fibre 4.2g; Sodium 35mg.

SORREL, SPINACH AND DILL SOUP

*THE WARM FLAVOUR OF HORSERADISH AND THE ANISEED FLAVOUR OF DILL MELD WITH SORREL AND
SPINACH TO MAKE THIS UNUSUAL RUSSIAN SOUP. AN EXCELLENT SUMMER SOUP, SERVED CHILLED.*

SERVES 6

INGREDIENTS

25g/1oz/2 tbsp butter
225g/8oz sorrel, stalks
  removed
225g/8oz young spinach,
  stalks removed
25g/1oz fresh horseradish,
  grated
750ml/1¼ pints/3 cups cider
1 pickled cucumber,
  finely chopped
30ml/2 tbsp chopped fresh dill
225g/8oz cooked fish, such
  as pike, perch or salmon, skinned
  and boned
salt and ground black pepper
sprig of dill, to garnish

1 Melt the butter in a large pan.
Add the prepared sorrel and spinach
leaves together with the grated
fresh horseradish.

2 Cover the pan and allow to cook
gently for 3–4 minutes, or until the
sorrel and spinach leaves have wilted.

3 Tip into a food processor or blender
and process to a fine purée (paste).
Ladle into a tureen or bowl and stir in
the cider, cucumber and dill.

4 Chop the fish into bitesize pieces.
Add to the soup, then season well.
Chill for at least 3 hours before serving,
garnished with a sprig of dill.

Energy 156kcal/653kJ; Protein 11.4g; Carbohydrate 4.8g, of which sugars 4.7g; Fat 6.6g, of which saturates 2.8g; Cholesterol 19mg; Calcium 201mg; Fibre 1.9g; Sodium 324mg.

CHILLED TOMATO <u>AND</u> BASIL-FLOWER SOUP

*THIS IS A REALLY FRESH-TASTING SOUP, PACKED WITH THE COMPLEMENTARY FLAVOURS OF TOMATO
AND BASIL, AND TOPPED WITH PRETTY PINK AND PURPLE SWEET BASIL FLOWERS.*

SERVES 4

INGREDIENTS
    15ml/1 tbsp olive oil
    1 onion, finely chopped
    1 garlic clove, crushed
    600ml/1 pint/2½ cups
      vegetable stock
    900g/2lb tomatoes, roughly chopped
    20 fresh basil leaves
    a few drops of balsamic vinegar
    juice of ½ lemon
    150ml/¼ pint/⅔ cup natural
      (plain) yogurt
    granulated sugar and salt, to taste
For the garnish
    30ml/2 tbsp natural (plain) yogurt
    8 small basil leaves
    10ml/2 tsp basil flowers, all green
      parts removed

COOK'S TIP
Basil flowers may be small but they
certainly have a beautifully aromatic
flavour and are surprisingly sweet. They
can be used fresh in all sorts of ways by
being added with basil leaves to tomato
salads or pizza toppings, sprinkled on
pastas, or used as flavourings in tomato
juice. To remove the flowers from the
stem, simply pull – they will come away
easily. Purple-leaved basil has a pretty
mauve flower, which is delicious too.

1 Heat the oil in a pan and add the
finely chopped onion and garlic. Fry
the onion and garlic in the oil for
2–3 minutes until soft and transparent,
stirring occasionally.

2 Add 300ml/½ pint/1¼ cups of the
vegetable stock and the chopped
tomatoes to the pan. Bring to the
boil, then lower the heat and simmer
the mixture for 15 minutes. Stir it
occasionally to prevent it from sticking
to the base of the pan.

3 Allow the mixture to cool slightly,
then transfer it to a food processor and
process until smooth. Press through a
sieve placed over a bowl to remove the
tomato skins and seeds.

4 Return the mixture to the food
processor and add the remainder of the
stock, half the basil leaves, the vinegar,
lemon juice and yogurt. Season with
sugar and salt to taste. Process until
smooth. Pour into a bowl and chill.

5 Just before serving, finely shred the
remaining basil leaves and add them
to the soup. Pour the chilled soup into
individual bowls. Garnish with yogurt
topped with a few small basil leaves
and a sprinkling of basil flowers.

Energy 89kcal/377kJ; Protein 3.7g; Carbohydrate 11g, of which sugars 10.6g; Fat 3.8g, of which saturates 0.8g; Cholesterol 1mg; Calcium 91mg; Fibre 2.5g; Sodium 52mg.

CUCUMBER AND YOGURT SOUP WITH WALNUTS

THIS IS A PARTICULARLY REFRESHING COLD SOUP, USING A CLASSIC COMBINATION OF CUCUMBER AND YOGURT. IF YOU PREFER IT SMOOTH, BLEND IT IN A FOOD PROCESSOR BEFORE SERVING.

SERVES 5–6

INGREDIENTS
  1 cucumber
  4 garlic cloves
  2.5ml/½ tsp salt
  75g/3oz/¾ cup walnut pieces
  40g/1½oz day-old bread, torn into
    pieces
  30ml/2 tbsp walnut or
    sunflower oil
  400ml/14fl oz/1⅔ cups natural
    (plain) yogurt
  120ml/4fl oz/½ cup cold water
    or chilled still mineral water
  5–10ml/1–2 tsp lemon juice
For the garnish
  40g/1½oz/scant ½ cup walnuts,
    coarsely chopped
  25ml/1½ tbsp olive oil
  sprigs of fresh dill

1 Cut the cucumber in half and peel one half of it. Dice the cucumber flesh and set aside.

2 Using a large mortar and pestle, crush together the garlic and salt well, then add the walnuts and bread.

3 When the mixture is smooth, slowly add the walnut or sunflower oil.

4 Transfer the mixture to a large bowl and beat in the yogurt and diced cucumber. Add the cold water or mineral water and lemon juice to taste.

5 Pour the soup into chilled soup bowls to serve. Garnish with the chopped walnuts and drizzle with the olive oil. Finally, arrange the sprigs of dill on top and serve immediately.

Energy 175kcal/728kJ; Protein 6g; Carbohydrate 9.2g, of which sugars 6g; Fat 13.1g, of which saturates 1.5g; Cholesterol 1mg; Calcium 152mg; Fibre 0.7g; Sodium 92mg.

BABY CHERRY TOMATO SOUP
WITH ROCKET PESTO

FOR THEIR SIZE, BABY TOMATOES ARE A POWERHOUSE OF SWEETNESS AND FLAVOUR. HERE THEY ARE
COMPLEMENTED BEAUTIFULLY BY A RICH PASTE OF PEPPERY ROCKET.

SERVES 4

INGREDIENTS
    225g/8oz baby cherry
      tomatoes, halved
    225g/8oz baby plum tomatoes, halved
    225g/8oz vine-ripened
      tomatoes, halved
    2 shallots, roughly chopped
    25ml/1½ tbsp sun-dried
      tomato paste
    600ml/1 pint/2½ cups
      vegetable stock
    salt and ground black pepper
    ice cubes, to serve
For the pesto
    15g/½oz rocket (arugula) leaves
    75ml/5 tbsp olive oil
    15g/½oz/2 tbsp pine nuts
    1 garlic clove
    25g/1oz/⅓ cup freshly grated
      Parmesan cheese

1 Purée all the tomatoes and the shallots in a food processor or blender. Add the sun-dried tomato paste and process until smooth. Press the purée through a sieve (strainer) into a pan.

2 Add the vegetable stock, bring to the boil and simmer gently for 4–5 minutes. Season well with salt and black pepper. Leave to cool, then chill in the refrigerator for at least 4 hours.

3 To make the pesto, purée the rocket, oil, pine nuts and garlic using a mortar and pestle. Alternatively, use a food processor.

4 Stir the Parmesan cheese into the pesto mix, grinding it well.

5 Ladle the soup into bowls and add a few ice cubes to each. Spoon some of the rocket pesto into the centre of each portion and serve.

VARIATION
The pesto can be made with other soft-leaved herbs in place of rocket. Try fresh basil, coriander (cilantro) or mint, or use a mixture of herb leaves, if you like. Parsley and mint are a good flavour combination and make delicious pesto.

Energy 197kcal/819kJ; Protein 4.9g; Carbohydrate 7.9g, of which sugars 7.6g; Fat 16.5g, of which saturates 3.3g; Cholesterol 6mg; Calcium 101mg; Fibre 2.4g; Sodium 105mg.

CHILLED TOMATO AND SWEET PEPPER SOUP

A RECIPE INSPIRED BY THE SPANISH GAZPACHO, WHERE RAW INGREDIENTS ARE COMBINED TO MAKE A CHILLED SOUP. IN THIS RECIPE THE INGREDIENTS ARE COOKED FIRST AND THEN CHILLED.

SERVES 4

INGREDIENTS

  2 red (bell) peppers, halved
  45ml/3 tbsp olive oil
  1 onion, finely chopped
  2 garlic cloves, crushed
  675g/1½lb ripe, well-flavoured
    tomatoes
  150ml/¼ pint/⅔ cup red wine
  600ml/1 pint/2½ cups vegetable stock
  salt and ground black pepper
  chopped fresh chives, to garnish
For the croûtons
  2 slices day-old white bread,
    crusts removed
  60ml/4 tbsp olive oil

COOK'S TIP
Any juice that accumulates in the pan after grilling (broiling) the peppers, or in the bowl, should be stirred into the soup. It will add a delectable flavour.

1 Cut each pepper half into quarters and seed. Place skin-side up on a grill (broiler) rack and cook until the skins have charred. Transfer to a bowl and cover with a plate.

2 Heat the oil in a large pan. Add the onion and garlic, and cook until soft. Meanwhile, remove the skin from the peppers and roughly chop them. Cut the tomatoes into chunks.

3 Add the peppers and tomatoes to the pan, then cover and cook gently for 10 minutes. Add the red wine and cook for a further 5 minutes, then add the stock and salt and pepper, and simmer for 20 minutes.

4 To make the croûtons, cut the bread into cubes. Heat the oil in a small frying pan, add the bread and fry until golden. Drain on paper towels, cool, then store in an airtight box.

5 Process the soup in a blender or food processor until smooth. Pour into a clean glass or ceramic bowl and leave to cool thoroughly before chilling for at least 3 hours. When the soup is cold, season to taste.

6 Serve the soup in bowls, topped with the croûtons and garnished with chopped chives.

Energy 292kcal/1216kJ; Protein 3.4g; Carbohydrate 18.8g, of which sugars 11.8g; Fat 20.4g, of which saturates 3g; Cholesterol 0mg; Calcium 40mg; Fibre 3.5g; Sodium 92mg.

CHILLED ALMOND SOUP

UNLESS YOU ARE PREPARED TO SPEND TIME POUNDING ALL THE INGREDIENTS BY HAND, A FOOD PROCESSOR IS ESSENTIAL FOR THIS SPANISH SOUP.

SERVES 6

INGREDIENTS
    115g/4oz fresh white bread
    750ml/1¼ pints/3 cups
      cold water
    115g/4oz/1 cup blanched
      almonds
    2 garlic cloves, sliced
    75ml/5 tbsp olive oil
    25ml/1½ tbsp sherry vinegar
    salt and ground black pepper
For the garnish
    toasted flaked (sliced) almonds
    seedless green and black grapes,
      halved and skinned

1 Break the bread into a bowl and pour 150ml/¼ pint/⅔ cup of the water on top. Leave for 5 minutes.

2 Put the almonds and garlic in a blender or food processor and process until finely ground. Blend the soaked bread into the mixture.

3 Gradually add the oil until the mixture forms a smooth paste. Add the sherry vinegar then the remaining cold water and process until smooth.

4 Transfer to a bowl and season to taste. Chill for 2–3 hours. Garnish with the toasted almonds and grapes.

Energy 366kcal/1523kJ; Protein 6.8g; Carbohydrate 24.2g, of which sugars 8.2g; Fat 26.7g, of which saturates 2.9g; Cholesterol 0mg; Calcium 74mg; Fibre 1.9g; Sodium 177mg.

LIGHT AND REFRESHING SOUPS

As an appetizer before the main meal, a light and refreshing soup is a good choice. Tomatoes, peas, carrots, asparagus and mushrooms, teamed with fresh herbs such as basil, tarragon and coriander, make appetizing soups that are full of flavour. For an international flavour, try Balinese Vegetable Soup, or Light and Fragrant Broth with Stuffed Cabbage Leaves, which in Vietnam is often served at New Year celebrations.

ITALIAN PEA AND BASIL SOUP

THE PUNGENT FLAVOUR OF BASIL LIFTS THIS APPETIZING ITALIAN SOUP, WHILE THE ONION AND GARLIC GIVE DEPTH. SERVE IT WITH GOOD CRUSTY BREAD TO ENJOY IT AT ITS BEST.

2 Add the peas and stock to the pan and bring to the boil. Reduce the heat, add the basil and seasoning, then simmer for 10 minutes.

3 Spoon the soup into a food processor or blender (you may have to do this in batches) and process until the soup is smooth.

4 Return the soup to the rinsed pan and reheat gently until piping hot. Ladle into warm bowls, sprinkle with shaved Parmesan and garnish with basil.

VARIATION
You can also use mint or a mixture of parsley, mint and chives in place of the basil, if you like.

SERVES 4

INGREDIENTS
    75ml/5 tbsp olive oil
    2 large onions, chopped
    1 celery stick, chopped
    1 carrot, chopped
    1 garlic clove, finely chopped
    400g/14oz/3½ cups frozen
      petits pois (baby peas)
    900ml/1½ pints/3¾ cups
      vegetable stock
    25g/1oz/1 cup fresh basil leaves,
      roughly torn, plus extra to garnish
    salt and ground black pepper
    shaved Parmesan cheese,
      to serve

1 Heat the oil in a large pan and add the onions, celery, carrot and garlic. Cover the pan and cook over a low heat for 45 minutes, or until the vegetables are soft, stirring occasionally to prevent the vegetables sticking.

Energy 261kcal/1078kJ; Protein 8.8g; Carbohydrate 22.9g, of which sugars 10.9g; Fat 15.7g, of which saturates 2.3g; Cholesterol 0mg; Calcium 73mg; Fibre 7.3g; Sodium 16mg

FRESH TOMATO SOUP

THE COMBINATION OF INTENSELY FLAVOURED SUN-RIPENED AND FRESH TOMATOES NEEDS LITTLE EMBELLISHMENT IN THIS TASTY ITALIAN SOUP. CHOOSE THE RIPEST-LOOKING TOMATOES.

SERVES 6

INGREDIENTS

1.3–1.6kg/3–3½lb ripe tomatoes
400ml/14fl oz/1⅔ cups chicken or
  vegetable stock
45ml/3 tbsp sun-dried tomato
  purée (paste)
30–45ml/2–3 tbsp balsamic vinegar
10–15ml/2–3 tsp sugar
a small handful of fresh basil leaves,
  plus extra to garnish
salt and ground black pepper
toasted cheese croûtes and crème
  fraîche, to serve

COOK'S TIP
Use a sharp knife to cut a cross in the base of each tomato before plunging it into the boiling water. The skin will then peel back easily from the crosses.

1 Plunge the tomatoes into boiling water for 30 seconds, then refresh in cold water. Peel off the skins and quarter the tomatoes. Put them in a large pan and pour over the chicken or vegetable stock. Bring just to the boil, reduce the heat, cover and simmer gently for 10 minutes until the tomatoes are pulpy.

2 Stir in the tomato purée, vinegar, sugar and basil. Season with salt and pepper, then cook gently, stirring, for 2 minutes. Process the soup in a blender or food processor, then return to a clean pan and reheat gently. Serve in bowls, topped with one or two toasted cheese croûtes and a spoonful of crème fraîche, garnished with basil leaves.

Energy 52kcal/225kJ; Protein 1.9g; Carbohydrate 10.4g, of which sugars 10.4g; Fat 0.7g, of which saturates 0.2g; Cholesterol 0mg; Calcium 19mg; Fibre 2.4g; Sodium 38mg.

CARROT AND ORANGE SOUP

THIS TRADITIONAL BRIGHT AND SUMMERY SOUP IS ALWAYS POPULAR FOR ITS WONDERFULLY CREAMY CONSISTENCY AND VIBRANTLY FRESH CITRUS FLAVOUR. USE A GOOD, HOME-MADE CHICKEN OR VEGETABLE STOCK IF YOU CAN, FOR THE BEST RESULTS.

SERVES 4

INGREDIENTS
   50g/2oz/¼ cup butter
   3 leeks, sliced
   450g/1lb carrots, sliced
   1.2 litres/2 pints/5 cups chicken or
      vegetable stock
   rind and juice of 2 oranges
   2.5ml/½ tsp freshly grated nutmeg
   150ml/¼ pint/⅔ cup Greek
      (US strained plain) yogurt
   salt and ground black pepper
   fresh sprigs of coriander (cilantro),
      to garnish

1 Melt the butter in a large pan. Add the leeks and carrots and stir well, coating the vegetables with the butter. Cover and cook for about 10 minutes, until the vegetables are beginning to soften but not colour.

2 Pour in the stock and the orange rind and juice. Add the nutmeg and season to taste with salt and pepper. Bring to the boil, lower the heat, cover and simmer for about 40 minutes, or until the vegetables are tender.

3 Leave to cool slightly, then purée the soup in a food processor or blender until smooth.

4 Return the soup to the pan and add 30ml/2 tbsp of the yogurt, then taste the soup and adjust the seasoning, if necessary. Reheat gently.

5 Ladle the soup into warm individual bowls and put a swirl of yogurt in the centre of each. Sprinkle the fresh sprigs of coriander over each bowl to garnish, and serve immediately.

Energy 206kcal/856kJ; Protein 5g; Carbohydrate 15.8g, of which sugars 14.2g; Fat 14.4g, of which saturates 8.3g; Cholesterol 27mg; Calcium 111mg; Fibre 5.8g; Sodium 131mg.

LIGHT AND FRAGRANT BROTH WITH STUFFED CABBAGE LEAVES

THE ORIGINS OF THIS VIETNAMESE SOUP, CANH BAP CUON, COULD BE ATTRIBUTED TO THE FRENCH DISH, CHOU FARCI, OR TO THE CHINESE TRADITION OF COOKING DUMPLINGS IN A CLEAR BROTH.

SERVES 4

INGREDIENTS
    10 Chinese leaves (Chinese cabbage)
    or Savoy cabbage leaves, halved,
    main ribs removed
    4 spring onions (scallions), green
    tops left whole, white part
    chopped
    5 or 6 dried cloud ears (wood ears),
    soaked in hot water for 15 minutes
    115g/4oz minced (ground) pork
    115g/4oz prawns (shrimp), shelled,
    deveined and finely chopped
    1 Thai chilli, seeded and chopped
    30ml/2 tbsp *nuoc mam*
    15ml/1 tbsp soy sauce
    4cm/1½in fresh root ginger, peeled
    and very finely sliced
    chopped fresh coriander (cilantro),
    to garnish
For the stock
    1 meaty chicken carcass
    2 onions, peeled and quartered
    4 garlic cloves, crushed
    4cm/1½in fresh root ginger, chopped
    30ml/2 tbsp *nuoc mam*
    30ml/2 tbsp soy sauce
    6 black peppercorns
    a few sprigs of fresh thyme
    sea salt

1 To make the stock, put the chicken carcass into a deep pan. Add the other stock ingredients and cover with water. Bring to the boil, skim off any foam, then reduce the heat and simmer gently with the lid on for 1½–2 hours. Remove the lid and simmer for a further 30 minutes to reduce the stock. Skim off any fat, then strain the stock and measure out 1.5 litres/2½ pints/6¼ cups.

2 Blanch the cabbage leaves in boiling water for 2 minutes. Remove with tongs or a slotted spoon and refresh under cold water. Add the green tops of the spring onions to the boiling water and blanch for 1 minute, then drain and refresh under cold water. Tear each piece into five thin strips and set aside.

3 Squeeze the cloud ear dry, then trim and finely chop and mix with the pork, prawns, spring onion whites, chilli, *nuoc mam* and soy sauce. Lay a cabbage leaf flat and put a teaspoon of the filling 1cm/½in from the bottom edge. Fold the edge over the filling, then fold in the sides. Roll all the way to the top of the leaf to form a tight bundle. Tie a piece of blanched spring onion green around the bundle. Repeat with the remaining leaves and filling.

4 Bring the stock to the boil in a wok or deep pan. Stir in the finely sliced ginger, then reduce the heat and drop in the cabbage bundles. Bubble very gently over a medium heat for about 20 minutes to ensure that the filling is thoroughly cooked.

5 Ladle into bowls and sprinkle with fresh coriander leaves.

Energy 87kcal/362kJ; Protein 11.8g; Carbohydrate 3.1g, of which sugars 3g; Fat 3.2g, of which saturates 1.1g; Cholesterol 75mg; Calcium 54mg; Fibre 1.2g; Sodium 527mg.

BALINESE VEGETABLE SOUP

THE BALINESE BASE THIS POPULAR SOUP ON BEANS, BUT ANY SEASONAL VEGETABLES CAN BE ADDED OR SUBSTITUTED. THE RECIPE ALSO INCLUDES SHRIMP PASTE, WHICH IS KNOWN LOCALLY AS TERASI.

2 Finely grind the chopped garlic, macadamia nuts or almonds, shrimp paste (blachan) and the coriander seeds to a paste using a pestle and mortar or in a food processor.

3 Heat the oil in a wok, and fry the onion until transparent. Remove with a slotted spoon. Add the nut paste to the wok and fry it for 2 minutes without allowing it to brown.

SERVES 8

INGREDIENTS
225g/8oz green beans
1.2 litres/2 pints/5 cups lightly
  salted water
1 garlic clove, roughly
  chopped
2 macadamia nuts or 4 almonds,
  finely chopped
1cm/1/2in cube shrimp paste
  (blachan)
10–15ml/2–3 tsp coriander seeds,
  dry fried
30ml/2 tbsp vegetable oil
1 onion, finely sliced
400ml/14fl oz can coconut milk
2 bay leaves
225g/8oz/4 cups beansprouts
8 thin lemon wedges
30ml/2 tbsp lemon juice
salt and ground black pepper

1 Top and tail the beans, then cut them into small pieces. Bring the lightly salted water to the boil, add the beans to the pan and cook for 3–4 minutes. Drain, reserving the cooking water. Set the beans aside.

COOK'S TIP
Dry-fry the coriander seeds for about 2 minutes until the aroma is released.

4 Pour in the reserved vegetable water. Spoon off 45–60ml/3–4 tbsp of the cream from the top of the coconut milk and set it aside. Add the remaining coconut milk to the wok, bring to the boil and add the bay leaves. Cook, uncovered, for 15–20 minutes.

5 Just before serving, reserve a few beans, fried onions and beansprouts to garnish and stir the rest into the soup. Add the lemon wedges, reserved coconut cream, lemon juice and seasoning; stir well. Pour into individual soup bowls and serve, garnished with the reserved beans, onion and beansprouts.

Energy 54kcal/224kJ; Protein 2.1g; Carbohydrate 5.2g, of which sugars 4.2g; Fat 2.8g, of which saturates 0.4g; Cholesterol 0mg; Calcium 38mg; Fibre 1.3g; Sodium 57mg.

PEA SOUP WITH GARLIC

THIS DELICIOUS SOUP HAS A WONDERFULLY SWEET TASTE AND SMOOTH TEXTURE, AND IS GREAT SERVED WITH CRUSTY BREAD AND GARNISHED WITH MINT.

SERVES 4

INGREDIENTS
  25g/1oz/2 tbsp butter
  1 garlic clove, crushed
  900g/2lb/8 cups frozen peas
  1.2 litres/2 pints/5 cups
    chicken stock
  salt and ground black pepper

1 Heat the butter in a large pan and add the garlic. Fry gently for 2–3 minutes, until softened, then add the peas. Cook for 1–2 minutes more, then pour in the stock.

COOK'S TIP
If you keep a bag of frozen peas in the freezer, you can rustle up this soup at very short notice.

2 Bring the soup to the boil, then reduce the heat to a simmer. Cover and cook for 5–6 minutes, until the peas are tender. Leave to cool slightly, then transfer the mixture to a food processor and process until smooth (you may have to do this in two batches).

3 Return the soup to the pan and heat through gently. Season with salt and pepper to taste.

Energy 233kcal/965kJ; Protein 15.6g; Carbohydrate 25.5g, of which sugars 5.2g; Fat 8.5g, of which saturates 3.9g; Cholesterol 13mg; Calcium 49mg; Fibre 10.6g; Sodium 40mg.

SUMMER HERB SOUP WITH CHARGRILLED RADICCHIO

THE SWEETNESS OF SHALLOTS AND LEEKS IN THIS SOUP IS BALANCED BEAUTIFULLY BY THE SLIGHTLY ACIDIC SORREL WITH ITS HINT OF LEMON, AND A BOUQUET OF SUMMER HERBS.

SERVES 4–6

INGREDIENTS
  30ml/2 tbsp dry white wine
  2 shallots, finely chopped
  1 garlic clove, crushed
  2 leeks, sliced
  1 large potato, about 225g/8oz,
    roughly chopped
  2 courgettes (zucchini), chopped
  600ml/1 pint/2½ cups water
  115g/4oz sorrel, torn
  large handful of fresh chervil
  large handful of fresh flat leaf parsley
  large handful of fresh mint
  1 round (butterhead) lettuce,
    separated into leaves
  600ml/1 pint/2½ cups
    vegetable stock
  1 small head of radicchio
  5ml/1 tsp groundnut (peanut) oil
  salt and ground black pepper

1 Put the wine, shallots and garlic into a heavy-based pan and bring to the boil. Cook for 2–3 minutes, until softened.

2 Add the leeks, potato and courgette with enough of the water to come about halfway up the vegetables. Lay a wetted piece of greaseproof paper over the vegetables and put a lid on the pan, then cook for 10–15 minutes, until soft.

3 Remove the paper and add the fresh herbs and lettuce. Cook for 1–2 minutes, or until wilted.

4 Pour in the remaining water and the vegetable stock and simmer for 10–12 minutes. Cool the soup slightly, then process it in a food processor or blender until smooth. Return the soup to the rinsed-out pan and season well.

5 Cut the radicchio into thin wedges that hold together, then brush the cut sides with the oil. Heat a ridged griddle or frying pan until very hot and add the radicchio wedges.

6 Cook the radicchio for 1 minute on each side until slightly charred. Reheat the soup over a low heat, then ladle it into warmed shallow bowls. Serve a wedge of charred radicchio on top.

Energy 102kcal/428kJ; Protein 5g; Carbohydrate 15.1g, of which sugars 5.7g; Fat 2.2g, of which saturates 0.4g; Cholesterol 0mg; Calcium 135mg; Fibre 4.9g; Sodium 57mg.

TOMATO, CIABATTA AND BASIL OIL SOUP

THROUGHOUT EUROPE, BREAD IS A POPULAR INGREDIENT FOR THICKENING SOUP, AND THIS RECIPE SHOWS HOW WONDERFULLY QUICK AND EASY THIS METHOD CAN BE.

SERVES 4

INGREDIENTS

45ml/3 tbsp olive oil
1 red onion, chopped
6 garlic cloves, chopped
300ml/½ pint/1¼ cups white wine
150ml/¼ pint/⅔ cup water
12 plum tomatoes, quartered
2 x 400g/14oz cans plum tomatoes
2.5ml/½ tsp sugar
½ ciabatta loaf
salt and ground black pepper
basil leaves, to garnish
For the basil oil
115g/4oz basil leaves
120ml/4fl oz/½ cup olive oil

1 For the basil oil, process the basil and oil in a food processor or blender to make a paste. Line a bowl with muslin (cheesecloth) and scrape the paste into it. Gather up the muslin and squeeze firmly to extract all the oil. Set aside.

2 Heat the oil in a large pan and cook the onion and garlic for 4–5 minutes until softened.

3 Add the wine, water, fresh and canned tomatoes. Bring to the boil, reduce the heat and cover the pan, then simmer for 3–4 minutes. Add the sugar and season well with salt and black pepper.

4 Break the bread into bite-sized pieces and stir into the soup.

5 Ladle the soup into bowls. Garnish with basil and drizzle the basil oil over each portion.

Energy 332kcal/1396kJ; Protein 7.8g; Carbohydrate 35.4g, of which sugars 16.3g; Fat 13.4g, of which saturates 2g; Cholesterol 0mg; Calcium 98mg; Fibre 5g; Sodium 306mg.

SPINACH AND RICE SOUP

USE VERY FRESH, YOUNG SPINACH LEAVES AND ITALIAN RISOTTO RICE TO PREPARE THIS SURPRISINGLY LIGHT, REFRESHING SOUP.

SERVES 4

INGREDIENTS

675g/1½lb fresh spinach, washed
45ml/3 tbsp extra virgin olive oil
1 small onion, finely chopped
2 garlic cloves, finely chopped
1 small fresh red chilli, seeded and finely chopped
115g/4oz/generous ½ cup risotto rice
1.2 litres/2 pints/5 cups vegetable stock
salt and ground black pepper
60ml/4 tbsp grated Pecorino cheese, to serve

1 Place the spinach in a large pan with just the water that clings to its leaves after washing. Add a large pinch of salt. Heat gently until the spinach has wilted, then remove from the heat and drain, reserving any liquid. Chop finely.

2 Heat the oil in a large pan and cook the onion, garlic and chilli for 4–5 minutes until softened. Stir in the rice until well coated, then pour in the stock and reserved spinach liquid.

3 Bring to the boil, lower the heat and simmer for 10 minutes. Add the spinach and cook for 5–7 minutes more, until the rice is tender. Season with salt and freshly ground pepper and serve with the Pecorino cheese.

COOK'S TIP
Pecorino is an Italian cheese made with ewe's milk. If it is unavailable, use grated Parmesan cheese instead.

Energy 293kcal/1215kJ; Protein 13g; Carbohydrate 26.8g, of which sugars 3.4g; Fat 14.7g, of which saturates 4.4g; Cholesterol 15mg; Calcium 476mg; Fibre 3.8g; Sodium 400mg.

TOMATO AND FRESH BASIL SOUP

THIS IS THE PERFECT SOUP FOR SERVING IN LATE SUMMER, WHEN FRESH TOMATOES ARE AT THEIR RIPEST AND MOST FLAVOURSOME.

SERVES 4–6

INGREDIENTS

    15ml/1 tbsp olive oil
    25g/1oz/2 tbsp butter
    1 medium onion, finely chopped
    900g/2lb ripe tomatoes,
      roughly chopped
    1 garlic clove, roughly chopped
    about 750ml/1¼ pints/3 cups
      chicken or vegetable stock
    120ml/4fl oz/½ cup dry white wine
    30ml/2 tbsp sun-dried tomato
      purée (paste)
    30ml/2 tbsp shredded fresh basil,
      plus a few whole leaves to garnish
    150ml/¼ pint/⅔ cup double
      (heavy) cream
    salt and ground black pepper

1 Heat the oil and butter in a large pan until foaming. Add the onion and cook gently for about 5 minutes, stirring frequently, until softened, but do not allow to brown.

2 Stir in the chopped tomatoes and garlic, then add the stock, white wine and sun-dried tomato purée, with salt and pepper to taste. Bring to the boil, then lower the heat, half-cover the pan and simmer gently for 20 minutes, stirring occasionally to stop the tomatoes sticking to the base.

COOK'S TIP
For best results, choose Italian plum tomatoes, but other ripe full-flavoured tomatoes may be used.

3 Pour the soup into a food processor or blender. Add the shredded basil and blend to a purée. Using a wooden spoon, press the purée through a sieve (strainer) into a clean pan. Discard tomato seeds left in the sieve and put the pan back on the stove.

4 Add the double cream and heat through, stirring. Do not allow the soup to boil. Check the consistency and add more stock, if necessary. Adjust the seasoning, pour into heated bowls and garnish with whole basil leaves. Serve immediately.

Energy 218kcal/901kJ; Protein 1.9g; Carbohydrate 6.7g, of which sugars 6.5g; Fat 19.2g, of which saturates 10.9g; Cholesterol 43mg; Calcium 30mg; Fibre 1.8g; Sodium 57mg.

ROASTED PEPPER SOUP

GRILLING INTENSIFIES THE FLAVOUR OF SWEET RED AND YELLOW PEPPERS AND HELPS THIS DELICIOUS SOUP TO KEEP ITS STUNNING COLOUR.

SERVES 4

INGREDIENTS
    3 red (bell) peppers
    1 yellow (bell) pepper
    1 medium onion, chopped
    1 garlic clove, crushed
    750ml/1¼ pints/3 cups vegetable
      stock
    15ml/1 tbsp plain (all-purpose) flour
    salt and ground black pepper
    diced red and yellow (bell) pepper,
      to garnish

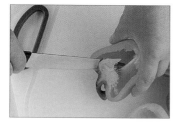

1 Preheat the grill (boiler) to hot. Cut the peppers in half, remove their stalks, cores and white pith, and scrape out the seeds.

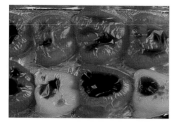

2 Line a grill pan with foil and arrange the halved peppers, skin side up, in a single layer on the foil. Grill (broil) for 8–10 minutes, until the skins have blackened and blistered.

VARIATION
If you prefer, garnish the soup before serving with a swirl of natural (plain) yogurt or crème fraîche instead of the diced peppers.

3 Transfer the peppers to a plastic bag and leave until cool, then peel away their skins and discard. Roughly chop the pepper flesh.

4 Put the onion, garlic clove and 150ml/¼ pint/⅔ cup of the stock in a large pan. Boil for about 5 minutes until the stock has reduced in volume. Reduce the heat and stir until softened and just beginning to colour.

5 Sprinkle the flour over the onion, then gradually add the remaining stock, stirring to prevent lumps forming.

6 Add the chopped, roasted peppers and bring to the boil. Cover and simmer for a further 5 minutes.

7 Leave to cool slightly, then purée in a food processor or blender until smooth. Season to taste with salt and ground black pepper.

8 Return to the pan and reheat until the soup is piping hot.

9 Ladle into four soup bowls and garnish each with a sprinkling of diced peppers before serving.

COOK'S TIP
Stir any juice that accumulates in the pan after grilling (broiling) the peppers into the soup for extra flavour.

Energy 87kcal/364kJ; Protein 2.7g; Carbohydrate 18.1g, of which sugars 13.5g; Fat 0.9g, of which saturates 0.2g; Cholesterol 0mg; Calcium 32mg; Fibre 3.6g; Sodium 9mg.

CARROT AND CORIANDER SOUP

USE A GOOD HOME-MADE STOCK FOR THIS SOUP — IT ADDS A FAR GREATER DEPTH OF FLAVOUR THAN STOCK MADE FROM CUBES.

2 Stir in the ground coriander and cook for about 1 minute. Pour in the stock and season with salt and pepper to taste. Bring to the boil, cover and simmer for about 20 minutes, until the leeks and carrots are tender.

3 Leave to cool slightly, then purée the soup in a blender until smooth. Return the soup to the pan and add 30ml/ 2 tbsp of the yogurt, then taste the soup and adjust the seasoning. Reheat gently, but do not boil.

SERVES 4

INGREDIENTS
50g/2oz/4 tbsp butter
3 leeks, sliced
450g/1lb carrots, sliced
15ml/1tbsp ground coriander
1.2 litres/2 pints/5 cups
  chicken stock
150ml/¼ pint/⅔ cup Greek
  (US strained plain) yogurt
salt and ground black pepper
30–45ml/2–3 tbsp chopped fresh
  coriander (cilantro), to garnish

1 Melt the butter in a large pan. Add the leeks and carrots and stir well to coat with the butter. Cover and cook for 10 minutes, until the vegetables are beginning to soften.

4 Ladle the soup into bowls and put a tablespoonful of the remaining yogurt in the centre of each. Sprinkle over the chopped coriander and serve immediately.

Energy 209kcal/865kJ; Protein 5.6g; Carbohydrate 14.1g, of which sugars 12.5g; Fat 15.2g, of which saturates 8.7g; Cholesterol 27mg; Calcium 123mg; Fibre 6g; Sodium 134mg.

CARROT SOUP WITH GINGER

THE ZING OF FRESH GINGER IS AN IDEAL COMPLEMENT TO THE SWEETNESS OF COOKED CARROTS IN THIS REFRESHING SOUP.

SERVES 6

INGREDIENTS

25g/1oz/2 tbsp butter or margarine
1 onion, chopped
1 celery stick, chopped
1 medium potato, chopped
675g/1½lb carrots, chopped
10ml/2 tsp finely chopped fresh
  root ginger
1.2 litres/2 pints/5 cups
  chicken stock
105ml/7 tbsp whipping cream
a good pinch of freshly
  grated nutmeg
salt and ground black pepper

1 Melt the butter or margarine, add the onion and celery and cook for 5 minutes.

2 Stir in the potato, carrots, ginger and stock. Bring to the boil. Reduce the heat to low, cover and simmer for about 20 minutes.

3 Pour the soup into a food processor or blender and process until it is smooth. Alternatively, use a vegetable mill to purée the soup. Return the soup to the pan. Stir in the cream and nutmeg and add salt and pepper to taste. Reheat gently to serve.

Energy 163kcal/675kJ; Protein 1.7g; Carbohydrate 15.2g, of which sugars 9.8g; Fat 10.9g, of which saturates 6.7g; Cholesterol 27mg; Calcium 46mg; Fibre 3.2g; Sodium 65mg

BEETROOT AND APRICOT SWIRL

THIS SOUP IS MOST ATTRACTIVE IF YOU SWIRL TOGETHER THE TWO DIFFERENTLY COLOURED
MIXTURES, BUT IF YOU PREFER THEY CAN BE MIXED TOGETHER TO SAVE TIME AND WASHING UP.

SERVES 4

INGREDIENTS

4 large cooked beetroots (beets),
  roughly chopped
1 small onion, roughly chopped
600ml/1 pint/2½ cups chicken stock
200g/7oz/1 cup ready-to-eat dried
  apricots
250ml/8fl oz/1 cup orange juice
salt and ground black pepper

1 Place the beetroot and half the onion in a pan with the stock. Bring to the boil, reduce the heat, cover and simmer for 10 minutes. Purée until smooth in a food processor or blender.

2 Place the rest of the onion in a pan with the apricots and orange juice, cover and simmer gently for about 15 minutes, until tender. Purée in a food processor or blender to the same consistency as the beetroot mixture.

3 Return the two mixtures to the pans and reheat. Season to taste with salt and pepper. To serve, swirl the two mixtures together in individual soup bowls for a marbled effect. Serve while still hot.

Energy 143kcal/609kJ; Protein 4.2g; Carbohydrate 32.5g, of which sugars 31.6g; Fat 0.5g, of which saturates 0g; Cholesterol 0mg; Calcium 67mg; Fibre 5.3g; Sodium 80mg.

TAMARIND SOUP <u>WITH</u> VEGETABLES

KNOWN IN INDONESIA AS SAYUR ASAM, THIS IS A COLOURFUL AND REFRESHING SOUP FROM JAKARTA WITH MORE THAN A HINT OF SHARPNESS.

SERVES 4 AS AN APPETIZER OR 8 AS
PART OF A BUFFET

INGREDIENTS
   5 shallots or 1 medium red
     onion, sliced
   3 garlic cloves, crushed
   2.5cm/1in galangal, peeled
     and sliced
   1 or 2 fresh red chillies, seeded
     and sliced
   25g/1oz/¼ cup raw peanuts
   1cm/½in cube shrimp paste,
     prepared
   1.2 litres/2 pints/5 cups well-
     flavoured stock
   50–75g/2–3oz/½–¾ cup salted
     peanuts, lightly crushed
   15–30ml/1–2 tbsp soft dark
     brown sugar
   5ml/1 tsp tamarind pulp, soaked
     in 75ml/5 tbsp warm water for
     15 minutes
   salt
For the vegetables
   1 *chayote*, thinly peeled, seeds
     removed, flesh finely sliced
   115g/4oz French (green) beans,
     trimmed and finely sliced
   50g/2oz corn kernels (optional)
   a handful of green leaves, such as
     watercress, rocket (arugula) or
     Chinese leaves (Chinese cabbage),
     finely shredded
   1 fresh green chilli, sliced,
     to garnish

1 Put the shallots or onion, garlic, galangal, chillies, raw peanuts and shrimp paste in a food processor or pestle and mortar and grind to a paste.

2 Pour in some of the stock to moisten and then pour this mixture into a pan or wok, adding the rest of the stock. Cook for 15 minutes with the crushed salted peanuts and sugar.

3 Strain the tamarind pulp, discarding the seeds, and reserve the juice.

4 About 5 minutes before serving, add the *chayote* slices, beans and corn, if using, to the soup and cook fairly rapidly. At the last minute, add the green leaves and salt to taste. Add the tamarind juice and adjust the seasoning. Serve immediately, garnished with slices of green chilli.

Energy 80kcal/334kJ; Protein 3.8g; Carbohydrate 6.2g, of which sugars 4.9g; Fat 4.6g, of which saturates 0.9g; Cholesterol 0mg; Calcium 46mg; Fibre 1.7g; Sodium 19mg.

FRESH MUSHROOM SOUP WITH TARRAGON

THIS IS A LIGHT MUSHROOM SOUP, SUBTLY FLAVOURED WITH TARRAGON. ADD A COUPLE OF SPOONFULS OF DRY SHERRY FOR A SPECIAL DINNER PARTY.

SERVES 6

INGREDIENTS

15g/½oz/1 tbsp butter or margarine
4 shallots, finely chopped
450g/1lb/6 cups chestnut
   mushrooms, finely chopped
300ml/½ pint/1¼ cups vegetable
   stock
300ml/½ pint/1¼ cups semi-
   skimmed (low-fat) milk
15–30ml/1–2 tbsp chopped fresh
   tarragon
30ml/2 tbsp dry sherry (optional)
salt and ground black pepper
sprigs of fresh tarragon, to garnish

VARIATION
If you prefer, use a mixture of wild and button (white) mushrooms instead.

1 Melt the butter or margarine in a pan, add the shallots and cook gently for 5 minutes, stirring occasionally. Add the mushrooms and cook for 3 minutes, stirring. Add the stock and milk.

2 Bring to the boil, cover and simmer gently for 20 minutes. Stir in the tarragon and season to taste.

3 Allow the soup to cool slightly, then purée in a blender or food processor, in batches if necessary, until smooth. Return to the rinsed-out pan and reheat gently.

4 Stir in the sherry, if using, then ladle the soup into warmed soup bowls and serve garnished with sprigs of tarragon.

Energy 55kcal/230kJ; Protein 3.2g; Carbohydrate 3.5g, of which sugars 3.1g; Fat 3.3g, of which saturates 1.9g; Cholesterol 8mg; Calcium 68mg; Fibre 1g; Sodium 41mg.

AVOCADO, SPINACH AND SORREL SOUP

*SORREL, WITH ITS SHARP LEMONY FLAVOUR, GROWS WILD THROUGHOUT THE UK, EUROPE, NORTH
AMERICA AND ASIA. IN SOME PARTS OF SCOTLAND IT IS KNOWN AS 'SOUROCKS'.*

SERVES 4

INGREDIENTS
  30ml/2 tbsp olive oil
  2 onions, chopped
  1kg/2¼lb fresh spinach
  900ml/1½ pints/3¾ cups light
  chicken stock
  4 garlic cloves, crushed with salt
  1 bunch sorrel leaves
  2 avocados, peeled and stoned
  (pitted)

1 Pour the olive oil into a large heavy
pan and sweat the onions over a gentle
heat until soft but not coloured.

2 Meanwhile, wash the spinach
thoroughly and remove the stalks.

3 Add the spinach to the onions and
cook for 2 minutes, stirring, to wilt the
leaves. Cover, increase the heat slightly
and cook for 3 minutes. Add the stock,
cover and simmer for about 10 minutes.

4 Add the garlic, sorrel and avocados
and heat gently. Remove from the heat.

5 Allow the soup to cool then purée in a
blender. Reheat the soup before serving
with warmed crusty bread.

COOK'S TIPS
• Crushing garlic in salt helps to bring
out the oils of the garlic and also stops
any being wasted in a garlic press. Use a
coarse salt and try to keep a chopping
board or at least a corner of one for this
sole purpose, as it is hard to get rid of
the scent of garlic and it can taint
other foods.
• When using avocados in soup do not
let them boil as this makes them taste
bitter. They are best added at the end
and just heated through.
• This soup freezes for up to a month.
Freeze it the day you make it.

Energy 282kcal/1161kJ; Protein 9.3g; Carbohydrate 11.4g, of which sugars 8.3g; Fat 22.1g, of which saturates 4.1g; Cholesterol 0mg; Calcium 452mg; Fibre 8.9g; Sodium 357mg.

DUCK CONSOMMÉ

THE VIETNAMESE COMMUNITY IN FRANCE HAS INFLUENCED FRENCH COOKING, AS THIS SOUP BEARS WITNESS — IT IS LIGHT AND RICH AT THE SAME TIME, WITH FLAVOURS OF SOUTH-EAST ASIA.

SERVES 4

INGREDIENTS
    1 duck carcass (raw or cooked), plus
    2 legs or any giblets, trimmed of as
    much fat as possible
    1 large onion, unpeeled, with root
    end trimmed
    2 carrots, cut into 5cm/2in pieces
    1 parsnip, cut into 5cm/2in pieces
    1 leek, cut into 5cm/2in pieces
    2–4 garlic cloves, crushed
    2.5cm/1in piece fresh root ginger,
    peeled and sliced
    15ml/1 tbsp black peppercorns
    4–6 sprigs of fresh thyme or
    5ml/1 tsp dried
    1 small bunch of coriander (cilantro),
    leaves and stems separated
For the garnish
    1 small carrot
    1 small leek, halved lengthways
    4–6 shiitake mushrooms,
    thinly sliced
    soy sauce
    2 spring onions (scallions), sliced
    watercress or finely shredded Chinese
    leaves (Chinese cabbage)
    ground black pepper

1 Put the duck carcass and legs or giblets, onion, carrots, parsnip, leek and garlic in a large, heavy pan or flameproof casserole. Add the ginger, peppercorns, thyme and coriander stems, cover with cold water and bring to the boil over a medium-high heat, skimming off any foam that rises to the surface.

2 Reduce the heat and simmer for 1½–2 hours, then strain through a muslin-lined (cheesecloth-lined) sieve (strainer) into a bowl, discarding the bones and vegetables. Cool and chill overnight. Skim off any congealed fat and blot the surface with kitchen paper.

3 To make the garnish, cut the carrot and leek into 5cm/2in pieces. Cut each piece lengthways in thin slices, then stack and slice into thin julienne strips. Place in a large pan with the sliced mushrooms.

4 Pour over the stock and add a few dashes of soy sauce and some pepper. Bring to the boil over a medium-high heat, skimming any foam that rises to the surface. Adjust the seasoning. Stir in the spring onions and watercress or Chinese leaves.

5 Ladle the consommé into warmed bowls and sprinkle with the coriander leaves before serving.

Energy 12kcal/51kJ; Protein 1.4g; Carbohydrate 1.9g, of which sugars 1.6g; Fat 0.6g, of which saturates 0.2g; Cholesterol 0mg; Calcium 13mg; Fibre 1g; Sodium 550mg

CHINESE CHICKEN AND ASPARAGUS SOUP

THIS IS A VERY DELICATE AND DELICIOUS SOUP. ITS TASTE IS VASTLY SUPERIOR IF YOU USE HOME-MADE CHICKEN STOCK.

SERVES 4

INGREDIENTS
  140g/5oz chicken breast fillet
  pinch of salt
  5ml/1 tsp egg white
  5ml/1 tsp cornflour (cornstarch), mixed
    to a paste with 15ml/1 tsp water
  115g/4oz asparagus
  700ml/1¼ pints/3 cups
    chicken stock
  salt and ground black pepper
  fresh coriander (cilantro) leaves,
    to garnish

1 Cut the chicken meat into thin slices, each about the size of a postage stamp. Mix with a pinch of salt, then add the egg white, and finally the cornflour paste.

2 Cut off and discard the tough stems of the asparagus, and diagonally cut the tender spears into short, even lengths.

COOK'S TIP
When fresh asparagus is not in season, canned white asparagus is an acceptable substitute. You do not need to cook it for 2 minutes at step 3.

3 In a wok or large pan, bring the stock to a rolling boil, add the asparagus and bring back to the boil, cooking for 2 minutes.

4 Add the chicken, stir to separate and bring back to the boil once more. Taste and adjust the seasonings. Serve hot, garnished with fresh coriander leaves.

Energy 49kcal/208kJ; Protein 9.4g; Carbohydrate 1.7g, of which sugars 0.6g; Fat 0.6g, of which saturates 0.1g; Cholesterol 25mg; Calcium 10mg; Fibre 0.5g; Sodium 24mg.

CLEAR SOUP WITH SEAFOOD STICKS

THIS DELICATE JAPANESE SOUP, WHICH IS OFTEN EATEN WITH SUSHI, IS VERY QUICK TO MAKE IF YOU PREPARE THE FIRST DASHI BEFOREHAND OR IF YOU USE FREEZE-DRIED DASHI-NO-MOTO.

SERVES 4

INGREDIENTS

4 mitsuba sprigs or 4 chives
  and a few sprigs of mustard and
  cress
4 seafood sticks
400ml/14fl oz/1⅔ cups first dashi
  stock, or the same amount of water
  and 5ml/1 tsp dashi-no-moto
15ml/1 tbsp Japanese soy
  sauce (shoyu)
7.5ml/1½ tsp salt
grated rind of yuzu (optional),
  to garnish

1 Mitsuba leaves are normally sold with the stems and roots on to retain freshness. Cut off the root, then cut 5cm/2in from the top, retaining both the long straw-like stem and the leaf.

2 Blanch the stems in hot water from the kettle. If you use chives, choose them at least 10cm/4in in length and blanch them, too.

3 Take a seafood stick and carefully tie around the middle with a mitsuba stem or chive, holding it in place with a knot. Do not pull too tightly, as the bow will easily break. Repeat the process to make four tied seafood sticks.

4 Hold one seafood stick in your hand. With your finger, carefully loosen both ends to make it look like a tassel.

5 Place one seafood stick in each soup bowl, then put the four mitsuba leaves or mustard and cress on top.

6 Heat the stock in a pan and bring to the boil. Add shoyu and salt to taste. Pour the stock gently over the mitsuba and seafood stick. Sprinkle with grated yuzu rind, if using.

COOK'S TIPS
• Mitsuba is a member of the parsley family and is available from Asian stores.
• Dashi stock can be bought as instant dashi-no-moto, or you can make your own.
• Yuzu is a popular Japanese citrus fruit, about the same size as a clementine, with a firm, thick, yellow skin.

Energy 9kcal/36kJ; Protein 1.1g; Carbohydrate 1g, of which sugars 0.3g; Fat 0.1g, of which saturates 0g; Cholesterol 4mg; Calcium 2mg; Fibre 0g; Sodium 1025mg.

CHINESE CHICKEN AND CHILLI SOUP

GINGER AND LEMON GRASS ADD AN AROMATIC NOTE TO THIS TASTY, REFRESHING SOUP, WHICH CAN BE SERVED AS A LIGHT LUNCH OR APPETIZER.

SERVES 4

INGREDIENTS

150g/5oz boneless chicken breast
  portion, cut into thin strips
2.5cm/1in piece fresh root ginger,
  finely chopped
5cm/2in piece lemon grass stalk,
  finely chopped
1 red chilli, seeded and
  thinly sliced
8 baby corn cobs, halved lengthways
1 large carrot, cut into thin sticks
1 litre/1¾ pints/4 cups hot
  chicken stock
4 spring onions (scallions),
  thinly sliced
12 small shiitake mushrooms, sliced
115g/4oz/1 cup vermicelli
  rice noodles
30ml/2 tbsp soy sauce
salt and ground black pepper

2 Place the Chinese sand pot in an unheated oven. Set the temperature to 200°C/400°F/Gas 6 and cook the soup for 30–40 minutes, or until the stock is simmering and the chicken and vegetables are tender.

3 Add the spring onions and the mushrooms, cover and return the pot to the oven for 10 minutes.

4 Meanwhile place the noodles in a large bowl and cover with boiling water. Soak for the required time, following the packet instructions.

5 Stir the soy sauce into the soup, taste for seasoning and add salt and pepper as required.

6 Drain the noodles and divide them among four warmed serving bowls. Divide the soup between the bowls and serve immediately.

1 Place the chicken strips, chopped ginger, chopped lemon grass and sliced chilli in a Chinese sand pot. Add the halved baby corn and the carrot sticks. Pour over the hot chicken stock and cover the pot.

COOK'S TIP
Rice noodles are available in a variety of thicknesses and can be bought in straight lengths or in coils or loops. They are a creamy white colour and very brittle in texture. Rice noodles are pre-cooked so they only require a very short soaking time – check the packet for exact timings. Vermicelli rice noodles are very fine and will only need to be soaked for a few minutes.

Energy 165kcal/693kJ; Protein 13.3g; Carbohydrate 26g, of which sugars 3.1g; Fat 0.9g, of which saturates 0.2g; Cholesterol 26mg; Calcium 23mg; Fibre 1.4g; Sodium 852mg.

CHICKEN RICE SOUP WITH LEMON GRASS

SHNOR CHROOK IS CAMBODIA'S ANSWER TO THE CHICKEN NOODLE SOUP OF THE WEST. LIGHT AND REFRESHING, IT IS A PERFECT DISH FOR A HOT DAY, AS WELL AS A GREAT PICK-ME-UP WHEN YOU ARE FEELING LOW OR TIRED. THE FRESH, CITRUS AROMA OF LEMON GRASS AND LIME, COMBINED WITH THE WARMTH OF THE CHILLIES, IS INVIGORATING AND AWAKENS THE SENSES.

SERVES 4

INGREDIENTS

For the stock
   1 small chicken or 2 meaty
   chicken legs
   1 onion, quartered
   2 garlic cloves, crushed
   25g/1oz fresh root ginger, sliced
   2 lemon grass stalks
   2 dried red chillies
   30ml/2 tbsp *nuoc mam*

For the soup
   2 lemon grass stalks, trimmed and
   cut into 3 pieces
   15ml/1 tbsp Thai fish sauce
   90g/3½oz/½ cup short grain rice,
   rinsed
   sea salt and ground black pepper
   a small bunch of coriander (cilantro)
   leaves, finely chopped, and 1 green
   or red chilli, to garnish
   1 lime, quartered, to serve

1 Put the chicken into a deep pan and add all the other stock ingredients.

2 Bring the water to the boil for a few minutes, then reduce the heat and simmer gently with the lid on for about 2 hours, until the chicken is tender.

3 Skim off any fat from the stock, strain and reserve. Remove the skin from the chicken and shred the meat. Set aside while you make the soup.

4 Bruise the lemon grass stalks with the blunt edge of a chopping knife.

5 Pour the stock back into the deep pan and bring to the boil. Reduce the heat and stir in the bruised lemon grass stalks and the fish sauce.

6 Stir in the rice and simmer, uncovered, for about 40 minutes. Add the shredded chicken and season to taste with salt and black pepper.

7 Slice the chilli in half, remove the seeds and cut the flesh into very thin strips. It is a good idea to wear gloves when handling chillies.

8 Ladle the soup into individual bowls, garnish with coriander and the thin strips of chilli and serve with lime wedges to squeeze over.

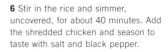

Energy 124kcal/519kJ; Protein 10.9g; Carbohydrate 18.1g, of which sugars 0g; Fat 0.7g, of which saturates 0.1g; Cholesterol 26mg; Calcium 8mg; Fibre 0g; Sodium 226mg.

HOT AND SPICY SOUPS

Make your taste buds tingle with these hot and spicy soups
from all around the world. In the recipes in this section,
chillies, ginger, cayenne pepper and garlic add punch to
vegetables, legumes, meat and shellfish. Choose from exotic
dishes such as the richly flavoured Thai-style Lentil and
Coconut Soup, traditional North African Spiced Soup known as
Harira, Goan Potato Soup with Spiced Pea Samosas, or
Mexican Beef Chilli with Monterey Jack Nachos.

CURRIED PARSNIP SOUP WITH CROÛTONS

THE MILD SWEETNESS OF PARSNIPS AND MANGO CHUTNEY IS GIVEN AN EXCITING LIFT WITH A BLEND OF SPICES IN THIS SIMPLE SOUP GARNISHED WITH NAAN CROÛTONS.

SERVES 4

INGREDIENTS
  30ml/2 tbsp olive oil
  1 onion, chopped
  1 garlic clove, crushed
  1 small green chilli, seeded and
    finely chopped
  15ml/1 tbsp grated fresh
    root ginger
  5 large parsnips, diced
  5ml/1 tsp cumin seeds
  5ml/1 tsp ground coriander
  2.5ml/½ tsp ground turmeric
  30ml/2 tbsp mango chutney
  1.2 litres/2 pints/5 cups water
  juice of 1 lime
  salt and ground black pepper
  60ml/4 tbsp natural (plain) yogurt
    and mango chutney, to serve
  chopped fresh coriander (cilantro),
    to garnish (optional)

For the sesame naan croûtons
  45ml/3 tbsp olive oil
  1 large naan
  15ml/1 tbsp sesame seeds

1 Heat the oil in a large pan and add the onion, garlic, chilli and ginger. Cook for 4–5 minutes, until the onion has softened. Add the parsnips and cook for 2–3 minutes. Sprinkle in the cumin seeds, coriander and turmeric and cook for 1 minute, stirring constantly.

2 Add the chutney and the water. Season well and bring to the boil. Reduce the heat and simmer for 15 minutes, until the parsnips are soft.

3 Cool the soup slightly, then process it in a food processor or blender until smooth, and return it to the saucepan. Stir in the lime juice.

4 For the naan croûtons, cut the naan into small dice. Heat the oil in a large frying pan and cook until golden all over. Remove from the heat and drain off any excess oil. Add the sesame seeds and return to the heat for 30 seconds, until the seeds are golden.

5 Ladle the soup into bowls. Add a little yogurt and top with mango chutney and naan croûtons.

Energy 189kcal/792kJ; Protein 4g; Carbohydrate 26.6g, of which sugars 15.5g; Fat 8.2g, of which saturates 1.2g; Cholesterol 0mg; Calcium 101mg; Fibre 7.5g; Sodium 110mg.

SPICED LENTIL SOUP WITH PARSLEY CREAM

CRISPY SHALLOTS AND A PARSLEY CREAM TOP THIS RICH SOUP, WHICH IS INSPIRED BY THE DHALS OF INDIAN COOKING. CHUNKS OF SMOKED BACON ADD TEXTURE.

SERVES 6

INGREDIENTS

   5ml/1 tsp cumin seeds
   2.5ml/½ tsp coriander seeds
   5ml/1 tsp ground turmeric
   30ml/2 tbsp olive oil
   1 onion, chopped
   2 garlic cloves, chopped
   1 smoked bacon hock
   1.2 litres/2 pints/5 cups
     vegetable stock
   275g/10oz/1¼ cups red lentils
   400g/14oz can chopped tomatoes
   15ml/1 tbsp vegetable oil
   3 shallots, thinly sliced
For the parsley cream
   45ml/3 tbsp chopped
     fresh parsley
   150ml/¼ pint/⅔ cup Greek
     (US strained plain) yogurt
   salt and ground black pepper

1 Heat a frying pan and add the cumin and coriander seeds. Roast them over a high heat for a few seconds, shaking the pan until they smell aromatic. Transfer to a mortar and crush using a pestle. Mix in the turmeric. Set aside.

2 Heat the oil in a large pan. Add the onion and garlic and cook for 4–5 minutes, until softened.

3 Add the spice mixture and cook for 2 minutes, stirring continuously.

COOK'S TIP
Tip lentils into a sieve (strainer) or colander and pick them over to remove any pieces of grit before rinsing.

4 Place the bacon in the pan and pour in the stock. Bring to the boil, cover and simmer gently for 30 minutes.

5 Add the red lentils and cook for 20 minutes or until the lentils and bacon hock are tender. Stir in the tomatoes and cook for a further 5 minutes.

6 Remove the bacon from the pan and set it aside until cool enough to handle. Leave the soup to cool slightly, then process in a food processor or blender until almost smooth. Return the soup to the rinsed-out pan. Cut the meat from the hock, discarding skin and fat, then stir it into the soup and reheat.

7 Heat the oil in a frying pan and fry the shallots for 10 minutes until crisp and golden. Remove using a slotted spoon and drain on kitchen paper.

8 To make the parsley cream, stir the chopped parsley into the yogurt and season well. Ladle the soup into bowls and add a dollop of the parsley cream to each. Pile some crisp shallots on to each portion and serve at once.

Energy 235kcal/991kJ; Protein 13g; Carbohydrate 28.4g, of which sugars 3.7g; Fat 8.8g, of which saturates 2.2g; Cholesterol 0mg; Calcium 66mg; Fibre 2.9g; Sodium 40mg.

TOMATO SOUP WITH RED PEPPER CREAM

THIS DAZZLING SOUP CAN BE MADE AS FIERY OR AS MILD AS YOU LIKE BY INCREASING OR REDUCING THE NUMBER OF CHILLIES.

SERVES 4

INGREDIENTS
    1.5kg/3–3½lb plum tomatoes, halved
    5 red chillies, seeded
    1 red (bell) pepper, halved
      and seeded
    2 red onions, roughly chopped
    6 garlic cloves, crushed
    30ml/2 tbsp sun-dried tomato paste
    45ml/3 tbsp olive oil
    400ml/14fl oz/1⅔ cups
      vegetable stock
    salt and ground black pepper
    wild rocket (arugula), to garnish
For the pepper cream
    1 red pepper, halved and
      seeded
    10ml/2 tsp olive oil
    120ml/4fl oz/½ cup crème fraîche
    a few drops of Tabasco sauce

1 Preheat the oven to 200°C/400°F/ Gas 6. Place the tomatoes, chillies, red pepper, onions, garlic and tomato paste in a roasting tin (pan). Toss all the vegetables, drizzle with the oil and toss again, then roast for 40 minutes, until tender and the pepper skin is slightly charred.

2 Meanwhile make the pepper cream. Lay the red pepper halves skin side up on a baking tray and brush with the olive oil.

3 Roast with the mixed vegetables for about 30–40 minutes, until blistered.

COOK'S TIP
The pepper cream may be a bit runny when first processed, but it firms up when chilled.

4 Transfer the pepper for the pepper cream to a bowl as soon as it is cooked. Cover with clear film (plastic wrap) and leave to cool. Peel away the skin and purée the flesh in a food processor or blender with half the crème fraîche. Pour into a bowl and stir in the remaining crème fraîche. Season and add a dash of Tabasco sauce. Chill in the refrigerator until required.

5 Process the roasted vegetables in batches, adding a ladleful of stock to each batch to make a smooth, thick purée. Depending on how juicy the tomatoes are, you may not need all the vegetable stock.

6 Press the purée through a sieve (strainer) into a pan and stir in more stock if you want to thin the soup. Heat gently and season well. Ladle the soup into bowls and spoon red pepper cream into the centre of each bowl. Pile wild rocket leaves on top to garnish.

Energy 319kcal/1330kJ; Protein 5.3g; Carbohydrate 23.5g, of which sugars 22g; Fat 23.4g, of which saturates 10g; Cholesterol 34mg; Calcium 67mg; Fibre 6.2g; Sodium 72mg.

NORTH AFRICAN SPICED SOUP

CLASSICALLY KNOWN AS HARIRA, *THIS SOUP IS OFTEN SERVED IN THE EVENING DURING* RAMADAN, *THE* MUSLIM *RELIGIOUS FESTIVAL WHEN FOLLOWERS FAST DURING THE DAYTIME FOR A MONTH.*

SERVES 6

INGREDIENTS

1 large onion, chopped
1.2 litres/2 pints/5 cups stock
5ml/1 tsp ground cinnamon
5ml/1 tsp turmeric
15ml/1 tbsp grated ginger
pinch of cayenne pepper
2 carrots, diced
2 celery sticks, diced
400g/14oz can chopped tomatoes
450g/1lb floury potatoes, diced
5 strands saffron
400g/14oz can chickpeas, drained
30ml/2 tbsp chopped fresh
    coriander (cilantro)
15ml/1 tbsp lemon juice
salt and ground black pepper
fried wedges of lemon, to serve

1 Place the chopped onion in a large pot with 300ml/½ pint/1¼ cups of the vegetable stock. Bring the mixture to the boil and simmer gently for about 10 minutes.

2 Meanwhile, mix together the cinnamon, turmeric, ginger, cayenne pepper and 30ml/2 tbsp of stock to form a paste. Stir into the onion mixture with the carrots, celery and remaining stock.

3 Bring the mixture to a boil, reduce the heat, then cover and gently simmer for 5 minutes.

4 Add the tomatoes and potatoes and simmer gently, covered, for 20 minutes. Add the saffron, chickpeas, coriander and lemon juice. Season to taste and when piping hot serve with fried wedges of lemon.

Energy 158kcal/668kJ; Protein 7.2g; Carbohydrate 28.4g, of which sugars 7g; Fat 2.5g, of which saturates 0.4g; Cholesterol 0mg; Calcium 64mg; Fibre 5.4g; Sodium 173mg.

CURRIED CAULIFLOWER SOUP

THIS SPICY, CREAMY SOUP IS PERFECT FOR LUNCH ON A COLD WINTER'S DAY SERVED WITH CRUSTY BREAD AND GARNISHED WITH FRESH CORIANDER.

SERVES 4

INGREDIENTS
    750ml/1¼ pints/3 cups milk
    1 large cauliflower
    15ml/1 tbsp garam masala
    salt and ground black pepper

1 Pour the milk into a large pan and place over a medium heat. Cut the cauliflower into florets and add to the milk with the garam masala and season with salt and pepper.

2 Bring the milk to the boil, then reduce the heat, partially cover the pan with a lid and simmer for about 20 minutes, or until the cauliflower is tender.

3 Let the mixture cool for a few minutes, then transfer to a food processor and process until smooth (you may have to do this in two separate batches).

4 Return the purée to the pan and heat through gently without boiling, checking and adjusting the seasoning to taste. Serve immediately.

Energy 143kcal/601kJ; Protein 12g; Carbohydrate 13.9g, of which sugars 12.6g; Fat 4.8g, of which saturates 2.3g; Cholesterol 11mg; Calcium 271mg; Fibre 3.2g; Sodium 104mg.

CORN <u>AND</u> RED CHILLI CHOWDER

CORN AND CHILLIES MAKE GOOD BEDFELLOWS, AND HERE THE COOL COMBINATION OF CREAMED CORN AND MILK IS THE PERFECT FOIL FOR THE RAGING HEAT OF THE CHILLIES.

SERVES 6

INGREDIENTS

2 tomatoes, skinned
1 onion, roughly chopped
375g/13oz can creamed corn
2 red (bell) peppers, halved
and seeded
15ml/1 tbsp olive oil, plus extra
for brushing
3 red chillies, seeded and
sliced
2 garlic cloves, chopped
5ml/1 tsp ground cumin
5ml/1 tsp ground coriander
600ml/1 pint/2½ cups milk
350ml/12fl oz/1½ cups
chicken stock
3 cobs of corn, kernels removed
450g/1lb potatoes, finely diced
60ml/4 tbsp double (heavy) cream
60ml/4 tbsp chopped fresh parsley
salt and ground black pepper

1 Process the tomatoes and onion in a food processor or blender to a smooth purée. Add the creamed corn and process again, then set aside. Preheat the grill (broiler) to high.

2 Put the peppers, skin sides up, on a grill rack and brush with oil. Grill (broil) for 8–10 minutes, until the skins blacken and blister. Transfer to a bowl and cover with clear film (plastic wrap), then leave to cool. Peel and dice the peppers, then set them aside.

3 Heat the oil in a large pan and add the chillies and garlic. Cook, stirring, for 2–3 minutes, until softened.

4 Add the ground cumin and coriander, and cook for a further 1 minute. Stir in the corn purée and cook for about 8 minutes, stirring occasionally.

5 Pour in the milk and stock, then stir in the corn kernels, potatoes, red pepper and seasoning to taste. Cook for 15–20 minutes, until the corn and potatoes are tender.

6 Pour into deep bowls and add the cream, then sprinkle over the chopped parsley and serve at once.

Energy 343kcal/1448kJ; Protein 9.4g; Carbohydrate 55.4g, of which sugars 23.2g; Fat 10.9g, of which saturates 5.1g; Cholesterol 20mg; Calcium 147mg; Fibre 4g; Sodium 383mg.

FRAGRANT BEETROOT AND VEGETABLE SOUP WITH SPICED LAMB KUBBEH

THE JEWISH COMMUNITY FROM COCHIN IN INDIA IS SCATTERED NOW BUT IS STILL FAMOUS FOR ITS CUISINE. THIS TANGY SOUP IS SERVED WITH DUMPLINGS MADE OF BRIGHT YELLOW PASTA WRAPPED AROUND A SPICY LAMB FILLING, AND A DOLLOP OF FRAGRANT GREEN HERB PASTE.

SERVES 6–8

INGREDIENTS

15ml/1 tbsp vegetable oil
½ onion, finely chopped
6 garlic cloves
1 carrot, diced
1 courgette (zucchini), diced
½ celery stick, diced (optional)
4–5 cardamom pods
2.5ml/½ tsp curry powder
4 vacuum-packed beetroot (beets)
    (cooked not pickled), finely diced
    and juice reserved
1 litre/1¾ pints/4 cups
    vegetable stock
400g/14oz can chopped tomatoes
45–60ml/3–4 tbsp chopped fresh
    coriander (cilantro) leaves
2 bay leaves
15ml/1 tbsp sugar
salt and ground black pepper
15–30ml/1–2 tbsp white wine
    vinegar, to serve
For the kubbeh
2 large pinches of saffron threads
15ml/1 tbsp hot water
15ml/1 tbsp vegetable oil
1 large onion, chopped
250g/9oz lean minced (ground) lamb
5ml/1 tsp vinegar
½ bunch fresh mint, chopped
115g/4oz/1 cup plain (all-purpose) flour
2–3 pinches of salt
2.5–5ml/½–1 tsp ground turmeric
45–60ml/3–4 tbsp cold water
For the ginger and coriander paste
4 garlic cloves, chopped
15–25ml/1–1½ tbsp chopped
    fresh root ginger
½–4 fresh mild chillies
½ large bunch fresh coriander
    (cilantro)
30ml/2 tbsp white wine vinegar
extra virgin olive oil

COOK'S TIP
Serve any leftover paste with meatballs
or spread on sandwiches.

1 For the paste, process the garlic, ginger and chillies in a food processor. Add the coriander, vinegar, oil and salt and process to a purée. Set aside.

2 To make the kubbeh filling, place the saffron and hot water in a small bowl and leave to infuse (steep). Meanwhile, heat the oil in a pan and fry the onion until softened. Put the onion and saffron water in a food processor and blend. Add the lamb, season and blend. Add the vinegar and mint, then chill.

3 To make the kubbeh dough, put the flour, salt and ground turmeric in a food processor, then gradually add the water, processing until it forms a sticky dough. Knead on a floured surface for 5 minutes, wrap in a plastic bag and leave to stand for 30 minutes.

4 Divide the dough into 10–15 pieces. Roll each into a ball, then, using a pasta machine, roll into very thin rounds.

5 Lay the rounds on a well-floured surface. Place a spoonful of filling in the middle of each. Dampen the edges of the dough, then bring them together and seal. Set aside on a floured surface.

6 To make the soup, heat the oil in a pan, add the onion and fry for about 10 minutes, or until softened but not browned. Add half the garlic, the carrot, courgette, celery (if using), cardamom pods and curry powder, and cook for 2–3 minutes.

7 Add three of the diced beetroot, the stock, tomatoes, coriander, bay leaves and sugar to the pan. Bring to the boil, then reduce the heat and simmer for about 20 minutes.

8 Add the remaining beetroot, beetroot juice and garlic to the soup. Season with salt and pepper to taste and set aside until ready to serve.

9 To serve, reheat the soup and poach the dumplings in a large pan of salted boiling water for about 4 minutes. Using a slotted spoon, remove the dumplings from the water as they are cooked and place on a plate to keep warm.

10 Ladle the soup into bowls, adding a dash of vinegar to each bowl, then add two or three dumplings and a small spoonful of the ginger and coriander paste to each. Serve immediately.

GOAN POTATO SOUP WITH SPICED PEA SAMOSAS

IN GOA THIS SOUP WOULD BE SERVED AS A COMPLETE MEAL. BOTH SOUP AND SAMOSAS ARE SIMPLE TO PREPARE, AND MAKE A SUBSTANTIAL VEGETARIAN LUNCH.

SERVES 4

INGREDIENTS
 60ml/4 tbsp sunflower oil
 10ml/2 tsp black mustard seeds
 1 large onion, chopped
 1 red chilli, seeded and chopped
 2.5ml/½ tsp ground turmeric
 1.5ml/¼ tsp cayenne pepper
 900g/2lb potatoes, cut into cubes
 4 fresh curry leaves
 750ml/1¼ pint/3 cups water
 225g/8oz spinach leaves, torn if large
 400ml/14fl oz/1⅔ cups coconut milk
 handful of fresh coriander
  (cilantro) leaves
 salt and ground black pepper
For the samosa dough
 275g/10oz/2½ cups plain
  (all-purpose) flour
 1.5ml/¼ tsp salt
 30ml/2 tbsp sunflower oil
 150ml/¼ pint/⅔ cup warm water
For the samosa filling
 60ml/4 tbsp sunflower oil
 1 small onion, finely chopped
 175g/6oz/1½ cups frozen peas,
  thawed
 15ml/1 tbsp grated fresh root ginger
 1 green chilli, seeded and
  finely chopped
 45ml/3 tbsp water
 350g/12oz cooked potatoes,
  finely diced
 7.5ml/1½ tsp ground coriander
 5ml/1 tsp garam masala
 7.5ml/1½ tsp ground cumin
 1.5ml/¼ tsp cayenne pepper
 10ml/2 tsp lemon juice
 30ml/2 tbsp chopped fresh
  coriander
 vegetable oil, for deep frying

1 Make the samosa dough. Mix the flour and salt in a bowl and make a well in the middle. Add the oil and water and mix in the flour to make a soft dough. Knead briefly on a lightly floured surface. Wrap in clear film (plastic wrap) and chill for 30 minutes.

2 To make the filling, heat the oil in a frying pan and add the onion. Cook for 6–7 minutes until golden. Add the peas, ginger, chilli and water. Cover and simmer for 5–6 minutes, until the peas are cooked. Add the potatoes, spices and lemon juice. Cook over a low heat for 2–3 minutes. Stir in the coriander and season well. Leave to cool.

3 Divide the dough into eight. On a floured surface, roll out one piece into an 18cm/7in round. Keep the remaining dough covered. Cut the round in half and place 30ml/2 tbsp of the filling on each half towards one corner.

4 Dampen the edges and fold the dough over the filling. Pinch the edges together to form triangles. Repeat with the remaining dough and filling.

5 Heat the oil for deep frying to 190°C/375°F, or until a cube of bread rises and sizzles in 30 seconds. Fry the samosas for 4–5 minutes, turning once. Drain on kitchen paper.

6 To make the soup, heat the oil in a large pan. Add the mustard seeds, cover and cook until they begin to pop. Add the onion and chilli and cook for 5–6 minutes, until softened. Stir in the turmeric, cayenne, potatoes, curry leaves and water. Cover and cook over a low heat for 15 minutes, stirring occasionally, until the potatoes are soft.

7 Add the spinach and cook for 5 minutes. Stir in the coconut milk and cook for a further 5 minutes. Season and add the coriander leaves before ladling the soup into bowls. Serve with the vegetable samosas.

Energy 836kcal/3503kJ; Protein 16.7g; Carbohydrate 112g, of which sugars 8.6g; Fat 38.7g, of which saturates 4.9g; Cholesterol 0mg; Calcium 227mg; Fibre 8.9g; Sodium 117mg.

MEXICAN BEEF CHILLI WITH MONTEREY JACK NACHOS

STEAMING BOWLS OF BEEF CHILLI SOUP, PACKED WITH BEANS, ARE DELICIOUS TOPPED WITH CRUSHED TORTILLAS AND CHEESE. POP THE BOWLS UNDER THE GRILL TO MELT THE CHEESE, IF YOU WISH.

SERVES 4

INGREDIENTS
45ml/3 tbsp olive oil
350g/12oz rump steak, cut into
  small pieces
2 onions, chopped
2 garlic cloves, crushed
2 green chillies, seeded and
  finely chopped
30ml/2 tbsp mild chilli powder
5ml/1 tsp ground cumin
2 bay leaves
30ml/2 tbsp tomato purée (paste)
900ml/1½ pints/3¾ cups beef stock
2 x 400g/14oz cans mixed beans,
  drained and rinsed
45ml/3 tbsp chopped fresh coriander
  (cilantro) leaves
salt and ground black pepper
For the topping
  bag of plain tortilla chips,
    lightly crushed
  225g/8oz/2 cups Monterey Jack
    cheese, grated

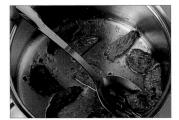

1 Heat the oil in a large pan over a high heat and cook the meat all over until golden. Use a slotted spoon to remove it from the pan.

2 Reduce the heat and add the onions, garlic and chillies, then cook for 4–5 minutes, until softened.

VARIATION
Use Cheddar cheese instead of Monterey Jack if you prefer.

3 Add the chilli powder and ground cumin, and cook for a further 2 minutes. Return the meat to the pan, then stir in the bay leaves, tomato purée and beef stock. Bring to the boil.

4 Reduce the heat, cover the pan and simmer for about 45 minutes, or until the meat is tender.

5 Put a quarter of the beans into a bowl and mash with a potato masher. Stir these into the soup to thicken it slightly. Add the remaining beans and simmer for about 5 minutes. Season and stir in the chopped coriander. Ladle the soup into warmed bowls and spoon tortilla chips on top. Pile grated cheese over the tortilla chips and serve.

Energy 749kcal/3135kJ; Protein 50g; Carbohydrate 54.1g, of which sugars 10.3g; Fat 37.2g, of which saturates 16.1g; Cholesterol 106mg; Calcium 609mg; Fibre 14.5g; Sodium 1473mg.

SPICY TOMATO AND CORIANDER SOUP

HEART-WARMING TOMATO SOUP IS ALWAYS A FAVOURITE. DELICIOUSLY SPICY, IT IS ALSO THE PERFECT SOUP TO PREPARE FOR A COLD WINTER'S DAY.

SERVES 4

INGREDIENTS

675g/1½lb tomatoes
30ml/2 tbsp vegetable oil
1 bay leaf
4 spring onions (scallions), chopped
5ml/1 tsp salt
2.5ml/½ tsp crushed garlic
5ml/1 tsp crushed black peppercorns
30ml/2 tbsp chopped fresh coriander
  (cilantro)
750ml/1¼ pints/3 cups water
15ml/1 tbsp cornflour (cornstarch)
30ml/2 tbsp single (light) cream,
  to serve

2 In a medium pan, heat the oil and fry the chopped tomatoes, bay leaf and chopped spring onions for a few minutes until soft and translucent, but not browned.

5 Remove the soup from the heat and press through a sieve (strainer) over a bowl. Discard the sieved vegetables.

1 To peel the tomatoes, plunge them into very hot water, then lift them out more or less straight away using a slotted spoon. The skin should now peel off quickly and easily. Once this is done, chop the tomatoes roughly.

3 Gradually add the salt, garlic, peppercorns and fresh coriander to the tomato mixture, finally adding the water.

4 Bring to the boil, lower the heat and simmer for 15–20 minutes. Meanwhile, dissolve the cornflour in a little cold water, and set aside.

6 Return to the pan, add the cornflour mixture and simmer over a gentle heat, stirring continuously, for about 3 minutes until thickened.

7 Pour into individual warmed soup bowls and serve piping hot, with a swirl of cream.

VARIATION
Instead of cream, add a dollop of natural (plain) yogurt or crème fraîche to the individual servings.

COOK'S TIP
The best tomatoes to use for this soup are ripe Italian plum tomatoes. If the only fresh tomatoes available are rather pale and under-ripe, add 15ml/1 tbsp tomato purée (paste) to the pan with the chopped tomatoes. This will enhance the colour and flavour of the soup.

Energy 63kcal/267kJ; Protein 2g; Carbohydrate 9.5g, of which sugars 6g; Fat 2.2g, of which saturates 1.1g; Cholesterol 4mg; Calcium 48mg; Fibre 2.5g; Sodium 24mg.

SPICY CARROT SOUP WITH GARLIC CROÛTONS

CARROT SOUP IS GIVEN A HINT OF SPICE WITH CORIANDER, CUMIN AND CHILLI POWDER. THE FINAL TOUCH COMES WITH A GARNISH OF GARLIC CROÛTONS.

SERVES 6

INGREDIENTS

15ml/1 tbsp olive oil
1 large onion, chopped
675g/1½lb/3¾ cups carrots, sliced
5ml/1 tsp each ground coriander,
  ground cumin and hot chilli powder
900ml/1½ pints/3¾ cups vegetable
  stock
salt and ground black pepper
fresh coriander (cilantro), to garnish
For the garlic croûtons
  a little olive oil
  2 garlic cloves, crushed
  4 slices bread, crusts removed, cut
    into 1cm/½in cubes

1 To make the soup, heat the oil in a large pan, add the onion and carrots and cook gently for 5 minutes, stirring occasionally. Add the ground spices and cook gently for 1 minute, continuing to stir.

2 Stir in the stock, bring to the boil, then cover and cook gently for about 45 minutes until the carrots are tender.

3 Meanwhile, make the garlic croûtons. Heat the oil in a frying pan, add the garlic and cook for 30 seconds. Add the bread cubes, turn them over in the oil and fry until crisp and golden brown all over, turning frequently. Drain on kitchen paper and keep warm.

4 Purée the soup in a blender or food processor. Return it to the rinsed-out pan, season and reheat gently. Serve hot, sprinkled with garlic croûtons and garnished with coriander sprigs.

Energy 124kcal/517kJ; Protein 2.5g; Carbohydrate 19.7g, of which sugars 10.6g; Fat 4.4g, of which saturates 0.6g; Cholesterol 0mg; Calcium 55mg; Fibre 3.4g; Sodium 116mg.

ROASTED GARLIC AND BUTTERNUT SQUASH SOUP WITH TOMATO SALSA

THIS IS A WONDERFUL, RICHLY FLAVOURED DISH. A SPOONFUL OF THE HOT AND SPICY TOMATO SALSA GIVES BITE TO THE SWEET-TASTING SQUASH AND GARLIC SOUP.

SERVES 4–5

INGREDIENTS

2 garlic bulbs, outer skin removed
75ml/5 tbsp olive oil
a few fresh thyme sprigs
1 large butternut squash, halved
  and seeded
2 onions, chopped
5ml/1 tsp ground coriander
1.2 litres/2 pints/5 cups vegetable
  or chicken stock
30–45ml/2–3 tbsp chopped fresh
  oregano or marjoram
salt and ground black pepper
For the salsa
4 large ripe tomatoes, halved
  and seeded
1 red (bell) pepper, halved
  and seeded
1 large fresh red chilli, halved
  and seeded
30–45ml/2–3 tbsp extra virgin
  olive oil
15ml/1 tbsp balsamic vinegar
pinch of caster (superfine) sugar

1 Preheat the oven to 220°C/425°F/Gas 7. Place the garlic bulbs on a piece of foil and pour over half the olive oil. Add the thyme sprigs, then fold the foil around the garlic bulbs to enclose them completely. Place the foil parcel on a baking sheet with the butternut squash and brush the squash with 15ml/1 tbsp of the remaining olive oil. Add the tomatoes, red pepper and fresh chilli for the salsa.

2 Roast the vegetables for 25 minutes, then remove the tomatoes, pepper and chilli. Reduce the temperature to 190°C/375°F/Gas 5 and cook the squash and garlic for 20–25 minutes more, or until the squash is tender.

3 Heat the remaining oil in a large, heavy-based pan and cook the onions and ground coriander gently for about 10 minutes, or until softened.

4 Skin the pepper and chilli and process in a food processor or blender with the tomatoes and 30ml/2 tbsp olive oil. Stir in the vinegar and seasoning to taste, adding a pinch of caster sugar. Add the remaining oil if you think the salsa needs it.

5 Squeeze the roasted garlic out of its papery skin into the onions and scoop the squash out of its skin, adding it to the pan. Add the stock, 5ml/1 tsp salt and plenty of black pepper. Bring to the boil and simmer for 10 minutes.

6 Stir in half the oregano or marjoram and cool the soup slightly, then process it in a blender or food processor. Alternatively, press the soup through a fine sieve (strainer).

7 Reheat the soup without allowing it to boil, then taste for seasoning before ladling it into warmed bowls. Top each with a spoonful of salsa and sprinkle over the remaining chopped oregano or marjoram. Serve immediately.

Energy 303kcal/1256kJ; Protein 4.2g; Carbohydrate 20.7g, of which sugars 16.6g; Fat 23.2g, of which saturates 3.5g; Cholesterol 0mg; Calcium 107mg; Fibre 5.7g; Sodium 15mg.

CURRIED CELERY SOUP

AN UNUSUAL BUT STIMULATING COMBINATION OF FLAVOURS, THIS WARMING SOUP IS AN EXCELLENT WAY TO TRANSFORM CELERY. SERVE WITH WARM WHOLEMEAL BREAD ROLLS.

SERVES 4–6

INGREDIENTS

10ml/2 tsp olive oil
1 onion, chopped
1 leek, sliced
675g/1½lb celery, chopped
15ml/1 tbsp medium or hot curry
    powder
225g/8oz unpeeled potatoes, washed
    and diced
900ml/1½ pints/3¾ cups vegetable
    stock
1 bouquet garni
30ml/2 tbsp chopped fresh mixed
    herbs
salt
celery seeds and leaves, to garnish

1 Heat the oil in a large pan. Add the onion, leek and celery, cover and cook gently for about 10 minutes, stirring occasionally.

2 Add the curry powder and cook gently for 2 minutes, stirring from time to time to prevent it sticking to the pan.

3 Add the potatoes, stock and bouquet garni, cover and bring to the boil. Simmer for about 20 minutes, until the vegetables are tender but not too soft.

4 Remove and discard the bouquet garni and set the soup aside to cool slightly before it is processed.

COOK'S TIP
For a change, use celeriac and sweet potatoes for this soup in place of celery and standard potatoes.

5 Transfer the soup to a blender or food processor and process in batches until smooth.

6 Add the mixed herbs, season to taste with salt and process briefly again. Return to the pan and reheat gently until piping hot.

7 Ladle into bowls and garnish each one with a sprinkling of celery seeds and a few celery leaves before serving.

Energy 50kcal/212kJ; Protein 1.8g; Carbohydrate 8.7g, of which sugars 2.7g; Fat 1.2g, of which saturates 0.2g; Cholesterol 0mg; Calcium 58mg; Fibre 2.4g; Sodium 73mg.

YOGURT SOUP

MAKE THIS TRADITIONAL INDIAN SOUP AS HOT AS YOU LIKE BY ADDING MORE OR LESS SPICE. SOME COMMUNITIES IN INDIA ADD SUGAR.

SERVES 4–6

INGREDIENTS

450ml/¾ pint/scant 2 cups natural
  (plain) yogurt, beaten
25g/1oz/¼ cup gram flour
2.5ml/½ tsp chilli powder
2.5ml/½ tsp turmeric
2 or 3 fresh green chillies, chopped
60ml/4 tbsp vegetable oil
1 whole dried red chilli
5ml/1 tsp cumin seeds
3 or 4 curry leaves
3 garlic cloves, crushed
5cm/2in piece fresh root ginger,
  peeled and crushed
salt
30ml/2 tbsp chopped fresh coriander
  (cilantro). to garnish

1 Mix together the yogurt, flour, chilli powder, turmeric and salt and strain into a pan.

2 Add the green chillies and cook gently for about 10 minutes, stirring occasionally. Be careful not to let the soup boil over.

3 Heat the oil in a frying pan and fry the remaining spices with the garlic and ginger until the dried chilli turns black. Stir in 15ml/1 tbsp of the coriander.

4 Add the spices to the soup, cover and leave to rest for 5 minutes. Reheat. Serve hot, garnished with coriander.

Energy 125kcal/520kJ; Protein 4.5g; Carbohydrate 9.1g, of which sugars 5.9g; Fat 8.2g, of which saturates 1.2g; Cholesterol 1mg; Calcium 165mg; Fibre 0.6g; Sodium 65mg.

SPICY CHICKEN AND MUSHROOM SOUP

THIS CREAMY CHICKEN SOUP MAKES A HEARTY MEAL. SERVE IT PIPING HOT WITH FRESH GARLIC BREAD AND GARNISHED WITH CHOPPED CORIANDER.

SERVES 4

INGREDIENTS

75g/3oz/6 tbsp unsalted butter
2.5ml/½ tsp crushed garlic
5ml/1 tsp garam masala
5ml/1 tsp crushed black
   peppercorns
5ml/1 tsp salt
1.5ml/¼ tsp freshly grated nutmeg
225g/8oz chicken, skinned and
   boned
1 medium leek, sliced
75g/3oz/generous 1 cup mushrooms,
   sliced
50g/2oz/⅓ cup corn kernels
300ml/½ pint/1¼ cups water
250ml/8fl oz/1 cup single (light)
   cream
30ml/2 tbsp chopped fresh coriander
   (cilantro)
5ml/1 tsp crushed dried red chillies,
   to garnish (optional)

1 Melt the butter in a medium pan. Lower the heat slightly and add the garlic and garam masala. Lower the heat even further and add the black peppercorns, salt and nutmeg.

2 Cut the chicken pieces into very fine strips and add to the pan with the leek, mushrooms and corn. Cook for 5–7 minutes until the chicken is cooked through, stirring constantly.

COOK'S TIP
Any type of mushrooms may be used for this soup, for example field (portabello), Paris Browns or button (white).

3 Remove the pan from the heat and allow to cool slightly.

4 Transfer three-quarters of the mixture into a food processor or blender. Add the water and process for about 1 minute.

5 Pour the purée back into the pan and bring to the boil over a medium heat. Lower the heat and stir in the cream.

6 Add the fresh coriander. Taste and adjust the seasoning. Serve garnished with crushed red chillies, if you like.

Energy 335kcal/1388kJ; Protein 17.1g; Carbohydrate 3.1g, of which sugars 2.7g; Fat 28.3g, of which saturates 17.6g; Cholesterol 114mg; Calcium 75mg; Fibre 1.4g; Sodium 310mg.

LIGHTLY SPICED TOMATO SOUP

*SIMPLE AND QUICK TO MAKE, THIS TOMATO SOUP WILL SOON BECOME ONE OF YOUR FIRM FAVOURITES.
SERVE SPRINKLED WITH PLENTY OF COARSELY GROUND BLACK PEPPER IF YOU LIKE IT REALLY SPICY.*

SERVES 4

INGREDIENTS

　15ml/1 tbsp corn or groundnut
　　(peanut) oil
　1 onion, finely chopped
　900g/2lb tomatoes, peeled, seeded
　　and chopped
　475ml/16fl oz/2 cups chicken stock
　2 sprigs of fresh coriander (cilantro)
　salt
　coarsely ground black pepper

1 Heat the oil in a large pan and fry the
onion for about 5 minutes until it is soft
and transparent but not brown.

2 Add the chopped tomatoes, chicken
stock and coriander to the pan. Bring to
the boil, then lower the heat, cover the
pan and simmer gently for 15 minutes
or until the tomatoes are soft.

3 Remove and discard the coriander.
Press the soup through a sieve
(strainer) and return it to the clean pan.
Season and heat through. Serve
sprinkled with coarsely ground pepper.

Energy 71kcal/299kJ; Protein 2g; Carbohydrate 8.4g, of which sugars 8g; Fat 3.6g, of which saturates 0.6g; Cholesterol 0mg; Calcium 35mg; Fibre 2.8g; Sodium 23mg.

MUSHROOM, CELERY AND GARLIC SOUP

A ROBUST SOUP IN WHICH THE DOMINANT FLAVOUR OF MUSHROOMS IS ENHANCED WITH GARLIC, WHILE CELERY INTRODUCES A CONTRASTING NOTE.

SERVES 4

INGREDIENTS

350g/12oz/4½ cups chopped
  mushrooms
4 celery sticks, chopped
3 garlic cloves
45ml/3 tbsp dry sherry or white wine
750ml/1¼ pints/3 cups chicken
  stock
30ml/2 tbsp Worcestershire sauce
5ml/1 tsp freshly grated nutmeg
salt and ground black pepper
celery leaves, to garnish

1 Place the mushrooms, celery and garlic in a pan and stir in the sherry or wine. Cover and cook over a low heat for 30–40 minutes until the vegetables are tender.

COOK'S TIP
Any type of mushrooms may be used for this soup, for example field (portabello), Paris Browns or button (white).

2 Add half the stock and purée in a food processor or blender until smooth. Return to the pan and add the remaining stock, the Worcestershire sauce and nutmeg.

3 Bring to the boil and season to taste with salt and pepper.

4 Ladle into warmed soup bowls and serve hot, garnished with celery leaves.

Energy 26kcal/109kJ; Protein 1.9g; Carbohydrate 1.9g, of which sugars 1.6g; Fat 0.5g, of which saturates 0.1g; Cholesterol 0mg; Calcium 33mg; Fibre 1.3g; Sodium 113mg.

HOT-AND-SOUR PRAWN SOUP <u>WITH</u> LEMON GRASS

THIS CLASSIC SEAFOOD SOUP, KNOWN AS TOM YAM GOONG, *IS PROBABLY THE MOST POPULAR AND BEST-KNOWN SOUP FROM* THAILAND.

SERVES 4–6

INGREDIENTS
   450g/1lb king prawns
   1 litre/1¾ pints/4 cups chicken stock
     or water
   3 lemon grass stalks
   10 kaffir lime leaves, torn in half
   225g/8oz can straw mushrooms,
     drained
   45ml/3 tbsp Thai fish sauce
   50ml/2fl oz/¼ cup lime juice
   30ml/2 tbsp chopped spring onion
     (scallion)
   15ml/1 tbsp fresh coriander (cilantro)
     leaves
   4 fresh red chillies, seeded
     and chopped
   2 spring onions (scallions), finely
     chopped, to garnish

1 Shell and devein the prawns and set aside. Rinse the prawn shells, place in a large pan with the stock or water and bring to the boil.

2 Bruise the lemon grass stalks with the blunt edge of a chopping knife and add them to the stock, together with half the lime leaves. Simmer gently for 5–6 minutes until the stalks change colour.

3 Strain the stock, return to the pan and reheat. Add the mushrooms and prawns, then cook until the prawns turn pink.

4 Stir in the fish sauce, lime juice, spring onion, coriander, red chillies and the rest of the lime leaves. Taste and adjust the seasoning. The soup should be sour, salty, spicy and hot. Garnish with finely chopped spring onions.

Energy 63kcal/268kJ; Protein 14g; Carbohydrate 0.4g, of which sugars 0.3g; Fat 0.7g, of which saturates 0.1g; Cholesterol 146mg; Calcium 64mg; Fibre 0.5g; Sodium 145mg.

PORK ᴬᴺᴰ PICKLED MUSTARD GREENS SOUP

THIS HIGHLY FLAVOURED SOUP MAKES AN INTERESTING START TO A MEAL. ADD MORE SLICED FRESH CHILLIES TO GARNISH IF YOU REALLY WANT TO PACK A PUNCH.

SERVES 4–6

INGREDIENTS
   225g/8oz pickled mustard leaves,
      soaked
   50g/2oz cellophane noodles, soaked
   15ml/1 tbsp vegetable oil
   4 garlic cloves, finely sliced
   1 litre/1¾ pints/4 cups chicken stock
   450g/1lb pork ribs, cut into large
      chunks
   30ml/2 tbsp Thai fish sauce
   a pinch of sugar
   ground black pepper
   2 fresh chillies, seeded and finely
      sliced, to garnish

3 Heat the oil in a small frying pan, add the garlic and stir-fry until golden. Transfer to a bowl and set aside.

4 Pour the stock into a pan, bring to the boil, then add the pork ribs and simmer gently for 10–15 minutes.

5 Add the pickled mustard leaves and cellophane noodles. Bring back to the boil. Season to taste with Thai fish sauce, sugar and ground black pepper.

6 Garnish with the fried garlic and the red chillies and serve hot.

1 Cut the pickled mustard leaves into bite-size pieces. Taste to check the seasoning. If they are too salty, soak them for a little longer.

2 Drain the cellophane noodles, discarding the soaking water, and cut them into pieces about 5cm/2in long.

COOK'S TIP
The colour of Thai fish sauce can vary. Lighter sauces are considered to be better than darker vesions.

Energy 218kcal/910kJ; Protein 24.5g; Carbohydrate 7.8g, of which sugars 0.9g; Fat 9.7g, of which saturates 3g; Cholesterol 74mg; Calcium 90mg; Fibre 0.8g; Sodium 454mg.

SPICED PARSNIP SOUP

*THIS PALE, CREAMY-TEXTURED SOUP IS GIVEN A SPECIAL TOUCH WITH AN AROMATIC, SPICED GARLIC
AND CORIANDER GARNISH.*

SERVES 4–6

INGREDIENTS

40g/1½oz/3 tbsp butter
1 onion, chopped
675g/1½lb parsnips, diced
5ml/1 tsp ground coriander
2.ml/½ tsp ground cumin
2.5ml/½ tsp ground turmeric
1.5ml/¼ tsp chilli powder
1.2 litres/2 pints/5 cups stock
150ml/¼ pint/⅔ cup single (light)
  cream
15ml/1 tbsp sunflower oil
1 garlic clove, cut into julienne strips
10ml/2 tsp yellow mustard seeds
salt and ground black pepper

1 Melt the butter in a large pan, add the chopped onion and parsnips and fry gently for about 3 minutes.

2 Stir in the spices and cook for 1 minute more.

3 Add the stock, season and bring to the boil. Reduce the heat, cover and simmer for 45 minutes, or until tender.

4 Cool slightly, then purée in a blender or food processor until smooth.

5 Return the soup to the pan, add the cream and heat through gently.

6 Heat the oil in a small pan, add the julienne strips of garlic and the yellow mustard seeds and fry quickly until the garlic is beginning to brown and the mustard seeds start to pop and splutter.

7 Ladle the soup into warmed soup bowls and pour a little of the spice mixture over each one. Serve hot.

Energy 191kcal/795kJ; Protein 3.1g; Carbohydrate 15.6g, of which sugars 7.6g; Fat 13.4g, of which saturates 7g; Cholesterol 28mg; Calcium 72mg; Fibre 5.4g; Sodium 59mg.

LEEK, PARSNIP AND GINGER SOUP

A FLAVOURSOME WINTER WARMER, WITH THE ADDED SPICINESS OF FRESH GINGER. GARNISH WITH A SWIRL OF FROMAGE BLANC AND A SPRINKLING OF PAPRIKA.

SERVES 4–6

INGREDIENTS

30ml/2 tbsp olive oil
225g/8oz/2 cups leeks, sliced
25g/1oz fresh root ginger, peeled and finely chopped
675g/1½lb/5 cups parsnips, roughly chopped
300ml/½ pint/1¼ cups dry white wine
1.2 litres/2 pints/5 cups vegetable stock or water
salt and ground black pepper
fromage blanc and paprika, to garnish

1 Heat the oil in a large pan and add the leeks and ginger. Cook gently, stirring, for 2–3 minutes until the leeks start to soften.

2 Add the parsnips and cook for a further 7–8 minutes until they are beginning to soften.

VARIATION
Double (heavy) cream, crème fraîche or natural (plain) yogurt may be used to garnish in place of fromage blanc.

3 Pour in the wine and stock or water and bring to the boil. Reduce the heat and simmer for 20–30 minutes or until the parsnips are tender.

4 Purée in a blender or food processor until smooth. Season to taste. Reheat and garnish with a swirl of fromage blanc and a light dusting of paprika.

Energy 146kcal/613kJ; Protein 2.7g; Carbohydrate 15.5g, of which sugars 7.5g; Fat 5.1g, of which saturates 0.8g; Cholesterol 0mg; Calcium 60mg; Fibre 6g; Sodium 14mg.

SPICY BEAN SOUP

A FILLING SOUP MADE WITH TWO KINDS OF BEANS FLAVOURED WITH CUMIN. SERVE IT GARNISHED WITH A SWIRL OF SOUR CREAM AND CHOPPED FRESH CORIANDER.

<u>SERVES 6–8</u>

INGREDIENTS

    175g/6oz/1 cup dried black beans,
      soaked overnight and drained
    175g/6oz/1 cup dried kidney beans,
      soaked overnight and drained
    2 bay leaves
    90ml/6 tbsp coarse salt
    30ml/2 tbsp olive or vegetable oil
    3 carrots, chopped
    1 onion, chopped
    1 celery stick
    1 garlic clove, crushed
    5ml/1 tsp ground cumin
    1.5–2.5ml/¼–½ tsp cayenne pepper
    2.5ml/½ tsp dried oregano
    50ml/2fl oz/¼ cup red wine
    1.2 litres/2 pints/5 cups beef stock
    250ml/8fl oz/1 cup water
    salt and ground black pepper
For the garnish
    sour cream
    chopped fresh coriander (cilantro)

1 Put the black beans and kidney beans in two separate pans with cold water to cover and a bay leaf in each. Boil rapidly for 10 minutes, then cover and simmer for 20 minutes.

2 Add 45ml/3 tbsp coarse salt to each pan and continue simmering for a further 30 minutes until the beans are tender. Drain.

COOK'S TIP
Beans toughen with age so, although they will keep for up to a year in a cool, dry place, it is best to buy small quantities from a store with a regular turnover.

3 Heat the oil in a large heavy pan or flameproof casserole. Add the carrots, onion, celery and garlic and cook over a low heat for 8–10 minutes, stirring, until softened.

4 Stir in the cumin, cayenne, oregano and salt to taste.

5 Add the wine, stock and water and stir to mix all the ingredients together. Remove the bay leaves from the cooked beans and add the beans to the casserole.

6 Bring to the boil, reduce the heat, then cover and simmer for about 20 minutes, stirring occasionally to prevent sticking to the base of the pan.

7 Transfer half the soup (including most of the solids) to a food processor or blender. Process until smooth. Return to the pan and stir to combine well.

8 Reheat the soup and adjust the seasoning. Serve hot, garnished with sour cream and chopped coriander.

Energy 161kcal/681kJ; Protein 9.9g; Carbohydrate 23g, of which sugars 3g; Fat 3.5g, of which saturates 0.6g; Cholesterol 0mg; Calcium 47mg; Fibre 5.6g; Sodium 506mg.

CURRIED CARROT AND APPLE SOUP

THE COMBINATION OF CARROT, CURRY AND APPLE IS A HIGHLY SUCCESSFUL ONE. CURLS OF FRESH
CARROT MAKE AN ATTRACTIVE GARNISH.

SERVES 4

INGREDIENTS

    10ml/2 tsp sunflower oil
    15ml/1 tbsp mild Korma curry
      powder
    500g/1¼lb carrots, chopped
    1 large onion, chopped
    1 cooking apple, chopped
    750ml/1¼ pints/3 cups chicken
      stock
    salt and ground black pepper
    natural (plain) yogurt and carrot
      curls, to garnish

1 Heat the oil in a large, heavy pan and very gently fry the curry powder for 2–3 minutes.

2 Add the chopped carrots and onion and the cooking apple, stir well until coated with the curry powder, then cover the pan. Cook over a low heat for about 15 minutes, shaking the pan occasionally to prevent sticking to the base of the pan, until softened.

3 Spoon the vegetable mixture into a food processor or blender, then add half the stock and process until smooth.

4 Return to the pan and pour in the remaining stock. Bring the soup to the boil and adjust the seasoning before serving in bowls, garnished with a swirl of yogurt and a few curls of raw carrot.

Energy 90kcal/376kJ; Protein 1.7g; Carbohydrate 17.3g, of which sugars 15g; Fat 2.1g, of which saturates 0.3g; Cholesterol 0mg; Calcium 51mg; Fibre 4.3g; Sodium 34mg.

SPICY PEANUT SOUP

A THICK AND WARMING VEGETABLE SOUP, EXCITINGLY FLAVOURED WITH CHILLI AND PEANUTS. ADD A SPRINKLING OF ROUGHLY CHOPPED PEANUTS AS A CRUNCHY GARNISH.

SERVES 6

INGREDIENTS
30ml/2 tbsp oil
1 large onion, finely chopped
2 garlic cloves, crushed
5ml/1 tsp mild chilli powder
2 red (bell) peppers, seeded and
  finely chopped
225g/8oz carrots, finely chopped
225g/8oz potatoes, finely chopped
3 celery sticks, sliced
900ml/1½ pints/3¾ cups vegetable
  stock
90ml/6 tbsp crunchy peanut butter
115g/4oz/⅔ cup corn
salt and ground black pepper
roughly chopped unsalted roasted
  peanuts, to garnish

1 Heat the oil in a large pan and cook the onion and garlic for about 3 minutes. Add the chilli powder and cook for a further 1 minute.

2 Add the red peppers, carrots, potatoes and celery. Stir well, then cook for a further 4 minutes, stirring occasionally.

3 Add the vegetable stock, followed by the peanut butter and corn. Stir until thoroughly combined.

4 Season well. Bring to the boil, cover and simmer for about 20 minutes until all the vegetables are tender. Serve garnished with chopped peanuts.

Energy 211kcal/880kJ; Protein 6.3g; Carbohydrate 20.5g, of which sugars 12g; Fat 12.1g, of which saturates 2.5g; Cholesterol 0mg; Calcium 46mg; Fibre 4.4g; Sodium 298mg.

SOUTH INDIAN PEPPER WATER

THIS IS A HIGHLY SOOTHING BROTH FOR COLD WINTER EVENINGS. SERVE WITH THE WHOLE SPICES OR STRAIN AND REHEAT IF YOU SO WISH. THE LEMON JUICE MAY BE ADJUSTED TO TASTE.

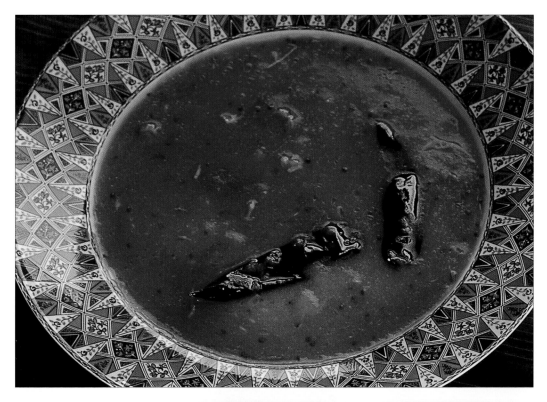

SERVES 2–4

INGREDIENTS
30ml/2 tbsp vegetable oil
2.5ml/½ tsp ground black pepper
5ml/1 tsp cumin seeds
2.5ml/½ tsp mustard seeds
1.5ml/¼ tsp asafoetida powder
2 whole dried red chillies
4–6 curry leaves
2.5ml/½ tsp ground turmeric
2 garlic cloves, crushed
300ml/½ pint/1¼ cups tomato juice
juice of 2 lemons
120ml/4fl oz/½ cup water
salt
fresh coriander (cilantro) leaves,
  chopped, to garnish

1 In a large frying pan, heat the vegetable oil and fry the spices and garlic until the chillies are nearly black and the garlic is a golden brown.

COOK'S TIP
Asafoetida can smell unpleasant but this disappears when added to your cooking.

2 Lower the heat and add the tomato juice, lemon juice, water and salt to taste. Bring to the boil, then simmer for 10 minutes.

3 Ladle the soup into warmed bowls, garnish with chopped coriander and serve piping hot.

Energy 63kcal/262kJ; Protein 0.7g; Carbohydrate 2.6g, of which sugars 2.3g; Fat 5.6g, of which saturates 0.7g; Cholesterol 0mg; Calcium 16mg; Fibre 0.8g; Sodium 178mg.

SPICED RED LENTIL SOUP
WITH COCONUT MILK

A SUBTLE BLEND OF SPICES TAKES THIS WARMING SOUP TO NEW HEIGHTS. SERVE IT WITH CRUSTY BREAD FOR A FILLING AND SATISFYING LUNCH.

SERVES 6

INGREDIENTS

  2 onions, finely chopped
  2 garlic cloves, crushed
  4 tomatoes, roughly chopped
  2.5ml/½ tsp ground turmeric
  5ml/1 tsp ground cumin
  6 cardamom pods
  ½ cinnamon stick
  225g/8oz/1 cup red lentils, rinsed
    and drained
  900ml/1½ pints/3¾ cups water
  400g/14oz can coconut milk
  15ml/1 tbsp lime juice
  salt and ground black pepper
  cumin seeds, to garnish

COOK'S TIP
Unlike other legumes, lentils do not need soaking before being cooked.

1 Put the onions, garlic, tomatoes, turmeric, cumin, cardamom pods, cinnamon, lentils and water into a large pan. Bring to the boil, lower the heat, cover and simmer gently for 20 minutes or until the lentils are soft.

2 Remove the cardamom pods and cinnamon stick, then purée the mixture in a blender or food processor.

3 Press the soup through a sieve (strainer), then return to the clean pan.

4 Reserve a little of the coconut milk for the garnish and add the remainder to the pan with the lime juice. Stir well and season with salt and pepper. Reheat the soup gently without boiling. Swirl in the reserved coconut milk, garnish with cumin seeds and serve piping hot.

Energy 163kcal/694kJ; Protein 10.2g; Carbohydrate 30.4g, of which sugars 9g; Fat 1g, of which saturates 0.3g; Cholesterol 0mg; Calcium 56mg; Fibre 3.2g; Sodium 94mg.

SPICY ROASTED PUMPKIN SOUP WITH PUMPKIN CRISPS

THE PUMPKIN IS ROASTED WHOLE, THEN SPLIT OPEN AND SCOOPED OUT TO MAKE THIS DELICIOUS SOUP; TOPPED WITH CRISP STRIPS OF FRIED PUMPKIN, IT IS A REAL TREAT.

SERVES 6–8

INGREDIENTS
    1.5kg/3–3½lb pumpkin
    90ml/6 tbsp olive oil
    2 onions, chopped
    3 garlic cloves, chopped
    7.5cm/3in piece fresh root
      ginger, grated
    5ml/1 tsp ground coriander
    2.5ml/½ tsp ground turmeric
    pinch of cayenne pepper
    1 litre/1¾ pints/4 cups
      vegetable stock
    salt and ground black pepper
    15ml/1 tbsp sesame seeds and
      fresh coriander (cilantro) leaves,
      to garnish
For the pumpkin crisps
    wedge of fresh pumpkin, seeded
    120ml/4fl oz/½ cup olive oil

1 Preheat the oven to 200°C/400°F/ Gas 6. Prick the pumpkin around the top several times with a fork. Brush the pumpkin with plenty of the oil and bake for 45 minutes or until tender. Leave until cool enough to handle.

2 Take care when cutting the pumpkin as there may still be a lot of hot steam inside. When cool enough to handle, scoop out and discard the seeds. Scoop out and chop the flesh.

3 Heat 60ml/4 tbsp of the remaining oil (you may not have to use all of it) in a large pan and add the onions, garlic and ginger, then cook gently for 4–5 minutes. Add the coriander, turmeric and cayenne, and cook for 2 minutes. Stir in the pumpkin flesh and stock. Bring to the boil, reduce the heat and simmer for 20 minutes.

COOK'S TIP
If only large pumpkins are available, cut off two or three large wedges weighing 1.5kg/3–3½lb in total. Brush with oil and roast for 20–30 minutes until tender.

4 Cool the soup slightly, then purée it in a food processor or blender until smooth. Return the soup to the rinsed pan and season well.

5 Meanwhile, prepare the pumpkin crisps. Using a swivel-blade potato peeler, pare off long thin strips.

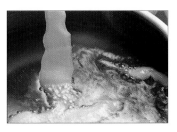

6 Heat the oil in a small pan and fry the strips in batches for 2–3 minutes, until crisp. Drain on kitchen paper.

7 Reheat the soup and ladle it into bowls. Top with the pumpkin crisps and garnish each portion with sesame seeds and coriander leaves.

Energy 271kcal/1119kJ; Protein 3.1g; Carbohydrate 11.1g, of which sugars 8.2g; Fat 24.1g, of which saturates 3.6g; Cholesterol 0mg; Calcium 110mg; Fibre 3.8g; Sodium 3mg.

CASTILIAN GARLIC SOUP

THIS RICH, DARK GARLIC SOUP COMES FROM LA MANCHA IN CENTRAL SPAIN, AND IS SIMILAR TO PORTUGUESE GARLIC SOUP. THE REGION IS FAMOUS FOR ITS SUMMER SUNSHINE, AND THE LOCAL SOUP HAS A HARSH, STRONG TASTE TO MATCH THE CLIMATE.

SERVES 4

INGREDIENTS
    30ml/2 tbsp olive oil
    4 large garlic cloves, peeled
    4 slices stale country bread
    20ml/4 tbsp paprika
    1 litre/1¾ pints/4 cups
      beef stock
    1.5ml/¼ tsp ground cumin
    4 free-range (farm-fresh) eggs
    salt and ground black pepper
    chopped fresh parsley, to garnish

VARIATION
If you prefer, you can simply whisk the eggs into the hot soup.

1 Preheat the oven to 230°C/450°F/ Gas 8. Heat the olive oil in a large pan. Add the whole peeled garlic cloves and cook until they are golden, then remove and set aside. Fry the slices of bread in the oil until golden, then set these aside.

2 Add 15ml/1 tbsp of the paprika to the pan, and fry for a few seconds. Stir in the beef stock, cumin and remaining paprika, then add the reserved garlic, crushing the cloves with the back of a wooden spoon. Season to taste, then cook for about 5 minutes.

3 Break up the slices of fried bread into bitesize pieces and stir them into the soup. Ladle the soup into four ovenproof bowls. Carefully break an egg into each bowl of soup and place in the oven for about 3 minutes, until the eggs are set. Sprinkle the soup with chopped fresh parsley and serve immediately.

Energy 202kcal/843kJ; Protein 9.3g; Carbohydrate 15.3g, of which sugars 1.5g; Fat 12.2g, of which saturates 2.4g; Cholesterol 190mg; Calcium 69mg; Fibre 0.6g; Sodium 202mg.

THAI-STYLE LENTIL AND COCONUT SOUP

HOT, SPICY AND RICHLY FLAVOURED, THIS SUBSTANTIAL SOUP IS ALMOST A MEAL IN ITSELF. IF YOU ARE REALLY HUNGRY, SERVE WITH CHUNKS OF WARMED NAAN BREAD OR THICK SLICES OF TOAST.

SERVES 4

INGREDIENTS

30ml/2 tbsp sunflower oil
2 red onions, finely chopped
1 bird's eye chilli, seeded and
   finely sliced
2 garlic cloves, chopped
2.5cm/1in piece fresh lemon grass,
   outer layers removed and inside
   finely sliced
200g/7oz/scant 1 cup red
   lentils, rinsed
5ml/1 tsp ground coriander
5ml/1 tsp paprika
400ml/14fl oz/1⅔ cups coconut milk
juice of 1 lime
3 spring onions (scallions), chopped
20g/¾oz/scant 1 cup fresh coriander
   (cilantro), finely chopped
salt and freshly ground black pepper

1 Heat the oil in a large pan and add the onions, chilli, garlic and lemon grass. Cook for 5 minutes or until the onions have softened but not browned, stirring occasionally.

COOK'S TIP
When using canned coconut milk, shake it before opening. This ensures that the layers of milk are well combined.

2 Add the lentils and spices. Pour in the coconut milk and 900ml/1½ pints/3¾ cups water, and stir. Bring to the boil, reduce the heat and simmer for 40–45 minutes, until the lentils are soft.

3 Pour in the lime juice and add the spring onions and coriander, reserving a little of each for the garnish. Season, ladle into bowls and garnish.

Energy 245kcal/1034kJ; Protein 12.9g; Carbohydrate 35.8g, of which sugars 8.1g; Fat 6.6g, of which saturates 1g; Cholesterol 0mg; Calcium 75mg; Fibre 3.2g; Sodium 131mg.

CREAMY
VEGETABLE SOUPS

A bowl of smooth and creamy vegetable soup served with some crusty bread makes an excellent light lunch at any time of year. Choose whichever vegetables are fresh and in season — tomatoes and herbs in the summer, pumpkins and squash for the autumn, leeks and root vegetables during the winter months. In this section you will find Simple Cream of Onion Soup and Parsnip Soup from Ireland alongside exotic dishes such as Creamy Heart of Palm Soup and Jersusalem Artichoke Soup.

CREAMY HEART OF PALM SOUP

THIS DELICATE SOUP HAS A LUXURIOUS, CREAMY, ALMOST VELVETY TEXTURE. THE SUBTLE YET DISTINCTIVE FLAVOUR OF THE PALM HEARTS IS LIKE NO OTHER, ALTHOUGH IT IS MILDLY REMINISCENT OF ARTICHOKES AND ASPARAGUS. SERVE WITH FRESH BREAD FOR A SATISFYING LUNCH.

SERVES 4

INGREDIENTS
25g/1oz/2 tbsp butter
10ml/2 tsp olive oil
1 onion, finely chopped
1 large leek, finely sliced
15ml/1 tbsp plain (all-purpose) flour
1 litre/1¾ pints/4 cups
  well-flavoured chicken stock
350g/12oz potatoes, peeled
  and cubed
2 x 400g/14oz cans hearts of palm,
  drained and sliced
250ml/8fl oz/1 cup double
  (heavy) cream
salt and ground black pepper
cayenne pepper and chopped fresh
  chives, to garnish

1 Heat the butter and oil in a large pan over a low heat. Add the onion and leek and stir well until coated in butter. Cover and cook for 5 minutes until softened and translucent.

2 Sprinkle over the flour. Cook, stirring, for 1 minute.

3 Pour in the stock and add the potatoes. Bring to the boil, then lower the heat and simmer for 10 minutes. Stir in the hearts of palm and the cream, and simmer gently for 10 minutes.

4 Process in a blender or food processor until smooth. Return the soup to the pan and heat gently, adding a little water if necessary. The consistency should be thick but not too heavy. Season with salt and ground black pepper.

5 Ladle the soup into heated bowls and garnish each with a pinch of cayenne pepper and a scattering of fresh chives. Serve immediately.

VARIATION
For a richer, buttery flavour, add the flesh of a ripe avocado when blending.

Energy 486kcal/2016kJ; Protein 4.9g; Carbohydrate 25.9g, of which sugars 3g; Fat 41.1g, of which saturates 24.4g; Cholesterol 99mg; Calcium 127mg; Fibre 3.7g; Sodium 97mg.

PARSNIP SOUP

THIS LIGHTLY SPICED SOUP HAS BECOME VERY POPULAR IN IRELAND IN RECENT YEARS, AND MANY VARIATIONS ABOUND, INCLUDING THIS TRADITIONAL IRISH COMBINATION WHERE PARSNIP AND APPLE ARE USED IN EQUAL PROPORTIONS.

SERVES 6

INGREDIENTS
900g/2lb parsnips
50g/2oz/¼ cup butter
1 onion, chopped
2 garlic cloves, crushed
10ml/2 tsp ground cumin
5ml/1 tsp ground coriander
about 1.2 litres/2 pints/5 cups hot
  chicken stock
150ml/¼ pint/⅔ cup single
  (light) cream
salt and ground black pepper
chopped fresh chives or parsley
  and/or croûtons, to garnish

COOK'S TIP
Parsnips taste best after the first frost as the cold converts their starches into sugar, enhancing their sweetness.

1 Peel and thinly slice the parsnips. Heat the butter in a large heavy pan and add the peeled parsnips and chopped onion with the crushed garlic. Cook until softened but not coloured, stirring occasionally. Add the ground cumin and ground coriander to the vegetable mixture and cook, stirring, for 1–2 minutes, and then gradually blend in the hot chicken stock and mix well.

2 Cover and simmer for about 20 minutes, or until the parsnip is soft. Purée the soup, adjust the texture with extra stock or water if it seems too thick, and check the seasoning. Add the cream and reheat without boiling.

3 Serve immediately, sprinkled with chopped chives or parsley and/or croûtons, to garnish.

Energy 215kcal/899kJ; Protein 3.9g; Carbohydrate 21.3g, of which sugars 10.6g; Fat 13.3g, of which saturates 7.7g; Cholesterol 32mg; Calcium 92mg; Fibre 7.3g; Sodium 74mg.

CREAM OF MUSHROOM SOUP WITH GOAT'S CHEESE CROSTINI

CLASSIC CREAM OF MUSHROOM SOUP IS STILL A FIRM FAVOURITE, ESPECIALLY WITH THE ADDITION OF LUXURIOUSLY CRISP AND GARLICKY CROÛTES.

SERVES 6

INGREDIENTS
 25g/1oz/2 tbsp butter
 1 onion, chopped
 1 garlic clove, chopped
 450g/1lb/6 cups button (white),
   chestnut or brown cap mushrooms,
   roughly chopped
 15ml/1 tbsp plain (all-purpose) flour
 45ml/3 tbsp dry sherry
 900ml/1½ pints/3¾ cups
   vegetable stock
 150ml/¼ pint/⅔ cup double
   (heavy) cream
 salt and ground black pepper
 fresh chervil sprigs, to garnish
For the crostini
 15ml/1 tbsp olive oil, plus extra
   for brushing
 1 shallot, chopped
 115g/4oz/1½ cups button (white)
   mushrooms, finely chopped
 15ml/1 tbsp chopped fresh parsley
 6 brown cap (cremini) mushrooms
 6 slices baguette
 1 small garlic clove
 115g/4oz/1 cup soft goat's cheese

1 Melt the butter in a pan and cook the onion and garlic for 5 minutes. Stir in the mushrooms, cover and cook for 10 minutes, stirring occasionally.

2 Stir in the flour and cook for 1 minute. Stir in the sherry and stock and bring to the boil, then simmer for 15 minutes. Cool slightly, then purée the soup in a food processor or blender until smooth.

3 Meanwhile, prepare the crostini. Heat the oil in a small pan. Add the shallot and button mushrooms, and cook for 8–10 minutes, until softened. Drain well and transfer to a food processor. Add the parsley and process until finely chopped.

4 Preheat the grill (broiler). Brush the brown cap mushrooms with oil and cook for 5–6 minutes.

5 Toast the slices of baguette, rub with the garlic and put a spoonful of cheese on each. Top the grilled (broiled) mushrooms with the mushroom mixture and place on the crostini.

6 Return the soup to the pan and stir in the cream. Season, then reheat gently. Ladle the soup into six bowls. Float a crostini in the centre of each and garnish with chervil.

Energy 313kcal/1305kJ; Protein 6.2g; Carbohydrate 26.8g, of which sugars 2.5g; Fat 20g, of which saturates 11g; Cholesterol 43mg; Calcium 75mg; Fibre 2.2g; Sodium 283mg.

ASPARAGUS AND PEA SOUP WITH PARMESAN CHEESE

THIS BRIGHT AND TASTY SOUP USES EVERY INCH OF THE ASPARAGUS, INCLUDING THE WOODY ENDS, WHICH ARE USED FOR MAKING THE STOCK.

SERVES 6

INGREDIENTS

350g/12oz asparagus
2 leeks
1 bay leaf
1 carrot, roughly chopped
1 celery stick, chopped
few stalks of fresh parsley
1.75 litres/3 pints/7½ cups
  cold water
25g/1oz/2 tbsp butter
150g/5oz fresh garden peas
15ml/1 tbsp chopped fresh parsley
120ml/4fl oz/½ cup double
  (heavy) cream
grated rind of ½ lemon
salt and ground black pepper
shavings of Parmesan cheese,
  to serve

1 Cut the woody ends from the asparagus, then set the spears aside. Roughly chop the woody ends and place them in a large pan. Cut off and chop the green parts of the leeks and add to the asparagus stalks with the bay leaf, carrot, celery, parsley stalks and the cold water. Bring to the boil and simmer for 30 minutes. Strain the stock and discard the vegetables.

2 Cut the tips off the asparagus and set aside, then cut the stems into short pieces. Chop the remainder of the leeks.

3 Melt the butter in a large pan and add the leeks. Cook for 3–4 minutes until softened, then add the asparagus stems, peas and chopped parsley. Pour in 1.2 litres/2 pints/5 cups of the asparagus stock. Bring to the boil, reduce the heat and cook for 6–8 minutes, until all the vegetables are tender. Season well.

4 Cool the soup slightly, then purée it in a food processor or blender until smooth. Press the purée through a very fine sieve into the rinsed pan. Stir in the cream and lemon rind.

5 Bring a small pan of water to the boil and cook the asparagus tips for about 2–3 minutes until just tender. Drain and refresh under cold water. Reheat the soup, but do not allow it to boil.

6 Ladle the soup into six warmed bowls and garnish with the asparagus tips. Serve immediately, with shavings of Parmesan cheese and plenty of ground black pepper.

VARIATION
For a lighter soup, you could replace the cream with low-fat milk, but the finished dish will not taste as rich.

Energy 221kcal/912kJ; Protein 8.1g; Carbohydrate 7.1g, of which sugars 4.3g; Fat 18g, of which saturates 10.8g; Cholesterol 45mg; Calcium 151mg; Fibre 3.8g; Sodium 129mg.

POTATO AND FENNEL SOUP WITH WARM ROSEMARY SCONES

THE SIMPLE FLAVOURS IN THIS FINE SOUP ARE ENHANCED BY THE DELICATE PERFUME OF HERB FLOWERS, AND COMPLEMENTED BY ROSEMARY-SEASONED SCONES.

SERVES 4

INGREDIENTS

75g/3oz/6 tbsp butter
2 onions, chopped
5ml/1 tsp fennel seeds, crushed
3 fennel bulbs, coarsely chopped
900g/2lb potatoes, thinly sliced
1.2 litres/2 pints/5 cups chicken
    stock
150ml/¼ pint/⅔ cup double
    (heavy) cream
salt and ground black pepper
fresh herb flowers and 15ml/
    1 tbsp chopped fresh chives,
    to garnish

For the rosemary scones (biscuits)
    225g/8oz/2 cups self-raising
        (self-rising) flour
    2.5ml/½ tsp salt
    5ml/1 tsp baking powder
    10ml/2 tsp chopped fresh
        rosemary
    50g/2oz/¼ cup butter
    150ml/¼ pint/⅔ cup milk
    1 egg, beaten, to glaze

1 Melt the butter in a pan. Add the onions and cook gently for 10 minutes, stirring occasionally, until very soft. Add the fennel seeds and cook for 2–3 minutes. Stir in the fennel and potatoes.

2 Cover the vegetables with a sheet of wet baking parchment and put a lid on the pan. Cook gently for 10 minutes until very soft.

3 Remove the parchment. Pour in the stock, bring to the boil, cover and simmer for 35 minutes.

4 Meanwhile, make the scones. Preheat the oven to 230°C/450°F/Gas 8 and grease a baking tray. Sift the flour, salt and baking powder into a bowl. Stir in the rosemary, then rub in the butter. Add the milk and mix to form a soft dough.

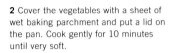

5 Knead very lightly on a floured surface. Roll out to 2cm/¾in thick. Stamp out 12 rounds with a cutter.

6 Brush with the egg and bake on the prepared baking tray for 8–10 minutes, until risen and golden. Cool on a wire rack until warm.

7 Leave the soup to cool slightly, then purée it in a food processor or blender until smooth. Press through a sieve (strainer) into the rinsed pan.

8 Stir in the cream with seasoning to taste. Reheat gently but do not boil.

9 Ladle the soup into four warmed soup bowls and scatter a few herb flowers and chopped chives over each. Serve immediately with the warm rosemary scones.

Energy 797kcal/3332kJ; Protein 12.3g; Carbohydrate 84.1g, of which sugars 8.8g; Fat 48.1g, of which saturates 29.6g; Cholesterol 120mg; Calcium 316mg; Fibre 7.6g; Sodium 703mg.

ARTICHOKE SOUP WITH ANCHOVY AND ARTICHOKE BRUSCHETTA

JERUSALEM ARTICHOKES ORIGINATE FROM NORTH AMERICA, YET LEND THEMSELVES BEAUTIFULLY TO THE METHODS AND FLAVOURS OF MEDITERRANEAN COOKING.

SERVES 6

INGREDIENTS
squeeze of lemon juice
450g/1lb Jerusalem artichokes
65g/2½oz/5 tbsp butter
175g/6oz potatoes, roughly diced
1 small onion, chopped
1 garlic clove, chopped
1 celery stick, chopped
1 small fennel bulb, halved, cored
    and chopped
1.2 litres/2 pints/5 cups vegetable
    stock
300ml/½ pint/1¼ cups double
    (heavy) cream
pinch of freshly grated nutmeg
salt and ground black pepper
basil leaves, to garnish

For the artichoke and anchovy bruschetta
6 thick slices French bread
1 garlic clove
50g/2oz/¼ cup unsalted butter
400g/14oz can artichoke hearts,
    drained and halved
45ml/3 tbsp tapenade
9 salted anchovy fillets, halved
    lengthways

1 Prepare a large bowl of cold water with a squeeze of lemon juice added. Peel and dice the Jerusalem artichokes, adding them to the water as soon as each one is prepared. This will prevent them from discolouring.

2 Melt the butter in a large, heavy-based saucepan. Drain the artichokes and add to the pan with the potatoes, onion, garlic, celery and fennel. Stir well and cook for 10 minutes, stirring occasionally, until beginning to soften.

3 Pour in the stock and bring to the boil, then simmer for 10–15 minutes, until all the vegetables are softened. Cool the soup slightly, then process in a food processor or blender until smooth. Press it through a sieve (strainer) into a clean pan. Add the cream and nutmeg, and season well.

4 To make the bruschetta, lightly toast the French bread slices on both sides. Rub each slice with the garlic clove and set aside. Melt the butter in a small pan. Add the artichoke hearts and cook for 3–4 minutes, turning once.

5 Spread the tapenade on the toast and arrange pieces of artichoke heart on top. Top with anchovy fillets and garnish with basil leaves.

6 Reheat the artichoke soup without allowing it to boil, then ladle it into bowls. Serve the bruschetta with the soup.

Energy 790kcal/3303kJ; Protein 14.3g; Carbohydrate 85.6g, of which sugars 16.4g; Fat 45.8g, of which saturates 27.3g; Cholesterol 111mg; Calcium 232mg; Fibre 7.6g; Sodium 1030mg.

SIMPLE CREAM OF ONION SOUP

THIS WONDERFULLY SOOTHING SOUP HAS A DEEP, BUTTERY FLAVOUR THAT IS COMPLEMENTED BY CRISP CROÛTONS OR CHOPPED CHIVES, SPRINKLED OVER JUST BEFORE SERVING.

SERVES 4

INGREDIENTS

   115g/4oz/½ cup unsalted butter
   1kg/2¼lb yellow onions, sliced
   1 fresh bay leaf
   105ml/7 tbsp dry white vermouth
   1 litre/1¾ pints/4 cups good chicken
     or vegetable stock
   150ml/¼ pint/⅔ cup double
     (heavy) cream
   a little lemon juice (optional)
   salt and ground black pepper
   croûtons or chopped fresh chives,
     to garnish

COOK'S TIP

Adding the second batch of onions gives texture and a buttery flavour to this soup. Make sure they do not brown.

1 Melt 75g/3oz/6 tbsp of the butter in a large heavy-based pan. Set about 200g/7oz of the onions aside and add the rest to the pan with the bay leaf. Stir to coat in the butter, then cover and cook very gently for about 30 minutes. The onions should be very soft and tender, but not browned.

2 Add the vermouth, increase the heat and boil rapidly until the liquid has evaporated. Add the stock, 5ml/1 tsp salt and pepper to taste. Bring to the boil, lower the heat and simmer for 5 minutes, then remove from the heat.

3 Leave to cool, then discard the bay leaf and process the soup in a blender or food processor. Return the soup to the rinsed pan.

4 Meanwhile, melt the remaining butter in another pan and cook the remaining onions slowly, covered, until soft but not browned. Uncover and continue to cook gently until golden yellow.

5 Add the cream to the soup and reheat it gently until hot, but do not allow it to boil. Taste and adjust the seasoning, adding a little lemon juice if liked. Add the buttery onions and stir for 1–2 minutes, then ladle the soup into bowls. Sprinkle with croûtons or chopped chives and serve.

Energy 519kcal/2139kJ; Protein 3.8g; Carbohydrate 21.4g, of which sugars 15.6g; Fat 44.3g, of which saturates 27.5g; Cholesterol 113mg; Calcium 88mg; Fibre 3.5g; Sodium 193mg.

CREAM OF CAULIFLOWER SOUP

THIS SOUP IS LIGHT IN FLAVOUR YET SATISFYING ENOUGH FOR A LUNCHTIME SNACK.
YOU CAN TRY GREEN CAULIFLOWER FOR A COLOURFUL CHANGE.

SERVES 6

INGREDIENTS

30ml/2 tbsp olive oil
2 large onions, finely diced
1 garlic clove, crushed
3 large floury potatoes, finely diced
3 celery sticks, finely diced
1.75 litres/3 pints/7½ cups stock
2 carrots, finely diced
1 medium cauliflower, chopped
15ml/1 tbsp chopped fresh dill
15ml/1 tbsp lemon juice
5ml/1 tsp mustard powder
1.5ml/¼ tsp caraway seeds
300ml/½ pint/1¼ cups single
 (light) cream
salt and ground black pepper
shredded spring onions (scallions)

3 Add the cauliflower, fresh dill, lemon juice, mustard powder and caraway seeds to the pan and simmer gently for 20 minutes, until the vegetables are just tender.

4 Process the soup in a blender or food processor until smooth, return to the pan and stir in the cream. Season to taste and serve garnished with shredded spring onions.

1 Heat the oil in a large pan, add the onions and garlic and fry them for a few minutes until they soften. Add the potatoes, celery and stock and simmer for 10 minutes.

2 Add the carrots and simmer for a further 10 minutes.

Energy 258kcal/1075kJ; Protein 6.9g; Carbohydrate 26.9g, of which sugars 9.8g; Fat 14.4g, of which saturates 6.9g; Cholesterol 28mg; Calcium 95mg; Fibre 3.8g; Sodium 46mg.

CAULIFLOWER AND WALNUT CREAM

EVEN THOUGH THERE'S NO CREAM ADDED TO THIS SOUP, THE CAULIFLOWER GIVES IT A DELICIOUS, RICH, CREAMY TEXTURE, FOR PLEASURE WITHOUT THE CALORIES.

SERVES 4

INGREDIENTS
1 medium cauliflower
1 medium onion, roughly chopped
450ml/¾ pint/scant 2 cups chicken
  or vegetable stock
450ml/¾ pint/scant 2 cups
  skimmed milk
45ml/3 tbsp walnut pieces
salt and ground black pepper
paprika and chopped walnuts,
  to garnish

VARIATION
If you prefer, you can make this soup
using broccoli instead of cauliflower.

1 Trim the cauliflower of outer leaves
and break into small florets. Place the
cauliflower, onion and stock in a pan.

2 Bring to the boil, cover and simmer
for about 15 minutes until soft. Add the
milk and walnut pieces, then purée in a
blender or food processor until smooth.

3 Season the soup to taste with salt and
black pepper, then reheat and bring to
the boil.

4 Serve sprinkled with a dusting of
paprika and chopped walnuts.

Energy 175kcal/727kJ; Protein 10g; Carbohydrate 14.3g, of which sugars 12g; Fat 9.1g, of which saturates 1g; Cholesterol 4mg; Calcium 188mg; Fibre 3.3g; Sodium 62mg.

BROCCOLI AND ALMOND SOUP

THE CREAMINESS OF THE TOASTED ALMONDS COMBINES PERFECTLY WITH THE SLIGHTLY BITTER TASTE OF THE BROCCOLI IN THIS APPETIZING SOUP.

SERVES 4–6

INGREDIENTS

50g/2oz/½ cup ground almonds
675g/1½lb broccoli
900ml/1½ pints/3¾ cups vegetable
 stock or water
300ml/½ pint/1¼ cups skimmed
 milk
salt and ground black pepper

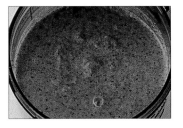

3 Place the remaining toasted almonds, broccoli, stock or water and milk in a blender and blend until smooth.

4 Season to taste with salt and pepper. Reheat and serve sprinkle with the reserved toasted almonds.

1 Preheat the oven to 180°C/350°F/ Gas 4. Spread the ground almonds evenly on a baking sheet and toast in the oven for about 10 minutes until golden. Reserve one quarter of the almonds and set aside to garnish the finished dish.

2 Cut the broccoli into small florets and steam for about 6–7 minutes until just tender.

COOK'S TIP
Make sure that you choose broccoli that has bright, compact florets. Yellowing florets, a limp woody stalk and a pungent smell are an indication of over-maturity and loss of flavour.

Energy 104kcal/435kJ; Protein 8.4g; Carbohydrate 4.8g, of which sugars 4.2g; Fat 5.8g, of which saturates 0.7g; Cholesterol 2mg; Calcium 144mg; Fibre 3.6g; Sodium 32mg.

JERUSALEM ARTICHOKE SOUP

TOPPED WITH SAFFRON CREAM, THIS DELICOUSLY CREAMY SOUP IS WONDERFUL ON A CHILLY DAY.
THE SAFFRON GIVES IT AN ATTRACTIVE COLOUR.

SERVES 4

INGREDIENTS

50g/2oz/4 tbsp butter
1 onion, chopped
450g/1lb Jerusalem artichokes,
  peeled and cut into chunks
900ml/1½ pints/3¾ cups chicken
  stock
150ml/¼ pint/⅔ cup milk
150ml/¼ pint/⅔ cup double
  (heavy) cream
a good pinch of saffron powder
salt and ground black pepper
chopped fresh chives, to garnish

1 Melt the butter in a large, heavy pan
and cook the onion for 5–8 minutes
until soft but not browned, stirring from
time to time.

2 Add the Jerusalem artichokes to the
pan and stir until coated in the butter.
Cover and cook gently for 10–15
minutes, being careful not to allow the
artichokes to brown. Pour in the
chicken stock and milk, then cover and
simmer for 15 minutes. Cool slightly,
then process in a blender or food
processor until smooth.

3 Strain the soup back into the pan.
Add half the cream, season to taste
and reheat gently. Lightly whip the
remaining cream and the saffron
powder. Ladle the soup into warmed
soup bowls and put a spoonful of
saffron cream in the centre of each.
Sprinkle the chopped chives over the
top and serve at once.

Energy 310kcal/1277kJ; Protein 2.7g; Carbohydrate 4.7g, of which sugars 4.3g; Fat 31.3g, of which saturates 19.4g; Cholesterol 80mg; Calcium 116mg; Fibre 1.5g; Sodium 168mg.

FRESH PEA SOUP ST GERMAIN

THIS SOUP TAKES ITS NAME FROM A SUBURB OF PARIS WHERE PEAS USED TO BE CULTIVATED IN MARKET GARDENS. SERVE IT IN EARLY SUMMER, WHEN FRESH PEAS ARE AT THEIR BEST.

SERVES 2–3

INGREDIENTS
  a small knob (pat) of butter
  2 or 3 shallots, finely chopped
  400g/14oz/3 cups shelled fresh
    peas (from about 1.5kg/3lb
    garden peas)
  500ml/17fl oz/2¼ cups water
  45–60ml/3–4 tbsp whipping cream
    (optional)
  salt and ground black pepper
  croûtons, to garnish

1 Melt the butter in a heavy pan or flameproof casserole. Add the shallots and cook for about 3 minutes, stirring them occasionally.

2 Add the peas and water and season with salt and a little pepper. Cover and simmer for about 12 minutes for young peas and up to 18 minutes for large or older peas, stirring occasionally.

COOK'S TIP
If fresh peas are not available, use frozen peas, but thaw and rinse them before use.

3 When the peas are tender, ladle them into a food processor or blender with a little of the cooking liquid and process until smooth.

4 Strain the soup into the pan or casserole, stir in the cream, if using, and heat through without boiling. Add the seasoning and serve hot, garnished with croûtons.

Energy 143kcal/591kJ; Protein 9.5g; Carbohydrate 16.7g, of which sugars 4.2g; Fat 4.8g, of which saturates 2.1g; Cholesterol 7mg; Calcium 34mg; Fibre 6.5g; Sodium 22mg.

CREAM OF SPINACH SOUP

THIS IS A DELICIOUSLY CREAMY SOUP THAT YOU WILL FIND YOURSELF MAKING OVER AND OVER AGAIN.
TOP WITH SOME CHOPPED CHIVES AS AN ATTRACTIVE GARNISH.

2 Pour the spinach mixture into a blender or food processor and add a little of the stock. Blend until smooth.

3 Return the mixture to the pan and add the remaining stock and the coconut cream or creamed coconut, with salt, pepper and nutmeg to taste. Simmer for 15 minutes to thicken.

SERVES 4

INGREDIENTS
    25g/1oz/2 tbsp butter
    1 small onion, chopped
    675g/1½lb fresh spinach, chopped
    1.2 litres/2 pints/5 cups vegetable
      stock
    50ml/2fl oz/½ cup coconut cream or
      15g/½oz creamed coconut
    freshly grated nutmeg
    250ml/8fl oz/1 cup single
      (light) cream
    salt and ground black pepper
    fresh chopped chives, to garnish

1 Melt the butter in a pan over a moderate heat and sauté the onion for a few minutes until soft. Add the spinach, cover the pan and cook gently for 10 minutes, until the spinach has wilted and reduced.

4 Add the cream to the pan, stir well and heat through, but do not boil. Serve hot, garnished with long strips of chives.

VARIATION
For a lighter soup, you could replace the cream with low-fat milk, but the finished dish will not taste as rich.

Energy 298kcal/1231kJ; Protein 7.8g; Carbohydrate 6.2g, of which sugars 5.7g; Fat 27.1g, of which saturates 18.4g; Cholesterol 48mg; Calcium 350mg; Fibre 3.8g; Sodium 297mg.

WATERCRESS SOUP

SERVE THIS DELICIOUS CREAMY SOUP WITH CRUSTY BREAD FOR A NUTRITIOUS MEAL, OR ON ITS OWN AS AN APPETIZER BEFORE A MAIN MEAL. ADD SOUR CREAM AND LEMON JUICE TO TASTE.

SERVES 4

INGREDIENTS

15ml/1 tbsp sunflower oil
15g/½oz/1 tbsp butter
1 medium onion, finely chopped
1 medium potato, diced
about 175g/6oz watercress
400ml/14fl oz/1⅔ cups vegetable stock
400ml/14fl oz/1⅔ cups milk

5 Process the soup in a food processor or blender.

6 Pour into a clean pan and heat gently with the reserved watercress leaves. Taste the soup when hot, add a little lemon juice and adjust the seasoning.

7 Pour the soup into warmed soup bowls and garnish with a little sour cream in the centre just before serving.

COOK'S TIP
Provided you leave out the sour cream, this is a low-calorie soup.

1 Heat the oil and butter in a large pan and fry the onion over a gentle heat until soft but not browned.

2 Add the potato, fry gently for 2–3 minutes and then cover and sweat for 5 minutes over a gentle heat, stirring from time to time.

3 Strip the watercress leaves from the stalks and roughly chop the stalks.

4 Add the stock and milk to the pan, stir in the chopped stalks and season. Bring to the boil and simmer gently, partially covered, for 10–12 minutes until the potatoes are tender. Add all but a few of the watercress leaves and simmer for 2 minutes more.

Energy 68kcal/280kJ; Protein 1.5g; Carbohydrate 1.4g, of which sugars 1g; Fat 6.3g, of which saturates 2.4g; Cholesterol 8mg; Calcium 79mg; Fibre 0.9g; Sodium 45mg.

CREAM ^{OF} RED PEPPER SOUP

GRILLING PEPPERS GIVES THEM A SWEET, SMOKY FLAVOUR, WHICH IS DELICIOUS IN SALADS OR, AS HERE, IN A VELVETY SOUP WITH A SECRET FLAVOURING OF ROSEMARY TO ADD AROMATIC DEPTH.

SERVES 4

INGREDIENTS

4 red (bell) peppers
25g/1oz/2 tbsp butter
1 onion, finely chopped
1 sprig of fresh rosemary
1.2 litres/2 pints/5 cups chicken or
   light vegetable stock
45ml/3 tbsp tomato purée (paste)
120ml/4fl oz/½ cup double
   (heavy) cream
paprika
salt and ground black pepper

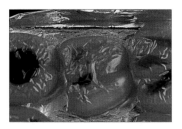

1 Preheat the grill (broiler). Line the grill pan with foil. Put the peppers in the grill pan under the grill and turn them regularly until the skins have blackened all round.

2 Put the peppers into polythene bags, sealing them tightly, and leave them for 20 minutes.

3 Peel off the blackened skins. Avoid rinsing them under the tap as this loses some of the natural oil and flavour.

4 Halve the peppers, removing the seeds, stalks and pith, then roughly chop the flesh.

5 Melt the butter in a deep pan. Add the onion and rosemary and cook gently over a low heat for about 5 minutes. Remove the rosemary and discard.

6 Add the peppers and stock to the onion, bring to the boil and simmer for 15 minutes. Stir in the tomato purée, then process or strain the soup to a smooth purée.

7 Stir in half the cream and season with paprika, salt, if necessary, and pepper.

8 Serve the soup hot or chilled, with the remaining cream swirled delicately on top. Speckle the cream very lightly with a pinch of paprika.

Energy 265kcal/1097kJ; Protein 3g; Carbohydrate 14.5g, of which sugars 13.7g; Fat 22g, of which saturates 13.5g; Cholesterol 54mg; Calcium 38mg; Fibre 3.3g; Sodium 79mg.

CREAMY TOMATO SOUP

TOMATO SOUP IS AN OLD FAVOURITE. THIS VERSION IS MADE SPECIAL BY THE ADDITION OF FRESH HERBS AND CREAM.

SERVES 4

INGREDIENTS

    25g/1oz/2 tbsp butter or margarine
    1 onion, chopped
    900g/2lb tomatoes, peeled and
      quartered
    2 carrots, chopped
    450ml/¾ pint/scant 2 cups chicken
      stock
    30ml/2 tbsp chopped fresh parsley
    2.5ml/½ tsp fresh thyme leaves, plus
      extra to garnish
    75ml/5 tbsp whipping cream
      (optional)
    salt and ground black pepper

COOK'S TIP
Meaty and flavourful, ripe Italian plum tomatoes are the best choice for making this soup.

1 Melt the butter or margarine in a large pan. Add the onion and cook for 5 minutes until softened.

2 Stir in the tomatoes, chopped carrots, chicken stock, parsley and thyme. Bring to the boil. Reduce the heat to low, cover the pan, and simmer gently for 15–20 minutes until the vegetables are tender.

3 Purée the soup in a vegetable mill until it is smooth. Return the puréed soup to the pan.

4 Stir in the cream, if using, and reheat gently. Season the soup to taste with salt and freshly ground black pepper. Ladle into warmed soup bowls and serve piping hot, garnished with fresh thyme leaves.

Energy 107kcal/447kJ; Protein 2.3g; Carbohydrate 11.4g, of which sugars 10.9g; Fat 6.1g, of which saturates 3.5g; Cholesterol 13mg; Calcium 50mg; Fibre 3.9g; Sodium 71mg.

CREAM OF SPRING ONION SOUP

THE ONIONY FLAVOUR OF THIS SOUP IS SURPRISINGLY DELICATE, AND RELIES ON THE USE OF A GOOD-QUALITY STOCK. IT IS EQUALLY DELICIOUS SERVED HOT OR COLD.

3 Add the potatoes and the stock. Bring to the boil, then cover again and simmer over moderately low heat for about 30 minutes. Cool slightly.

4 Purée the soup in a blender or food processor.

5 If serving the soup hot, pour it back into the pan. Add the cream and season with salt and pepper. Reheat gently, stirring occasionally. Add the lemon juice.

SERVES 4–6

INGREDIENTS
25g/1oz/2 tbsp butter
1 small onion, chopped
150g/5oz/1¾ cups spring onions, (scallions) chopped
225g/8oz potatoes, peeled and chopped
600ml/1 pint/2½ cups vegetable stock
350ml/12fl oz/1½ cups single (light) cream
30ml/2 tbsp lemon juice
salt and ground white pepper
chopped spring onion greens or fresh chives, to garnish

1 Melt the butter in a large pan and add all the onions. Stir to coat with the melted butter.

2 Cover and cook over very low heat for about 10 minutes or until softened.

6 If serving the soup cold, pour it into a bowl. Stir in the cream and lemon juice and season with salt and pepper. Cover the bowl and chill for at least 1 hour. Sprinkle with the chopped spring onion greens or chives before serving.

Energy 179kcal/744kJ; Protein 3.2g; Carbohydrate 8.9g, of which sugars 3.1g; Fat 14.8g, of which saturates 9.3g; Cholesterol 41mg; Calcium 67mg; Fibre 0.9g; Sodium 48mg.

CREAM OF MUSHROOM SOUP

A GOOD MUSHROOM SOUP MAKES THE MOST OF THE SUBTLE AND SOMETIMES RATHER ELUSIVE FLAVOUR OF MUSHROOMS. BUTTON MUSHROOMS ARE USED HERE FOR THEIR PALE COLOUR.

SERVES 4

INGREDIENTS

275g/10oz button (white) mushrooms
15ml/1 tbsp sunflower oil
40g/1½oz/3 tbsp butter
1 small onion, finely chopped
15ml/1 tbsp plain (all-purpose) flour
450ml/¾ pint/scant 2 cups vegetable
  stock
450ml/¾ pint/scant 2 cups milk
a pinch of dried basil
30–45ml/2–3 tbsp single (light)
  cream (optional)
salt and ground black pepper
fresh basil leaves, to garnish

1 Separate the mushroom caps from the stalks. Finely slice the caps and finely chop the stalks.

2 Heat the oil and half the butter in a heavy pan. Add the onion, mushroom stalks and about three-quarters of the mushroom caps. Fry for about 1–2 minutes, stirring frequently, then cover and sweat over gentle heat for 6–7 minutes, stirring from time to time.

3 Stir in the flour and cook for about 1 minute. Gradually add the stock and milk, to make a smooth, thin sauce. Add the dried basil, and season to taste. Bring to the boil and simmer, partly covered, for 15 minutes.

VARIATION
Chestnut or field (portabello) mushrooms may be used instead of button (white) mushrooms. They give a fuller flavour but turn the soup brown.

4 Pour into a food processor or blender and process until smooth.

5 Melt the rest of the butter in a frying pan and fry the remaining mushroom caps gently for 3–4 minutes until they are just tender.

6 Pour the soup into a clean pan and stir in the fried mushrooms. Heat until very hot and adjust the seasoning. Add the cream, if using.

7 Sprinkle with fresh basil leaves and serve hot.

Energy 178kcal/742kJ; Protein 5.7g; Carbohydrate 9.7g, of which sugars 6.4g; Fat 13.3g, of which saturates 6.8g; Cholesterol 28mg; Calcium 150mg; Fibre 1.1g; Sodium 113mg.

CREAMY CORN SOUP

THIS MEXICAN-STYLE SOUP IS SIMPLE TO PREPARE YET FULL OF FLAVOUR. IT IS SOMETIMES MADE WITH SOUR CREAM AND CREAM CHEESE.

SERVES 4

INGREDIENTS
- 30ml/2 tbsp corn oil
- 1 onion, finely chopped
- 1 red (bell) pepper, seeded and chopped, plus ½, seeded and finely diced, to garnish
- 450g/1lb/2⅔ cups corn kernels, thawed if frozen
- 750ml/1¼ pints/3 cups chicken stock
- 250ml/8fl oz/1 cup single (light) cream
- salt and ground black pepper

VARIATION
Poblano chillies may be added to this soup, but these are rather difficult to locate outside Mexico.

1 Heat the oil in a frying pan and sauté the onion and chopped red pepper for about 5 minutes, until soft. Add the corn and sauté for 2 minutes.

2 Carefully transfer the contents of the pan to a food processor or blender. Process until smooth, scraping down the sides of the blender and adding a little of the stock, if necessary.

3 Transfer the mixture to a pan and stir in the stock. Season to taste with salt and pepper, bring to a simmer and cook for 5 minutes.

4 Gently stir in the cream. Serve the soup hot or chilled, sprinkled with the diced red pepper. If serving hot, reheat gently after adding the cream, but do not allow the soup to boil.

Energy 327kcal/1367kJ; Protein 6g; Carbohydrate 35.3g, of which sugars 15.7g; Fat 19g, of which saturates 8.7g; Cholesterol 34mg; Calcium 68mg; Fibre 2.5g; Sodium 324mg.

CREAM OF AVOCADO SOUP

AVOCADOS MAKE WONDERFUL SOUP — PRETTY, DELICIOUS AND REFRESHING. THIS SOUP TASTES JUST AS GOOD SERVED CHILLED AS IT DOES HOT.

SERVES 4

INGREDIENTS

    2 large ripe avocados
    1 litre/1¾ pints/4 cups chicken
      stock
    250ml/8fl oz/1 cup single
      (light) cream
    salt and ground white pepper
    15ml/1 tbsp finely chopped fresh
      coriander (cilantro), to garnish
      (optional)

COOK'S TIP

It is important to choose really ripe avocadoes for this soup. To test whether an avocado is ripe, gently press the stalk end with your thumb and forefinger to see if it is soft.

1 Cut the avocados in half, remove the stones and mash the flesh.

2 Put the flesh into a sieve (strainer) and press it through the sieve with a wooden spoon into a warm soup bowl.

3 Heat the chicken stock with the cream in a pan.

4 When the mixture is hot, but not boiling, whisk it into the puréed avocado in the bowl.

5 Season to taste with salt and pepper. Serve immediately, sprinkled with chopped fresh coriander, if you like.

Energy 263kcal/1087kJ; Protein 3.5g; Carbohydrate 2.8g, of which sugars 1.8g; Fat 26.4g, of which saturates 10.7g; Cholesterol 34mg; Calcium 64mg; Fibre 2.6g; Sodium 23mg.

PUMPKIN SOUP

*THE SWEET FLAVOUR OF PUMPKIN IS EXCELLENT IN SOUPS, TEAMING WELL WITH OTHER SAVOURY
INGREDIENTS SUCH AS ONIONS AND POTATOES TO MAKE A WARM AND COMFORTING DISH.*

SERVES 4–6

INGREDIENTS
    15ml/1 tbsp sunflower oil
    25g/1oz/2 tbsp butter
    1 large onion, sliced
    675g/1½lb pumpkin, cut into
      large chunks
    450g/1lb potatoes, sliced
    600ml/1 pint/2½ cups
      vegetable stock
    a good pinch of freshly grated
      nutmeg
    5ml/1 tsp chopped fresh
      tarragon
    600ml/1 pint/2½ cups milk
    about 5–10ml/1–2 tsp lemon juice
    salt and ground black pepper

1 Heat the oil and butter in a heavy pan
and fry the onion for 4–5 minutes over a
gentle heat until soft but not browned,
stirring frequently.

2 Add the pumpkin and sliced potatoes,
stir well, then cover and sweat over a
low heat for about 10 minutes until the
vegetables are almost tender, stirring
occasionally to stop them sticking
to the pan.

3 Stir in the stock, nutmeg, tarragon
and seasoning. Bring to the boil and
simmer for 10 minutes until tender.

COOK'S TIP
For added flavour, try roasting the
pumpkin before adding to the soup.

4 Allow to cool slightly, then pour into a
food processor or blender and process
until smooth. Pour back into a clean
pan and add the milk. Heat gently and
then taste, adding the lemon juice and
extra seasoning, if necessary. Serve
piping hot.

Energy 173kcal/726kJ; Protein 5.9g; Carbohydrate 21.9g, of which sugars 9.5g; Fat 7.5g, of which saturates 3.7g; Cholesterol 15mg; Calcium 166mg; Fibre 2.4g; Sodium 78mg.

ROOT VEGETABLE SOUP

SIMMER A SELECTION OF POPULAR WINTER ROOT VEGETABLES TOGETHER FOR A WARMING AND SATISFYING SOUP. ITS CREAMY TASTE COMES FROM ADDING CRÈME FRAÎCHE JUST BEFORE SERVING.

SERVES 6

INGREDIENTS

   3 medium carrots, chopped
   1 large potato, chopped
   1 large parsnip, chopped
   1 large turnip or small swede
     (rutabaga), chopped
   1 onion, chopped
   30ml/2 tbsp sunflower oil
   25g/1oz/2 tbsp butter
   1.5 litres/2½ pints/6¼ cups water
   1 piece fresh root ginger, peeled
     and grated
   300ml/½ pint/1¼ cups milk
   45ml/3 tbsp crème fraîche or
     fromage frais
   30ml/2 tbsp chopped fresh dill
   15ml/1 tbsp lemon juice
   salt and ground black pepper
   sprigs of fresh dill, to garnish

3 Strain the vegetables, reserving the stock, add the ginger and vegetables to a food processor or blender and purée until smooth. Return the puréed mixture and stock to the pan. Add the milk and stir while the soup gently reheats.

4 Remove from the heat and stir in the crème fraîche or fromage frais, plus the dill and lemon juice. Season if necessary. Reheat the soup but do not allow it to boil or it may curdle. Serve garnished with sprigs of dill.

1 Put the carrots, potato, parsnip, turnip or swede and onion into a large pan with the oil and butter. Fry lightly, then cover and sweat the vegetables on a low heat for 15 minutes, shaking the pan occasionally.

2 Pour in the water, bring to the boil and season well. Cover and simmer for 20 minutes until the vegetables are soft.

VARIATION
Dill makes an attractive garnish for this soup, but you could use other herbs instead. Try using sprigs of fresh tarragon, coriander (cilantro), parsley or thyme for a different flavour.

Energy 168kcal/702kJ; Protein 3.3g; Carbohydrate 14.2g, of which sugars 7.1g; Fat 11.4g, of which saturates 5.3g; Cholesterol 20mg; Calcium 91mg; Fibre 2.3g; Sodium 63mg.

BUTTERNUT SQUASH BISQUE

THIS IS A FRAGRANT, CREAMY AND DELICATELY FLAVOURED SOUP WITH A WONDERFUL COLOUR.
SUBSTITUTE VEGETABLE STOCK IF YOU ARE CATERING FOR VEGETARIANS.

SERVES 4

INGREDIENTS

25g/1oz/2 tbsp butter or margarine
2 small onions, finely chopped
450g/1lb butternut squash, peeled,
  seeded and cubed
1.2 litres/2 pints/5 cups chicken
  stock
225g/8oz potatoes, cubed
5ml/1 tsp paprika
120ml/4fl oz/½ cup whipping cream
  (optional)
25ml/1½ tbsp chopped fresh chives,
  plus a few whole chives to garnish
salt and ground black pepper

1 Melt the butter or margarine in a large pan. Add the onions and cook for about 5 minutes until soft.

2 Add the squash, stock, potatoes and paprika. Bring to the boil. Reduce the heat to low, cover the pan and simmer for about 35 minutes until all the vegetables are soft.

3 Pour the soup into a food processor or blender and process until smooth. Return the soup to the pan.

4 Stir in the cream, if using. Season with salt and pepper and reheat gently. Stir in the chopped chives just before serving. Garnish each serving with a few whole chives.

Energy 106kcal/443kJ; Protein 2g; Carbohydrate 12.8g, of which sugars 3.5g; Fat 5.6g, of which saturates 3.4g; Cholesterol 13mg; Calcium 41mg; Fibre 1.9g; Sodium 45mg.

PEAR AND WATERCRESS SOUP

THIS UNUSUAL SOUP COMBINES SWEET PEARS WITH SLIGHTLY SHARP WATERCRESS. A MORE TRADITIONAL PARTNER, STILTON CHEESE, APPEARS IN THE FORM OF CRISP CROÛTONS.

SERVES 6

INGREDIENTS
    1 bunch of watercress
    4 medium pears, sliced
    900ml/1½ pints/3¾ cups chicken
      stock, preferably home-made
    120ml/4fl oz/½ cup double
      (heavy) cream
    juice of 1 lime
    salt and ground black pepper
For the Stilton croûtons
    25g/1oz/2 tbsp butter
    15ml/1 tbsp olive oil
    200g/7oz/3 cups cubed stale bread
    115g/4oz/1 cup Stilton cheese,
      chopped

1 Place two-thirds of the watercress leaves and all the stalks in a pan with the pears, stock and a little seasoning. Simmer for about 15–20 minutes.

2 Reserving some of the watercress leaves for the garnish, add the rest to the soup and immediately blend in a food processor until smooth.

3 Put the mixture into a bowl and stir in the cream and the lime juice to mix the flavours thoroughly. Season again with salt and pepper to taste.

4 Pour the soup back into the pan and reheat, stirring gently, until warmed through but not boiling.

5 To make the Stilton croûtons, melt the butter and oil and fry the cubes of bread until golden brown. Drain on kitchen paper. Sprinkle the cheese on top and heat under a hot grill (broiler) until bubbling.

6 Pour the soup into warmed bowls. Divide the Stilton croûtons and reserved watercress among the bowls and serve piping hot.

Energy 351kcal/1463kJ; Protein 9g; Carbohydrate 27g, of which sugars 11.4g; Fat 23.6g, of which saturates 13.6g; Cholesterol 55mg; Calcium 177mg; Fibre 3.2g; Sodium 373mg.

SQUASH SOUP WITH HORSERADISH CREAM

THE COMBINATION OF CREAM, CURRY POWDER AND HORSERADISH MAKES A WONDERFUL TOPPING FOR THIS BEAUTIFUL GOLDEN SOUP.

SERVES 6

INGREDIENTS
    1 butternut squash
    1 cooking apple
    25g/1oz/2 tbsp butter
    1 onion, finely chopped
    5–10ml/1–2 tsp curry powder,
      plus extra to garnish
    900ml/1½ pints/3¾ cups
      vegetable stock
    5ml/1 tsp chopped fresh sage
    150ml/¼ pint/⅔ cup apple juice
    salt and ground black pepper
    lime rind, shredded, to garnish
      (optional)
For the horseradish cream
    60ml/4 tbsp double (heavy) cream
    10ml/2 tsp horseradish sauce
    2.5ml/½ tsp curry powder

1 Peel the squash, remove the seeds and chop the flesh. Peel, core and chop the apple.

2 Heat the butter in a large pan. Add the onion and cook, stirring, for 5 minutes until soft. Stir in the curry powder. Cook to bring out the flavour, stirring constantly, for 2 minutes.

3 Add the stock, squash, apple and sage. Bring to the boil, lower the heat, cover and simmer for 20 minutes until the squash and apple are soft.

4 Meanwhile, make the horseradish cream. Whip the cream in a bowl until stiff, then stir in the horseradish sauce and curry powder. Cover and chill in the refrigerator until required.

5 Purée the soup in a blender or food processor. Return to the clean pan and add the apple juice. Season to taste. Reheat gently, without boiling.

6 Serve the soup in bowls, topped with a spoonful of horseradish cream and a dusting of curry powder. Garnish with a shredded lime rind, if you like.

Energy 118kcal/489kJ; Protein 1.3g; Carbohydrate 7.7g, of which sugars 6.7g; Fat 9.3g, of which saturates 5.7g; Cholesterol 23mg; Calcium 50mg; Fibre 1.7g; Sodium 44mg.

WILD MUSHROOM SOUP

DRIED PORCINI HAVE AN INTENSE FLAVOUR, SO ONLY A SMALL QUANTITY IS NEEDED. IF YOU PREFER A REALLY CREAMY SOUP, PUT ALL OF IT INTO THE FOOD PROCESSOR OR BLENDER.

SERVES 4

INGREDIENTS
    25g/1oz/2 cups dried porcini
      mushrooms
    250ml/8fl oz/1 cup warm water
    30ml/2 tbsp olive oil
    15g/½oz/1 tbsp butter
    2 leeks, finely sliced
    2 shallots, roughly chopped
    1 garlic clove, roughly chopped
    225g/8oz fresh wild mushrooms
    1.2 litres/2 pints/5 cups beef stock
    2.5ml/½ tsp dried thyme
    150ml/¼ pint/⅔ cup double (heavy)
      cream
    salt and ground black pepper
    sprigs of fresh thyme, to garnish

3 Chop or slice the fresh mushrooms and add to the pan. Stir over a medium heat for a few minutes until they begin to soften. Pour in the beef stock and bring to the boil. Add the porcini, soaking liquid, dried thyme and salt and pepper. Lower the heat, half-cover the pan and simmer gently for 30 minutes, stirring occasionally.

4 Pour about three-quarters of the soup into a food processor or blender and process until smooth. Return to the soup remaining in the pan, stir in the double cream and heat through. Check the consistency, adding more stock or water if the soup is too thick. Adjust the seasoning. Serve hot, garnished with sprigs of fresh thyme.

1 Put the dried porcini in a bowl, add the warm water and leave to soak for 20–30 minutes. Lift out of the liquid and squeeze to remove as much of the soaking liquid as possible. Strain all the liquid and reserve to use later in the recipe. Finely chop the porcini.

2 Heat the oil and butter in a large pan until foaming. Add the leeks, shallots and garlic and cook gently for about 5 minutes, stirring frequently, until softened but not coloured.

COOK'S TIP
Beef stock may seem unusual in a vegetable soup, but it helps to strengthen the earthy flavour of the mushroom. Use a vegetable stock if you are catering for vegetarians.

CREAMY BEETROOT SOUP

A SIMPLY STUNNING COLOUR, THIS DELICIOUSLY CREAMY BEETROOT SOUP IS THE PERFECT DISH TO SERVE WHEN YOU WANT TO OFFER SOMETHING A LITTLE DIFFERENT.

SERVES 6

INGREDIENTS

1 onion, chopped
450g/1lb raw beetroot (beet), peeled
  and chopped
2 celery sticks, chopped
½ red (bell) pepper, chopped
115g/4oz mushrooms, chopped
1 large cooking apple, chopped
25g/1oz/2 tbsp butter
30ml/2 tbsp sunflower oil
2 litres/3½ pints/9 cups stock
  or water
5ml/1 tsp cumin seeds
a pinch of dried thyme
1 large bay leaf
fresh lemon juice, to taste
salt and ground black pepper
For the garnish
150ml/¼ pint/⅔ cup sour cream
a few sprigs of fresh dill

1 Place the chopped vegetables and apple in a large pan with the butter, oil and 45ml/3 tbsp of the stock or water. Cover and cook gently for about 15 minutes, shaking the pan occasionally.

2 Stir in the cumin seeds and cook for 1 minute, then add the remaining stock or water, the thyme, bay leaf and lemon juice and seasoning to taste.

3 Bring the mixture to the boil, then cover the pan and turn down the heat to a gentle simmer. Cook for about 30 minutes.

4 Strain the vegetables and reserve the liquid. Process the vegetables in a food processor or blender until they are smooth and creamy.

COOK'S TIP
The flavour of this marvellous soup matures and improves if it is made the day before it is needed.

5 Return the vegetables to the pan, add the reserved stock and reheat. Check the seasoning.

6 Divide between individual serving bowls. Garnish each with swirls of sour cream and top with a few sprigs of fresh dill.

Energy 162kcal/674kJ; Protein 2.9g; Carbohydrate 10.5g, of which sugars 9.7g; Fat 12.4g, of which saturates 5.8g; Cholesterol 24mg; Calcium 50mg; Fibre 2.5g; Sodium 94mg.

CREAM OF CELERIAC AND SPINACH SOUP

CELERIAC HAS A WONDERFUL FLAVOUR THAT IS REMINISCENT OF CELERY, BUT ALSO ADDS A SLIGHTLY NUTTY TASTE. HERE IT IS COMBINED WITH SPINACH TO MAKE A DELICIOUS SOUP.

SERVES 6

INGREDIENTS
  1 litre/1¾ pints/4 cups water
  250ml/8fl oz/1 cup dry white wine
  1 leek, thickly sliced
  500g/1¼lb celeriac, diced
  200g/7oz fresh spinach leaves
  freshly grated nutmeg
  salt and ground black pepper
  25g/1oz/¼ cup pine nuts, to garnish

COOK'S TIP
If the soup is too thick, thin it with a little water or semi-skimmed (low-fat) milk when puréeing.

1 Mix the water and wine in a jug. Place the leek, celeriac and spinach in a deep pan and pour the liquid over the top. Bring to the boil, lower the heat and simmer for 10–15 minutes until the vegetables are soft.

2 Pour the celeriac mixture into a blender or food processor and purée until smooth, in batches if necessary. Return to the clean pan and season to taste with salt, ground black pepper and nutmeg. Reheat gently.

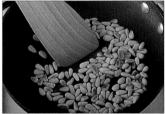

3 Heat a non-stick frying pan (do not add any oil) and add the pine nuts. Roast until golden brown, stirring occasionally so that they do not stick. Sprinkle them over the soup and serve.

Energy 77kcal/319kJ; Protein 2.4g; Carbohydrate 2.6g, of which sugars 2.3g; Fat 3.4g, of which saturates 0.3g; Cholesterol 0mg; Calcium 102mg; Fibre 2.3g; Sodium 99mg.

APPLE SOUP

A DELICIOUS SOUP THAT MAKES THE MOST OF FRESHLY PICKED APPLES. SERVE IT WITH LEMON WEDGES TO ENHANCE THE FLAVOUR, AND SOME FRESH CRUSTY BREAD.

SERVES 6

INGREDIENTS
  45ml/3 tbsp oil
  1 kohlrabi, diced
  3 carrots, diced
  2 celery sticks, diced
  1 green (bell) pepper, diced
  2 tomatoes, diced
  2 litres/3½ pints/9 cups chicken
    stock
  6 large green apples
  45ml/3 tbsp plain (all-purpose) flour
  150ml/¼ pint/⅔ cup double
    (heavy) cream
  15ml/1 tbsp granulated sugar
  30–45ml/2–3 tbsp lemon juice
  salt and ground black pepper
  lemon wedges, to serve

1 Heat the oil in a large pan. Add the kohlrabi, carrots, celery, green pepper and tomatoes and fry for 5–6 minutes until just softened.

2 Pour in the chicken stock, bring to the boil, then reduce the heat and simmer for about 45 minutes.

3 Meanwhile, peel and core the apples, then chop into small cubes. Add to the pan and simmer for 15 minutes.

4 Mix together the flour and cream and stir into the soup. Bring to the boil. Add the sugar, lemon juice and seasoning. Serve with lemon wedges.

Energy 278kcal/1159kJ; Protein 2.4g; Carbohydrate 24.8g, of which sugars 18.8g; Fat 19.5g, of which saturates 9.2g; Cholesterol 34mg; Calcium 63mg; Fibre 4.6g; Sodium 54mg.

CHUNKY VEGETABLE SOUPS

In this section you will find a collection of traditional soups using colourful Mediterranean vegetables, such as Greek Aubergine and Courgette Soup, Summer Minestrone, and Provençal Vegetable Soup. In winter root vegetables come into their own — now's the time to try Russian Spinach and Root Vegetable Soup with Dill, Winter Vegetable Soup, or Leek and Thyme Soup. And winter meets summer in Roast Vegetable Medley with Sun-Dried Tomato Bread.

GREEK AUBERGINE AND COURGETTE SOUP

A FUSION OF FLAVOURS FROM THE SUNNY GREEK ISLANDS CREATES THIS FABULOUS SOUP, WHICH IS SERVED WITH TZATZIKI, THE POPULAR COMBINATION OF CUCUMBER AND CREAMY YOGURT.

SERVES 4

INGREDIENTS

    2 large aubergines (eggplant),
        roughly diced
    4 large courgettes (zucchini),
        roughly diced
    1 onion, roughly chopped
    4 garlic cloves, roughly chopped
    45ml/3 tbsp olive oil
    1.2 litres/2 pints/5 cups
        vegetable stock
    15ml/1 tbsp chopped fresh oregano
    salt and ground black pepper
    mint sprigs, to garnish
For the tzatziki
    1 cucumber
    10ml/2 tsp salt
    2 garlic cloves, crushed
    5ml/1 tsp white wine vinegar
    225g/8oz/1 cup Greek (US strained
        plain) yogurt
    small bunch of fresh mint leaves,
        chopped

1 Preheat the oven to 200°C/400°F/Gas 6. Place the aubergines and courgettes in a roasting tin (pan). Add the onion and garlic, and drizzle over the olive oil. Roast for 35 minutes, turning once, until tender and slightly charred.

2 Place half the roasted vegetables in a food processor or blender. Add the stock and process until almost smooth. Pour into a large pan and add the remaining vegetables. Bring to the boil, season and stir in the chopped oregano.

3 For the tzatziki, peel, seed and dice the cucumber. Place the flesh in a colander and sprinkle with salt. Leave for 30 minutes. Mix the garlic with the vinegar and stir into the yogurt. Pat the cucumber dry on kitchen paper and fold it into the yogurt. Season to taste and stir in the mint. Chill until required.

4 Ladle the soup into bowls and garnish with mint sprigs. Hand round the bowl of tzatziki so that your guests can add a dollop or two to their soup.

Energy 188kcal/778kJ; Protein 6.9g; Carbohydrate 8.5g, of which sugars 7.3g; Fat 14.9g, of which saturates 4.3g; Cholesterol 0mg; Calcium 134mg; Fibre 3.6g; Sodium 1027mg.

CORN AND SWEET POTATO SOUP

THE COMBINATION OF CORN AND SWEET POTATO GIVES THIS SOUP A REAL DEPTH OF FLAVOUR AS WELL AS MAKING IT LOOK VERY COLOURFUL.

SERVES 6

INGREDIENTS
15ml/1 tbsp olive oil
1 onion, finely chopped
2 garlic cloves, crushed
1 small red chilli, seeded
  and finely chopped
1.75 litres/3 pints/7½ cups
  vegetable stock
10ml/2 tsp ground cumin
1 medium sweet potato,
  diced
½ red (bell) pepper, finely chopped
450g/1lb corn kernels
salt and ground black pepper
lime wedges, to serve

COOK'S TIP
Wear rubber gloves to protect your hands when seeding and chopping fresh chillies.

1 Heat the oil and fry the onion for 5 minutes until softened. Add the garlic and chilli and fry for a further 2 minutes.

2 In the same pan, add 300ml/½ pint/ 1¼ cups of the vegetable stock. Bring to the boil and simmer for 10 minutes.

3 Mix the cumin with a little stock to form a paste and then stir into the soup. Add the diced sweet potato, stir and simmer for 10 minutes. Season and stir again.

4 Add the pepper, corn and remaining stock and simmer for 10 minutes. Process half of the soup until smooth and then stir into the chunky soup. Season and serve with lime wedges for squeezing over.

Energy 146kcal/618kJ; Protein 2.9g; Carbohydrate 28.9g, of which sugars 10.7g; Fat 2.9g, of which saturates 0.5g; Cholesterol 0mg; Calcium 15mg; Fibre 2.3g; Sodium 217mg.

SUMMER VEGETABLE SOUP

THIS BRIGHTLY COLOURED, FRESH-TASTING TOMATO SOUP MAKES THE MOST OF SUMMER VEGETABLES IN SEASON. ADD LOTS OF RED AND YELLOW PEPPERS TO MAKE A SWEETER VERSION.

SERVES 4

INGREDIENTS
450g/1lb ripe plum tomatoes
225g/8oz ripe yellow tomatoes
45ml/3 tbsp olive oil
1 large onion, finely chopped
15ml/1 tbsp sun-dried tomato
  purée (paste)
225g/8oz courgettes (zucchini),
  trimmed and chopped
225g/8oz yellow courgettes,
  trimmed and chopped
3 waxy new potatoes, diced
2 garlic cloves, crushed
about 1.2 litres/2 pints/5 cups
  chicken stock or water
60ml/4 tbsp shredded fresh basil
50g/2oz/⅔ cup freshly grated
  (shredded) Parmesan cheese
sea salt and freshly ground
  black pepper

1 Plunge all the tomatoes in boiling water for 30 seconds, refresh in cold water, then peel and chop finely. Heat the oil in a large pan, add the onion and cook gently for about 5 minutes, stirring constantly, until softened. Stir in the sun-dried tomato purée, chopped tomatoes, courgettes, diced potatoes and garlic. Mix well and cook gently for 10 minutes, shaking the pan often.

2 Pour in the stock or water. Bring to the boil, lower the heat, half cover the pan and simmer gently for 15 minutes or until the vegetables are just tender. Add more stock or water if necessary.

3 Remove the pan from the heat and stir in the basil and half the cheese. Taste for seasoning. Serve hot, sprinkled with the remaining cheese.

Energy 243kcal/1012kJ; Protein 10.3g; Carbohydrate 20.9g, of which sugars 12g; Fat 13.7g, of which saturates 4.1g; Cholesterol 13mg; Calcium 215mg; Fibre 4.3g; Sodium 169mg.

CORN AND POTATO CHOWDER

THIS CREAMY YET CHUNKY SOUP IS RICH WITH THE SWEET TASTE OF CORN. IT'S EXCELLENT SERVED
WITH THICK CRUSTY BREAD AND TOPPED WITH SOME MELTED CHEDDAR CHEESE.

SERVES 4

INGREDIENTS

1 onion, chopped
1 garlic clove, crushed
1 medium baking potato, chopped
2 celery sticks, sliced
1 small green (bell) pepper, seeded,
  halved and sliced
30ml/2 tbsp sunflower oil
25g/1oz/2 tbsp butter
600ml/1 pint/2½ cups stock or water
300ml/½ pint/1¼ cups milk
200g/7oz can flageolet beans
300g/11oz can corn kernels
good pinch dried sage
salt and ground black pepper
Cheddar cheese, grated, to serve

1 Put the onion, garlic, potato, celery
and green pepper into a large heavy-
based pan with the oil and butter.

2 Heat the ingredients until sizzling
then reduce the heat to low. Cover
and cook gently for about 10 minutes,
shaking the pan occasionally to prevent
the ingredients sticking.

3 Pour in the stock or water, season
with salt and pepper to taste and bring
to the boil. Reduce the heat, cover
again and simmer gently for about 15
minutes until the vegetables are tender.

4 Add the milk, beans and corn –
including their liquids – and the sage.
Simmer, uncovered, for 5 minutes.
Check the seasoning and serve hot,
sprinkled with grated cheese.

Energy 251kcal/1052kJ; Protein 9.7g; Carbohydrate 25.9g, of which sugars 9.3g; Fat 12.9g, of which saturates 4.9g; Cholesterol 18mg; Calcium 128mg; Fibre 5.5g; Sodium 1154mg.

ROAST VEGETABLE MEDLEY WITH SUN-DRIED TOMATO BREAD

WINTER MEETS SUMMER IN THIS SOUP RECIPE FOR CHUNKY ROASTED ROOTS. SERVE IT WITH BREAD BAKED WITH A HINT OF ADDED SUMMER FLAVOUR IN THE FORM OF SUN-DRIED TOMATOES.

SERVES 4

INGREDIENTS

4 parsnips, quartered lengthways
2 red onions, cut into thin wedges
4 carrots, thickly sliced
2 leeks, thickly sliced
1 small swede (rutabaga), cut into
   bite-size pieces
4 potatoes, cut into chunks
60ml/4 tbsp olive oil
few sprigs of fresh thyme
1 garlic bulb, broken into
   cloves, unpeeled
1 litre/1¾ pints/4 cups
   vegetable stock
salt and ground black pepper
fresh thyme sprigs, to garnish
For the sun-dried tomato bread
   1 ciabatta loaf (about 275g/10oz)
   75g/3oz/6 tbsp butter, softened
   1 garlic clove, crushed
   4 sun-dried tomatoes, finely chopped
   30ml/2 tbsp chopped fresh parsley

1 Preheat the oven to 200°C/400°F/ Gas 6. Cut the thick ends of the parsnip quarters into four, then place them in a large roasting tin (pan). Add the onions, carrots, leeks, swede and potatoes, and spread them in an even layer.

2 Drizzle the olive oil over the vegetables. Add the thyme sprigs and the unpeeled garlic cloves. Toss well to coat with oil and roast for about 45 minutes, until all the vegetables are tender and slightly charred.

3 Meanwhile, to make the sun-dried tomato bread, cut diagonal slits along the loaf, taking care not to cut right through it. Mix the butter with the garlic, sun-dried tomatoes and parsley. Spread the mixture into each slit, then press the bread back together. Wrap the loaf in foil and bake for 15 minutes, opening the foil for the last 5 minutes.

4 Discard the thyme from the roasted vegetables. Squeeze the garlic cloves from their skins over the vegetables.

5 Process about half the vegetables with the stock in a food processor or blender until almost smooth. Pour into a pan and add the remaining vegetables. Bring to the boil and season well with salt and black pepper.

6 Ladle the soup into bowls and garnish with fresh thyme leaves. Serve the hot bread with the soup.

Energy 511kcal/2146kJ; Protein 13.9g; Carbohydrate 72.6g, of which sugars 18.9g; Fat 20.4g, of which saturates 10.6g; Cholesterol 40mg; Calcium 218mg; Fibre 12.1g; Sodium 521mg.

SWEET AND SOUR CABBAGE, BEETROOT AND TOMATO BORSCHT

THERE ARE MANY VARIATIONS OF THIS CLASSIC JEWISH SOUP, WHICH MAY BE SERVED HOT OR COLD. THIS VERSION INCLUDES PLENTIFUL AMOUNTS OF CABBAGE, TOMATOES AND POTATOES.

SERVES 6

INGREDIENTS

1 onion, chopped
1 carrot, chopped
4–6 raw or vacuum-packed (cooked,
   not pickled) beetroot (beets),
   3–4 diced and 1–2 coarsely grated
400g/14oz can tomatoes
4–6 new potatoes, cut into
   bitesize pieces
1 small white cabbage, thinly sliced
1 litre/1¾ pints/4 cups vegetable stock
45ml/3 tbsp sugar
30–45ml/2–3 tbsp white wine, cider
   vinegar or sour salt (citric acid)
45ml/3 tbsp chopped fresh dill, plus
   extra to garnish
salt and ground black pepper
sour cream, to garnish
buttered rye bread, to serve

1 Put the onion, carrot, diced beetroot, tomatoes, potatoes, cabbage and stock in a large pan. Bring to the boil, reduce the heat and simmer for 30 minutes, or until the potatoes are tender.

VARIATION
To make meat borscht, place 1kg/2¼lb chopped beef in a large pan. Pour over water to cover and crumble in 1 beef stock (bouillon) cube. Bring to the boil, then reduce the heat and simmer until tender. Skim any fat from the surface, then add the vegetables and proceed as above. For Kashrut, omit the sour cream and serve with unbuttered rye bread.

2 Add the grated beetroot, sugar and wine, vinegar or sour salt to the soup and cook for 10 minutes. Taste for a good sweet-sour balance and add more sugar and/or vinegar if necessary. Season.

3 Stir the chopped dill into the soup and ladle into warmed bowls immediately. Garnish each bowl with a generous spoonful of sour cream and more dill and serve with buttered rye bread.

Energy 111kcal/470kJ; Protein 3.2g; Carbohydrate 24.6g, of which sugars 17.8g; Fat 0.6g, of which saturates 0.1g; Cholesterol 0mg; Calcium 65mg; Fibre 3.8g; Sodium 52mg.

LEEK AND THYME SOUP

THIS IS A FILLING, HEART-WARMING SOUP, WHICH CAN BE LIQUIDIZED TO A SMOOTH PURÉE OR SERVED AS IT IS HERE, IN ITS ORIGINAL PEASANT STYLE.

SERVES 4

INGREDIENTS
  900g/2lb leeks
  450g/1lb potatoes
  115g/4oz/½ cup butter
  1 large sprig fresh thyme, plus extra
    to garnish (optional)
  300ml/½ pint/1¼ cups milk
  salt and ground black pepper
  60ml/4 tbsp double (heavy) cream,
    to serve

1 Trim the leeks. If you are using big winter leeks, strip away all the coarse outer leaves, then cut the leeks into thick slices. Wash thoroughly under cold running water.

2 Cut the potatoes into rough dice, about 2.5cm/1in, and dry thoroughly on kitchen paper.

3 Melt the butter in a large pan and add the leeks and 1 sprig of thyme. Cover and cook for 4–5 minutes until softened. Add the potato pieces and just enough cold water to cover the vegetables. Re-cover and cook over a low heat for 30 minutes.

4 Pour in the milk and season with salt and pepper. Cover and simmer for a further 30 minutes. You will find that some of the potato breaks up, leaving you with a semi-puréed and rather lumpy soup.

5 Remove the sprig of thyme (the leaves will have fallen into the soup) and serve, adding 15ml/1 tbsp cream and a garnish of thyme to each bowl.

COOK'S TIP
Leeks need meticulous cleaning to remove any grit and earth between the layers of leaves. Slice the green part of the leek and separate the leaves before washing under cold running water.

Energy 377kcal/1570kJ; Protein 8.2g; Carbohydrate 28.3g, of which sugars 10.1g; Fat 26.4g, of which saturates 16.1g; Cholesterol 66mg; Calcium 156mg; Fibre 6.1g; Sodium 223mg.

WINTER VEGETABLE SOUP

NO FEWER THAN EIGHT VARIETIES OF VEGETABLE ARE PACKED INTO THIS HEARTY AND NUTRITIOUS SOUP. SERVE IT FOR LUNCH ON A COLD WINTER'S DAY, WITH PLENTY OF CRUSTY BREAD.

SERVES EIGHT

INGREDIENTS
    1 medium Savoy cabbage, quartered
        and cored
    30ml/2 tbsp corn oil
    4 carrots, finely sliced
    2 celery stalks, finely sliced
    2 parsnips, diced
    1.5 litres/2½ pints/6¼ cups
        chicken stock
    3 medium potatoes, diced
    2 courgettes (zucchini), sliced
    1 red (bell) pepper, seeded and diced
    115g/4oz/2 cups cauliflower florets
    2 tomatoes, seeded and diced
    2.5ml/½ tsp fresh thyme leaves or
        1.5ml/¼ tsp dried thyme
    30ml/2 tbsp chopped fresh parsley
    salt and ground black pepper

1 Using a sharp knife, slice the cabbage quarters into thin strips across the leaves.

2 Heat the oil in a large pan. Add the cabbage, carrots, celery and parsnips and cook for 10–15 minutes over medium heat, stirring frequently to prevent the vegetables from sticking.

3 Stir the stock into the vegetables and bring to the boil, skimming off any foam that rises to the surface.

4 Add the potatoes, courgettes, pepper, cauliflower and tomatoes, with the herbs, and salt and pepper to taste.

5 Bring back to the boil. Reduce the heat to low, cover the pan and simmer for 15–20 minutes until the vegetables are tender. Serve hot.

VARIATION
Other vegetables can be used for this soup in place of the ones listed. White winter cabbage, sweet potato, leeks, swede (rutabaga) and turnip would all be good choices.

Energy 105kcal/441kJ; Protein 3.4g; Carbohydrate 15.4g, of which sugars 8.2g; Fat 3.7g, of which saturates 0.6g; Cholesterol 0mg; Calcium 56mg; Fibre 3.9g; Sodium 23mg.

VEGETABLE AND HERB CHOWDER

A MEDLEY OF FRESH VEGETABLES AND HERBS COMBINES TO MAKE A DELICIOUS LUNCHTIME SOUP TO SERVE WITH SOME CRUSTY BREAD.

SERVES 4

INGREDIENTS

25g/1oz/2 tbsp butter
1 onion, finely chopped
1 leek, finely sliced
1 celery stick, diced
1 yellow or green (bell) pepper,
  seeded and diced
30ml/2 tbsp chopped fresh parsley
15ml/1 tbsp plain (all-purpose) flour
1.2 litres/2 pints/5 cups vegetable
  stock
350g/12oz potatoes, diced
a few sprigs of fresh thyme or
  2.5ml/½ tsp dried thyme
1 bay leaf
115g/4oz/1 cup young runner (green)
  beans, diagonally sliced
120ml/4fl oz/½ cup milk
salt and ground black pepper

1 Melt the butter in a heavy pan or flameproof casserole and add the onion, leek, celery, yellow or green pepper and parsley. Cover and cook gently over low heat until the vegetables are soft.

2 Add the flour and stir until well blended. Gradually stir in the stock. Bring the mixture to the boil, stirring frequently.

3 Add the potatoes, thyme and bay leaf. Simmer, uncovered, for 10 minutes.

4 Add the beans and simmer for a further 10–15 minutes until all the vegetables are tender.

5 Stir in the milk. Season with salt and pepper. Heat through. Before serving, discard the thyme stalks and bay leaf.

Energy 172kcal/723kJ; Protein 4.9g; Carbohydrate 24.9g, of which sugars 8g; Fat 6.6g, of which saturates 3.8g; Cholesterol 15mg; Calcium 80mg; Fibre 3.7g; Sodium 68mg

VEGETABLE SOUP WITH COCONUT

THE COCONUT COMPLEMENTS THE VEGETABLES IN THIS FINE SOUP, AND THE VARIOUS GROUND SPICES ADD ADDITIONAL FLAVOUR.

SERVES 4

INGREDIENTS

   25g/1oz/2 tbsp butter or margarine
   ½ red onion, finely chopped
   175g/6oz each turnip, sweet potato
     and pumpkin, roughly diced
   5ml/1 tsp dried marjoram
   2.5ml/½ tsp ground ginger
   1.5ml/¼ tsp ground cinnamon
   15ml/1 tbsp chopped spring onion
     (scallion)
   1 litre/1¾ pints/4 cups well-flavoured
     vegetable stock
   30ml/2 tbsp flaked (sliced) almonds
   1 fresh chilli, seeded and chopped
   5ml/1 tsp sugar
   25g/1oz creamed coconut or
     25ml/1½ tbsp coconut cream
   salt and ground black pepper
   coriander (cilantro), to garnish

3 Add the vegetable stock, flaked almonds, chilli and sugar and stir well to mix. Cover and simmer gently for 10–15 minutes until the vegetables are just tender.

4 Add the creamed coconut ot coconut cream to the soup and stir to mix thoroughly. Spoon into warmed bowls, sprinkle with chopped coriander and serve immediately.

1 Melt the butter or margarine in a large, non-stick pan. Fry the onion for 4–5 minutes.

2 Add the diced vegetables and fry for 3–4 minutes. Add the marjoram, ginger, cinnamon, spring onion and fry over a low heat for about 10 minutes, stirring.

Energy 227kcal/953kJ; Protein 3.5g; Carbohydrate 27.4g, of which sugars 8.3g; Fat 12.3g, of which saturates 5.9g; Cholesterol 13mg; Calcium 54mg; Fibre 3.7g; Sodium 88mg.

BROAD BEAN AND RICE SOUP

THIS THICK SOUP MAKES THE MOST OF FRESH BROAD BEANS WHILE THEY ARE IN SEASON. IT WORKS WELL WITH FROZEN BEANS FOR THE REST OF THE YEAR.

SERVES 4

INGREDIENTS
1kg/2¼lb broad (fava) beans in
  their pods
90ml/6 tbsp olive oil
1 medium onion, finely chopped
2 medium tomatoes, peeled and
  finely chopped
225g/8oz/1 cup arborio or other
  non-parboiled rice
25g/1oz/2 tbsp butter
1 litre/1¾ pints/4 cups boiling water
salt and ground black pepper
grated Parmesan cheese, to serve
  (optional)

COOK'S TIP
If fresh broad (fava) beans are not in
season, use 400g/14oz frozen shelled
broad beans, thawed, instead.

1 Bring a large pan of water to the boil
and blanch the beans for 3–4 minutes.
Drain and rinse under cold water. Peel
off the skins.

2 Heat the oil in a large pan. Add the
onion and cook over low to moderate
heat until it softens. Stir in the beans
and cook for about 5 minutes, stirring to
coat them with the oil.

3 Season with salt and pepper. Add the
tomatoes and cook for 5 minutes more,
stirring. Add the rice and cook for a
further 1–2 minutes, stirring constantly.

4 Add the butter and stir until it melts.
Pour in the water, a little at a time.
Adjust the seasoning to taste. Continue
cooking until the rice is tender. Serve
with grated Parmesan, if you like.

ITALIAN VEGETABLE SOUP

THE SUCCESS OF THIS CLEAR SOUP DEPENDS ON THE QUALITY OF THE STOCK, SO USE HOME-MADE VEGETABLE STOCK RATHER THAN STOCK OR BOUILLON CUBES.

SERVES 4

INGREDIENTS

  1 small carrot
  1 baby leek
  1 celery stick
  50g/2oz green cabbage
  900ml/1½ pints/3¾ cups
    vegetable stock
  1 bay leaf
  115g/4oz/1 cup cooked
    cannellini beans
  25g/1oz/¼ cup soup pasta, such as
    tiny shells, bows, stars or elbows
  salt and ground black pepper
  chopped fresh chives, to garnish

1 Cut the carrot, leek and celery into 5cm/2in long julienne strips. Finely shred the cabbage.

2 Put the stock and bay leaf into a large pan and bring to the boil. Add the carrot, leek and celery, cover and simmer for 6 minutes, until the vegetables are softened, but not tender.

VARIATION
Cooked flageolet (small cannellini) beans can be used to vary this recipe.

3 Add the cabbage, beans and pasta, then simmer, uncovered, for a further 4–5 minutes, or until the vegetables are tender and the pasta is *al dente*.

4 Remove the bay leaf and season to taste. Ladle the soup into four warmed soup bowls and garnish with chopped chives. Serve immediately.

Energy 55kcal/234kJ; Protein 3.1g; Carbohydrate 10.1g, of which sugars 3g; Fat 0.5g, of which saturates 0.1g; Cholesterol 0mg; Calcium 28mg; Fibre 2.7g; Sodium 133mg.

FRESH TOMATO AND BEAN SOUP

THIS IS A RICH, CHUNKY TOMATO SOUP, WITH BEANS AND CORIANDER. SERVE WITH OLIVE CIABATTA FOR A SATISFYING SUMMER LUNCH DISH.

SERVES 4

INGREDIENTS

    900g/2lb ripe plum tomatoes
    30ml/2 tbsp olive oil
    275g/10oz onions, roughly chopped
    2 garlic cloves, crushed
    900ml/1½ pints/3¾ cups vegetable
      stock
    30ml/2 tbsp sun-dried tomato
      purée (paste)
    10ml/2 tsp paprika
    15ml/1 tbsp cornflour (cornstarch)
    425g/15oz can cannellini beans,
      rinsed and drained
    30ml/2 tbsp chopped fresh coriander
      (cilantro)
    salt and ground black pepper
    olive ciabatta, to serve

1 First, peel the tomatoes. Using a sharp knife, make a small cross in each one and place in a bowl. Pour over boiling water to cover and leave to stand for 30–60 seconds.

2 Drain the tomatoes and cover with cold water. When they are cool enough to handle, drain again. Using a sharp knife, peel off the skins. Quarter them and then cut each piece in half again.

3 Heat the oil in a large pan and cook the chopped onions and garlic for about 3 minutes or until they are just beginning to soften.

4 Add the tomatoes to the onions and stir in the stock, sun-dried tomato purée and paprika. Season with a little salt and pepper.

5 Bring to the boil and simmer gently for about 10 minutes until the tomatoes are softened.

6 In a small bowl, mix the cornflour to a smooth paste with 30ml/2 tbsp cold water. Stir the beans into the soup with the cornflour paste. Cook for a further 5 minutes.

7 Taste and adjust the seasoning if necessary. Stir in the chopped coriander just before serving with chunks of olive ciabatta.

Energy 216kcal/911kJ; Protein 9.3g; Carbohydrate 31g, of which sugars 13.3g; Fat 7g, of which saturates 1.1g; Cholesterol 0mg; Calcium 70mg; Fibre 8.8g; Sodium 492mg.

PROVENÇAL VEGETABLE SOUP

THIS SATISFYING CHUNKY VEGETABLE SOUP CAPTURES ALL THE FLAVOURS OF SUMMER IN PROVENCE. THE BASIL AND GARLIC PURÉE, PISTOU, GIVES IT EXTRA COLOUR AND A WONDERFUL AROMA — SO DON'T LEAVE IT OUT.

SERVES 6–8

INGREDIENTS

275g/10oz/1½ cups shelled fresh broad (fava) beans or 175g/6oz/ ¾ cup dried haricot (navy) beans, soaked overnight
2.5ml/½ tsp dried *herbes de Provence*
2 garlic cloves, finely chopped
15ml/1 tbsp olive oil
1 onion, finely chopped
1 large leek, finely sliced
1 celery stick, finely sliced
2 carrots, finely diced
2 small potatoes, finely diced
115g/4oz French (green) beans
1.2 litres/2 pints/5 cups water
2 small courgettes (zucchini), finely chopped
3 medium tomatoes, peeled, seeded and finely chopped
115g/4oz/1 cup shelled garden peas
a handful of spinach leaves, cut into thin ribbons
salt and ground black pepper
sprigs of fresh basil, to garnish
For the *pistou*
1 or 2 garlic cloves, finely chopped
15g/½oz/½ cup (packed) basil leaves
60ml/4 tbsp grated Parmesan cheese
60ml/4 tbsp extra virgin olive oil

1 To make the *pistou*, put the garlic, basil and Parmesan cheese in a food processor and process until smooth, scraping down the sides once. With the machine running, slowly add the olive oil through the feed tube.

2 To make the soup, if using dried haricot beans, drain them, place in a pan and cover with water. Boil vigorously for 10 minutes and drain.

3 Place the par-boiled beans, or fresh beans if using, in a pan with the *herbes de Provence* and one of the garlic cloves. Add water to cover by 2.5cm/ 1in. Bring to the boil, reduce the heat and simmer over medium-low heat until tender, about 10 minutes for fresh beans or 1 hour for dried beans. Set aside in the cooking liquid.

4 Heat the oil in a large pan or flameproof casserole. Add the onion and leek and cook for 5 minutes, stirring occasionally, until they are beginning to soften.

COOK'S TIPS
• Both the *pistou* and the soup can be made 1 or 2 days in advance and chilled. To serve, reheat gently, stirring occasionally to prevent sticking.
• Alternatively, you can pound the garlic, basil and cheese for the pistou with a mortar and pestle. Then stir in the oil.

5 Add the celery, carrots and the remaining garlic clove and cook, covered, for 10 minutes, stirring occasionally.

6 Add the potatoes, French beans and water, then season lightly with salt and pepper. Bring to the boil, skimming any foam that rises to the surface, then reduce the heat, cover and simmer gently for 10 minutes.

7 Add the courgettes, tomatoes and peas, together with the reserved beans and their cooking liquid, and simmer for about 25–30 minutes until all the vegetables are tender. Add the spinach and simmer for 5 minutes.

8 Season the soup and swirl a spoonful of *pistou* into each bowl. Garnish with fresh basil and serve.

Energy 168kcal/700kJ; Protein 8.2g; Carbohydrate 11.7g, of which sugars 4.4g; Fat 10.2g, of which saturates 2.7g; Cholesterol 8mg; Calcium 136mg; Fibre 4.7g; Sodium 95mg.

MIXED MUSHROOM SOLYANKA WITH PICKLED CUCUMBER

THE TART FLAVOURS OF PICKLED CUCUMBER, CAPERS AND LEMON ADD EXTRA BITE TO THIS TRADITIONAL RUSSIAN SOUP. THIS IS THE PERFECT DISH TO SERVE WHEN YOU WANT TO OFFER SOMETHING A LITTLE DIFFERENT.

SERVES 4

INGREDIENTS
2 onions, chopped
1.2 litres/2 pints/5 cups
 vegetable stock
450g/1lb/6 cups mushrooms, sliced
20ml/4 tsp tomato purée (paste)
1 pickled cucumber, chopped
1 bay leaf
15ml/1 tbsp capers in brine, drained
pinch of salt
6 peppercorns, crushed
lemon rind curls, green olives and
 sprigs of flat leaf parsley, to garnish

2 Add the remaining vegetable stock with the sliced mushrooms, bring to the boil, cover and simmer gently for about 30 minutes.

3 In a small bowl, blend the tomato purée with 30ml/2 tbsp of stock.

4 Add the tomato purée to the pan with the pickled cucumber, bay leaf, capers, salt and peppercorns. Cook gently for a further 10 minutes.

5 Ladle the soup into warmed bowls and sprinkle lemon rind curls, a few olives and a sprig of flat leaf parsley over each bowl before serving.

1 Put the onions in a large pan with 50ml/2fl oz/¼ cup of the stock. Cook, stirring occasionally, until all the liquid has evaporated.

COOK'S TIP
Using a mixture of mushrooms gives this soup its character. Try using varieties such as Paris Browns, field (portabello) and button (white) mushrooms.

Energy 35kcal/147kJ; Protein 3g; Carbohydrate 4.6g, of which sugars 3.6g; Fat 0.7g, of which saturates 0.1g; Cholesterol 0mg; Calcium 20mg; Fibre 2g; Sodium 34mg.

RUSSIAN SPINACH AND ROOT VEGETABLE SOUP WITH DILL

THIS IS A TYPICAL RUSSIAN SOUP, TRADITIONALLY PREPARED WHEN THE FIRST VEGETABLES OF SPRINGTIME APPEAR. EARTHY ROOT VEGETABLES, COOKED WITH FRESH SPINACH LEAVES, ARE ENLIVENED WITH A TART, FRESH TOPPING OF DILL, LEMON AND SOUR CREAM.

SERVES 4–6

INGREDIENTS
  1 small turnip, cut into chunks
  2 carrots, sliced or diced
  1 small parsnip, cut into large dice
  1 potato, peeled and diced
  1 onion, chopped or cut into chunks
  1 garlic clove, finely chopped
  ¼ celeriac bulb, diced
  1 litre/1¾ pints/4 cups vegetable
    or chicken stock
  200g/7oz spinach, washed and
    roughly chopped
  1 small bunch fresh dill, chopped
  salt and ground black pepper
For the garnish
  2 hard-boiled eggs, sliced
  1 lemon, cut into slices
  250ml/8fl oz/1 cup sour cream
  30ml/2 tbsp fresh parsley and dill

1 Put the turnip, carrots, parsnip, potato, onion, garlic, celeriac and stock into a large pan. Bring to the boil, then simmer for 25–30 minutes, or until the vegetables are very tender.

COOK'S TIP
For the best results, use a really good-quality vegetable stock.

2 Add the spinach to the pan and cook for a further 5 minutes, or until the spinach is tender but still green and leafy. Season with salt and pepper.

3 Stir the dill into the soup, then ladle into bowls and serve garnished with egg, lemon, sour cream and a sprinkling of parsley and dill.

Energy 229kcal/952kJ; Protein 7.8g; Carbohydrate 14.3g, of which sugars 9.2g; Fat 16.2g, of which saturates 8.7g; Cholesterol 133mg; Calcium 197mg; Fibre 4.1g; Sodium 148mg.

PISTOU

SERVE THIS DELICIOUS TRADITIONAL VEGETABLE SOUP, FROM NICE IN THE SOUTH OF FRANCE, WITH A SPOONFUL OF SUN-DRIED TOMATO PESTO STIRRED INTO EACH BOWL, AND HAND ROUND A BOWL OF FRESH PARMESAN CHEESE. ANY TYPE OF SMALL PASTA SHAPES MAY BE USED, SUCH AS TINY SHELLS, BOWS, STARS OR ELBOWS.

SERVES 4

INGREDIENTS
    1 courgette (zucchini), diced
    1 small potato, diced
    1 shallot, chopped
    1 carrot, diced
    225g/8oz can chopped tomatoes
    1.2 litres/2 pints/5 cups vegetable
        stock
    50g/2oz French (green) beans, cut
        into 1cm/½in lengths
    50g/2oz/½ cup frozen petits pois
        (baby peas)
    50g/2oz/½ cup small pasta shapes
    60–90ml/4–6 tbsp pesto
    15ml/1 tbsp sun-dried tomato
        purée (paste)
salt and ground black pepper
grated Parmesan cheese, to serve

1 Place the courgette, potato, shallot, carrot and tomatoes in a large pan. Add the vegetable stock and season with salt and pepper. Bring to the boil, then cover and simmer for 20 minutes.

2 Add the French beans, petits pois and pasta shapes. Cook for a further 10 minutes, until the pasta is tender.

3 Taste the soup and adjust the seasoning as necessary. Ladle the soup into individual bowls. Mix together the pesto and sun-dried tomato purée, and stir a spoonful into each serving.

4 Serve, handing round a bowl of grated Parmesan cheese for sprinkling into each bowl.

Energy 156kcal/651kJ; Protein 4.1g; Carbohydrate 21.3g, of which sugars 6.1g; Fat 6.3g, of which saturates 1g; Cholesterol 0mg; Calcium 36mg; Fibre 2.9g; Sodium 16mg.

GRANDFATHER'S SOUP

*THIS TRADITIONAL EASTERN EUROPEAN SOUP DERIVES ITS NAME FROM THE FACT THAT IT IS
EASILY DIGESTED AND THEREFORE THOUGHT TO BE SUITABLE FOR THE ELDERLY. TO GET THE
CORRECT TEXTURE FOR THE DISH, USE OLD POTATOES OF A FLOURY TEXTURE, SUCH AS KING
EDWARD, MARIS PIPER OR ESTIMA.*

SERVES 4

INGREDIENTS
    1 large onion, finely sliced
    25g/1oz/2 tbsp butter
    350g/12oz potatoes, peeled
      and diced
    900ml/1½ pints/3¾ cups
      beef stock
    1 bay leaf
    salt and ground black pepper
For the drop noodles
    75g/3oz/⅔ cup self-raising
      (self-rising) flour
    pinch of salt
    15g/½oz/1 tbsp butter
    15ml/1 tbsp chopped fresh parsley,
      plus a little extra to garnish
    1 egg, beaten
    chunks of bread, to serve

1 In a wide heavy-based pan, cook
the onion gently in the butter for
10 minutes, or until it begins to soften
and go golden brown.

2 Add the diced potatoes and cook
for 2–3 minutes, then pour in the stock.
Add the bay leaf, salt and pepper. Bring
to the boil, then reduce the heat, cover
and simmer for about 10 minutes.

3 To make the noodles, sift the flour and
salt into a bowl and rub in the butter.
Stir in the parsley, then add the egg
and mix to a soft dough.

4 Drop half-teaspoonfuls of the dough
into the simmering soup. Cover and
simmer gently for a further 10 minutes.
Ladle into warmed soup bowls, sprinkle
over a little parsley, and serve.

Energy 239kcal/1001kJ; Protein 5.5g; Carbohydrate 33.3g, of which sugars 5g; Fat 10.2g, of which saturates 5.7g; Cholesterol 69mg; Calcium 96mg; Fibre 2.3g; Sodium 157mg.

WINTER WARMING SOUPS

A hot soup is the ideal dish for a cold winter day. The soups
in this section are hearty and nourishing, made with
ingredients such as potatoes, root vegetables, leeks and
pumpkins. Bread and oatmeal are used to add body and texture
— for example in Broccoli and Bread Soup, Tomato and Bread
Soup, Irish Yellow Broth, and Leek and Oatmeal Soup. Garlic
is thought to help ward off winter colds, so why not try it in
Garlic Soup or Potato and Roasted Garlic Broth.

POTATO AND ROASTED GARLIC BROTH

ROASTED GARLIC TAKES ON A SUBTLE, SWEET FLAVOUR IN THIS DELICIOUS VEGETARIAN SOUP. SERVE IT PIPING HOT WITH MELTED CHEDDAR OR GRUYÈRE CHEESE ON FRENCH BREAD, AS A WINTER WARMER.

SERVES 4

INGREDIENTS
  2 small or 1 large whole head of
    garlic (about 20 cloves)
  4 medium potatoes (about 500g/
    1¼lb in total), diced
  1.75 litres/3 pints/7½ cups
    good-quality hot vegetable stock
  salt and ground black pepper
  chopped flat leaf parsley, to garnish

COOK'S TIP
Choose floury potatoes such as Maris
Piper, Estima, Cara or King Edward to
give the soup a delicious velvety texture.

VARIATION
Use chicken or beef stock for a slightly
different flavour, if you like.

1 Preheat the oven to 190°C/375°F/
Gas 5. Place the unpeeled garlic bulbs
or bulb in a small roasting pan and
bake in the oven for 30 minutes until
soft in the centre.

2 Meanwhile, par-boil the potatoes in a
large pan of lightly salted boiling water
for 10 minutes.

3 Simmer the stock in another pan for
5 minutes. Drain the potatoes and add
them to the stock.

4 Squeeze the garlic pulp into the soup,
reserving a few whole cloves, stir and
season to taste. Simmer for 15 minutes
and serve topped with the whole garlic
cloves and parsley.

Energy 115kcal/488kJ; Protein 4.3g; Carbohydrate 24.3g, of which sugars 2.1g; Fat 0.7g, of which saturates 0.2g; Cholesterol 0mg; Calcium 14mg; Fibre 2.3g; Sodium 219mg.

GREEN PEA SOUP <u>WITH</u> SPINACH

THIS LOVELY GREEN SOUP WAS INVENTED BY THE WIFE OF A 17TH-CENTURY BRITISH MEMBER OF PARLIAMENT, AND IT HAS STOOD THE TEST OF TIME.

SERVES 6

INGREDIENTS

450g/1lb/generous 3 cups podded
   fresh or frozen peas
1 leek, finely sliced
2 garlic cloves, crushed
2 rindless lean back bacon rashers
   (strips), diced
1.2 litres/2 pints/5 cups ham or
   chicken stock
30ml/2 tbsp olive oil
50g/2oz fresh spinach, shredded
40g/1½oz/⅓ cup white cabbage,
   finely shredded
½ small lettuce, finely shredded
1 celery stick, finely chopped
a large handful of parsley, chopped
20ml/4 tsp chopped fresh mint
a pinch of ground mace
salt and ground black pepper

3 About 5 minutes before the pea mixture is ready, heat the oil in a deep frying pan. Add the spinach, cabbage, lettuce, celery and herbs. Cover and sweat the mixture until soft.

4 Add the processed pea mixture to the vegetables and herbs, and heat through.

5 Season with mace, and salt and pepper, and serve hot.

1 Put the peas, leek, garlic and bacon in a large pan. Add the stock, bring to the boil, then lower the heat and simmer for 20 minutes.

2 Transfer to a blender or food processor and process until smooth.

Energy 127kcal/527kJ; Protein 7.7g; Carbohydrate 10.1g, of which sugars 2.8g; Fat 6.5g, of which saturates 1.3g; Cholesterol 4mg; Calcium 58mg; Fibre 4.6g; Sodium 146mg.

MUSHROOM SOUP

USING A MIXTURE OF MUSHROOMS GIVES THIS SOUP CHARACTER. THIS MAKES A FLAVOURSOME LIGHT MEAL SERVED WITH FRESH CRUSTY BREAD.

SERVES 4–6 AS A LIGHT MEAL
OR 6–8 AS A SOUP COURSE

INGREDIENTS
    20g/¾oz/1½ tbsp butter
    15ml/1 tbsp oil
    1 onion, roughly chopped
    4 potatoes, about 250–350g/9–12oz,
        roughly chopped
    350g/12oz mixed mushrooms, such
        as Paris Browns, field (portabello)
        and button (white), cleaned and
        roughly chopped
    1 or 2 garlic cloves, crushed
    150ml/¼ pint/⅔ cup white wine or
        dry (hard) cider
    1.2 litres/2 pints/5 cups good
        chicken stock
    bunch of fresh parsley, chopped
    salt and ground black pepper
    whipped or sour cream,
        to garnish

1 Heat the butter and oil in a large pan over medium heat. Add the chopped onion, turning it in the butter until well coated. Stir in the potatoes. Cover and sweat over a low heat for 5–10 minutes until softened but not browned.

2 Add the mushrooms, garlic and white wine or cider and stock. Season, bring to the boil and cook for 15 minutes, until all the ingredients are tender.

3 Put the mixture through a mouli-legume (food mill), using the coarse blade, or liquidize (blend). Return the soup to the rinsed pan, and add three-quarters of the parsley. Bring back to the boil, season, and garnish with cream and the remaining parsley.

GARLIC SOUP

THIS INTERESTING AND SURPRISINGLY SUBTLY FLAVOURED IRISH SOUP MAKES GOOD USE OF AN ANCIENT INGREDIENT THAT IS NOT ONLY DELICIOUS BUT ALSO BELIEVED TO HAVE HEALTH-GIVING PROPERTIES. IT CERTAINLY BRINGS A GREAT SENSE OF WELL-BEING AND IS A REAL TREAT FOR GARLIC-LOVERS. SERVE IT WITH SOME CRUSTY BREAD AS A REAL WINTER WARMER.

SERVES 8

INGREDIENTS
    12 large garlic cloves, peeled
    15ml/1 tbsp olive oil
    15ml/1 tbsp melted butter
    1 small onion, finely chopped
    15g/½oz/2 tbsp plain
        (all-purpose) flour
    15ml/1 tbsp white wine vinegar
    1 litre/1¾ pints/4 cups good
        chicken stock
    2 egg yolks, lightly beaten
    bread croûtons, fried in butter,
        to serve

VARIATION
Grilled croûtes make a nice change in place of the croûtons. Toast small slices of baguette, top with grated Cheddar and grill (broil) until the cheese melts.

1 Crush the garlic. Put the oil and butter into a pan, add the garlic and onion, and cook them gently for 20 minutes, until soft but not brown.

2 Add the flour and stir to make a roux. Cook for a few minutes, then stir in the wine vinegar, stock and 1 litre/1¾ pints/4 cups water. Simmer for about 30 minutes.

3 When ready to serve the soup, whisk in the lightly beaten egg yolks. Put the croûtons into eight soup bowls and pour over the hot soup.

COOK'S TIP
When adding egg yolks to thicken a soup, reheat the soup gently but do not bring it back to the boil, otherwise the egg will curdle.

Top: Energy 155kcal/648kJ; Protein 3.2g; Carbohydrate 13.6g, of which sugars 3.4g; Fat 7.6g, of which saturates 3.2g; Cholesterol 11mg; Calcium 23mg; Fibre 2.1g; Sodium 44mg.
Bottom: Energy 55kcal/229kJ; Protein 1.6g; Carbohydrate 3.6g, of which sugars 0.6g; Fat 4g, of which saturates 1.3g; Cholesterol 53mg; Calcium 13mg; Fibre 0.4g; Sodium 11mg.

ROASTED ROOT VEGETABLE SOUP

ROASTING THE VEGETABLES GIVES THIS WINTER SOUP A WONDERFUL DEPTH OF FLAVOUR. YOU CAN USE OTHER VEGETABLES, IF YOU WISH, OR ADAPT THE QUANTITIES DEPENDING ON WHAT'S IN SEASON.

SERVES 6

INGREDIENTS

50ml/2fl oz/¼ cup olive oil
1 small butternut squash, peeled, seeded and cubed
2 carrots, cut into thick rounds
1 large parsnip, cubed
1 small swede (rutabaga), cubed
2 leeks, thickly sliced
1 onion, quartered
3 bay leaves
4 thyme sprigs, plus extra to garnish
3 rosemary sprigs
1.2 litres/2 pints/5 cups
 vegetable stock
salt and freshly ground black pepper
soured cream, to serve

1 Preheat the oven to 200°C/400°F/ Gas 6.

2 Pour the olive oil into a large bowl. Add the prepared vegetables and toss thoroughly with a spoon until they are all coated in the oil.

3 Spread out the vegetables in a single layer on one large or two small baking sheets. Tuck the bay leaves and the thyme and rosemary sprigs amongst the vegetables.

4 Roast the vegetables for about 50 minutes until tender, turning them occasionally to make sure they brown evenly. Remove from the oven, discard the herbs and transfer the vegetables to a large pan.

5 Pour the stock into the pan and bring to the boil. Reduce the heat, season to taste, then simmer for 10 minutes. Transfer the soup to a food processor or blender (or use a hand blender) and process for a few minutes until thick and smooth.

6 Return the soup to the pan to heat through. Season and serve with a swirl of soured cream. Garnish each serving with a sprig of thyme.

COOK'S TIP
Dried herbs can be used in place of fresh; sprinkle 2.5ml/½ tsp of each type over the vegetables in step 2 above.

Energy 65kcal/272kJ; Protein 2.5g; Carbohydrate 11.3g, of which sugars 8.8g; Fat 1.3g, of which saturates 0.3g; Cholesterol 0mg; Calcium 93mg; Fibre 4.4g; Sodium 13mg.

LEEK, POTATO AND ROCKET SOUP

ROCKET ADDS ITS DISTINCTIVE, PEPPERY TASTE TO THIS WONDERFULLY SATISFYING SOUP.
SERVE IT HOT, GARNISHED WITH A GENEROUS SPRINKLING OF TASTY CIABATTA CROÛTONS.

SERVES 4–6

INGREDIENTS
50g/2oz/4 tbsp butter
1 onion, chopped
3 leeks, chopped
2 medium floury potatoes, diced
900ml/1½ pints/3¾ cups light
 chicken stock or water
2 large handfuls rocket (arugula)
150ml/¼ pint/⅔ cup double
 (heavy) cream
salt and ground black pepper
garlic-flavoured ciabatta croûtons,
 to serve

1 Melt the butter in a large heavy-based pan, then add the onion, leeks and potatoes and stir until the vegetables are coated in butter. Heat the ingredients until sizzling then reduce the heat to low.

2 Cover and sweat the vegetables for 15 minutes. Pour in the stock or water and bring to the boil then reduce the heat, cover again and simmer for 20 minutes until the vegetables are tender.

3 Press the soup through a sieve (strainer) or pass through a food mill and return to the rinsed pan. (When puréeing the soup, don't use a blender or food processor, as these will give it a gluey texture.) Chop the rocket, add it to the pan and cook the soup gently, uncovered, for 5 minutes.

4 Stir in the cream, then season to taste and reheat gently. Ladle the soup into warmed soup bowls and serve with a scattering of garlic-flavoured ciabatta croûtons in each.

Energy 393kcal/1631kJ; Protein 5.2g; Carbohydrate 23.6g, of which sugars 7.1g; Fat 31.5g, of which saturates 19.3g; Cholesterol 78mg; Calcium 87mg; Fibre 4.5g; Sodium 116mg.

PUMPKIN SOUP <u>WITH</u> RICE

PUMPKIN IS SO FULL OF COLOUR AND FLAVOUR THAT IT INSPIRES YOU TO BUY IT, GO HOME AND START COOKING THIS DELICIOUS WINTER SOUP.

SERVES 4

INGREDIENTS

1.1kg/2lb 7oz pumpkin
750ml/1¼ pints/3 cups
  chicken stock
750ml/1¼ pints/3 cups semi-
  skimmed (low-fat) milk
10–15ml/2–3 tsp sugar
75g/3oz/½ cup cooked white rice
salt and ground black pepper
5ml/1 tsp ground cinnamon,
  to serve

1 Remove the seeds from the pumpkin, cut off the peel and chop the flesh.

2 Place in a pan and add the stock, milk, sugar and seasoning. Bring to the boil, then reduce the heat and simmer for about 20 minutes, or until the pumpkin is tender. Drain the pumpkin, reserving the liquid, and purée it in a food processor, then return it to the pan with the liquid.

3 Bring the soup back to the boil, throw in the rice and simmer for a few minutes. Check the seasoning, pour into bowls and dust with cinnamon.

Energy 202kcal/856kJ; Protein 9.7g; Carbohydrate 33.1g, of which sugars 15.6g; Fat 4.4g, of which saturates 2.5g; Cholesterol 11mg; Calcium 315mg; Fibre 2.8g; Sodium 82mg.

MOROCCAN VEGETABLE SOUP

CREAMY PARSNIP AND PUMPKIN GIVE THIS SOUP A WONDERFULLY RICH TEXTURE. ADD A GOOD PINCH OF PAPRIKA FOR WARMTH AND COLOUR.

SERVES 4

INGREDIENTS

15ml/1 tbsp olive or sunflower oil
15g/½oz/1 tbsp butter
1 onion, chopped
225g/8oz carrots, chopped
225g/8oz parsnips, chopped
225g/8oz pumpkin
about 900ml/1½ pints/3¾ cups
  vegetable or chicken stock
lemon juice, to taste
salt and ground black pepper
For the garnish
7.5ml/1½ tsp olive oil
½ garlic clove, finely chopped
45ml/3 tbsp chopped fresh parsley
  and coriander (cilantro), mixed
a good pinch of paprika

1 Heat the oil and butter in a large pan and fry the onion for 3 minutes until softened. Add the carrots and parsnips, cover and cook for a further 5 minutes.

2 Cut the pumpkin into chunks. Discard the seeds and pith and stir into the pan. Cook for 5 minutes, then add the stock and seasoning and bring to the boil. Cover and simmer for 35–40 minutes.

3 Allow the soup to cool slightly, then pour in to a food processor or blender and purée until smooth, adding a little extra water if the soup seems too thick. Pour back into the clean pan and reheat gently without boiling.

4 To make the garnish, heat the oil in a small pan and fry the garlic and herbs for 1–2 minutes. Add the paprika and stir well.

5 Adjust the seasoning of the soup and stir in lemon juice to taste. Pour into bowls and spoon a little of the prepared garnish on top, which should then be swirled carefully into the soup.

COOK'S TIP
Parsnips are best purchased after the first frost of the year, as the cold converts their starches into sugar, enhancing their sweetness. Scrub well and peel only if the skin is tough.

Energy 141kcal/585kJ; Protein 2.3g; Carbohydrate 14.2g, of which sugars 9.5g; Fat 8.7g, of which saturates 2.8g; Cholesterol 8mg; Calcium 80mg; Fibre 5.3g; Sodium 47mg.

CABBAGE AND POTATO SOUP WITH CARAWAY

EARTHY FLOURY POTATOES ARE ESSENTIAL TO THE SUCCESS OF THIS SOUP, SO CHOOSE YOUR VARIETY CAREFULLY. CARAWAY SEEDS COME FROM A PLANT IN THE PARSLEY FAMILY. THEY ARE AROMATIC AND NUTTY, WITH A DELICATE ANISE FLAVOUR, ADDING A SUBTLE ACCENT TO THIS SATISFYING DISH.

SERVES 4

INGREDIENTS
  30ml/2 tbsp olive oil
  2 small onions, sliced
  6 garlic cloves, halved
  350g/12oz/3 cups shredded green
    cabbage
  4 potatoes, unpeeled
  5ml/1 tsp caraway seeds
  5ml/1 tsp sea salt
  1.2 litres/2 pints/5 cups water

COOK'S TIP
Use floury potatoes to achieve the correct texture for this soup. King Edward or Maris Piper (US Russet or Idaho) are excellent choices.

1 Pour the olive oil into a large pan and cook the onion for 3–4 minutes, until soft. Add the garlic and the cabbage and cook over a low heat for a further 10 minutes, stirring occasionally to prevent the cabbage from sticking to the base of the pan.

2 Add the potatoes, caraway seeds, sea salt and water. Bring to the boil then simmer until the vegetables are cooked.

3 Remove from the heat and allow to cool slightly before serving, strained or mashed into a purée.

Energy 144kcal/601kJ; Protein 3.1g; Carbohydrate 20.4g, of which sugars 8.1g; Fat 6g, of which saturates 0.9g; Cholesterol 0mg; Calcium 60mg; Fibre 3.3g; Sodium 507mg.

PEANUT AND POTATO SOUP

PEANUT SOUP IS A FIRM FAVOURITE THROUGHOUT CENTRAL AND SOUTH AMERICA, AND IS PARTICULARLY POPULAR IN BOLIVIA AND ECUADOR. AS IN MANY LATIN AMERICAN RECIPES, THE GROUND NUTS ARE USED AS A THICKENING AGENT, WITH UNEXPECTEDLY DELICIOUS RESULTS.

SERVES 6

INGREDIENTS

60ml/4 tbsp groundnut (peanut) oil
1 onion, finely chopped
2 garlic cloves, crushed
1 red (bell) pepper, seeded
 and chopped
250g/9oz potatoes, peeled and diced
2 fresh red chillies, seeded
 and chopped
200g/7oz canned chopped tomatoes
150g/5oz/1¼ cups unsalted peanuts
1.5 litres/2½ pints/6¼ cups beef stock
salt and ground black pepper
30ml/2 tbsp chopped fresh coriander
 (cilantro), to garnish

1 Heat the oil in a large heavy pan over a low heat. Stir in the onion and cook for 5 minutes, until beginning to soften. Add the garlic, pepper, potatoes, chillies and tomatoes. Stir well to coat the vegetables evenly in the oil, cover and cook for 5 minutes, until softened.

2 Meanwhile, toast the peanuts by gently cooking them in a large dry frying pan over a medium heat. Keep a close eye on them, moving the peanuts around the pan until they are evenly golden. Take care not to burn them.

COOK'S TIP
Replace the unsalted peanuts with peanut butter if you like. Use equal quantities of chunky and smooth peanut butter for the ideal texture.

3 Set 30ml/2 tbsp of the peanuts aside, to use as garnish. Transfer the remaining peanuts to a food processor and process until finely ground. Add the vegetables and process again until smooth.

4 Return the mixture to the pan and stir in the beef stock. Bring to the boil, then lower the heat and simmer for 10 minutes.

5 Pour the soup into heated bowls. Garnish with a generous scattering of coriander and the remaining peanuts.

Energy 260kcal/1079kJ; Protein 8g; Carbohydrate 14.7g, of which sugars 6.2g; Fat 19.2g, of which saturates 3.6g; Cholesterol 0mg; Calcium 30mg; Fibre 3g; Sodium 20mg.

TOMATO SOUP WITH BLACK OLIVE
CIABATTA TOASTS

TOMATO SOUP IS EVERYBODY'S FAVOURITE, PARTICULARLY WHEN MADE WITH FRESH SUN-RIPENED TOMATOES. THIS DELICIOUS SOUP IS WONDERFULLY WARMING AND HAS AN EARTHY RICHNESS.

SERVES 6

INGREDIENTS
   450g/1lb very ripe fresh tomatoes
   30ml/2 tbsp olive oil
   1 onion, chopped
   1 garlic clove, crushed
   30ml/2 tbsp sherry vinegar
   30ml/2 tbsp tomato purée (paste)
   15ml/1 tbsp cornflour (cornstarch)
      or potato flour
   300ml/½ pint/1¼ cups passata
      (bottled strained tomatoes)
   1 bay leaf
   900ml/1½ pints/3¾ cups vegetable
      or chicken stock
   200ml/7fl oz/scant 1 cup crème fraîche
   salt and ground black pepper
   basil leaves, to garnish
For the black olive ciabatta toasts
   1 plain or black olive ciabatta
   1 small red (bell) pepper
   3 whole garlic cloves, skins on
   225g/8oz black olives (preferably
      a wrinkly Greek variety)
   30–45ml/2–3 tbsp salted capers or
      capers in vinegar
   12 drained canned anchovy fillets
      or 1 small can tuna in oil, drained
   about 150ml/¼ pint/⅔ cup good-
      quality olive oil
   fresh lemon juice and ground black
      pepper, to taste
   45ml/3 tbsp chopped fresh basil

1 Make the ciabatta toasts first. Preheat the oven to 200ºC/400ºF/Gas 6. Split the ciabatta in half and cut each half into nine fingers to give 18 in total. Arrange on a baking sheet and bake for 10–15 minutes until golden and crisp.

2 Place the whole pepper and garlic cloves under a hot grill (broiler) and cook for 15 minutes, turning, until charred all over. If you prefer, you can bake them in the oven for about 25 minutes. Once charred, put the garlic and pepper in a plastic bag, seal and leave to cool for about 10 minutes.

3 When the pepper is cool, peel off the skin (do not wash) and remove the stalk and seeds. Peel the skin off the garlic. Stone (pit) the olives. Rinse the capers under running water to remove the salt or vinegar. Place the prepared ingredients in a food processor with the anchovies or tuna and process until roughly chopped.

4 With the machine running, slowly add the olive oil until you have a fairly smooth dark paste. Alternatively, just stir in the olive oil for a chunkier result. Season to taste with lemon juice and pepper. Stir in the basil.

5 Spread the paste on the finger toasts, or, if not using immediately, transfer to a jar, cover with a layer of olive oil and keep in the refrigerator for up to three weeks.

6 For the soup, cut the tomatoes in half and remove the seeds and pulp using a lemon squeezer. Press the pulp through a sieve (strainer) and reserve the liquid.

7 Heat the oil in a pan and add the onion, garlic, sherry vinegar, tomato purée and the tomato halves. Stir, then cover the pan and cook over a low heat for 1 hour, stirring occasionally. When done, process the soup in a blender or food processor until smooth, then pass through a sieve to remove any pieces of skin. Return to the pan.

8 Mix the cornflour or potato flour with the reserved tomato pulp, then stir into the hot soup with the passata, bay leaf and stock. Simmer for 30 minutes. Stir in the crème fraîche and garnish with the basil leaves. Serve piping hot, with the ciabatta toasts.

Energy 532kcal/2211kJ; Protein 11.9g; Carbohydrate 29.3g, of which sugars 7.6g; Fat 41.7g, of which saturates 13.2g; Cholesterol 50mg; Calcium 120mg; Fibre 3.5g; Sodium 1352mg.

RUSSIAN BORSCHT WITH *KVAS* AND SOUR CREAM

BEETROOT IS THE MAIN INGREDIENT OF BORSCHT, AND ITS FLAVOUR AND COLOUR DOMINATE THIS WELL-KNOWN SOUP. IT IS A CLASSIC OF BOTH RUSSIA AND POLAND.

SERVES 4–6

INGREDIENTS
900g/2lb uncooked beetroot, peeled
2 carrots, peeled
2 celery sticks
40g/1½oz/3 tbsp butter
2 onions, sliced
2 garlic cloves, crushed
4 tomatoes, peeled, seeded
   and chopped
1 bay leaf
1 large parsley sprig
2 cloves
4 whole peppercorns
1.2 litres/2 pints/5 cups beef or
   chicken stock
150ml/¼ pint/⅔ cup beetroot *kvas*
   (see Cook's Tip) or the liquid from
   pickled beetroot
salt and ground black pepper
sour cream, garnished with chopped
   fresh chives or sprigs of dill, to serve

1 Cut the beetroot, carrots and celery into thick strips. Melt the butter in a pan and cook the onions over a low heat for 5 minutes, stirring occasionally.

2 Add the beetroot, carrots and celery and cook for a further 5 minutes.

COOK'S TIP
Beetroot *kvas* adds an intense colour and a slight tartness. If unavailable, peel and grate 1 beetroot, add 150ml/¼ pint/⅔ cup stock and 10ml/2 tsp lemon juice. Bring to the boil, cover and leave for 30 minutes. Strain before using.

3 Add the crushed garlic and chopped tomatoes to the pan and cook, stirring, for 2 more minutes.

4 Place the bay leaf, parsley, cloves and peppercorns in a piece of muslin (cheesecloth) and tie with string.

5 Add the muslin bag to the pan with the stock. Bring to the boil, reduce the heat, cover and simmer for 1¼ hours, until the vegetables are tender. Discard the bag. Stir in the beetroot *kvas* and season. Ladle into bowls and serve with soured cream. Garnish with chives or dill.

Energy 125kcal/532kJ; Protein 5.3g; Carbohydrate 26.2g, of which sugars 23.5g; Fat 0.7g, of which saturates 0.1g; Cholesterol 0mg; Calcium 71mg; Fibre 6.6g; Sodium 166mg.

BROCCOLI AND BREAD SOUP

BROCCOLI GROWS ABUNDANTLY AROUND ROME AND IS SERVED IN THIS SOUP WITH GARLIC TOASTS, SPRINKLED WITH PARMESAN CHEESE.

SERVES 6

INGREDIENTS
675g/1½lb broccoli spears
1.75 litres/3 pints/7½ cups chicken
  or vegetable stock
15ml/1 tbsp lemon juice
salt and ground black pepper
To serve
6 slices white bread
1 large garlic clove, cut in half
grated Parmesan cheese (optional)

COOK'S TIP
Choose broccoli that has bright, compact florets. Yellowing florets, a limp woody stalk and a pungent smell are an indication of overmaturing, and the flavour will not be so good.

1 Using a small, sharp knife, peel the broccoli stems, starting from the base and pulling gently up towards the florets. (The peel should come off easily.) Chop the broccoli into small chunks.

2 Bring the stock to the boil in a large pan. Add the broccoli and simmer for about 10 minutes until soft.

3 Purée about half of the soup and mix into the rest of the soup. Season with salt, pepper and lemon juice.

4 Reheat the soup. Toast the bread, rub with garlic and cut into quarters. Place 3 or 4 pieces of toast in the bottom of each soup plate. Ladle on the soup. Serve immediately, with Parmesan if you like.

TOMATO AND BREAD SOUP

THIS COLOURFUL FLORENTINE RECIPE WAS CREATED TO USE UP STALE BREAD. IT CAN BE MADE WITH VERY RIPE FRESH OR CANNED PLUM TOMATOES.

SERVES 4

INGREDIENTS
90ml/6 tbsp olive oil
small piece dried chilli, crumbled
  (optional)
175g/6oz/1½ cups stale bread, cut
  into 2.5cm/1in cubes
1 medium onion, finely chopped
2 garlic cloves, finely chopped
675g/1½lb ripe tomatoes, peeled and
  chopped, or 2 x 400g/14oz cans
  peeled plum tomatoes, chopped
45ml/3 tbsp chopped fresh basil
1.5 litres/2½ pints/6¼ cups light
  meat stock or water, or a
  combination
salt and ground black pepper
extra virgin olive oil, to serve
  (optional)

1 Heat 60ml/4 tbsp of the oil in a large pan. Add the chilli, if using, and stir for 1–2 minutes.

2 Add the bread cubes and cook until golden, then remove to a plate and drain on kitchen paper.

3 Add the remaining oil, the onion and garlic to the pan and cook until the onion softens.

4 Stir in the tomatoes, basil and the reserved bread cubes. Season with salt. Cook over a moderate heat, stirring occasionally, for about 15 minutes.

5 Meanwhile, heat the stock or water to simmering point. Add it to the tomato mixture and stir well. Bring to the boil. Lower the heat slightly and simmer gently for 20 minutes.

6 Remove the soup from the heat. Use a fork to mash together the tomatoes and bread. Season with pepper, and more salt if necessary. Allow to stand for 10 minutes.

7 Just before serving, swirl in a little extra virgin olive oil, if you like.

Top: Energy 101kcal/426kJ; Protein 7.2g; Carbohydrate 15.3g, of which sugars 2.4g; Fat 1.5g, of which saturates 0.2g; Cholesterol 0mg; Calcium 93mg; Fibre 3.3g; Sodium 149mg.
Bottom: Energy 289kcal/1210kJ; Protein 5.4g; Carbohydrate 28.3g, of which sugars 7.5g; Fat 18g, of which saturates 2.5g; Cholesterol 0mg; Calcium 86mg; Fibre 3.1g; Sodium 247mg.

MUSHROOM AND BREAD SOUP WITH PARSLEY

*THICKENED WITH BREAD, THIS RICH MUSHROOM SOUP WILL WARM YOU UP ON A COLD WINTER DAY.
IT MAKES A TERRIFIC HEARTY LUNCH.*

SERVES 8

INGREDIENTS

75g/3oz/6 tbsp unsalted
  (sweet) butter
900g/2lb field (portobello)
  mushrooms, sliced
2 onions, roughly chopped
600ml/1 pint/2½ cups milk
8 slices white bread
60ml/4 tbsp chopped fresh parsley
300ml/½ pint/1¼ cups double
  (heavy) cream
salt and ground black pepper

1 Melt the butter and sauté the sliced mushrooms and chopped onions over gentle heat for about 10 minutes until soft but not browned.

2 Pour the milk into the pan.

2 Tear the bread into pieces, add to the pan and leave to soak for 15 minutes. Purée the soup and return it to the pan. Add 45ml/3 tbsp of the parsley, the cream and seasoning. Reheat and garnish with the remaining parsley.

Energy 314kcal/1298kJ; Protein 5.5g; Carbohydrate 6.7g, of which sugars 5.9g; Fat 29.7g, of which saturates 18.3g; Cholesterol 76mg; Calcium 123mg; Fibre 1.6g; Sodium 104mg.

BEETROOT AND BUTTER BEAN SOUP

THIS SOUP IS A SIMPLIFIED VERSION OF BORSCHT AND IS PREPARED IN A FRACTION OF THE TIME. SERVE WITH A SPOONFUL OF SOUR CREAM AND A SPRINKLING OF CHOPPED FRESH PARSLEY.

SERVES FOUR

INGREDIENTS
30ml/2 tbsp vegetable oil
1 medium onion, sliced
5ml/1 tsp caraway seeds
finely grated rind of ½ orange
250g/9oz cooked beetroot (beet)
1.2 litres/2 pints/5 cups beef stock
  or *rassol* (see Cook's Tip)
400g/14oz can butter (lima) beans,
  drained and rinsed
15ml/1 tbsp wine vinegar
60ml/4 tbsp sour cream
60ml/4 tbsp chopped fresh parsley,
  to garnish

1 Heat the oil in a large pan and cook the onion, caraway seeds and orange rind until soft but not coloured.

COOK'S TIP
Rassol is a beetroot (beet) broth, which is used to impart a strong beetroot colour and flavour. You are most likely to find it in Kosher food stores.

2 Grate the beetroot and add to the pan with the stock or *rassol*, butter beans and vinegar. Simmer on a low heat for a further 10 minutes.

3 Divide the soup between four bowls, add a spoonful of sour cream to each, sprinkle with chopped parsley and serve piping hot.

Energy 189kcal/790kJ; Protein 7.9g; Carbohydrate 19.8g, of which sugars 7.1g; Fat 9.2g, of which saturates 2.6g; Cholesterol 9mg; Calcium 65mg; Fibre 6.5g; Sodium 471mg.

MUSHROOM AND HERB POTAGE

DO NOT WORRY IF THIS SOUP IS NOT COMPLETELY SMOOTH — IT IS ESPECIALLY NICE WHEN IT HAS A SLIGHTLY NUTTY, TEXTURED CONSISTENCY. THE SHERRY INTENSIFIES THE FLAVOUR OF THE STOCK AND ADDS A LITTLE PUNCH.

SERVES 4

INGREDIENTS
   50g/2oz smoked streaky (fatty) bacon
   1 onion, chopped
   15ml/1 tbsp sunflower oil
   350g/12oz open field (portabello)
     mushrooms or a mixture of wild and
     brown mushrooms
   600ml/1 pint/2½ cups good meat
     stock
   30ml/2 tbsp sweet sherry
   30ml/2 tbsp chopped fresh mixed
     herbs, such as sage, rosemary,
     thyme and marjoram, or 10ml/2 tsp
     mixed dried herbs
   salt and ground black pepper
   a few sprigs of fresh sage or
     marjoram, to garnish
   60ml/4 tbsp Greek-style (US strained
     plain) yogurt or crème fraîche

1 Roughly chop the bacon and place in a large pan. Cook gently until all the fat comes out.

COOK'S TIP
For the best flavour, use home-made meat stock for this soup (see page 32). Once it is made, the stock will keep in the refrigerator for up to 4 days, or in the freezer for up to 3 months.

2 Add the onion and soften, adding oil if necessary. Wipe the mushrooms clean, roughly chop and add to the pan. Cover and sweat until they have completely softened and their liquid has run out.

3 Add the stock, sherry, herbs and seasoning, cover and simmer for 10–12 minutes. Process the soup in a food processor or blender until smooth, but don't worry if you still have a slightly textured result.

4 Check the seasoning and heat through. Serve with a dollop of yogurt or crème fraîche and a sprig of fresh sage or marjoram in each bowl.

Energy 111kcal/460kJ; Protein 4.7g; Carbohydrate 2g, of which sugars 1.4g; Fat 8.7g, of which saturates 2.4g; Cholesterol 8mg; Calcium 33mg; Fibre 1.2g; Sodium 174mg.

LEEK <u>AND</u> POTATO SOUP

THIS IS A HEARTY SCOTTISH STAPLE, SUITABLE FOR EVERYTHING FROM A WARMING LUNCH TO A HOT DRINK FROM A FLASK ON A COLD AFTERNOON. THE CHOPPED VEGETABLES PRODUCE A CHUNKY SOUP. IF YOU PREFER A SMOOTH TEXTURE, PRESS THE MIXTURE THROUGH A SIEVE.

SERVES 4

INGREDIENTS
50g/2oz/¼ cup butter
2 leeks, washed thoroughly and chopped
1 small onion, peeled and finely chopped
350g/12oz potatoes, peeled and chopped
900ml/1½ pints/3¾ cups chicken or vegetable stock
salt and ground black pepper

1 Heat 25g/1oz/2 tbsp of the butter in a large pan over a medium heat. Add the leeks and onion and cook gently, for about 7 minutes, until they are softened.

2 Add the potatoes to the pan and cook for about 2–3 minutes, then add the stock and bring to the boil. Cover and simmer for 30–35 minutes, until the potatoes are tender.

COOK'S TIP
This soup tastes better if you make your own chicken or vegetable stock (see pages 30–1).

3 Season to taste and remove the pan from the heat. Chop up and stir in the remaining butter. Serve hot, with fresh crusty bread.

Energy 179kcal/747kJ; Protein 3.2g; Carbohydrate 17.9g, of which sugars 4g; Fat 11g, of which saturates 6.7g; Cholesterol 27mg; Calcium 32mg; Fibre 3g; Sodium 88mg.

YELLOW BROTH

THIS IS ONE OF MANY VERSIONS OF THIS FAMOUS NORTHERN IRISH SOUP, WHICH IS BOTH THICKENED WITH, AND GIVEN ITS FLAVOUR BY, OATMEAL. IT'S THE PERFECT SOUP TO SERVE ON A REALLY COLD WINTER'S DAY, GARNISHED WITH CHOPPED FRESH PARSLEY.

SERVES 4

INGREDIENTS
  25g/1oz/2 tbsp butter
  1 onion, finely chopped
  1 celery stick, finely chopped
  1 carrot, finely chopped
  25g/1oz/¼ cup plain (all-purpose)
    flour
  900ml/1½ pints/3¾ cups chicken
    stock
  25g/1oz/¼ cup medium oatmeal
  115g/4oz spinach, chopped
  30ml/2 tbsp cream
  salt and ground black pepper
  chopped fresh parsley, to garnish

1 Melt the butter in a large pan. Add the onion, celery and carrot and stir to coat with the melted butter. Cook for about 2 minutes until the onion is beginning to soften.

2 Stir in the flour and cook gently for a further 1 minute, stirring constantly. Pour in the chicken stock, bring to the boil and cover. Reduce the heat and simmer for 30 minutes until the vegetables are tender.

3 Stir in the oatmeal and chopped spinach and cook for a further 15 minutes, stirring from time to time.

4 Stir in the cream and season well. Serve hot, garnished with chopped fresh parsley.

Energy 127kcal/530kJ; Protein 2.8g; Carbohydrate 12.8g, of which sugars 3g; Fat 7.5g, of which saturates 4.2g; Cholesterol 17mg; Calcium 81mg; Fibre 2g; Sodium 92mg.

LEEK <u>AND</u> OATMEAL SOUP

THIS TRADITIONAL IRISH SOUP IS KNOWN AS BROTCHÁN FOLTCHEP *OR* BROTCHÁN ROY, *AND COMBINES LEEKS, OATMEAL AND MILK — THREE INGREDIENTS THAT HAVE BEEN STAPLE FOODS IN IRELAND FOR CENTURIES. SERVE WITH FRESHLY BAKED BREAD AND BUTTER.*

SERVES 4–6

INGREDIENTS
about 1.2 litres/2 pints/5 cups
chicken stock and milk, mixed
30ml/2 tbsp medium pinhead
oatmeal
25g/1oz/2 tbsp butter
6 large leeks, sliced into 2cm/¾in
pieces and washed
pinch of ground mace
30ml/2 tbsp chopped fresh parsley
sea salt and ground black pepper
single (light) cream and chopped
fresh parsley or chives, to garnish
(optional)

1 Bring the stock and milk mixture to the boil over medium heat and sprinkle in the oatmeal. Stir well to prevent lumps forming, and then simmer gently.

2 Melt the butter in a separate pan and cook the leeks over a gentle heat until softened slightly, then add them to the stock. Simmer for 15–20 minutes, until the oatmeal is cooked.

VARIATION
Make nettle and oatmeal soup in the spring, when the nettle tops are young and tender. Strip 275g/10oz leaves from the stems, chop and add to the leeks.

3 Season with salt, pepper and mace, stir in the parsley and serve in warmed bowls. Decorate with a swirl of cream and some chopped fresh parsley or chives, if you like.

Energy 121kcal/505kJ; Protein 4.2g; Carbohydrate 11.3g, of which sugars 4.5g; Fat 6.8g, of which saturates 3.5g; Cholesterol 13mg; Calcium 53mg; Fibre 4.9g; Sodium 44mg

IRISH POTATO SOUP

THIS MOST IRISH OF ALL SOUPS IS NOT ONLY EXCELLENT AS IT IS, BUT VERSATILE TOO, AS IT CAN BE USED AS A BASE FOR NUMEROUS OTHER SOUPS. USE A FLOURY POTATO, SUCH AS GOLDEN WONDER.

SERVES 6–8

INGREDIENTS

50g/2oz/¼ cup butter
2 large onions, peeled and
　finely chopped
675g/1½lb potatoes, diced
about 1.75 litres/3 pints/7½ cups
　hot chicken stock
a little milk, if necessary
sea salt and ground black pepper
chopped fresh chives, to garnish

1 Melt the butter in a large heavy pan and add the onions, turning them in the butter until well coated. Cover and leave to sweat over a very low heat for about 10 mintues.

2 Add the potatoes to the pan, and mix well with the butter and onions. Season with salt and pepper, cover and cook without colouring over a gentle heat for about 10 minutes. Add the stock, bring to the boil and simmer for 25 minutes, or until the vegetables are tender.

3 Remove from the heat and allow to cool slightly. Purée the soup in batches in a blender or food processor.

4 Reheat the soup over a low heat and adjust the seasoning. If the soup seems too thick, add a little extra stock or milk to achieve the right consistency.

5 Serve the soup very hot, sprinkled with chopped chives.

COOK'S TIP
The best potatoes to use in soups are the floury ones, because they cook more quickly and disintegrate easily. Choose varieties such as Golden Wonder, Maris Piper, Estima and King Edward.

Energy 167kcal/699kJ; Protein 2.9g; Carbohydrate 23.5g, of which sugars 5.3g; Fat 7.5g, of which saturates 4.5g; Cholesterol 18mg; Calcium 26mg; Fibre 2.1g; Sodium 201mg.

NETTLE SOUP

A COUNTRY-STYLE SOUP WHICH IS A TASTY VARIATION OF THE CLASSIC IRISH POTATO SOUP. USE WILD NETTLES IF YOU CAN FIND THEM, OR A WASHED HEAD OF ROUND LETTUCE IF YOU PREFER.

SERVES 4

INGREDIENTS

   115g/4oz/½ cup butter
   450g/1lb onions, sliced
   450g/1lb potatoes, cut into chunks
   750ml/1¼ pints/3 cups chicken
     stock
   25g/1oz nettle leaves, removed from
     the stalks
   a small bunch of chives, chopped
   salt and ground black pepper
   double (heavy) cream, to serve

COOK'S TIP
Wear rubber gloves when handling the nettle leaves to avoid being stung. The leaves lose their sting when cooked.

1 Melt the butter in a large pan and add the sliced onions. Cover and cook for about 5 minutes until just softened.

2 Add the potatoes to the pan with the chicken stock. Cover and cook for 25 minutes, until soft.

3 Wash the nettle leaves and add to the pan. Cook for 5 minutes.

4 Purée the soup in a blender or food processor. Return it to the pan, season and stir in the chives. Serve with a swirl of cream and a sprinkle of pepper.

Energy 338kcal/1404kJ; Protein 3.9g; Carbohydrate 27.6g, of which sugars 8.3g; Fat 24.4g, of which saturates 15.1g; Cholesterol 61mg; Calcium 71mg; Fibre 3.3g; Sodium 202mg.

SWEET POTATO AND RED PEPPER SOUP

AS COLOURFUL AS IT IS GOOD TO EAT, THIS SOUP IS A SURE WINNER. SERVE IT WITH SOME FRESH COUNTRY BREAD FOR A WARMING WINTER TREAT.

SERVES 6

INGREDIENTS

2 red (bell) peppers (about 22g/8oz)
   seeded and cubed
500g/1¼lb sweet potatoes, cubed
1 onion, roughly chopped
2 large garlic cloves, roughly chopped
300ml/½ pint/1¼ cups dry white
   wine
1.2 litres/2 pints/5 cups vegetable
   stock
Tabasco sauce, to taste
salt and ground black pepper
fresh country bread, to serve

1 Dice a small quantity of red pepper for the garnish and set aside. Put the rest into a pan with the sweet potato, onion, garlic, wine and vegetable stock. Bring to the boil, lower the heat and simmer for 30 minutes or until all the vegetables are quite soft.

2 Transfer the mixture to a blender or food processor and process until smooth. Season to taste with salt, pepper and a generous dash of Tabasco. Cool slightly. Garnish with the reserved diced red pepper and serve warm or at room temperature.

Energy 124kcal/526kJ; Protein 1.6g; Carbohydrate 21.8g, of which sugars 8.6g; Fat 0.5g, of which saturates 0.1g; Cholesterol 0mg; Calcium 29mg; Fibre 2.9g; Sodium 38mg.

SWEET POTATO AND PARSNIP SOUP

THE SWEETNESS OF THE TWO ROOT VEGETABLES COMES THROUGH STRONGLY IN THIS DELICIOUS SOUP.
ROASTED VEGETABLE STRIPS ADD AN UNUSUAL GARNISH.

SERVES 6

INGREDIENTS
    15ml/1 tbsp sunflower oil
    1 large leek, sliced
    2 celery sticks, chopped
    450g/1lb sweet potatoes, diced
    225g/8oz/1½ cups parsnips, diced
    900ml/1½ pints/3¾ cups vegetable
      stock
    salt and ground black pepper
For the garnish
    15ml/1 tbsp chopped fresh parsley
    roasted strips of sweet potatoes
      and parsnips

1 Heat the oil in a large pan and add the leek, celery, sweet potatoes and parsnips. Cook gently for about 5 minutes, stirring to prevent them browning or sticking to the pan.

2 Stir in the vegetable stock and bring to the boil, then cover and simmer gently for about 25 minutes, or until the vegetables are tender, stirring occasionally. Season to taste. Remove the pan from the heat and allow the soup to cool slightly.

COOK'S TIP
Cut some narrow strips of sweet potato and parsnip, drizzle with olive oil and roast in a hot oven for 10–15 minutes.

3 Purée the soup in a blender or food processor until smooth, then return the soup to the pan and reheat gently.

4 To serve, sprinkle over the chopped parsley and roasted strips of sweet potatoes and parsnips.

Energy 113kcal/479kJ; Protein 2.1g; Carbohydrate 21.6g, of which sugars 7.2g; Fat 2.6g, of which saturates 0.4g; Cholesterol 0mg; Calcium 45mg; Fibre 4.3g; Sodium 40mg.

LEGUME SOUPS

Soups made with legumes — peas, beans and lentils — are very nutritious as they contain protein, fibre, minerals and B vitamins, and are low in fat. The recipes in this section are particularly suitable for vegetarians, if made with vegetarian stock. For a quick and easy lunch, try a simple Potage of Lentil, or Catalan Potato and Broad Bean Soup. On special occasions, impress your guests with cinnamon-scented Moroccan Chickpea and Lentil Soup with Honey Buns.

CATALAN POTATO AND BROAD BEAN SOUP

BROAD BEANS ARE ALSO KNOWN AS FAVA BEANS. WHILE THEY ARE IN SEASON, FRESH BEANS ARE IDEAL, BUT TINNED OR FROZEN WILL MAKE A PERFECTLY GOOD SUBSTITUTE.

SERVES 6

INGREDIENTS
    30ml/2 tbsp olive oil
    2 onions, chopped
    3 large floury potatoes, diced
    450g/1lb fresh broad (fava) beans
    1.75 litres/3 pints/7½ cups
        vegetable stock
    1 bunch coriander (cilantro),
        finely chopped
    150ml/¼ pint/⅔ cup single
        (light) cream
    salt and ground black pepper
    fresh coriander, to garnish

COOK'S TIP
Broad (fava) beans sometimes have a tough outer skin, particularly if they are large. To remove this, first cook the beans briefly, peel off the skin, and add the tender centre part to the soup.

1 Heat the oil in a large pan and fry the onions, stirring occasionally, for about 5 minutes until softened but not brown.

2 Add the potatoes, beans (reserving a few for garnishing) and stock to the mixture in the pan and bring to the boil, then simmer for 5 minutes.

3 Stir in the coriander and simmer for a further 10 minutes.

4 Process the mixture in a blender or food processor (you may have to do this in batches) then return the soup to the pan.

5 Stir in the cream (reserving a little for garnishing). Season to taste with salt and pepper, and bring to a simmer.

6 Serve garnished with more coriander leaves, beans and cream.

Energy 187kcal/784kJ; Protein 8.1g; Carbohydrate 19.2g, of which sugars 3.5g; Fat 9.2g, of which saturates 3.7g; Cholesterol 14mg; Calcium 89mg; Fibre 6.1g; Sodium 22mg.

BROAD BEAN MINESTRONE

THE CLASSIC, WINTRY MINESTRONE SOUP TAKES ON A SUMMER-FRESH IMAGE IN THIS LIGHT RECIPE.
ANY SMALL PASTA SHAPES CAN BE USED INSTEAD OF THE SPAGHETTINI IF YOU PREFER.

SERVES 6

INGREDIENTS

30ml/2 tbsp olive oil
2 onions, peeled and finely chopped
2 garlic cloves, peeled and
  finely chopped
2 carrots, very finely chopped
1 celery stick, very finely chopped
1.27 litres/2¼ pints/5⅔ cups
  boiling water
450g/1lb shelled fresh broad
  (fava) beans
225g/8oz mangetouts (snow peas),
  cut into fine strips
3 tomatoes, peeled and chopped
5ml/1 tsp tomato purée (paste)
50g/2oz spaghettini, broken into
  4cm/1½ in lengths
225g/8oz baby spinach
30ml/2 tbsp chopped fresh parsley
handful of fresh basil leaves
salt and ground black pepper
basil sprigs, to garnish
freshly grated Parmesan cheese,
  to serve

4 Bring the pan of water back to the boil, add the mangetouts and cook for 1 minute until just tender. Drain, then refresh under cold water and set aside.

5 Add the tomatoes and the tomato purée to the soup. Cook for 1 minute. Purée two or three large ladlefuls of the soup and a quarter of the broad beans in a food processor or blender until smooth. Set aside.

6 Add the spaghettini to the remaining soup and cook for 6–8 minutes, until tender. Stir in the purée and spinach and cook for 2–3 minutes. Add the rest of the broad beans, the mangetouts and parsley, and season well.

7 When you are ready to serve the soup, stir in the basil leaves, ladle the soup into deep cups or bowls and garnish with sprigs of basil. Serve a little grated Parmesan with the soup.

1 Heat the oil in a pan and add the chopped onions and garlic. Cook over a low heat for 4–5 minutes, until softened but not browned.

2 Add the carrots and celery, and cook for 2–3 minutes. Add the boiling water and simmer for 15 minutes, until the vegetables are tender.

3 Cook the broad beans in boiling salted water for 4–5 minutes. Remove with a slotted spoon, refresh under cold water and set aside.

Energy 162kcal/682kJ; Protein 9.9g; Carbohydrate 20.8g, of which sugars 6.5g; Fat 4.9g, of which saturates 0.7g; Cholesterol 0mg; Calcium 137mg; Fibre 7.9g; Sodium 72mg.

POTAGE <u>OF</u> LENTILS

*THIS TRADITIONAL JEWISH SOUP IS SOMETIMES KNOWN AS ESAU'S SOUP. RED LENTILS AND VEGETABLES
ARE COOKED AND PURÉED, THEN SHARPENED WITH LOTS OF LEMON JUICE.*

<u>SERVES 4</u>

INGREDIENTS
    45ml/3 tbsp olive oil
    1 onion, chopped
    2 celery sticks, chopped
    1 or 2 carrots, sliced
    8 garlic cloves, chopped
    1 potato, peeled and diced
    250g/9oz/generous 1 cup red lentils,
      picked over and rinsed
    1 litre/1¾ pints/4 cups
      vegetable stock
    2 bay leaves
    1 or 2 lemons, halved
    2.5ml/½ tsp ground cumin, or
      to taste
    cayenne pepper or Tabasco sauce,
      to taste
    salt and ground black pepper
    lemon slices and chopped
      fresh flat leaf parsley, to serve

1 Heat the oil in a large pan. Add the
onion and cook for about 5 minutes, or
until softened. Stir in the celery, carrots,
half the garlic and all the potato. Cook for
a few minutes until beginning to soften.

2 Add the lentils and stock to the pan
and bring to the boil. Reduce the heat,
cover and simmer for about 30 minutes,
until the potato and lentils are tender.

3 Add the bay leaves, remaining garlic
and half the lemons to the pan and
cook the soup for a further 10 minutes.
Remove the bay leaves. Squeeze the
juice from the remaining lemons, then
stir into the soup, to taste.

4 Pour the soup into a food processor
or blender and process until smooth.
(You may need to do this in batches.)
Tip the soup back into the pan, stir in
the cumin, cayenne pepper or Tabasco
sauce, and season with salt and pepper.

5 Ladle the soup into bowls and top
each portion with lemon slices and
a sprinkling of chopped fresh flat
leaf parsley.

VARIATION
On a hot day, serve this soup cold, with
even more lemon juice.

Energy 330kcal/1391kJ; Protein 16.3g; Carbohydrate 48.1g, of which sugars 4.7g; Fat 9.4g, of which saturates 1.4g; Cholesterol 0mg; Calcium 50mg; Fibre 4.5g; Sodium 44mg.

BEAN AND PISTOU SOUP

THIS HEARTY VEGETARIAN SOUP IS A TYPICAL PROVENÇAL-STYLE SOUP, RICHLY FLAVOURED WITH A HOME-MADE GARLIC AND FRESH BASIL PISTOU SAUCE.

SERVES 4–6

INGREDIENTS

150g/5oz/scant 1 cup dried haricot
  (navy) beans, soaked overnight
150g/5oz/scant 1 cup dried flageolet
  or cannellini beans, soaked overnight
1 onion, chopped
1.2 litres/2 pints/5 cups hot
  vegetable stock
2 carrots, roughly chopped
225g/8oz Savoy cabbage, shredded
1 large potato, about 225g/8oz,
  roughly chopped
225g/8oz French (green) beans,
  chopped
salt and ground black pepper
basil leaves, to garnish
For the pistou
  4 garlic cloves
  8 large sprigs basil leaves
  90ml/6 tbsp olive oil
  60ml/4 tbsp freshly grated
    Parmesan cheese

3 Add the chopped carrots, shredded cabbage, chopped potato and French beans to the bean pot. Season with salt and pepper, cover and return the pot to the oven. Reduce the oven temperature to 180°C/350°F/Gas 4 and cook for 1 hour, or until all the vegetables are cooked right through.

4 Meanwhile place the garlic and basil in a mortar and pound with a pestle, then gradually beat in the oil. Stir in the grated Parmesan. Stir half the pistou into the soup and then ladle into warmed soup bowls. Top each bowl of soup with a spoonful of the remaining pistou and serve garnished with basil.

1 Soak a bean pot in cold water for 20 minutes, then drain. Drain the soaked haricot and flageolet or cannellini beans and place in the bean pot. Add the chopped onion and pour over sufficient cold water to come 5cm/2in above the beans. Cover and place the pot in an unheated oven. Set the oven to 200°C/400°F/Gas 6 and cook for about 1½ hours, or until the beans are tender.

2 Drain the beans and onions. Place half the beans and onions in a food processor or blender and process to a paste. Return the beans and paste to the bean pot. Add the vegetable stock.

Energy 286kcal/1214kJ; Protein 19.8g; Carbohydrate 50.9g, of which sugars 11.1g; Fat 1.8g, of which saturates 0.3g; Cholesterol 0mg; Calcium 142mg; Fibre 16.1g; Sodium 36mg.

BUTTER BEAN, SUN-DRIED TOMATO AND PESTO SOUP

THIS SOUP IS SO QUICK AND EASY TO MAKE, AND USING PLENTY OF PESTO AND SUN-DRIED TOMATO PASTE GIVES IT A RICH, MINESTRONE-LIKE FLAVOUR.

SERVES 4

INGREDIENTS
900ml/1½ pints/3¾ cups chicken
    or vegetable stock
2 x 400g/14oz cans butter
    (lima) beans
60ml/4 tbsp sun-dried tomato
    purée (paste)
75ml/5 tbsp pesto

COOK'S TIP
Use a good-quality home-made or bought fresh stock for the best results. Vegetarians should use vegetable stock.

VARIATION
As an alternative to butter (lima) beans, use haricot (navy) or cannellini beans.

1 Drain and rinse the butter beans. Put the drained beans in a large pan with the stock and bring just to the boil.

2 Reduce the heat and stir in the tomato purée and pesto. Cover, bring back to simmering point and cook gently for 5 minutes.

3 Transfer six ladlefuls of the soup to a blender or food processor, scooping up plenty of the beans. Process until smooth, then return to the pan.

4 Heat gently, stirring frequently, for 5 minutes, then season if necessary. Ladle into four warmed soup bowls.

Energy 264kcal/1109kJ; Protein 14.8g; Carbohydrate 27.4g, of which sugars 3.6g; Fat 11.3g, of which saturates 2.7g; Cholesterol 6mg; Calcium 109mg; Fibre 9.5g; Sodium 932mg.

AMERICAN RED BEAN SOUP
WITH GUACAMOLE SALSA

THIS SOUP IS IN TEX-MEX STYLE, AND IT IS SERVED WITH A COOLING AVOCADO AND LIME SALSA. IF YOU RELISH CHILLIES, ADD A LITTLE MORE CAYENNE FOR A TRULY FIERY EXPERIENCE.

SERVES 6

INGREDIENTS
30ml/2 tbsp olive oil
2 onions, chopped
2 garlic cloves, chopped
10ml/2 tsp ground cumin
1.5ml/¼ tsp cayenne pepper
15ml/1 tbsp paprika
15ml/1 tbsp tomato purée (paste)
2.5ml/½ tsp dried oregano
400g/14oz can chopped tomatoes
2 x 400g/14oz cans red kidney
 beans, drained and rinsed
900ml/1½ pints/3¾ cups water
salt and ground black pepper
Tabasco sauce, to serve
For the guacamole salsa
2 avocados
1 small red onion, finely chopped
1 green chilli, seeded and chopped
15ml/1 tbsp chopped fresh
 coriander (cilantro)
juice of 1 lime

1 Heat the oil in a pan and add the onions and garlic. Cook for 4–5 minutes, until softened. Add the cumin, cayenne and paprika, and cook for 1 minute.

2 Stir in the tomato purée and cook for a few seconds, then stir in the oregano. Add the chopped tomatoes, kidney beans and water. Bring to the boil and simmer for 15–20 minutes.

4 To make the guacamole salsa, halve, stone (pit) and peel the avocados, then dice them finely. Place in a small bowl and gently, but thoroughly, mix with the finely chopped red onion and chilli, and the coriander and lime juice.

3 Cool the soup slightly, then purée it in a food processor or blender until smooth. Return to the pan and season.

5 Reheat the soup and ladle into bowls. Spoon a little guacamole salsa into the middle of each and serve, offering Tabasco sauce separately.

Energy 244kcal/1023kJ; Protein 10.5g; Carbohydrate 27.5g, of which sugars 7.4g; Fat 11g, of which saturates 2g; Cholesterol 0mg; Calcium 108mg; Fibre 10g; Sodium 535mg.

BLACK-EYED BEAN
AND TOMATO BROTH

THIS DELICIOUS BLACK-EYED BEAN SOUP – KNOWN AS LUBIYA IN ISRAEL – IS FLAVOURED WITH TANGY LEMON AND SPECKLED WITH CHOPPED FRESH CORIANDER. IT IS IDEAL FOR SERVING AT PARTIES; SIMPLY MULTIPLY THE QUANTITIES AS REQUIRED.

SERVES 4

INGREDIENTS
175g/6oz/1 cup black-eyed
  beans (peas)
15ml/1 tbsp olive oil
2 onions, chopped
4 garlic cloves, chopped
1 medium-hot or 2–3 mild fresh
  chillies, chopped
5ml/1 tsp ground cumin
5ml/1 tsp ground turmeric
250g/9oz fresh or canned
  tomatoes, diced
600ml/1 pint/2½ cups chicken,
  beef or vegetable stock
25g/1oz fresh coriander (cilantro)
  leaves, roughly chopped
juice of ½ lemon
pitta bread, to serve

1 Put the beans in a pan, cover with cold water, bring to the boil and cook for 5 minutes. Remove from the heat, cover and leave to stand for 2 hours. Drain the beans, return to the pan, cover with fresh cold water, then simmer for 35–40 minutes, or until the beans are tender. Drain and set aside.

2 Heat the oil in a pan, add the onions, garlic and chilli and cook for 5 minutes, or until the onion is soft. Stir in the cumin, turmeric, tomatoes, stock, half the coriander and the beans and simmer for 20–30 minutes. Stir in the lemon juice and remaining coriander and serve at once with pitta bread.

Energy 168kcal/712kJ; Protein 10.7g; Carbohydrate 25g, of which sugars 2.3g; Fat 3.6g, of which saturates 0.6g; Cholesterol 0mg; Calcium 52mg; Fibre 4.1g; Sodium 10mg.

MOROCCAN CHICKPEA <u>AND</u> LENTIL SOUP <u>WITH</u> HONEY BUNS

THIS THICK PULSE AND VEGETABLE SOUP IS SAID TO ORIGINATE FROM A SEMOLINA GRUEL THAT THE BERBERS ATE DURING THE COLD WINTERS IN THE ATLAS MOUNTAINS. TODAY, IT IS SERVED IN RESTAURANTS AND CAFÉS AS A HEARTY SNACK WITH HONEY-SWEETENED SPICED BREAD OR BUNS.

SERVES 8

INGREDIENTS

30–45ml/2–3 tbsp olive oil
2 onions, halved and sliced
2.5ml/½ tsp ground ginger
2.5ml/½ tsp ground turmeric
5ml/1 tsp ground cinnamon
pinch of saffron threads
2 x 400g/14oz cans chopped
  tomatoes
5–10ml/1–2 tsp caster
  (superfine) sugar
175g/6oz/¾ cup brown or green
  lentils, picked over and rinsed
about 1.75 litres/3 pints/7½ cups
  meat or vegetable stock, or water
200g/7oz/1 generous cup dried
  chickpeas, soaked overnight,
  drained and boiled until tender
200g/7oz/1 generous cup dried broad
  (fava) beans, soaked overnight,
  drained and boiled until tender
small bunch of fresh coriander
  (cilantro), chopped
small bunch of flat leaf
  parsley, chopped
salt and ground black pepper
for the buns
2.5ml/½ tsp dried yeast
300g/11oz/1¼ cups unbleached
  strong white bread flour
15–30ml/1–2 tbsp clear honey
5ml/1 tsp fennel seeds
250ml/8fl oz/1 cup milk
1 egg yolk, stirred with a little milk
salt

1 Make the buns. Dissolve the yeast in about 15ml/1 tbsp lukewarm water. Sift the flour and a pinch of salt into a bowl. Make a well in the centre and add the dissolved yeast, honey and fennel seeds. Gradually pour in the milk, using your hands to work it into the flour along with the honey and yeast, until the mixture forms a dough – if the dough becomes too sticky to handle, add more flour.

2 Turn the dough out on to a floured surface and knead well for about 10 minutes, until it is smooth and elastic. Flour the surface under the dough and cover it with a damp cloth, then leave the dough to rise until it has doubled in size.

3 Preheat the oven to 230°C/450°F/ Gas 8. Grease two baking sheets. Divide the dough into 12 balls. On a floured surface, flatten the balls of dough with the palm of your hand, then place them on a baking sheet. Brush the tops of the buns with egg yolk and bake for about 15 minutes until they are risen slightly and sound hollow when tapped underneath. Transfer to a wire rack to cool.

4 To make the soup, heat the olive oil in a stockpot or large pan. Add the onions and stir for about 15 minutes, or until they are soft.

5 Add the ginger, turmeric, cinnamon, saffron, tomatoes and sugar. Stir in the lentils and pour in the stock or water. Bring to the boil, then reduce the heat, cover and simmer for about 25 minutes, or until the lentils are tender.

6 Stir in the cooked chickpeas and beans, bring back to the boil, then cover and simmer for a further 10–15 minutes. Stir in the fresh herbs and season the soup to taste. Serve piping hot, with the honey buns.

Energy 368kcal/1558kJ; Protein 18.3g; Carbohydrate 64.9g, of which sugars 9.7g; Fat 5.7g, of which saturates 1g; Cholesterol 2mg; Calcium 172mg; Fibre 7.5g; Sodium 74mg.

TUSCAN CANNELLINI BEAN SOUP
WITH CAVOLO NERO

CAVOLO NERO IS A VERY DARK GREEN CABBAGE WITH A NUTTY FLAVOUR FROM TUSCANY AND SOUTHERN ITALY. IT IS IDEAL FOR THIS TRADITIONAL RECIPE.

SERVES 4

INGREDIENTS
   2 x 400g/14oz cans chopped
     tomatoes with herbs
   250g/9oz cavolo nero leaves, or
     Savoy cabbage
   400g/14oz can cannellini beans,
     drained and rinsed
   60ml/4 tbsp extra virgin olive oil
   salt and ground black pepper

1 Pour the tomatoes into a large pan and add a can of cold water. Season with salt and pepper and bring to the boil, then reduce the heat to a simmer.

2 Roughly shred the cabbage leaves and add them to the pan. Partially cover the pan and simmer gently for about 15 minutes, or until the cabbage is tender.

3 Add the cannellini beans to the pan and warm through for a few minutes. Check and adjust the seasoning, then ladle the soup into bowls, drizzle each one with a little olive oil and serve.

Energy 227kcal/950kJ; Protein 8.2g; Carbohydrate 22.3g, of which sugars 10.4g; Fat 12.2g, of which saturates 1.9g; Cholesterol 0mg; Calcium 60mg; Fibre 7.9g; Sodium 443mg.

OLD COUNTRY MUSHROOM, BEAN AND BARLEY SOUP

THIS HEARTY JEWISH SOUP IS PERFECT ON A FREEZING COLD DAY. SERVE IN WARMED BOWLS, WITH PLENTY OF RYE OR PUMPERNICKEL BREAD.

SERVES 6–8

INGREDIENTS

30–45ml/2–3 tbsp small haricot
  (navy) beans, soaked overnight
45–60ml/ 3–4 tbsp green split peas
45–60ml/3–4 tbsp yellow split peas
90–105ml/6–7 tbsp pearl barley
1 onion, chopped
2 carrots, sliced
3 celery sticks, diced or sliced
1/2 baking potato, peeled and cut
  into chunks
10g/1/4oz or 45ml/3 tbsp mixed
  flavourful dried mushrooms
5 garlic cloves, sliced
2 litres/3½ pints/8 cups water
2 vegetable stock (bouillon) cubes
salt and ground black pepper
30–45ml/2–3 tbsp chopped fresh
  parsley, to garnish

1 In a large pan, put the beans, green and yellow split peas, pearl barley, onion, carrots, celery, potato, mushrooms, garlic and water.

2 Bring the mixture to the boil, then reduce the heat, cover and simmer gently for about 1½ hours, or until the beans are tender.

3 Crumble the stock cubes into the soup and taste for seasoning. Ladle into warmed bowls, garnish with parsley and serve with rye or pumpernickel bread.

COOK'S TIP
Do not add the stock (bouillon) cubes until the end of cooking as the salt will stop the beans from becoming tender.

Energy 171kcal/726kJ; Protein 7.7g; Carbohydrate 35.4g, of which sugars 3.7g; Fat 0.8g, of which saturates 0.1g; Cholesterol 0mg; Calcium 37mg; Fibre 3.3g; Sodium 27mg.

RUSSIAN PEA AND BARLEY SOUP

THIS THICK AND WARMING SOUP, GROCHOWKA, MAKES A SUBSTANTIAL APPETIZER, OR IT MAY BE SERVED AS A MEAL IN ITS OWN RIGHT, EATEN WITH HOT CRUSTY BREAD.

3 Dry-fry the bacon cubes in a frying pan for 5 minutes, or until well browned and crispy. Remove from the pan with a slotted spoon, leaving the fat behind, and set aside.

4 Add the butter to the frying pan, add the onion and garlic and cook gently for 5 minutes. Add the celeriac and cook for a further 5 minutes, or until the onion is just starting to colour.

SERVES 6

INGREDIENTS
    225g/8oz/1¼ cups yellow split peas, rinsed in cold water
    25g/1oz/¼ cup pearl barley, rinsed in cold water
    1.75 litres/3 pints/7½ cups vegetable or ham stock
    50g/2oz smoked streaky (fatty) bacon, cubed
    25g/1oz/2 tbsp butter
    1 onion, finely chopped
    2 garlic cloves, crushed
    225g/8oz celeriac, cubed
    15ml/1 tbsp roughly chopped fresh marjoram
    salt and ground black pepper
    bread, to serve

1 Put the peas and barley in a bowl, cover with plenty of water and leave to soak overnight.

2 The next day, drain and rinse the peas and barley. Put them in a large pan, pour in the stock and bring to the boil. Turn down the heat and simmer gently for 40 minutes.

5 Add the softened vegetables and bacon to the pan of stock, peas and barley. Season lightly with salt and pepper, then cover and simmer for 20 minutes, or until the soup is thick. Stir in the marjoram, add extra black pepper to taste and serve with bread.

Energy 189kcal/799kJ; Protein 11g; Carbohydrate 25.8g, of which sugars 1.8g; Fat 5.5g, of which saturates 2.8g; Cholesterol 13mg; Calcium 39mg; Fibre 2.4g; Sodium 190mg.

LENTIL AND BACON SOUP

THIS IS A WONDERFULLY HEARTY GERMAN SOUP. A LIGHTER VERSION CAN BE MADE BY OMITTING THE FRANKFURTERS, IF YOU PREFER.

SERVES 6

INGREDIENTS

    225g/8oz/1 cup brown lentils
    15ml/1 tbsp sunflower oil
    1 onion, finely chopped
    1 leek, finely chopped
    1 carrot, finely diced
    2 celery sticks, chopped
    115g/4oz piece lean bacon
    2 bay leaves
    1.5 litres/2½ pints/6¼ cups water
    30ml/2 tbsp chopped fresh parsley,
      plus extra to garnish
    225g/8oz frankfurters, sliced
    salt and ground black pepper

1 Rinse the lentils thoroughly under cold running water, then drain.

2 Heat the oil in a large pan and gently fry the onion for 5 minutes until soft. Add the leek, carrot, celery, bacon and bay leaves.

3 Add the lentils. Pour in the water, then slowly bring to the boil. Skim the surface, then simmer, half-covered, for about 45–50 minutes, or until the lentils are soft.

4 Remove the piece of bacon from the soup and cut into small cubes. Trim off any fat.

5 Return the bacon to the soup with the parsley and sliced frankfurters, and season well with salt and freshly ground black pepper. Simmer for 2–3 minutes, then remove the bay leaves.

6 Transfer to individual soup bowls and serve garnished with chopped parsley.

COOK'S TIP
Unlike most legumes, brown lentils do not need to be soaked before cooking.

Energy 260kcal/1091kJ; Protein 14.8g; Carbohydrate 24.6g, of which sugars 3.8g; Fat 12.1g, of which saturates 3.8g; Cholesterol 29mg; Calcium 41mg; Fibre 3.2g; Sodium 370mg.

WHITE BEAN SOUP

*USE EITHER HARICOT (NAVY) BEANS OR BUTTER (LIMA) BEANS FOR THIS VELVETY SOUP. DRIED BEANS
NEED TO BE SOAKED IN COLD WATER OVERNIGHT BEFORE THEY ARE COOKED.*

SERVES 4

INGREDIENTS

175g/6oz/¾ cup dried white beans,
    soaked in cold water overnight
30–45ml/2–3 tbsp oil
2 large onions, chopped
4 celery sticks, chopped
1 parsnip, chopped
1 litre/1¾ pints/4 cups chicken stock
salt and ground black pepper
chopped fresh coriander (cilantro)
    and paprika, to garnish

1 Drain the beans and boil rapidly in
fresh water for 10 minutes. Drain, cover
with fresh water and simmer for 1–2
hours until soft. Reserve the liquid and
discard any bean skins on the surface.

2 Heat the oil in a heavy pan and
sauté the onions, celery and parsnip
for 3 minutes.

3 Add the cooked beans and stock and
continue cooking until the vegetables
are tender.

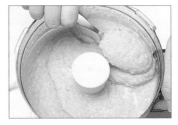

4 Allow the soup to cool slightly and,
using a food processor or hand
blender, purée the soup until it is
velvety smooth.

5 Reheat the soup gently, gradually
adding some of the bean liquid or a
little water if it is too thick. Season to
taste with salt and pepper.

6 To serve, transfer the soup into wide
bowls. Garnish with fresh coriander and
a sprinkling of paprika. Serve hot.

VARIATIONS
• You can, if you prefer, use a 400g/
14oz can cannellini or butter (lima)
beans instead of dried beans. Drain and
rinse them before adding to the dish.
• Garnish the soup with chopped parsley
instead of coriander (cilantro), and
sprinkle with a little cayenne pepper.

Energy 220kcal/926kJ; Protein 11.5g; Carbohydrate 30.6g, of which sugars 8.4g; Fat 6.7g, of which saturates 0.9g; Cholesterol 0mg; Calcium 91mg; Fibre 9.8g; Sodium 32mg.

BLACK AND WHITE BEAN SOUP

ALTHOUGH THIS SOUP TAKES A WHILE TO PREPARE, THE RESULTS ARE SO STUNNING THAT IT IS WELL WORTH THE EFFORT.

SERVES 8

INGREDIENTS
350g/12oz/2 cups dried black beans, soaked overnight and drained
2.4 litres/4¼ pints/10½ cups water
6 garlic cloves, crushed
350g/12oz/2 cups dried white beans, soaked overnight and drained
90ml/6 tbsp balsamic vinegar
4 jalapeño peppers, seeded and chopped
6 spring onions (scallions), finely chopped
juice of 1 lime
50ml/2fl oz/¼ cup olive oil
15g/½oz/¼ cup chopped fresh coriander (cilantro), plus extra to garnish
salt and ground black pepper

1 Drain and rinse the black beans under cold running water. Place in a large pan with half the water and garlic. Bring to the boil. Reduce the heat to low, cover the pan, and simmer for about 1½ hours until the beans are soft.

2 Meanwhile, drain and rinse the white beans and put in another pan with the remaining water and garlic. Bring to the boil, cover the pan and simmer for about 1 hour until soft.

3 Purée the cooked white beans in a food processor or blender. Stir in the vinegar, jalapeños, and half of the spring onions. Return to the pan and reheat gently.

4 Purée the cooked black beans in the food processor or blender. Return them to the pan and stir in the lime juice, olive oil, coriander and remaining spring onions. Reheat gently.

5 Season both soups with salt and freshly ground black pepper. To serve, place a ladleful of each puréed soup in each soup bowl, side by side. Swirl the two soups together with a cocktail stick (toothpick) or skewer. Garnish with fresh coriander and serve hot.

Energy 281kcal/1189kJ; Protein 19.7g; Carbohydrate 40.2g, of which sugars 3.7g; Fat 5.7g, of which saturates 0.8g; Cholesterol 0mg; Calcium 92mg; Fibre 14.2g; Sodium 17mg.

SPLIT PEA AND PUMPKIN SOUP

THIS IS A TASTY VEGETARIAN VERSION OF A TRADITIONAL PEA SOUP. THE SPLIT PEAS NEED TO BE SOAKED IN COLD WATER OVERNIGHT.

2 In a separate pan, melt the butter and sauté the onion until it is soft but not browned.

3 Add the pumpkin, tomatoes, tarragon, coriander, cumin and chilli powder, and crumble in the stock cube. Bring to the boil over high heat.

4 Stir the vegetable mixture into the cooked split peas and their liquid. Simmer over a gentle heat for about 20 minutes or until the vegetables are tender. If the soup is too thick, add another 150ml/¼ pint/⅔ cup water and reheat.

5 Ladle into warm bowls and serve hot, garnished with sprigs of coriander.

SERVES 4

INGREDIENTS

225g/8oz/1 cup split peas
1.2 litres/2 pints/5 cups water
25g/1oz/2 tbsp butter
1 onion, finely chopped
225g/8oz pumpkin, chopped
3 tomatoes, peeled and chopped
5ml/1 tsp dried tarragon, crushed
15ml/1 tbsp chopped fresh coriander
  (cilantro)
2.5ml/½ tsp ground cumin
chilli powder, to taste
1 vegetable stock (bouillon) cube
sprigs of fresh coriander, to garnish

1 Soak the split peas overnight in enough water to cover them completely, then drain. Place them in a large pan, add the water and boil for about 30 minutes until tender.

Energy 251kcal/1061kJ; Protein 14.5g; Carbohydrate 36.5g, of which sugars 5.5g; Fat 6.2g, of which saturates 3.5g; Cholesterol 13mg; Calcium 55mg; Fibre 4.3g; Sodium 65mg.

CAULIFLOWER, FLAGEOLET AND FENNEL SOUP

THE SWEET, ANISE-LIQUORICE FLAVOUR OF THE FENNEL SEEDS GIVES A DELICIOUS EDGE TO THIS HEARTY VEGETARIAN SOUP.

SERVES 4–6

INGREDIENTS

15ml/1 tbsp olive oil
1 garlic clove, crushed
1 onion, chopped
10ml/2 tsp fennel seeds
1 cauliflower, cut into small florets
2 x 400g/14oz cans flageolet or
  cannellini beans, drained and rinsed
1.2 litres/2 pints/5 cups vegetable
  stock or water
salt and ground black pepper
chopped fresh parsley, to garnish
toasted slices of French bread,
  to serve

3 Bring the mixture to the boil. Reduce the heat and simmer for about 10 minutes or until the cauliflower is tender. Pour the soup into a blender or food processor and blend until smooth.

4 Stir in the remaining beans and season to taste. Reheat and pour into bowls. Sprinkle with chopped parsley and serve with toasted slices of French bread.

1 Heat the olive oil. Add the garlic, onion and fennel seeds and cook gently for 5 minutes or until softened.

2 Add the cauliflower florets, half the beans and the vegetable stock or water.

COOK'S TIP
When purchasing a cauliflower, look for one with cream-coloured, compact, firm florets, or curds, encased in large, bright green leaves.

Energy 170kcal/719kJ; Protein 11.1g; Carbohydrate 26g, of which sugars 6.6g; Fat 3.1g, of which saturates 0.5g; Cholesterol 0mg; Calcium 108mg; Fibre 9.3g; Sodium 525mg.

EASTERN EUROPEAN CHICKPEA SOUP

CHICKPEAS FORM PART OF THE STAPLE DIET IN THE BALKANS, WHERE THIS SOUP ORIGINATES. IT IS ECONOMICAL TO MAKE, AND IS A HEARTY AND SATISFYING DISH.

SERVES 4–6

INGREDIENTS
  500g/1¼lb/5 cups chickpeas,
    soaked overnight
  2 litres/3½ pints/9 cups vegetable
    stock
  3 large waxy potatoes, cut into
    bite-size chunks
  50ml/2fl oz/¼ cup olive oil
  225g/8oz spinach leaves
  salt and ground black pepper
  spicy sausage, cooked (optional)

1 Drain the chickpeas and rinse under cold water. Place in a large pan with the vegetable stock. Bring to the boil, then reduce the heat and cook gently for about 1 hour.

2 Add the potatoes, olive oil and salt and pepper to taste. Cook for 20 minutes until the potatoes are tender.

COOK'S TIP
Dried chickpeas toughen with age so, although they will keep for up to a year in a cool dry place, it is best to buy them in small quantities.

3 Add the spinach and sliced, cooked sausage (if using) 5 minutes before the end of cooking. Serve the soup in individual warmed soup bowls.

CHICKPEA AND SPINACH SOUP WITH GARLIC

THIS DELICIOUS, THICK AND CREAMY SOUP IS RICHLY FLAVOURED AND PERFECT FOR VEGETARIANS.
SERVED WITH SOME FRESH CRUSTY BREAD IT MAKES A COMPLETE MEAL.

SERVES 4

INGREDIENTS
30ml/2 tbsp olive oil
4 garlic cloves, crushed
1 onion, roughly chopped
10ml/2 tsp ground cumin
10ml/2 tsp ground coriander
1.2 litres/2 pints/5 cups vegetable
  stock
350g/12oz potatoes, finely chopped
425g/15oz can chickpeas, drained
15ml/1 tbsp cornflour (cornstarch)
150ml/¼ pint/⅔ cup double
  (heavy) cream
30ml/2 tbsp light tahini
200g/7oz spinach, shredded
cayenne pepper
salt and ground black pepper

1 Heat the oil in a large pan and cook the garlic and onion for about 5 minutes or until the onion is softened and golden brown.

2 Stir in the ground cumin and coriander and cook for 1 minute. Add the stock and potatoes. Bring to the boil and simmer for 10 minutes.

3 Add the chickpeas and simmer for a further 5 minutes or until the potatoes are just tender.

4 Blend together the cornflour, cream, tahini and plenty of seasoning. Stir into the soup a little at a time. Add the shredded spinach.

5 Bring to the boil, stirring, and simmer for a further 2 minutes. Adjust the seasoning with salt, pepper and cayenne pepper to taste.

6 Spoon into four warmed bowls and serve sprinkled with a little extra cayenne pepper.

COOK'S TIPS
• Tahini is a paste made with sesame seeds and is available from many health food stores.
• You can use dried chickpeas instead of canned ones if you prefer, but remember that they will need soaking overnight.
• For a lighter soup, use semi-skimmed (low-fat) milk instead of cream, but the result will not be so rich and creamy.

Energy 496kcal/2066kJ; Protein 12.7g; Carbohydrate 37.3g, of which sugars 3.8g; Fat 33.9g, of which saturates 14.4g; Cholesterol 51mg; Calcium 210mg; Fibre 7.1g; Sodium 326mg.

CHICKPEA AND PARSLEY SOUP

PARSLEY AND A HINT OF LEMON BRING FRESHNESS TO CHICKPEAS. USE VEGETABLE STOCK INSTEAD OF CHICKEN STOCK FOR THIS SOUP IF YOU ARE CATERING FOR VEGETARIANS.

2 Place the onion and parsley in a food processor or blender and process until finely chopped.

3 Heat the olive and sunflower oils in a large pan or flameproof casserole and fry the onion mixture for about 4 minutes over a low heat until the onion is slightly softened.

4 Add the chickpeas, cook gently for 1–2 minutes then add the stock. Season well. Bring the soup to the boil, then cover and simmer for 20 minutes.

SERVES 6

INGREDIENTS
   225g/8oz/1⅓ cups chickpeas,
      soaked overnight
   1 small onion
   1 bunch of fresh parsley (about
      40g/1½oz)
   30ml/2 tbsp olive and sunflower
      oils, mixed
   1.2 litres/2 pints/5 cups chicken
      stock
   juice of ½ lemon
   salt and ground black pepper
   lemon wedges and finely pared strips
      of rind, to garnish

1 Drain the chickpeas and rinse under cold running water. Place in a large pan covered with fresh water, bring to the boil and cook for 1–1½ hours until tender. Drain and peel.

5 Allow the soup to cool a little and then mash the chickpeas using a fork until the soup is thick but still quite chunky.

6 Reheat the soup and add the lemon juice. Serve garnished with lemon wedges and rind.

VARIATIONS
• This soup is equally good made with coriander (cilantro) instead of parsley.
• If you do not have time to soak dried chickpeas overnight, use canned ones instead – drain before adding to the soup.

Energy 159kcal/668kJ; Protein 8.3g; Carbohydrate 19.6g, of which sugars 1.7g; Fat 5.8g, of which saturates 0.6g; Cholesterol 0mg; Calcium 76mg; Fibre 4.5g; Sodium 17mg.

GREEN LENTIL SOUP

LENTIL SOUP IS AN EASTERN MEDITERRANEAN CLASSIC, VARYING IN ITS SPICINESS ACCORDING TO THE REGION IT COMES FROM.

SERVES 4–6

INGREDIENTS

  225g/8oz/1 cup green lentils
  75ml/5 tbsp olive oil
  3 onions, finely chopped
  2 garlic cloves, finely sliced
  10ml/2 tsp cumin seeds, crushed
  1.5ml/¼ tsp ground turmeric
  600ml/1 pint/2½ cups vegetable
    stock
  600ml/1 pint/2½ cups water
  salt and ground black pepper
  30ml/2 tbsp roughly chopped fresh
    coriander (cilantro), to garnish
  warm crusty bread, to serve

1 Put the lentils in a pan and cover with cold water. Boil for 10 minutes. Drain.

2 Heat 30ml/2 tbsp of the oil and fry two-thirds of the onions with the garlic, cumin and turmeric for 3 minutes.

3 Add the lentils, stock and water. Bring to the boil, reduce the heat, cover and simmer for 30 minutes until the lentils are soft.

4 Heat the remaining oil and fry the rest of the onion until golden brown, stirring frequently.

5 Use a potato masher to lightly mash the lentils and make the soup pulpy in texture. Reheat gently and season with salt and freshly ground pepper to taste.

6 Pour the soup into warmed bowls. Stir the fresh coriander into the fried onion and sprinkle over the soup as a garnish. Serve hot with warm crusty bread.

COOK'S TIP
Red or Puy lentils make an equally good substitute for green lentils. The lentils do not need to be soaked before cooking.

Energy 220kcal/921kJ; Protein 9.5g; Carbohydrate 25.1g, of which sugars 3.7g; Fat 9.8g, of which saturates 1.4g; Cholesterol 0mg; Calcium 32mg; Fibre 2.5g; Sodium 15mg.

GARLICKY LENTIL SOUP

HIGH IN FIBRE, LENTILS MAKE A PARTICULARLY TASTY SOUP. UNLIKE MANY PULSES, THEY DO NOT NEED TO BE SOAKED BEFORE BEING COOKED.

SERVES 6

INGREDIENTS

    225g/8oz/1 cup red lentils, rinsed
      and drained
    2 onions, finely chopped
    2 large garlic cloves, finely chopped
    1 carrot, finely chopped
    30ml/2 tbsp olive oil
    2 bay leaves
    a generous pinch of dried marjoram
      or oregano
    1.5 litres/2½ pints/6¼ cups
      vegetable stock
    30ml/2 tbsp red wine vinegar
    salt and ground black pepper
    celery leaves, to garnish
    crusty bread rolls, to serve

1 Put all the ingredients except for the vinegar, seasoning and garnish in a large, heavy pan. Bring to the boil over a medium heat, then lower the heat and simmer for 1½ hours, stirring the soup occasionally to prevent the lentils from sticking to the bottom.

2 Remove the bay leaves and add the red wine vinegar, with salt and pepper to taste. If the soup is too thick, thin it with a little extra vegetable stock or water. Serve the soup in heated bowls, garnished with celery leaves. Serve with warmed crusty rolls.

Energy 176kcal/742kJ; Protein 9.6g; Carbohydrate 26.4g, of which sugars 4.9g; Fat 4.3g, of which saturates 0.6g; Cholesterol 0mg; Calcium 36mg; Fibre 2.9g; Sodium 19mg.

LENTIL SOUP WITH ROSEMARY

A CLASSIC RUSTIC ITALIAN SOUP FLAVOURED WITH ROSEMARY, THIS IS DELICIOUS SERVED WITH GARLIC BREAD.

SERVES 4

INGREDIENTS

225g/8oz/1 cup dried green or brown lentils
45ml/3 tbsp extra virgin olive oil
3 rindless streaky (fatty) bacon rashers (strips), cut into small dice
1 onion, finely chopped
2 celery sticks, finely chopped
2 carrots, finely chopped
2 sprigs fresh rosemary, finely chopped
2 bay leaves
400g/14oz can plum tomatoes
1.75 litres/3 pints/7½ cups vegetable stock
salt and ground black pepper
fresh bay leaves and sprigs of fresh rosemary, to garnish

1 Place the lentils in a bowl and cover with cold water. Leave to soak for at least 2 hours. Rinse and drain well.

2 Heat the oil in a large pan. Add the bacon and cook for about 3 minutes, then stir in the onion and cook for 5 minutes until softened.

3 Stir in the celery, carrots, rosemary, bay leaves and lentils. Toss over the heat for 1 minute until coated in the oil.

COOK'S TIP
Look out for the small green lentils in Italian groceries or delicatessens. If you buy your lentils loose, remember to put them in a sieve (strainer) or colander and pick them over, removing any pieces of grit, before rinsing them.

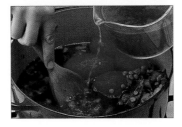

4 Stir in the tomatoes and stock, and bring to the boil. Lower the heat, half-cover the pan and simmer gently for about 1 hour until the lentils are perfectly tender.

5 Remove the bay leaves, add salt and freshly ground black pepper to taste and serve with a garnish of fresh bay leaves and sprigs of rosemary.

Energy 334kcal/1403kJ; Protein 18.2g; Carbohydrate 38.1g, of which sugars 7.3g; Fat 13.1g, of which saturates 2.8g; Cholesterol 12mg; Calcium 53mg; Fibre 4.7g; Sodium 392mg.

SPLIT PEA AND HAM SOUP

THE MAIN INGREDIENT FOR THIS DISH IS BACON HOCK, WHICH IS THE NARROW PIECE OF BONE CUT FROM A LEG OF HAM. YOU COULD USE A PIECE OF PORK BELLY INSTEAD, IF YOU PREFER.

SERVES 4

INGREDIENTS
  450g/1lb/2½ cups green split peas
  4 rindless bacon rashers (strips)
  1 onion, roughly chopped
  2 carrots, sliced
  1 celery stick, sliced
  2.4 litres/4¼ pints/10½ cups cold
    water
  1 sprig of fresh thyme
  2 bay leaves
  1 large potato, roughly diced
  1 bacon hock
  ground black pepper

1 Put the split peas into a bowl, cover with cold water and leave to soak overnight.

2 Cut the bacon into small pieces. In a large pan, dry-fry the bacon for 4–5 minutes or until crisp. Remove from the pan with a slotted spoon.

3 Add the chopped onion, carrots and celery to the fat in the pan and cook for 3–4 minutes until the onion is softened but not brown. Return the bacon to the pan with the water.

4 Drain the split peas and add to the pan with the thyme, bay leaves, potato and bacon hock. Bring to the boil, reduce the heat, cover and cook gently for 1 hour.

5 Remove the thyme, bay leaves and hock. Process the soup in a blender or food processor until smooth. Return to a clean pan. Cut the meat from the hock, add to the soup and heat through gently. Season with plenty of freshly ground black pepper. Ladle into warm soup bowls and serve.

Energy 466kcal/1974kJ; Protein 32.2g; Carbohydrate 75.6g, of which sugars 6.2g; Fat 5.9g, of which saturates 1.9g; Cholesterol 13mg; Calcium 75mg; Fibre 7g; Sodium 443mg.

TUSCAN BEAN SOUP

THIS ITALIAN SOUP IS KNOWN AS RIBOLLITA. IT IS RATHER LIKE MINESTRONE, BUT MADE WITH BEANS INSTEAD OF PASTA, AND IS TRADITIONALLY LADLED OVER A RICH GREEN VEGETABLE, SUCH AS SPINACH.

SERVES 6

INGREDIENTS
45ml/3 tbsp olive oil
2 onions, chopped
2 carrots, sliced
4 garlic cloves, crushed
2 celery sticks, thinly sliced
1 fennel bulb, trimmed and chopped
2 large courgettes (zucchini),
  thinly sliced
400g/14oz can chopped tomatoes
30ml/2 tbsp home-made or
  bought pesto
900ml/1½ pints/3¾ cups
  vegetable stock
400g/14oz can haricot (navy) or
  borlotti beans, drained
salt and ground black pepper
For the base
15ml/1 tbsp extra virgin olive oil,
  plus extra for drizzling
450g/1lb fresh young spinach
ground black pepper

1 Heat the oil in a large pan. Add the chopped onions, carrots, crushed garlic, celery and fennel and fry gently for about 10 minutes. Add the courgettes and fry for a further 2 minutes.

2 Stir in the chopped tomatoes, pesto, stock and beans and bring to the boil. Lower the heat, cover and simmer gently for 25–30 minutes, until the vegetables are completely tender. Season with salt and black pepper to taste.

3 Heat the oil in a frying pan and fry the spinach for 2 minutes, or until wilted. Spoon the spinach into heated soup bowls, then ladle the soup over the spinach. Just before serving, drizzle with olive oil and sprinkle with ground black pepper.

VARIATION
Use other dark greens, such as chard or cabbage, instead of the spinach; simply shred and cook until tender, then ladle the soup over the top.

Energy 197kcal/822kJ; Protein 6.8g; Carbohydrate 20.8g, of which sugars 10.3g; Fat 10.2g, of which saturates 1.5g; Cholesterol 0mg; Calcium 93mg; Fibre 7.7g; Sodium 287mg.

PASTA SOUPS

In Italy hearty pasta soups are often served with bread for a
light supper. There are hundreds of little pasta shapes, called
pastina, to choose from — which means an endless variety of
dishes is possible. Most of the soups in this section are rustic
Italian classics such as Borlotti Bean and Pasta Soup, and
Meatballs in Pasta Soup with Basil. For something more
unusual, try Tomato Soup with Israeli Couscous — a toasted
round pasta much larger than regular couscous.

LENTIL AND PASTA SOUP

THIS RUSTIC VEGETARIAN SOUP MAKES A FILLING LUNCH OR SUPPER AND GOES WELL WITH GRANARY OR CRUSTY ITALIAN BREAD.

SERVES 4–6

INGREDIENTS

175g/6oz/¾ cup brown lentils
3 garlic cloves
1 litre/1¾ pints/4 cups water
45ml/3 tbsp olive oil
25g/1oz/2 tbsp butter
1 onion, finely chopped
2 celery sticks, finely chopped
30ml/2 tbsp sun-dried tomato paste
1.75 litres/3 pints/7½ cups vegetable
  stock
a few fresh marjoram leaves, plus
  extra to garnish
a few fresh basil leaves
leaves from a sprig of fresh thyme
50g/2oz/½ cup small pasta shapes,
  such as tubetti
salt and ground black pepper

1 Put the lentils in a large pan. Smash one of the garlic cloves (there's no need to peel it first) and add it to the lentils. Pour in the water and bring to the boil. Lower the heat to a gentle simmer and cook for about 20 minutes, stirring occasionally, until the lentils are just tender.

2 Drain the lentils, then remove the cooked garlic clove and set it aside.

3 Rinse the lentils under cold water, then leave them to drain again. Heat 30ml/2 tbsp of the oil with half the butter in a large pan. Add the onion and celery and cook over low heat, stirring frequently to prevent sticking, for 5–7 minutes until softened.

4 Crush the remaining garlic and peel and mash the reserved cooked garlic clove. Add to the vegetables with the remaining oil, the tomato paste and lentils. Stir to mix.

5 Add the stock, herbs and salt and pepper to taste. Bring to the boil, stirring, and simmer for 30 minutes.

6 Add the pasta and bring to the boil, stirring. Simmer, stirring frequently, for 7–8 minutes or according to the instructions on the packet, until the pasta is *al dente*.

7 Add the remaining butter and adjust the seasoning.

8 Ladle into warmed bowls and garnish with marjoram leaves. Serve hot.

COOK'S TIPS
• Use green lentils instead of brown, if you like, but the orange or red ones are not so good for this soup because they tend to go mushy.
• Put lentils in a sieve (strainer) or colander and pick them over to remove any pieces of grit before rinsing.

Energy 206kcal/865kJ; Protein 8.1g; Carbohydrate 23.5g, of which sugars 1.7g; Fat 9.5g, of which saturates 3g; Cholesterol 9mg; Calcium 24mg; Fibre 1.9g; Sodium 42mg.

BORLOTTI BEAN AND PASTA SOUP

A COMPLETE MEAL IN A BOWL, THIS IS A VERSION OF A CLASSIC ITALIAN SOUP. TRADITIONALLY, THE
PERSON WHO FINDS THE BAY LEAF IS HONOURED WITH A KISS FROM THE COOK.

SERVES 4

INGREDIENTS
   1 onion, chopped
   1 celery stick, chopped
   2 carrots, chopped
   75ml/5 tbsp olive oil
   1 bay leaf
   1 glass white wine (optional)
   1 litre/1¾ pints/4 cups
      vegetable stock
   400g/14oz can chopped tomatoes
   300ml/½ pint/1¼ cups passata
      (bottled strained tomatoes)
   175g/6oz/1½ cups dried pasta shapes,
      such as farfalle or conchiglie
   400g/14oz can borlotti
      beans, drained
   salt and ground black pepper
   250g/9oz spinach, washed
      and drained
   50g/2oz/⅔ cup freshly grated
      Parmesan cheese, to serve

VARIATION
Other pulses, such as cannellini beans,
haricot (navy) beans or chickpeas, are
equally good in this soup.

1 Place the chopped onion, celery and
carrots in a large pan with the olive
oil. Cook over a medium heat for
5 minutes or until the vegetables soften,
stirring occasionally.

2 Add the bay leaf, wine, vegetable
stock, tomatoes and passata, and bring
to the boil. Lower the heat and simmer
for 10 minutes until the vegetables are
just tender.

3 Add the pasta and beans, and bring
the soup back to the boil, then simmer
for 8 minutes until the pasta is *al dente*.
Stir frequently to prevent the pasta
from sticking.

4 Season to taste with salt and pepper.
Remove any thick stalks from the
spinach and add it to the mixture. Cook
for a further 2 minutes. Serve in heated
soup bowls sprinkled with the freshly
grated Parmesan.

VARIATIONS
• This soup is also delicious with chunks
of cooked spicy sausage or pieces of
crispy cooked pancetta or bacon – simply
add to the soup at the end of Step 3 and
stir in, ensuring that the meat is piping
hot before serving.
• For vegetarians, you could use fried
chunks of smoked or marinated tofu as
an alternative to meat.

Energy 488kcal/2049kJ; Protein 20.5g; Carbohydrate 59.8g, of which sugars 14.1g; Fat 20.1g, of which saturates 4.9g; Cholesterol 13mg; Calcium 366mg; Fibre 11.1g; Sodium 808mg.

BROCCOLI, ANCHOVY AND PASTA SOUP

THIS SOUP IS FROM APULIA IN THE SOUTH OF ITALY, WHERE ANCHOVIES AND BROCCOLI ARE USED TOGETHER IN MANY DELICIOUS DISHES.

SERVES 4

INGREDIENTS

30ml/2 tbsp olive oil
1 small onion, finely chopped
1 garlic clove, finely chopped
¼–⅓ fresh red chilli, seeded and
  finely chopped
2 canned anchovy fillets, drained
200ml/7fl oz/scant 1 cup passata
  (bottled strained tomatoes)
45ml/3 tbsp dry white wine
1.2 litres/2 pints/5 cups vegetable
  stock
300g/11oz/2 cups broccoli florets
200g/7oz/1¾ cups orecchiette
salt and ground black pepper
grated Pecorino cheese, to serve

COOK'S TIP
Wear rubber gloves to protect your hands
when seeding and chopping the chilli.

1 Heat the oil in a large pan. Add the onion, garlic, chilli and anchovies and cook over a low heat, stirring all the time, for 5–6 minutes.

2 Add the passata and white wine, with salt and ground black pepper to taste. Bring to the boil, cover the pan, then cook over a low heat, stirring occasionally to prevent sticking, for 12–15 minutes.

3 Pour in the stock. Bring to the boil, then add the broccoli and simmer for about 5 minutes. Add the pasta and bring back to the boil, stirring. Simmer for 7–8 minutes or according to the instructions on the packet, stirring frequently, until the pasta is *al dente*.

4 Taste and adjust the seasoning. Serve hot, in individual warmed bowls. Hand round the Pecorino cheese separately.

Energy 268kcal/1131kJ; Protein 10.3g; Carbohydrate 41.2g, of which sugars 5.2g; Fat 7.3g, of which saturates 1.1g; Cholesterol 1mg; Calcium 69mg; Fibre 3.9g; Sodium 182mg.

PASTA, BEAN AND VEGETABLE SOUP

THIS IS A CALABRIAN SPECIALITY KNOWN AS MILLECOSEDDE. THE NAME COMES FROM THE ITALIAN WORD MILLECOSE, MEANING "A THOUSAND THINGS". LITERALLY ANYTHING EDIBLE CAN GO IN THIS SOUP.

SERVES 4–6

INGREDIENTS

75g/3oz/scant ½ cup brown lentils
15g/½oz dried mushrooms
60ml/4 tbsp olive oil
1 carrot, diced
1 celery stick, diced
1 onion, finely chopped
1 garlic clove, finely chopped
a little chopped fresh flat leaf parsley
a good pinch of crushed red
  chillies (optional)
1.5 litres/2½ pints/6¼ cups
  vegetable stock
150g/5oz/scant 1 cup each canned
  red kidney beans, cannellini beans
  and chickpeas, rinsed and drained
115g/4oz/1 cup dried small pasta
  shapes, such as rigatoni, penne
  or penne rigate
salt and ground black pepper
freshly grated Pecorino cheese,
  to serve
chopped flat leaf parsley, to garnish

1 Put the lentils in a medium pan, add 475ml/16fl oz/2 cups water and bring to the boil over a high heat. Lower the heat to a gentle simmer and cook, stirring occasionally, for 15–20 minutes or until the lentils are just tender. Meanwhile, soak the dried mushrooms in 175ml/6fl oz/¾ cup warm water for 15–20 minutes.

2 Put the lentils in a sieve (strainer) to drain, then rinse under the cold tap. Drain the soaked mushrooms and reserve the soaking liquid. Finely chop the mushrooms and set aside.

3 Heat the oil in a large pan and add the carrot, celery, onion, garlic, parsley and chillies, if using. Cook over a low heat, stirring constantly, for 5–7 minutes, until the vegetables are soft.

4 Add the stock, then the mushrooms and their soaking liquid. Bring to the boil, then add the beans, chickpeas and lentils. Season to taste. Cover, and simmer gently for 20 minutes.

5 Add the pasta and bring back to the boil, stirring. Simmer for 7–8 minutes, until the pasta is *al dente*. Season, then serve hot in soup bowls, with grated Pecorino and chopped parsley.

COOK'S TIP
You can freeze the soup at the end of Step 4. Thaw and bring to the boil, add the pasta and simmer until tender.

Energy 668kcal/2831kJ; Protein 41.4g; Carbohydrate 100.8g, of which sugars 7.5g; Fat 14g, of which saturates 2g; Cholesterol 0mg; Calcium 178mg; Fibre 26.1g; Sodium 44mg.

TOMATO SOUP WITH ISRAELI COUSCOUS

NEWLY POPULAR ISRAELI COUSCOUS IS A TOASTED, ROUND PASTA WHICH IS MUCH LARGER THAN REGULAR COUSCOUS. IT MAKES A WONDERFUL ADDITION TO THIS WARM AND COMFORTING SOUP. IF YOU LIKE YOUR SOUP REALLY GARLICKY, ADD AN EXTRA CLOVE OF CHOPPED GARLIC BEFORE SERVING.

SERVES 4–6

INGREDIENTS
  30ml/2 tbsp olive oil
  1 onion, chopped
  1 or 2 carrots, diced
  400g/14oz can chopped tomatoes
  6 garlic cloves, roughly chopped
  1.5 litres/2½ pints/6¼ cups
    vegetable or chicken stock
  200–250g/7–9oz/1–1½ cups
    Israeli couscous
  2 or 3 mint sprigs, chopped, or
    several pinches of dried mint
  1.5ml/¼ tsp ground cumin
  ¼ bunch fresh coriander (cilantro),
    or about 5 sprigs, chopped
  cayenne pepper, to taste
  salt and ground black pepper

1 Heat the oil in a large pan, add the onion and carrots and cook gently for about 10 minutes until softened. Add the tomatoes, half the garlic, stock, couscous, mint, ground cumin, coriander, and cayenne pepper, salt and pepper to taste.

2 Bring the soup to the boil, add the remaining chopped garlic, then reduce the heat slightly and simmer gently for 7–10 minutes, stirring occasionally, or until the couscous is just tender. Serve piping hot, ladled into individual serving bowls.

Energy 191kcal/797kJ; Protein 4.2g; Carbohydrate 31.3g, of which sugars 5g; Fat 6.2g, of which saturates 0.8g; Cholesterol 0mg; Calcium 30mg; Fibre 1.4g; Sodium 44mg.

MEATBALLS IN PASTA SOUP WITH BASIL

THESE HOME-MADE MEATBALLS ARE DELICIOUS — SCENTED WITH ORANGE AND GARLIC, THEY ARE SERVED IN A RUSTIC PASTA SOUP, WHICH IS THICKENED WITH PURÉED CANNELLINI BEANS. THE DISH IS A FILLING AND SATISFYING ITALIAN CLASSIC.

SERVES 4

INGREDIENTS

    400g/14oz can cannellini beans,
      drained and rinsed
    1 litre/1¾ pints/4 cups
      vegetable stock
    45ml/3 tbsp olive oil
    1 onion, finely chopped
    2 garlic cloves, chopped
    1 small red chilli, seeded and chopped
    2 celery sticks, finely chopped
    1 carrot, finely chopped
    15ml/1 tbsp tomato purée (paste)
    300g/11oz small pasta shapes
    large handful of fresh basil, torn
    salt and ground black pepper
    basil leaves, to garnish
    freshly grated Parmesan cheese,
      to serve
For the meatballs
    1 thick slice white bread,
      crusts removed
    60ml/4 tbsp milk
    350g/12oz lean minced (ground)
      beef or veal
    30ml/2 tbsp chopped fresh parsley
    grated rind of 1 orange
    2 garlic cloves, crushed
    1 egg, beaten
    30ml/2 tbsp olive oil

1 First prepare the meatballs. Break the bread into small pieces and place them in a bowl. Add the milk and leave to soak for about 10 minutes. Add the minced beef or veal, parsley, orange rind and garlic, and season well. Mix well with your hands.

2 When the bread is thoroughly incorporated with the meat, add enough beaten egg to bind the mixture. Shape small spoonfuls of the mixture into balls about the size of a large olive.

COOK'S TIP
Choose hollow pasta shapes for this soup, which will scoop up the soup as you eat. Look for small and medium-size shapes that are made especially for soup.

3 Heat the oil in a frying pan and fry the meatballs in batches for 6–8 minutes until browned all over. Use tongs or a draining spoon to remove them from the pan, and set them aside.

4 Purée the cannellini beans with a little of the stock in a food processor or blender until smooth. Set aside.

5 Heat the olive oil in a large pan. Add the chopped onion and garlic, chilli, celery and carrot, and cook for 4–5 minutes. Cover and cook gently for a further 5 minutes.

6 Stir in the tomato purée, the bean purée and the remaining vegetable stock. Bring the soup to the boil and cook for about 10 minutes.

7 Stir in the pasta shapes and simmer for 8–10 minutes, until the pasta is tender, but not soft. Add the meatballs and basil and cook for a further 5 minutes. Season the soup well before ladling it into warmed bowls. Garnish each bowl of soup with a basil leaf, and serve freshly grated Parmesan cheese with the soup.

Energy 718kcal/3014kJ; Protein 35g; Carbohydrate 80.9g, of which sugars 10g; Fat 30.5g, of which saturates 8.5g; Cholesterol 53mg; Calcium 152mg; Fibre 9.7g; Sodium 529mg.

AVGOLEMONO WITH PASTA

THIS IS THE MOST POPULAR OF GREEK SOUPS. THE NAME MEANS EGG AND LEMON, THE TWO MOST IMPORTANT INGREDIENTS, WHICH PRODUCE A LIGHT, NOURISHING SOUP. ORZO IS A GREEK RICE-SHAPED PASTA, BUT YOU CAN USE ANY SMALL SOUP PASTA.

SERVES 4–6

INGREDIENTS

    1.75 litres/3 pints/7½ cups
      chicken stock
    115g/4oz/½ cup orzo pasta
    3 eggs
    juice of 1 large lemon
    salt and ground black pepper
    lemon slices, to garnish

COOK'S TIP

This egg and lemon combination is also widely used in Greece as a sauce for pasta or with meatballs.

1 Pour the stock into a large pan, and bring it to a rolling boil. Add the pasta and cook for 5 minutes.

2 Beat the eggs until frothy, then add the lemon juice and 15ml/ 1 tbsp of cold water. Slowly stir in a ladleful of the hot chicken stock, then add one or two more.

3 Return this mixture to the pan, remove from the heat and stir well. (Do not let the soup boil once the eggs have been added or it will curdle.)

4 Season the soup to taste with salt and freshly ground black pepper and serve immediately, garnished with a few lemon slices.

Energy 154kcal/648kJ; Protein 8.1g; Carbohydrate 21.3g, of which sugars 1g; Fat 4.7g, of which saturates 1.2g; Cholesterol 143mg; Calcium 29mg; Fibre 0.8g; Sodium 53mg.

OLD-FASHIONED CHICKEN NOODLE SOUP

THIS IS A REALLY TRADITIONAL CHICKEN NOODLE SOUP — CLEAR, GOLDEN AND WARMING, AND FILLED WITH LIGHTLY COOKED PASTA. IT IS GUARANTEED TO MAKE YOU FEEL BETTER WHENEVER YOU HAVE A COLD. THE SECRET LIES IN BEGINNING WITH A GOOD-QUALITY STOCK.

SERVES 4–6

INGREDIENTS
    2kg/4½lb boiling fowl (stewing
      chicken) with the giblets (except
      the liver)
    1 large onion, peeled and halved
    2 large carrots, halved lengthways
    6 celery sticks, roughly chopped
    1 bay leaf
    175g/6oz vermicelli pasta
    45ml/3 tbsp chopped fresh parsley
      or whole parsley leaves
    salt and ground black pepper

1 Put the chicken into a large pan with all the vegetables and the bay leaf. Cover with 2.4 litres/4 pints/10 cups cold water. Bring slowly to the boil, carefully skimming off any scum that rises to the top. Add 5ml/1 tsp salt and some ground black pepper.

2 Turn down the heat and simmer the soup slowly for at least 2 hours, or until the fowl is tender. When simmering, the surface of the liquid should just tremble. If it is allowed to boil, the soup will become cloudy.

3 When tender, remove the bird from the broth and strip the flesh off the carcass. (Use the meat in sandwiches or a risotto.) Return the bones to the soup and simmer for another hour.

VARIATION
For a change you can use the same weight of guinea fowl and chicken wings and thighs, mixed.

4 Strain the soup into a bowl, cool, then chill overnight. The next day the soup should have set to a solid jelly and will be covered with a thin layer of solidified chicken fat. Carefully remove the fat.

5 To serve the soup, reheat in a large pan. Add the vermicelli and chopped parsley, and simmer for 6–8 minutes until the pasta is cooked. Taste and season well. Serve piping hot.

Energy 176kcal/748kJ; Protein 6.3g; Carbohydrate 37.5g, of which sugars 5.7g; Fat 1.2g, of which saturates 0.1g; Cholesterol 0mg; Calcium 66mg; Fibre 3.4g; Sodium 39mg.

FARMHOUSE SOUP

ROOT VEGETABLES FORM THE BASE OF THIS CHUNKY, MINESTRONE-STYLE, MAIN-MEAL SOUP. SERVE IT WITH CRUSTY BREAD FOR A FILLING AND SATISFYING LUNCH DISH.

SERVES 4

INGREDIENTS

30ml/2 tbsp olive oil
1 onion, roughly chopped
3 carrots, cut into large chunks
175–200g/6–7oz turnips, chopped
175g/6oz swede (rutabaga), chopped
400g/14oz can chopped tomatoes
15ml/1 tbsp tomato purée (paste)
5ml/1 tsp dried mixed herbs
5ml/1 tsp dried oregano
50g/2oz/½ cup dried peppers, finely
  sliced (optional)
1.5 litres/2½ pints/6¼ cups
  vegetable stock or water
50g/2oz/½ cup small macaroni or
  conchiglie
400g/14oz can red kidney beans,
  rinsed and drained
30ml/2 tbsp chopped flat leaf parsley
salt and ground black pepper
grated Parmesan cheese, to serve

1 Heat the oil in a large pan, add the onion and cook over a low heat for about 5 minutes until softened.

2 Add the fresh vegetables, canned tomatoes, tomato purée, dried herbs and dried peppers, if using. Stir in salt and pepper to taste.

3 Pour in the stock or water and bring to the boil. Stir well, cover, lower the heat and simmer for 30 minutes, stirring occasionally.

COOK'S TIPS
• Packets of dried Italian peppers are sold in many supermarkets and in delicatessens. They are piquant and firm with a 'meaty' bite to them, which makes them ideal for adding substance to vegetarian soups.
• You can vary the vegetables according to what you have to hand.

4 Add the pasta and bring to the boil, stirring. Lower the heat and simmer, uncovered, for about 5 minutes or according to the instructions on the packet, until the pasta is just *al dente*.

5 Stir in the beans. Heat through for 2–3 minutes, then remove from the heat and stir in the parsley. Taste and adjust the seasoning. Serve hot in warmed soup bowls and hand round the grated Parmesan separately.

Energy 262kcal/1101kJ; Protein 10.4g; Carbohydrate 41.5g, of which sugars 17.6g; Fat 7.1g, of which saturates 1.1g; Cholesterol 0mg; Calcium 148mg; Fibre 11.5g; Sodium 432mg.

PASTA SOUP <u>WITH</u> CHICKEN LIVERS

THIS SOUP CAN BE SERVED AS A FIRST OR MAIN COURSE. YOU WILL FIND THAT THE FRIED CHICKEN
LIVERS ARE REALLY DELICIOUS, EVEN IF YOU DO NOT NORMALLY LIKE THEM.

<u>SERVES 4–6</u>

INGREDIENTS

115g/4oz/½ cup chicken livers,
  thawed if frozen
15ml/1 tbsp olive oil
a knob (pat) of butter
4 garlic cloves, crushed
3 sprigs each fresh parsley, marjoram
  and sage, chopped
1 sprig fresh thyme, chopped
5 or 6 fresh basil leaves, chopped
15–30ml/1–2 tbsp dry white wine
2 x 300g/11oz cans condensed
  chicken consommé
225g/8oz/2 cups frozen peas
50g/2oz/½ cup small pasta shapes,
  such as farfalle
2 or 3 spring onions (scallions), sliced
salt and ground black pepper

2 Empty both cans of chicken consommé into a large pan and add water to the condensed soup as directed on the labels. Add an extra can of water, then stir in a little salt and pepper to taste and bring to the boil.

3 Add the frozen peas to the pan and simmer for about 5 minutes, then add the small pasta shapes and bring the soup back to the boil, stirring. Allow to simmer, stirring frequently to prevent sticking, for about 5 minutes or according to the instructions on the packet, until the pasta is *al dente*.

4 Add the fried chicken livers and spring onions and heat through for 2–3 minutes. Taste and adjust the seasoning. Serve hot, in warmed bowls.

1 Cut the chicken livers into pieces with scissors. Heat the oil and butter in a frying pan, add the garlic, herbs, and seasoning, and fry for a few minutes. Add the livers, increase the heat to high and stir-fry until they change colour and become dry. Add the wine, cook until it evaporates, then remove from the heat.

Energy 105kcal/440kJ; Protein 7.7g; Carbohydrate 11.1g, of which sugars 1.5g; Fat 3.5g, of which saturates 0.5g; Cholesterol 73mg; Calcium 33mg; Fibre 2.5g; Sodium 426mg

CHICKEN STELLETTE SOUP

SIMPLE AND QUICK TO PREPARE, PROVIDED YOU HAVE SOME GOOD STOCK TO HAND, THIS LIGHT, CLEAR SOUP IS EASY ON THE PALATE AND THE EYE.

SERVES 4–6

INGREDIENTS

    900ml/1½ pints/3¾ cups chicken
      stock
    1 bay leaf
    4 spring onions (scallions), sliced
    225g/8oz button (white) mushrooms,
      sliced
    115g/4oz cooked chicken breast
    50g/2oz small soup pasta (stellette)
    150ml/¼ pint/⅔ cup dry white wine
    15ml/1 tbsp chopped parsley
    salt and ground black pepper

COOK'S TIP
This soup tastes best if you make your own chicken stock rather than using a stock (bouillon) cube.

1 Put the stock and bay leaf into a large pan and bring to the boil. Add the sliced spring onions and mushrooms.

2 Remove the skin from the chicken and discard. Slice the chicken, add to the soup and season to taste with salt and pepper. Heat for 2–3 minutes.

3 Add the pasta to the soup, cover and leave to simmer for 7–8 minutes until the pasta is *al dente*.

4 Just before serving, add the wine and chopped parsley and heat through for 2–3 minutes. Pour into individual warmed soup bowls and serve hot.

Energy 72kcal/303kJ; Protein 6.4g; Carbohydrate 6.7g, of which sugars 0.7g; Fat 0.6g, of which saturates 0.1g; Cholesterol 13mg; Calcium 10mg; Fibre 0.8g; Sodium 15mg.

COURGETTE SOUP WITH PASTA

THIS IS A PRETTY, FRESH-TASTING SOUP, WHICH IS ALWAYS A WELCOME DISH IN HOT WEATHER. ADD A DECORATIVE SWIRL OF SOUR CREAM TO FINISH.

SERVES 4–6

INGREDIENTS

60ml/4 tbsp olive or sunflower oil
2 onions, finely chopped
1.5 litres/2½ pints/6¼ cups chicken
  stock
900g/2lb courgettes (zucchini)
115g/4oz small soup pasta
  (stellette)
a little lemon juice
30ml/2 tbsp chopped fresh chervil
salt and ground black pepper
sour cream, to serve

1 Heat the oil in a large pan and add the onions. Cover and cook gently for about 20 minutes, stirring occasionally, until soft but not coloured.

2 Add the stock to the pan and bring the mixture to the boil.

3 Meanwhile, grate the courgettes and stir into the boiling stock with the pasta. Reduce the heat, cover the pan and simmer for 15 minutes until the pasta is tender, or *al dente*.

4 Season to taste with lemon juice, salt and pepper. Stir in the chopped fresh chervil. Pour into bowls and add a swirl of sour cream before serving.

VARIATION
You can use cucumber instead of courgettes (zucchini), if you prefer, and other soup pasta such as tiny shells.

Energy 183kcal/765kJ; Protein 5.9g; Carbohydrate 22.2g, of which sugars 7g; Fat 8.4g, of which saturates 1.2g; Cholesterol 0mg; Calcium 64mg; Fibre 3g; Sodium 5mg.

BEETROOT SOUP WITH RAVIOLI

BEETROOT AND PASTA MAKE AN UNUSUAL COMBINATION, BUT THIS SOUP IS NO LESS GOOD FOR THAT. SERVE IT WITH SOME CRUSTY BREAD.

SERVES 4–5

INGREDIENTS
1 quantity of basic pasta dough
  (see page 251)
1 egg white, beaten, for brushing
flour, for dusting
1 small onion or shallot, chopped
2 garlic cloves, crushed
5ml/1 tsp fennel seeds
600ml/1 pint/2½ cups chicken or
  vegetable stock
225g/8oz cooked beetroot (beet)
30ml/2 tbsp fresh orange juice
fresh fennel or dill leaves, to garnish
For the filling
115g/4oz mushrooms, finely chopped
1 shallot or small onion, chopped
1 or 2 garlic cloves, crushed
5ml/1 tsp chopped fresh thyme
15ml/1 tbsp chopped fresh parsley
90ml/6 tbsp fresh white breadcrumbs
salt and ground black pepper
a large pinch of grated nutmeg

1 Process all the filling ingredients in a food processor or blender.

2 Roll the pasta into thin sheets. Lay one piece over a ravioli tray and put 5ml/1 tsp of the filling into each depression. Brush around the edges of each ravioli with egg white. Cover with another sheet of pasta and press the edges together well to seal. Transfer to a floured dish towel and leave to rest for one hour before cooking.

3 Cut into individual ravioli. Cook in boiling, salted water for 2 minutes (in batches to stop them sticking together). Remove and drop into a bowl of cold water for 5 seconds before placing on a tray. (You can make these a day in advance and store in the refrigerator.)

4 Put the onion, garlic and fennel seeds into a pan with 150ml/¼ pint/⅔ cup of the stock. Bring to the boil, cover and simmer for 5 minutes until tender.

5 Peel and finely dice the beetroot, reserving 60ml/4 tbsp for the garnish. Add the rest of it to the soup with the remaining stock, and bring to the boil.

6 Add the orange juice and cooked ravioli and simmer for 2 minutes.

7 Serve in shallow soup bowls, garnished with the reserved diced beetroot and fresh fennel or dill leaves.

Energy 260kcal/1101kJ; Protein 9.8g; Carbohydrate 51g, of which sugars 6.1g; Fat 3.3g, of which saturates 0.7g; Cholesterol 76mg; Calcium 108mg; Fibre 3.1g; Sodium 198mg.

CHUNKY PASTA SOUP

SERVE THIS HEARTY, MAIN-MEAL SOUP WITH TASTY, PESTO-TOPPED FRENCH BREAD CROÛTONS. ANY KIND OF PASTA SHAPE CAN BE USED - SHELLS, SPIRALS OR TUBES.

SERVES 4

INGREDIENTS

115g/4oz/½ cup dried beans – a
   mixture of red kidney and haricot
   (navy) beans – soaked overnight
1.2 litres/2 pints/5 cups water
15ml/1 tbsp oil
1 onion, chopped
2 celery sticks, finely sliced
2 or 3 garlic cloves, crushed
2 leeks, finely sliced
1 vegetable stock (bouillon) cube
400g/14oz can or jar pimientos
45–60ml/3–4 tbsp tomato purée
   (paste)
115g/4oz pasta shapes
4 slices French bread
15ml/1 tbsp pesto sauce
115g/4oz/1 cup baby corn cobs,
   halved
50g/2oz each broccoli and
   cauliflower florets
a few drops of Tabasco sauce
salt and ground black pepper

1 Drain the beans and place in a large pan with the water. Bring to the boil and simmer for about 1 hour, or until nearly tender.

2 When the beans are almost ready, heat the oil in a large pan and fry the vegetables for 2 minutes. Add the stock cube and the beans with about 600ml/1 pint/2½ cups of their liquid. Cover and simmer for 10 minutes.

COOK'S TIP
Make your own stock (see page 30) instead of using a stock (bouillon) cube.

3 Meanwhile, purée the pimientos with a little of their liquid and add to the pan. Stir in the tomato purée and pasta and cook for 15 minutes.

4 Preheat the oven to 200°C/400°F/Gas 6.

5 Meanwhile, make the pesto croûtons. Spread the French bread with the pesto sauce and bake in the preheated oven for 10 minutes or until crisp.

6 When the pasta is just cooked, add the corn, broccoli and cauliflower florets, Tabasco sauce and seasoning to taste. Heat through for 2–3 minutes.

7 Ladle into warmed soup bowls and serve immediately with the croûtons.

Energy 387kcal/1641kJ; Protein 20.1g; Carbohydrate 70.3g, of which sugars 14.9g; Fat 4.7g, of which saturates 1.2g; Cholesterol 3mg; Calcium 185mg; Fibre 12.5g; Sodium 654mg.

TINY PASTA IN BROTH

IN ITALY THIS SOUP IS OFTEN SERVED WITH BREAD FOR A LIGHT SUPPER. HAND ROUND A BOWL OF GRATED PARMESAN CHEESE FOR SPRINKLING ON TOP.

SERVES 4

INGREDIENTS

1.2 litres/2 pints/5 cups beef stock
75g/3oz/¾ cup small soup pasta,
  such as stellette
2 pieces bottled roasted red (bell)
  pepper (about 50g/2oz)
salt and ground black pepper
grated Parmesan cheese, to serve

1 Bring the beef stock to the boil in a large pan. Add salt and pepper to taste, then drop in the soup pasta. Stir well and bring the stock back to the boil.

2 Lower the heat to a simmer and cook for 7–8 minutes, or according to the packet instructions, until the pasta is *al dente*. Stir often during cooking to prevent the pasta shapes from sticking together.

3 Drain the pieces of bottled roasted pepper and dice them finely. Place them in the bottom of four warmed soup plates, and set them aside.

4 Taste the soup and adjust the seasoning. Ladle into the soup plates and serve immediately, with grated Parmesan handed round separately.

LITTLE STUFFED HATS IN BROTH

THIS SOUP IS SERVED IN NORTHERN ITALY ON SANTO STEFANO (ST STEPHEN'S DAY – OUR BOXING DAY) AND ON NEW YEAR'S DAY. IT MAKES A WELCOME CHANGE FROM ALL THE SPECIAL CELEBRATION FOOD AT THIS TIME OF YEAR. IT IS TRADITIONALLY MADE WITH THE CHRISTMAS CAPON CARCASS, BUT CHICKEN STOCK WORKS EQUALLY WELL.

SERVES 4

INGREDIENTS

1.2 litres/2 pints/5 cups
  chicken stock
90–115g/3½–4oz/1 cup fresh or
  dried cappelletti
30ml/2 tbsp dry white wine
  (optional)
about 15ml/1 tbsp finely chopped
  fresh flat leaf parsley (optional)
salt and ground black pepper
about 30ml/2 tbsp grated Parmesan
  cheese, to serve

1 Pour the chicken stock into a large pan and bring to the boil. Add a little salt and pepper to taste, then drop in the pasta. Stir well to separate the pasta and bring back to the boil.

2 Lower the heat to a simmer and cook according to the instructions on the packet, until the pasta is *al dente*. Stir frequently during cooking to ensure the pasta cooks evenly.

3 Swirl in the wine and parsley, if using, then taste and adjust the seasoning.

4 Ladle into four warmed soup plates, then sprinkle with grated Parmesan. Serve immediately.

COOK'S TIP
Cappelletti is just another name for tortellini, which come from Romagna. You can either buy them ready-made or make your own.

Top: Energy 68kcal/290kJ; Protein 2.6g; Carbohydrate 14.7g, of which sugars 1.4g; Fat 0.5g, of which saturates 0.1g; Cholesterol 0mg; Calcium 6mg; Fibre 0.8g; Sodium 183mg.
Bottom: Energy 77kcal/328kJ; Protein 2.9g; Carbohydrate 16.7g, of which sugars 0.8g; Fat 0.5g, of which saturates 0.1g; Cholesterol 0mg; Calcium 6mg; Fibre 0.7g; Sodium 183mg.

ROASTED TOMATO AND PASTA SOUP

WHEN THE ONLY TOMATOES YOU CAN BUY ARE NOT PARTICULARLY FLAVOURSOME, MAKE THIS SOUP.
THE ROASTING COMPENSATES FOR LACK OF FLAVOUR, AND THE SOUP HAS A LOVELY SMOKY TASTE.

SERVES 4

INGREDIENTS
  450g/1lb ripe Italian plum tomatoes,
  halved lengthways
  1 large red (bell) pepper, quartered
  lengthways and seeded
  1 large red onion, quartered
  lengthways
  2 garlic cloves, unpeeled
  15ml/1 tbsp olive oil
  1.2 litres/2 pints/5 cups vegetable
  stock or water
  a good pinch of granulated sugar
  90g/3½oz/scant 1 cup small pasta
  shapes, such as tubetti or small
  macaroni
salt and ground black pepper
fresh basil leaves, to garnish

1 Preheat the oven to 190°C/375°F/
Gas 5. Spread out the tomatoes, red
pepper, onion and garlic in a roasting
pan and drizzle with the olive oil.

2 Roast for 30–40 minutes until the
vegetables are soft and charred, turning
them halfway through cooking.

3 Transfer the vegetables to a food
processor, add about 250ml/8fl oz/
1 cup of the stock or water, and process
until puréed. Scrape into a sieve
(strainer) placed over a large pan and
press the purée through into the pan.

4 Add the remaining stock or water,
the sugar and salt and pepper to taste.
Bring to the boil.

5 Add the pasta and simmer for
7–8 minutes (or according to the
instructions on the packet), stirring
frequently, until *al dente*. Taste and
adjust the seasoning with salt and
freshly ground black pepper. Serve hot
in warmed bowls, garnished with the
fresh basil leaves.

COOK'S TIP
You can roast the vegetables in advance,
allow them to cool, then leave them in a
covered bowl in the refrigerator overnight
before puréeing.

Energy 128kcal/543kJ; Protein 4.5g; Carbohydrate 26.9g, of which sugars 9.7g; Fat 1g, of which saturates 0.2g; Cholesterol 0mg; Calcium 30mg; Fibre 3.2g; Sodium 14mg.

PASTA <u>AND</u> CHICKPEA SOUP

THIS IS A SIMPLE, FILLING, COUNTRY-STYLE SOUP. THE SHAPE OF THE PASTA AND THE BEANS COMPLEMENT ONE ANOTHER BEAUTIFULLY.

<u>SERVES 4–6</u>

INGREDIENTS

60ml/4 tbsp olive oil
1 onion, finely chopped
2 carrots, finely chopped
2 celery sticks, finely chopped
400g/14oz can chickpeas, rinsed
   and drained
200g/7oz can cannellini beans,
   rinsed and drained
150ml/¼ pint/⅔ cup passata
120ml/4fl oz/½ cup water
1.5 litres/2½ pints/6¼ cups
   vegetable or chicken stock
1 sprig fresh rosemary, plus a few
   leaves to garnish
200g/7oz/scant 2 cups dried
   conchiglie
salt and ground black pepper
shavings of Parmesan cheese,
   to serve

1 Heat the oil in a large pan, add the vegetables and cook over a low heat, stirring frequently, for 5–7 minutes.

2 Add the chickpeas and cannellini beans, stir well to mix, then cook for 5 minutes. Stir in the passata and water. Cook, stirring, for 2–3 minutes.

3 Add 475ml/16fl oz/2 cups of the stock, the rosemary sprig, and salt and freshly ground black pepper to taste. Bring to the boil, cover, then simmer gently, stirring occasionally, for 1 hour.

COOK'S TIP
If you use dried chickpeas, soak them overnight and boil until tender.

4 Pour in the remaining stock, add the pasta and bring to the boil. Lower the heat and simmer for 7–8 minutes (or according to the instructions on the packet), until the pasta is *al dente*. Remove the rosemary sprig. Serve the soup sprinkled with rosemary leaves and Parmesan shavings.

VARIATION
You can use other pasta shapes, but conchiglie are ideal because they scoop up the chickpeas and beans.

Energy 317kcal/1336kJ; Protein 12g; Carbohydrate 45.6g, of which sugars 5.4g; Fat 11g, of which saturates 1.4g; Cholesterol 0mg; Calcium 71mg; Fibre 6.2g; Sodium 290mg.

PASTA SQUARES AND PEAS IN BROTH

THIS THICK SOUP IS FROM LAZIO, WHERE IT IS TRADITIONALLY MADE WITH FRESH HOME-MADE PASTA AND PEAS. IN THIS MODERN VERSION, READY-MADE PASTA IS USED WITH FROZEN PEAS TO SAVE TIME.

SERVES 4–6

INGREDIENTS

25g/1oz/2 tbsp butter
50g/2oz/⅓ cup pancetta or rindless
   smoked streaky (fatty) bacon,
   roughly chopped
1 small onion, finely chopped
1 celery stick, finely chopped
400g/14oz/3½ cups frozen peas
5ml/1 tsp tomato purée (paste)
5–10ml/1–2 tsp finely chopped fresh
   flat leaf parsley
1 litre/1¾ pints/4 cups chicken stock
300g/11oz fresh lasagne sheets
about 50g/2oz/⅓ cup prosciutto, cut
   into cubes
salt and ground black pepper
grated Parmesan cheese, to serve

1 Melt the butter in a large pan and add the pancetta or bacon, onion and celery. Cook over a low heat for 5 minutes.

2 Add the peas and cook for 3 minutes. Stir in the tomato purée, parsley, stock and seasoning. Bring to the boil, cover and simmer gently for 10 minutes.

3 Cut the lasagne sheets into 2cm/¾in squares. Taste the soup and adjust the seasoning. Drop in the pasta, stir and bring to the boil. Simmer for 2–3 minutes or until the pasta is *al dente*, then stir in the prosciutto. Serve hot in warmed bowls, with grated Parmesan handed round separately.

Energy 240kcal/1013kJ; Protein 9.2g; Carbohydrate 38.4g, of which sugars 2.7g; Fat 6.6g, of which saturates 3.1g; Cholesterol 19mg; Calcium 20mg; Fibre 1.7g; Sodium 241mg.

CONSOMMÉ <u>WITH</u> AGNOLOTTI

PRAWNS, CRAB AND CHICKEN JOSTLE FOR THE UPPER HAND IN THIS RICH AND SATISFYING CONSOMMÉ.
GARNISH WITH COOKED PRAWNS AND FRESH CORIANDER LEAVES.

SERVES 4–6

INGREDIENTS
- 75g/3oz cooked peeled prawns (shrimp)
- 75g/3oz canned crab meat, drained
- 5ml/1 tsp finely grated fresh root ginger
- 15ml/1 tbsp fresh white breadcrumbs
- 5ml/1 tsp light soy sauce
- 1 spring onion (scallion), finely chopped
- 1 garlic clove, crushed
- 1 egg white, beaten
- 400g/14oz can chicken or fish consommé
- 30ml/2 tbsp sherry or vermouth
- salt and ground black pepper

For the pasta
- 200g/7oz/1¾ cups plain (all-purpose) flour
- 2 eggs
- 10ml/2 tsp cold water

For the garnish
- 50g/2oz cooked peeled prawns (shrimp)
- fresh coriander (cilantro) leaves

1 For the pasta, sift the flour and a pinch of salt on to a work surface and make a well in the centre with your hand. Put the eggs and water into the well. Using a fork, beat the eggs gently together, then draw in the flour from the sides to make a thick paste.

2 When the mixture becomes too stiff to use a fork, use your hands to mix to a firm dough. Knead the dough for about 5 minutes until smooth. Wrap in clear film (plastic wrap) to prevent it drying out and leave to rest for 20–30 minutes.

3 Meanwhile, put the prawns, crab meat, ginger, breadcrumbs, soy sauce, spring onion, garlic and seasoning into a food processor or blender and process until smooth.

4 Roll the rested pasta into thin sheets. Stamp out 32 x 5cm/2in rounds using a fluted pastry (cookie) cutter.

5 Place 5ml/1 tsp of the filling in the centre of half the pasta rounds. Brush the edges of each round with egg white and sandwich with a second round on top. Pinch the edges together to stop the filling seeping out.

6 Cook the pasta in a large pan of boiling, salted water for 5 minutes (in batches to stop them sticking together). Remove and drop into a bowl of cold water for 5 seconds before placing on a tray. (You can make these pasta shapes a day in advance. Cover with clear film and store in the refrigerator.)

7 Heat the consommé in a pan with the sherry or vermouth. Add the cooked pasta shapes to the soup and simmer for 1–2 minutes.

8 Serve the pasta in soup bowls covered with hot consommé. Garnish with peeled prawns and coriander leaves.

Energy 179kcal/756kJ; Protein 11.6g; Carbohydrate 28g, of which sugars 0.7g; Fat 2.6g, of which saturates 0.6g; Cholesterol 113mg; Calcium 92mg; Fibre 1.1g; Sodium 225mg.

NOODLE SOUPS

Noodles are a key ingredient in many Asian soups. Beef Noodle soup, Pho, is the essence of Vietnam. This popular dish is sold as fast food on street corners and eaten by everyone from workers to families. Thailand is represented by Thai Chicken Noodle Soup with Little Crab Cakes, and Thai Cellophane Noodle Soup. From Myanmar comes Chiang Mai Noodle Soup. And from Japan there is Tokyo-style Ramen Noodles in Soup, and Soba Noodles in Hot Soup with Tempura.

BEEF NOODLE SOUP

Some would say that this classic noodle soup, pho, is Vietnam in a bowl. Made with beef (pho bo) or chicken (pho ga), it is Vietnamese fast food, street food, working men's food and family food. It is cheap and filling, and makes an intensely satisfying meal at any time of day or night. In the south, in particular, it is popular for breakfast. Everyone has their own recipe for pho, or their favourite place to enjoy it.

SERVES 6

INGREDIENTS
  250g/9oz beef sirloin
  500g/1¼lb dried rice sticks
  (vermicelli), soaked in lukewarm
  water for 20 minutes
  1 onion, halved and finely sliced
  6–8 spring onions (scallions), cut
  into long pieces
  2 or 3 red Thai chillies, seeded and
  finely sliced
  115g/4oz/½ cup beansprouts
  1 large bunch each fresh coriander
  (cilantro) and mint, stalks removed,
  leaves chopped
  2 limes, quartered, and hoisin sauce,
  nuoc mam or *nuoc cham* to serve
For the stock
  1.5kg/3lb 5oz oxtail, trimmed of fat
  and cut into thick pieces
  1kg/2¼lb beef shank or brisket
  2 large onions, peeled and quartered
  2 carrots, peeled and cut into chunks
  7.5cm/3in fresh root ginger, chopped
  6 cloves
  2 cinnamon sticks
  6 star anise
  5ml/1 tsp black peppercorns
  30ml/2 tbsp soy sauce
  45–60ml/3–4 tbsp *nuoc mam*
  salt

1 To make the stock, put the oxtail into a large, deep pan and cover it with water. Bring it to the boil and blanch the meat for 10–15 minutes. Drain the meat, rinsing off any scum, and clean out the pan. Put the blanched oxtail back into the pan with the other stock ingredients, apart from the *nuoc mam* and salt, and cover with about 3 litres/5¼ pints/12 cups water. Bring it to the boil, reduce the heat and simmer, covered, for 2–3 hours.

2 Remove the lid and simmer for another hour, until the stock has reduced to about 2 litres/3½ pints/8 cups. Skim off any fat and then strain the stock into another pan.

3 Cut the beef sirloin against the grain into very thin pieces, the size of the heel of a hand. Bring the stock to the boil once more, stir in the *nuoc mam*, season to taste with salt, then reduce the heat and leave the stock simmering gently until ready to use.

COOK'S TIPS
• The key to *pho* is a tasty, light stock flavoured with ginger, cinnamon, cloves and star anise, so it is worth cooking it slowly and leaving it to stand overnight to allow the flavours to develop fully.
• The fine slices of rare, tender beef cook gently under the steaming stock that is spooned over the top. Use chopsticks to lift the noodles through the layers of flavouring and slurp them up.

4 Meanwhile, bring a pan filled with water to the boil, drain the rice sticks and add to the water. Cook for about 5 minutes or until tender – you may need to separate them with a pair of chopsticks if they look as though they are sticking together.

5 Drain the rice sticks and divide them equally among six wide soup bowls. Top each serving with the slices of beef, onions, spring onions and chillies. Ladle the hot stock over the top of these ingredients, top with the beansprouts and fresh herbs and serve with the lime wedges to squeeze over. Pass around the hoisin sauce, *nuoc mam* or *nuoc cham* for those who like a little sweetening, fish flavouring or extra fire.

Energy 180kcal/748kJ; Protein 10.8g; Carbohydrate 4.8g, of which sugars 4.1g; Fat 4.2g, of which saturates 1.6g; Cholesterol 24mg; Calcium 35mg; Fibre 1g; Sodium 219mg.

CHICKEN AND CRAB NOODLE SOUP
WITH CORIANDER OMELETTE

THE CHICKEN MAKES A DELICIOUS STOCK FOR THIS LIGHT NOODLE SOUP WITH ITS ELUSIVE HINT OF ENTICING AROMATIC CHINESE FLAVOURS.

SERVES 6

INGREDIENTS
  2 chicken legs, skinned
  1.75 litres/3 pints/7½ cups water
  bunch of spring onions (scallions)
  2.5cm/1in piece fresh root
    ginger, sliced
  5ml/1 tsp black peppercorns
  2 garlic cloves, halved
  75g/3oz rice noodles
  115g/4oz fresh white crab meat
  30ml/2 tbsp light soy sauce
  salt and ground black pepper
  coriander (cilantro) leaves, to garnish
For the omelettes
  4 eggs
  30ml/2 tbsp chopped fresh
    coriander leaves
  15ml/1 tbsp extra virgin olive oil

1 Put the chicken and water in a pan. Bring to the boil, reduce the heat and cook gently for 20 minutes; skim the surface occasionally.

2 Slice half the spring onions and add to the pan with the ginger, peppercorns, garlic and salt to taste. Cover and simmer for 1½ hours.

3 Meanwhile, soak the noodles in boiling water for 4 minutes, or according to the packet instructions. Drain and refresh under cold water. Shred the remaining spring onions and set aside.

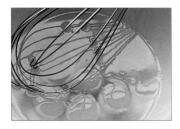

4 To make the omelettes, beat the eggs with the coriander and seasoning.

5 Heat a little of the olive oil in a small frying pan. Add a third of the egg and swirl the pan to coat the base evenly. Cook for 1 minute. Flip over and cook for 30 seconds. Turn the omelette out on to a plate and leave to cool. Repeat twice more to make three omelettes.

6 Roll up the omelettes tightly one at a time and slice thinly.

7 Remove the chicken from the stock and leave to cool. Strain the stock through a sieve (strainer) lined with muslin (cheesecloth) into a clean pan. When the chicken is cool enough to handle, remove and finely shred the meat, discarding the bones.

8 Bring the stock to the boil. Add the noodles, chicken, spring onions and crab meat, then simmer for 1–2 minutes. Stir in the soy sauce and season. Ladle the soup into bowls, top each with sliced omelette and coriander leaves, and serve.

Energy 159kcal/664kJ; Protein 13.5g; Carbohydrate 10.6g, of which sugars 0.4g; Fat 6.9g, of which saturates 1.7g; Cholesterol 157mg; Calcium 46mg; Fibre 0g; Sodium 526mg.

THAI CHICKEN NOODLE SOUP
WITH LITTLE CRAB CAKES

THIS SOUP IS A MEAL IN ITSELF. LOOK FOR STORES THAT SELL BUNCHES OF CORIANDER WITH THE ROOTS STILL ATTACHED, AS THEY ADD EXCELLENT FLAVOUR TO THE STOCK.

SERVES 6

INGREDIENTS
  8 garlic cloves
  small bunch of coriander (cilantro),
    with roots on
  1.2–1.4kg/2½–3lb chicken
  2 star anise
  2 carrots, chopped
  2 celery sticks, chopped
  1 onion, chopped
  30ml/2 tbsp soy sauce
  150g/5oz egg noodles
  30ml/2 tbsp vegetable oil
  60ml/4 tbsp Thai fish sauce
  1.5ml/¼ tsp chilli powder
  150g/5oz/1½ cups beansprouts
  2 spring onions (scallions), sliced
  herb sprigs, to garnish
  salt and ground black pepper
For the crab cakes
  5ml/1 tsp Thai red curry paste
  5ml/1 tsp cornflour (cornstarch)
  5ml/1 tsp Thai fish sauce
  1 small egg yolk
  15ml/1 tbsp chopped fresh
    coriander
  175g/6oz white crab meat
  50g/2oz/1 cup fresh white
    breadcrumbs
  30ml/2 tbsp vegetable oil

1 Chop four of the garlic cloves, thinly slice the remainder and set aside. Cut the roots off the coriander stems and place in a large pan with the garlic. Pick the coriander leaves off their stems and set aside; discard the stems. Place the chicken in the pan and add the star anise, carrots, celery and onion and soy sauce. Pour in enough water to cover the chicken. Bring to the boil, reduce the heat, cover and simmer for 1 hour.

2 For the crab cakes, mix the curry paste, cornflour, fish sauce and egg yolk in a bowl. Add the coriander, crab meat, breadcrumbs and seasoning, then mix well. Divide the mixture into 12 portions and form each into a small cake.

3 Cook the egg noodles according to the packet instructions. Drain and set aside. Heat the oil in a small pan and fry the sliced garlic until golden brown. Drain and set aside.

4 Remove the chicken from its stock and leave until cool enough to handle. (Reserve the stock.) Discard the chicken skin, take the meat off the bones and tear it into large strips. Set aside. Strain the stock and pour 1.2 litres/2 pints/5 cups into a pan. Stir in the fish sauce, chilli powder and seasoning, then bring to the boil. Reduce the heat and keep hot.

5 To cook the crab cakes, heat the vegetable oil in a large frying pan and fry the crab cakes for 2–3 minutes on each side until golden.

6 Divide the cooked noodles, fried garlic slices, beansprouts, sliced spring onions and chicken strips among six shallow soup bowls.

7 Arrange two of the crab cakes on top of the noodles, then ladle the hot chicken broth into the bowls. Sprinkle a few fresh coriander leaves over the soups, then garnish with the herb sprigs and serve immediately.

Energy 250kcal/1049kJ; Protein 10.9g; Carbohydrate 28.8g, of which sugars 3.5g; Fat 10.9g, of which saturates 1.8g; Cholesterol 62mg; Calcium 74mg; Fibre 1.9g; Sodium 638mg.

UDON NOODLES WITH EGG BROTH AND GINGER

IN THIS DISH, CALLED ANKAKE UDON, *THE SOUP FOR THE UDON IS THICKENED WITH CORNFLOUR AND RETAINS ITS HEAT FOR A LONG TIME. A PERFECT LUNCH FOR A FREEZING COLD DAY.*

2 Heat at least 2 litres/3½ pints/9 cups water in a large pan, and cook the udon for 8 minutes or according to the packet instructions. Drain under cold running water and wash off the starch with your hands. Leave in the sieve (strainer).

3 Pour the soup into a large pan and bring to the boil. Blend the cornflour with 60ml/4 tbsp water. Reduce the heat to medium and gradually add the cornflour mixture to the hot soup. Stir constantly. The soup will thicken after a few minutes. Reduce the heat to low.

SERVES 4

INGREDIENTS
    400g/14oz dried udon noodles
    30ml/2 tbsp cornflour (cornstarch)
    4 eggs, beaten
    50g/2oz mustard and cress
    2 spring onions (scallions),
        finely chopped
    2.5cm/1in fresh root ginger, peeled
        and finely grated, to garnish
For the soup
    1 litre/1¾ pints/4 cups water
    40g/1½oz kezuri-bushi
    25ml/1½ tbsp mirin
    25ml/1½ tbsp Japanese soy
        sauce (shoyu)
    7.5ml/1½ tsp salt

1 To make the soup, place the water and the soup ingredients in a pan and bring to the boil on a medium heat. Remove from the heat when it starts boiling. Stand for 1 minute, then strain through muslin (cheesecloth). Check the taste and add more salt if required.

4 Mix the egg, mustard and cress, and spring onions in a small bowl. Stir the soup once again to create a whirlpool. Pour the eggs slowly into the soup pan.

5 Reheat the udon with hot water from a kettle. Divide among four bowls and pour the soup over the top. Garnish with the ginger and serve hot.

COOK'S TIPS
• You can use ready-made noodle soup, available from Japanese food stores.
• Kezuri-bushi, or shaved, dried fish, is available in various graded packets.

Energy 487kcal/2038kJ; Protein 15.5g; Carbohydrate 92.8g, of which sugars 0.6g; Fat 6.1g, of which saturates 1.6g; Cholesterol 190mg; Calcium 61mg; Fibre 0.2g; Sodium 1359mg.

POT-COOKED UDON IN MISO SOUP

UDON IS A WHITE WHEAT NOODLE EATEN WITH VARIOUS HOT AND COLD SOUPS. IN THIS DISH, KNOWN AS MISO NIKOMI UDON, THE NOODLES ARE COOKED IN A CLAY POT WITH A RICH MISO SOUP.

SERVES 4

INGREDIENTS

200g/7oz chicken breast portion,
  boned and skinned
10ml/2 tsp sake
2 abura-age
900ml/1½ pints/3¾ cups second
  dashi stock, or the same amount
  of water and 7.5ml/1½ tsp
  dashi-no-moto
6 large fresh shiitake mushrooms,
  stalks removed, quartered
4 spring onions (scallions), trimmed
  and chopped into 3mm/⅛in lengths
30ml/2 tbsp mirin
about 90g/3½oz aka miso or
  hatcho miso
300g/11oz dried udon noodles
4 eggs
shichimi togarashi (optional)

1 Cut the chicken into bitesize pieces. Sprinkle with sake and leave to marinate for 15 minutes.

2 Put the abura-age in a sieve (strainer) and thoroughly rinse with hot water from the kettle to wash off the oil. Drain on kitchen paper and cut each abura-age into 4 squares.

3 To make the soup, heat the second dashi stock in a large pan. When it has come to the boil, add the chicken pieces, shiitake mushrooms and abura-age and cook for 5 minutes. Remove the pan from the heat and add the spring onions.

COOK'S TIPS
Look for the traditional ingredients in Japanese food stores:
• Abura-age is a thin deep-fried tofu, used in traditional Japanese soups.
• Dashi-no-moto are freeze-dried granules of dashi fish stock.
• Hatcho miso is a paste made from soybeans using traditional methods.
• Shichimi togarashi is a peppery condiment made of seven seasonings.

4 Put the mirin and miso paste into a small bowl. Scoop 30ml/2 tbsp soup from the pan and mix this in well.

5 To cook the udon, boil at least 2 litres/3½ pints/9 cups water in a large pan. The water should not come higher than two-thirds the depth of the pan. Cook the udon for 6 minutes and drain.

6 Put the udon in one large flameproof clay pot or casserole (or divide among four small pots). Mix the miso paste into the soup and check the taste. Add more miso if required. Ladle in enough soup to cover the udon, and arrange the soup ingredients on top of the udon.

7 Put the soup on a medium heat and break an egg on top. When the soup bubbles, wait for 1 minute, then cover and remove from the heat. Leave to stand for 2 minutes. Serve with shichimi togarashi, if you like.

Energy 431kcal/1819kJ; Protein 28.6g; Carbohydrate 54.7g, of which sugars 2.2g; Fat 12.6g, of which saturates 3.5g; Cholesterol 248mg; Calcium 60mg; Fibre 2.9g; Sodium 594mg.

AROMATIC BROTH WITH ROAST DUCK, PAK CHOI AND EGG NOODLES

THIS CHINESE-INSPIRED VIETNAMESE SOUP, MI VIT TIM, MAKES A DELICIOUS AUTUMN OR WINTER MEAL. IN A VIETNAMESE HOUSEHOLD, A BOWL OF FRESH OR MARINATED CHILLIES MIGHT BE PRESENTED AS A FIERY SIDE DISH TO CHEW ON, BUT HERE THEY ARE SLICED AND SPRINKLED OVER THE SOUP WITH HERBS. THIS RECIPE CAN BE MADE USING CHICKEN STOCK AND LEFTOVER MEAT FROM A ROASTED DUCK OR BY ROASTING A DUCK, SLICING OFF THE BREAST AND THIGH MEAT FOR THE SOUP, AND THEN USING THE MEATY CARCASS TO MAKE A STOCK.

SERVES 4

INGREDIENTS
    15ml/1 tbsp vegetable oil
    2 shallots, thinly sliced
    4cm/1½in fresh root ginger, peeled
      and sliced
    15ml/1 tbsp soy sauce
    5ml/1 tsp five-spice powder
    10ml/2 tsp sugar
    175g/6oz pak choi (bok choy)
    450g/1lb fresh egg noodles
    350g/12oz roast duck, thinly sliced
    sea salt
For the stock
    1 chicken or duck carcass
    2 carrots, peeled and quartered
    2 onions, peeled and quartered
    4cm/1½in fresh root ginger, peeled
      and cut into chunks
    2 lemon grass stalks, chopped
    30ml/2 tbsp *nuoc mam*
    15ml/1 tbsp soy sauce
    6 black peppercorns
For the garnish
    4 spring onions (scallions), sliced
    1 or 2 red Serrano chillies, sliced
    1 bunch each coriander (cilantro)
      and basil leaves, chopped

1 To make the stock, put the chicken or duck carcass into a deep pan. Add all the other stock ingredients and pour in 2.5 litres/4½ pints/10¼ cups water.

2 Bring to the boil and boil for a few minutes. Skim off any foam, reduce the heat and simmer gently with the lid on for 2–3 hours. Remove the lid and continue to simmer for 30 minutes to reduce the stock. Skim off any fat, season with salt, then strain the stock. Measure out 2 litres/3½ pints/8 cups.

3 Heat the oil in a wok or deep pan and add the shallots and ginger. Stir in the soy sauce, five-spice powder, sugar and stock and bring to the boil. Season with a little salt, reduce the heat and simmer for 10–15 minutes.

4 Cut the pak choi diagonally into wide strips and blanch in boiling water. Drain and refresh under cold running water to prevent them cooking any further. Bring a large pan of water to the boil, then add the fresh noodles. Cook for 5 minutes, then drain well.

5 Separate the noodles into four soup bowls, lay some of the pak choi and sliced duck over them, and then ladle over generous amounts of the simmering broth. Garnish with the spring onions, chillies and herbs, and serve immediately.

COOK'S TIP
If you can't find fresh egg noodles, you can use dried ones instead. Soak them in lukewarm water for about 20 minutes, then cook, one portion at a time, in a sieve (strainer) lowered into boiling water. Use a chopstick to untangle the noodles as they soften.

Energy 620kcal/2616kJ; Protein 37.3g; Carbohydrate 82.9g, of which sugars 3.9g; Fat 19.7g, of which saturates 4.4g; Cholesterol 158mg; Calcium 124mg; Fibre 4.4g; Sodium 655mg.

THAI CELLOPHANE NOODLE SOUP

*THE THAI NOODLES USED IN THIS SOUP GO BY VARIOUS NAMES: GLASS NOODLES, CELLOPHANE
NOODLES, BEAN THREAD OR TRANSPARENT NOODLES. THEY ARE MADE FROM MUNG BEAN FLOUR,
AND ARE ESPECIALLY VALUED FOR THEIR BRITTLE TEXTURE.*

SERVES 4

INGREDIENTS

    4 large dried shiitake mushrooms
    15g/½oz dried lily buds
    ½ cucumber, coarsely chopped
    2 garlic cloves, halved
    90g/3½oz white cabbage, chopped
    1.2 litres/2 pints/5 cups boiling water
    115g/4oz cellophane noodles
    30ml/2 tbsp soy sauce
    15ml/1 tbsp palm sugar or light
      muscovado (brown) sugar
    90g/3½oz block silken tofu, diced
    fresh coriander (cilantro), to garnish

1 Soak the shiitake mushrooms and
dried lily buds in two separate bowls
of warm water for 30 minutes.

COOK'S TIP
Dried lily buds are the unopened flowers
of day lilies. They must always be soaked
in warm water before use.

2 Meanwhile, put the chopped
cucumber, garlic and cabbage in
a food processor or blender and
process to a smooth paste. Scrape
the mixture into a large pan and
add the measured boiling water.

3 Bring to the boil, then reduce the
heat and cook for 2 minutes, stirring
the mixture occasionally. Strain this
warm stock into another pan, return
to a low heat and gently bring to
simmering point.

4 Drain the soaked lily buds, rinse
under cold running water, then drain
again. Cut off any hard ends. Add the
lily buds to the stock with the noodles,
soy sauce and sugar and cook for
5 minutes more.

5 Strain the liquid from the soaked
mushrooms into the soup. Discard the
mushroom stems, then slice the caps.
Divide them and the tofu among four
bowls. Pour the soup over, garnish with
fresh coriander leaves and serve.

Energy 143kcal/598kJ; Protein 4.9g; Carbohydrate 28.3g, of which sugars 5.6g; Fat 1.1g, of which saturates 0.1g; Cholesterol 0mg; Calcium 137mg; Fibre 0.6g; Sodium 362mg.

CHIANG MAI NOODLE SOUP

NOWADAYS A SIGNATURE DISH OF THE CITY OF CHIANG MAI, THIS DELICIOUS NOODLE SOUP ORIGINATED IN BURMA, NOW CALLED MYANMAR, WHICH LIES ONLY A LITTLE TO THE NORTH OF THE CITY. IT IS ALSO THE THAI EQUIVALENT OF THE FAMOUS MALAYSIAN "LAKSA".

SERVES 4–6

INGREDIENTS
  600ml/1 pint/2½ cups coconut milk
  30ml/2 tbsp Thai red curry paste
  5ml/1 tsp ground turmeric
  450g/1lb chicken thighs, boned and
    cut into bitesize chunks
  600ml/1 pint/2½ cups
    chicken stock
  60ml/4 tbsp Thai fish sauce
  15ml/1 tbsp dark soy sauce
  juice of ½–1 lime
  450g/1lb fresh egg noodles, blanched
    briefly in boiling water
  salt and ground black pepper
To garnish
  3 spring onions (scallions), chopped
  4 fresh red chillies, chopped
  4 shallots, chopped
  60ml/4 tbsp sliced pickled mustard
    leaves, rinsed
  30ml/2 tbsp fried sliced garlic
  coriander (cilantro) leaves
  4–6 fried noodle nests (optional)

1 Pour about one-third of the coconut milk into a large, heavy pan or wok. Bring to the boil over a medium heat, stirring frequently with a wooden spoon until the milk separates.

2 Add the curry paste and ground turmeric, stir to mix completely and cook until the mixture is fragrant.

3 Add the chunks of chicken and toss over the heat for about 2 minutes, making sure that all the chunks are thoroughly coated with the paste.

4 Add the remaining coconut milk, the chicken stock, fish sauce and soy sauce. Season with salt and pepper to taste. Bring to simmering point, stirring frequently, then lower the heat and cook gently for 7–10 minutes. Remove from the heat and stir in lime juice to taste.

5 Reheat the fresh egg noodles in boiling water, drain and divide among four to six warmed bowls. Divide the chunks of chicken among the bowls and ladle in the hot soup. Top each serving with spring onions, chillies, shallots, pickled mustard leaves, fried garlic, coriander leaves and a fried noodle nest, if using. Serve immediately.

Energy 679kcal/2873kJ; Protein 43.2g; Carbohydrate 88.7g, of which sugars 10.1g; Fat 19.4g, of which saturates 5.6g; Cholesterol 180mg; Calcium 95mg; Fibre 3.4g; Sodium 769mg.

TOKYO-STYLE RAMEN NOODLES IN SOUP

RAMEN IS A HYBRID CHINESE NOODLE DISH PRESENTED IN A JAPANESE WAY, AND THERE ARE MANY REGIONAL VARIATIONS FEATURING LOCAL SPECIALITIES. THIS IS A LEGENDARY TOKYO VERSION.

SERVES 4

INGREDIENTS
   250g/9oz dried ramen noodles
For the soup stock
   4 spring onions (scallions)
   7.5cm/3in fresh root ginger, quartered
   raw bones from 2 chickens, washed
   1 large onion, quartered
   4 garlic cloves, peeled
   1 large carrot, roughly chopped
   1 egg shell
   120ml/4fl oz/½ cup sake
   about 60ml/4 tbsp Japanese soy
   sauce (shoyu)
   2.5ml/½ tsp salt
For the *cha-shu* (pot-roast pork)
   500g/1¼lb pork shoulder, boned
   30ml/2 tbsp vegetable oil
   2 spring onions (scallions), chopped
   2.5cm/1in fresh root ginger, peeled
   and sliced
   15ml/1 tbsp sake
   45ml/3 tbsp Japanese soy sauce
   15ml/1 tbsp caster (superfine) sugar
For the toppings
   2 hard-boiled eggs
   150g/5oz menma, soaked for
   30 minutes and drained
   ½ nori sheet, broken into pieces
   2 spring onions (scallions), chopped
   ground white pepper
   sesame oil or chilli oil

1 To make the soup stock, bruise the spring onions and ginger by hitting with the side of a large knife. Pour 1.5 litres/ 2½ pints/6¼ cups water into a wok and bring to the boil. Add the chicken bones and boil until meat changes colour. Discard the water and wash the bones.

2 Wash the wok, bring 2 litres/ 3½ pints/ 9 cups water to the boil and add the bones and other stock ingredients, except the soy sauce and salt. Reduce the heat to low, and simmer until the water has reduced by half, skimming off any scum. Strain into a bowl through a sieve (strainer) lined with muslin (cheesecloth). This will take 1–2 hours.

3 Make the *cha-shu*. Roll the meat up tightly, 8cm/3½in in diameter, and tie it with kitchen string.

4 Wash the wok and dry over a high heat. Heat the oil to smoking point in the wok and add the chopped spring onions and ginger. Cook briefly, then add the meat. Turn often to brown the outside evenly.

5 Sprinkle with sake and add 400ml/ 14fl oz/1⅔ cups water, the soy sauce and sugar. Boil, then reduce the heat to low and cover. Cook for 25–30 minutes, turning every 5 minutes. Remove from the heat.

6 Slice the pork into 12 fine slices. Use any leftover pork for another recipe.

7 Shell and halve the boiled eggs, and sprinkle some salt on to the yolks.

8 Pour 1 litre/1¾ pints/4 cups soup stock from the bowl into a large pan. Boil and add the soy sauce and salt. Check the seasoning; add more sauce if required.

9 Wash the wok again and bring 2 litres/ 3½ pints/9 cups water to the boil. Cook the ramen noodles according to the packet instructions until just soft. Stir constantly to prevent sticking. If the water bubbles up, pour in 50ml/2fl oz/ ¼ cup cold water. Drain well and divide among four bowls.

10 Pour the soup over the noodles to cover. Arrange half a boiled egg, pork slices, menma and nori on top, and sprinkle with spring onions. Serve with pepper and sesame or chilli oil. Season to taste with a little salt, if you like.

COOK'S TIPS
• Sake, made from fermented rice, can be stored in the refrigerator for at least 3 weeks in a sealed container.
• Menma are pickled bamboo shoots, and need soaking before use.

Energy 466kcal/1947kJ; Protein 35.1g; Carbohydrate 49.9g, of which sugars 0.9g; Fat 13.9g, of which saturates 3.2g; Cholesterol 175mg; Calcium 43mg; Fibre 0.3g; Sodium 489mg.

SOBA NOODLES IN HOT SOUP WITH TEMPURA

WHEN YOU COOK JAPANESE NOODLE DISHES, EVERYONE SHOULD BE READY AT THE DINNER TABLE, BECAUSE COOKED NOODLES START TO SOFTEN AND LOSE THEIR TASTE AND TEXTURE QUITE QUICKLY.

SERVES 4

INGREDIENTS
    400g/14oz dried soba noodles
    1 spring onion (scallion), sliced
    shichimi togarashi (optional)
For the tempura
    16 medium raw tiger or king prawns
    (jumbo shrimp), heads and shell
    removed, tails intact
    400ml/14fl oz/1⅔ cups ice-cold water
    1 large (US extra large) egg, beaten
    200g/7oz/scant 2 cups plain
    (all-purpose) flour
    vegetable oil, for deep-frying
For the soup
    150ml/¼ pint/⅔ cup mirin
    150ml/¼ pint/⅔ cup shoyu
    900ml/1½ pints/3¾ cups water
    25g/1oz kezuri-bushi or 2 × 15g/
    ½oz packets
    15ml/1 tbsp caster (superfine) sugar
    5ml/1 tsp salt
    900ml/1½ pints/3¾ cups first dashi
    stock or the same amount of water
    and 12.5ml/2½ tsp dashi-no-moto

1 To make the soup, put the mirin in a large pan. Bring to the boil, then add the rest of the soup ingredients apart from the dashi stock. Bring back to the boil, then reduce the heat to low. Skim off the scum and cook for 2 minutes. Strain the soup and put back into a clean pan with the dashi stock.

2 Remove the vein from the prawns, then make five shallow cuts into each prawn's belly. Clip the tip of the tail with scissors and squeeze out any moisture from the tail.

3 To make the batter, pour the ice-cold water into a bowl and mix in the beaten egg. Sift in the flour and stir briefly; it should remain fairly lumpy.

4 Heat the oil in a wok or deep-fryer to 180°C/350°F. Hold the tail of a prawn, dunk it in the batter, then plunge it into the hot oil. Deep-fry two prawns at a time until crisp and golden. Drain on kitchen paper and keep warm.

5 Put the noodles in a large pan with at least 2 litres/3½ pints/9 cups rapidly boiling water, and stir frequently to stop them sticking.

6 When the water foams, pour in about 50ml/2fl oz/¼ cup cold water to lower the temperature. Repeat when the water foams once again. The noodles should be slightly softer than *al dente* pasta.

7 Tip the noodles into a sieve (strainer) and wash under cold water with your hands to rinse off any oil.

8 Heat the soup. Warm the noodles with hot water, and divide among individual serving bowls. Place the prawns attractively on the noodles and add the soup. Sprinkle with sliced spring onion and some shichimi togarashi, if you like. Serve immediately.

COOK'S TIPS
• Shichimi togarashi is a peppery condiment made of seven seasonings.
• Kezuri-bushi is ready-shaved dried fish, one of the main ingredients used in dashi stock.
• Dashi is a fish stock that is frequently used in Japanese cooking. Freeze-dried granules are called dashi-no-moto, and these can be used to make a quick dashi.

Energy 728kcal/3053kJ; Protein 30.7g; Carbohydrate 121.8g, of which sugars 5.3g; Fat 14g, of which saturates 1.9g; Cholesterol 218mg; Calcium 173mg; Fibre 1.6g; Sodium 728mg.

SAPPORO-STYLE RAMEN NOODLES IN SOUP

THIS IS A RICH AND TANGY SOUP FROM SAPPORO, THE CAPITAL OF HOKKAIDO, WHICH IS JAPAN'S MOST NORTHERLY ISLAND. RAW GRATED GARLIC AND CHILLI OIL ARE ADDED TO WARM THE BODY.

SERVES 4

INGREDIENTS
250g/9oz dried ramen noodles
For the soup stock
    4 spring onions (scallions)
    6cm/2½in fresh root ginger, quartered
    raw bones from 2 chickens, washed
    1 large onion, quartered
    4 garlic cloves
    1 large carrot, roughly chopped
    1 egg shell
    120ml/4fl oz/½ cup sake
    90ml/6 tbsp miso (any colour)
    30ml/2 tbsp Japanese soy sauce
       (shoyu)
For the toppings
    115g/4oz pork belly
    5cm/2in carrot
    12 mangetouts (snow peas)
    8 baby corn cobs
    15ml/1 tbsp sesame oil
    1 dried red chilli, seeded and crushed
    225g/8oz/1 cup beansprouts
    2 spring onions, chopped
    2 garlic cloves, finely grated
    chilli oil
    salt

1 To make the soup stock, bruise the spring onions and ginger by hitting with a rolling pin. Boil 1.5 litres/2½ pints/ 6¼ cups water in a heavy pan, add the bones, and cook until the meat changes colour. Discard the water and wash the bones under running water.

2 Wash the pan and boil 2 litres/3½ pints/ 9 cups water, then add the bones and other stock ingredients except for the miso and soy sauce. Reduce the heat to low, and simmer for 2 hours, skimming any scum off. Strain into a bowl through a sieve (strainer) lined with muslin (cheesecloth); this will take about 1–2 hours. Do not squeeze the muslin.

3 Cut the pork into 5mm/¼in slices. Peel and halve the carrot lengthways then cut into 3mm/⅛in thick, 5cm/2in long slices. Boil the carrot, mangetouts and corn for 3 minutes in water. Drain.

4 Heat the sesame oil in a wok and fry the pork slices and chilli. When the colour of the meat has changed, add the beansprouts. Reduce the heat to medium and add 1 litre/1¾ pints/4 cups soup stock. Cook for 5 minutes.

5 Scoop 60ml/4 tbsp soup stock from the wok and mix well with the miso and soy sauce in a bowl. Stir back into the soup. Reduce the heat to low.

6 Bring 2 litres/3½ pints/9 cups water to the boil. Cook the noodles until just soft, following the instructions on the packet. Stir constantly. If the water bubbles up, pour in 50ml/2fl oz/¼ cup cold water. Drain well and divide among four bowls.

7 Pour the hot soup on to the noodles and heap the beansprouts and pork on top. Add the carrot, mangetouts and corn. Sprinkle with the spring onions and serve with garlic and chilli oil.

Energy 365kcal/1522kJ; Protein 12.5g; Carbohydrate 54.1g, of which sugars 3.9g; Fat 10.9g, of which saturates 3.9g; Cholesterol 21mg; Calcium 43mg; Fibre 1.7g; Sodium 569mg.

PORK AND NOODLE BROTH WITH PRAWNS

THIS DELICATELY FLAVOURED SOUP FROM VIETNAM IS QUICK AND EASY TO MAKE, WHILE TASTING REALLY SPECIAL. THE NOODLES MAKE THE SOUP INTO A SATISFYING AND WHOLESOME DISH.

SERVES 4–6

INGREDIENTS
- 350g/12oz pork chops or fillet (tenderloin)
- 225g/8oz raw prawn (shrimp) tails or cooked prawns
- 150g/5oz thin egg noodles
- 15ml/1 tbsp vegetable oil
- 10ml/2 tsp sesame oil
- 4 shallots or 1 medium onion, sliced
- 15ml/1 tbsp finely sliced fresh root ginger
- 1 garlic clove, crushed
- 5ml/1 tsp sugar
- 1.5 litres/2½ pints/6¼ cups chicken stock
- 2 kaffir lime leaves
- 45ml/3 tbsp Thai fish sauce
- juice of ½ lime

For the garnish
- 4 sprigs of fresh coriander (cilantro)
- 2 spring onions (scallions), green parts only, chopped

1 If you are using pork chops rather than fillet, remove any fat and the bones. Slice and set aside.

2 If using raw prawn tails, peel and devein the prawns.

3 Bring a large pan of salted water to the boil and simmer the egg noodles until softened, or according to the instructions on the packet. Drain and refresh under cold running water. Set the noodles to one side.

4 Pre-heat a wok. Add the vegetable and sesame oils and heat through. When the oil is hot, add the shallots or onion and stir-fry for 3–4 minutes, until evenly browned. Remove from the wok and set aside.

5 Add the ginger, garlic, sugar and chicken stock to the wok and bring to a simmer. Add the lime leaves, fish sauce and lime juice. Add the pork, then simmer for 15 minutes.

6 Add the prawns and noodles and simmer for 3–4 minutes, or longer if using raw prawns to ensure that they are cooked. Add the shallots or onion.

7 Serve garnished with coriander sprigs and the green parts of the spring onion.

VARIATION
This quick and delicious recipe can be made with 200g/7oz boneless chicken breast instead of pork fillet (tenderloin).

COOK'S TIP
Place the pork in the freezer for 30 minutes to firm, but not freeze it. The cold makes the meat easier to slice thinly.

Energy 223kcal/936kJ; Protein 22.2g; Carbohydrate 18.1g, of which sugars 0.7g; Fat 7.3g, of which saturates 1.8g; Cholesterol 117mg; Calcium 41mg; Fibre 0.7g; Sodium 335mg.

JAPANESE-STYLE NOODLE SOUP

THIS DELICATE, FRAGRANT SOUP IS FLAVOURED WITH JUST A SUBTLE HINT OF CHILLI. IT IS BEST SERVED AS A LIGHT LUNCH OR FIRST COURSE.

SERVES 4

INGREDIENTS

45ml/3 tbsp mugi miso
200g/7oz/scant 2 cups udon noodles,
  soba noodles or Chinese noodles
30ml/2 tbsp sake or dry sherry
15ml/1 tbsp rice or wine vinegar
45ml/3 tbsp Japanese soy sauce
115g/4oz asparagus tips or
  mangetouts (snow peas), thinly
  sliced diagonally
50g/2oz/scant 1 cup shiitake
  mushrooms, stalks removed and
  thinly sliced
1 carrot, sliced into julienne strips
3 spring onions (scallions), thinly
  sliced diagonally
salt and ground black pepper
5ml/1 tsp dried chilli flakes, to serve

1 Bring 1 litre/1¾ pints/4 cups water to the boil in a pan. Pour 150ml/¼ pint/⅔ cup boiling water over the miso and stir until dissolved, then set aside.

2 Meanwhile, bring another large pan of lightly salted water to the boil, add the noodles and cook until just tender.

3 Drain the noodles in a colander. Rinse under cold running water, then drain again. Set aside.

COOK'S TIPS
• Mugi miso is the fermented paste of soybeans and barley.
• If fresh shiitake mushrooms are not available, use dried ones instead. Put them in a bowl, pour over boiling water and leave to stand for 30 minutes.

4 Add the sake or sherry, rice or wine vinegar and soy sauce to the pan of boiling water. Boil gently for 3 minutes or until the alcohol has evaporated, then reduce the heat and stir in the miso mixture.

5 Add the asparagus or mangetouts, mushrooms, carrot and spring onions, and simmer for 2 minutes until the vegetables are tender. Season to taste.

6 Divide the noodles among four warm bowls and pour the soup over the top. Sprinkle with the chilli flakes to serve.

Energy 220kcal/929kJ; Protein 7.9g; Carbohydrate 39.7g, of which sugars 4.4g; Fat 4.3g, of which saturates 1.2g; Cholesterol 15mg; Calcium 37mg; Fibre 2.8g; Sodium 898mg.

NOODLE, PAK CHOI AND SALMON RAMEN

THIS LIGHTLY SPICED JAPANESE NOODLE SOUP IS ENHANCED BY SLICES OF SEARED FRESH SALMON AND CRISP VEGETABLES. THE CONTRASTS IN TEXTURE ARE AS APPEALING AS THE DELICIOUS TASTE.

SERVES 4

INGREDIENTS

1.5 litres/2½ pints/6 cups good
    vegetable stock
2.5cm/1in piece fresh root ginger,
    finely sliced
2 garlic cloves, crushed
6 spring onions (scallions), sliced
45ml/3 tbsp soy sauce
45ml/3 tbsp sake
450g/1lb salmon fillet, skinned
5ml/1 tsp groundnut (peanut) oil
350g/12oz ramen or udon noodles
4 small heads pak choi (bok choy),
    broken into leaves
1 fresh red chilli, seeded and sliced
50g/2oz/1 cup beansprouts
salt and ground black pepper

1 Pour the stock into a large pan and add the ginger, garlic, and a third of the spring onions.

2 Add the soy sauce and sake. Bring to the boil, then reduce the heat and simmer for 30 minutes.

3 Meanwhile, remove any pin bones from the salmon using tweezers, then cut the salmon on the slant into 12 slices, using a very sharp knife.

4 Brush a ridged griddle or frying pan with the oil and heat until very hot. Sear the salmon slices for 1–2 minutes on each side until tender and marked by the ridges of the pan. Set aside.

COOK'S TIP
To obtain the distinctive stripes on the slices of salmon, it is important that the ridged pan or griddle is very hot before they are added. Avoid moving the slices, or the stripes will become blurred.

5 Cook the ramen or udon noodles in a large pan of boiling water for 4–5 minutes or according to the instructions on the packet. Tip into a colander, drain well and refresh under cold running water. Drain again and set aside.

6 Strain the broth into a clean pan and season, then bring to the boil. Add the pak choi. Using a fork, twist the noodles into four nests and put these into deep bowls. Divide the salmon slices, spring onions, chilli and beansprouts among the bowls. Ladle in the broth.

Energy 569kcal/2394kJ; Protein 34.6g; Carbohydrate 65.6g, of which sugars 4.1g; Fat 20.5g, of which saturates 4.3g; Cholesterol 83mg; Calcium 70mg; Fibre 3.5g; Sodium 746mg.

NOODLES IN SOUP

IN CHINA, NOODLES IN SOUP (TANG MEIN) ARE FAR MORE POPULAR THAN FRIED NOODLES (CHOW MEIN). YOU CAN ADAPT THIS BASIC RECIPE BY USING DIFFERENT INGREDIENTS FOR THE 'DRESSING'.

SERVES 4

INGREDIENTS

225g/8oz chicken breast fillet, pork
   fillet (tenderloin) or cooked meat
3 or 4 shiitake mushrooms
115g/4oz canned sliced bamboo
   shoots, drained
115g/4oz spinach leaves
2 spring onions (scallions)
350g/12oz dried egg noodles
600ml/1 pint/2½ cups stock
30ml/2 tbsp vegetable oil
5ml/1 tsp salt
2.5ml/½ tsp light brown sugar
15ml/1 tbsp light soy sauce
10ml/2 tsp Chinese rice wine or dry
   sherry
a few drops of sesame oil
red chilli sauce, to serve

1 Place the mushrooms in a bowl and cover with boiling water. Set aside and leave to soak for 30 minutes.

2 Thinly shred the meat. Squeeze dry the shiitake mushrooms and discard any hard stalks. Then thinly shred the mushrooms, bamboo shoots, greens and spring onions.

3 Cook the noodles in boiling water according to the instructions on the packet, then drain and rinse under cold water. Place in a serving bowl.

4 Bring the stock to the boil and pour over the noodles. Set aside and keep warm.

5 Heat the oil in a preheated wok, add about half of the spring onions and the meat, and stir-fry for about 1 minute.

VARIATIONS
• Use lettuce hearts or Chinese leaves (Chinese cabbage) in place of spinach.
• Use fresh shiitake mushrooms if they are available. They will not need to be soaked before adding to the soup.

6 Add the mushrooms, bamboo shoots and greens and stir-fry for 1 minute. Add the salt, sugar, soy sauce and rice wine or sherry and blend well.

7 Pour the 'dressing' over the noodles, garnish with the remaining spring onions, and sprinkle over a few drops of sesame oil. Divide between individual bowls and serve with red chilli sauce.

Energy 482kcal/2032kJ; Protein 26.4g; Carbohydrate 65g, of which sugars 3.3g; Fat 13.8g, of which saturates 2.9g; Cholesterol 66mg; Calcium 87mg; Fibre 3.9g; Sodium 994mg.

CRAB SOUP WITH CORIANDER RELISH

PREPARED FRESH CRAB IS READILY AVAILABLE, HIGH QUALITY AND CONVENIENT — PERFECT FOR CREATING AN EXOTIC SEAFOOD AND NOODLE SOUP IN MINUTES. HERE IT IS ACCOMPANIED BY A HOT CORIANDER AND CHILLI RELISH THAT GIVES IT A SPICY TANG.

SERVES 4

INGREDIENTS
45ml/3 tbsp olive oil
1 red onion, finely chopped
2 red chillies, seeded and
  finely chopped
1 garlic clove, finely chopped
450g/1lb fresh white crab meat
30ml/2 tbsp chopped fresh parsley
30ml/2 tbsp chopped fresh
  coriander (cilantro)
juice of 2 lemons
1 lemon grass stalk
1 litre/1¾ pints/4 cups good fish
  or chicken stock
15ml/1 tbsp Thai fish sauce
150g/5oz vermicelli or angel hair
  pasta, broken into 5–7.5cm/
  2–3in lengths
salt and ground black pepper
For the relish
  50g/2oz/1 cup fresh coriander
    (cilantro) leaves
  1 green chilli, seeded and
    chopped
  15ml/1 tbsp sunflower oil
  25ml/1½ tbsp lemon juice
  2.5ml/½ tsp ground roasted
    cumin seeds

1 Heat the oil in a pan and add the onion, chillies and garlic. Cook over a gentle heat for 10 minutes until the onion is very soft.

2 Transfer the cooked onion and chillies to a bowl and stir in the crab meat, parsley, coriander and lemon juice, then set aside.

3 Lay the lemon grass on a chopping board and bruise it with a rolling pin or pestle. Pour the stock and fish sauce into a pan. Add the lemon grass and bring to the boil, then add the pasta. Simmer, uncovered, for 3–4 minutes or until the pasta is just tender.

4 Meanwhile, make the relish. Using a mortar and pestle, make a coarse paste with the fresh coriander, chilli, oil, lemon juice and cumin.

5 Remove and discard the lemon grass from the soup. Stir the chilli and crab mixture into the soup and season it well. Bring to the boil, then reduce the heat and simmer for 2 minutes.

6 Ladle the soup into four deep, warmed bowls and put a spoonful of the coriander relish in the centre of each. Serve at once.

Energy 425kcal/1773kJ; Protein 26.7g; Carbohydrate 50.7g, of which sugars 1.4g; Fat 12.6g, of which saturates 1.6g; Cholesterol 81mg; Calcium 198mg; Fibre 1.3g; Sodium 632mg.

SHIITAKE MUSHROOM LAKSA

"NOODLES" OF FINELY SLICED RED ONIONS ENHANCE THE TRADITIONAL FLOUR NOODLES IN THIS SOUP, WHICH IS BASED ON THE CLASSIC MALAYSIAN SOUP KNOWN AS PENANG LAKSA.

SERVES 6

INGREDIENTS

150g/5oz/2½ cups dried shiitake
 mushrooms
1.2 litres/2 pints/5 cups boiling
 vegetable stock
30ml/2 tbsp tamarind paste
250ml/8fl oz/1 cup hot water
6 large dried red chillies, stems
 removed and seeded
2 lemon grass stalks, finely sliced
5ml/1 tsp ground turmeric
15ml/1 tbsp grated fresh galangal
1 onion, chopped
5ml/1 tsp dried shrimp paste
30ml/2 tbsp oil
10ml/2 tsp palm sugar
175g/6oz rice vermicelli
1 red onion, peeled and very
 finely sliced
1 small cucumber, seeded and
 cut into strips
handful of fresh mint leaves,
 to garnish

4 Process the lemon grass, turmeric, galangal, onion, soaked chillies and shrimp paste in a food processor or blender, adding a little soaking water from the chillies to form a paste.

5 Heat the oil in a large, heavy-based pan and cook the paste over a low heat for 4–5 minutes until fragrant. Add the tamarind liquid and bring to the boil, then simmer for 5 minutes. Remove from the heat.

6 Drain the mushrooms and reserve the stock. Discard the stems, then halve or quarter the mushrooms, if large. Add the mushrooms to the pan with their soaking liquid, the remaining stock and the palm sugar. Simmer for 25–30 minutes or until tender.

7 Put the rice vermicelli into a large bowl and cover with boiling water, then leave to soak for 4 minutes or according to the packet instructions. Drain well, then divide among six bowls. Top with onion and cucumber, then ladle in the boiling shiitake soup. Add a small bunch of mint leaves to each bowl and serve immediately.

1 Place the mushrooms in a bowl and pour in enough boiling stock to cover them. Set aside and leave to soak for 30 minutes.

2 Put the tamarind paste into a small bowl and pour in the hot water. Mash the paste against the side of the bowl with a fork to extract as much flavour as possible, then strain and reserve the liquid, discarding the pulp.

3 Soak the chillies in enough hot water to cover for 5 minutes, then drain, reserving the liquid.

Energy 152kcal/635kJ; Protein 3.2g; Carbohydrate 25.9g, of which sugars 2.6g; Fat 4g, of which saturates 0.5g; Cholesterol 0mg; Calcium 14mg; Fibre 0.6g; Sodium 4mg.

SEAFOOD LAKSA

FOR A DELICIOUS MEAL, SERVE CREAMY RICE NOODLES IN A SPICY COCONUT-FLAVOURED SOUP, TOPPED WITH SEAFOOD. THERE IS A FAIR AMOUNT OF WORK INVOLVED IN THE PREPARATION, BUT YOU CAN MAKE THE SOUP BASE IN ADVANCE.

SERVES 4

INGREDIENTS

4 fresh red chillies, seeded and
   roughly chopped
1 onion, roughly chopped
1 piece shrimp paste, the size of a
   stock (bouillon) cube
1 lemon grass stalk, chopped
1 small piece fresh root ginger,
   peeled and roughly chopped
6 macadamia nuts or almonds
60ml/4 tbsp vegetable oil
5ml/1 tsp paprika
5ml/1 tsp ground turmeric
475ml/16fl oz/2 cups fish stock
600ml/1 pint/2½ cups coconut milk
a dash of Thai fish sauce, to taste
12 king prawns (shrimp), peeled and
   deveined
8 scallops
225g/8oz prepared squid, cut
   into rings
350g/12oz rice vermicelli or rice
   noodles, soaked in warm water
   until soft
salt and ground black pepper
lime halves, to serve
For the garnish
   ¼ cucumber, cut into matchsticks
   2 fresh red chillies, seeded and
      finely sliced
   30ml/2 tbsp mint leaves
   30ml/2 tbsp fried shallots or onions

1 In a blender or food processor,
process the chillies, onion, shrimp
paste, lemon grass, ginger and nuts
until smooth in texture.

2 Heat 45ml/3 tbsp of the oil in a
large pan. Add the chilli paste and fry
for 6 minutes, stirring. Stir in the
paprika and turmeric and fry for about
2 minutes more.

COOK'S TIP
Wear rubber gloves when preparing the
chillies to prevent any juice from getting
on to your hands.

3 Add the stock and the coconut milk to
the pan. Bring to the boil, then simmer
gently for 15–20 minutes. Season with
fish sauce.

4 Season the seafood with salt and
pepper. Fry quickly in the remaining oil
for 2–3 minutes until cooked.

5 Add the noodles to the soup and heat
through. Divide among individual
serving bowls.

6 Place the fried seafood on top, then
garnish with the cucumber, chillies,
mint and fried shallots or onions. Serve
with the limes.

Energy 348kcal/1456kJ; Protein 24.3g; Carbohydrate 12.8g, of which sugars 10.9g; Fat 13.1g, of which saturates 2g; Cholesterol 236mg; Calcium 111mg; Fibre 0.2g; Sodium 378mg.

NOODLE SOUP WITH PORK AND SICHUAN PICKLE

THIS SOUP IS A MEAL IN ITSELF AND THE HOT PICKLE GIVES IT A DELICIOUS TANG.

SERVES 4

INGREDIENTS

    1 litre/1¾ pints/4 cups chicken stock
    350g/12oz egg noodles
    15ml/1 tbsp dried prawns (shrimp),
      soaked in water
    30ml/2 tbsp vegetable oil
    225g/8oz lean pork, finely shredded
    15ml/1 tbsp yellow bean paste
    15ml/1 tbsp soy sauce
    115g/4oz Sichuan hot pickle, rinsed,
      drained and shredded
    a pinch of sugar
    2 spring onions (scallions), finely
      sliced, to garnish

1 Bring the stock to the boil in a pan. Add the noodles and cook until almost tender. Drain the noodles. Drain the dried prawns, rinse them under cold water, drain again and add to the stock.

2 Lower the heat and simmer for a further 2 minutes. Keep hot.

3 Heat the oil in a frying pan or wok. Add the pork and stir-fry over a high heat for 3 minutes.

4 Add the bean paste and soy sauce to the pork and stir-fry for 1 minute. Add the hot pickle with a pinch of sugar. Stir-fry for 1 minute further.

5 Divide the noodles and soup among individual serving bowls. Spoon the pork mixture on top, then sprinkle with the spring onions and serve immediately.

Energy 480kcal/2022kJ; Protein 25.2g; Carbohydrate 64.8g, of which sugars 3.2g; Fat 15.1g, of which saturates 3.5g; Cholesterol 81mg; Calcium 81mg; Fibre 2.9g; Sodium 1023mg.

TOFU SOUPS

Nutritious and satisfying, tofu is added to Asian soups to make them into a complete meal. Tom Yam Gung with Tofu is a famous Thai speciality that is ideal as a light lunch or supper. Tofu Soup with Mushrooms, Tomato, Ginger and Coriander is a typical Canh, *or clear broth, from the north of Vietnam. Hot-and-Sour Soup is a classic Chinese dish. Japanese soups include Miso Broth with Spring Onions and Tofu, and Japanese Crushed Tofu Soup.*

MISO BROTH <u>WITH</u> SPRING ONIONS <u>AND</u> TOFU

THE JAPANESE EAT MISO BROTH, A SIMPLE BUT HIGHLY NUTRITIOUS SOUP, ALMOST EVERY DAY — IT IS STANDARD BREAKFAST FARE AND IT IS EATEN WITH RICE OR NOODLES LATER IN THE DAY.

SERVES 4

INGREDIENTS

1 bunch of spring onions (scallions)
  or 5 baby leeks
15g/½oz fresh coriander (cilantro)
3 thin slices fresh root ginger
2 star anise
1 small dried red chilli
1.2 litres/2 pints/5 cups dashi stock
  or vegetable stock
225g/8oz pak choi (bok choy) or
  other Asian greens, thickly sliced
200g/7oz firm tofu, cut into
  2.5cm/1in cubes
60ml/4 tbsp red miso
30–45ml/2–3 tbsp Japanese soy
  sauce (shoyu)
1 fresh red chilli, seeded and
  shredded (optional)

1 Cut the coarse green tops off the spring onions or baby leeks and slice the rest of the spring onions or leeks finely on the diagonal. Place the coarse green tops in a large pan with the coriander stalks, fresh root ginger, star anise, dried chilli and dashi or vegetable stock.

2 Heat the mixture gently until boiling, then lower the heat and simmer for 10 minutes. Strain, return to the pan and reheat until simmering. Add the green portion of the sliced spring onions or leeks to the soup with the pak choi or greens and tofu. Cook for 2 minutes.

3 Mix 45ml/3 tbsp of the miso with a little of the hot soup in a bowl, then stir it into the soup. Taste the soup and add more miso with soy sauce to taste.

4 Coarsely chop the coriander leaves and stir most of them into the soup with the white part of the spring onions or leeks. Cook for 1 minute, then ladle the soup into warmed serving bowls. Sprinkle with the remaining coriander and the fresh red chilli, if using, and serve immediately.

COOK'S TIP
Dashi is available powdered in Asian and Chinese stores. Alternatively, make your own by gently simmering 10–15cm/ 4–6in kombu seaweed in 1.2 litres/ 2 pints/5 cups water for 10 minutes. Do not boil vigorously as this makes the dashi bitter. Remove the kombu, then add 15g/½oz dried bonito flakes and bring to the boil. Strain immediately through a fine sieve (strainer).

Energy 60kcal/252kJ; Protein 5.5g; Carbohydrate 4.4g, of which sugars 4.1g; Fat 2.3g, of which saturates 0.3g; Cholesterol 0mg; Calcium 294mg; Fibre 1.6g; Sodium 453mg.

HOT AND SWEET VEGETABLE AND TOFU SOUP

THIS SOOTHING, NUTRITIOUS SOUP TAKES ONLY MINUTES TO MAKE AS THE SPINACH AND SILKEN TOFU ARE SIMPLY PLACED IN BOWLS AND COVERED WITH THE FLAVOURED HOT STOCK.

SERVES 4

INGREDIENTS

1.2 litres/2 pints/5 cups
    vegetable stock
5–10ml/1–2 tsp Thai red
    curry paste
2 kaffir lime leaves, torn
40g/1½oz/3 tbsp palm sugar or light
    muscovado (brown) sugar
30ml/2 tbsp soy sauce
juice of 1 lime
1 carrot, cut into thin batons
50g/2oz baby spinach leaves, any
    coarse stalks removed
225g/8oz block silken tofu, diced

1 Heat the stock in a large pan, then add the red curry paste. Stir constantly over a medium heat until the paste has dissolved. Add the lime leaves, sugar and soy sauce and bring to the boil.

2 Add the lime juice and carrot to the pan. Reduce the heat and simmer for 5–10 minutes. Place the spinach and tofu in four individual serving bowls and pour the hot stock on top to serve.

Energy 105kcal/439kJ; Protein 5.3g; Carbohydrate 13.2g, of which sugars 12.8g; Fat 3.8g, of which saturates 0.5g; Cholesterol 0mg; Calcium 320mg; Fibre 0.7g; Sodium 559mg.

INDONESIAN TOFU LAKSA

THIS SPICY SOUP, WITH DEEP-FRIED TOFU, IS NOT A DISH YOU CAN THROW TOGETHER IN A FEW MINUTES, BUT IT IS MARVELLOUS PARTY FOOD. GUESTS SPOON NOODLES INTO WIDE SOUP BOWLS, ADD ACCOMPANIMENTS OF THEIR CHOICE, TOP UP WITH SOUP AND TAKE PRAWN CRACKERS TO NIBBLE.

SERVES 6

INGREDIENTS
675g/1½lb small clams, scrubbed
2 x 400ml/14fl oz cans coconut milk
50g/2oz *ikan bilis* (dried anchovies)
900ml/1½ pints/3¾ cups water
115g/4oz shallots, finely chopped
4 garlic cloves, chopped
6 macadamia nuts or blanched
  almonds, chopped
3 lemon grass stalks, root trimmed
90ml/6 tbsp sunflower oil
1cm/½in cube shrimp paste
25g/1oz/2 tbsp mild curry powder
a few curry leaves
2 or 3 aubergines (eggplants), total
  weight about 675g/1½lb, trimmed
675g/1½lb raw peeled prawns
  (shrimp)
10ml/2 tsp sugar
1 head Chinese leaves (Chinese
  cabbage), thinly sliced
115g/4oz/2 cups beansprouts, rinsed
2 spring onions (scallions), chopped
50g/2oz crispy fried onions
115g/4oz deep-fried tofu
675g/1½lb mixed noodles (*laksa,
  mee* and *behoon*) or one type only
prawn (shrimp) crackers, to serve

1 Put the clams in a large pan with 1cm/½in water. Bring to the boil, cover and steam over a high heat for about 3–4 minutes, until all the clams have opened. Discard any that remain shut. Make up the coconut milk to 1.2 litres/2 pints/5 cups with water. Put the *ikan bilis* in a pan and add the water. Bring to the boil and simmer for 20 minutes.

2 Meanwhile, put the shallots, garlic and nuts into a mortar. Cut off the lower 5cm/2in of two of the lemon grass stalks, chop finely and add to the mortar. Pound the mixture to a paste.

3 Heat the oil in a large heavy pan, add the shallot paste and cook, stirring constantly, for 1–2 minutes, until the mixture gives off a rich aroma. Bruise the remaining lemon grass stalk and add to the pan. Toss over the heat to release its flavour. Mix the shrimp paste and curry powder to a paste with a little of the coconut milk, add to the pan and toss the mixture over the heat for 1 minute, stirring constantly, and keeping the heat low. Stir in the remaining coconut milk. Add the curry leaves and leave the mixture to simmer while you prepare the accompaniments.

VARIATION
You could substitute mussels for clams if you like. Scrub them thoroughly, removing any beards, and cook them in lightly salted water for about 5 minutes, until they open. As with clams, discard any mussels that remain closed.

4 Strain the stock into a pan. Discard the *ikan bilis*, bring to the boil, then add the aubergines. Cook for about 10 minutes, or until tender and the skins can be peeled off easily. Lift out of the stock, peel and cut into thick strips.

5 Arrange the aubergines on a serving platter. Sprinkle the prawns with sugar, add to the stock and cook for about 2–4 minutes, until they have just turned pink. Remove with a slotted spoon and place next to the aubergines. Add the Chinese leaves, beansprouts, spring onions and crispy fried onions to the platter, together with the clams.

6 Gradually stir the remaining *ikan bilis* stock into the pan of soup and bring to the boil. Rinse the fried tofu in boiling water, cool slightly and squeeze to remove excess oil. Cut each piece in half and add to the soup. Lower the heat to a very gentle simmer.

7 Cook the noodles according to the instructions of the packet, drain and pile in a dish. Remove the curry leaves and lemon grass from the soup and discard. Place the noodles, soup and the platter of seafood and vegetables on the table, along with a bowl of prawn crackers, so that guests can help themselves to the various accompaniments.

COOK'S TIP
Dried shrimp or prawn paste, also called *blachan*, is sold in small blocks and is available from Asian supermarkets.

Energy 882kcal/3714kJ; Protein 61.5g; Carbohydrate 96.9g, of which sugars 14.9g; Fat 30.2g, of which saturates 5.3g; Cholesterol 333mg; Calcium 602mg; Fibre 7.5g; Sodium 2185mg.

THAI HOT-AND-SOUR SOUP

THIS LIGHT AND INVIGORATING SOUP, WITH ITS FINELY BALANCED COMBINATION OF FLAVOURS, IS BEST SERVED AT THE BEGINNING OF A MEAL TO STIMULATE THE APPETITE.

SERVES 4

INGREDIENTS
  2 carrots
  900ml/1½ pints/3¾ cups
    vegetable stock
  2 Thai chillies, seeded and
    finely sliced
  2 lemon grass stalks, outer leaves
    removed and each stalk cut into
    3 pieces
  4 kaffir lime leaves
  2 garlic cloves, finely chopped
  4 spring onions (scallions),
    finely sliced
  5ml/1 tsp sugar
  juice of 1 lime
  45ml/3 tbsp chopped fresh
    coriander (cilantro)
  130g/4½oz/1 cup Japanese
    tofu, sliced
  salt

1 To make carrot flowers, cut each carrot in half crossways, then cut four v-shaped channels lengthways. Slice into thin rounds and set aside.

2 Pour the stock into a large pan. Reserve 2.5ml/½ tsp of the chillies and add the rest to the pan with the lemon grass, lime leaves, garlic and half the spring onions. Bring to the boil, reduce the heat and simmer for 20 minutes.

3 Strain the stock and discard the flavourings. Return the stock to the pan, add the reserved chillies and spring onions, the sugar, lime juice, coriander and salt to taste.

4 Simmer over a gentle heat for 5 minutes, then add the carrot flowers and the tofu, and cook for a further 2 minutes until the carrot is just tender. Ladle into bowls and serve hot.

Energy 40kcal/169kJ; Protein 3.3g; Carbohydrate 3.4g, of which sugars 3.1g; Fat 1.6g, of which saturates 0.2g; Cholesterol 0mg; Calcium 197mg; Fibre 1.2g; Sodium 11mg

JAPANESE CRUSHED TOFU SOUP

THE MAIN INGREDIENT FOR THIS TRADITIONAL JAPANESE SOUP IS CRUSHED TOFU, WHICH IS BOTH NUTRITIOUS AND SATISFYING.

SERVES 4

INGREDIENTS

   150g/5oz fresh tofu, weighed
     without water
   2 dried shiitake mushrooms
   50g/2oz gobo
   5ml/1 tsp rice vinegar
   ½ black or white konnyaku (about
     115g/4oz)
   30ml/2 tbsp sesame oil
   115g/4oz mooli (daikon), finely sliced
   50g/2oz carrot, finely sliced
   750ml/1¼ pints/3 cups kombu and
     bonito stock or instant dashi
   a pinch of salt
   30ml/2 tbsp sake or dry white wine
   7.5ml/1½ tsp mirin
   45ml/3 tbsp white or red miso paste
   a dash of soy sauce
   6 mangetouts (snow peas), trimmed,
     boiled and finely sliced, to garnish

1 Crush the tofu roughly by hand until it resembles lumpy scrambled egg in texture – do not crush it too finely. Wrap the tofu in a clean dish towel and put it in a sieve (strainer), then pour over plenty of boiling water. Leave the tofu to drain thoroughly for 10 minutes.

2 Soak the dried shiitake mushrooms in tepid water for 20 minutes, then drain them. Remove their stems and cut the caps into 4–6 pieces.

3 Scrub the skin off the gobo and slice it into thin shavings. Soak the shavings for 5 minutes in plenty of cold water with the vinegar added to remove any bitter taste. Drain.

4 Put the konnyaku in a small pan and cover with water. Bring to the boil, then drain and cool.

5 Tear the konnyaku into 2cm/¾in lumps: do not use a knife, as smooth cuts will prevent it from absorbing any flavour.

6 Heat the sesame oil in a deep pan. Add all the shiitake mushrooms, gobo, mooli, carrot and konnyaku. Stir-fry for 1 minute, then add the tofu and stir well.

7 Pour in the stock or dashi and add the salt, sake or wine and **mirin**. Bring to the boil. Skim the broth and simmer it for 5 minutes.

8 In a small bowl, dissolve the miso paste in a little of the soup, then return it to the pan. Simmer the soup gently for 10 minutes, until the vegetables are soft. Add the soy sauce, then remove from the heat. Serve immediately, garnished with the mangetouts.

Energy 85kcal/355kJ; Protein 4.8g; Carbohydrate 11.7g, of which sugars 10.9g; Fat 2.3g, of which saturates 0.5g; Cholesterol 0mg; Calcium 241mg; Fibre 3.7g; Sodium 678mg.

SPINACH AND TOFU SOUP

THIS IS AN EXTREMELY DELICATE AND MILD-FLAVOURED SOUP, WHICH CAN BE USED TO
COUNTERBALANCE THE HEAT FROM A HOT THAI CURRY.

SERVES 4–6

INGREDIENTS

30ml/2 tbsp dried shrimps
1 litre/1¾ pints/4 cups chicken
stock
225g/8oz fresh tofu, drained and
cut into 2cm/¾in cubes
30ml/2 tbsp Thai fish sauce
350g/12oz fresh spinach, washed
ground black pepper
2 spring onions (scallions), finely
sliced, to garnish

1 Rinse the dried shrimps under cold
running water and drain. Combine the
shrimps with the chicken stock in a
large pan and bring to the boil.

2 Add the tofu and simmer for about
5 minutes. Season with fish sauce and
black pepper to taste.

3 Tear the spinach leaves into pieces.
Add to the soup and cook for a further
1–2 minutes.

4 Pour the soup into warmed bowls,
sprinkle the chopped spring onions on
top to garnish, and serve.

Energy 55kcal/231kJ; Protein 7.6g; Carbohydrate 1.4g, of which sugars 1.1g; Fat 2.2g, of which saturates 0.3g; Cholesterol 25mg; Calcium 352mg; Fibre 1.3g; Sodium 300mg.

CHINESE TOFU AND LETTUCE SOUP

THIS LIGHT, CLEAR SOUP IS BRIMFUL OF COLOURFUL, TASTY VEGETABLES. FOR THIS SOUP YOU NEED SMOKED OR MARINATED TOFU, WHICH HAS ADDED FLAVOUR.

SERVES 4

INGREDIENTS
 30ml/2 tbsp groundnut (peanut) or
  sunflower oil
 200g/7oz smoked or marinated tofu,
  cubed
 3 spring onions (scallions), sliced
 2 garlic cloves, cut into thin strips
 1 carrot, finely sliced into rounds
 1 litre/1¾ pints/4 cups vegetable
  stock
 30ml/2 tbsp soy sauce
 15ml/1 tbsp dry sherry or vermouth
 5ml/1 tsp sugar
 115g/4oz Cos lettuce, shredded
 salt and ground black pepper

1 Heat the oil in a preheated wok, then stir-fry the tofu cubes until browned, stirring continuously. Drain on kitchen paper and set aside.

2 Add the spring onions, garlic and carrot to the wok and stir-fry for 2 minutes. Add the stock, soy sauce, sherry or vermouth, sugar, lettuce and fried tofu. Heat through gently for 1 minute, season to taste and serve.

Energy 106kcal/439kJ; Protein 4.8g; Carbohydrate 3.2g, of which sugars 2.8g; Fat 7.8g, of which saturates 1g; Cholesterol 0mg; Calcium 272mg; Fibre 0.8g; Sodium 543mg.

THAI MIXED VEGETABLE SOUP

IN THAILAND, THIS TYPE OF SOUP IS USUALLY MADE IN LARGE QUANTITIES AND THEN REHEATED FOR CONSUMPTION OVER SEVERAL DAYS. IF YOU WOULD LIKE TO DO THE SAME, DOUBLE OR TREBLE THE QUANTITIES. CHILL LEFTOVER SOUP RAPIDLY AND REHEAT THOROUGHLY BEFORE SERVING.

SERVES 4

INGREDIENTS
30ml/2 tbsp groundnut (peanut) oil
15ml/1 tbsp magic paste (see Cook's Tip)
90g/3½oz Savoy cabbage or Chinese leaves (Chinese cabbage), finely shredded
90g/3½oz mooli (daikon), finely diced
1 medium cauliflower, coarsely chopped
4 celery sticks, coarsely chopped
1.2 litres/2 pints/5 cups vegetable stock
130g/4½oz fried tofu, cut into 2.5cm/1in cubes
5ml/1 tsp palm sugar or light muscovado (brown) sugar
45ml/3 tbsp light soy sauce

1 Heat the groundnut oil in a large, heavy pan or wok. Add the magic paste and cook over a low heat, stirring frequently, until it gives off its aroma. Add the shredded Savoy cabbage or Chinese leaves, mooli, cauliflower and celery. Pour in the vegetable stock, increase the heat to medium and bring to the boil, stirring occasionally. Gently stir in the tofu cubes.

2 Add the sugar and soy sauce. Reduce the heat and simmer for 15 minutes, until the vegetables are cooked and tender. Taste and add a little more soy sauce if needed. Serve hot.

COOK'S TIP
Magic paste is a mixture of crushed garlic, white pepper and coriander (cilantro). Look for it at Thai markets.

Energy 167kcal/693kJ; Protein 10.4g; Carbohydrate 4.9g, of which sugars 4.2g; Fat 11.9g, of which saturates 0.8g; Cholesterol 0mg; Calcium 521mg; Fibre 1.9g; Sodium 832mg.

TOM YAM GUNG WITH TOFU

ONE OF THE MOST REFRESHING AND HEALTHY SOUPS, THIS FRAGRANT DISH IS A FAMOUS THAI SPECIALITY, AND WOULD MAKE AN IDEAL LIGHT LUNCH OR SUPPER.

SERVES 4

INGREDIENTS

30ml/2 tbsp groundnut (peanut) oil
300g/11oz firm tofu, cut into small
bite-size pieces
1.2 litres/2 pints/5 cups good
vegetable stock
15ml/1 tbsp Thai chilli jam (*nam
pick pow*)
grated rind of 1 kaffir lime
1 shallot, finely sliced
1 garlic clove, peeled and
finely chopped
2 kaffir lime leaves, shredded
3 red chillies, seeded and shredded
1 lemon grass stalk, finely chopped
6 shiitake mushrooms, thinly sliced
4 spring onions (scallions), finely
shredded
45ml/3 tbsp Thai fish sauce
45ml/3 tbsp lime juice
5ml/1 tsp caster (superfine) sugar
45ml/3 tbsp chopped fresh coriander
(cilantro) leaves
salt and ground black pepper

1 Heat the oil in a wok and fry the tofu for 4–5 minutes until golden, turning occasionally to brown on all sides. Use a slotted spoon to remove the tofu and set aside. Tip the oil from the wok into a large, heavy-based pan.

COOK'S TIP
Kaffir lime leaves have a distinct citrus flavour. Fresh leaves can be bought from Asian shops, and some supermarkets sell them dried. Thai fish sauce (*nam pla*) and chilli jam (*nam pick pow*) are available from some supermarkets.

2 Add the stock, chilli jam, kaffir lime rind, shallot, garlic, lime leaves, two-thirds of the chillies and the lemon grass to the pan. Bring to the boil and simmer for 20 minutes.

3 Strain the stock into a clean pan. Stir in the remaining chilli, the shiitake mushrooms, spring onions, fish sauce, lime juice and sugar. Simmer for 3 minutes. Add the fried tofu and heat through for 1 minute. Mix in the chopped coriander and season to taste. Serve at once in warmed bowls.

Energy 122kcal/506kJ; Protein 7.1g; Carbohydrate 3.6g, of which sugars 2.9g; Fat 8.9g, of which saturates 1.5g; Cholesterol 0mg; Calcium 395mg; Fibre 0.7g; Sodium 273mg.

CHINESE HOT-AND-SOUR SOUP

A classic Chinese soup, this is a warming and flavoursome start to a meal. Garnish it with spring onion rings for an attractive finish.

SERVES 4

INGREDIENTS

1g/¼oz dried cloud ears (wood ears)
8 fresh shiitake mushrooms
75g/3oz tofu
50g/2oz/½ cup sliced, drained, canned bamboo shoots
900ml/1½ pints/3¾ cups vegetable stock
15ml/1 tbsp caster (superfine) sugar
45ml/3 tbsp rice vinegar
15ml/1 tbsp light soy sauce
1.5ml/¼ tsp chilli oil
2.5ml/½ tsp salt
a large pinch of ground white pepper
15ml/1 tbsp cornflour (cornstarch)
15ml/1 tbsp cold water
1 egg white
5ml/1 tsp sesame oil
2 spring onions (scallions), cut into fine rings, to garnish

1 Soak the cloud ears in hot water for 30 minutes or until soft. Drain, trim off and discard the hard base from each, and chop the cloud ears roughly.

COOK'S TIPS
• To transform this tasty soup into a nutritious light lunch or supper, simply add extra mushrooms, tofu and bamboo shoots.
• Use dried shiitake mushrooms if fresh ones are not available. Soak them in boiling water for 20 minutes to reconstitute them before use.
• Use marinated deep-fried tofu if you want some extra flavour.

2 Remove and discard the stalks from the shiitake mushrooms. Cut the caps into thin strips.

3 Cut the tofu into 1cm/½in cubes and shred the bamboo shoots finely.

4 Place the stock, mushrooms, tofu, bamboo shoots and cloud ears in a large pan. Bring the stock to the boil, lower the heat and simmer for about 5 minutes.

5 Stir in the sugar, vinegar, soy sauce, chilli oil, salt and pepper.

6 Mix the cornflour to a thin paste with the water. Add the mixture to the soup, stirring until it thickens slightly.

7 Lightly beat the egg white, then pour it slowly into the soup in a steady stream, stirring constantly. Cook, stirring, until the egg white changes colour.

8 Add the sesame oil just before serving. Ladle the soup into heated bowls and garnish each portion with spring onion rings.

MINESTRONE WITH MARINATED FRIED TOFU

THIS SATISFYING AND APPEALING SOUP IS A MEAL IN ITSELF AND CAN BE ADAPTED TO USE WHATEVER VEGETABLES ARE AVAILABLE.

SERVES 6

INGREDIENTS

15ml/1 tbsp olive oil
2 leeks, finely chopped
2 celery sticks, finely diced
2 garlic cloves, finely chopped
2 courgettes (zucchini), finely diced
450g/1lb carrots, finely diced
200g/7oz green beans, finely sliced
5ml/1 tsp dried Mediterranean herbs
1.2 litres/2 pints/5 cups vegetable stock
400g/14oz can chopped tomatoes
300g/11oz marinated deep-fried tofu pieces
20g/¾oz bunch fresh flat leaf parsley or basil, chopped
sea salt and ground black pepper

1 Preheat the oven to 200°C/400°F/ Gas 6. Heat the oil in a large pan then sauté the leeks, celery and garlic for 7–8 minutes, or until softened and beginning to turn golden.

2 Add the other vegetables and dried herbs. Stir to mix well, then pour over the vegetable stock and tomatoes. Bring to the boil, then simmer for 20–25 minutes, until the vegetables are tender.

3 Meanwhile, place the tofu pieces on a baking sheet and bake for 8–10 minutes to warm through.

4 Add the chopped parsley or basil to the soup and season to taste with sea salt and pepper.

5 Stir in the warmed tofu and serve immediately sprinkled with a grinding of extra black pepper.

Energy 122kcal/510kJ; Protein 7.6g; Carbohydrate 12.2g, of which sugars 10.8g; Fat 5.1g, of which saturates 0.8g; Cholesterol 0mg; Calcium 328mg; Fibre 5.2g; Sodium 36mg.

TOFU SOUP <u>WITH</u> MUSHROOMS, TOMATO, GINGER <u>AND</u> CORIANDER

THIS IS A TYPICAL CANH — A CLEAR BROTH FROM THE NORTH OF VIETNAM. IT IS DESIGNED TO BE LIGHT, TO BALANCE A MEAL THAT MAY INCLUDE SOME HEAVIER MEAT OR POULTRY DISHES.

SERVES 4

INGREDIENTS

115g/4oz/scant 2 cups dried shiitake
  mushrooms, soaked in water for
  20 minutes
15ml/1 tbsp vegetable oil
2 shallots, halved and sliced
2 Thai chillies, seeded and sliced
4cm/1½in fresh root ginger, peeled
  and grated or finely chopped
15ml/1 tbsp *nuoc mam*
350g/12oz tofu, rinsed, drained and
  cut into bitesize cubes
4 tomatoes, skinned, seeded and cut
  into thin strips
salt and ground black pepper
1 bunch coriander (cilantro),
  stalks removed, finely chopped, to
  garnish
For the stock
1 meaty chicken carcass or
  500g/1¼lb pork ribs
25g/1oz dried squid or shrimp,
  soaked in water for 15 minutes
2 onions, peeled and quartered
2 garlic cloves, crushed
7.5cm/3in fresh root ginger, coarsely
  chopped
15ml/1 tbsp *nuoc mam*
6 black peppercorns
2 star anise
4 cloves
1 cinnamon stick
sea salt

1 To make the stock, put the chicken carcass or pork ribs in a deep pan. Drain and rinse the dried squid or shrimp. Add to the pan with the remaining stock ingredients, except the salt, and pour in 2 litres/3½ pints/8 cups water. Bring the water to the boil, and boil for a few minutes, skim off any foam, then reduce the heat and simmer gently with the lid on for 1½–2 hours. Remove the lid and continue simmering for a further 30 minutes to reduce. Skim off any fat, season with salt, strain and measure out 1.5 litres/2½ pints/6¼ cups.

2 Squeeze dry the soaked shiitake mushrooms, remove the stems and slice the caps into thin strips. Heat the oil in a large pan or wok and stir in the shallots, chilli and ginger. As the fragrance begins to rise, stir in the *nuoc mam*, followed by the stock.

3 Add the tofu, mushrooms and tomatoes and bring the stock to the boil. Reduce the heat and simmer for 5–10 minutes. Season to taste and sprinkle the finely chopped fresh coriander over the top. Serve piping hot.

Energy 127kcal/532kJ; Protein 9.9g; Carbohydrate 6.1g, of which sugars 5.1g; Fat 7.3g, of which saturates 0.9g; Cholesterol 0mg; Calcium 483mg; Fibre 2.5g; Sodium 554mg.

CHICKEN AND DUCK SOUPS

A substantial chicken soup such as Chicken, Leek and Celery Soup, Chicken Soup with Knaidlach, or Pumpkin, Rice and Chicken Soup can be a meal in itself, served with crusty bread and some fresh fruit to follow. Chicken soups from Asia are usually lighter and refreshing, often served as an appetizer or as part of a meal. Duck makes a rich soup, and there are several recipes to try, including Cream of Duck Soup with Blueberry Relish, and Duck and Nut Soup with Jujubes.

SOUTHERN AMERICAN SUCCOTASH SOUP WITH CHICKEN

BASED ON A VEGETABLE DISH FROM THE SOUTHERN STATES OF AMERICA, THIS SOUP INCLUDES SUCCULENT FRESH CORN KERNELS, WHICH GIVE IT A RICHNESS THAT COMPLEMENTS THE CHICKEN.

SERVES 4

INGREDIENTS

750ml/1¼ pints/3 cups chicken stock
4 boneless, skinless chicken breasts
50g/2oz/¼ cup butter
2 onions, chopped
115g/4oz piece rindless smoked
  streaky (fatty) bacon, chopped
25g/1oz/¼ cup plain
  (all-purpose) flour
4 corn cobs
300ml/½ pint/1¼ cups milk
400g/14oz can butter (lima)
  beans, drained
45ml/3 tbsp chopped fresh parsley
salt and ground black pepper

6 Cut the chicken into bite-size pieces and stir into the soup. Stir in the butter beans and the remaining milk. Bring to the boil and cook for 5 minutes, then season well and stir in the parsley.

1 Bring the chicken stock to the boil in a large pan. Add the chicken breasts and bring back to the boil. Reduce the heat and cook for 12–15 minutes, until cooked through and tender. Use a slotted spoon to remove the chicken from the pan and leave to cool. Reserve the stock.

2 Melt the butter in a pan. Add the onions and cook for 4–5 minutes, until softened but not brown.

3 Add the bacon and cook for 5–6 minutes, until beginning to brown. Sprinkle in the flour and cook for 1 minute, stirring continuously.

4 Gradually stir in the hot stock and bring to the boil, stirring until thickened. Remove from the heat.

5 Using a sharp knife, remove the kernels from the corn cobs. Stir the kernels into the pan with half the milk. Return to the heat and cook, stirring occasionally, for 12–15 minutes, until the corn is tender.

VARIATION
Canned corn can be used instead of fresh corn.

MOROCCAN CHICKEN SOUP
WITH CHARMOULA BUTTER

THIS TASTY SOUP, INSPIRED BY THE INGREDIENTS OF NORTH AFRICA, IS SPICED WITH CHILLI AND
SERVED WITH A RICH AND PUNGENT LEMON BUTTER CREAMED WITH CRISP BREADCRUMBS.

SERVES 6

INGREDIENTS
  50g/2oz/¼ cup butter
  450g/1lb chicken breasts, cut
    into strips
  1 onion, chopped
  2 garlic cloves, crushed
  7.5ml/1½ tsp plain (all-purpose) flour
  15ml/1 tbsp harissa
  1 litre/1¾ pints/4 cups chicken stock
  400g/14oz can chopped tomatoes
  400g/14oz can chickpeas, drained
    and rinsed
  salt and ground black pepper
  lemon wedges, to serve
For the charmoula
  50g/2oz/¼ cup slightly salted butter,
    at room temperature
  30ml/2 tbsp chopped fresh
    coriander (cilantro)
  2 garlic cloves, crushed
  5ml/1 tsp ground cumin
  1 red chilli, seeded and chopped
  pinch of saffron strands
  finely grated rind of ½ lemon
  5ml/1 tsp paprika
  25g/1oz/1 cup dried breadcrumbs

1 Melt the butter in a large, heavy-based pan. Add the chicken strips and cook for 5–6 minutes, turning with a wooden spatula, until beginning to brown. Use a slotted spoon to remove the chicken from the pan and set aside.

2 Add the onion and garlic to the pan and cook over a gentle heat for 4–5 minutes, until softened but not brown.

3 Stir in the flour and cook for 3–4 minutes, stirring continuously, until beginning to brown.

4 Stir in the harissa and cook for a further 1 minute. Gradually pour in the stock and cook for 2–3 minutes, until slightly thickened. Stir in the tomatoes.

5 Return the chicken to the soup and add the chickpeas. Cover and cook over a low heat for 20 minutes. Season well with salt and black pepper.

6 Meanwhile, to make the charmoula, put the butter into a bowl and beat in the coriander, garlic, cumin, chilli, saffron strands, lemon rind and paprika. When the mixture is well combined, stir in the coarse breadcrumbs.

7 Ladle the soup into six warmed bowls. Spoon a little of the charmoula into the centre of each and leave for a few seconds to allow the butter to melt into the soup before serving with lemon wedges.

Energy 313kcal/1312kJ; Protein 25g; Carbohydrate 18.3g, of which sugars 3.3g; Fat 16.1g, of which saturates 9g; Cholesterol 88mg; Calcium 53mg; Fibre 3.6g; Sodium 207mg.

CHICKEN, LEEK AND CELERY SOUP

THIS MAKES A SUBSTANTIAL MAIN COURSE SOUP WITH FRESH CRUSTY BREAD. YOU WILL NEED NOTHING MORE THAN A SALAD AND CHEESE, OR JUST FRESH FRUIT TO FOLLOW THIS DISH.

SERVES 4–6

INGREDIENTS

1.4kg/3lb free-range chicken
1 small head of celery, trimmed
1 onion, coarsely chopped
1 fresh bay leaf
a few fresh parsley stalks
a few fresh tarragon sprigs
2.4 litres/4 pints/10 cups cold water
3 large leeks
65g/2½oz/5 tbsp butter
2 potatoes, cut into chunks
150ml/¼ pint/⅔ cup dry white wine
30–45ml/2–3 tbsp single (light)
  cream (optional)
salt and ground black pepper
90g/3½oz pancetta, grilled until
  crisp, to garnish

1 Cut the breasts off the chicken and set aside. Chop the rest of the chicken carcass into 8–10 pieces and place in a large pan.

2 Chop 4–5 of the outer sticks of the celery and add them to the pan with the onion. Tie the bay leaf, parsley and tarragon together and add to the pan. Pour in the cold water to cover the ingredients and bring to the boil. Reduce the heat and cover the pan, then simmer for 1½ hours.

3 Remove the chicken and cut off and reserve the meat. Strain the stock, then return it to the pan and boil rapidly until it has reduced to about 1.5 litres/2½ pints/6¼ cups.

4 Meanwhile, set about 150g/5oz of the leeks aside. Slice the remaining leeks and the remaining celery, reserving any celery leaves. Chop the celery leaves and set aside to garnish the soup.

5 Melt half the butter in a large, heavy-based pan. Add the sliced leeks and celery, cover and cook over a low heat for about 10 minutes, or until softened but not browned. Add the potatoes, wine and 1.2 litres/2 pints/5 cups of the stock.

6 Season well with salt and pepper, bring to the boil and reduce the heat. Part-cover the pan and simmer the soup for 15–20 minutes, or until the potatoes are cooked.

7 Meanwhile, skin the reserved chicken breasts and cut the flesh into small pieces. Melt the remaining butter in a frying pan, add the chicken and fry for 5–7 minutes, until cooked.

8 Thickly slice the remaining leeks, add to the pan and cook, stirring occasionally, for a further 3–4 minutes, until just cooked.

9 Process the soup with the cooked chicken from the stock in a blender or food processor. Taste and adjust the seasoning, and add more stock if the soup is very thick.

10 Stir in the cream, if using, and the chicken and leek mixture. Reheat gently and serve in warmed bowls. Crumble the pancetta over the soup and sprinkle with the chopped celery leaves.

Energy 294kcal/1246kJ; Protein 40.5g; Carbohydrate 22.1g, of which sugars 5.9g; Fat 2.8g, of which saturates 0.7g; Cholesterol 105mg; Calcium 69mg; Fibre 4.9g; Sodium 124mg.

COCK-A-LEEKIE WITH PUY LENTILS AND THYME

THIS ANCIENT SCOTTISH SOUP IS MADE WITH BOTH BEEF AND CHICKEN TO FLAVOUR THE BROTH. THE ADDITION OF PUY LENTILS GIVES THIS VERSION EVEN MORE EARTHINESS.

SERVES 4

INGREDIENTS

2 leeks, cut into 5cm/2in julienne
115g/4oz/½ cup Puy lentils
1 bay leaf
a few sprigs of fresh thyme
115g/4oz minced (ground) beef
2 skinless, boneless chicken breasts
900ml/1½ pints/3¾ cups good
   home-made beef stock
8 ready-to-eat prunes, cut into strips
salt and ground black pepper
fresh thyme sprigs, to garnish

1 Bring a small pan of salted water to the boil and cook the julienne of leeks for 1–2 minutes. Drain and refresh under cold running water. Drain again and set aside.

COOK'S TIP

To cut fine and even julienne strips, cut the leek into 5cm/2in lengths. Cut each piece in half lengthways, then with the cut side down, cut the leek into thin strips.

2 Pick over the lentils to check for any small stones or grit. Put into a pan with the bay leaf and thyme and cover with cold water. Bring to the boil and cook for 25–30 minutes until tender. Drain and refresh under cold water.

3 Put the minced beef and chicken breasts in a pan and pour over enough stock to cover them. Bring to the boil and cook gently for 15–20 minutes, or until tender. Using a slotted spoon, remove the chicken from the stock and leave to cool.

4 When the chicken is cool enough to handle, cut it into strips. Return it to the stock in the pan and add the lentils and the remaining stock. Bring just to the boil and add seasoning to taste.

5 Divide the leeks and prunes among four warmed bowls. Ladle over the hot chicken and lentil broth. Garnish each portion with a few fresh thyme sprigs and serve immediately.

Energy 275kcal/1160kJ; Protein 32.3g; Carbohydrate 23.5g, of which sugars 7.4g; Fat 6.4g, of which saturates 2.4g; Cholesterol 70mg; Calcium 47mg; Fibre 4.1g; Sodium 82mg.

CHICKEN AND LEEK SOUP
WITH PRUNES AND BARLEY

THIS RECIPE IS BASED ON THE TRADITIONAL SCOTTISH SOUP, COCK-A-LEEKIE. THE UNUSUAL COMBINATION OF LEEKS AND PRUNES IS SURPRISINGLY DELICIOUS.

SERVES 6

INGREDIENTS

1 chicken, weighing about 2kg/4¼lb
900g/2lb leeks
1 fresh bay leaf
a few fresh parsley stalks and
   thyme sprigs
1 large carrot, thickly sliced
2.4 litres/4 pints/10 cups chicken
   or beef stock
115g/4oz/generous ½ cup
   pearl barley
400g/14oz ready-to-eat prunes
salt and ground black pepper
chopped fresh parsley, to garnish

1 Cut the breasts off the chicken and set aside. Place the remaining chicken carcass in a large pan. Cut half the leeks into 5cm/2in lengths and add them to the pan. Tie the bay leaf, parsley and thyme into a bouquet garni and add to the pan with the carrot and the stock. Bring to the boil, then reduce the heat and cover. Simmer gently for 1 hour. Skim off any scum when the water first boils and occasionally during simmering.

2 Add the chicken breasts and cook for another 30 minutes, until they are just cooked. Leave until cool enough to handle, then strain the stock. Reserve the chicken breasts and meat from the chicken carcass. Discard all the skin, bones, cooked vegetables and herbs. Skim as much fat as you can from the stock, then return it to the pan.

3 Meanwhile, rinse the pearl barley thoroughly in a sieve (strainer) under cold running water, then cook it in a large pan of boiling water for about 10 minutes. Drain, rinse well again and drain thoroughly.

4 Add the pearl barley to the stock. Bring to the boil over a medium heat, then lower the heat and cook very gently for 15–20 minutes, until the barley is just cooked and tender. Season the soup with 5ml/1 tsp salt and black pepper.

5 Add the prunes. Slice the remaining leeks and add them to the pan. Bring to the boil, then simmer for 10 minutes or until the leeks are just cooked.

6 Slice the chicken breasts and add them to the soup with the remaining chicken meat, sliced or cut into neat pieces. Reheat if necessary, then ladle the soup into deep plates and sprinkle with chopped parsley.

Energy 359kcal/1526kJ; Protein 41.7g; Carbohydrate 44g, of which sugars 26.9g; Fat 3g, of which saturates 0.6g; Cholesterol 105mg; Calcium 73mg; Fibre 7.4g; Sodium 104mg.

CHICKEN SOUP WITH KNAIDLACH

A BOWL OF CHICKEN SOUP CAN HEAL THE SOUL AS WELL AS THE BODY, AS ANYONE WHO HAS EVER SUFFERED FROM FLU AND BEEN COMFORTED, OR SUFFERED GRIEF AND BEEN CONSOLED, WILL KNOW. THIS SOUP IS SERVED WITH KNAIDLACH — DUMPLINGS MADE OF MATZO, EGGS AND CHICKEN FAT.

SERVES 6–8

INGREDIENTS
1–1.5kg/2¼–3¼lb chicken, cut
  into portions
2 or 3 onions
3–4 litres/5–7 pints/12–16 cups water
3–5 carrots, thickly sliced
3–5 celery sticks, thickly sliced
1 small parsnip, cut in half
30–45ml/2–3 tbsp roughly chopped
  fresh parsley
30–45ml/2–3 tbsp chopped fresh dill
1 or 2 pinches ground turmeric
2 chicken stock (bouillon) cubes
2 garlic cloves, finely chopped
  (optional)
salt and ground black pepper
For the knaidlach
175g/6oz/¾ cup medium matzo meal
2 eggs, lightly beaten
45ml/3 tbsp vegetable oil or rendered
  chicken fat
1 garlic clove, finely chopped (optional)
30ml/2 tbsp chopped fresh parsley,
  plus extra to garnish
½ onion, finely grated
1 or 2 pinches of chicken stock
  (bouillon) cube or powder (optional)
about 90ml/6 tbsp water
salt and ground black pepper

1 Put the chicken pieces in a very large pan. Keeping them whole, cut a large cross in the stem end of each onion and add to the pan with the water, carrots, celery, parsnip, parsley, half the fresh dill, the turmeric, and salt and black pepper.

2 Cover the pan and bring to the boil, then immediately lower the heat to a simmer. Skim and discard the scum that rises to the top. (Scum will continue to form but it is only the first scum that rises that will detract from the clarity and flavour of the soup.)

3 Add the crumbled stock cubes and simmer for 2–3 hours. When the soup is flavourful, skim off the fat. Alternatively, chill the soup and remove the layer of solid fat that forms.

4 To make the knaidlach, combine the matzo meal with the eggs, oil or fat, chopped garlic, if using, parsley, onion, salt and pepper in a large bowl. Add only a little chicken stock cube or powder, if using, as these are salty. Add the water and mix together until the mixture is of the consistency of a thick, soft paste.

5 Cover the matzo batter and chill for 30 minutes, during which time the mixture will become firm.

6 Bring a pan of water to the boil and have a bowl of water next to the stove. Dip two tablespoons into the water, then take a spoonful of the matzo batter. With wet hands, roll it into a ball, then slip it into the boiling water and reduce the heat so that the water simmers. Continue with the remaining matzo batter, working relatively quickly, then cover the pan and cook for 15–20 minutes.

7 Remove the knaidlach from the pan with a slotted spoon and transfer to a plate for about 20 minutes to firm up.

8 Reheat the soup, adding the remaining dill and the garlic, if using. Season to taste. Put two or three knaidlach in each bowl, pour over the soup and garnish.

VARIATIONS
• Instead of knaidlach, the soup can be served over rice or noodles.
• To make lighter knaidlach, separate the eggs and add the yolks to the matzo mixture. Whisk the whites until stiff, then fold into the mixture.

Energy 455kcal/1890kJ; Protein 26.9g; Carbohydrate 33.4g, of which sugars 10.1g; Fat 23.7g, of which saturates 5.4g; Cholesterol 173mg; Calcium 65mg; Fibre 3.9g; Sodium 136mg.

THAI CHICKEN SOUP

THIS MAKES FULL USE OF THE CHARACTERISTIC THAI FLAVOURS OF GARLIC, COCONUT, LEMON,
PEANUT BUTTER, FRESH CORIANDER AND CHILLI.

SERVES 4

INGREDIENTS

15ml/1 tbsp vegetable oil
1 garlic clove, finely chopped
2 skinless, boneless chicken breasts
  (175g/6oz each) chopped
2.5ml/½ tsp ground turmeric
1.5ml/¼ tsp hot chilli powder
75g/3oz/½ cup creamed coconut
900ml/1½ pints/3¾ cups hot
  chicken stock
30ml/2 tbsp lemon or lime juice
30ml/2 tbsp crunchy peanut butter
50g/2oz/1 cup thread egg noodles,
  broken into small pieces
15ml/1 tbsp chopped spring
  onions (scallions)
15ml/1 tbsp chopped fresh
  coriander (cilantro)
salt and ground black pepper
desiccated (dry unsweetened
  shredded) coconut and finely
  chopped fresh red chilli, to garnish

1 Heat the oil in a large pan and fry the garlic for 1 minute until lightly golden. Add the chicken and spices. Stir-fry for 3–4 minutes.

2 Crumble the creamed coconut into the hot chicken stock and stir until dissolved. Pour the liquid on to the chicken breasts and add the lemon or lime juice, peanut butter and thread egg noodles.

COOK'S TIP
If creamed coconut is not available, use coconut cream instead and reduce the quantity of chicken stock.

3 Cover the pan and simmer for 15 minutes. Add the spring onions and fresh coriander, season well with salt and ground black pepper and cook gently for a further 5 minutes.

4 Meanwhile, heat the desiccated coconut and chilli in a small frying pan for 2–3 minutes, stirring frequently, until the coconut is lightly browned.

5 Pour the soup into bowls and serve sprinkled with coconut and chilli.

Energy 338kcal/1411kJ; Protein 25.4g; Carbohydrate 11.4g, of which sugars 2.2g; Fat 21.6g, of which saturates 13g; Cholesterol 65mg; Calcium 17mg; Fibre 0.8g; Sodium 107mg.

THAI-STYLE CHICKEN NOODLE SOUP

*A FRAGRANT BLEND OF COCONUT MILK, LEMON GRASS, GINGER AND LIME MAKES A DELICIOUS SOUP,
WITH JUST A HINT OF WARMING CHILLI.*

SERVES 4

INGREDIENTS
5ml/1 tsp oil
1 or 2 fresh red chillies, seeded
  and chopped
2 garlic cloves, crushed
1 large leek, finely sliced
600ml/1 pint/2½ cups chicken stock
400ml/14fl oz/1⅔ cups coconut milk
450g/1lb skinless, boneless chicken
  thighs, cut into bite-size pieces
30ml/2 tbsp Thai fish sauce
1 lemon grass stalk, split
2.5cm/1in fresh root ginger, peeled
  and finely chopped
5ml/1 tsp sugar
4 kaffir lime leaves (optional)
75g/3oz/¾ cup frozen peas, thawed
45ml/3 tbsp chopped fresh coriander
  (cilantro)

1 Heat the oil in a large pan and cook the chillies and garlic for about 2 minutes.

2 Add the sliced leek and cook for a further 2 minutes.

3 Stir in the stock and coconut milk and bring to the boil over a medium-high heat.

COOK'S TIP
• Wear rubber gloves to protect your hands when seeding and chopping fresh chillies.
• The colour of Thai fish sauce can vary considerably. The lighter-coloured sauces are more expensive but are considered to be better than darker versions.

4 Add the chicken, fish sauce, lemon grass, ginger, sugar and lime leaves, if using. Lower the heat and simmer, covered, for 15 minutes until the chicken is tender, stirring occasionally.

5 Add the peas and cook for a further 3 minutes.

6 Remove the lemon grass and stir in the coriander just before serving.

Energy 177kcal/750kJ; Protein 29.3g; Carbohydrate 9.3g, of which sugars 7.4g; Fat 2.8g, of which saturates 0.8g; Cholesterol 79mg; Calcium 50mg; Fibre 1.9g; Sodium 179mg.

CHICKEN AND ALMOND SOUP

THIS SOUP MAKES AN EXCELLENT LUNCH OR SUPPER DISH WHEN SERVED WITH NAAN BREAD. THE GROUND ALMONDS GIVE IT A LOVELY CREAMY TEXTURE.

SERVES 4

INGREDIENTS

75g/3oz/6 tbsp unsalted (sweet) butter
1 medium leek, chopped
2.5ml/½ tsp shredded fresh
   root ginger
75g/3oz/¾ cup ground almonds
5ml/1 tsp salt
2.5ml/½ tsp crushed black
   peppercorns
1 fresh green chilli, chopped
1 medium carrot, sliced
50g/2oz/½ cup frozen peas
115g/4oz/1 cup chicken, skinned,
   boned and cubed
30ml/2 tbsp chopped fresh
   coriander (cilantro)
450ml/¾ pint/scant 2 cups water
250ml/8fl oz/1 cup single (light)
   cream
4 sprigs of fresh coriander (cilantro)

1 Melt the unsalted butter in a deep, round-bottomed frying pan, and sauté the chopped leek and the root ginger until soft but only just turning brown.

2 Lower the heat and add the ground almonds, salt, peppercorns, chilli, carrot, peas and chicken. Fry for about 10 minutes or until the chicken is completely cooked, stirring constantly. Add the chopped fresh coriander.

COOK'S TIP
Ground almonds can be used as a thickener in soups, and they add extra flavour as well as texture. Their very delicate flavour blends particularly well with chicken-based soups.

3 Remove from the heat and allow to cool slightly.

4 Transfer the mixture to a food processor or blender and process for about 1½ minutes. Pour in the water and blend for a further 30 seconds.

5 Pour back into the pan and bring to the boil, stirring occasionally. Once it has boiled, lower the heat and gradually stir in the cream. Cook gently for a further 2 minutes, stirring from time to time. Serve garnished with the sprigs of fresh coriander.

Energy 425kcal/1760kJ; Protein 14.6g; Carbohydrate 5.5g, of which sugars 3.5g; Fat 38.5g, of which saturates 18.4g; Cholesterol 94mg; Calcium 119mg; Fibre 3g; Sodium 153mg.

CHICKEN, TOMATO AND CHRISTOPHENE SOUP

CHICKEN BREASTS AND SMOKED HADDOCK TAKE ON THE FLAVOURS OF HERBS AND SPICES TO PRODUCE THIS WELL-FLAVOURED SOUP.

SERVES 4

INGREDIENTS

225g/8oz skinless, boneless chicken
   breasts, diced
1 garlic clove, crushed
a pinch of freshly grated nutmeg
25g/1oz/2 tbsp butter or margarine
½ onion, finely chopped
15ml/1 tbsp tomato purée (paste)
400g/14oz can tomatoes, puréed
1.2 litres/2 pints/5 cups chicken
   stock
1 fresh chilli, seeded and chopped
1 christophene, peeled and diced
   (about 350g/12oz)
5ml/1 tsp dried oregano
2.5ml/½ tsp dried thyme
50g/2oz smoked haddock fillet,
   skinned and diced
salt and ground black pepper
chopped fresh chives, to garnish

3 Add the tomato purée, puréed tomatoes, stock, chilli, christophene and herbs. Bring to the boil, cover and simmer gently for 35 minutes or until the christophene is tender.

4 Add the smoked fish and simmer for a further 5 minutes or until the fish is cooked through. Adjust the seasoning and pour into warmed soup bowls. Garnish with a sprinkling of chopped fresh chives and serve piping hot.

1 Dice the chicken, place in a bowl and season with salt, pepper, garlic and nutmeg. Mix well to flavour and then set aside for about 30 minutes.

2 Melt the butter or margarine in a large pan, add the chicken and sauté over a moderate heat for 5–6 minutes. Stir in the onion and fry gently for a further 5 minutes or until the onion is slightly softened.

COOK'S TIP
This soup tastes even better using home-made stock (see page 31). Once made, chicken stock will keep in an airtight container in the refrigerator for 3–4 days.

Energy 145kcal/609kJ; Protein 17.2g; Carbohydrate 5.1g, of which sugars 4.8g; Fat 6.3g, of which saturates 3.5g; Cholesterol 57mg; Calcium 53mg; Fibre 2.2g; Sodium 229mg.

PUMPKIN, RICE AND CHICKEN SOUP

THIS IS A WARM, COMFORTING SOUP WHICH, DESPITE THE SPICE AND BASMATI RICE, IS QUINTESSENTIALLY ENGLISH. FOR AN EVEN MORE SUBSTANTIAL MEAL, ADD A LITTLE MORE RICE AND MAKE SURE YOU USE ALL THE CHICKEN FROM THE STOCK.

SERVES 4

INGREDIENTS
1 wedge of pumpkin, about 450g/1lb
15ml/1 tbsp sunflower oil
25g/1oz/2 tbsp butter
6 green cardamom pods
2 leeks, chopped
115g/4oz/generous ½ cup basmati
  rice, soaked
350ml/12fl oz/1½ cups milk
salt and ground black pepper
generous strips of pared orange rind,
  to garnish
For the chicken stock
2 chicken quarters
1 onion, quartered
2 carrots, chopped
1 celery stalk, chopped
6–8 peppercorns
900ml/1½ pints/3¾ cups water

1 First make the chicken stock. Place the chicken quarters, onion, carrots, celery stalk and peppercorns in a large pan. Pour in the water and slowly bring to the boil. Skim the surface of the stock if necessary, then lower the heat, cover and simmer gently for 1 hour.

2 Strain the chicken stock into a clean, large bowl, discarding the vegetables. Skin and bone one or both chicken pieces and cut the flesh into strips. (If not using both chicken pieces for the soup, reserve the other piece for another recipe.)

3 Skin the pumpkin and remove all the seeds and pith, so that you have about 350g/12oz flesh. Cut the flesh into 2.5cm/1in cubes.

4 Heat the oil and butter in a pan and fry the cardamom pods for 2–3 minutes until slightly swollen. Add the leeks and pumpkin. Cook, stirring, for 3–4 minutes over a medium heat, then lower the heat, cover and sweat for 5 minutes more or until the pumpkin is quite soft, stirring once or twice.

5 Measure out 600ml/1 pint/2½ cups of the stock and add to the pumpkin mixture. Bring to the boil, then lower the heat, cover and simmer gently for 10–15 minutes, until the pumpkin is soft.

6 Pour the remaining stock into a measuring jug and make up with water to 300ml/½ pint/1¼ cups. Drain the rice and put it into a pan. Pour in the stock, bring to the boil, then simmer for about 10 minutes until the rice is tender. Add seasoning to taste.

7 Remove the cardamom pods, then process the soup in a blender or food processor until smooth. Pour back into a clean pan and stir in the milk, chicken and rice (with any stock that has not been absorbed). Heat until simmering. Garnish with the strips of pared orange rind and freshly ground black pepper, and serve with granary or wholemeal bread.

COOK'S TIP
Once made, chicken stock will keep in an airtight container in the refrigerator for 3–4 days.

Energy 315kcal/1320kJ; Protein 24.6g; Carbohydrate 29.9g, of which sugars 6.3g; Fat 10.8g, of which saturates 4.9g; Cholesterol 71mg; Calcium 140mg; Fibre 2.1g; Sodium 122mg.

CHICKEN AND COCONUT SOUP

THIS RECIPE COMBINES THE ORIENTAL FLAVOURS OF THAILAND IN A SMOOTH EUROPEAN-STYLE SOUP, AND THE FINISHED DISH IS COMPLEMENTED BY A TOPPING OF CRISP SHALLOTS.

SERVES 6

INGREDIENTS
40g/1½oz/3 tbsp butter
1 onion, finely chopped
2 garlic cloves, chopped
2.5cm/1in piece fresh root ginger,
  finely chopped
10ml/2 tsp Thai green curry paste
2.5ml/½ tsp turmeric
400ml/14fl oz can coconut milk
475ml/16fl oz/2 cups
  chicken stock
2 lime leaves, shredded
1 lemon grass stalk, finely chopped
8 skinless, boneless chicken thighs
350g/12oz spinach, roughly chopped
10ml/2 tsp Thai fish sauce
30ml/2 tbsp lime juice
30ml/2 tbsp vegetable oil
2 shallots, thinly sliced
salt and ground black pepper
small handful of Thai purple
  basil leaves, to garnish

1 Melt the butter in a large, heavy-based pan. Add the onion, garlic and ginger. Cook for 4–5 minutes, until soft.

2 Stir in the curry paste and turmeric, and cook for a further 2–3 minutes, stirring continuously.

3 Pour in two-thirds of the coconut milk; cook for 5 minutes. Add the stock, lime leaves, lemon grass and chicken. Heat until simmering; cook for 15 minutes or until the chicken is tender.

4 Use a slotted spoon to remove the chicken thighs. Set them aside to cool.

5 Add the spinach to the pan and cook for 3–4 minutes. Stir in the remaining coconut milk and seasoning, then process the soup in a food processor or blender until almost smooth. Return the soup to the rinsed-out pan. Cut the chicken thighs into bite-size pieces and stir these into the soup with the fish sauce and lime juice.

6 Reheat the soup gently until hot, but do not let it boil. Meanwhile, heat the oil in a frying pan and cook the shallots for 6–8 minutes, until crisp and golden, stirring occasionally. Drain on kitchen paper. Ladle the soup into bowls, then top with the basil leaves and fried shallots, and serve.

Energy 136kcal/570kJ; Protein 14.1g; Carbohydrate 5.2g, of which sugars 4.9g; Fat 6.7g, of which saturates 3.8g; Cholesterol 49mg; Calcium 125mg; Fibre 1.4g; Sodium 344mg.

GINGER, CHICKEN AND COCONUT SOUP

THIS AROMATIC SOUP IS RICH WITH COCONUT MILK AND INTENSELY FLAVOURED WITH GALANGAL, LEMON GRASS AND KAFFIR LIME LEAVES.

SERVES 4–6

INGREDIENTS
  750ml/1¼ pints/3 cups coconut milk
  475ml/16fl oz/2 cups chicken stock
  4 lemon grass stalks, bruised and chopped
  2.5cm/1in piece galangal, finely sliced
  10 black peppercorns, crushed
  10 kaffir lime leaves, torn
  300g/11oz skinless boneless chicken, cut into thin strips
  115g/4oz button (white) mushrooms
  50g/2oz/½ cup baby corn cobs
  60ml/4 tbsp lime juice
  45ml/3 tbsp Thai fish sauce
For the garnish
  2 red chillies, chopped
  4 spring onions (scallions), chopped
  chopped fresh coriander (cilantro)

1 Bring the coconut milk and chicken stock to the boil in a pan. Add the lemon grass, galangal, peppercorns and half the kaffir lime leaves. Reduce the heat and simmer gently for 10 minutes.

2 Strain the stock into a clean pan. Return to the heat and add the chicken, mushrooms and corn. Cook for 5–7 minutes until the chicken is tender.

3 Stir in the lime juice, fish sauce to taste and the rest of the lime leaves.

4 Ladle into warm soup bowls and serve hot, garnished with red chillies, spring onions and coriander.

COOK'S TIP
Wear rubber gloves to protect your hands when handling fresh chillies.

Energy 87kcal/371kJ; Protein 13.1g; Carbohydrate 6.8g, of which sugars 6.7g; Fat 1.1g, of which saturates 0.4g; Cholesterol 35mg; Calcium 42mg; Fibre 0.3g; Sodium 620mg.

JALAPEÑO-STYLE SOUP

CHICKEN, CHILLI AND AVOCADO COMBINE TO MAKE THIS SIMPLE BUT UNUSUAL SOUP. THE CHILLI IS
REMOVED BEFORE SERVING, LEAVING JUST A HINT OF SPICINESS.

SERVES 6

INGREDIENTS

1.5 litres/2½ pints/6¼ cups
   chicken stock
2 cooked chicken breast fillets,
   skinned and cut into large strips
1 drained canned chipotle or
   jalapeño chilli, rinsed
1 avocado

COOK'S TIPS
• When using canned chillies, it is
important to rinse them thoroughly
before adding them to a dish so as to
remove the flavour of any pickling liquid.
• The soup tastes best if you use home-
made stock (see page 31). Once made, it
will keep in an airtight container in the
refrigerator for 3–4 days.

1 Heat the stock in a large pan and add
the chicken and chilli. Simmer over a
very gentle heat for 5 minutes to heat
the chicken through and release the
flavour from the chilli.

2 Cut the avocado in half, remove the
stone and peel off the skin. Slice the
avocado flesh neatly lengthways.

3 Using a slotted spoon, remove the
chilli from the stock and discard it.
Pour the soup into heated serving
bowls, distributing the chicken evenly
among them.

4 Carefully add a few avocado slices
to each bowl and serve the soup
immediately, piping hot.

Energy 95kcal/400kJ; Protein 14.7g; Carbohydrate 0.4g, of which sugars 0.1g; Fat 4g, of which saturates 0.9g; Cholesterol 41mg; Calcium 8mg; Fibre 0.6g; Sodium 134mg.

CREAM OF DUCK SOUP WITH BLUEBERRY RELISH

THIS DELICIOUS, RICH SOUP IS IDEAL FOR SMART OCCASIONS. YOU CAN USE A WHOLE DUCK, BUT COOKING WITH DUCK BREASTS AND LEGS IS EASIER.

SERVES 4

INGREDIENTS

2 duck breasts
4 rindless streaky (fatty) bacon
  rashers (strips), chopped
1 onion, chopped
1 garlic clove, chopped
2 carrots, diced
2 celery sticks, chopped
4 large open mushrooms, chopped
15ml/1 tbsp tomato purée (paste)
2 duck legs
15ml/1 tbsp plain (all-purpose) flour
45ml/3 tbsp brandy
150ml/¼ pint/⅔ cup port
300ml/½ pint/1¼ cups red wine
900ml/1½ pints/3¾ cups
  chicken stock
1 bay leaf
2 sprigs fresh thyme
15ml/1 tbsp redcurrant jelly
150ml/¼ pint/⅔ cup double
  (heavy) cream
salt and ground black pepper
For the blueberry relish
150g/5oz/1¼ cups blueberries
15ml/1 tbsp caster (superfine) sugar
grated rind and juice of 2 limes
15ml/1 tbsp chopped fresh parsley
15ml/1 tbsp balsamic vinegar

1 Use a sharp knife to score the skin and fat on the duck breasts.

2 Preheat a heavy pan. Place the duck breasts in the pan, skin sides down, and cook for 8–10 minutes, until golden. Turn and cook for a further 5–6 minutes.

3 Remove the duck from the pan and set aside. Drain off some of the fat, leaving about 45ml/3 tbsp in the pan.

4 Add the bacon, onion, garlic, carrots, celery and mushrooms to the pan and cook for 10 minutes, stirring occasionally. Stir in the tomato purée and cook for 2 minutes. Remove the skin and bones from the duck legs and chop the flesh. Add to the pan and cook for 5 minutes.

5 Stir in the flour and cook for 1 minute. Gradually stir in the brandy, port, wine and stock and bring to the boil, stirring. Add the bay leaf, thyme and redcurrant jelly, then stir until the jelly melts. Reduce the heat and simmer for 1 hour.

6 Meanwhile, make the relish. Put the blueberries, caster sugar, lime rind and juice, parsley and vinegar in a small bowl. Very lightly bruise the blueberries with a fork, leaving some of the berries whole. Set aside until required.

7 Strain the soup through a colander, then through a fine sieve (strainer) into a clean pan. Bring to the boil, reduce the heat and simmer for 10 minutes.

8 Meanwhile, remove and discard the skin and fat from the duck breasts and cut the meat into thin strips. Add the meat strips to the soup with the double cream and season well. Bring just to boiling point.

9 Ladle the soup into warmed bowls and top each serving with a dollop of the blueberry relish. Serve piping hot.

Energy 642kcal/2673kJ; Protein 39.2g; Carbohydrate 14.2g, of which sugars 13.6g; Fat 35g, of which saturates 17.2g; Cholesterol 252mg; Calcium 83mg; Fibre 2.8g; Sodium 384mg.

DUCK BROTH <u>WITH</u> ORANGE SPICED DUMPLINGS

USING A DELICATE TOUCH WHEN BRINGING TOGETHER THE MIXTURE FOR THE DUMPLINGS WILL CREATE A LIGHT TEXTURE TO MATCH THEIR DELICIOUS FLAVOUR.

SERVES 4

INGREDIENTS
    1 duckling, about 1.75kg/4–4½lb,
      with liver
    1 large onion, halved
    2 carrots, thickly sliced
    ½ garlic bulb
    1 bouquet garni
    3 cloves
    30ml/2 tbsp chopped chives,
      to garnish
For the spiced dumplings
    2 thick slices white bread
    60ml/4 tbsp milk
    2 rashers (strips) rindless streaky
      (fatty) bacon
    1 shallot, finely chopped
    1 garlic clove, crushed
    1 egg yolk, beaten
    grated rind of 1 orange
    2.5ml/½ tsp paprika
    50g/2oz/½ cup plain
      (all-purpose) flour
    salt and ground black pepper

1 Set the duck liver aside. Using a sharp knife, cut off the breasts from the duckling and set them aside.

2 Put the carcass into a large, heavy-based pan and pour in enough water to cover the carcass. Bring to the boil and skim the scum off the surface.

3 Add the onion, carrots, garlic, bouquet garni and cloves. Reduce the heat and cover the pan, then simmer for 2 hours, skimming occasionally to remove scum.

4 Lift the carcass from the broth and leave to cool. Strain the broth, and skim it to remove any fat. Return the broth to the pan and simmer gently, uncovered, until reduced to 1.2 litres/2 pints/5 cups.

5 Remove all the meat from the duck carcass and shred it finely. Set aside.

6 For the dumplings, soak the bread in the milk for 5 minutes. Remove the skin and fat from the duck breasts. Mince (grind) the meat with the liver and bacon. Squeeze the milk from the bread, then add the bread to the meat with the shallot, garlic, egg yolk, orange rind, paprika, flour and seasoning, and mix.

7 Form a spoonful of the mixture into a ball, a little smaller than a walnut. Repeat with the remaining mixture to make 20 small dumplings.

8 Bring a large pan of lightly salted water to the boil and poach the dumplings for 4–5 minutes, until they are just tender.

9 Bring the duck broth back to the boil and add the dumplings.

10 Divide the shredded duck meat between four warmed bowls and ladle in the broth and dumplings. Garnish with chives.

Energy 289kcal/1214kJ; Protein 29.9g; Carbohydrate 19g, of which sugars 2.8g; Fat 13g, of which saturates 3.1g; Cholesterol 196mg; Calcium 63mg; Fibre 1.3g; Sodium 373mg.

DUCK AND PRESERVED LIME SOUP

THIS RICH CAMBODIAN SOUP, SAMLAW TIAH, ORIGINATES IN THE CHIU CHOW REGION OF SOUTHERN CHINA. THIS RECIPE IS ADAPTED FROM THE WONDERFUL BOOK ESSENTIALS OF ASIAN CUISINE, *WRITTEN BY CORINNE TRANG WHOSE CAMBODIAN GRANDMOTHER WAS OF CHIU CHOW ANCESTRY.*

SERVES 4–6

INGREDIENTS
    1 lean duck, weighing roughly
      1.5kg/3lb 5oz
    2 preserved limes
    25g/1oz fresh root ginger, thinly
      sliced
    sea salt and ground black pepper
For the garnish
    vegetable oil, for frying
    25g/1oz fresh root ginger, thinly
      sliced into strips
    2 garlic cloves, thinly sliced
      into strips
    2 spring onions (scallions),
      finely sliced

COOK'S TIP
Preserved limes have a distinctive
bitter flavour. Look out for them in
Asian markets.

1 Place the duck in a large pan with enough water to cover. Season with salt and pepper and bring the water to the boil. Reduce the heat, cover the pot, and simmer for 1½ hours.

2 Add the preserved limes and ginger to the cooking liquid. Continue to simmer for another hour, skimming off the fat from time to time, until the liquid has reduced a little and the duck is so tender, it almost falls off the bone.

3 Meanwhile heat some vegetable oil in a wok. Stir in the ginger and garlic strips and fry until gold and crispy. Drain well on kitchen paper and keep aside for garnishing.

4 Transfer the duck to a large dish and shred the meat into individual bowls. Check the broth for seasoning, then ladle it over the duck. Sprinkle the spring onions with the fried ginger and garlic over the top and serve immediately.

Energy 114kcal/479kJ; Protein 14g; Carbohydrate 0.4g, of which sugars 0.4g; Fat 6.4g, of which saturates 1.7g; Cholesterol 75mg; Calcium 11mg; Fibre 0.1g; Sodium 78mg.

DUCK AND NUT SOUP WITH JUJUBES

THIS NORTHERN VIETNAMESE DISH IS RICH AND DELICIOUS. PACKED WITH NUTS AND SWEETENED WITH JUJUBES (DRIED CHINESE RED DATES), IT RESEMBLES NEITHER A SOUP NOR A STEW, BUT SOMEWHERE IN BETWEEN. SERVED ON ITS OWN, OR WITH RICE AND PICKLES, IT IS A MEAL IN ITSELF.

SERVES 4

INGREDIENTS

30–45ml/2–3 tbsp vegetable oil
4 duck legs, split into thighs and
    drumsticks
juice of 1 coconut
60ml/4 tbsp *nuoc mam*
4 lemon grass stalks, bruised
12 chestnuts, peeled
90g/3½oz unsalted cashew nuts,
    roasted
90g/3½oz unsalted almonds, roasted
90g/3½oz unsalted peanuts, roasted
12 jujubes
sea salt and ground black pepper
a small bunch of fresh basil leaves,
    to garnish

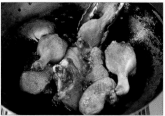

1 Heat the oil in a heavy pan. Brown the duck pieces in the oil and drain on kitchen paper.

2 Bring 2 litres/3½ pints/7¾ cups water to the boil. Reduce the heat and add the coconut juice, *nuoc mam*, lemon grass and duck legs. Cover the pan and simmer over a gentle heat for 2–3 hours.

3 Add the nuts and jujubes and cook for 40–45 minutes, until the chestnuts are soft and the duck is tender. Skim off any fat, season to taste. Sprinkle the basil leaves over the top to serve.

COOK'S TIP
To extract the coconut juice, pierce the eyes on top and turn the coconut upside down over a bowl.

Energy 664kcal/2767kJ; Protein 36.1g; Carbohydrate 29.3g, of which sugars 15.4g; Fat 47.2g, of which saturates 7.4g; Cholesterol 110mg; Calcium 112mg; Fibre 5.5g; Sodium 731mg

MEAT SOUPS

Nourishing meaty soups are just the thing for warming you up on cold winter days. This section includes soups from all around the world — Irish Kidney and Bacon Soup, Mediterranean Sausage and Pesto Soup, Chinese Pork and Rice Porridge, and Japanese Miso Soup with Pork and Vegetables. For a special occasion, serve the delicious traditional Khmer dish, Spicy Beef and Aubergine Soup, or exotic Vietnamese Pork and Lotus Root Broth.

SPICY BEEF AND AUBERGINE SOUP

A WONDERFUL KHMER DISH, THIS SOUP, SAMLAW MACHOU KROEUNG, IS SWEET, SPICY AND TANGY. THE FLAVOUR IS MAINLY DERIVED FROM THE CAMBODIAN HERBAL CONDIMENT, KROEUNG, AND THE FERMENTED FISH EXTRACT, TUK TREY.

SERVES 6

INGREDIENTS

For the stock
   1kg/2¼lb beef shanks or brisket
   2 large onions, quartered
   2–3 carrots, cut into chunks
   90g/3½oz fresh root ginger, sliced
   2 cinnamon sticks
   4 star anise
   5ml/1 tsp black peppercorns
   30ml/2 tbsp soy sauce
   45–60ml/3–4 tbsp *tuk trey*

For the soup
   4 dried New Mexico chillies
   15ml/1 tbsp vegetable oil
   75ml/5 tbsp *kroeung*
   2 or 3 fresh or dried red Thai chillies
   75ml/5 tbsp tamarind extract
   15–30ml/1–2 tbsp *tuk trey*
   30ml/2 tbsp palm sugar
   12 Thai aubergines (eggplants),
      stems removed, cut into bitesize
      chunks
   a bunch of watercress, trimmed
   a handful of fresh curry leaves
   sea salt and ground black pepper

2 Soak the New Mexico chillies in water for 30 minutes. Split them open, remove the seeds and scrape out the pulp with a teaspoon.

3 Take the lid off the stock and stir in the remaining two ingredients. Simmer, uncovered, for another hour, until the stock has reduced to about 2 litres/ 3½ pints/7¾ cups.

4 Skim off any fat, strain the stock into a bowl and put aside. Lift the meat on to a plate, tear it into thin strips and put half of it aside for the soup.

7 Meanwhile, dry-fry the curry leaves. Heat a small heavy pan over a high heat, add the curry leaves and cook them until they begin to crackle. Transfer them to a plate and set aside.

8 Season the soup to taste. Stir in half the curry leaves and ladle the soup into individual bowls. Sprinkle the remaining curry leaves over the top and serve.

1 To make the stock, put the beef shanks into a deep pan with all the other stock ingredients, apart from the soy sauce and *tuk trey*. Cover with 3 litres/5 pints/12 cups water and bring to the boil. Reduce the heat and simmer, covered, for 2–3 hours.

COOK'S TIP
Thai chillies and aubergines, and also tamarind extract and *tuk trey*, can be found in South-east Asian markets.

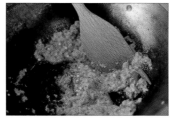

5 Heat the oil in a heavy pan. Stir in the *kroeung* along with the pulp from the New Mexico chillies and the whole Thai chillies. Stir the spicy paste as it sizzles, until it begins to darken. Add the tamarind extract, *tuk trey*, sugar and the reserved stock. Stir well and bring the liquid to the boil.

6 Reduce the heat and add the reserved beef, aubergines and watercress. Cook for about 20 minutes to allow the flavours to mingle.

Energy 303kcal/1276kJ; Protein 37g; Carbohydrate 16.5g, of which sugars 14.5g; Fat 10.6g, of which saturates 4.2g; Cholesterol 90mg; Calcium 35mg; Fibre 2.4g; Sodium 0.3mg.

BEEF AND BARLEY SOUP

THIS TRADITIONAL IRISH FARMHOUSE SOUP MAKES A WONDERFULLY RESTORATIVE DISH ON A COLD DAY. THE FLAVOURS DEVELOP PARTICULARLY WELL IF IT IS MADE IN ADVANCE AND REHEATED.

SERVES 6–8

INGREDIENTS
450–675g/1–1½lb rib steak, or
    other stewing beef on the bone
2 large onions
50g/2oz/¼ cup pearl barley
50g/2oz/¼ cup green split peas
3 large carrots, chopped
2 white turnips, peeled and diced
3 celery sticks, chopped
1 large or 2 medium leeks, thinly
    sliced and thoroughly washed in
    cold water
sea salt and ground black pepper
chopped fresh parsley, to serve

1 Bone the meat and put the bones and half an onion, roughly sliced, into a large pan. Cover with cold water, season and bring to the boil. Skim if necessary, then simmer until needed.

2 Meanwhile, trim any fat or gristle from the meat and cut into small pieces. Chop the remaining onions finely. Drain the stock from the bones, make it up with water to 2 litres/3½ pints/9 cups, and return to the rinsed pan with the meat, onions, barley and split peas.

3 Season, bring to the boil, and skim if necessary. Reduce the heat, cover and simmer for about 30 minutes.

4 Add the rest of the vegetables and simmer for 1 hour, or until the meat is tender. Check the seasoning.

5 Serve in large warmed bowls, generously sprinkled with parsley.

Energy 167kcal/705kJ; Protein 16g; Carbohydrate 21.4g, of which sugars 7.8g; Fat 2.6g, of which saturates 0.8g; Cholesterol 34mg; Calcium 54mg; Fibre 3.6g; Sodium 58mg.

ROAST LAMB SHANKS <u>IN</u> BARLEY BROTH

SUCCULENT ROASTED LAMB SHANKS STUDDED WITH GARLIC AND ROSEMARY MAKE A FABULOUS MEAL WHEN SERVED IN A HEARTY VEGETABLE, BARLEY AND TOMATO BROTH.

<u>SERVES 4</u>

INGREDIENTS

    4 small lamb shanks
    4 garlic cloves, cut into slivers
    handful of fresh rosemary sprigs
    30ml/2 tbsp olive oil
    2 carrots, diced
    2 celery sticks, diced
    1 large onion, chopped
    1 bay leaf
    few sprigs of fresh thyme
    1.2 litres/2 pints/5 cups
       lamb stock
    50g/2oz pearl barley
    450g/1lb tomatoes, peeled and
       roughly chopped
    grated rind of 1 large lemon
    30ml/2 tbsp chopped fresh parsley
    salt and ground black pepper

4 Remove the lamb shanks from the casserole using a slotted spoon.

5 Skim the fat from the surface of the roasted vegetables, then add them to the broth. Stir in the tomatoes, lemon rind and parsley.

6 Bring the soup back to the boil. Reduce the heat and simmer for 5 minutes. Add the lamb shanks and heat through, then season. Put a lamb shank into each of four large bowls, then ladle the barley broth over the meat and serve at once.

1 Preheat the oven to 150°C/300°F/ Gas 2. Make small cuts all over the lamb and insert slivers of garlic and sprigs of rosemary into them.

2 Heat the oil in a flameproof casserole and brown the shanks two at a time. Remove and set aside. Add the carrots, celery and onion in batches and cook until lightly browned. Put all the vegetables in the casserole with the bay leaf and thyme. Pour in stock to cover, place the lamb shanks on top and roast for 2 hours.

3 Meanwhile, pour the remaining stock into a large saucepan. Add the pearl barley, then bring to the boil. Reduce the heat, cover and simmer for 1 hour, or until the barley is tender.

Energy 287kcal/1199kJ; Protein 22.5g; Carbohydrate 19.5g, of which sugars 7.6g; Fat 13.7g, of which saturates 0.9g; Cholesterol 0mg; Calcium 35mg; Fibre 2.3g; Sodium 24mg.

SOUR BROTH WITH WATER SPINACH AND BEEF

WATER SPINACH IS A POPULAR VEGETABLE IN VIETNAM. WHEN COOKED, THE STEMS REMAIN CRUNCHY WHILE THE LEAVES SOFTEN, LENDING A CONTRAST OF TEXTURE. SERVED AS AN APPETIZER, OR PALATE CLEANSER, THIS IS A LIGHT SOUP WITH TENDER BITES OF RARE BEEF AND SOUR NOTES OF LEMON.

SERVES 4–6

INGREDIENTS

30ml/2 tbsp *nuoc mam*
5ml/1 tsp sugar
175g/6oz beef fillet (tenderloin),
   finely sliced against the grain into
   2.5cm/1in strips
1.2 litres/2 pints/5 cups beef or
   chicken stock
175g/6oz water spinach, trimmed,
   rinsed, leaves and stalks
   separated
juice of 1 lemon
ground black pepper
1 red or green chilli, seeded and
   finely sliced, to garnish

1 Stir the *nuoc mam* with the sugar, toss in the beef and marinate for 30 minutes.

2 Bring the stock to the boil, reduce the heat and add the water spinach. Stir in the lemon juice and season with pepper.

3 Place the meat strips in individual bowls and ladle the piping hot broth over the top. (The meat will cook in the hot broth.) Garnish each serving with sliced chillies, and serve.

Energy 61kcal/254kJ; Protein 7.4g; Carbohydrate 1.2g, of which sugars 1.1g; Fat 3g, of which saturates 1.1g; Cholesterol 17mg; Calcium 51mg; Fibre 0.6g; Sodium 0.06mg.

PORK AND LOTUS ROOT BROTH

THIS VIETNAMESE SOUP IS FROM THE CENTRAL REGION OF THE COUNTRY WHERE THE LOTUS, OR WATER LILY, IS USED IN MANY DISHES. IN THIS CLEAR BROTH, WHICH IS SERVED AS AN APPETIZER, THE THIN, ROUND SLICES OF FRESH LOTUS ROOT LOOK LIKE PRETTY, DELICATE FLOWERS FLOATING IN WATER.

SERVES 4–6

INGREDIENTS

For the stock

    450g/1lb pork ribs

    1 onion, quartered

    2 carrots, cut into chunks

    25g/1oz dried squid or dried shrimp, soaked in water for 30 minutes, rinsed and drained

    15ml/1 tbsp *nuoc mam*

    15ml/1 tbsp soy sauce

    6 black peppercorns

    sea salt

For the broth

    450g/1lb fresh lotus roots, peeled and thinly sliced

    ground black pepper

    1 red chilli, seeded and finely sliced, and a small bunch of basil leaves, to garnish

1 Put the ribs into a deep pan and cover with water. Add the other stock ingredients and bring to the boil. Reduce the heat and simmer for 1 hour.

2 Take off the lid and simmer for a further 30 minutes to reduce the stock. Strain the stock – you should have roughly 1.2 litres/2 pints/5 cups – and shred the meat off the pork ribs.

3 Pour the stock back into the pan and bring it to the boil. Reduce the heat and add the lotus root. Partially cover the pan and simmer gently for 30–40 minutes, until the lotus root is tender.

4 Stir in the shredded meat and season the broth with salt and pepper. Ladle into warmed serving bowls and garnish with the chilli and basil leaves.

Energy 181kcal/756kJ; Protein 23.8g; Carbohydrate 4g, of which sugars 3.1g; Fat 7.8g, of which saturates 2.7g; Cholesterol 74mg; Calcium 65mg; Fibre 1.4g; Sodium 0.27mg.

MISO SOUP WITH PORK AND VEGETABLES

THIS IS QUITE A RICH AND FILLING SOUP. ITS JAPANESE NAME, TANUKI JIRU, MEANS RACCOON SOUP FOR HUNTERS, BUT AS RACCOONS ARE NOT EATEN NOWADAYS, PORK IS USED INSTEAD.

SERVES 4

INGREDIENTS

200g/7oz lean boneless pork
15cm/6in piece gobo or 1 parsnip
50g/2oz mooli (daikon)
4 fresh shiitake mushrooms
½ konnyaku or 125g/4½oz tofu
a little sesame oil, for stir-frying
600ml/1 pint/2½ cups second dashi
   stock, or the same amount of water
   and 10ml/2 tsp dashi-no-moto
70ml/4½ tbsp miso
2 spring onions (scallions), chopped
5ml/1 tsp sesame seeds

1 Press the meat down on a chopping board using the palm of your hand and slice horizontally into very thin long strips, then cut the strips crossways into stamp-size pieces. Set the pork aside.

2 Peel the gobo, if using, with a potato peeler, then cut diagonally into 1cm/½in thick slices. Quickly plunge the slices into a bowl of cold water to stop them discolouring. If you are using parsnip, peel, cut it in half lengthways, then cut it into 1cm/½in thick half-moon-shaped slices.

3 Peel and slice the mooli into 1.5cm/⅔in thick discs. Cut the discs into 1.5cm/⅔in cubes. Remove the shiitake stalks and cut the caps into quarters.

4 Place the konnyaku, if using, in a pan of boiling water and cook for 1 minute. Drain and cool. Cut in quarters lengthways, then crossways into 3mm/⅛in thick pieces.

5 Heat a little sesame oil in a heavy cast-iron or enamelled pan until purple smoke rises. Stir-fry the pork, then add the konnyaku or tofu and all the vegetables except for the spring onions. When the colour of the meat has changed, add the stock.

6 Bring to the boil over a medium heat, and skim off the foam until the soup looks fairly clear. Reduce the heat, cover and simmer for 15 minutes.

7 Put the miso in a small bowl and mix with 60ml/4 tbsp hot stock to make a smooth paste. Stir one-third of the miso into the soup; taste and add more if required. Add the spring onion and remove from the heat. Serve very hot in individual soup bowls, sprinkled with sesame seeds.

COOK'S TIPS
• Gobo is burdock root, and can be substituted with parsnip in this recipe.
• Mooli, also known as daikon, is a long, white vegetable which is a member of the radish family.
• Konnyaku is a gelatinous cake made from a relative of the sweet potato.

Energy 110kcal/459kJ; Protein 16g; Carbohydrate 1.3g, of which sugars 0.9g; Fat 4.5g, of which saturates 1g; Cholesterol 32mg; Calcium 29.5mg; Fibre 0.4g; Sodium 573mg.

SWEET-AND-SOUR PORK SOUP

THIS VERY QUICK, SHARP AND TANGY SOUP IS PERFECT FOR AN INFORMAL SUPPER. IT CAN ALSO BE MADE WITH SHREDDED CHICKEN BREAST INSTEAD OF PORK.

SERVES 6–8

INGREDIENTS
900g/2lb pork fillet, trimmed
1 unripe papaya, halved, seeded,
  peeled and shredded
3 shallots, chopped
5 garlic cloves, chopped
5ml/1 tsp crushed black peppercorns
15ml/1 tbsp shrimp paste
30ml/2 tbsp vegetable oil
1.5 litres/2½ pints/6¼ cups
  chicken stock
2.5cm/1in piece fresh root
  ginger, grated
120ml/4fl oz/½ cup tamarind water
15ml/1 tbsp honey
juice of 1 lime
2 small red chillies, seeded
  and sliced
4 spring onions (scallions), sliced
salt and ground black pepper

1 Cut the pork into very fine strips, 5cm/2in long. Mix with the papaya and set aside. Process the shallots, garlic, peppercorns and shrimp paste in a food processor or blender to form a paste.

2 Heat the oil in a heavy pan and fry the paste for 1–2 minutes. Add the stock and bring to the boil. Reduce the heat. Add the pork and papaya, ginger and tamarind water.

3 Simmer the soup for 7–8 minutes, until the pork is tender.

4 Stir in the honey, lime juice, and most of the sliced chillies and spring onions. Season to taste with salt and ground black pepper.

5 Ladle the soup into bowls and serve immediately, garnished with the remaining chillies and onions.

Energy 229kcal/963kJ; Protein 32.8g; Carbohydrate 11.1g, of which sugars 10.9g; Fat 6.2g, of which saturates 2.1g; Cholesterol 95mg; Calcium 37mg; Fibre 2.3g; Sodium 111mg.

PORK AND RICE PORRIDGE

ORIGINATING IN CHINA, THIS DISH HAS NOW SPREAD THROUGHOUT THE WHOLE OF SOUTH-EAST ASIA AND IS LOVED FOR ITS COMFORTING BLANDNESS. IT IS INVARIABLY SERVED WITH A FEW STRONGLY FLAVOURED ACCOMPANIMENTS.

2 Pour the stock into a large pan. Bring to the boil and add the rice. Season the minced pork. Add it by taking small teaspoons and tapping the spoon on the side of the pan so that the meat falls into the soup in small lumps.

3 Stir in the fish sauce and pickled garlic and simmer for 10 minutes, until the pork is cooked. Stir in the celery.

4 Serve the rice porridge in individual warmed bowls. Sprinkle the prepared garlic and shallots on top and season with plenty of ground pepper.

COOK'S TIP
Pickled garlic has a distinctive flavour and is available from Asian food stores.

SERVES 2

INGREDIENTS
  900ml/1½ pints/3¾ cups
    vegetable stock
  200g/7oz/1¾ cups cooked rice
  225g/8oz minced (ground) pork
  15ml/1 tbsp Thai fish sauce
  2 heads pickled garlic,
    finely chopped
  1 celery stick, finely diced
  salt and ground black pepper
To garnish
  30ml/2 tbsp groundnut (peanut) oil
  4 garlic cloves, thinly sliced
  4 small red shallots, finely sliced

1 Make the garnishes by heating the groundnut oil in a frying pan and cooking the garlic and shallots over a low heat until brown. Drain on kitchen paper and reserve.

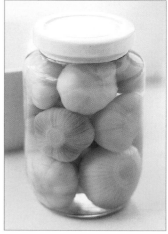

Energy 375kcal/1574kJ; Protein 26.8g; Carbohydrate 31.1g, of which sugars 0.2g; Fat 16.8g, of which saturates 4g; Cholesterol 71mg; Calcium 32mg; Fibre 0.3g; Sodium 89mg.

MEDITERRANEAN SAUSAGE AND PESTO SOUP

THIS DELICIOUS SOUP MAKES A SATISFYING ONE-POT MEAL THAT BRINGS THE SUMMERY FLAVOUR OF BASIL TO MIDWINTER MEALS. THE LENTILS ENHANCE THE FLAVOUR OF THE SMOKED SAUSAGE. THICK SLICES OF WARM CRUSTY BREAD MAKE THE PERFECT ACCOMPANIMENT.

SERVES 4

INGREDIENTS

15ml/1 tbsp olive oil, plus extra
  for frying
1 red onion, chopped
450g/1lb smoked pork sausages
225g/8oz/1 cup red lentils
400g/14oz can chopped tomatoes
1 litre/1¾ pints/4 cups water
oil, for deep-frying
salt and ground black pepper
60ml/4 tbsp pesto and fresh basil
  sprigs, to garnish

1 Heat the oil in a large pan and cook the onion until softened. Coarsely chop all but one of the sausages and add them to the pan. Cook for 5 minutes, stirring, or until the sausages are cooked.

2 Stir in the lentils, tomatoes and water, and bring to the boil. Reduce the heat, cover and simmer for about 20 minutes. Cool the soup slightly before puréeing it in a blender. Return the soup to the rinsed pan.

3 Cook the remaining sausage in a little oil in a small frying pan, turning it often, for 10 minutes, or until lightly browned and firm. Transfer to a chopping board or plate and leave to cool slightly, then slice thinly.

4 Heat the oil for deep-frying to 190°C/375°F or until a cube of day-old bread browns in about 60 seconds. Deep-fry the sausage slices and basil briefly until the sausages are brown and the basil leaves are crisp.

5 Lift them out using a slotted spoon and drain on kitchen paper.

6 Reheat the soup, add seasoning to taste, then ladle into warmed individual soup bowls. Sprinkle with the deep-fried sausage slices and basil and swirl a little pesto through each portion. Serve with warm crusty bread.

Energy 656kcal/2741kJ; Protein 30.9g; Carbohydrate 46.7g, of which sugars 8.2g; Fat 39.7g, of which saturates 13.1g; Cholesterol 75mg; Calcium 250mg; Fibre 4.8g; Sodium 1109mg.

LAMB <u>AND</u> VEGETABLE BROTH

THIS IS A GOOD MODERN ADAPTATION OF THE TRADITIONAL RECIPE FOR IRISH MUTTON BROTH, KNOWN LOCALLY AS BRACHÁN CAOIREOLA, AND IS DELICIOUS SERVED WITH WHOLEMEAL BREAD TO MAKE A FILLING LUNCH DISH ON A COLD WINTER'S DAY.

SERVES 6

INGREDIENTS

675g/1½lb best end of neck of lamb
   on the bone (cross rib)
1 large onion
2 bay leaves
3 carrots, chopped
½ white turnip, diced
½ small white cabbage, shredded
2 large leeks, thinly sliced
15ml/1 tbsp tomato purée (paste)
30ml/2 tbsp chopped fresh parsley
salt and ground black pepper

COOK'S TIP

Best end of neck (cross rib) is the rib joint between the middle neck and loin. It is the best cut to use for this soup.

1 Trim any excess fat from the meat. Chop the onion, and put the lamb and bay leaves in a large pan. Add 1.5 litres/2½ pints/6¼ cups water and bring to the boil. Skim the surface and then simmer for about 1½–2 hours. Remove the lamb on to a board and leave to cool until ready to handle.

2 Remove the meat from the bones and cut into small pieces. Discard the bones and return the meat to the broth. Add the vegetables, tomato purée and parsley, and season well. Simmer for another 30 minutes, until the vegetables are just tender. Ladle into warmed soup bowls and serve piping hot.

Energy 167kcal/696kJ; Protein 14.6g; Carbohydrate 10.5g, of which sugars 9g; Fat 7.6g, of which saturates 3.4g; Cholesterol 48mg; Calcium 58mg; Fibre 3.7g; Sodium 81mg.

BEEF AND LAMB STEW

THIS TRADITIONAL JEWISH CHAMIM IS MADE WITH SAVOURY MEATS AND CHICKPEAS, BAKED IN A VERY LOW OVEN FOR SEVERAL HOURS. A PARCEL OF RICE IS OFTEN ADDED TO THE BROTH PART WAY THROUGH COOKING, WHICH PRODUCES A LIGHTLY PRESSED RICE WITH A SLIGHTLY CHEWY TEXTURE.

SERVES 8

INGREDIENTS

250g/9oz/1 cup chickpeas,
  soaked overnight
45ml/3 tbsp olive oil
1 onion, chopped
10 garlic cloves, chopped
1 parsnip, sliced
3 carrots, sliced
5–10ml/1–2 tsp ground cumin
2.5ml/½ tsp ground turmeric
15ml/1 tbsp chopped fresh root ginger
2 litres/3½ pints/8 cups beef stock
1 potato, peeled and cut into chunks
½ marrow (large zucchini), sliced or
  cut into chunks
400g/14oz fresh or canned
  tomatoes, diced
45–60ml/3–4 tbsp brown or
  green lentils
2 bay leaves
250g/9oz salted meat such as
  salt (corned) beef (or double the
  quantity of lamb)
250g/9oz piece of lamb
½ large bunch fresh coriander
  (cilantro), chopped
200g/7oz/1 cup long grain rice
1 lemon, cut into wedges, and a
  spicy sauce or finely chopped fresh
  chillies, to serve

1 Preheat the oven to 120°C/250°F/ Gas ½. Drain the chickpeas.

2 Heat the oil in a large flameproof casserole, add the onion, garlic, parsnip, carrots, cumin, turmeric and ginger and cook for 2–3 minutes. Add the chickpeas, stock, potato, marrow, tomatoes, lentils, bay leaves, salted meat, lamb and coriander. Cover and cook in the oven for about 3 hours.

COOK'S TIP
Add 1 or 2 pinches of bicarbonate of soda (baking soda) to the soaking chickpeas to make them tender, but do not add too much as it can make them mushy.

3 Put the rice on a double thickness of muslin (cheesecloth) and tie together at the corners, allowing enough room for the rice to expand while it is cooking.

4 Two hours before the end of cooking, remove the casserole from the oven. Place the rice parcel in the casserole, anchoring the edge of the muslin parcel under the lid so that the parcel is held above the soup and allowed to steam. Return the casserole to the oven and continue cooking for a further 2 hours.

5 Carefully remove the lid and the rice. Skim any fat off the top of the soup and ladle the soup into bowls with a scoop of the rice and one or two pieces of meat. Serve with lemon wedges and a spoonful of hot sauce or chopped fresh chillies.

Energy 385kcal/1621kJ; Protein 25.6g; Carbohydrate 48.6g, of which sugars 5.3g; Fat 10.8g, of which saturates 2.7g; Cholesterol 24mg; Calcium 116mg; Fibre 5.4g; Sodium 54mg.

THREE-DELICACY SOUP

THIS DELICIOUS SOUP COMBINES THE THREE INGREDIENTS OF CHICKEN, HAM AND PRAWNS. THEIR DIFFERENT FLAVOURS ARE RETAINED IN THE SIMPLE CHICKEN STOCK.

SERVES 4

INGREDIENTS
    115g/4oz chicken breast fillet
    115g/4oz honey-roast ham
    115g/4oz peeled prawns (shrimp)
    700ml/1¼ pints/3 cups chicken stock
    salt
    chopped spring onions (scallions), to
        garnish

1 Thinly slice the chicken breast and ham into small pieces. If the prawns are large, cut them in half lengthways.

COOK'S TIP
Fresh, uncooked prawns (shrimp) impart the best flavour. If unavailable, use ready-cooked prawns. Add towards the end of cooking, to prevent over-cooking.

2 In a wok or large pan, bring the stock to a rolling boil and add the chicken, ham and prawns. Bring back to the boil, add salt to taste and simmer for a further 1 minute.

3 Ladle into individual soup bowls. Serve hot, garnished with chopped spring onions.

LAMB AND CUCUMBER SOUP

THIS IS A VERY SIMPLE SOUP TO PREPARE, BUT IT TASTES DELICIOUS NEVERTHELESS. YOU CAN USE EITHER CHICKEN OR VEGETABLE STOCK.

SERVES 4

INGREDIENTS
    225g/8oz lamb steak
    15ml/1 tbsp light soy sauce
    10ml/2 tsp Chinese rice wine
    2.5ml/½ tsp sesame oil
    7.5cm/3in piece cucumber
    750ml/1¼ pints/3 cups chicken or
        vegetable stock
    15ml/1 tbsp rice vinegar
    salt and ground white pepper

COOK'S TIPS
• If Chinese rice wine is not available, use dry sherry instead.
• Vegetable or chicken stock may be used for this dish. Home-made stock (see pages 30 and 31) tastes much better than a stock (bouillon) cube. Once made, it can be kept in the refrigerator for 3–4 days, or frozen for longer storage.

1 Using a sharp knife, trim off any excess fat from the lamb steaks. Thinly slice the lamb into small pieces.

2 Combine the soy sauce, wine or sherry and sesame oil in a small bowl. Add the sliced lamb and marinate for 25–30 minutes. Discard the marinade.

3 Halve the cucumber piece lengthways (do not peel it), then cut into thin slices diagonally.

4 In a wok or large pan, bring the stock to a rolling boil, add the lamb and stir to separate the slices.

5 Return to the boil, then add the cucumber slices, vinegar and seasoning. Bring back to the boil and serve immediately.

Top: Energy 83kcal/351kJ; Protein 17.7g; Carbohydrate 0.3g, of which sugars 0.3g; Fat 1.7g, of which saturates 0.5g; Cholesterol 93mg; Calcium 27mg; Fibre 0g; Sodium 781mg.
Bottom: Energy 105kcal/438kJ; Protein 11.2g; Carbohydrate 0.4g, of which sugars 0.3g; Fat 6.6g, of which saturates 3g; Cholesterol 43mg; Calcium 6mg; Fibre 0g; Sodium 316mg.

INDIAN LAMB SOUP WITH RICE AND COCONUT

THIS MEATY SOUP THICKENED WITH LONG GRAIN RICE AND FLAVOURED WITH CUMIN AND CORIANDER SEEDS IS BASED ON THE CLASSIC INDIAN MULLIGATAWNY SOUP.

SERVES 6

INGREDIENTS
  2 onions, chopped
  6 garlic cloves, crushed
  5cm/2in piece fresh root
    ginger, grated
  90ml/6 tbsp olive oil
  30ml/2 tbsp black poppy seeds
  5ml/1 tsp cumin seeds
  5ml/1 tsp coriander seeds
  2.5ml/½ tsp ground turmeric
  450g/1lb boneless lamb chump
    chops, trimmed and cut into
    bite-size pieces
  1.5ml/¼ tsp cayenne pepper
  1.2 litres/2 pints/5 cups
    lamb stock
  50g/2oz/generous ⅓ cup long
    grain rice
  30ml/2 tbsp lemon juice
  60ml/4 tbsp coconut milk
  salt and ground black pepper
  fresh coriander (cilantro) sprigs and
    toasted flaked coconut, to garnish

1 Process the onions, garlic, ginger and 15ml/1 tbsp of the oil in a food processor or blender to form a paste. Set aside.

2 Heat a small, heavy frying pan. Add the poppy, cumin and coriander seeds and toast for a few seconds, shaking the pan, until they begin to release their aroma.

3 Transfer the toasted seeds to a mortar and grind them to a powder with a pestle. Stir in the ground turmeric. Set aside.

4 Heat the rest of the oil in a heavy pan. Fry the lamb in batches over a high heat for about 4–5 minutes until browned all over. Remove the lamb and set aside.

5 Add the onion, garlic and ginger paste to the pan and cook for 1–2 minutes, stirring continuously. Stir in the ground spices and cook for 1 minute. Return the meat to the pan with any meat juices that have seeped out while it has been standing. Add the cayenne, stock and seasoning.

6 Bring to the boil, cover and simmer for 30–35 minutes or until the lamb is tender.

7 Stir in the rice, then cover and cook for a further 15 minutes.

8 Add the lemon juice and coconut milk and simmer for a further 2 minutes.

9 Ladle the soup into six warmed bowls and garnish with sprigs of coriander and lightly toasted flaked coconut. Serve piping hot.

BULGARIAN SOUR LAMB SOUP

THIS TRADITIONAL SOUR SOUP USES LAMB, THOUGH PORK AND POULTRY ARE POPULAR ALTERNATIVES.
THE PAPRIKA BUTTER MAKES AN UNUSUAL GARNISH.

SERVES 4–5

INGREDIENTS
    30ml/2 tbsp oil
    450g/1lb lean lamb, trimmed
      and cubed
    1 onion, diced
    30ml/2 tbsp plain (all-purpose) flour
    15ml/1 tbsp paprika
    1 litre/1¾ pints/4 cups hot lamb
      stock
    3 sprigs of fresh parsley
    4 spring onions (scallions)
    4 sprigs of fresh dill
    25g/1oz/scant ¼ cup long grain rice
    2 eggs, beaten
    30–45ml/2–3 tbsp vinegar or
      lemon juice
    salt and ground black pepper
For the garnish
    25g/1oz/2 tbsp butter, melted
    5ml/1 tsp paprika
    a little fresh parsley or lovage
      and dill

1 In a large pan heat the oil and fry the meat until brown. Add the onion and cook until it has softened. Sprinkle in the flour and paprika. Stir well, add the stock and cook for 10 minutes.

2 Tie the parsley, spring onions and dill together with string and add to the large pan with the rice and seasoning. Bring to the boil, then simmer for about 30–40 minutes, or until the lamb is tender.

COOK'S TIP
Add extra vinegar or lemon juice if you want a more piquant flavour.

3 Remove the pan from the heat and stir in the eggs. Add the vinegar or lemon juice. Discard the tied herbs and season to taste.

4 For the garnish, melt the butter in a pan and add the paprika. Ladle the soup into warmed serving bowls. Garnish with the herbs and a little red paprika butter.

Energy 314kcal/1309kJ; Protein 21.6g; Carbohydrate 10.1g, of which sugars 1.2g; Fat 21.1g, of which saturates 8.4g; Cholesterol 155mg; Calcium 49mg; Fibre 0.8g; Sodium 139mg.

SOUP OF TOULOUSE SAUSAGE WITH BORLOTTI BEANS AND BREADCRUMBS

A BIG-FILLER SOUP, THIS RECIPE IS BASED LOOSELY ON CASSOULET. FRENCH SAUSAGES AND ITALIAN BEANS CONTRIBUTE FLAVOUR AND SUBSTANCE, AND THE SOUP IS TOPPED WITH GOLDEN BREADCRUMBS.

SERVES 6

INGREDIENTS
250g/9oz/generous 1¼ cups
  borlotti beans
115g/4oz piece pancetta,
  finely chopped
6 Toulouse sausages, thickly sliced
1 large onion, finely chopped
2 garlic cloves, chopped
2 carrots, finely diced
2 leeks, finely chopped
6 tomatoes, peeled, seeded
  and chopped
30ml/2 tbsp tomato purée (paste)
1.27 litres/2¼ pints/5⅔ cups
  vegetable stock
175g/6oz spring greens, roughly
  shredded
25g/1oz/2 tbsp butter
115g/4oz/2 cups fresh white
  breadcrumbs
50g/2oz/⅔ cup freshly grated
  Parmesan cheese
salt and ground black pepper

1 Put the borlotti beans in a large bowl, cover with plenty of cold water and leave to soak overnight.

2 Next day, place the beans in a pan, cover with plenty of cold water and bring to the boil, then boil for 10 minutes. Drain well.

3 Heat a large pan and dry fry the pancetta until browned and the fat runs. Add the sausages and cook for 4–5 minutes, stirring occasionally, until beginning to brown.

4 Add the onion and garlic and cook for 3–4 minutes until softened. Add the beans, carrots, leeks, tomatoes and tomato purée, then add the stock. Stir, bring to the boil and cover. Simmer for about 1¼ hours or until the beans are tender, then stir in the spring greens and cook for 12–15 minutes more. Season well.

5 Meanwhile, melt the butter in a frying pan and fry the breadcrumbs, stirring, for 4–5 minutes, until golden, then stir in the Parmesan.

6 Ladle the soup into six warmed bowls. Sprinkle the fried breadcrumb mixture over each portion. Serve with some warm crusty bread.

VARIATION
Toulouse sausage, which is flavoured with garlic, can be substituted with Polish kielbasa or Italian sweet sausage.

Energy 574kcal/2405kJ; Protein 29g; Carbohydrate 47.7g, of which sugars 10.2g; Fat 31g, of which saturates 12.5g; Cholesterol 75mg; Calcium 284mg; Fibre 10.7g; Sodium 1179mg.

BRAISED CABBAGE SOUP WITH BEEF AND HORSERADISH CREAM

THIS BRILLIANT WINTER SOUP REALLY IS A COMPLETE MAIN COURSE IN A BOWL. THE JOINT OF BEEF CAN BE COOKED AS RARE OR AS WELL DONE AS YOU LIKE.

SERVES 6

INGREDIENTS
900g/2lb red cabbage, hard core
    discarded and leaves shredded
2 onions, finely sliced
1 large cooking apple, peeled, cored
    and chopped
45ml/3 tbsp soft light brown sugar
2 garlic cloves, crushed
1.5ml/¼ tsp grated nutmeg
2.5ml/½ tsp caraway seeds
45ml/3 tbsp red wine vinegar
1 litre/1¾ pints/4 cups beef stock
675kg/1½lb sirloin joint
30ml/2 tbsp olive oil
salt and ground black pepper
watercress, to garnish
For the horseradish cream
    15–30ml/1–2 tbsp fresh horseradish
    10ml/2 tsp wine vinegar
    2.5ml/½ tsp Dijon mustard
    150ml/¼ pint/⅔ cup double
        (heavy) cream

1 Preheat the oven to 150°C/300°F/ Gas 2. Mix together the first eight ingredients and 45ml/3 tbsp of the stock. Add plenty of seasoning, then put into a large buttered casserole and cover with a tight-fitting lid.

2 Bake for 2½ hours, checking every 30 minutes or so to ensure that the cabbage is not becoming too dry. If necessary, add a few more tablespoons of the stock. Remove the casserole from the oven and set aside. Increase the oven temperature to 230°C/450°F/ Gas 8.

3 Trim off most of the fat from the sirloin, leaving a thin layer. Tie the joint with string. Heat the oil in a heavy frying pan until smoking. Add the beef and cook until well browned all over.

4 Transfer to a roasting tin and roast for about 15–20 minutes for medium-rare or 25–30 minutes for well-done beef.

5 For the horseradish cream, grate the horseradish and mix with the wine vinegar, mustard and seasoning into 45ml/3 tbsp of the cream. Lightly whip the remaining cream and fold in the horseradish mixture. Chill until required.

6 Spoon the braised cabbage into a saucepan and pour in the remaining stock. Bring just to boiling point.

7 Remove the beef from the oven and leave to rest for 5 minutes, then remove the string and carve into slices.

8 Ladle the soup into bowls and divide the beef among them, resting on the cabbage. Spoon a little horseradish cream on to each serving of beef, and garnish with small bunches of watercress. Serve at once.

Energy 395kcal/1645kJ; Protein 29.4g; Carbohydrate 19.4g, of which sugars 18.5g; Fat 22.5g, of which saturates 11.1g; Cholesterol 92mg; Calcium 104mg; Fibre 3.8g; Sodium 97mg.

IRISH BACON BROTH

A HEARTY MEAL IN A SOUP BOWL. THE BACON HOCK CONTRIBUTES FLAVOUR AND SOME MEAT TO THIS DISH, BUT IT MAY BE SALTY SO REMEMBER TO TASTE AND ADD EXTRA SALT ONLY IF REQUIRED.

SERVES 6–8

INGREDIENTS

1 bacon hock, about 900g/2lb
75g/3oz/⅓ cup pearl barley
75g/3oz/⅓ cup lentils
2 leeks, sliced, or onions, diced
4 carrots, diced
200g/7oz swede (rutabaga), diced
3 potatoes, diced
small bunch of herbs (thyme, parsley, bay leaf)
1 small cabbage, trimmed and quartered or sliced
salt and ground black pepper
chopped fresh parsley, to garnish
brown bread, to serve

COOK'S TIP
Traditionally, the cabbage is simply trimmed and quartered, although it may be sliced if you prefer.

1 Soak the bacon in cold water overnight. Next morning, drain, put into a large pan and cover with cold water. Bring to the boil and skim off any scum. Add the barley and lentils. Bring back to the boil and simmer for 15 minutes.

2 Add the vegetables, some black pepper and the herbs. Bring back to the boil, reduce the heat and simmer gently for 1½ hours, or until the meat is tender.

3 Lift the bacon hock from the pan with a slotted spoon. Remove the skin, then take the meat off the bones and break it into bitesize pieces. Return to the pan with the cabbage. Discard the herbs and cook for a little longer until the cabbage is cooked to your liking.

4 Adjust the seasoning and ladle into serving bowls, garnish with parsley and serve with freshly baked brown bread.

Energy 276kcal/1166kJ; Protein 26.6g; Carbohydrate 33.6g, of which sugars 8.4g; Fat 4.8g, of which saturates 1.6g; Cholesterol 13mg; Calcium 87mg; Fibre 4.8g; Sodium 765mg.

IRISH KIDNEY AND BACON SOUP

ALTHOUGH THERE IS A MODERN TWIST IN THE SEASONINGS, THE TWO MAIN INGREDIENTS OF THIS MEATY SOUP ARE STILL VERY TRADITIONALLY IRISH.

SERVES 4–6

INGREDIENTS

225g/8oz ox (beef) kidney
15ml/1 tbsp vegetable oil
4 streaky (fatty) bacon rashers
  (strips), chopped
1 large onion, chopped
2 garlic cloves, finely chopped
15ml/1 tbsp plain (all-purpose) flour
1.5 litres/2½ pints/6¼ cups water
a good dash of Worcestershire sauce
a good dash of soy sauce
15ml/1 tbsp chopped fresh thyme,
  or 5ml/1 tsp dried
75g/3oz/¾ cup grated cheese
4–6 slices French bread, toasted
salt and ground black pepper

1 Wash the kidney in cold, salted water. Drain, dry well on kitchen paper and chop into small pieces.

COOK'S TIP
Ox (beef) kidneys are tougher than veal or lamb, so need to be cooked more slowly.

2 Heat the vegetable oil in a large pan over a medium heat. Add the chopped streaky bacon and sauté for a few minutes. Add the prepared kidney and continue cooking until nicely browned. Stir in the chopped onion and chopped garlic, and cook until the onion is just soft but not browned.

3 Add the flour and cook for 2 minutes. Gradually add the water, stirring constantly. Add the sauces, thyme and seasoning to taste. Reduce the heat and simmer gently for 30–35 minutes.

4 Sprinkle the cheese on to the toast and grill until it is bubbling. Pour the soup into bowls, and top with the bread.

Energy 379kcal/1592kJ; Protein 23.7g; Carbohydrate 34g, of which sugars 3.2g; Fat 17g, of which saturates 7.1g; Cholesterol 184mg; Calcium 225mg, Fibre 1.6g; Sodium 1167mg.

GOLDEN CHORIZO AND CHICKPEA SOUP

THIS HEARTY SPANISH SOUP IS SUBSTANTIAL ENOUGH TO MAKE A COMPLETE MEAL. SMALL UNCOOKED CHORIZO SAUSAGES ARE AVAILABLE FROM SPANISH DELICATESSENS, BUT READY-TO-EAT CHORIZO CAN BE CUT INTO CHUNKS AND USED INSTEAD.

SERVES 4

INGREDIENTS
115g/4oz/⅔ cup dried chickpeas
pinch of saffron strands
45ml/3 tbsp olive oil
450g/1lb uncooked mini chorizo
  sausages
5ml/1 tsp dried chilli flakes
6 garlic cloves, finely chopped
450g/1lb tomatoes, roughly chopped
350g/12oz new potatoes, quartered
2 bay leaves
450ml/¾ pint/scant 2 cups water
60ml/4 tbsp chopped fresh parsley
salt and ground black pepper
30ml/2 tbsp extra virgin olive oil,
  to garnish
crusty bread, to serve

1 Put the chickpeas in a large bowl, cover with plenty of cold water and leave to soak overnight.

2 Next day, drain and place in a large pan. Cover with plenty of fresh water and bring to the boil, skimming off any scum as it forms. Cover and simmer for 2–3 hours, until tender. Add more boiling water, if necessary, to keep the chickpeas well covered during cooking. Drain, reserving the cooking liquid.

3 Heat the oil in a large, deep frying pan. Add the chorizo sausages and fry over a medium heat for 5 minutes, until a lot of oil has seeped out of the sausages and they are pale golden brown. Drain and set aside.

4 Soak the saffron strands in a little warm water.

5 Add the chilli flakes and garlic to the fat in the frying pan and cook for a few seconds. Stir in the saffron with its soaking water, the chopped tomatoes, chickpeas, potatoes, chorizo sausages and bay leaves. Pour in 450ml/¾ pint/ scant 2 cups of the chickpea cooking liquor and the water, and stir in salt and pepper to taste.

6 Bring to the boil, then reduce the heat and simmer for 45–50 minutes, stirring gently occasionally, until the potatoes are tender and the soup has thickened slightly.

7 Add the chopped parsley to the soup and adjust the seasoning. Ladle the soup into four large, warmed soup plates and drizzle a little extra virgin olive oil over each portion. Serve with crusty bread.

Energy 642kcal/2674kJ; Protein 21.7g; Carbohydrate 42.3g, of which sugars 8.1g; Fat 44g, of which saturates 12.5g; Cholesterol 68mg; Calcium 174mg; Fibre 6.1g; Sodium 997mg.

KALE, CHORIZO AND POTATO SOUP

THIS HEARTY WINTER SOUP HAS A SPICY KICK TO IT, WHICH COMES FROM THE CHORIZO SAUSAGE.
THE SOUP BECOMES MORE POTENT IF CHILLED OVERNIGHT. IT IS WORTH BUYING THE BEST POSSIBLE
CHORIZO SAUSAGE TO IMPROVE THE FLAVOUR.

SERVES 6–8

INGREDIENTS
  225g/8oz kale, stems removed
  225g/8oz chorizo sausage
  675g/1½lb red potatoes
  1.75 litres/3 pints/7½ cups
    vegetable stock
  5ml/1 tsp ground black pepper
  pinch cayenne pepper (optional)
  12 slices French bread, grilled
    (broiled)
  salt and ground black pepper

1 Process the kale in a food processor
for a few seconds to chop it finely.

2 Prick the sausages and place in
a pan with enough water to cover.
Simmer for 15 minutes. Drain and
cut into thin slices.

3 Cook the potatoes in lightly salted
boiling water for about 15 minutes or
until tender. Drain and place in a bowl,
then mash, adding a little of the cooking
liquid to form a thick paste.

COOK'S TIP
Chorizo sausage is usually sold whole or
cut into lengths or rounds.

4 Bring the vegetable stock to the boil
and add the kale. Add the chorizo and
simmer for 5 minutes. Add the paste
gradually, and simmer for 20 minutes.
Season with black pepper and cayenne.

5 Place bread slices in each bowl, and
pour over the soup. Serve, generously
sprinkled with pepper.

Energy 411kcal/1740kJ; Protein 13.2g; Carbohydrate 69.3g, of which sugars 6.2g; Fat 11g, of which saturates 4.1g; Cholesterol 15mg; Calcium 140mg; Fibre 4g; Sodium 812mg.

CELERIAC SOUP WITH CABBAGE, BACON AND HERBS

VERSATILE, YET OFTEN OVERLOOKED, CELERIAC IS A WINTER VEGETABLE THAT MAKES EXCELLENT SOUP. IT TASTES WONDERFUL TOPPED WITH A COMPLEMENTARY SEASONAL VERSION OF A SALSA.

SERVES 4

INGREDIENTS
  50g/2oz butter
  2 onions, chopped
  675g/1½lb celeriac,
    roughly diced
  450g/1lb potatoes, roughly diced
  1.2 litres/2 pints/5 cups
    vegetable stock
  150ml/¼ pint/⅔ cup single
    (light) cream
  salt and ground black pepper
  sprigs of fresh thyme, to garnish
For the cabbage and bacon topping
  1 small savoy cabbage
  50g/2oz/¼ cup butter
  175g/6oz rindless streaky (fatty)
    bacon, roughly chopped
  15ml/1 tbsp chopped fresh thyme
  15ml/1 tbsp chopped fresh rosemary

1 Melt the butter in a pan. Add the onions and cook for 4–5 minutes, until softened. Add the celeriac. Cover the vegetables with a wetted piece of baking parchment, then put a lid on the pan and cook gently for 10 minutes.

2 Remove the paper. Stir in the potatoes and stock, bring to the boil, reduce the heat and simmer for 20 minutes. Leave to cool slightly. Using a slotted spoon, remove half the celeriac and potatoes from the soup and set them aside.

3 Purée the soup in a food processor or blender. Return the soup to the pan with the reserved celeriac and potatoes.

4 Prepare the cabbage and bacon mixture. Discard the tough outer leaves from the cabbage. Roughly tear the remaining leaves, discarding any hard stalks, and blanch them in boiling salted water for 2–3 minutes. Refresh under cold running water and drain.

5 Melt the butter in a large frying pan and cook the bacon for 3–4 minutes. Add the cabbage, thyme and rosemary, and stir-fry for 5–6 minutes, until tender. Season well.

6 Add the cream to the soup and season it well, then reheat gently until piping hot.

7 Ladle the soup into warmed bowls and pile the cabbage mixture in the centre of each portion. Garnish with sprigs of fresh thyme.

VARIATION
Savoy cabbage is used for the topping in this dish, but other greens, such as kale or spring greens, would also be suitable.

Energy 462kcal/1919kJ; Protein 12.3g; Carbohydrate 24.3g, of which sugars 7.3g; Fat 35.7g, of which saturates 20.4g; Cholesterol 97mg; Calcium 144mg; Fibre 4.3g; Sodium 954mg.

BACON <u>AND</u> CHICKPEA SOUP
<u>WITH</u> TORTILLA CHIPS

THIS SILKY-SMOOTH NUTTY SOUP IS ABSOLUTELY DELICIOUS AND SO EASY TO MAKE. TAKE IT TO THE SOFA WITH A BOWL OF WARM AND SPICY TORTILLA CHIPS AND DIP, CRUNCH AND SLURP YOUR WAY THROUGH YOUR FAVOURITE TELEVISION FIX.

SERVES 4–6

INGREDIENTS
  400g/14oz/2 cups dried chickpeas,
    soaked overnight in cold water
  115g/4oz/½ cup butter
  150g/5oz pancetta or streaky (fatty)
    bacon, roughly chopped
  2 onions, finely chopped
  1 carrot, chopped
  1 celery stick, chopped
  15ml/1 tbsp chopped fresh rosemary
  2 fresh bay leaves
  2 garlic cloves, halved
For the tortilla chips
  75g/3oz/6 tbsp butter
  2.5ml/½ tsp sweet paprika
  1.5ml/¼ tsp ground cumin
  175g/6oz plain tortilla chips
  salt and ground black pepper

1 Drain the chickpeas, put them in a large pan and cover with plenty of cold water. Bring to the boil and simmer for about 20 minutes. Strain and set aside.

2 Melt the butter in a large pan and add the pancetta or bacon. Fry over a medium heat until just beginning to turn golden. Add the chopped vegetables and cook for 5–10 minutes until soft.

COOK'S TIP
Packets of diced bacon are available in most supermarkets, and these are ideal for adding to soups.

3 Add the chickpeas to the pan with the rosemary, bay leaves, garlic cloves and enough water to cover completely. Bring to the boil, half cover, turn down the heat and simmer for 45–60 minutes, stirring occasionally. (The chickpeas should start to disintegrate and will thicken the soup.)

4 Allow the soup to cool slightly, then pour it into a blender or food processor and process until smooth. Return the soup to the rinsed-out pan, taste and season with salt and plenty of black pepper. Reheat gently.

5 To make the tortilla chips, preheat the oven to 180°C/350°F/Gas 4. Melt the butter with the paprika and cumin in a pan, then lightly brush the mixture over the tortilla chips. Reserve any leftover spiced butter.

6 Spread the chips out on a baking sheet and warm through in the oven for 5 minutes.

7 Ladle the soup into bowls, pour some of the reserved spiced butter over each and sprinkle with a little paprika. Serve with the warm tortilla chips.

Energy 996kcal/4154kJ; Protein 31.4g; Carbohydrate 80.1g, of which sugars 6.6g; Fat 63.3g, of which saturates 30.1g; Cholesterol 126mg; Calcium 252mg; Fibre 14.3g; Sodium 1186mg.

INDIAN BEEF AND BERRY SOUP

THE FRESH BERRIES GIVE THIS UNUSUAL SOUP A PLEASANT KICK. THIS IS AN IDEAL SOUP TO SERVE ON A REALLY COLD DAY, AS IT IS WARMING AND FILLING WITH A COMFORTING SWEETNESS.

SERVES 4

INGREDIENTS

30ml/2 tbsp vegetable oil
450g/1lb tender beef steak
2 medium onions, finely sliced
25g/1oz/2 tbsp butter
1 litre/1¾ pints/4 cups good beef
   stock or bouillon
2.5ml/½ tsp salt
115g/4oz/1 cup fresh huckleberries,
   blueberries or blackberries, lightly
   mashed
15ml/1 tbsp honey

1 Heat the oil in a heavy pan until almost smoking. Add the steak and brown on both sides over a medium-high heat. Remove the steak from the pan and set aside.

2 Reduce the heat to low and add the sliced onions and butter to the pan. Stir well, scraping up the meat juices. Cook over a low heat until the onions are soft.

3 Add the beef stock or bouillon and salt and bring to the boil, stirring well. Mix in the mashed berries and the honey. Simmer for 20 minutes.

4 Meanwhile, cut the steak into thin, bite-size slivers. Taste the soup and add more salt or honey if necessary. Add the steak to the pan. Cook gently for 30 seconds, stirring, then serve hot.

COOK'S TIP
For best results, use a good home-made beef stock (see page 32).

Energy 338kcal/1404kJ; Protein 26.8g; Carbohydrate 10.3g, of which sugars 8.6g; Fat 21.3g, of which saturates 8.2g; Cholesterol 79mg; Calcium 38mg; Fibre 2g; Sodium 113mg.

TOMATO AND BEEF SOUP

FRESH TOMATOES AND SPRING ONIONS GIVE THIS LIGHT BEEF BROTH A SUPERB FLAVOUR AND APPEARANCE. GARNISH THE SOUP WITH SHREDDED SPRING ONIONS.

SERVES 4

INGREDIENTS

75g/3oz rump (round) steak,
  trimmed of fat
900ml/1½ pints/3¾ cups beef stock
30ml/2 tbsp tomato purée (paste)
6 tomatoes, halved, seeded
  and chopped
10ml/2 tsp caster (superfine) sugar
15ml/1 tbsp cornflour (cornstarch)
15ml/1 tbsp cold water
1 egg white
2.5ml/½ tsp sesame oil
2 spring onions (scallions), shredded
salt and ground black pepper

1 Cut the beef into thin strips and place it in a pan. Pour over boiling water to cover. Cook for 2 minutes, then drain thoroughly and set aside.

2 Bring the stock to the boil in a clean pan. Stir in the tomato purée, then the tomatoes and sugar. Add the beef, allow the stock to boil again, then lower the heat and simmer for 2 minutes.

3 Mix the cornflour to a thin paste with the cold water. Add the paste to the soup, stirring constantly until it thickens slightly but does not become lumpy.

4 Lightly beat the egg white in a small bowl.

5 Pour the egg white into the soup in a steady stream, stirring all the time. As soon as the egg white changes colour, add salt and pepper, stir the soup and pour it into heated bowls.

6 Drizzle sesame oil on each portion, sprinkle with spring onions and serve.

Energy 79kcal/337kJ; Protein 6.2g; Carbohydrate 11.1g, of which sugars 7.6g; Fat 1.5g, of which saturates 0.5g; Cholesterol 11mg; Calcium 16mg; Fibre 1.5g; Sodium 58mg.

CLEAR SOUP <u>WITH</u> MEATBALLS

A CHINESE-STYLE SOUP, IN WHICH TINY MEATBALLS ARE COMBINED WITH LIGHTLY COOKED VEGETABLES IN A TASTY AND FRAGRANT STOCK.

SERVES 8

INGREDIENTS
    4–6 Chinese mushrooms, soaked in
      warm water for 30 minutes
    30ml/2 tbsp groundnut (peanut) oil
    1 large onion, finely chopped
    2 garlic cloves, finely crushed
    1cm/½in piece fresh root ginger,
      bruised
    2 litres/3½ pints/9 cups beef or
      chicken stock, including soaking
      liquid from the mushrooms
    30ml/2 tbsp soy sauce
    115g/4oz curly kale, spinach or
      Chinese leaves (Chinese cabbage),
      shredded
For the meatballs
    175g/6oz/¾ cup finely minced
      (ground) beef
    1 small onion, finely chopped
    1 or 2 garlic cloves, crushed
    15ml/1 tbsp cornflour (cornstarch)
    a little egg white, lightly beaten
    salt and ground black pepper

1 First prepare the meatballs. Mix the beef with the onion, garlic, cornflour and seasoning in a food processor and then bind with sufficient egg white to make a firm mixture. With wet hands, roll into tiny, bite-size balls and set aside.

2 Drain the mushrooms. Add the soaking liquid to the stock. Trim off and discard the stalks. Slice the caps finely and set aside.

3 Heat a wok or large pan and add the oil. Fry the onion, garlic and ginger for 2–3 minutes to bring out the flavour, but do not allow to brown.

4 When the onion is soft, pour in the stock. Bring to the boil, then stir in the soy sauce and mushroom slices and simmer for 10 minutes.

5 Add the meatballs and cook for a further 10 minutes.

6 Just before serving, remove the ginger. Stir in the shredded curly kale, spinach or Chinese leaves. Heat through for 1 minute only – no longer or the leaves will be overcooked. Ladle the soup into warmed bowls and serve immediately, piping hot.

SPINACH AND LEMON SOUP WITH MEATBALLS

THIS SOUP, KNOWN AS AARSHE SAAK, *IS ALMOST STANDARD FARE IN MANY PARTS OF THE* MIDDLE
EAST. IN GREECE, *IT IS MADE WITHOUT THE MEATBALLS AND IS SIMPLY CALLED* AVGOLEMONO.

SERVES 6

INGREDIENTS
2 large onions
45ml/3 tbsp oil
15ml/1 tbsp ground turmeric
115g/4oz/½ cup yellow split peas
1.2 litres/2 pints/5 cups water
225g/8oz minced (ground) lamb
450g/1lb spinach, chopped
50g/2oz/½ cup rice flour
juice of 2 lemons
1 or 2 garlic cloves, finely chopped
30ml/2 tbsp chopped fresh mint
4 eggs
salt and ground black pepper
sprigs of fresh mint, to garnish

1 Chop one of the onions and fry in
30ml/2 tbsp of the oil in a large pan
until golden. Add the turmeric, peas
and water and bring to the boil. Simmer
for 20 minutes.

2 Grate the other onion into a bowl, add
the lamb and seasoning and mix well.
Using your hands, form the mixture into
small balls, about the size of walnuts.
Carefully add to the pan and simmer for
10 minutes, then add the spinach,
cover and simmer for 20 minutes.

3 Mix the flour with about 250ml/
8fl oz/1 cup cold water to make a
smooth paste, then slowly add to the
pan, stirring all the time. Add the lemon
juice, season and cook over a gentle
heat for 20 minutes.

4 Meanwhile, heat the remaining oil in a
small pan and fry the garlic briefly until
golden. Stir in the mint and remove the
pan from the heat.

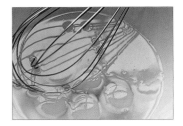

5 Break the eggs into a small bowl and
beat with an egg whisk.

6 Remove the soup from the heat
and stir in the beaten eggs. Ladle into
warmed soup bowls.

7 Sprinkle the prepared garlic and mint
mixture over the soup, garnish with
mint sprigs and serve immediately.

Energy 316kcal/1318kJ; Protein 19.8g; Carbohydrate 25.7g, of which sugars 6.3g; Fat 15.3g, of which saturates 4.1g; Cholesterol 156mg; Calcium 203mg; Fibre 3.9g; Sodium 189mg.

ONION <u>AND</u> PANCETTA SOUP

THIS SOUP COMES FROM UMBRIA, WHERE IT IS SOMETIMES THICKENED WITH BEATEN EGGS AND PLENTY OF GRATED PARMESAN CHEESE. IT IS THEN SERVED ON TOP OF HOT TOASTED CROÛTES.

SERVES 4

INGREDIENTS
  115g/4oz pancetta rashers (strips),
    rinds removed, roughly chopped
  30ml/2 tbsp olive oil
  15g/½oz/1 tbsp butter
  675g/1½lb onions, finely sliced
  10ml/2 tsp granulated sugar
  about 1.2 litres/2 pints/5 cups
    chicken stock
  350g/12oz ripe Italian plum
    tomatoes, peeled and roughly
    chopped
  a few fresh basil leaves, shredded
  salt and ground black pepper
  grated Parmesan cheese, to serve

1 Put the chopped pancetta in a large pan and heat gently, stirring constantly, until the fat runs. Increase the heat to medium, add the oil, butter, sliced onions and sugar and stir well to mix all the ingredients.

2 Half-cover the pan and cook the onions gently for about 20 minutes until golden. Stir frequently and lower the heat if necessary.

3 Add the stock, tomatoes and salt and pepper and bring to the boil, stirring. Lower the heat, half-cover the pan and simmer, stirring occasionally, for about 30 minutes.

4 Check the consistency of the soup and add a little more stock or water if it is too thick.

5 Just before serving, stir in most of the basil and adjust the seasoning to taste. Serve hot, garnished with the remaining shredded basil. Hand round the freshly grated Parmesan separately.

COOK'S TIP
Look for Vidalia onions to make this soup. They are available at large supermarkets, and have a sweet flavour and attractive, yellowish flesh.

BEEF CHILLI SOUP

THIS IS A HEARTY DISH BASED ON A TRADITIONAL CHILLI RECIPE. IT IS IDEAL SERVED WITH FRESH, CRUSTY BREAD AS A WARMING START TO ANY MEAL.

SERVES 4

INGREDIENTS
   15ml/1 tbsp oil
   1 onion, chopped
   175g/6oz/¾ cup minced
      (ground) beef
   2 garlic cloves, chopped
   1 fresh red chilli, sliced
   25g/1oz/¼ cup plain (all-purpose)
      flour
   400g/14oz can chopped tomatoes
   600ml/1 pint/2½ cups beef stock
   225g/8oz/2 cups canned kidney
      beans, drained
   30ml/2 tbsp chopped fresh parsley
   salt and ground black pepper
   crusty bread, to serve

1 Heat the oil in a large pan. Fry the onion and minced beef for 5 minutes until brown and sealed.

2 Add the garlic, chilli and flour. Cook for 1 minute. Add the tomatoes and pour in the stock. Bring to the boil.

COOK'S TIPS
• For a milder flavour, remove the seeds from the chilli after slicing it. Wear rubber gloves to protect your skin when handling chillies.
• You can use dried red kidney beans instead of canned ones, but they must be soaked overnight in cold water. Next day, boil them rapidly for 15 minutes before reducing the heat and simmering for at least an hour until tender.
• Use home-made beef stock (see page 32) for a better flavour.

3 Stir in the drained kidney beans and add salt and pepper to taste. Cook for 20 minutes.

4 Add the chopped parsley, reserving a little to garnish the finished dish. Pour the soup into warm bowls, sprinkle with the reserved parsley and serve with crusty bread.

Energy 226kcal/946kJ; Protein 14.2g; Carbohydrate 19.4g, of which sugars 6.2g; Fat 10.7g, of which saturates 3.5g; Cholesterol 26mg; Calcium 79mg; Fibre 5.3g; Sodium 267mg.

WONTON SOUP

IN CHINA, WONTON SOUP IS SERVED AS A SNACK, OR DIM SUM, RATHER THAN AS A SOUP COURSE DURING A LARGE MEAL. IT IS A FRESH-TASTING, DELICATELY FLAVOURED SOUP.

SERVES 4

INGREDIENTS
175g/6oz pork, not too lean, roughly chopped
50g/2oz peeled prawns (shrimp), finely chopped
5ml/1 tsp light brown sugar
15ml/1 tbsp Chinese rice wine or dry sherry
15ml/1 tbsp light soy sauce
5ml/1 tsp finely chopped spring onions (scallions)
5ml/1 tsp finely chopped fresh root ginger
24 ready-made wonton wrappers
about 750ml/1¼ pints/3 cups stock
15ml/1 tbsp light soy sauce
finely chopped spring onions (scallions), to garnish

1 In a bowl, thoroughly mix the chopped pork and prawns with the sugar, rice wine or sherry, soy sauce, spring onions and ginger. Set aside for 25–30 minutes for the flavours to blend.

COOK'S TIP
Use a vegetable or light chicken stock (see pages 30–1) for this soup.

2 Place about 5ml/1 tsp of the pork and prawn mixture in the centre of each wonton wrapper.

3 Wet the edges of each filled wonton wrapper with a little water and press them together with your fingers to seal. Fold each wonton parcel over.

4 To cook, bring the stock to a rolling boil in a wok, add the wontons and cook for 4–5 minutes. Season with the soy sauce and add the spring onions.

5 Ladle into warmed individual soup bowls and serve hot.

Energy 134kcal/568kJ; Protein 13.6g; Carbohydrate 16.3g, of which sugars 1.9g; Fat 2.1g, of which saturates 0.7g; Cholesterol 52mg; Calcium 42mg; Fibre 0.6g; Sodium 589mg.

PORK AND VEGETABLE SOUP

THE UNUSUAL INGREDIENTS IN THIS INTERESTING JAPANESE SOUP ARE AVAILABLE FROM SPECIALIST
FOOD STORES AND JAPANESE SUPERMARKETS.

SERVES FOUR

INGREDIENTS
   50g/2oz gobo (optional)
   5ml/1 tsp rice vinegar
   ½ black konnyaku (about 115g/4oz)
   10ml/2 tsp oil
   200g/7oz pork belly, cut into thin
     3–4cm/1¼–½ in-long strips
   115g/4oz mooli (daikon), peeled and
     thinly sliced
   50g/2oz carrot, thinly sliced
   1 medium potato, thinly sliced
   4 shiitake mushrooms, stems
     removed and thinly sliced
   800ml/scant 1½ pints/3½ cups
     kombu and bonito stock or
     instant dashi
   15ml/1 tbsp *sake* or dry white wine
   45ml/3 tbsp red or white miso paste
For the garnish
   2 spring onions, thinly sliced
   seven-spice flavour (shichimi)

1 Scrub the skin off the gobo, if using, with a vegetable brush. Slice the vegetable into fine shavings. Soak the prepared gobo for 5 minutes in plenty of water with the vinegar added to remove any bitter taste, then drain.

2 Put the piece of konnyaku in a small pan and add enough water just to cover it. Bring to the boil over a moderate heat, then drain and allow to cool. This removes any bitter taste.

3 Using your hands, tear the konnyaku into 2cm/¾in lumps. Do not use a knife as a smooth cut surface will not absorb any flavour.

4 Heat the oil in a large pan and quickly stir-fry the pork. Add the gobo, if using, mooli, carrot, potato, shiitake mushrooms and konnyaku, then stir-fry for 1 minute. Pour in the stock and sake or wine.

5 Bring the soup to the boil, then skim it and simmer for 10 minutes, until the vegetables have softened.

6 Ladle a little of the soup into a small bowl and dissolve the miso paste in it. Pour back into the pan and bring to the boil once more. Do not continue to boil or the flavour will be lost. Remove from the heat, then pour into individual warmed serving bowls.

7 Sprinkle with the spring onions and seven-spice flavour (shichimi) and serve.

Energy 245kcal/1017kJ; Protein 9.7g; Carbohydrate 8.8g, of which sugars 2.2g; Fat 19g, of which saturates 6.8g; Cholesterol 36mg; Calcium 19mg; Fibre 1.6g; Sodium 51mg.

FISH SOUPS

Fish soups are always delicious and can be eaten either as a first course or as an entire meal. Chunky, hearty soups such as Matelote, Smoked Haddock and Potato Soup, and Fish Soup with Tomatoes and Mushrooms are perfect for a winter lunch or supper. Sophisticated soups such as Pad Thai Red Monkfish Soup, Bourride of Red Mullet and Fennel, and Soup Niçoise with Seared Tuna are great for entertaining and sure to impress your guests.

FISH SOUP WITH TOMATOES AND MUSHROOMS

WITH SOME FRESH CRUSTY HOME-MADE BROWN BREAD OR GARLIC BREAD, THIS QUICK-AND-EASY SOUP CAN BE SERVED LIKE A STEW AND WILL MAKE A DELICIOUS FIRST COURSE OR SUPPER.

SERVES 6

INGREDIENTS
25g/1oz/2 tbsp butter
1 onion, finely chopped
1 garlic clove, crushed
1 small red (bell) pepper, chopped
2.5ml/½ tsp sugar
a dash of Tabasco sauce
25g/1oz/¼ cup plain
  (all-purpose) flour
600ml/1 pint/2½ cups fish stock
400g/14oz can chopped tomatoes
115g/4oz/1½ cups mushrooms,
  chopped
about 300ml/½ pint/1¼ cups milk
225g/8oz white fish, cut into cubes
115g/4oz smoked haddock or cod,
  skinned, and cut into bitesize cubes
12–18 mussels, cleaned (optional)
salt and ground black pepper
chopped fresh parsley, to garnish

1 Melt the butter in a large heavy pan and cook the chopped onion and crushed garlic gently in it until they are softened but not browned.

2 Add the chopped red pepper. Season with salt and pepper, the sugar and Tabasco sauce.

3 Sprinkle the flour over and cook gently for 2 minutes, stirring.

4 Gradually stir in the stock and add the canned tomatoes, with their juices and the mushrooms.

5 Bring to the boil over medium heat, stir well, then reduce the heat and simmer gently until the vegetables are soft. Add the milk and bring back to the boil. Add the fish to the pan and simmer for 3 minutes.

6 Add the mussels, if using, and cook for another 3–4 minutes, or until the fish is just tender but not breaking up. Discard any mussels that remain closed. Adjust the consistency with a little extra fish stock or milk, if necessary. Check the seasoning.

7 Ladle the soup into six warmed bowls and serve piping hot, garnished with chopped parsley.

Energy 132kcal/556kJ; Protein 15.6g; Carbohydrate 8g, of which sugars 4.5g; Fat 4.4g, of which saturates 2.4g; Cholesterol 40mg; Calcium 29mg; Fibre 1.6g; Sodium 341mg.

FISH SOUP WITH ROUILLE

MAKING THIS SOUP IS SIMPLICITY ITSELF, YET THE FLAVOUR SUGGESTS IT IS THE PRODUCT OF PAINSTAKING PREPARATION AND COOKING.

SERVES 6

INGREDIENTS
    1kg/2¼lb mixed fish
    30ml/2 tbsp olive oil
    1 onion, chopped
    1 carrot, chopped
    1 leek, chopped
    2 large ripe tomatoes, chopped
    1 red (bell) pepper, seeded
      and chopped
    2 garlic cloves, peeled
    150g/5oz/⅔ cup tomato
      purée (paste)
    1 large fresh bouquet garni
    300ml/½ pint/1¼ cups dry
      white wine
    salt and ground black pepper
For the rouille
    2 garlic cloves, roughly chopped
    5ml/1 tsp coarse salt
    1 thick slice of white bread, crust
      removed, soaked in water and
      squeezed dry
    1 fresh red chilli, seeded and
      roughly chopped
    45ml/3 tbsp olive oil
    salt and cayenne pepper
For the garnish
    12 slices of baguette, toasted in
      the oven
    50g/2oz Gruyère cheese,
      finely grated

1 Cut the fish into 7.5cm/3in chunks, removing any obvious bones. Heat the oil in a large pan, then add the fish and chopped vegetables. Stir until these begin to colour.

2 Add all the other soup ingredients, then pour in just enough cold water to cover the mixture. Season well and bring to just below boiling point, then lower the heat to a bare simmer, cover and cook for 1 hour.

3 Meanwhile, make the rouille. Put the garlic and coarse salt in a mortar and crush to a paste with a pestle. Add the soaked bread and chilli and pound until smooth, or purée in a food processor. Whisk in the olive oil, a drop at a time, to make a smooth, shiny sauce that resembles mayonnaise. Season with salt and add a pinch of cayenne if you like a fiery taste. Set the rouille aside.

4 Lift out and discard the bouquet garni from the soup. Purée the soup in batches in a food processor, then strain through a fine sieve (strainer) placed over a clean pan, pushing the solids through with the back of a ladle.

5 Reheat the soup without letting it boil. Check the seasoning and ladle into individual bowls. Top each serving with two slices of toasted baguette, a spoonful of rouille and some grated Gruyère.

COOK'S TIP
Any firm fish can be used for this recipe. If you use whole fish, include the heads, which enhance the flavour of the soup.

THAI FISH BROTH

LEMON GRASS, CHILLIES AND GALANGAL ARE AMONG THE FLAVOURINGS USED IN THIS FRAGRANT SOUP.

SERVES 2–3

INGREDIENTS

1 litre/1¾ pints/4 cups fish or
   light chicken stock
4 lemon grass stalks
3 limes
2 small fresh hot red chillies,
   seeded and thinly sliced
2cm/¾ in piece fresh galangal,
   peeled and thinly sliced
6 coriander (cilantro) stalks and leaves
2 kaffir lime leaves, coarsely
   chopped (optional)
350g/12oz monkfish fillet, skinned
   and cut into 2.5cm/1in pieces
15ml/1 tbsp rice vinegar
45ml/3 tbsp Thai fish sauce
30ml/2 tbsp chopped coriander
   leaves, to garnish

1 Pour the stock into a pan and bring it to the boil. Meanwhile, slice the bulb end of each lemon grass stalk diagonally into pieces about 3mm/⅛in thick. Peel off four wide strips of lime rind with a potato peeler, taking care to avoid the white pith underneath which would make the soup bitter. Squeeze the limes and reserve the juice.

2 Add the sliced lemon grass, lime rind, chillies, galangal and coriander stalks to the stock, with the kaffir lime leaves, if using. Simmer for 1–2 minutes.

VARIATIONS
• Prawns (shrimp), scallops, squid or sole can be substituted for the monkfish.
• If you use kaffir lime leaves, you will need the juice of only 2 limes.

3 Add the monkfish, rice vinegar and fish sauce, with half the reserved lime juice. Simmer for about 3 minutes, until the fish is just cooked. Lift out and discard the coriander stalks, taste the broth and add more lime juice if necessary; the soup should taste quite sour. Sprinkle with the coriander leaves and serve very hot.

Energy 124kcal/529kJ; Protein 28.3g; Carbohydrate 0.7g, of which sugars 0.6g; Fat 1g, of which saturates 0.2g; Cholesterol 25mg; Calcium 64mg; Fibre 1.3g; Sodium 40mg.

PAD THAI RED MONKFISH SOUP

THIS LIGHT COCONUT SOUP IS BASED ON THAILAND'S CLASSIC STIR-FRIED NOODLE DISH.

SERVES 4

INGREDIENTS
175g/6oz flat rice noodles
30ml/2 tbsp vegetable oil
2 garlic cloves, chopped
15ml/1 tbsp red curry paste
450g/1lb monkfish tail, cut into
  bite-size pieces
300ml/½ pint/1¼ cups
  coconut cream
750ml/1¼ pints/3 cups hot
  chicken stock
45ml/3 tbsp Thai fish sauce
15ml/1 tbsp palm sugar
60ml/4 tbsp roughly chopped
  roasted peanuts
4 spring onions (scallions),
  shredded lengthways
50g/2oz beansprouts
large handful of fresh Thai
  basil leaves
salt and ground black pepper
1 red chilli, seeded and cut
  lengthways into slivers,
  to garnish

1 Soak the noodles in boiling water for 10 minutes, or according to the packet instructions. Drain.

2 Heat the oil in a wok or saucepan over a high heat. Add the garlic and cook for 2 minutes. Stir in the curry paste and cook for 1 minute.

COOK'S TIP
Thai fish sauce (*nam pla*) is made from salted, fermented fish. The colour of the sauce can vary considerably. Look for a light-coloured sauce, as it is considered better than the darker version.

3 Add the monkfish and stir-fry over a high heat for 4–5 minutes, until just tender. Pour in the coconut cream and stock. Stir in the fish sauce and sugar, and bring just to the boil. Add the drained noodles and cook for 1–2 minutes, until tender.

4 Stir in half the peanuts, half the spring onions, half the beansprouts, the basil and seasoning. Ladle the soup into deep bowls and sprinkle over the remaining peanuts. Garnish with the rest of the spring onions and beansprouts, and the red chilli.

Energy 379kcal/1589kJ; Protein 25.5g; Carbohydrate 41.2g, of which sugars 4.7g; Fat 12g, of which saturates 2g; Cholesterol 18mg; Calcium 49mg; Fibre 0.9g; Sodium 111mg.

SALMON CHOWDER

DILL IS THE PERFECT PARTNER FOR SALMON IN THIS CREAMY SOUP FROM THE USA. IT TAKES ITS INSPIRATION FROM THE SATISFYING SOUPS THAT ARE TYPICAL OF THE EASTERN SEABOARD OF THE COUNTRY, AND IS BEST SERVED IMMEDIATELY AFTER COOKING, WHEN THE SALMON IS JUST TENDER.

SERVES 4

INGREDIENTS
  20g/³⁄₄oz/1¹⁄₂ tbsp butter
  1 onion, finely chopped
  1 leek, finely chopped
  1 small fennel bulb, finely chopped
  25g/1oz/¹⁄₄ cup plain
    (all-purpose) flour
  1.75 litres/3 pints/7 cups fish stock
  2 medium potatoes, cut into
    1cm/¹⁄₂in cubes
  450g/1lb salmon fillet, skinned and
    cut into 2cm/³⁄₄in cubes
  175ml/6fl oz/³⁄₄ cup milk
  120ml/4fl oz/¹⁄₂ cup whipping cream
  30ml/2 tbsp chopped fresh dill
  salt and ground black pepper

1 Melt the butter in a large pan. Add the onion, leek and chopped fennel and cook for 6 minutes until softened.

2 Stir in the flour. Reduce the heat to low and cook for 3 minutes, stirring occasionally with a wooden spoon.

3 Add the fish stock and potatoes to the mixture in the pan. Season with a little salt and ground black pepper. Bring to the boil, then reduce the heat, cover and simmer gently for about 20 minutes or until the potatoes are tender when tested with a fork.

4 Add the cubed salmon fillet and simmer gently for 3–5 minutes until it is just cooked.

5 Stir the milk, cream and chopped dill into the contents of the pan. Cook until just warmed through, stirring occasionally, but do not allow to boil. Adjust the seasoning to taste, then ladle into warmed soup bowls to serve.

Energy 464kcal/1934kJ; Protein 27.9g; Carbohydrate 22.1g, of which sugars 6.5g; Fat 30g, of which saturates 12.9g; Cholesterol 101mg; Calcium 131mg; Fibre 3.1g; Sodium 122mg.

CURRIED SALMON SOUP

A HINT OF MILD CURRY PASTE REALLY ENHANCES THE FLAVOUR OF THIS SOUP, WITHOUT MAKING IT TOO SPICY. GRATED CREAMED COCONUT ADDS A LUXURY TOUCH, WHILE HELPING TO AMALGAMATE THE FLAVOURS. SERVED WITH CHUNKS OF WARM BREAD, THIS MAKES A SUBSTANTIAL APPETIZER.

SERVES 4

INGREDIENTS

50g/2oz/¼ cup butter
2 onions, roughly chopped
10ml/2 tsp mild curry paste
475ml/16fl oz/2 cups water
150ml/¼ pint/⅔ cup white wine
300ml/½ pint/1¼ cups double
  (heavy) cream
50g/2oz/½ cup creamed coconut,
  grated, or 120ml/4fl oz/½ cup
  coconut cream
2 potatoes, about 350g/12oz, cubed
450g/1lb salmon fillet, skinned
  and cut into bitesize pieces
60ml/4 tbsp chopped fresh
  flat leaf parsley
salt and ground black pepper

1 Melt the butter in a large pan, add the onions and cook for 3–4 minutes, until beginning to soften. Stir in the curry paste. Cook for 1 minute more.

2 Add the water, wine, cream and creamed coconut or coconut cream, with seasoning. Bring to the boil, stirring until the coconut has dissolved.

3 Add the potatoes to the pan. Simmer, covered, for about 15 minutes or until they are almost tender. Do not allow them to break down into the mixture.

4 Add the fish gently so as not to break it up. Simmer for 2–3 minutes until just cooked. Add the parsley and adjust the seasoning. Serve immediately.

Energy 837kcal/3466kJ; Protein 26.3g; Carbohydrate 16.6g, of which sugars 3.6g; Fat 71.8g, of which saturates 41.2g; Cholesterol 186mg; Calcium 74mg; Fibre 0.9g; Sodium 158mg.

SALMON SOUP WITH SALSA AND ROUILLE

THIS SMART FISH SOUP IS THE PERFECT CHOICE FOR SUMMER ENTERTAINING. SORREL IS A GOOD
PARTNER FOR SALMON, BUT DILL OR FENNEL ARE EQUALLY DELICIOUS ALTERNATIVES.

SERVES 4

INGREDIENTS

 90ml/6 tbsp olive oil
 1 onion, chopped
 1 leek, chopped
 1 celery stick, chopped
 1 fennel bulb, roughly chopped
 1 red (bell) pepper, seeded
  and sliced
 3 garlic cloves, chopped
 grated rind and juice of 2 oranges
 1 bay leaf
 400g/14oz can chopped tomatoes
 1.2 litres/2 pints/5 cups fish stock
 pinch of cayenne pepper
 800g/1¾lb salmon fillet, skinned
 300ml/½ pint/1¼ cups double
  (heavy) cream
 salt and ground black pepper
 4 thin slices baguette, to serve

For the ruby salsa
 2 tomatoes, peeled, seeded
  and diced
 ½ small red onion, very
  finely chopped
 15ml/1 tbsp cod's roe
 15ml/1 tbsp chopped fresh sorrel

For the rouille
 120ml/4fl oz/½ cup mayonnaise
 1 garlic clove, crushed
 5ml/1 tsp sun-dried tomato paste

1 Heat the oil in a large pan and add the chopped onion, leek, celery, fennel, pepper and garlic. Cover the pan and cook gently for 20 minutes or until all the vegetables have softened. Do not allow the onion and garlic to brown.

2 Add the orange rind and juice, bay leaf and tomatoes. Cover and cook for 4–5 minutes, stirring occasionally. Add the stock and cayenne, cover the pan and simmer for 30 minutes.

3 Add the salmon and cook gently for 8–10 minutes, until just cooked. Using a slotted spoon, remove the salmon and place it on a large plate.

4 Flake the salmon into large pieces, and remove any bones that were missed when the fish was originally filleted. Put the flaked salmon in a dish and set it aside.

COOK'S TIP
For a smart presentation, choose wide, shallow soup plates, so that there is plenty of room for the rouille-topped toast on top of the flaked salmon. The ruby salsa adds the finishing touch.

5 Meanwhile, make the salsa. Put the tomatoes in a bowl and add the finely chopped red onion. Stir in the cod's roe and the chopped fresh sorrel. Transfer the mixture to a serving dish and set it aside.

6 To make the rouille to top the toast, mix the mayonnaise with the crushed garlic and the sun-dried tomato paste in a bowl.

7 Leave the soup to cool slightly, then remove and discard the bay leaf. Purée the soup in a food processor or blender until smooth, then press it through a fine sieve (strainer) into the rinsed pan.

8 Stir in the cream and season well, then add the flaked salmon. Toast the baguette slices under a hot grill (broiler) on both sides and set aside.

9 Reheat the soup gently without letting it boil. Ladle it into bowls and float the toasted baguette slices on top. Add a spoonful of rouille to each slice of baguette and spoon some ruby salsa on top. Serve immediately.

Energy 1153kcal/4772kJ; Protein 44.9g; Carbohydrate 13.7g, of which sugars 12.5g; Fat 102.5g, of which saturates 34.9g; Cholesterol 225mg; Calcium 127mg; Fibre 4.7g; Sodium 268mg.

MATELOTE

THIS FISHERMEN'S CHUNKY SOUP IS TRADITIONALLY MADE FROM FRESHWATER FISH, INCLUDING EEL.
ANY FIRM FISH CAN BE USED, BUT TRY TO INCLUDE AT LEAST SOME EEL, AND USE A ROBUST DRY
WHITE OR RED WINE FOR EXTRA FLAVOUR.

SERVES 6

INGREDIENTS
    1kg/2¼ lb mixed fish, including
        450g/1lb conger eel if possible
    50g/2oz/¼ cup butter
    1 onion, thickly sliced
    2 celery sticks, thickly sliced
    2 carrots, thickly sliced
    1 bottle dry white or red wine
    1 fresh bouquet garni containing
        parsley, bay leaf and chervil
    2 cloves
    6 black peppercorns
    beurre manié for thickening, see
        Cook's Tip
    salt and cayenne pepper
For the garnish
    25g/1oz/2 tbsp butter
    12 baby onions, peeled
    12 button (white) mushrooms
    chopped flat leaf parsley

1 Cut all the fish into thick slices, removing any obvious bones. Melt the butter in a large pan, put in the fish and sliced vegetables and stir over a medium heat until lightly browned. Pour in the wine and enough cold water to cover. Add the bouquet garni and spices and season. Bring to the boil, lower the heat and simmer gently for 20–30 minutes, until the fish is tender, skimming the surface occasionally.

2 Meanwhile, prepare the garnish. Heat the butter in a deep frying pan and sauté the baby onions until golden and tender. Add the mushrooms and fry until golden. Season and keep hot.

3 Strain the soup through a large sieve (strainer) into a clean pan. Discard the herbs and spices in the sieve, then divide the fish among deep soup plates (you can skin the fish if you wish, but this is not essential) and keep hot.

4 Reheat the soup until it boils. Lower the heat and whisk in the *beurre manié* little by little until the soup thickens. Season it and pour over the fish. Garnish each portion with the fried baby onions and mushrooms and sprinkle with chopped parsley.

COOK'S TIP
To make the *beurre manié* for thickening, mix 15g/½oz/1 tbsp softened butter with 15ml/1 tbsp plain (all-purpose) flour. Add to the boiling soup a pinch at a time, whisking all the time.

Energy 323kcal/1346kJ; Protein 31.4g; Carbohydrate 2.3g, of which sugars 1.9g; Fat 11.6g, of which saturates 6.7g; Cholesterol 103mg; Calcium 35mg; Fibre 0.8g; Sodium 192mg.

SMOKED MACKEREL AND TOMATO SOUP

ALL THE INGREDIENTS FOR THIS UNUSUAL SOUP ARE COOKED IN A SINGLE PAN, SO IT IS NOT ONLY QUICK AND EASY TO PREPARE, BUT REDUCES THE CLEARING UP. SMOKED MACKEREL GIVES THE SOUP A ROBUST FLAVOUR, BUT THIS IS TEMPERED BY THE CITRUS TONES IN THE LEMON GRASS AND TAMARIND.

SERVES 4

INGREDIENTS

200g/7oz smoked mackerel fillets
4 tomatoes
1 litre/1¾ pints/4 cups
    vegetable stock
1 lemon grass stalk, finely chopped
5cm/2in piece fresh galangal,
    finely diced
4 shallots, finely chopped
2 garlic cloves, finely chopped
2.5ml/½ tsp dried chilli flakes
15ml/1 tbsp Thai fish sauce
5ml/1 tsp palm sugar or light
    muscovado (brown) sugar
45ml/3 tbsp thick tamarind juice,
    made by mixing tamarind paste
    with warm water
small bunch of fresh chives or spring
    onions (scallions), to garnish

1 Prepare the smoked mackerel fillets. Remove and discard the skin, if necessary, then chop the flesh into large pieces. Remove any stray bones with your fingers or a pair of tweezers.

2 Cut the tomatoes in half, squeeze out most of the seeds with your fingers, then finely dice the flesh with a sharp knife. Set aside.

3 Pour the stock into a large pan and add the lemon grass, galangal, shallots and garlic. Bring to the boil, reduce the heat and simmer for 15 minutes.

4 Add the fish, tomatoes, chilli flakes, fish sauce, sugar and tamarind juice. Simmer for 4–5 minutes, until the fish and tomatoes are heated through. Serve garnished with chives or spring onions.

Energy 203kcal/845kJ; Protein 10.3g; Carbohydrate 5.3g, of which sugars 5g; Fat 15.8g, of which saturates 3.3g; Cholesterol 53mg; Calcium 21mg; Fibre 1.2g; Sodium 385mg.

CARIBBEAN SALT COD AND OKRA SOUP

INSPIRED BY INGREDIENTS POPULARLY USED IN CARIBBEAN COOKING, THIS COLOURFUL, CHUNKY SOUP IS SERVED IN DEEP BOWLS AROUND A CHIVE-FLAVOURED SWEET YAM MASH. OKRA GIVES THE DISH A FLAVOUR THAT IS A CROSS BETWEEN ASPARAGUS AND AUBERGINE.

2 Heat the oil in a heavy-based pan. Add the garlic, onion and chilli, and cook for 4–5 minutes until softened.

3 Add the salt cod and cook for 3–4 minutes, until it begins to colour. Stir in the tomatoes, wine and bay leaves and bring to the boil. Pour in the water, bring to the boil, reduce the heat and simmer for 10 minutes.

4 Meanwhile, trim the stalk ends off the okra and cut the pods into chunks. Add to the soup and cook for 10 minutes. Stir in the callaloo or spinach and cook for 5 minutes, until the okra is tender.

5 Meanwhile, prepare the creamed yam. Peel the yam and cut it into large dice, then place in a saucepan with the lemon juice and add cold water to cover. Bring to the boil and cook for 15–20 minutes, until tender. Drain well, then return the yam to the pan and dry it out over the heat for a few seconds. Mash with the butter and cream, and season well. Stir in the chives.

6 Season the soup and stir in the chopped parsley. Spoon portions of creamed yam into the centres of six soup bowls and ladle the soup around it. Serve immediately.

SERVES 6

INGREDIENTS
200g/7oz salt cod, soaked for
  24 hours, changing the water
  several times
15ml/1 tbsp olive oil
1 garlic clove, chopped
1 onion, chopped
1 green chilli, seeded and chopped
6 plum tomatoes, peeled and
  chopped
250ml/8fl oz/1 cup white wine
2 bay leaves
900ml/1½ pints/3¾ cups water
225g/8oz okra

225g/8oz callaloo or spinach
30ml/2 tbsp chopped fresh parsley
salt and ground black pepper

For the creamed yam
675g/1½lb yam
juice of 1 lemon
50g/2oz/¼ cup butter
30ml/2 tbsp double (heavy) cream
15ml/1 tbsp chopped fresh
  chives

1 Drain and skin the salt cod, then rinse it under cold running water. Cut the flesh into bite-size pieces, removing any bones, and set aside.

COD, BROAD BEAN AND SPINACH CHOWDER

FRESH COD AND VEGETABLES ARE ABUNDANT IN THIS THICK AND CREAMY SOUP, WHICH IS FINISHED WITH CRISP GRANARY CROÛTONS TO SOAK UP THE DELICIOUS LIQUID. MAKE IT EARLY IN THE SUMMER TO TAKE ADVANTAGE OF THE YOUNGEST, SWEETEST FRESH BEANS.

SERVES 6

INGREDIENTS

1 litre/1¾ pints/4 cups milk
150ml/¼ pint/⅔ cup double (heavy) cream
675g/1½lb cod fillet, skinned and boned
45ml/3 tbsp olive oil
1 onion, sliced
2 garlic cloves, finely chopped
450g/1lb potatoes, thickly sliced
450g/1lb fresh broad (fava) beans, podded
225g/8oz baby spinach leaves
pinch of grated nutmeg
30ml/2 tbsp chopped fresh chives
salt and ground black pepper
fresh chives, to garnish

For the croûtons
60ml/4 tbsp olive oil
6 slices Granary (whole-wheat) bread, crusts removed, cut into large cubes

1 Pour the milk and cream into a large pan and bring to the boil. Add the cod and bring back to the boil. Reduce the heat and simmer for 2–3 minutes, then remove from the heat and leave to stand for about 6 minutes, until the fish is just cooked. Use a slotted spoon to remove the fish from the cooking liquid.

2 Using a fork, flake the cooked cod into chunky pieces, removing any bones or skin, then cover and set aside.

3 Heat the olive oil in a large pan and add the onion and garlic. Cook for about 5 minutes, until softened, stirring occasionally. Add the potatoes, stir in the milk mixture and bring to the boil. Reduce the heat and cover the pan. Cook for 10 minutes. Add the broad beans; cook for 10 minutes more or until the beans are tender and the potatoes just begin to break up.

4 Meanwhile, to make the croûtons, heat the oil in a frying pan and add the bread cubes. Cook over a medium heat, stirring often, until golden all over. Remove using a slotted spoon and leave to drain on kitchen paper.

5 Add the cod to the soup and heat through gently. Just before serving, add the spinach and stir for 1–2 minutes, until wilted. Season the soup well and stir in the nutmeg and chives.

6 Ladle the soup into six warmed soup bowls and pile the croûtons on top. Garnish with fresh chives and serve immediately.

COOK'S TIP
When fresh broad (fava) beans are out of season, frozen beans are acceptable as an alternative. Make sure that you cook them for the time recommended on the packet.

Energy 603kcal/2525kJ; Protein 37.9g; Carbohydrate 44.7g, of which sugars 12.2g; Fat 31.6g, of which saturates 12.4g; Cholesterol 96mg; Calcium 398mg; Fibre 7.6g; Sodium 375mg.

CAMBODIAN BAMBOO, FISH AND RICE SOUP

THIS IS A REFRESHING KHMER SOUP MADE WITH FRESHWATER FISH. A SPECIALITY OF PHNOM PENH,
SAMLAW TRAPEANG IS FLAVOURED WITH COCONUT MILK, THE FERMENTED FISH EXTRACT, TUK
PRAHOC, LEMON GRASS AND GALANGAL – SOME OF CAMBODIA'S PRINCIPAL INGREDIENTS.

SERVES 4

INGREDIENTS
For the stock
    675g/1½lb pork ribs
    1 onion, quartered
    225g/8oz carrots, cut into chunks
    25g/1oz dried squid or dried shrimp,
      soaked in water for 30 minutes,
      rinsed and drained
    15ml/1 tbsp *nuoc mam*
    15ml/1 tbsp soy sauce
    6 black peppercorns
    salt
For the soup
    75g/3oz/scant ½ cup long grain rice,
      well rinsed
    250ml/8fl oz/1 cup coconut milk
    30ml/2 tbsp *tuk prahoc*
    2 lemon grass stalks, trimmed and
      crushed
    25g/1oz galangal, thinly sliced
    2 or 3 Thai chillies
    4 garlic cloves, crushed
    15ml/1 tbsp palm sugar
    1 fresh bamboo shoot, peeled,
      boiled in water for 10 minutes,
      and sliced
    450g/1lb freshwater fish fillets, such
      as carp or catfish, skinned and cut
      into bitesize pieces
    a small bunch fresh basil leaves
    a small bunch fresh coriander
      (cilantro), finely chopped, and 1
      green chilli, finely sliced, to garnish
    rice or noodles, to serve

1 To prepare the stock, put the ribs in a large pan and cover with 2.5 litres/4¼ pints/10 cups water. Bring the water to the boil, skim off any fat, and add the remaining stock ingredients. Cover the pan and simmer for 1 hour, then skim off any foam or fat.

2 Continue to simmer the stock for a further 1–1½ hours, until it has reduced. Check the seasoning and strain the stock into another pan. There should be approximately 2 litres/3½ pints/7¾ cups of stock.

3 Bring the pan of stock to the boil. Stir in the rice and reduce the heat. Add the coconut milk, *tuk prahoc*, lemon grass, galangal, chillies, garlic and sugar. Simmer for about 10 minutes to let the flavours mingle.

4 Add the bamboo shoot and fish. Simmer for about 5 minutes, until the fish is cooked. Check the seasoning and stir in the basil. Ladle the soup into individual bowls, garnish with the chopped coriander and sliced chilli and serve with the rice or noodles.

Energy 181kcal/763kJ; Protein 22.8g; Carbohydrate 19.6g, of which sugars 4.3g; Fat 1.3g, of which saturates 0.2g; Cholesterol 52mg; Calcium 64mg; Fibre 0.9g; Sodium 145mg.

JAMAICAN RICE AND BEAN SOUP WITH SALT COD

BASED ON THE CLASSIC CARIBBEAN DISH OF RICE AND PEAS, THIS RECIPE IS MADE WITH BLACK-EYED BEANS, BUT KIDNEY BEANS OR, MORE TRADITIONALLY, PIGEON PEAS CAN BE USED INSTEAD. THIS IS A VERY HEARTY SOUP THAT CAN BE SERVED AS A COMPLETE MEAL.

SERVES 6

INGREDIENTS

15ml/1 tbsp sunflower oil
75g/3oz/6 tbsp butter
115g/4oz thick rindless bacon
  rashers (strips), cut into lardons
1 onion, chopped
2 garlic cloves, chopped
1 red chilli, seeded and chopped
225g/8oz/generous 1 cup long
  grain rice
2 fresh thyme sprigs
1 cinnamon stick
400g/14oz can black-eyed beans
  (peas), drained and rinsed
900ml/1½ pints/3¾ cups water
350g/12oz salt cod, soaked for
  24 hours, changing the water
  several times
plain (all-purpose) flour, for dusting
400g/14oz can coconut milk
175g/6oz baby spinach leaves
30ml/2 tbsp chopped fresh parsley
salt and ground black pepper

1 Heat the oil and 25g/1oz/2 tbsp of the butter in a large, heavy-based pan. Add the bacon strips and cook for 3–4 minutes, until golden. Stir in the onion, garlic and chilli and cook for a further 4–5 minutes.

2 Stir in the rice. Cook for 1–2 minutes, until the grains are translucent. Stir in the thyme, cinnamon stick and black-eyed beans and cook for 1–2 minutes. Pour in the water and bring to the boil. Reduce the heat to low and cook for 25–30 minutes.

3 Meanwhile, wash the soaked salt cod under cold running water. Pat dry with kitchen paper and remove the skin. Cut into large bite-size pieces and toss in the flour until evenly coated. Shake off the excess flour.

4 Melt the remaining butter in a large, heavy-based frying pan. Add the cod, in batches if necessary, and cook for 4–5 minutes until tender and golden. Remove the cod and set aside.

5 Stir the coconut milk into the cooked rice and beans. Remove the cinnamon stick and cook for 2–3 minutes. Stir in the spinach and cook for a further 2–3 minutes. Add the cod and chopped parsley, season and heat through. Ladle the soup into bowls and serve.

COOK'S TIP
Lardons are thicker and slightly longer than matchsticks. Cut them from thick bacon or gammon (smoked ham).

Energy 443kcal/1852kJ; Protein 30g; Carbohydrate 43.2g, of which sugars 5.1g; Fat 16.8g, of which saturates 8.3g; Cholesterol 71mg; Calcium 105mg; Fibre 3.8g; Sodium 999mg.

SMOKED COD AND POTATO SOUP

THIS THICK, CREAMY SOUP HAS A RICH, SMOKY FISH FLAVOUR. USE FLOURY POTATOES THAT WILL DISINTEGRATE EASILY AND THICKEN THE SOUP.

SERVES 6

INGREDIENTS

350g/12oz smoked cod fillet
1 onion, chopped
bouquet garni
900ml/1½ pints/3¾ cups water
500g/1¼lb floury potatoes,
    quartered
600ml/1 pint/2½ cups milk
40g/1½oz/3 tbsp butter
salt and ground black pepper
chopped chives, to garnish
crusty bread, to serve

1 Put the cod, onion, bouquet garni and water into a large heavy-based pan and bring to the boil. Skim the scum from the surface, then cover, reduce the heat and poach gently for 10–15 minutes, until the haddock flakes easily.

2 Lift the cod from the pan, cool slightly, then remove the skin and bones. Flake the flesh and put to one side. Return the skin and bones to the pan and simmer for 30 minutes.

3 Strain the fish stock and return to the pan, then add the potatoes and simmer for about 25 minutes. Remove the potatoes from the pan. Add the milk to the pan and bring to the boil.

4 Mash the potatoes with the butter, then whisk into the soup. Add the flaked fish to the pan and heat through. Season. Ladle into soup bowls, sprinkle with chives and serve with crusty bread.

Energy 205kcal/864kJ; Protein 16.1g; Carbohydrate 19g, of which sugars 6.4g; Fat 7.8g, of which saturates 4.7g; Cholesterol 41mg; Calcium 142mg; Fibre 1g; Sodium 536mg.

BOURRIDE ᵒᶠ RED MULLET ᴬᴺᴰ FENNEL

THIS FISH SOUP FROM PROVENCE IN FRANCE IS MADE WITH FRESH MAYONNAISE. THE SECRET OF SUCCESS IS TO COOK THE SOUP GENTLY.

SERVES 4

INGREDIENTS

25ml/1½ tbsp olive oil
1 onion, chopped
3 garlic cloves, chopped
2 fennel bulbs, halved, cored and
  thinly sliced
4 tomatoes, chopped
1 bay leaf
1 fresh thyme sprig
1.2 litres/2 pints/5 cups fish stock
675g/1½lb red mullet or snapper
8 baguette slices
1 garlic clove
30ml/2 tbsp sun-dried tomato paste
12 black olives, pitted and quartered
salt and ground black pepper
fresh fennel fronds, to garnish
For the mayonnaise
  2 egg yolks
  10ml/2 tsp white wine vinegar
  300ml/½ pint/1¼ cups extra virgin
    olive oil

1 Heat the olive oil in a large, heavy pan. Add the onion and garlic and cook for 5 minutes, until softened. Add the fennel and cook for a further 2–3 minutes. Stir in the tomatoes, bay leaf, thyme and fish stock. Bring the mixture to the boil, then reduce the heat and simmer for 30 minutes.

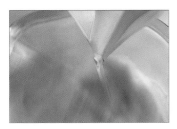

2 Meanwhile, make the mayonnaise. Put the egg yolks and vinegar in a bowl. Season and whisk well. Whisk in the oil, a little at a time, increasing the speed from a few drops at a time to a slow trickle. Transfer to a bowl and set aside.

3 Scale and fillet the mullet. Cut each fillet into two or three pieces, then add them to the soup and cook gently for 5 minutes. Use a slotted spoon to remove the mullet, and set aside.

4 Strain the cooking liquid through a fine sieve (strainer), pressing the vegetables with a ladle to extract as much of the flavour as possible.

5 Whisk about a ladleful of the soup into the mayonnaise, then whisk in the remaining soup in one go.

6 Return the soup to a clean pan and cook very gently, whisking continuously, until the mixture is slightly thickened. Add the fish to the soup and set aside.

7 Toast the baguette slices on both sides. Rub each slice with the clove of garlic and spread with sun-dried tomato paste. Divide the olives among the toasted bread slices.

8 Reheat the soup, but do not allow it to boil. Ladle it into bowls and top each with two toasts. Garnish with fennel.

Energy 322kcal/1354kJ; Protein 35.3g; Carbohydrate 17.5g, of which sugars 6.4g; Fat 12.9g, of which saturates 1g; Cholesterol 0mg; Calcium 173mg; Fibre 4.4g; Sodium 299mg.

FISH AND SWEET POTATO SOUP

THE SUBTLE SWEETNESS OF THE POTATO, COMBINED WITH THE FISH AND THE AROMATIC FLAVOUR OF
OREGANO, MAKES THIS AN APPETIZING SOUP.

SERVES 4

INGREDIENTS
  ½ onion, chopped
  175g/6oz sweet potato, peeled
   and diced
  175g/6oz boneless white fish fillet,
   skinned
  50g/2oz carrot, chopped
  5ml/1 tsp chopped fresh oregano or
   2.5ml/½ tsp dried oregano
  2.5ml/½ tsp ground cinnamon
  1.5 litres/2½ pints/6¼ cups fish
   stock
  75ml/5 tbsp single (light) cream
  chopped fresh parsley, to garnish

VARIATION
Garnish with chopped fresh tarragon
instead of parsley.

1 Put the chopped onion, diced sweet
potato, white fish, chopped carrot,
oregano, cinnamon and half the fish
stock in a pan. Bring to the boil, then
simmer for 20 minutes or until the
potato is cooked.

2 Allow to cool, then process in a
blender or food processor until smooth.

3 Return the soup to the pan, then add
the remaining fish stock and gently
bring to the boil. Reduce the heat to
low and add the single cream, then
gently heat through without boiling,
stirring occasionally.

4 Serve hot in warmed soup bowls,
garnished with chopped fresh parsley.

Energy 119kcal/501kJ; Protein 9.4g; Carbohydrate 11.9g, of which sugars 4.7g; Fat 4.1g, of which saturates 2.4g; Cholesterol 30mg; Calcium 38mg; Fibre 1.6g; Sodium 53mg.

FISHERMAN'S SOUP

*THERE IS SOMETHING TRULY DELICIOUS ABOUT THE COMBINED FLAVOURS OF BACON AND FISH. THIS
HEARTY SOUP IS IDEAL FOR A WINTER LUNCH OR SUPPER.*

SERVES 4

INGREDIENTS

6 streaky (fatty) bacon rashers
(strips), chopped
15g/½oz/1 tbsp butter
1 large onion, chopped
1 garlic clove, finely chopped
30ml/2 tbsp chopped fresh parsley
5ml/1 tsp fresh thyme leaves or
2.5ml/½ tsp dried thyme
450g/1lb tomatoes, peeled, seeded
and chopped
150ml/¼ pint/⅔ cup dry vermouth or
white wine
450ml/¾ pint/scant 2 cups fish stock
300g/11oz potatoes, diced
675–900g/1½–2lb skinless white
fish fillets, cut into large chunks
salt and ground black pepper
fresh flat leaf parsley, to garnish

1 Fry the bacon in a large pan over
moderate heat until lightly browned but
not crisp. Remove from the pan and
drain on kitchen paper.

2 Add the butter to the pan and cook
the onion, stirring occasionally, for
3–5 minutes until soft. Add the garlic
and herbs and continue cooking for
1 minute, stirring. Add the tomatoes,
vermouth or wine and stock and bring
to the boil.

3 Reduce the heat, cover and simmer
the stew for 15 minutes. Add the
potatoes, cover again and simmer for a
further 10–12 minutes or until the
potatoes are almost tender.

4 Add the chunks of fish and the bacon
pieces. Simmer gently, uncovered, for
5 minutes or until the fish is just cooked
and the potatoes are tender. Adjust the
seasoning, garnish with flat leaf parsley
and serve.

COOK'S TIP
In winter, when fresh tomatoes are
lacking in flavour, you can substitute
canned chopped tomatoes.

Energy 368kcal/1543kJ; Protein 39.1g; Carbohydrate 17g, of which sugars 5.6g; Fat 13.7g, of which saturates 5.4g; Cholesterol 110mg; Calcium 38mg; Fibre 2.1g; Sodium 617mg.

TOMATO SOUP <u>WITH</u> CHILLI SQUID

ORIENTAL-STYLE SEARED SQUID MINGLES WITH THE PUNGENT TOMATO AND GARLIC FLAVOURS OF THE MEDITERRANEAN IN THIS SUPERLATIVE SOUP.

SERVES 4

INGREDIENTS

    4 small squid (or 1 or 2 large squid)
    60ml/4 tbsp olive oil
    2 shallots, chopped
    1 garlic clove, crushed
    1.2kg/2½lb ripe tomatoes, roughly
      chopped
    15ml/1 tbsp sun-dried tomato paste
    450ml/¾ pint/2 scant cups vegetable
      stock
    about 2.5ml/½ tsp sugar
    2 red chillies, seeded and chopped
    30ml/2 tbsp chopped fresh tarragon
    salt and ground black pepper
    crusty bread, to serve

1 To clean the squid, grasp the head and tentacles in one hand and pull the body away with the other. Discard the intestines that come away with the head. Cut the tentacles away from the head in one piece and reserve them; discard the head. Pull the plastic-like quill out of the main body and remove any roe which may be present. Pull off the fins from either side of the body pouch and rub off the semi-transparent, mottled skin. Wash the prepared squid under cold running water.

2 Cut the squid into rings and set these aside with the tentacles.

3 Heat 30ml/2 tbsp of the oil in a pan. Add the shallots and garlic, and cook for 4–5 minutes, until just softened. Stir in the tomatoes and tomato paste, and season. Cover and cook for 3 minutes. Add half the stock and simmer for 5 minutes, until the tomatoes are very soft.

4 Cool the soup, then rub it through a sieve (strainer) and return it to the rinsed-out pan. Stir in the remaining stock and the sugar, and reheat gently.

5 Meanwhile, heat the remaining oil in a large frying pan. Add the squid rings and tentacles, and the chillies. Cook for 4–5 minutes, stirring continuously, then remove from the heat and stir in the chopped tarragon.

6 Taste the soup and adjust the seasoning if necessary. If the soup tastes slightly sharp, add a little extra sugar. Ladle the soup into four bowls and spoon the chilli squid in the centre. Serve immediately with crusty bread.

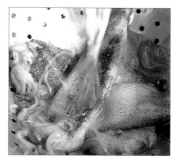

Energy 186kcal/777kJ; Protein 8.1g; Carbohydrate 10.9g, of which sugars 10.2g; Fat 12.6g, of which saturates 2g; Cholesterol 84mg; Calcium 30mg; Fibre 3.2g; Sodium 69mg.

SEAFARER'S STEW

ANY VARIETY OF FIRM FISH MAY BE USED IN THIS RECIPE, BUT BE SURE TO USE SMOKED HADDOCK AS WELL; IT IS ESSENTIAL FOR ITS DISTINCTIVE FLAVOUR.

SERVES 4

INGREDIENTS

   225g/8oz undyed smoked
     haddock fillet
   225g/8oz fresh monkfish fillet
   20 mussels, scrubbed
   2 streaky (fatty) bacon rashers (strips)
   15ml/1 tbsp olive oil
   1 shallot, finely chopped
   225g/8oz carrots, coarsely grated
   150ml/¼ pint/⅔ cup single (light) or
     double (heavy) cream
   115g/4oz cooked peeled prawns
     (shrimp)
   salt and ground black pepper
   30ml/2 tbsp chopped fresh parsley,
     to garnish

5 Stir in the cream together with the haddock, monkfish, mussels and prawns and heat gently, without boiling. Season and serve in large bowls, garnished with parsley.

1 In a large, heavy pan, simmer the haddock and monkfish in 1.2 litres/ 2 pints/5 cups water for 5 minutes, then add the mussels and cover the pan.

2 Cook for a further 5 minutes or until all the mussels have opened. Discard any that have not. Drain, reserving the liquid. Return the liquid to the rinsed pan and set aside.

3 Flake the haddock, removing any skin and bones, then cut the monkfish into large chunks. Cut the bacon into strips.

4 Heat the oil in a heavy frying pan and fry the shallot and bacon for 3–4 minutes or until the shallot is soft and the bacon lightly browned. Add to the strained fish broth, bring to the boil, then add the grated carrots and cook for 10 minutes.

Energy 255kcal/1070kJ; Protein 31.3g; Carbohydrate 7.1g, of which sugars 5.8g; Fat 11.5g, of which saturates 5.9g; Cholesterol 123mg; Calcium 101mg; Fibre 1.6g; Sodium 748mg.

SMOKED HADDOCK CHOWDER

BASED ON A TRADITIONAL SCOTTISH RECIPE, THIS SOUP HAS AMERICAN-STYLE SWEETNESS FROM THE SWEET POTATOES AND BUTTERNUT SQUASH, AND IS FLAVOURED WITH A HINT OF THAI BASIL.

SERVES 6

INGREDIENTS
  400g/14oz sweet potatoes
    (pink-fleshed variety)
  225g/8oz butternut squash
  50g/2oz/¼ cup butter
  1 onion, chopped
  450g/1lb smoked haddock fillets
  300ml/½ pint/1¼ cups water
  600ml/1 pint/2½ cups milk
  small handful of Thai basil leaves
  60ml/4 tbsp double (heavy) cream
  salt and ground black pepper

3 Use a sharp knife to skin the smoked haddock fillets.

4 Add the fillets and water to the pan. Bring to the boil, reduce the heat and simmer for 10 minutes, until the fish is cooked. Use a slotted spoon to lift the fish out of the pan, and leave to cool. Set the cooking liquid aside.

5 When cool enough to handle, carefully break the flesh into large flakes, discarding the skin and bones. Set the fish aside.

6 Press the sweet potatoes through a sieve (strainer) and beat in the remaining butter with seasoning to taste. Strain the reserved fish cooking liquid and return it to the rinsed pan, then whisk in the sweet potato. Stir in the milk and bring to the boil. Simmer for about 2–3 minutes.

7 Stir in the butternut squash, fish, Thai basil leaves and cream. Season the soup to taste and heat through without boiling. Ladle the soup into six warmed soup bowls and serve immediately.

1 Peel the sweet potatoes and butternut squash and cut into small, bitesize pieces. Cook them separately in boiling salted water for 15 minutes or until just tender. Drain both well.

2 Melt half the butter in a large, heavy pan. Add the onion and cook for 4–5 minutes, until soft.

COOK'S TIP
The best type of smoked fish to use in this recipe is Finnan haddock, but other types of smoked haddock can be used with almost equal success.

Energy 285kcal/1196kJ; Protein 19.1g; Carbohydrate 20.7g, of which sugars 9.9g; Fat 14.7g, of which saturates 8.9g; Cholesterol 64mg; Calcium 166mg; Fibre 2.1g; Sodium 173mg.

SOUP NIÇOISE <u>WITH</u> SEARED TUNA

INGREDIENTS FOR THE FAMOUS SALAD FROM NICE IN THE SOUTH OF FRANCE ARE TRANSFORMED INTO A SIMPLE, YET ELEGANT, SOUP BY ADDING A HOT GARLIC-INFUSED STOCK.

SERVES 4

INGREDIENTS
    12 bottled anchovy fillets, drained
    30ml/2 tbsp milk
    115g/4oz green beans, halved
    4 plum tomatoes
    16 black olives, pitted
    1 litre/1¾ pints/4 cups good
        vegetable stock
    3 garlic cloves, crushed
    30ml/2 tbsp lemon juice
    15ml/1 tbsp olive oil
    4 tuna steaks, about 75g/3oz each
    small bunch of spring onions
        (scallions), shredded lengthways
    handful of fresh basil leaves,
        finely shredded
    salt and ground black pepper
    fresh crusty bread, to serve

1 Soak the anchovies in the milk for 10 minutes. Drain well and dry on kitchen paper.

2 Cook the green beans in boiling salted water for 2–3 minutes. Drain, refresh under cold running water and drain. Split any thick beans diagonally lengthways. Wash the olives to remove any oil, then cut into quarters.

3 Peel, halve and seed the tomatoes, then cut into wedges. Set all the prepared ingredients aside.

4 Bring the stock to the boil in a large, heavy pan. Add the garlic, reduce the heat and simmer for 10 minutes. Season the stock well and add the lemon juice.

5 Meanwhile, brush a griddle pan or frying pan with the oil and heat until very hot. Season the tuna and cook for about 2 minutes on each side. Do not overcook the tuna or it will become dry.

6 Gently toss together the green beans, tomatoes, spring onions, anchovies, black olives and shredded basil leaves.

7 Put the seared tuna steaks into four bowls and pile the vegetable mixture on top. Carefully ladle the hot garlic stock around the ingredients. Serve at once, with crusty bread.

COOK'S TIP
Buy anchovy fillets that have been bottled in extra virgin olive oil if you can, as they have a far superior flavour to the smaller anchovy fillets.

Energy 217kcal/909kJ; Protein 27.4g; Carbohydrate 3g, of which sugars 2.7g; Fat 10.7g, of which saturates 2.2g; Cholesterol 34mg; Calcium 76mg; Fibre 2g; Sodium 829mg.

CULLEN SKINK

This is a traditional Scottish soup. A cullen is a seatown or port district of a town, while skink means stock or broth.

3 Strain the stock through a sieve (strainer) and return to the pan.

4 Add the potatoes and simmer for about 25 minutes, or until tender. Remove the potatoes from the pan using a slotted spoon.

5 Add the milk to the pan and bring to the boil.

6 Meanwhile, mash the potatoes with the butter, then whisk into the liquid in the pan until thick and creamy. Add the flaked fish to the pan and adjust the seasoning. Sprinkle with chives and serve immediately.

SERVES 6

INGREDIENTS
1 Finnan haddock, about 350g/12oz
1 onion, chopped
1 bouquet garni
900ml/1½ pints/3¾ cups water
500g/1¼ lb potatoes, quartered
600ml/1 pint/2½ cups milk
40g/1½ oz/3 tbsp butter
salt and ground black pepper
chopped fresh chives, to garnish

1 Put the haddock, onion, bouquet garni and water into a pan and bring to the boil. Reduce the heat, cover and poach for 10–15 minutes.

2 Lift the cooked haddock from the pan, using a fish slice, and remove the skin and bones. Flake the flesh and reserve. Return the skin and bones to the pan and simmer, uncovered, for 30 minutes.

Energy 205kcal/864kJ; Protein 16.1g; Carbohydrate 19g, of which sugars 6.4g; Fat 7.8g, of which saturates 4.7g; Cholesterol 41mg; Calcium 137mg; Fibre 1g; Sodium 132mg.

SMOKED COD AND OKRA SOUP

*THE INSPIRATION FOR THIS SOUP CAME FROM A GHANAIAN RECIPE FOR OKRA SOUP. HERE IT IS
ENHANCED BY THE ADDITION OF SMOKED FISH.*

SERVES 4

INGREDIENTS

2 green bananas
50g/2oz/4 tbsp butter or margarine
1 onion, finely chopped
2 tomatoes, peeled and finely
  chopped
115g/4oz okra, trimmed
225g/8oz smoked cod fillet, cut into
  bite-size pieces
900ml/1½ pints/3¾ cups fish stock
1 fresh chilli, seeded and chopped
salt and ground black pepper
sprigs of fresh parsley, to garnish

3 Add the cod, fish stock, chilli and
seasoning. Bring to the boil, then
reduce the heat and simmer for about
20 minutes or until the cod is cooked
through and flakes easily.

4 Peel the cooked bananas and cut into
slices. Stir into the soup, heat through
for a few minutes and ladle into warmed
soup bowls. Garnish with sprigs of
parsley and serve piping hot.

1 Slit the skins of the green bananas
and place in a large pan. Cover with
water, bring to the boil and cook over a
moderate heat for 25 minutes until the
bananas are tender. Transfer to a plate
and leave to cool.

2 Melt the butter or margarine in a
large pan and sauté the onion for about
5 minutes until soft. Stir in the chopped
tomatoes and okra and fry gently for a
further 10 minutes.

Energy 230kcal/963kJ; Protein 12.6g; Carbohydrate 20.9g, of which sugars 18.6g; Fat 11.3g, of which saturates 6.8g; Cholesterol 53mg; Calcium 65mg; Fibre 2.6g; Sodium 741mg.

FISH BALL SOUP

The Japanese name for this soup is Tsumire-jiru. Tsumire *means, quite literally, sardine balls, and these are added to this delicious soup to impart their robust flavour.*

SERVES 4

INGREDIENTS
  100ml/3½fl oz/generous ⅓ cup sake
    or dry white wine
  1.2 litres/2 pints/5 cups instant
    dashi
  60ml/4 tbsp white miso paste
  150g/5oz shimeji mushrooms or
    6 shiitake mushrooms
  1 leek or large spring onion (scallion)
For the fish balls
  20g/¾oz fresh root ginger
  800g/1¾lb fresh sardines, gutted
    and heads removed
  30ml/2 tbsp white miso paste
  15ml/1 tbsp sake or dry white wine
  7.5ml/1½ tsp sugar
  1 egg
  30ml/2 tbsp cornflour (cornstarch)

1 First make the fish balls. To do this, grate the ginger and squeeze it well to yield 5ml/1 tsp ginger juice.

2 Rinse the sardines, then cut in half along the backbone. Remove all the bones. To skin a boned sardine, lay it skin-side down, then run a sharp knife along the skin from tail to head.

3 Coarsely chop the sardines and process with the ginger juice, miso, sake or wine, sugar and egg to a thick paste in a food processor or blender. Transfer to a bowl and mix in the cornflour until thoroughly blended.

4 Trim the shimeji mushrooms, or either separate each stem or remove the stems from the shiitake mushrooms. Shred the mushrooms. Cut the leek or spring onion into 4cm/1½in strips.

5 Bring the ingredients for the soup to the boil. Use 2 wet spoons to shape small portions of the sardine mixture into bite-size balls and drop them into the soup. Add the prepared mushrooms and leek or spring onion.

6 Simmer the soup until the sardine balls float to the surface. Ladle the soup into individual, deep soup bowls and serve immediately.

COOK'S TIP
If fresh shimeji or shiitake mushrooms are not available, use dried ones instead. Put them in a bowl, pour over boiling water and leave to stand for 30 minutes.

Energy 322kcal/1348kJ; Protein 33.9g; Carbohydrate 10.6g, of which sugars 3.3g; Fat 14.4g, of which saturates 4.1g; Cholesterol 48mg; Calcium 176mg; Fibre 1.3g; Sodium 462mg.

CREAMY FISH CHOWDER

A TRADITIONAL SOUP THAT NEVER FAILS TO PLEASE, WHETHER IT IS MADE WITH MILK OR, MORE LUXURIOUSLY, WITH A GENEROUS AMOUNT OF CREAM.

SERVES 4

INGREDIENTS

3 thick-cut bacon rashers (strips)
1 large onion
675g/1½ potatoes
1 litre/1¾ pints/4 cups fish stock
450g/1lb skinless haddock, cut into
  2.5cm/1in cubes
30ml/2 tbsp chopped fresh parsley
15ml/1 tbsp chopped fresh chives
300ml/½ pint/1¼ cups whipping
  cream or full cream (whole) milk
salt and ground black pepper

1 Remove the rind from the bacon and discard it; then cut the bacon into small pieces. Chop the onion and cut the potatoes into 2cm/¾in cubes.

2 Fry the bacon in a deep pan until the fat is rendered. Add the onion and potatoes and cook over low heat, without browning, for about 10 minutes. Season to taste.

3 Pour off excess bacon fat from the pan. Add the fish stock and bring to a boil. Simmer until the vegetables are tender, about 15–20 minutes.

4 Stir in the cubes of fish, the parsley and chives. Simmer for about 3–4 minutes, until the fish is just cooked.

5 Stir the cream or milk into the chowder and reheat gently, but do not bring to the boil. Season to taste.

6 Ladle into warmed soup bowls and serve immediately.

Energy 329kcal/1386kJ; Protein 30.3g; Carbohydrate 34.5g, of which sugars 8.4g; Fat 8.6g, of which saturates 3.7g; Cholesterol 63mg; Calcium 128mg; Fibre 2.4g; Sodium 364mg.

SMOKED COD CHOWDER

THE SHARP FLAVOUR OF THE SMOKED COD CONTRASTS WELL WITH THE CREAMY SOUP. SERVE THIS SOUP AS A SUBSTANTIAL APPETIZER BEFORE A LIGHT MAIN COURSE. WARM, CRUSTY WHOLEMEAL BREAD GOES WELL WITH IT.

SERVES 4–6

INGREDIENTS
    350g/12oz smoked cod fillet
    1 small onion, finely chopped
    1 bay leaf
    4 black peppercorns
    900ml/1½ pints/3¾ cups milk
    10ml/2 tsp cornflour (cornstarch)
    10ml/2 tsp cold water
    200g/7oz can corn kernels
    15ml/1 tbsp chopped fresh parsley
    crusty wholemeal (whole-wheat)
        bread, to serve

2 Bring to the boil. Reduce the heat and simmer very gently for 12–15 minutes, or until the fish is just cooked.

5 Drain the corn and add to the pan together with the flaked fish and chopped fresh parsley.

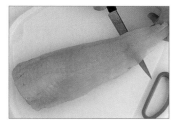

1 Skin the fish with a knife and put it into a large pan with the onion, bay leaf, black peppercorns and milk.

COOK'S TIP
The flavour of the chowder improves if it is made a day in advance. Chill in the refrigerator until required, then reheat gently to prevent the fish disintegrating.

3 Using a slotted spoon, lift out the fish and flake it into large chunks. Remove and discard the bay leaf and peppercorns.

4 Blend the cornflour with the water carefully until it forms a smooth paste, and add to the pan. Bring to the boil and simmer until slightly thickened.

VARIATION
Haddock fillets would be equally good in this chowder, or try smoked fillets for a stronger taste.

6 Reheat the soup until it is piping hot, but do not boil, taking care that the fish does not disintegrate.

7 Ladle into warmed soup bowls and serve immediately with plenty of warm crusty wholemeal bread.

Energy 166kcal/702kJ; Protein 16.9g; Carbohydrate 18.2g, of which sugars 10.8g; Fat 3.4g, of which saturates 1.7g; Cholesterol 36mg; Calcium 189mg; Fibre 0.6g; Sodium 191mg.

SPANISH FISH SOUP
WITH ORANGE

THE SPANISH NAME FOR THIS SOUP IS SOPA CACHORREÑA — *SEVILLE ORANGE SOUP — AND IT IS GOOD SERVED POST-CHRISTMAS, WHEN BITTER SEVILLE ORANGES ARE IN SEASON.*

2 Heat the oil in a large flameproof casserole over a high heat. Smash the garlic cloves with the flat of a knife and fry until they are well coloured. Discard them and turn down the heat. Fry the onion gently until it is softened, adding the tomato halfway through.

3 Strain in the hot fish stock (adding the orange spiral if you wish) and bring back to the boil. Add the potatoes to the pan and cook them for about 5 minutes.

4 Add the fish pieces to the soup, a few at a time, without letting it go off the boil. Cook for about 15 minutes. Add the squeezed orange juice and lemon juice, if using, and the paprika, with salt and pepper to taste. Serve in bowls, garnished with a little parsley.

SERVES 6

INGREDIENTS

   1kg/2¼lb small hake or whiting,
     whole but cleaned
   1.2 litres/2 pints/5 cups water
   4 bitter oranges or 4 sweet oranges
     and 2 lemons
   30ml/2 tbsp olive oil
   5 garlic cloves, unpeeled
   1 large onion, finely chopped
   1 tomato, peeled, seeded
     and chopped
   4 small potatoes, cut into rounds
   5ml/1 tsp paprika
   salt and ground black pepper
   15–30ml/1–2 tbsp finely chopped
     fresh parsley, to garnish

1 Fillet the fish and cut each fillet into three, reserving all the trimmings. Put the fillets on a plate, salt lightly and chill. Put the trimmings in a pan, add the water and a spiral of orange rind. Bring to a simmer, skim, then cover and cook gently for 30 minutes.

Energy 175kcal/738kJ; Protein 20.2g; Carbohydrate 18.8g, of which sugars 8.7g; Fat 2.6g, of which saturates 0.4g; Cholesterol 23mg; Calcium 59mg; Fibre 2.3g; Sodium 113mg.

MEDITERRANEAN LEEK <u>AND</u> FISH SOUP <u>WITH</u> TOMATOES

THIS CHUNKY SOUP, WHICH IS ALMOST A STEW, MAKES A ROBUST AND WONDERFULLY AROMATIC MEAL IN A BOWL. SERVE IT WITH CRISP-BAKED CROÛTES SPREAD WITH A TASTY GARLIC MAYONNAISE.

SERVES 4

INGREDIENTS
2 large thick leeks
30ml/2 tbsp olive oil
5ml/1 tsp crushed coriander seeds
a good pinch of dried red chilli flakes
300g/11oz small salad potatoes,
  peeled and thickly sliced
400g/14oz can chopped tomatoes
600ml/1 pint/2½ cups fish stock
150ml/¼ pint/⅔ cup white wine
1 fresh bay leaf
1 star anise
strip of pared orange rind
good pinch of saffron threads
450g/1lb white fish fillets, such as
  monkfish, sea bass, cod or haddock
450g/1lb small squid, cleaned
250g/9oz raw peeled prawns (shrimp)
30–45ml/2–3 tbsp chopped flat
  leaf parsley
salt and ground black pepper
To serve
1 short French loaf, sliced and toasted
garlic mayonnaise

1 Slice the leeks, keeping the green tops separate from the white bottom pieces. Wash the leek slices thoroughly in a colander and drain them well. Set the white slices aside for later.

2 Heat the oil in a heavy pan over a low heat, then add the green leek slices, the crushed coriander seeds and the dried red chilli flakes. Cook, stirring occasionally, for 5 minutes.

3 Add the potatoes and tomatoes, and pour in the stock and wine. Add the bay leaf, star anise, orange rind and saffron. Bring to the boil, lower the heat and partially cover the pan. Simmer for 20 minutes or until the potatoes are tender. Taste and adjust the seasoning.

4 Cut the white fish fillets into chunks. Cut the squid sacs into rectangles and score a criss-cross pattern into them without cutting right through.

5 Add the fish to the soup and cook gently for 4 minutes. Add the prawns and cook for 1 minute. Add the squid and the sliced white part of the leek and cook, stirring occasionally, for a further 2 minutes.

6 Finally, stir in the chopped parsley and serve immediately, ladling the soup into warmed bowls. Offer the toasted French bread and garlic mayonnaise with the soup.

Energy 340kcal/1437kJ; Protein 51.8g; Carbohydrate 7.2g, of which sugars 5.3g; Fat 9.2g, of which saturates 1.6g; Cholesterol 416mg; Calcium 111mg; Fibre 2.9g; Sodium 330mg.

ROCKET SOUP WITH KILN-SMOKED SALMON

KILN-SMOKED SALMON HAS ACTUALLY BEEN 'COOKED' DURING THE SMOKING PROCESS, PRODUCING A DELICIOUS FLAKY TEXTURE. THIS IS IN CONTRAST TO TRADITIONAL COLD-SMOKED SALMON, WHICH IS NOT ACTUALLY COOKED BUT DOES NOT SPOIL BECAUSE IT HAS BEEN PRESERVED FIRST IN BRINE.

2 Add the cream and stock, stir in gently and bring slowly to the boil. Allow to simmer gently for about 5 minutes.

3 Add the rocket, reserving a few leaves to garnish, and the basil, then return the soup briefly to the boil and turn off the heat. Add a little cold water and allow to cool for a few minutes.

SERVES 4

INGREDIENTS
  15ml/1 tbsp olive oil
  1 small onion, sliced
  1 garlic clove, crushed
  150ml/¼ pint/⅔ cup double
    (heavy) cream
  350ml/12fl oz/1½ cups vegetable
    stock
  350g/12oz rocket (arugula)
  4 fresh basil leaves
  salt and ground black pepper
  flaked kiln-smoked salmon and virgin
    olive oil, to garnish

1 Put the olive oil in a high-sided pan over medium heat and allow to heat up. Add the sliced onion and sweat for a few minutes, stirring continuously. Add the garlic and continue to sweat gently until soft and transparent, although you should not allow the onion to colour.

4 Purée in a blender until smooth, adding a little salt and pepper to taste. When ready to serve, reheat gently but do not allow to boil.

5 Serve in warmed bowls with a few flakes of salmon, a leaf or two of rocket and a drizzle of virgin olive oil over the top.

VARIATION
Cold-smoked salmon is also very good with this soup, and can be used if you can't find the kiln-smoked variety. Simply cut a few slices into medium to thick strips and add to the hot soup. Warming the smoked salmon for a few minutes increases the flavour.

Energy 258kcal/1063kJ; Protein 6.8g; Carbohydrate 3.2g, of which sugars 2.8g; Fat 24.3g, of which saturates 13.1g; Cholesterol 56mg; Calcium 174mg; Fibre 2.1g; Sodium 395mg.

HOT-AND-SOUR FISH SOUP

THIS UNUSUAL TANGY SOUP, CANH CHUA CA, CAN BE FOUND THROUGHOUT SOUTH-EAST ASIA – WITH THE BALANCE OF HOT, SWEET AND SOUR FLAVOURS VARYING FROM CAMBODIA TO THAILAND TO VIETNAM. CHILLIES PROVIDE THE HEAT, TAMARIND PRODUCES THE TARTNESS.

SERVES 4

INGREDIENTS
 1 catfish, sea bass or red snapper,
  about 1kg/2¼lb, filleted
 25g/1oz dried squid, soaked in water
  for 30 minutes
 15ml/1 tbsp vegetable oil
 2 spring onions (scallions), sliced
 2 shallots, sliced
 4cm/1½in fresh root ginger, peeled
  and chopped
 2 or 3 lemon grass stalks, cut into
  strips and crushed
 30ml/2 tbsp tamarind paste
 2 or 3 Thai chillies, seeded and sliced
 15ml/1 tbsp sugar
 30–45ml/2–3 tbsp *nuoc mam*
 225g/8oz fresh pineapple, peeled
  and diced
 3 tomatoes, skinned, seeded and
  roughly chopped
 50g/2oz canned sliced bamboo
  shoots, drained
 1 small bunch fresh coriander
  (cilantro), stalks removed, leaves
  finely chopped
 salt and ground black pepper
 115g/4oz/½cup beansprouts and
  1 bunch dill, fronds roughly
  chopped, to garnish
 lime quarters, to serve
For the marinade
 30ml/2 tbsp *nuoc mam*
 2 garlic cloves, finely chopped

1 Cut the fish into bitesize pieces. Reserve the head, tail and bones for the stock. In a bowl, mix together the marinade ingredients and add the fish pieces. Toss until well coated, cover and set aside. Drain and rinse the soaked dried squid.

COOK'S TIP
Depending on your mood, or your palate, you can adjust the balance of hot and sour by adding more chilli or tamarind to taste. Enjoyed as a meal in itself, the soup is usually served with plain steamed rice.

2 Heat the oil in a deep pan and stir in the spring onions, shallots, ginger, lemon grass and dried squid. Add the reserved fish head, tail and bones, and sauté for 1 minute. Add 1.2 litres/2 pints/5 cups water and bring to the boil. Reduce the heat and simmer for 30 minutes.

3 Strain the stock into another deep pan and bring the clear broth to the boil. Stir in the tamarind paste, chillies, sugar and *nuoc mam* and simmer for 2–3 minutes.

4 Add the pineapple, tomatoes and bamboo shoots and simmer for a further 2–3 minutes.

5 Finally stir in the fish pieces and the chopped fresh coriander, and cook until the fish turns opaque.

6 Season to taste and ladle the soup into hot bowls. Garnish with beansprouts and dill, and serve with the lime quarters to squeeze over.

Energy 335kcal/1415kJ; Protein 44g; Carbohydrate 24g, of which sugars 19g; Fat 7g, of which saturates 1g; Cholesterol 108mg; Calcium 138mg; Fibre 2.3g; Sodium 1.2g

SEAFOOD SOUP WITH ROUILLE

THIS IS A REALLY CHUNKY, AROMATIC MIXED FISH SOUP FROM FRANCE, FLAVOURED WITH PLENTY OF SAFFRON AND HERBS. ROUILLE, A FIERY HOT PASTE, IS SERVED SEPARATELY FOR EVERYONE TO SWIRL INTO THEIR SOUP TO FLAVOUR.

SERVES 6

INGREDIENTS
  3 gurnard or red mullet, scaled
    and gutted
  12 large prawns (shrimp)
  675g/1½lb white fish, such as cod,
    haddock, halibut or monkfish
  225g/8oz mussels
  1 onion, quartered
  1.2 litres/2 pints/5 cups water
  5ml/1 tsp saffron threads
  75ml/5 tbsp olive oil
  1 fennel bulb, roughly chopped
  4 garlic cloves, crushed
  3 strips pared orange rind
  4 sprigs of thyme
  675g/1½lb tomatoes or 400g/14oz
    can chopped tomatoes
  30ml/2 tbsp sun-dried tomato paste
  3 bay leaves
  salt and ground black pepper
For the *rouille*
  1 red (bell) pepper, seeded and
    roughly chopped
  1 fresh red chilli, seeded and sliced
  2 garlic cloves, chopped
  75ml/5 tbsp olive oil
  15g/½oz/¼ cup fresh breadcrumbs

1 To make the *rouille*, process the pepper, chilli, garlic, oil and breadcrumbs in a blender or food processor until smooth. Transfer to a serving dish and chill until required.

2 Fillet the gurnard or mullet by cutting away the flesh from the backbone. Reserve the heads and bones. Cut the fillets into small chunks. Shell half the prawns and reserve the trimmings to make the stock. Skin the white fish, discarding any bones, and cut into large chunks. Scrub the mussels well, discarding any that are open.

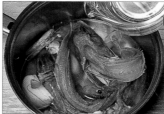

3 Put the fish trimmings and prawn trimmings in a pan with the onion and water. Bring to the boil, then simmer gently for 30 minutes. Cool slightly and strain.

4 Soak the saffron threads in 15ml/ 1 tbsp boiling water.

5 Heat 30ml/2 tbsp of the oil in a large sauté pan. Add the gurnard or mullet and white fish and fry over a high heat for 1 minute. Drain.

6 Heat the remaining oil and fry the fennel, garlic, orange rind and thyme until beginning to colour. Make up the strained stock to about 1.2 litres/ 2 pints/5 cups with water.

7 If using fresh tomatoes, plunge them into boiling water for 30 seconds, then refresh in cold water. Peel and chop. Add the stock to the pan with the saffron, tomatoes, tomato purée and bay leaves. Season, bring almost to the boil, then simmer gently, covered, for 20 minutes.

8 Stir in the gurnard or mullet, white fish, shelled and non-shelled prawns and mussels. Cover the pan and cook for 3–4 minutes. Discard any mussels that do not open.

9 Ladle the soup into warmed bowls and serve hot with the *rouille* in a separate serving dish.

Energy 349kcal/1462kJ; Protein 45.4g; Carbohydrate 9.6g, of which sugars 6.5g; Fat 14.5g, of which saturates 1.7g; Cholesterol 100mg; Calcium 117mg; Fibre 2.6g; Sodium 318mg.

SHELLFISH SOUPS

If you like shellfish, you will find some of the most delicious and luxurious soups in this section. Clam Chowder is a classic recipe from New England, while Soft-shell Crab, Prawn and Corn Gumbo is a favourite Louisiana dish. Or you could try traditional Mussel and Fennel Bree, or Shore Crab Soup, both from Scotland. From China there is Wonton and Prawn Tail Soup, and from Thailand comes Coconut and Seafood Soup, as well as Thai Prawn and Squash Soup.

SEAFOOD CHOWDER

CHOWDER TAKES ITS NAME FROM THE FRENCH WORD FOR CAULDRON — CHAUDIÈRE — THE TYPE OF POT TRADITIONALLY USED FOR SOUPS AND STEWS. LIKE MOST CHOWDERS, THIS IS A SUBSTANTIAL DISH, WHICH COULD EASILY BE SERVED WITH CRUSTY BREAD FOR A LUNCH OR SUPPER.

SERVES 4–6

INGREDIENTS

  200g/7oz/generous 1 cup drained,
    canned corn kernels
  600ml/1 pint/2½ cups milk
  15g/½oz/1 tbsp butter
  1 small leek, sliced
  1 small garlic clove, crushed
  2 rindless smoked streaky (fatty)
    bacon rashers (strips), chopped
  1 small green (bell) pepper, seeded
    and diced
  1 celery stalk, chopped
  115g/4oz/generous ½ cup white
    long grain rice
  5ml/1 tsp plain (all-purpose)
    flour
  about 450ml/¾ pint/scant 2 cups hot
    chicken or vegetable stock
  4 large scallops, preferably
    with corals
  115g/4oz white fish fillet, such
    as monkfish or plaice
  15ml/1 tbsp finely chopped
    fresh parsley
  a good pinch of cayenne pepper
  30–45ml/2–3 tbsp single (light)
    cream (optional)
  salt and ground black pepper

1 Place half the corn kernels in a food processor or blender. Add a little of the milk and process until thick and creamy.

VARIATION
Instead of monkfish or plaice, try this chowder with haddock or cod, which go well with cream, if you are using it.

2 Melt the butter in a large pan and gently fry the leek, garlic and bacon for 4–5 minutes until the leek has softened but not browned. Add the diced green pepper and chopped celery and sweat over a very gentle heat for 3–4 minutes more, stirring frequently.

3 Stir in the rice and cook for a few minutes until the grains begin to swell. Sprinkle over the flour. Cook, stirring occasionally, for about 1 minute, then gradually stir in the remaining milk and the stock.

4 Bring the mixture to the boil over a medium heat, then lower the heat and stir in the creamed corn mixture, with the whole corn kernels. Season well.

5 Cover the pan and simmer the chowder very gently for 20 minutes or until the rice is tender, stirring occasionally, and adding a little more chicken stock or water if the mixture thickens too quickly or the rice begins to stick to the bottom of the pan.

6 Pull the corals away from the scallops and slice the white flesh into 5mm/¼in pieces. Cut the fish fillet into bite-size chunks.

7 Stir the scallops and fish into the chowder, cook for 4 minutes, then stir in the corals, parsley and cayenne. Cook for a few minutes to heat through, then stir in the cream, if using. Adjust the seasoning and serve.

Energy 361kcal/1520kJ; Protein 21.9g; Carbohydrate 47.1g, of which sugars 13.6g; Fat 10.1g, of which saturates 4.9g; Cholesterol 41mg; Calcium 213mg; Fibre 2.1g; Sodium 437mg.

THAI PUMPKIN, PRAWN AND COCONUT SOUP

THE NATURAL SWEETNESS OF THE PUMPKIN IS HEIGHTENED BY THE ADDITION OF A LITTLE SUGAR IN THIS ATTRACTIVE SOUP, BUT THIS IS BALANCED BY THE CHILLIES, SHRIMP PASTE AND DRIED SHRIMP. COCONUT CREAM BLURS THE BOUNDARIES BEAUTIFULLY.

SERVES 4–6

INGREDIENTS
450g/1lb pumpkin
2 garlic cloves, crushed
4 shallots, finely chopped
2.5ml/½ tsp shrimp paste
1 lemon grass stalk, chopped
2 fresh green chillies, seeded
15ml/1 tbsp dried shrimp, soaked
 for 10 minutes in warm water
 to cover
600ml/1 pint/2½ cups
 chicken stock
600ml/1 pint/2½ cups
 coconut cream
30ml/2 tbsp Thai fish sauce
5ml/1 tsp granulated sugar
115g/4oz small cooked shelled
 prawns (shrimp)
salt and ground black pepper
To garnish
2 fresh red chillies, seeded and
 thinly sliced
10–12 fresh basil leaves

1 Peel the pumpkin and cut it into quarters with a sharp knife. Scoop out the seeds with a teaspoon and discard. Cut the flesh into chunks about 2cm/¾in thick and set aside.

2 Put the garlic, shallots, shrimp paste, lemon grass, green chillies and salt to taste in a mortar. Drain the dried shrimp, discarding the soaking liquid, and add them, then use a pestle to grind the mixture into a paste. Alternatively, place all the ingredients in a food processor and process to a paste.

3 Bring the chicken stock to the boil in a large pan. Add the ground paste and stir well to dissolve.

4 Add the pumpkin chunks and bring to a simmer. Simmer for 10–15 minutes, or until the pumpkin is tender.

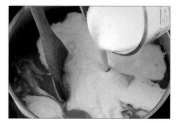

5 Stir in the coconut cream, then bring the soup back to simmering point. Do not let it boil. Add the fish sauce, sugar and ground black pepper to taste.

6 Add the prawns and cook for a further 2–3 minutes, until they are heated through. Serve in warmed soup bowls, garnished with chillies and basil leaves.

COOK'S TIP
Shrimp paste is made from ground shrimp fermented in brine.

Energy 73kcal/310kJ; Protein 6.5g; Carbohydrate 10.4g, of which sugars 9.8g; Fat 0.9g, of which saturates 0.5g; Cholesterol 56mg; Calcium 102mg; Fibre 1.3g; Sodium 399mg.

COCONUT AND SEAFOOD SOUP

THE LONG LIST OF INGREDIENTS COULD MISLEAD YOU INTO THINKING THAT THIS THAI SOUP IS COMPLICATED AND VERY TIME-CONSUMING TO PREPARE. IN FACT, IT IS EXTREMELY EASY TO PUT TOGETHER AND THE MARRIAGE OF FLAVOURS WORKS PERFECTLY.

SERVES 4

INGREDIENTS
600ml/1 pint/2½ cups fish stock
5 thin slices fresh galangal or fresh
  root ginger
2 lemon grass stalks, chopped
3 kaffir lime leaves, shredded
bunch of garlic chives, about 25g/1oz
small bunch of fresh coriander
  (cilantro), about 15g/½oz
15ml/1 tbsp vegetable oil
4 shallots, chopped
400ml/14fl oz can coconut milk
30–45ml/2–3 tbsp Thai fish sauce
45–60ml/3–4 tbsp Thai green
  curry paste
450g/1lb raw large prawns (shrimp),
  peeled and deveined
450g/1lb prepared squid
a little fresh lime juice (optional)
salt and ground black pepper
60ml/4 tbsp crisp fried shallot
  slices, to serve

2 Reserve a few garlic chives for the garnish, then chop the remainder. Add half the chopped garlic chives to the pan. Strip the coriander leaves from the stalks and set the leaves aside. Add the stalks to the pan. Bring to the boil, reduce the heat to low and cover the pan, then simmer gently for 20 minutes. Strain the stock into a bowl.

3 Rinse and dry the pan. Add the oil and shallots. Cook over a medium heat for 5–10 minutes, until the shallots are just beginning to brown.

4 Stir in the strained stock, coconut milk, the remaining kaffir lime leaves and 30ml/2 tbsp of the fish sauce. Heat gently until simmering and cook over a low heat for 5–10 minutes.

5 Stir in the curry paste and prawns, then cook for 3 minutes. Add the squid and cook for a further 2 minutes. Add the lime juice, if using, and season, adding more fish sauce to taste. Stir in the remaining chives and the reserved coriander leaves. Serve in bowls and sprinkle each portion with fried shallots and whole garlic chives.

1 Pour the fish stock into a large pan and add the slices of galangal or ginger, the lemon grass and half the shredded kaffir lime leaves.

VARIATIONS
• Instead of squid, you could add 400g/
14oz firm white fish, such as monkfish,
cut into small pieces.
• You could also replace the squid with
mussels. Steam 675g/1½lb live mussels
in a tightly covered pan for 3–4 minutes,
or until they have opened. Discard any
that remain shut, then remove them from
their shells and add to the soup.

Energy 205kcal/871kJ; Protein 37.7g; Carbohydrate 7.5g, of which sugars 5.8g; Fat 3g, of which saturates 0.8g; Cholesterol 473mg; Calcium 144mg; Fibre 0.4g; Sodium 449mg.

WONTON AND PRAWN TAIL SOUP

A WELL-FLAVOURED CHICKEN STOCK OR BROTH IS A MUST FOR THIS CLASSIC CHINESE SNACK, WHICH IS POPULAR ON FAST-FOOD STALLS IN TOWNS AND CITIES THROUGHOUT SOUTHERN CHINA. SERVE IT AS AN APPETIZER OR PART OF A MAIN MEAL.

SERVES 4

INGREDIENTS
200g/7oz minced (ground) pork
200g/7oz cooked, peeled prawns
   (shrimp), thawed if frozen
10ml/2 tsp rice wine or dry sherry
10ml/2 tsp light soy sauce
5ml/1 tsp sesame oil
24 thin wonton wrappers
1.2 litres/2 pints/5 cups
   chicken stock
12 tiger prawns, shelled, with
   tails still on
350g/12oz pak choi (bok choy),
   coarsely shredded
salt and ground black pepper
4 spring onions (scallions),
   sliced, and 1cm/½in piece fresh
   root ginger, finely shredded,
   to garnish

1 Put the pork, prawns, rice wine or sherry, soy sauce and sesame oil in a large bowl. Add plenty of seasoning and mix the ingredients thoroughly.

2 Put about 10ml/2 tsp of pork mixture in the centre of each wonton wrapper. Bring up the sides of the wrapper and pinch them together to seal the filling in a small bundle.

3 Bring a large pan of water to the boil. Add the wontons and cook for 3 minutes, then drain well and set aside.

4 Pour the stock into a pan and bring to the boil. Season to taste. Add the tiger prawns and cook for 2–3 minutes, until just tender. Add the wontons and pak choi and cook for 1–2 minutes. Garnish with spring onions and ginger to serve.

Energy 208kcal/874kJ; Protein 26.8g; Carbohydrate 11.8g, of which sugars 2.2g; Fat 6.2g, of which saturates 2g; Cholesterol 179mg; Calcium 234mg; Fibre 2.4g; Sodium 655mg.

CRAB AND ASPARAGUS SOUP WITH NUOC CHAM

IN THIS DELICIOUS VIETNAMESE SOUP, THE RECIPE HAS CLEARLY BEEN ADAPTED FROM THE CLASSIC
FRENCH ASPARAGUS VELOUTÉ TO PRODUCE A MEATIER VERSION THAT HAS MORE TEXTURE, AND THE
VIETNAMESE STAMP OF NUOC CHAM, A CHILLI DIPPING SAUCE.

SERVES 4

INGREDIENTS

15ml/1 tbsp vegetable oil
2 shallots, finely chopped
2 garlic cloves, finely chopped
15ml/1 tbsp rice flour or cornflour
    (cornstarch)
225g/8oz/1⅓ cups cooked crab meat,
    chopped into small pieces
450g/1lb preserved asparagus, finely
    chopped, or 450g/1lb fresh
    asparagus, trimmed and steamed
salt and ground black pepper
basil and coriander (cilantro) leaves,
    to garnish
nuoc cham, to serve
For the stock
1 meaty chicken carcass
25g/1oz dried shrimp, soaked in
    water for 30 minutes, rinsed and
    drained
2 onions, peeled and quartered
2 garlic cloves, crushed
15ml/1 tbsp *nuoc mam*
6 black peppercorns
sea salt

1 To make the stock, put the chicken carcass into a deep pan. Add all the other stock ingredients, except the salt, and pour in 2 litres/3½ pints/8 cups water. Boil for a few minutes, skim off any foam, then reduce the heat and simmer gently with the lid on for 1½–2 hours. Remove the lid and simmer for a further 30 minutes to reduce the stock. Skim off any fat, season with salt, then strain the stock and measure out roughly 1.5 litres/2½ pints/6¼ cups.

2 Heat the oil in a deep pan or wok. Stir in the shallots and garlic, until they begin to colour. Remove from the heat, stir in the flour, and then pour in the stock. Put the pan back over the heat and bring the liquid to the boil, stirring constantly, until smooth.

.COOK'S TIPS
• You can increase the quantity of crab meat as much as you like, to make a soup that is very rich and filling.
• Jars of asparagus preserved in brine are used for this recipe, or fresh asparagus that has been steamed until very soft and tender. It is best to avoid canned asparagus, because it tends to have a metallic taste.

3 Add the crab meat and asparagus, reduce the heat and leave to simmer for 15–20 minutes. Season to taste with salt and pepper, then ladle the soup into bowls, garnish with fresh basil and coriander leaves, and serve with a splash of *nuoc cham*.

Energy 142kcal/590kJ; Protein 17.1g; Carbohydrate 6.9g, of which sugars 3g; Fat 5.1g, of which saturates 0.6g; Cholesterol 72mg; Calcium 177mg; Fibre 2.1g; Sodium 584mg.

MUSSEL AND FENNEL BREE

BREE IS THE SCOTTISH WORD FOR A SOUP OR BROTH, MOST OFTEN ASSOCIATED WITH SHELLFISH RATHER LIKE A BISQUE OR BOUILLABAISSE. MUSSELS ARE PARTICULARLY GOOD PARTNERS FOR THE ANISE FLAVOUR OF PERNOD OR RICARD. TRY TO GET THE NATIVE SCOTTISH MUSSELS THAT ARE SMALLER WITH A GOOD FLAVOUR. YOU WILL NEED TWO PANS FOR THIS DISH, ONE TO COOK THE MUSSELS IN AND ONE FOR THE BREE.

SERVES 4

INGREDIENTS

1kg/2¼lb fresh mussels
1 fennel bulb
120ml/4fl oz/½ cup dry white wine
1 leek, finely sliced
olive oil
25g/1oz/2 tbsp butter
splash of Pernod or Ricard
150ml/¼ pint/⅔ cup double (heavy) cream
25g/1oz fresh parsley, chopped

2 Strip off the coarse outer leaves of the fennel and roughly chop them. Set to one side. Then take the central core of the fennel and chop it very finely. Set the chopped core aside in a separate dish or bowl.

3 Place the roughly chopped fennel leaves, the mussels and the wine in a large pan, cover and cook gently until all the mussels open, for about 5 minutes. Discard any mussels that remain closed.

6 Strain the liquor on to the leek mixture and bring to the boil. Add a little water and the pastis, and simmer for a few minutes.

7 Add the cream and parsley and bring back to the boil.

8 Place the mussels in a serving tureen and pour over the soup. Serve piping hot with crusty bread for mopping up the juices.

COOK'S TIP
Farmed or 'rope-grown' mussels are easier to clean. If you use mussels with lots of barnacles you will need to remove these first.

1 Clean the mussels thoroughly, removing any beards and scraping off any barnacles. Discard any that are broken or open.

4 In a second pan, heat the oil and butter, add the leek and finely chopped core of the fennel and cook gently, stirring continuously, until soft.

5 Meanwhile remove the mussels from the first pan and either leave in the shell or remove and discard the shells. Set aside while you make the bree.

Energy 392kcal/1624kJ; Protein 13.4g; Carbohydrate 5.7g, of which sugars 3g; Fat 33g, of which saturates 16.9g; Cholesterol 105mg; Calcium 95mg; Fibre 2.8g; Sodium 297mg.

THAI PRAWN AND SQUASH SOUP

THIS SQUASH SOUP COMES FROM NORTHERN THAILAND. IT IS QUITE HEARTY, SOMETHING OF A CROSS BETWEEN A SOUP AND A STEW. THE BANANA FLOWER ISN'T ESSENTIAL — YOU MAY FIND IT DIFFICULT TO OBTAIN — BUT IT DOES ADD A UNIQUE AND AUTHENTIC FLAVOUR.

SERVES 4

INGREDIENTS
    1 butternut squash, about 300g/11oz
    1 litre/1¾ pints/4 cups
        vegetable stock
    90g/3½oz/scant 1 cup green beans,
        cut into 2.5cm/1in pieces
    45g/1¾oz dried banana
        flower (optional)
    15ml/1 tbsp Thai fish sauce
    225g/8oz raw prawns (shrimp)
    small bunch fresh basil
    cooked rice, to serve
For the chilli paste
    115g/4oz shallots, sliced
    10 drained bottled green peppercorns
    1 small fresh green chilli, seeded
        and finely chopped
    2.5ml/½ tsp shrimp paste

1 Peel the butternut squash and cut it in half. Scoop out the seeds with a teaspoon and discard, then cut the flesh into neat cubes. Set aside.

2 Make the chilli paste by pounding the shallots, peppercorns, chilli and shrimp paste together using a mortar and pestle or puréeing them in a spice blender.

3 Heat the stock gently in a large pan, then stir in the chilli paste. Add the squash, beans and banana flower, if using. Bring to the boil and cook for 15 minutes.

4 Add the fish sauce, prawns and basil. Bring to simmering point, then simmer for 3 minutes. Serve in warmed bowls, accompanied by rice.

Energy 64kcal/271kJ; Protein 11.3g; Carbohydrate 3.4g, of which sugars 2.8g; Fat 0.7g, of which saturates 0.2g; Cholesterol 110mg; Calcium 82mg; Fibre 1.7g; Sodium 199mg.

SHORE CRAB SOUP

*THESE LITTLE CRABS HAVE A VELVET FEEL TO THEIR SHELL. THEY ARE MOSTLY CAUGHT OFF THE WEST
COAST OF SCOTLAND, AND CAN BE QUITE DIFFICULT TO FIND IN FISHMONGERS. IF YOU HAVE TROUBLE
FINDING THEM, YOU CAN ALSO USE COMMON OR BROWN CRABS FOR THIS RECIPE.*

SERVES 4

INGREDIENTS
    1kg/2¼lbs shore or velvet crabs
    50g/2oz/¼ cup butter
    50g/2oz leek, washed and chopped
    50g/2oz carrot, chopped
    30ml/2 tbsp brandy
    225g/8oz ripe tomatoes, chopped
    15ml/1 tbsp tomato purée (paste)
    120ml/4fl oz/½ cup dry white wine
    1.5 litres/2½ pints/6¼ cups fish
      stock
    sprig of fresh tarragon
    60ml/4 tbsp double (heavy) cream
    lemon juice

1 Bring a large pan of water to a rolling
boil and plunge the live crabs into it.
They will be killed very quickly, and the
bigger the pan and the more water
there is, the better. Once the crabs are
dead – a couple of minutes at most –
take them out of the water, place in a
large bowl and smash them up. This
can be done with either a wooden
mallet or the end of a rolling pin.

2 Melt the butter in a heavy pan, add
the leek and carrot and cook gently
until soft but not coloured.

COOK'S TIP
If you don't have fish stock then water
will do, or you could use some of the
water used to boil the crabs initially.

VARIATION
Crème fraîche may be used in place of
double (heavy) cream, if you prefer.

3 Add the crabs and continue cooking.
When very hot, pour in the brandy,
stirring to allow the flavour to pervade
the whole pan.

4 Add the tomatoes, tomato purée,
wine, stock and tarragon. Bring to
the boil and simmer gently for about
30 minutes.

5 Strain the soup through a metal sieve
(strainer), forcing as much of the
tomato mixture through as possible. (If
you like you could remove the big claws
and purée the remains in a blender.)

6 Return to the heat, simmer for a few
minutes then season to taste. Add the
cream and lemon juice, and serve.

Energy 419kcal/1741kJ; Protein 35.1g; Carbohydrate 3.8g, of which sugars 3.6g; Fat 25.7g, of which saturates 15.1g; Cholesterol 196mg; Calcium 252mg; Fibre 1.1g; Sodium 1122mg.

CLAM CHOWDER

IF FRESH CLAMS ARE HARD TO FIND, USE FROZEN OR CANNED CLAMS FOR THIS CLASSIC RECIPE FROM NEW ENGLAND. LARGE CLAMS SHOULD BE CUT INTO CHUNKY PIECES. RESERVE A FEW CLAMS IN THEIR SHELLS TO GARNISH, IF YOU LIKE. TRADITIONALLY, THE SOUP IS SERVED WITH SAVOURY BISCUITS CALLED SALTINE CRACKERS. YOU SHOULD BE ABLE TO FIND THESE IN ANY GOOD DELICATESSEN.

SERVES 4

INGREDIENTS

100g/3¾oz salt pork or thinly sliced
  unsmoked bacon, diced
1 large onion, chopped
2 potatoes, peeled and cut into cubes
1 bay leaf
1 fresh thyme sprig
300ml/½ pint/1¼ cups milk
400g/14oz cooked clams, cooking
  liquid reserved
150ml/¼ pint/⅔ cup double
  (heavy) cream
salt, ground white pepper and
  cayenne pepper
finely chopped fresh parsley, to garnish

1 Put the salt pork or unsmoked bacon in a pan, and heat gently, stirring frequently, until the fat runs and the meat is starting to brown. Add the chopped onion and fry over a low heat until softened but not browned.

2 Add the cubed potatoes, the bay leaf and thyme sprig, stir well to coat with fat, then pour in the milk and reserved clam liquid and bring to the boil. Lower the heat and simmer for about 10 minutes, until the potatoes are tender but still firm. Lift out the bay leaf and thyme sprig and discard.

3 Remove the shells from most of the clams. Add all the clams to the pan and season to taste with salt, pepper and cayenne. Simmer gently for 5 minutes more, then stir in the cream. Heat until the soup is very hot, but do not allow it to boil. Pour into a tureen, garnish with the chopped parsley and serve.

CHINESE CRAB AND CORN SOUP

FROZEN WHITE CRAB MEAT WORKS AS WELL AS FRESH IN THIS DELICATELY FLAVOURED SOUP.

SERVES 4

INGREDIENTS

600ml/1 pint/2½ cups fish or
  chicken stock
2.5cm/1in fresh root ginger, peeled
  and very finely sliced
400g/14oz can creamed corn
150g/5oz cooked white crab meat
15ml/1 tbsp arrowroot or
  cornflour (cornstarch)
15ml/1 tbsp rice wine or dry sherry
15–30ml/1–2 tbsp light soy sauce
1 egg white
salt and ground white pepper
shredded spring onions (scallions),
  to garnish

COOK'S TIP

This soup can be made with whole kernel corn, but creamed corn gives a better texture. If you can't find it in a can, use thawed frozen creamed corn instead; the result will be just as good.

1 Put the stock and ginger in a large pan and bring to the boil. Stir in the creamed corn and bring back to the boil.

2 Switch off the heat and add the crab meat. Put the arrowroot or cornflour in a cup and stir in the rice wine or sherry to make a smooth paste; stir this into the soup. Cook over a low heat for about 3 minutes until the soup has thickened and is slightly glutinous in consistency. Add light soy sauce, salt and white pepper to taste.

3 In a bowl, whisk the egg white to a stiff foam. Gradually fold it into the soup. Ladle the soup into heated bowls, garnish each portion with spring onions and serve.

VARIATION

To make prawn (shrimp) and corn soup, substitute 150g/5oz cooked peeled prawns for the crab meat. Chop the peeled prawns roughly and add to the soup at the beginning of step 2.

Top: Energy 392kcal/1631kJ; Protein 24.3g; Carbohydrate 15.3g, of which sugars 5.7g; Fat 26.3g, of which saturates 15.1g; Cholesterol 136mg; Calcium 191mg; Fibre 0.7g; Sodium 1632mg.
Bottom: Energy 184kcal/779kJ; Protein 10.6g; Carbohydrate 33.8g, of which sugars 9.9g; Fat 1.6g, of which saturates 0.3g; Cholesterol 27mg; Calcium 51mg; Fibre 1.4g; Sodium 762mg.

SCALLOP AND JERUSALEM ARTICHOKE SOUP

*THE SUBTLE SWEETNESS OF SCALLOPS COMBINES WELL WITH THE FLAVOUR OF JERUSALEM ARTICHOKES
IN THIS ATTRACTIVE AND SATISFYING GOLDEN SOUP.*

SERVES 6

INGREDIENTS

1kg/2¼lb Jerusalem artichokes
juice of ½ lemon
115g/4oz/½ cup butter
1 onion, finely chopped
600ml/1 pint/2½ cups fish stock
300ml/½ pint/1¼ cups milk
generous pinch of saffron threads
6 large or 12 small scallops, with
    their corals
150ml/¼ pint/⅔ cup
    whipping cream
salt and ground white pepper
45ml/3 tbsp flaked almonds and
    15ml/1 tbsp finely chopped
    fresh chervil, to garnish

1 Working quickly, scrub and peel the
Jerusalem artichokes, cut them into
2cm/¾in chunks and drop them
into a bowl of cold water which has
been acidulated with the lemon juice.
This will prevent the prepared
artichokes from discolouring.

2 Melt half the butter in a pan, add the
onion and cook over a low heat until
softened. Drain the artichokes and
add them to the pan. Cook gently for
5 minutes, stirring frequently. Pour in
the stock and milk, add the saffron and
bring to the boil. Lower the heat and
simmer until the artichokes are tender
but not mushy.

3 Meanwhile, carefully separate the
scallop corals from the white flesh.
Prick the corals and slice each scallop
in half horizontally. Heat half the
remaining butter in a frying pan, add
the scallops and corals and cook very
briefly (for about 1 minute) on each
side. Dice the scallops and corals,
keeping them separate, and set them
aside until needed.

4 When the artichokes are cooked, tip
the contents of the pan into a blender
or food processor. Add half the white
scallop meat and purée until very
smooth. Return the soup to the clean
pan, season with salt and white pepper
and keep hot over a low heat while you
prepare the garnish.

5 Heat the remaining butter in a frying
pan, add the almonds and toss over a
medium heat until golden brown. Add
the diced corals and cook for about
30 seconds.

6 Stir the cream into the soup and add
the remaining diced white scallop meat.
Ladle the soup into individual bowls and
garnish each serving with the almonds,
scallop corals and a sprinkling of chervil.

Energy 408kcal/1691kJ; Protein 12.8g; Carbohydrate 18.8g, of which sugars 16.4g; Fat 31.9g, of which saturates 17.5g; Cholesterol 86mg; Calcium 150mg; Fibre 4.7g; Sodium 247mg.

CRAB, COCONUT AND CORIANDER SOUP

QUICK AND EASY TO PREPARE, THIS SOUP HAS ALL THE FLAVOURS ASSOCIATED WITH THE BAHIA REGION OF BRAZIL: CREAMY COCONUT, PALM OIL, FRAGRANT CORIANDER AND CHILLI.

SERVES 4

INGREDIENTS
    30ml/2 tbsp olive oil
    1 onion, finely chopped
    1 celery stick, finely chopped
    2 garlic cloves, crushed
    1 fresh red chilli, seeded and
      chopped
    1 large tomato, peeled and chopped
    45ml/3 tbsp chopped fresh
      coriander (cilantro)
    1 litre/1¾ pints/4 cups fresh crab
      or fish stock
    500g/1¼lb crab meat
    250ml/8fl oz/1 cup coconut milk
    30ml/2 tbsp palm oil
    juice of 1 lime
    salt
    hot chilli oil and lime wedges,
      to serve

1 Heat the olive oil in a pan over a low heat. Stir in the onion and celery, and sauté gently for 5 minutes, until softened and translucent. Stir in the garlic and chilli and cook for a further 2 minutes.

2 Add the tomato and half the coriander and increase the heat. Cook, stirring, for 3 minutes, then add the stock. Bring to the boil, then simmer for 5 minutes.

3 Stir the crab, coconut milk and palm oil into the pan and simmer over a very low heat for a further 5 minutes. The consistency should be thick, but not stew-like, so add some water if needed.

4 Stir in the lime juice and remaining coriander, then season with salt to taste. Serve in heated bowls with the chilli oil and lime wedges on the side.

Energy 228kcal/951kJ; Protein 23.6g; Carbohydrate 5.4g, of which sugars 5g; Fat 12.6g, of which saturates 3.7g; Cholesterol 90mg; Calcium 199mg; Fibre 1.1g; Sodium 767mg.

THAI FISH SOUP

THAI FISH SAUCE, OR NAM PLA, *IS RICH IN B VITAMINS AND IS USED EXTENSIVELY IN THAI COOKING. IT IS AVAILABLE FROM THAI OR INDONESIAN STORES AND GOOD SUPERMARKETS.*

3 Prepare the scallops by cutting them in half, leaving the corals attached to one half.

4 Return the stock to a clean pan, add the prawns, mussels, monkfish and scallops and cook for 3 minutes. Remove from the heat and add the lime juice and fish sauce.

5 Serve garnished with the shredded lime leaf and finely sliced red chilli.

SERVES 4

INGREDIENTS
  350g/12oz raw large prawns (shrimp)
  15ml/1 tbsp groundnut (peanut) oil
  1.2 litres/2 pints/5 cups well-
    flavoured chicken or fish stock
  1 lemon grass stalk, bruised and cut
    into 2.5cm/1in lengths
  2 kaffir lime leaves, torn into pieces
  juice and finely grated rind of 1 lime
  ½ fresh green chilli, seeded and
    finely sliced
  4 scallops
  24 mussels, scrubbed
  115g/4oz monkfish fillet, cut into
    2cm/¾in chunks
  10ml/2 tsp Thai fish sauce
For the garnish
  1 kaffir lime leaf, shredded
  ½ fresh red chilli, finely sliced

1 Peel the prawns, reserving the shells, and remove the black vein running along their backs.

2 Heat the oil in a pan and fry the prawn shells until pink. Add the stock, lemon grass, lime leaves, lime rind and green chilli. Bring to the boil, simmer for 20 minutes, then strain through a sieve (strainer), reserving the liquid.

Energy 197kcal/830kJ; Protein 34.9g; Carbohydrate 3g, of which sugars 0.3g; Fat 5.1g, of which saturates 0.8g; Cholesterol 217mg; Calcium 108mg; Fibre 0g; Sodium 701mg.

SOFT-SHELL CRAB, PRAWN AND CORN GUMBO

A WELL-FLAVOURED CHICKEN AND SHELLFISH STOCK GIVES THIS DISH THE AUTHENTIC TASTE OF A TRADITIONAL LOUISIANA GUMBO. SERVE WITH SPOONS AND FORKS TO EAT THE CHUNKY CORN.

SERVES 6

INGREDIENTS

30ml/2 tbsp vegetable oil
1 onion, chopped
1 garlic clove, chopped
115g/4oz rindless streaky (fatty) bacon, chopped
40g/1½oz/⅓ cup plain (all-purpose) flour
1 celery stick, chopped
1 red (bell) pepper, seeded and chopped
1 red chilli, seeded and chopped
450g/1lb plum tomatoes, chopped
2 large corn cobs
4 soft-shell crabs, washed well
30ml/2 tbsp chopped fresh parsley
small bunch of spring onions (scallions), roughly chopped
salt and ground black pepper

For the stock

350g/12oz whole uncooked prawns (shrimp)
2 large chicken wings
1 carrot, thickly sliced
3 celery sticks, sliced
1 onion, sliced
handful of parsley stalks
2 bay leaves
1.5 litres/2½ pints/6¼ cups water

1 To make the stock, peel the prawns and put the shells in a pan. Set the prawns aside. Add the remaining ingredients to the pan. Bring to the boil and skim. Cover and cook for 1 hour.

2 To make the gumbo, heat the oil in a large pan, add the onion and garlic and cook for 3–4 minutes. Add the bacon and cook for 3 minutes. Stir in the flour and cook for 3–4 minutes.

3 When the mixture is turning golden, strain in the stock, stirring continuously. Add the celery, pepper, chilli and tomatoes, bring to the boil and simmer for 5 minutes.

4 Cut the corn cobs into 2.5cm/1in slices, and add to the gumbo.

5 To prepare the crabs, cut off the eyes and mouth, cut across the face and hook out the stomach with your fingers. Pull off the tail flap and pull out the gills or dead man's fingers. Quarter the crabs, then add to the gumbo with the prawns.

6 Simmer for 15 minutes until the crabs and corn are cooked. Season, then stir in the parsley and spring onions. Serve in deep bowls.

Energy 166kcal/694kJ; Protein 10.2g; Carbohydrate 11.1g, of which sugars 5.5g; Fat 9.3g, of which saturates 2.2g; Cholesterol 37mg; Calcium 94mg; Fibre 2.2g; Sodium 1280mg.

SAFFRON SEAFOOD SOUP

FILLING YET NOT TOO RICH, THIS GOLDEN SOUP WILL MAKE A DELICIOUS MEAL ON EARLY SUMMER EVENINGS, SERVED WITH LOTS OF HOT FRESH BREAD AND A GLASS OF FRUITY, DRY WHITE WINE. WHEN MUSSELS ARE NOT AVAILABLE USE PRAWNS (SHRIMP) IN THEIR SHELLS INSTEAD.

SERVES 4

INGREDIENTS
1 parsnip, quartered
2 carrots, quartered
1 onion, quartered
2 celery sticks, quartered
2 smoked bacon rashers (strips),
  rinds removed
juice of 1 lemon
pinch of saffron strands
450g/1lb fish heads
450g/1lb fresh mussels, scrubbed
1 leek, shredded
2 shallots, finely chopped
30ml/2 tbsp chopped dill, plus extra
  sprigs to garnish
450g/1lb haddock, skinned and boned
3 egg yolks
30ml/2 tbsp double (heavy) cream
salt and ground black pepper

1 Put the parsnip, carrots, onion, celery, bacon, lemon juice, saffron strands and fish heads in a large pan with 900ml/1½ pints/3¾ cups water and bring to the boil. Boil gently for about 20 minutes or until reduced by half.

COOK'S TIP
Fish stock freezes well and will keep for up to 6 months.

2 Discard any mussels that are open and don't close when tapped sharply. Add the rest to the pan of stock. Cook for about 4 minutes, until they have opened. Strain the soup and return the liquid to the pan. Discard any unopened mussels, then remove the remaining ones from their shells and set aside.

3 Add the leeks and shallots to the soup, bring to the boil and cook for 5 minutes. Add the dill and haddock, and simmer for a further 5 minutes until the fish is tender. Remove the haddock, using a slotted spoon, then flake it into a bowl, using a fork.

4 In another bowl, whisk together the eggs and double cream. Whisk in a little of the hot soup, then whisk the mixture back into the hot but not boiling liquid. Continue to whisk for several minutes as it heats through and thickens slightly, but do not let it boil.

5 Add the flaked haddock and mussels to the soup and check the seasoning. Garnish with tiny sprigs of dill and serve piping hot.

Energy 278kcal/1167kJ; Protein 33.2g; Carbohydrate 9.8g, of which sugars 8.5g; Fat 12.1g, of which saturates 4.8g; Cholesterol 222mg; Calcium 147mg; Fibre 3.4g; Sodium 377mg.

SAFFRON-FLAVOURED MUSSEL SOUP

THERE'S A FRAGRANT TASTE OF THE SEA OFF THE SPANISH COAST IN THIS CREAMY SOUP FILLED WITH THE JET BLACK SHELLS OF PLUMP MUSSELS. SAFFRON GOES WELL WITH SHELLFISH, AND GIVES THE SOUP A LOVELY PALE YELLOW COLOUR.

SERVES 4

INGREDIENTS

1.5kg/3–3½ lb fresh mussels
600ml/1 pint /2½ cups white wine
a few fresh parsley stalks
50g/2oz/¼ cup butter
2 leeks, finely chopped
2 celery sticks, finely chopped
1 carrot, chopped
2 garlic cloves, chopped
large pinch of saffron strands
600ml/1 pint/2½ cups double
   (heavy) cream
3 tomatoes, peeled, seeded
   and chopped
salt and ground black pepper
30ml/2 tbsp chopped fresh chives,
   to garnish

1 Clean the mussels and pull away the beards. Put into a large pan with the wine and parsley stalks. Cover, bring to the boil and cook for 4–5 minutes, shaking the pan occasionally, until the mussels have opened. Discard the stalks and any unopened mussels.

2 Drain the mussels over a large bowl, reserving the cooking liquid. When cool enough to handle, remove about half of the cooked mussels from their shells. Set aside with the remaining mussels in their shells.

COOK'S TIP
The most efficient way to clean fresh mussels is to scrub them under cold running water, using a stiff brush to remove any sand or dirt.

3 Melt the butter in a large pan, add the leeks, celery, carrot and garlic, and cook for 5 minutes until softened. Strain the reserved mussel cooking liquid through a fine sieve (strainer) or muslin (cheesecloth). Add to the pan and cook over a high heat for 8–10 minutes to reduce the liquid slightly. Strain into a clean pan, add the saffron strands and cook for 1 minute.

4 Add the cream and bring back to the boil. Season well. Add all the mussels and the tomatoes and heat gently to warm through. Ladle the soup into four bowls, then scatter with the chopped chives and serve immediately.

Energy 1054kcal/4359kJ; Protein 22.8g; Carbohydrate 7.5g, of which sugars 7.4g; Fat 93.4g, of which saturates 57.1g; Cholesterol 277mg; Calcium 327mg; Fibre 1.4g; Sodium 372mg.

PRAWN BISQUE

THE CLASSIC FRENCH METHOD FOR MAKING A BISQUE INVOLVES PUSHING THE SHELLFISH THROUGH A TAMIS, OR DRUM SIEVE. THIS RECIPE IS SIMPLER AND THE RESULT IS JUST AS SMOOTH.

SERVES 6–8

INGREDIENTS

675g/1½lb small or medium cooked
    prawns (shrimp) in their shells
25ml/1½ tbsp vegetable oil
2 onions, halved and sliced
1 large carrot, sliced
2 celery sticks, sliced
2 litres/3½ pints/9 cups water
a few drops of lemon juice
30ml/2 tbsp tomato purée (paste)
bouquet garni
50g/2oz/4 tbsp butter
50g/2oz/⅓ cup plain (all-purpose)
    flour
45–60ml/3–4 tbsp brandy
150ml/¼ pint/⅔ cup whipping
    cream

1 Remove the heads from the prawns and peel away the shells. Reserve the heads and shells for the stock. Place the prawns in a covered bowl and place in the refrigerator.

2 Heat the oil in a large pan, add the heads and shells and cook over a high heat, stirring, until they start to brown.

3 Reduce the heat to medium, add the vegetables and fry, stirring occasionally, for 5 minutes until the onions are soft but not browned.

4 Add the water, lemon juice, tomato purée and bouquet garni. Bring to the boil, then reduce the heat, cover and simmer gently for 25 minutes. Remove from the heat and strain the stock through a sieve (strainer).

5 Melt the butter in a heavy pan over a medium heat. Stir in the flour and cook until just golden, stirring occasionally to prevent it sticking to the base.

6 Add the brandy. Gradually pour in half the prawn stock, whisking vigorously until smooth, then whisk in the remaining liquid. Season if necessary.

7 Reduce the heat, cover and simmer for 5 minutes, stirring frequently.

8 Strain the soup into a clean pan. Add the cream and a little extra lemon juice to taste, then stir in most of the reserved prawns and cook over a medium heat, stirring frequently, until hot. Serve at once, garnished with the remaining reserved prawns.

COOK'S TIP
If you prefer, you may leave the brandy out of this dish and it will still taste delicious.

Energy 220kcal/915kJ; Protein 9g; Carbohydrate 9.7g, of which sugars 4g; Fat 15g, of which saturates 8.3g; Cholesterol 122mg; Calcium 73mg; Fibre 1.1g; Sodium 566mg.

SHRIMP AND CORN BISQUE

HOT PEPPER SAUCE BRINGS A TOUCH OF SPICE TO THIS MILD, CREAMY SOUP. IT LOOKS VERY ATTRACTIVE GARNISHED WITH SPRIGS OF FRESH DILL.

SERVES 4

INGREDIENTS

    30ml/2 tbsp olive oil
    1 onion, very finely chopped
    50g/2oz/4 tbsp butter or margarine
    25g/1oz/¼ cup flour
    750ml/1¼ pints/3 cups fish
      stock
    250ml/8fl oz/1 cup milk
    115g/4oz/1 cup peeled cooked small
      shrimps, deveined if necessary
    225g/8oz/1½ cups corn kernels
    2.5ml/½ tsp chopped fresh dill
      or thyme
    hot pepper sauce
    120ml/4fl oz/½ cup single
      (light) cream
    salt
    sprigs of fresh dill, to garnish

1 Heat the olive oil in a large heavy pan. Add the onion and cook over a low heat for 8–10 minutes until softened but not browned.

2 Meanwhile, melt the butter or margarine in a medium pan. Add the flour and cook for 1–2 minutes, stirring. Stir in the stock and milk, bring to the boil and cook for 5–8 minutes, stirring frequently.

3 Cut each shrimp into two or three pieces and add to the onion with the corn and dill or thyme. Cook for 2–3 minutes, then remove from the heat and set aside.

4 Add the sauce mixture to the shrimp and corn mixture, and mix well.

5 Remove 750ml/1¼ pints/3 cups of the soup and purée it in a blender or food processor. Return the purée to the rest of the soup in the pan and stir well. Season with salt and hot pepper sauce to taste.

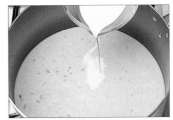

6 Add the cream and stir to blend. Heat the soup almost to boiling point, stirring frequently.

7 Divide into individual soup bowls and serve hot, garnished with sprigs of dill.

Energy 358kcal/1494kJ; Protein 12.4g; Carbohydrate 24.7g, of which sugars 10g; Fat 24.1g, of which saturates 11.9g; Cholesterol 84mg; Calcium 211mg; Fibre 1.2g; Sodium 1368mg.

CORN AND CRAB MEAT SOUP

THIS SOUP ORIGINATED IN THE USA BUT IT HAS SINCE BEEN INTRODUCED INTO CHINA. YOU MUST USE CREAMED CORN IN THE RECIPE TO ACHIEVE THE RIGHT CONSISTENCY.

SERVES 4

INGREDIENTS
    115g/4oz crab meat
    2.5ml/½ tsp finely chopped fresh
      root ginger
    30ml/2 tbsp milk
    15ml/1 tbsp cornflour (cornstarch)
    2 egg whites
    600ml/1 pint/2½ cups vegetable stock
    225g/8oz can creamed corn
    salt and ground black pepper
    chopped spring onions (scallions),
      to garnish

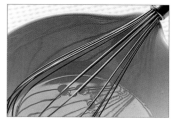

1 Flake the crab meat and mix with the ginger in a bowl. In another bowl, mix the milk and cornflour until smooth.

2 Beat the egg whites until frothy.

3 Add the milk and cornflour mixture and beat again until smooth. Blend with the crab meat.

4 In a wok or large pan, bring the vegetable stock to the boil. Add the creamed corn and bring back to the boil once more.

5 Stir in the crab meat and egg white mixture, adjust the seasoning and stir gently until well blended. Serve garnished with chopped spring onions.

VARIATION
You can use coarsely chopped chicken breast instead of crab meat.

Energy 115kcal/486kJ; Protein 8.6g; Carbohydrate 18.8g, of which sugars 5.8g; Fat 1.1g, of which saturates 0.2g; Cholesterol 21mg; Calcium 47mg; Fibre 0.8g; Sodium 346mg.

CORN AND SCALLOP CHOWDER

FRESH CORN IS IDEAL FOR THIS CHOWDER, ALTHOUGH CANNED OR FROZEN CORN ALSO WORKS WELL. THIS SOUP IS ALMOST A MEAL IN ITSELF AND MAKES A PERFECT LUNCH DISH.

SERVES 4–6

INGREDIENTS

2 corn cobs or 200g/7oz/
generous 1 cup frozen or
canned corn
600ml/1 pint/2½ cups milk
15g/½oz butter or margarine
1 small leek or onion, chopped
40g/1½oz/¼ cup smoked streaky
(fatty) bacon, finely chopped
1 small garlic clove, crushed
1 small green (bell) pepper, seeded
and diced
1 celery stick, chopped
1 medium potato, diced
15ml/1 tbsp plain (all-purpose) flour
300ml/½ pint/1¼ cups chicken or
vegetable stock
4 scallops
115g/4oz cooked fresh mussels
a pinch of paprika
150ml/¼ pint/⅔ cup single (light)
cream (optional)
salt and ground black pepper

1 Using a sharp knife, slice down the corn cobs, if using, to remove the kernels. Place half the kernels in a food processor or blender and process with a little of the milk. Set the other half aside.

2 Melt the butter or margarine in a large pan and gently fry the leek or onion, bacon and garlic for 4–5 minutes until the leek is soft but not browned. Add the green pepper, celery and potato and sweat over a gentle heat for a further 3–4 minutes, stirring frequently.

3 Stir in the flour and cook for about 1–2 minutes until golden and frothy. Stir in a little milk and the corn mixture, then add the stock, the remaining milk and corn kernels and seasoning.

4 Bring to the boil, and then simmer, partially covered, for 15–20 minutes until the vegetables are tender.

5 Pull the corals away from the scallops and slice the white flesh into 5mm/¼in slices. Stir the scallops into the soup, cook for 4 minutes and then stir in the corals, mussels and paprika. Heat through for a few minutes and then stir in the cream, if using. Check the seasoning and serve.

Energy 200kcal/845kJ; Protein 13g; Carbohydrate 23.6g, of which sugars 10.5g; Fat 6.7g, of which saturates 3.2g; Cholesterol 31mg; Calcium 150mg; Fibre 1.8g; Sodium 326mg.

CLAM AND CORN CHOWDER

THIS IS A RICH, CREAMY CHOWDER, MADE WITH DOUBLE CREAM. IT USES WHOLE BABY CORN, BABY NEW POTATOES AND ONIONS, AND SMALL CLAMS. SERVE IT WITH LIME WEDGES, IF YOU LIKE.

SERVES 4

INGREDIENTS
300ml/½ pint/1¼ cups double (heavy) cream
75g/3oz/6 tbsp unsalted (sweet) butter
1 small onion, finely chopped
1 apple, cored and sliced
1 garlic clove, crushed
45ml/3 tbsp mild curry powder
350g/12oz/3 cups baby corn cobs
225g/8oz cooked new potatoes
24 boiled baby onions
600ml/1 pint/2½ cups fish stock
40 small clams
salt and ground black pepper

1 Pour the cream into a small pan and cook over a high heat, stirring continuously, until it is reduced by half.

2 In a larger pan, melt half the butter. Add the onion, apple, garlic and curry powder. Sauté until the onion is translucent. Add the reduced cream and stir well.

3 In another pan, melt the remaining butter and add the baby corn, potatoes and baby onions. Cook for 5 minutes. Increase the heat and add the cream mixture and stock. Bring to the boil.

4 Add the clams. Cover and cook until the clams have opened. Discard any that do not open.

5 Season well to taste with salt and freshly ground black pepper. Ladle into soup bowls and serve piping hot.

COOK'S TIPS
• Canned or bottled clams in brine, once drained, can be used as an alternative to fresh ones in their shells. Discard any shells that remain closed during cooking as this means they were already dead when they were canned or bottled.
• Serve lime wedges with the soup as a garnish, if you like.

Energy 676kcal/2798kJ; Protein 18.2g; Carbohydrate 24.2g, of which sugars 11.3g; Fat 56.9g, of which saturates 35g; Cholesterol 193mg; Calcium 136mg; Fibre 3.8g; Sodium 2038mg.

LOBSTER BISQUE

BISQUE IS A LUXURIOUS, VELVETY SOUP WHICH CAN BE MADE WITH ANY CRUSTACEANS, SUCH AS CRAB OR SHRIMP. IF LOBSTER IS YOUR FAVOURITE SHELLFISH, THIS VERSION IS FOR YOU.

SERVES 6

INGREDIENTS

500g/1¼lb fresh lobster
75g/3oz/6 tbsp butter
1 onion, chopped
1 carrot, diced
1 celery stick, diced
45ml/3 tbsp brandy
250ml/8fl oz/1 cup dry white wine
1 litre/1¾ pints/4 cups fish stock
15ml/1 tbsp tomato purée (paste)
75g/3oz/scant ½ cup long grain rice
1 fresh bouquet garni
150ml/¼ pint/⅔ cup double (heavy) cream, plus extra to garnish
salt, ground white pepper and cayenne pepper

1 Cut the lobster into pieces. Melt half the butter in a large pan, add the vegetables and cook over a low heat until soft. Put in the lobster and stir gently until the shells turn red.

2 Pour over the brandy and set it alight. When the flames die down, add the wine and boil until reduced by half. Pour in the fish stock and simmer for 2–3 minutes. Remove the lobster.

3 Stir in the tomato purée and rice, add the bouquet garni and cook until the rice is tender, about 15 minutes. Meanwhile, remove the lobster meat from the shell and return the shells to the pan. Dice the meat and set it aside.

COOK'S TIP
It is best to buy a live lobster, chilling it in the freezer until it is comatose and then killing it just before cooking. If you can't face the procedure, use a cooked lobster; take care not to over-cook the flesh. Stir for only 30–60 seconds.

4 When the rice is cooked, discard all the larger bits of shell. Put the mixture in a blender or food processor and whizz to a purée. Press the purée through a fine sieve (strainer) over the clean pan. Stir the mixture, then heat until almost boiling. Season with salt, pepper and cayenne, then lower the heat and stir in the cream. Dice the remaining butter and whisk it into the bisque. Add the diced lobster meat and serve at once. If you like, pour a small spoonful of brandy into each soup bowl and swirl in a little extra cream.

Energy 347kcal/1438kJ; Protein 8.5g; Carbohydrate 12.9g, of which sugars 2.6g; Fat 24.3g, of which saturates 15g; Cholesterol 94mg; Calcium 48mg; Fibre 0.6g; Sodium 195mg.

CHILLI CLAM BROTH

THIS SOUP OF SUCCULENT CLAMS IN A TASTY STOCK COULD NOT BE EASIER TO PREPARE. POPULAR IN COASTAL AREAS OF COLOMBIA, IT MAKES THE PERFECT LUNCH ON A HOT SUMMER'S DAY.

SERVES 6

INGREDIENTS
30ml/2 tbsp olive oil
1 onion, finely chopped
3 garlic cloves, crushed
2 fresh red chillies, seeded and
  finely chopped
250ml/8fl oz/1 cup dry white wine
400ml/14fl oz can plum
  tomatoes, drained
1 large potato, about 250g/9oz,
  peeled and diced
400ml/14fl oz/1⅔ cups fish stock
1.3kg/3lb fresh clams
15ml/1 tbsp chopped fresh
  coriander (cilantro)
15ml/1 tbsp chopped fresh flat
  leaf parsley
salt
lime wedges, to garnish

1 Heat the oil in a pan. Add the onion and sauté for 5 minutes over a low heat. Stir in the garlic and chillies and cook for a further 2 minutes. Pour in the wine and bring to the boil, then simmer for 2 minutes.

2 Add the tomatoes, diced potato and stock. Bring to the boil, cover and lower the heat so that the soup simmers.

3 Season with salt and cook for 15 minutes, until the potatoes are beginning to break up and the tomatoes have made a rich sauce.

4 Meanwhile, wash the clams thoroughly under cold running water. Gently tap any that are open, and discard them if they do not close.

5 Add the clams to the soup, cover the pan and cook for about 3–4 minutes, or until the clams have opened, then stir in the chopped herbs. Season with salt to taste.

6 Check over the clams and throw away any that have failed to open. Ladle the soup into warmed bowls. Offer the lime wedges separately, to be squeezed over the soup just before eating.

Energy 290kcal/1217kJ; Protein 36.2g; Carbohydrate 14.1g, of which sugars 3.5g; Fat 7.2g, of which saturates 1.3g; Cholesterol 145mg; Calcium 184mg; Fibre 1.5g; Sodium 2614mg.

SPICED MUSSEL SOUP

CHUNKY AND COLOURFUL, THIS TURKISH FISH SOUP IS LIKE A CHOWDER IN ITS CONSISTENCY. IT IS FLAVOURED WITH HARISSA SAUCE, WHICH IS MORE FAMILIAR IN NORTH AFRICAN COOKERY.

SERVES 6

INGREDIENTS

1.5kg/3–3½lb fresh mussels
150ml/¼ pint/⅔ cup white wine
30ml/2 tbsp olive oil
1 onion, finely chopped
2 garlic cloves, crushed
2 celery sticks, finely sliced
bunch of spring onions (scallions)
  finely sliced
1 potato, diced
7.5ml/1½ tsp harissa sauce
3 tomatoes, peeled and diced
45ml/3 tbsp chopped fresh parsley
ground black pepper
thick natural (plain) yogurt, to serve
  (optional)

1 Scrub the mussels, discarding any damaged ones or any open ones that do not close when tapped with a knife.

2 Bring the wine to the boil in a large pan. Add the mussels and cover with a lid. Cook for 4–5 minutes until the mussels have opened wide. Discard any that remain closed.

3 Drain the mussels, reserving the cooking liquid. Reserve a few mussels in their shells to use as a garnish, and shell the rest.

4 Heat the oil in a pan and fry the onion, garlic, celery and spring onions for 5 minutes.

5 Add the shelled mussels, reserved liquid, potato, harissa sauce and tomatoes. Bring to the boil, reduce the heat and cover. Simmer gently for 25 minutes or until the potatoes are breaking up.

6 Stir in the parsley and pepper and add the reserved mussels in their shells. Heat through for 1 minute. Serve hot with a spoonful of yogurt, if you like.

Energy 153kcal/644kJ; Protein 14.5g; Carbohydrate 7.8g, of which sugars 3.2g; Fat 5.6g, of which saturates 0.9g; Cholesterol 30mg; Calcium 178mg; Fibre 1.5g; Sodium 175mg.

EGG AND CHEESE SOUPS

Omelettes are often used to add protein to light Oriental soups, and in this section you will find several examples, such as Thai Omelette Soup, Prawn and Egg-knot Soup, and Egg Flower Soup. Eggs are also an ingredient in many Mediterranean soups, for example Portuguese Garlic Soup and Greek Avgolemono. Cheese may also be included for added protein and flavour, as in the classic Roman Egg and Cheese Soup, and Irish Leek and Blue Cheese Soup.

PORTUGUESE GARLIC SOUP

THIS RECIPE IS BASED ON THE WONDERFUL BREAD SOUPS OR AÇORDAS OF PORTUGAL. BEING A SIMPLE SOUP IT SHOULD BE MADE WITH THE BEST INGREDIENTS — PLUMP GARLIC, FRESH CORIANDER, HIGH-QUALITY CRUSTY COUNTRY BREAD AND EXTRA VIRGIN OLIVE OIL.

SERVES 6

INGREDIENTS
25g/1oz fresh coriander (cilantro),
  leaves and stalks chopped separately
1.5 litres/2½ pints/6¼ cups vegetable
  or chicken stock, or water
5 or 6 plump garlic cloves, peeled
6 eggs
275g/10oz day-old bread, most
  of the crust removed, torn into
  bitesize pieces
salt and ground black pepper
90ml/6 tbsp extra virgin olive oil,
  plus extra to serve

1 Place the coriander stalks in a pan. Add the stock or water and bring to the boil. Lower the heat and simmer for 10 minutes, then process in a blender or food processor and sieve (strain) back into the pan.

2 Crush the garlic with 5ml/1 tsp salt, then stir in 120ml/4fl oz/½ cup hot soup. Return the mixture to the pan.

3 Meanwhile, poach the eggs in a frying pan of simmering water for about 3–4 minutes, until just set. Use a slotted spoon to remove them from the pan and transfer to a warmed plate. Trim off any untidy bits of white.

4 Bring the soup back to the boil and add seasoning. Stir in the chopped coriander leaves and remove from the heat.

5 Place the bread in six soup plates or bowls and drizzle the oil over it. Ladle in the soup and stir. Add a poached egg to each bowl and serve immediately, offering olive oil at the table so that it can be drizzled over the soup to taste.

Energy 299kcal/1249kJ; Protein 11.6g; Carbohydrate 24.6g, of which sugars 2.8g; Fat 18g, of which saturates 3.1g; Cholesterol 190mg; Calcium 170mg; Fibre 3g; Sodium 323mg.

THAI OMELETTE SOUP

THIS IS A SURPRISINGLY SATISFYING SOUP FROM THAILAND THAT IS VERY QUICK AND EASY TO PREPARE. IT IS A VERSATILE RECIPE, TOO, IN THAT YOU CAN VARY THE VEGETABLES YOU USE ACCORDING TO WHAT IS SEASONALLY AVAILABLE.

SERVES 4

INGREDIENTS
1 egg
15ml/1 tbsp groundnut (peanut) oil
900ml/1½ pints/3¾ cups
  vegetable stock
2 large carrots, finely diced
4 outer leaves Savoy
  cabbage, shredded
30ml/2 tbsp soy sauce
2.5ml/½ tsp granulated sugar
2.5ml/½ tsp ground black pepper
fresh coriander (cilantro) leaves,
  to garnish

VARIATION
Use pak choi (bok choy) instead of Savoy cabbage, if you like. In Thailand there are about forty different types of pak choi, including miniature versions.

1 Put the egg in a bowl and beat lightly with a fork. Heat the oil in a small frying pan until it is hot, but not smoking. Pour in the egg and swirl the pan so that it coats the base evenly. Cook over a medium heat until the omelette has set and the underside is golden. Slide it out of the pan and roll it up like a pancake. Slice into 5mm/¼in rounds and set aside for the garnish.

2 Put the stock into a large pan. Add the carrots and cabbage and bring to the boil. Reduce the heat and simmer for 5 minutes, then add the soy sauce, granulated sugar and pepper.

3 Stir well, then pour into warmed bowls. Lay a few omelette rounds on the surface of each portion and complete the garnish with the coriander leaves.

Energy 64kcal/264kJ; Protein 2.3g; Carbohydrate 4.3g, of which sugars 4.1g; Fat 4.3g, of which saturates 0.7g; Cholesterol 48mg; Calcium 27mg; Fibre 1.1g; Sodium 560mg.

FRENCH ONION SOUP
WITH GRUYÈRE CROÛTES

THIS IS PERHAPS THE MOST FAMOUS OF ALL ONION SOUPS. TRADITIONALLY, IT WAS SERVED AS A SUSTAINING EARLY MORNING MEAL TO THE PORTERS AND WORKERS OF LES HALLES MARKET IN PARIS.

SERVES 6

INGREDIENTS
  50g/2oz/¼ cup butter
  15ml/1 tbsp olive oil
  2kg/4½lb yellow onions, peeled
    and sliced
  5ml/1 tsp chopped fresh thyme
  5ml/1 tsp caster (superfine) sugar
  15ml/1 tbsp sherry vinegar
  1.5 litres/2½ pints/6¼ cups good
    beef, chicken or duck stock
  25ml/1½ tbsp plain (all-purpose) flour
  150ml/¼ pint/⅔ cup dry white wine
  45ml/3 tbsp brandy
  salt and ground black pepper
For the croûtes
  6–12 thick slices day-old French
    stick or baguette, about 2.5cm/
    1in thick
  1 garlic clove, halved
  15ml/1 tbsp French mustard
  115g/4oz/1 cup coarsely grated
    Gruyère cheese

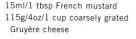

1 Melt the butter with the oil in a large pan. Add the onions and stir to coat them in the fat. Cook over a medium heat for 5–8 minutes, stirring once or twice, until the onions begin to soften. Stir in the thyme.

2 Reduce the heat to very low, cover the pan and cook the onions for 20–30 minutes, stirring frequently, until they are very soft and golden yellow.

3 Uncover the pan and increase the heat slightly. Stir in the sugar and cook for 5–10 minutes, until the onions start to brown. Add the sherry vinegar and increase the heat again, then continue cooking, stirring frequently, until the onions turn a deep, golden brown – this could take up to 20 minutes.

COOK'S TIP
The long slow cooking of the onions is the key to success with this soup. If the onions brown too quickly the soup will be bitter.

4 Meanwhile, bring the stock to the boil in another pan. Stir the flour into the onions and cook for about 2 minutes, then gradually pour in the hot stock. Add the wine and brandy and season the soup to taste with salt and pepper. Simmer for 10–15 minutes.

5 For the croûtes, preheat the oven to 150°C/300°F/Gas 2. Place the slices of bread on a greased baking tray and bake for 15–20 minutes, until dry and lightly browned. Rub the bread with the cut surface of the garlic and spread with the mustard, then sprinkle the grated Gruyère cheese over the slices.

6 Preheat the grill (broiler) on the hottest setting. Ladle the soup into a large flameproof pan or six flameproof bowls. Float the croûtes on the soup, then grill until the cheese melts, bubbles and browns. Serve immediately.

AVGOLEMONO

THIS IS A GREAT FAVOURITE IN GREECE AND IS A FINE EXAMPLE OF HOW JUST A FEW INGREDIENTS
CAN MAKE A MARVELLOUS DISH IF CAREFULLY CHOSEN AND COOKED. IT IS ESSENTIAL TO USE A
WELL-FLAVOURED STOCK. ADD AS LITTLE OR AS MUCH RICE AS YOU LIKE.

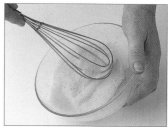

2 Whisk the egg yolks in a bowl, then add about 30ml/2 tbsp of the lemon juice, whisking constantly until the mixture is smooth and bubbly. Add a ladleful of soup and whisk again.

3 Remove the soup from the heat and slowly add the egg mixture, whisking all the time. The soup will turn a pretty lemon colour and will thicken slightly.

4 Taste and add more lemon juice if necessary. Stir in the parsley. Serve at once, without reheating, garnished with lemon slices and parsley sprigs.

SERVES 4

INGREDIENTS
900ml/1½ pints/3¾ cups chicken
   stock, preferably home-made
50g/2oz/generous ⅓ cup long
   grain rice
3 egg yolks
30–60ml/2–4 tbsp lemon juice
30ml/2 tbsp finely chopped fresh
   parsley
salt and ground black pepper
lemon slices and fresh parsley sprigs,
   to garnish

1 Pour the stock into a pan, bring to simmering point, then add the drained rice. Half cover and cook for about 12 minutes until the rice is just tender. Season with salt and pepper.

COOK'S TIP
The trick here is to add the egg mixture to the soup without it curdling. Avoid whisking the mixture into boiling liquid. It is safest to remove the soup from the heat entirely and then whisk in the mixture in a slow but steady stream. Do not reheat as curdling would be almost inevitable.

Energy 96kcal/404kJ; Protein 3.3g; Carbohydrate 10.9g, of which sugars 0.2g; Fat 4.7g, of which saturates 1.2g; Cholesterol 151mg; Calcium 39mg; Fibre 0.4g; Sodium 10mg.

SPICY TOMATO AND EGG DROP SOUP

POPULAR IN SOUTHERN VIETNAM AND CAMBODIA, THIS SPICY TOMATO SOUP WITH EGGS IS PROBABLY ADAPTED FROM THE TRADITIONAL CHINESE EGG DROP SOUP. ACCOMPANIED BY JASMINE OR GINGER RICE, THIS IS A TASTY DISH FOR A LIGHT LUNCH OR SUPPER.

SERVES 4

INGREDIENTS
    30ml/2 tbsp groundnut (peanut) or
      vegetable oil
    3 shallots, finely sliced
    2 garlic cloves, finely chopped
    2 Thai chillies, seeded and finely
      sliced
    25g/1oz galangal, shredded
    8 large, ripe tomatoes, skinned,
      seeded and finely chopped
    15ml/1 tbsp sugar
    30ml/2 tbsp *nuoc mam* or *tuk trey*
    4 lime leaves
    900ml/1½ pints/3¾ cups chicken
      stock
    15ml/1 tbsp wine vinegar
    4 eggs
    sea salt and ground black pepper
For the garnish
    chilli oil, for drizzling
    a small bunch of fresh coriander
      (cilantro), finely chopped
    a small bunch of fresh mint leaves,
      finely chopped

3 Stir the water clockwise with a spoon and drop an egg into the centre of the swirl. Follow with the others, or poach two at a time and keep the water boiling to throw the whites up over the yolks. Turn off the heat, cover the pan and leave to poach until firm enough to lift.

4 Using a slotted spoon, lift the eggs out of the water and slip them into the hot soup.

5 Drizzle a little chilli oil over the eggs, sprinkle with the coriander and mint, and serve piping hot.

1 Heat the oil in a wok or heavy pan. Stir in the shallots, garlic, chillies and galangal and cook until golden and fragrant. Add the tomatoes with the sugar, *nuoc mam* and lime leaves. Pour in the stock and bring to the boil. Reduce the heat and simmer for 30 minutes. Season to taste.

2 Just before serving, bring a wide pan of boiling water to the boil. Add the vinegar and a little salt. Break the eggs into individual cups or small bowls.

Energy 175kcal/732kJ; Protein 7.8g; Carbohydrate 10.9g, of which sugars 10.6g; Fat 11.6g, of which saturates 2.4g; Cholesterol 190mg; Calcium 47mg; Fibre 2.1g; Sodium 88mg.

EGG FLOWER SOUP

THIS SIMPLE, HEALTHY SOUP IS FLAVOURED WITH FRESH ROOT GINGER AND CHINESE FIVE-SPICE POWDER. IT IS QUICK AND DELICIOUS AND CAN BE MADE AT THE LAST MINUTE.

SERVES 4

INGREDIENTS

1.2 litres/2 pints/5 cups fresh
chicken or vegetable stock
10ml/2 tsp peeled, grated fresh
root ginger
10ml/2 tsp light soy sauce
5ml/1 tsp sesame oil
5ml/1 tsp Chinese five-spice powder
15ml/1 tbsp cornflour (cornstarch)
2 eggs
salt and ground black pepper
1 spring onion (scallion), very finely
sliced diagonally, and 15ml/1 tbsp
roughly chopped coriander (cilantro)
or flat leaf parsley, to garnish

COOK'S TIP
This soup is a good way of using up
leftover egg yolks or whites which have
been stored in the freezer.

1 Put the chicken or vegetable stock
into a large pan with the ginger, soy
sauce, oil and five-spice powder. Bring
to the boil and allow to simmer gently
for about 10 minutes.

2 Blend the cornflour in a measuring
jug with 60–75ml/4–5 tbsp water
and stir into the stock. Cook, stirring
constantly, until slightly thickened.
Season to taste with salt and pepper.

3 In a jug (pitcher), beat the eggs
together with 30ml/2 tbsp cold water
until the mixture becomes frothy.

4 Bring the soup back just to the boil
and drizzle in the egg mixture, stirring
vigorously with chopsticks. Choose a
jug with a fine spout to form a very thin
drizzle. Serve at once, sprinkled with
the sliced spring onions and chopped
coriander or parsley.

Energy 71kcal/298kJ; Protein 3.3g; Carbohydrate 7.1g, of which sugars 0.2g; Fat 3.6g, of which saturates 0.9g; Cholesterol 95mg; Calcium 16mg; Fibre 0g; Sodium 217mg.

PRAWN AND EGG-KNOT SOUP

OMELETTES AND PANCAKES ARE OFTEN USED TO ADD PROTEIN TO LIGHT ORIENTAL SOUPS. IN THIS RECIPE, THIN OMELETTES ARE TWISTED INTO LITTLE KNOTS AND ADDED AT THE LAST MINUTE.

SERVES 4

INGREDIENTS

    1 spring onion (scallion), shredded
    800ml/1⅓ pints/3½ cups well-
      flavoured stock or instant dashi
    5ml/1 tsp soy sauce
    dash of sake or dry white wine
    pinch of salt
For the prawn (shrimp) balls
    200g/7oz/generous 1 cup raw large
      prawns, shelled, thawed if frozen
    65g/2½oz cod fillet, skinned
    5ml/1 tsp egg white
    5ml/1 tsp sake or dry white wine,
      plus a dash extra
    22.5ml/4½ tsp cornflour (cornstarch)
      or potato flour
    2 or 3 drops soy sauce
    pinch of salt
For the omelette
    1 egg, beaten
    dash of mirin
    pinch of salt
    oil, for cooking

1 To make the prawn balls, use a pin to remove the black vein running down the back of each prawn. Place the prawns, cod, egg white, sake or dry white wine, cornflour or potato flour, soy sauce and a pinch of salt in a food processor or blender and process to a thick, sticky paste. Shape the mixture into 4 balls, place in a steaming basket and steam over a pan of vigorously boiling water for about 10 minutes.

2 To make the garnish, soak the spring onion shreds in iced water for about 5 minutes, until they curl, then drain.

3 To make the omelette, mix the egg with the mirin and salt. Heat a little oil in a frying pan and pour in the egg mixture, coating the pan evenly. When the omelette has set, turn it over and cook for 30 seconds. Leave to cool.

4 Cut the omelette into strips and tie each in a knot. Heat the stock or dashi, then add the soy sauce, sake or wine and salt. Divide the prawn balls and egg-knots among 4 bowls and add the soup. Garnish with the spring onion.

Energy 98kcal/412kJ; Protein 13.6g; Carbohydrate 7.1g, of which sugars 0.2g; Fat 1.9g, of which saturates 0.5g; Cholesterol 153mg; Calcium 51mg; Fibre 0.1g; Sodium 218mg.

EGG AND CHEESE SOUP

IN THIS CLASSIC ROMAN SOUP, EGGS AND CHEESE ARE BEATEN INTO HOT SOUP, PRODUCING THE
SLIGHTLY SCRAMBLED TEXTURE THAT IS CHARACTERISTIC OF THIS DISH.

SERVES 6

INGREDIENTS

   3 eggs
   45ml/3 tbsp fine semolina
   90ml/6 tbsp freshly grated
     Parmesan cheese
   pinch of nutmeg
   1.5 litres/2½ pints/6¼ cups cold
     meat or chicken stock
   salt and ground black pepper
   12 rounds of country bread or
     ciabatta, to serve

COOK'S TIP

Once added to the hot soup, the egg will
begin to cook and the soup will become
less smooth. Try not to overcook the soup
at this stage because it may cause the
egg to curdle.

1 Beat the eggs in a bowl, then beat
in the semolina and the cheese. Add
the nutmeg and beat in 250ml/8fl oz/
1 cup of the meat or chicken stock.
Pour the mixture into a measuring
jug (pitcher).

2 Pour the remaining stock into a large
pan and bring to a gentle simmer,
stirring occasionally.

3 A few minutes before you are ready to
serve the soup, whisk the egg mixture
into the hot stock. Raise the heat
slightly, and bring it barely to the boil.
Season and cook for 3–4 minutes.

4 To serve, toast the rounds of country
bread or ciabatta, place two in each
soup plate and ladle on the hot soup.
Serve immediately.

Energy 245kcal/1030kJ; Protein 14.1g; Carbohydrate 27.5g, of which sugars 1.3g; Fat 9.4g, of which saturates 4.1g; Cholesterol 110mg; Calcium 246mg; Fibre 1.1g; Sodium 424mg.

GARLIC SOUP WITH EGG AND CROÛTONS

SPANISH SOUP AND ITALIAN POLENTA MARRY WONDERFULLY WELL IN THIS RECIPE. THE DELICIOUS GARLIC SOUP ORIGINATES FROM ANDALUSIA IN SPAIN.

SERVES 4

INGREDIENTS

15ml/1 tbsp olive oil
1 garlic bulb, unpeeled and broken
  into cloves
4 slices day-old ciabatta bread,
  broken into pieces
1.2 litres/2 pints/5 cups
  chicken stock
pinch of saffron
15ml/1 tbsp white wine vinegar
4 eggs
salt and ground black pepper
chopped fresh parsley,
  to garnish
For the polenta
750ml/1¼ pints/3 cups milk
175g/6oz/1 cup quick-cook polenta
50g/2oz/¼ cup butter

1 Preheat the oven to 200°C/400°F/ Gas 6. Brush the oil over a roasting tin (pan), then add the garlic and bread, and roast for about 20 minutes, until the garlic is soft and the bread is dry. Leave until cool enough to handle.

2 Meanwhile, make the polenta. Bring the milk to the boil in a large, heavy-based pan and gradually pour in the polenta, stirring constantly. Cook for about 5 minutes, or according to the packet instructions, stirring frequently, until the polenta begins to come away from the side of the pan.

3 Spoon the polenta on to a chopping board and spread out to about 1cm/½in thick. Allow to cool and set, then cut into 1cm/½in dice.

4 Squeeze the garlic cloves from their skins into a food processor or blender. Add the bread and 300ml/½ pint/1¼ cups of the stock, then process until smooth. Pour into a pan. Pound the saffron in a mortar and stir in a little of the remaining stock, then add to the soup with enough of the remaining stock to thin the soup as required.

5 Melt the butter in a frying pan and cook the diced polenta over a high heat for 1–2 minutes, tossing until beginning to brown. Drain on kitchen paper.

6 Season the soup and reheat gently. Bring a large frying pan of water to the boil. Add the vinegar and reduce the heat to a simmer. Crack an egg on to a saucer. Swirl the water with a knife and drop the egg into the middle of the swirl. Repeat with the remaining eggs and poach for 2–3 minutes until set. Lift out the eggs using a draining spoon, then place one in each of four bowls.

7 Ladle the soup over the poached eggs, sprinkle polenta croûtons and parsley on top and serve.

Energy 415kcal/1731kJ; Protein 13.4g; Carbohydrate 43.9g, of which sugars 0.9g; Fat 20.8g, of which saturates 8.6g; Cholesterol 217mg; Calcium 57mg; Fibre 1.9g; Sodium 247mg.

CREAMY COURGETTE AND DOLCELATTE SOUP

THE BEAUTY OF THIS SOUP IS ITS DELICATE COLOUR, ITS CREAMY TEXTURE AND ITS SUBTLE TASTE. GARNISH IT WITH SOME SPRIGS OF FRESH OREGANO. IF YOU PREFER A MORE PRONOUNCED CHEESE FLAVOUR, USE GORGONZOLA INSTEAD OF DOLCELATTE.

2 Add the courgettes and oregano, with salt and pepper to taste. Cook over a medium heat for 10 minutes, stirring frequently to prevent sticking.

3 Pour in the stock and bring to the boil, stirring frequently. Lower the heat, half-cover the pan and simmer gently, stirring occasionally, for about 30 minutes.

4 Add the diced Dolcelatte, stirring until it is melted.

5 Process the soup in a blender or food processor until smooth, then press through a sieve into a clean pan.

6 Add two-thirds of the cream and stir over a low heat until hot, but not boiling. Check the consistency and add some more stock if the soup is too thick. Taste and adjust the seasoning if necessary.

7 Pour into heated bowls. Swirl in the remaining cream, garnish with fresh oregano and extra Dolcelatte cheese, crumbled, and serve.

SERVES 4–6

INGREDIENTS
  30ml/2 tbsp olive oil
  15g/½oz/1 tbsp butter
  1 medium onion, roughly chopped
  900g/2lb courgettes (zucchini),
    trimmed and sliced
  5ml/1 tsp dried oregano
  about 600ml/1 pint/2½ cups
    vegetable stock
  115g/4oz Dolcelatte cheese, diced
  300ml/½ pint/1¼ cups single (light)
    cream
  salt and ground black pepper
To garnish
  sprigs of fresh oregano
  extra Dolcelatte cheese

1 Heat the oil and butter in a large pan until foaming. Add the chopped onion and cook gently for about 5 minutes, stirring frequently, until the onion is softened but not brown.

Energy 250kcal/1031kJ; Protein 8.6g; Carbohydrate 5.8g, of which sugars 5.1g; Fat 21.5g, of which saturates 11.7g; Cholesterol 47mg; Calcium 182mg; Fibre 1.7g; Sodium 266mg.

IRISH LEEK AND BLUE CHEESE SOUP

THE BLUE CHEESE IS AN INTEGRAL PART OF THIS SUBSTANTIAL SOUP, WHICH MAKES FULL USE OF INGREDIENTS THAT HAVE ALWAYS BEEN IMPORTANT IN IRISH COOKING. IT CAN BE A GOOD WAY TO USE UP CHEESES LEFT OVER FROM THE CHEESEBOARD. SERVE WITH FRESHLY BAKED BROWN BREAD.

SERVES 6

INGREDIENTS

3 large leeks
50g/2oz/¼ cup butter
30ml/2 tbsp oil
115g/4oz Irish blue cheese,
    such as Cashel Blue
15g/½oz/2 tbsp plain
    (all-purpose) flour
15ml/1 tbsp wholegrain Irish
    mustard, or to taste
1.5 litres/2½ pints/6¼ cups
    chicken stock
ground black pepper
50g/2oz/½ cup grated cheese and
    chopped chives or spring onion
    (scallion) greens, to garnish

VARIATION
Any melting blue-veined cheese can be used in this recipe, such as Cabrales, Gorgonzola or Picon.

1 Slice the leeks thinly. Heat the butter and oil together in a large heavy pan and gently cook the leeks in it, covered, for 10–15 minutes, or until just softened but not brown.

2 Grate the cheese coarsely and add it to the pan, stirring over a low heat until it is melted. Add the flour and cook for 2 minutes, stirring constantly with a wooden spoon, then add ground black pepper and mustard to taste.

3 Gradually add the stock, stirring constantly and blending it in well; bring the soup to the boil.

4 Reduce the heat, cover and simmer very gently for about 15 minutes. Check the seasoning.

5 Serve the soup garnished with the extra grated cheese and the chopped chives or spring onion greens, and hand fresh bread around separately.

Energy 205kcal/852kJ; Protein 8.2g; Carbohydrate 7.9g, of which sugars 2.2g; Fat 15.7g, of which saturates 9.9g; Cholesterol 40mg; Calcium 188mg; Fibre 2.2g; Sodium 347mg.

AUBERGINE SOUP <u>WITH</u> MOZZARELLA <u>AND</u> GREMOLATA

GREMOLATA, A CLASSIC ITALIAN MIXTURE OF GARLIC, LEMON AND PARSLEY, ADDS A FLOURISH OF FRESH FLAVOUR TO THIS RICH CREAM SOUP.

SERVES 6

INGREDIENTS

30ml/2 tbsp olive oil
2 shallots, chopped
2 garlic cloves, chopped
1kg/2¼ lb aubergines (eggplants),
   trimmed and roughly chopped
1 litre/1¾ pints/4 cups
   chicken stock
150ml/¼ pint/⅔ cup double
   (heavy) cream
30ml/2 tbsp chopped
   fresh parsley
175g/6oz buffalo mozzarella,
   thinly sliced
salt and ground black pepper

For the gremolata
   2 garlic cloves, finely chopped
   grated rind of 2 lemons
   15ml/1 tbsp chopped fresh parsley

1 Heat the oil in a large pan and add the shallots and garlic. Cook for 4–5 minutes, until soft. Add the aubergines and cook for about 25 minutes, stirring occasionally, until soft and browned.

2 Pour in the stock and cook for about 5 minutes. Leave the soup to cool slightly, then purée in a food processor or blender until smooth. Return to the rinsed pan and season. Add the cream and parsley and bring to the boil.

3 Mix the ingredients for the gremolata in a small bowl.

4 Ladle the soup into bowls and lay the mozzarella on top. Sprinkle with the gremolata and serve.

Energy 261kcal/1079kJ; Protein 7.5g; Carbohydrate 4.9g, of which sugars 4.3g; Fat 23.7g, of which saturates 13.1g; Cholesterol 51mg; Calcium 137mg; Fibre 3.5g; Sodium 124mg.

BUTTERNUT SQUASH <u>AND</u> BLUE CHEESE RISOTTO SOUP

THIS IS, IN FACT, A VERY WET RISOTTO, BUT IT BEARS MORE THAN A PASSING RESEMBLANCE TO SOUP AND MAKES A VERY SMART FIRST COURSE FOR A DINNER PARTY.

SERVES 4

INGREDIENTS

25g/1oz/2 tbsp butter
30ml/2 tbsp olive oil
2 onions, finely chopped
½ celery stick, finely sliced
1 small butternut squash, peeled,
  seeded and cut into small cubes
15ml/1 tbsp chopped sage
300g/11oz/1½ cups risotto rice
1.2 litres/2 pints/5 cups hot
  chicken stock
30ml/2 tbsp double (heavy) cream
115g/4oz blue cheese, finely diced
30ml/2 tbsp olive oil
4 large sage leaves
salt and ground black pepper

1 Place the butter in a large pan with the oil and heat gently. Add the onions and celery, and cook for 4–5 minutes, until softened.

2 Stir in the butternut squash and cook for 3–4 minutes, then add the sage.

3 Add the rice and cook for 1–2 minutes, stirring, until the grains are slightly translucent. Add the chicken stock a ladleful at a time.

4 Cook until each ladleful of stock has been absorbed before adding the next. Continue adding the stock in this way until you have a very wet rice mixture. Season and stir in the cream.

5 Meanwhile, heat the oil in a frying pan and fry the sage leaves for a few seconds until crisp. Drain.

6 Stir the blue cheese into the risotto soup and ladle it into bowls. Garnish with a fried sage leaf.

Energy 505kcal/2100kJ; Protein 9.2g; Carbohydrate 63.7g, of which sugars 5.7g; Fat 23g, of which saturates 8.3g; Cholesterol 26mg; Calcium 110mg; Fibre 2.7g; Sodium 91mg.

BROCCOLI AND STILTON SOUP

THIS IS A REALLY EASY BUT RICH SOUP — CHOOSE SOMETHING SIMPLE TO FOLLOW, SUCH AS PLAINLY ROASTED OR GRILLED MEAT, POULTRY OR FISH.

2 Melt the butter in a large pan and cook the onion and leek until soft but not coloured. Add the broccoli and potato, then pour in the stock. Cover and simmer for 15–20 minutes, until the vegetables are tender.

3 Cool slightly then pour into a blender or food processor and purée until smooth. Strain the mixture through a sieve (strainer) back into the rinsed pan.

4 Add the milk and double cream to the pan. Season to taste with salt and ground black pepper. Reheat gently. At the last minute add the cheese, stirring until it just melts. Do not allow to boil.

SERVES 4

INGREDIENTS

  350g/12oz broccoli
  25g/1oz/2 tbsp butter
  1 onion, chopped
  1 leek, white part only, chopped
  1 small potato, cut into chunks
  600ml/1 pint/2½ cups hot chicken
    stock
  300ml/½ pint/1¼ cups milk
  45ml/3 tbsp double (heavy) cream
  115 g/4 oz Stilton cheese, rind
    removed, crumbled
  salt and ground black pepper

1 Cut the broccoli into florets, discarding any tough stems. Set aside two small florets to garnish the finished dish.

5 Meanwhile, blanch the reserved broccoli florets and cut them vertically into thin slices. Ladle the soup into warmed bowls and garnish with the sliced broccoli and a generous grinding of black pepper.

COOK'S TIP
Choose broccoli that has bright, compact florets. Yellowing florets and a pungent smell are an indication of overmaturity.

Energy 316kcal/1314kJ; Protein 14.7g; Carbohydrate 11.8g, of which sugars 7.2g; Fat 23.4g, of which saturates 14.7g; Cholesterol 60mg; Calcium 255mg; Fibre 3.7g; Sodium 310mg.

TOMATO AND BLUE CHEESE SOUP

THE CONCENTRATED FLAVOUR OF ROASTED TOMATOES STRIKES A GREAT BALANCE WITH THE STRONG
BLUE CHEESE AND THE BACON GARNISH.

SERVES 4

INGREDIENTS

1.5kg/3lb ripe tomatoes, peeled,
   quartered and seeded
2 garlic cloves, crushed
30ml/2 tbsp vegetable oil or butter
1 leek, chopped
1 carrot, chopped
1.2 litres/2 pints/5 cups chicken
   stock
115g/4oz blue cheese, crumbled
45ml/3 tbsp whipping cream
several large fresh basil leaves, or
   1 or 2 fresh parsley sprigs, plus
   extra to garnish
175g/6oz bacon, cooked and
   crumbled, to garnish
salt and ground black pepper

3 Stir in the stock and baked tomatoes.
Bring to the boil, then lower the heat,
cover and simmer for about 20 minutes,
until all the vegetables are soft.

4 Add the blue cheese, cream and basil
or parsley. Transfer to a food processor
or blender and process until smooth.
Taste and adjust the seasoning. Reheat
the soup, but do not boil. Garnish with
bacon and a sprig of fresh parsley.

1 Preheat the oven to 200°C/400°F/
Gas 6. Spread the tomatoes in a shallow
ovenproof dish. Sprinkle with the garlic
and some salt and pepper. Place in the
oven and bake for 35 minutes.

2 Heat the oil or butter in a large pan.
Add the leek and carrot and season
lightly with salt and pepper. Cook
over low heat, stirring often, for about
10 minutes, until softened.

Energy 365kcal/1519kJ; Protein 16.8g; Carbohydrate 14.7g, of which sugars 14.3g; Fat 27g, of which saturates 12.1g; Cholesterol 57mg; Calcium 191mg; Fibre 5.2g; Sodium 1067mg.

CAULIFLOWER AND BROCCOLI SOUP WITH CHEDDAR CHEESE CROÛTES

CREAMY CAULIFLOWER SOUP IS GIVEN REAL BITE BY ADDING CHUNKY CAULIFLOWER AND BROCCOLI FLORETS AND CRUSTY BREAD PILED HIGH WITH MELTING CHEDDAR CHEESE.

SERVES 4

INGREDIENTS

50g/2oz/¼ cup butter
1 onion, chopped
1 garlic clove, chopped
2 cauliflowers
1 large potato, cut into chunks
900ml/1½ pints/3¾ cups chicken
  stock
225g/8oz broccoli
150ml/¼ pint/⅔ cup single (heavy)
  cream
6 rindless streaky (fatty) bacon
  rashers (strips)
1 small baguette
225g/8oz/2 cups medium-mature
  (sharp) grated Cheddar cheese
salt and ground black pepper
chopped fresh parsley, to garnish

1 Melt the butter in a large pan and add the onion and garlic. Cook for 4–5 minutes, until softened.

2 Break the cauliflowers into florets and add about half and all the potato to the pan. Pour in the chicken stock and bring to the boil. Reduce the heat and simmer for 20 minutes, until very soft.

3 Meanwhile, cook the rest of the cauliflower in boiling salted water for about 6 minutes, or until just tender. Remove from the pan and refresh under cold running water, then drain well.

4 Chop the broccoli into florets and add to the boiling salted water. Cook for 3–4 minutes, until just tender. Drain and refresh under cold water. Add to the cauliflower and set aside.

5 Cool the soup slightly, then process it in a food processor or blender until smooth. Return the soup to the rinsed-out pan. Add the cream and salt and pepper to taste, then heat gently until piping hot. Add the blanched cauliflower and broccoli and heat through but do not boil.

6 Meanwhile, preheat the grill (broiler) to high. Grill (broil) the bacon until very crisp, then leave to cool slightly.

7 Ladle the soup into flameproof bowls. Tear the baguette into four ragged pieces and place one in the centre of each bowl. Sprinkle grated cheese over the bread and stand the bowls on one or two baking trays. Grill for 2–3 minutes, until the cheese is melted and bubbling. Take care when serving the hot bowls.

8 Roughly chop the bacon and sprinkle it over the melted cheese, then sprinkle the chopped parsley over the top and serve immediately.

Energy 737kcal/3071kJ; Protein 34.8g; Carbohydrate 45.5g, of which sugars 9.2g; Fat 46.2g, of which saturates 26.4g; Cholesterol 121mg; Calcium 589mg; Fibre 6.6g; Sodium 1206mg.

ONE-POT MEALS

A soup can be substantial enough to be a complete, one-pot meal, and in this section there are exciting dishes to serve on their own for lunch or supper. Gumbo is just such a dish, and here you will find recipes for Seafood and Sausage Gumbo, Louisiana Seafood Gumbo and Green Herb Gumbo. In Asian countries a laksa makes a complete meal — Malaysian Prawn Laksa is a good example. From the Mediterranean come Provençal Fish Soup with Pasta, and classic Bouillabaisse.

SEAFOOD AND SAUSAGE GUMBO

GUMBO IS A SOUP, BUT IS OFTEN SERVED OVER RICE AS A MAIN COURSE. THIS RECIPE IS ENOUGH FOR TEN TO TWELVE PEOPLE - SERVE IT FOR AN INFORMAL LUNCH OR SUPPER PARTY.

SERVES 10–12

INGREDIENTS

1.5kg/3lbs raw prawns (shrimp)
   in the shell
1.5 litres/2½ pints/6¼ cups water
4 medium onions, 2 of them
   quartered
4 bay leaves
175ml/6fl oz/3/4 cup vegetable oil
115g/4oz/1 cup flour
60ml/5 tbsp margarine or butter
2 green (bell) peppers, seeded and
   finely chopped
4 celery sticks, finely chopped
675g/1½lb Polish or andouille
   sausage, cut into 1cm/½in slices
450g/1lb fresh okra, cut into
   1cm/½in slices
3 garlic cloves, crushed
2.5ml/½ tsp fresh or dried thyme
   leaves
10ml/2 tsp salt
2.5ml/½ tsp ground black pepper
2.5ml/½ tsp white pepper
5ml/1 tsp cayenne pepper
30ml/2 tbsp hot pepper sauce
   (optional)
175g/6oz/2 cups chopped, peeled,
   fresh or canned plum tomatoes
450g/1lb fresh crab meat
boiled rice, to serve

1 Peel and devein the prawns; reserve the heads and shells. Cover and chill the prawns while you make the sauce.

2 Place the prawn heads and shells in a pan with the water, quartered onion and 1 bay leaf. Bring to the boil, then partly cover and simmer for 20 minutes. Strain and set aside.

3 To make a Cajun roux, heat the oil in a heavy frying pan. When the oil is hot, add the flour, a little at a time, and blend to a smooth paste.

4 Cook over a medium-low heat, stirring constantly for 25–40 minutes until the roux reaches the colour of peanut butter. Remove the pan from the heat and continue stirring until the roux has cooled and stopped cooking.

5 Melt the margarine or butter in a large, heavy pan or flameproof casserole. Finely chop the remaining onions and add to the pan with the chopped peppers and celery. Cook over medium-low heat for 6–8 minutes, until the onions are softened, stirring occasionally.

6 Add the sausage and mix well. Cook for 5 minutes more. Add the okra and garlic, stir, and cook until the okra stops producing white 'threads'.

7 Add the remaining bay leaves, the thyme, salt, black and white peppers, cayenne pepper, and hot pepper sauce to taste, if using. Mix thoroughly. Stir in 1.35 litres/2¼ pints/6 cups of the prawn stock and the chopped tomatoes. Bring to the boil, partly cover the pan, lower the heat and simmer for about 20 minutes.

8 Whisk in the Cajun roux. Increase the heat and bring to the boil, whisking well. Lower the heat again and simmer, uncovered, for a further 40–45 minutes, stirring occasionally.

9 Gently stir in the prawns and crab meat. Cook for 3–4 minutes until the prawns turn pink.

10 To serve, put a mound of hot boiled rice in each serving bowl and ladle on the gumbo, making sure each person gets some prawns, some crab meat and some sausage.

Energy 481kcal/2001kJ; Protein 28.7g; Carbohydrate 22.9g, of which sugars 8.8g; Fat 31.1g, of which saturates 6.6g; Cholesterol 96mg; Calcium 279mg; Fibre 4.1g; Sodium 1954mg.

LOUISIANA SEAFOOD GUMBO

GUMBO IS A SOUP, BUT IS SERVED OVER RICE AS A MAIN COURSE. IN LOUISIANA, OYSTERS ARE CHEAP AND PROLIFIC, AND WOULD BE USED HERE INSTEAD OF MUSSELS.

SERVES 6

INGREDIENTS

450g/1lb fresh mussels
450g/1lb prawns (shrimp), in the shell
1 cooked crab, about 1kg/2¼lb
a small bunch of parsley, leaves chopped and stalks reserved
150ml/¼ pint/⅔ cup vegetable oil
115g/4oz/1 cup plain (all-purpose) flour
1 green (bell) pepper, chopped
1 large onion, chopped
2 celery sticks, sliced
3 garlic cloves, finely chopped
75g/3oz smoked spiced sausage, skinned and sliced
275g/10oz/1½ cups white long grain rice
6 spring onions (scallions), shredded
cayenne pepper and Tabasco sauce
salt

3 Peel the prawns and set them aside, reserving a few for the garnish. Put the shells and heads into the pan.

4 Remove all the meat from the crab, separating the brown and white meat. Add all the pieces of shell to the pan with 5ml/2 tsp salt.

1 Wash the mussels in several changes of cold water, pulling away the black "beards". Discard any mussels that are broken or do not close when you tap them firmly.

2 Bring 250ml/8fl oz/1 cup water to the boil in a deep pan. Add the mussels, cover tightly and cook over a high heat, shaking frequently, for 3 minutes. As the mussels open, lift them out with tongs into a sieve (strainer) set over a bowl. Discard any that fail to open. Shell the mussels, discarding the shells. Return the liquid from the bowl to the pan and make the quantity up to 2 litres/3½ pints/8 cups with water.

5 Bring the shellfish stock to the boil, skimming it regularly. When there is no more froth on the surface, add the parsley stalks and simmer for 15 minutes. Cool the stock, then strain it into a measuring jug and make up to 2 litres/3½ pints/8 cups with water.

6 Heat the oil in a heavy pan and stir in the flour. Stir constantly over a medium heat with a wooden spoon or whisk until the roux reaches a golden-brown colour. Immediately add the pepper, onion, celery and garlic. Continue cooking for about 3 minutes until the onion is soft. Stir in the sausage. Reheat the stock.

7 Stir the brown crab meat into the roux, then ladle in the hot stock a little at a time, stirring constantly until it has all been smoothly incorporated. Bring to a low boil, partially cover the pan, then simmer the gumbo for 30 minutes.

8 Meanwhile, cook the rice in plenty of lightly salted boiling water until the grains are tender.

9 Add the prawns, mussels, white crab meat and spring onions to the gumbo. Return to the boil and season with salt if necessary, cayenne and a dash or two of Tabasco sauce. Simmer for a further minute, then add the chopped parsley leaves. Serve immediately, ladling the soup over the hot rice in soup plates.

COOK'S TIP
It is vital to stir constantly to darken the roux without burning. Should black specks appear at any stage of cooking, discard the roux and start again. Have the onion, green (bell) pepper and celery ready to add to the roux the minute it reaches the correct golden-brown stage, as this arrests its darkening.

MALAYSIAN PRAWN LAKSA

THIS SPICY PRAWN AND NOODLE SOUP TASTES JUST AS GOOD WHEN MADE WITH FRESH CRAB MEAT OR ANY FLAKED COOKED FISH INSTEAD OF THE PRAWNS. IF YOU ARE SHORT OF TIME, BUY READY-MADE LAKSA PASTE, WHICH YOU WILL FIND IN ORIENTAL STORES.

SERVES 2–3

INGREDIENTS
   115g/4oz rice vermicelli or stir-fry
      rice noodles
   15ml/1 tbsp vegetable or groundnut
      (peanut) oil
   600ml/1 pint/2½ cups fish stock
   400ml/14fl oz/1⅔ cups thin
      coconut milk
   30ml/2 tbsp Thai fish sauce
   ½ lime
   16–24 cooked peeled prawns
      (shrimp)
   salt
   cayenne pepper
   60ml/4 tbsp fresh coriander (cilantro)
      sprigs and leaves, chopped,
      to garnish
For the spicy paste
   2 lemon grass stalks,
      finely chopped
   2 fresh red chillies, seeded
      and chopped
   2.5cm/1in fresh root ginger, peeled
      and sliced
   2.5ml/½ tsp shrimp paste
   2 garlic cloves, chopped
   2.5ml/½ tsp ground turmeric
   30ml/2 tbsp tamarind paste

3 To make the spicy paste, place all the prepared ingredients in a mortar and pound with a pestle. Alternatively, put the ingredients in a food processor until a smooth paste is formed.

4 Heat the vegetable or groundnut oil in a large pan, add the spicy paste and fry, stirring constantly, for a few moments to release all the flavours. Be careful not to let it burn.

5 Add the fish stock and coconut milk and bring to the boil. Stir in the fish sauce, then simmer for 5 minutes. Season with salt and cayenne to taste, adding a squeeze of lime. Add the prawns and heat through for a few seconds.

6 Divide the noodles between two or three soup plates. Pour over the soup. Garnish each portion with fresh coriander and serve piping hot.

1 Cook the rice vermicelli or noodles in a large pan of boiling salted water for 3–4 minutes, or according to the instructions on the packet.

2 Transfer the noodles to a large sieve (strainer) or colander, then rinse under cold water and drain. Set aside.

Energy 436kcal/1830kJ; Protein 36.9g; Carbohydrate 55.3g, of which sugars 10.2g; Fat 7.6g, of which saturates 1.2g; Cholesterol 341mg; Calcium 239mg; Fibre 0.8g; Sodium 562mg.

PROVENÇAL FISH SOUP

THE ADDITION OF RICE MAKES THIS A SUBSTANTIAL MAIN-MEAL SOUP. BASMATI OR THAI RICE HAVE THE BEST FLAVOUR, BUT ANY LONG GRAIN RICE COULD BE USED. IF YOU PREFER A STRONGER TOMATO FLAVOUR, REPLACE THE WHITE WINE WITH EXTRA PASSATA.

SERVES 4–6

INGREDIENTS
    450g/1lb fresh mussels
    about 250ml/8fl oz/1 cup white wine
    675–900g/1½–2lb mixed white fish
        fillets, such as monkfish, plaice,
        flounder, cod or haddock
    6 large scallops
    30ml/2 tbsp olive oil
    3 leeks, chopped
    1 garlic clove, crushed
    1 red (bell) pepper, seeded and cut
        into 2.5cm/1in pieces
    1 yellow (bell) pepper, seeded and
        cut into 2.5cm/1in pieces
    175g/6oz fennel bulb, cut into
        4cm/1½in pieces
    400g/14oz can chopped tomatoes
    150ml/¼ pint/⅔ cup passata
        (bottled strained tomatoes)
    about 1 litre/1¾ pints/4 cups
        well-flavoured fish stock
    generous pinch of saffron threads,
        soaked in 15ml/1 tbsp hot water
    175g/6oz/scant 1 cup basmati
        rice, soaked
    8 large raw prawns (shrimp), peeled
        and deveined
    salt and ground black pepper
    30–45ml/2–3 tbsp fresh dill, to garnish

2 Strain, reserving the liquid. Discard any mussels that have not opened. Set aside half the mussels in their shells for the garnish; shell the rest and put them in a bowl.

3 Cut the fish into 2.5cm/1in cubes. Detach the corals from the scallops and slice the white flesh into three or four pieces. Add the scallops to the fish and the corals to the shelled mussels.

4 Heat the olive oil in a pan and fry the leeks and garlic for 3–4 minutes, until softened. Add the pepper chunks and fennel, and fry for 2 minutes more, until just softened.

COOK'S TIP
To make your own fish stock, place about 450g/1lb white fish trimmings – bones, heads, but not gills – in a large pan. Add a chopped onion, carrot, bay leaf, parsley sprig, 6 peppercorns and a piece of pared lemon rind. Pour in 1.2 litres/ 2 pints/5 cups water, bring to the boil, then simmer gently for 25–30 minutes. Strain through muslin (cheesecloth).

5 Add the tomatoes, passata, stock, saffron water, mussel liquid and wine. Season and cook for 5 minutes. Drain the rice, stir it into the mixture, cover and simmer for 10 minutes.

6 Carefully stir in the white fish and cook over a low heat for 5 minutes. Add the prawns, cook for 2 minutes, then add the scallop corals and shelled mussels and cook for 2–3 minutes more, until all the fish is tender. Add a little extra white wine or stock if needed. Spoon into warmed soup dishes, top with mussels in their shells and sprinkle with the dill. Serve immediately.

1 Clean the mussels, discarding any that do not close when tapped with a knife. Place them in a heavy pan. Add 90ml/6 tbsp of the wine, cover, bring to the boil over a high heat and cook for about 3 minutes or until all the mussels have opened.

Energy 568kcal/2385kJ; Protein 59.9g; Carbohydrate 50.5g, of which sugars 12.9g; Fat 9.7g, of which saturates 1.6g; Cholesterol 163mg; Calcium 182mg; Fibre 5.9g; Sodium 418mg.

CHICKEN SOUP WITH VERMICELLI

IN MOROCCO, THE COOK — WHO IS ALMOST ALWAYS THE MOST SENIOR FEMALE OF THE HOUSEHOLD — WOULD USE A WHOLE CHICKEN FOR THIS NOURISHING SOUP, TO SERVE TO HER FAMILY.

SERVES 4–6

INGREDIENTS

30ml/2 tbsp sunflower oil
15g/½oz/1 tbsp butter
1 onion, chopped
2 chicken legs or breast pieces,
   halved or quartered
flour, for dusting
2 carrots, cut into 4cm/1½in pieces
1 parsnip, cut into 4cm/1½in pieces
1.5 litres/2½ pints/6¼ cups chicken
   stock
1 cinnamon stick
a good pinch of paprika
a pinch of saffron
2 egg yolks
juice of ½ lemon
30ml/2 tbsp chopped fresh coriander
   (cilantro)
30ml/2 tbsp chopped fresh parsley
150g/5oz vermicelli
salt and ground black pepper

1 Heat the oil and butter in a pan or flameproof casserole, and fry the onion for 3–4 minutes until softened. Dust the chicken pieces in seasoned flour and fry gently until they are evenly browned.

2 Transfer the chicken to a plate and add the carrots and parsnip to the pan. Cook over a gentle heat for 3–4 minutes, stirring frequently. Return the chicken to the pan. Add the stock, cinnamon stick and paprika and season well.

3 Bring the soup to the boil, cover and simmer for 1 hour until the vegetables are very tender.

4 Meanwhile, blend the saffron in 30ml/2 tbsp boiling water. Beat the egg yolks with the lemon juice in a separate bowl and add the coriander and parsley. When the saffron water has cooled, stir into the egg and lemon mixture.

5 When the vegetables are tender, transfer the chicken to a plate. Increase the heat and stir in the noodles. Cook for 5–6 minutes until tender. Remove the skin and bones from the chicken and chop the flesh into bitesize pieces.

6 When the vermicelli is cooked, stir in the chicken pieces and the egg, lemon and saffron mixture. Cook over a low heat for 1–2 minutes, stirring all the time. Adjust the seasoning and serve.

Energy 236kcal/984kJ; Protein 15.8g; Carbohydrate 24.1g, of which sugars 3.3g; Fat 8.5g, of which saturates 2.5g; Cholesterol 108mg; Calcium 40mg; Fibre 1.6g; Sodium 60mg.

CHICKEN MINESTRONE

THIS IS A SPECIAL MINESTRONE MADE WITH FRESH CHICKEN. SERVED WITH CRUSTY ITALIAN BREAD, IT MAKES A HEARTY MEAL IN ITSELF.

SERVES 4–6

INGREDIENTS

15ml/1 tbsp olive oil
2 chicken thighs
3 rindless streaky (fatty) bacon rashers (strips), chopped
1 onion, finely chopped
a few fresh basil leaves, shredded
a few fresh rosemary leaves, finely chopped
15ml/1 tbsp chopped fresh flat leaf parsley
2 potatoes, cut into 1cm/½in cubes
1 large carrot, cut into 1cm/½in cubes
2 small courgettes (zucchini), cut into 1cm/½in cubes
1 or 2 celery sticks, cut into 1cm/½in cubes
1 litre/1¾ pints/4 cups chicken stock
200g/7oz/1¾ cups frozen peas
90g/3½oz/scant 1 cup stellette or other small soup pasta
salt and ground black pepper
Parmesan cheese shavings, to serve

1 Heat the oil in a large frying pan, add the chicken thighs and fry for about 5 minutes on each side. Remove with a slotted spoon and set aside.

2 Add the bacon, onion and herbs to the pan and cook gently, stirring constantly, for about 5 minutes. Add the potatoes, carrot, courgettes and celery and cook for 5–7 minutes more.

COOK'S TIP
This soup has more flavour if you use home-made chicken stock (see page 31).

3 Return the chicken thighs to the pan, add the stock and bring to the boil. Cover and cook over a low heat for 35–40 minutes, stirring the soup occasionally to prevent sticking.

4 Remove the chicken thighs with a slotted spoon and place them on a board. Stir the peas and pasta into the soup and bring back to the boil. Simmer, stirring, for 7–8 minutes or according to the instructions on the packet, until the pasta is just *al dente*.

5 Meanwhile, remove and discard the chicken skin, then remove the meat from the chicken bones and cut it into small (1cm/½in) pieces.

6 Return the chicken meat to the soup, stir well and heat through. Taste and add more salt and ground black pepper if necessary.

7 Ladle into warmed soup plates or bowls, top with Parmesan shavings and serve piping hot.

Energy 198kcal/833kJ; Protein 15.6g; Carbohydrate 23.3g, of which sugars 3.9g; Fat 5.4g, of which saturates 1.4g; Cholesterol 30mg; Calcium 31mg; Fibre 3.2g; Sodium 224mg.

GENOESE MINESTRONE

IN GENOA, THEY OFTEN MAKE MINESTRONE LIKE THIS, WITH PESTO STIRRED IN TOWARDS THE END OF COOKING. IT IS PACKED FULL OF VEGETABLES AND HAS A STRONG, HEADY FLAVOUR, MAKING IT AN EXCELLENT VEGETARIAN SUPPER DISH WHEN SERVED WITH BREAD.

SERVES 4–6

INGREDIENTS
   45ml/3 tbsp olive oil
   1 onion, finely chopped
   2 celery sticks, finely chopped
   1 large carrot, finely chopped
   150g/5oz French (green) beans, cut
      into 5cm/2in pieces
   1 courgette (zucchini), finely sliced
   1 potato, cut into 1cm/½in cubes
   ¼ Savoy cabbage, shredded
   1 small aubergine (eggplant), cut into
      1cm/½in cubes
   200g/7oz can cannellini beans,
      drained and rinsed
   2 Italian plum tomatoes, chopped
   1.2 litres/2 pints/5 cups vegetable
      stock
   90g/3½oz spaghetti or vermicelli
   salt and ground black pepper
For the pesto
   about 20 fresh basil leaves
   1 garlic clove
   10ml/2 tsp pine nuts
   15ml/1 tbsp freshly grated Parmesan
      cheese
   15ml/1 tbsp freshly grated pecorino
      cheese
   30ml/2 tbsp olive oil

1 Heat the oil in a large pan, add the onion, celery and carrot, and cook over a low heat, stirring, for 5–7 minutes.

2 Mix in the French beans, courgette, potato and cabbage. Stir-fry over a medium heat for 3 minutes. Add the aubergine, cannellini beans and plum tomatoes and stir-fry for 2–3 minutes.

3 Pour in the stock with salt and pepper to taste. Bring to the boil. Stir well, cover and lower the heat. Simmer for 40 minutes, stirring occasionally.

4 Meanwhile, put all the pesto ingredients in a food processor and process until the mixture forms a smooth sauce, adding 15–45ml/ 1–3 tbsp water through the feeder tube if the sauce seems too thick.

5 Break the pasta into small pieces and add it to the soup. Simmer, stirring frequently, for 5 minutes. Add the pesto sauce and stir it in well, then simmer for 2–3 minutes more, or until the pasta is *al dente*.

6 Check the seasoning and serve hot, in warmed soup plates or bowls.

Energy 222kcal/927kJ; Protein 8.2g; Carbohydrate 27.4g, of which sugars 6.6g; Fat 9.2g, of which saturates 2.1g; Cholesterol 5mg; Calcium 129mg; Fibre 4.9g; Sodium 203mg.

BEAN AND PASTA SOUP

THIS HEARTY, MAIN-MEAL SOUP SOMETIMES GOES BY THE SIMPLER NAME OF PASTA E FAGIOLI, *WHILE SOME ITALIANS REFER TO IT AS* MINESTRONE DI PASTA E FAGIOLI. *TRADITIONAL RECIPES USE DRIED BEANS AND A HAM BONE.*

SERVES 4–6

INGREDIENTS
30ml/2 tbsp olive oil
115g/4oz/⅔ cup pancetta or rindless smoked streaky (fatty) bacon, diced
1 onion
1 carrot
1 celery stick
1.75 litres/3 pints/7½ cups beef stock
1 cinnamon stick or a good pinch of ground cinnamon
90g/3½oz/scant 1 cup small pasta shapes, such as conchiglie or coralini
400g/14oz can borlotti beans, rinsed and drained
1 thick slice cooked ham (about 225g/8oz), diced
salt and ground black pepper
Parmesan cheese shavings, to serve

1 Heat the oil in a large pan, add the pancetta or bacon and cook, stirring, until lightly coloured.

2 Finely chop the vegetables, add to the pan and cook for about 10 minutes, stirring frequently, until lightly coloured.

3 Pour in the stock, add the cinnamon with salt and pepper to taste and bring to the boil. Cover and simmer gently for 15–20 minutes.

COOK'S TIP
This soup will have the best flavour if you use a good home-made beef stock (see page 32).

4 Add the pasta shapes. Bring back to the boil, lower the heat and simmer, stirring frequently, for 5 minutes. Add the borlotti beans and diced ham and simmer for 2–3 minutes, until the pasta is *al dente*.

5 Remove the cinnamon stick, if used, taste the soup and adjust the seasoning.

6 Spoon into warmed bowls and serve hot, sprinkled with Parmesan shavings.

VARIATIONS
• If you prefer, you can use spaghetti or tagliatelle instead of the small pasta shapes, breaking it into small pieces over the pan.
• Use cannellini or white haricot beans instead of the borlotti. Add them to the pan after the stock in step 1. If you like, add 15ml/1 tbsp tomato purée (paste) along with the beans.

Energy 240kcal/1010kJ; Protein 16.7g; Carbohydrate 25.1g, of which sugars 4.8g; Fat 8.8g, of which saturates 2.2g; Cholesterol 32mg; Calcium 60mg; Fibre 5g; Sodium 1009mg.

BACON AND LENTIL SOUP

SERVE THIS HEARTY AND FLAVOURSOME SOUP FOR A FAMILY LUNCH OR SUPPER WITH CHUNKS OF WARM, CRUSTY BREAD. IT'S JUST THE THING FOR A GOOD WINTER'S DAY.

SERVES 4

INGREDIENTS
    450g/1lb thick-sliced bacon, cubed
    1 onion, roughly chopped
    1 small turnip, roughly chopped
    1 celery stick, chopped
    1 potato, roughly chopped
    1 carrot, sliced
    75g/3oz/scant ½ cup lentils
    1 bouquet garni
    ground black pepper
    fresh flat leaf parsley, to garnish

COOK'S TIP
Use green or brown lentils for this soup as they retain their disc shape when cooked and do not disintegrate.

1 Heat a large pan and add the bacon. Cook for a few minutes, allowing the fat to run out.

2 Add the chopped onion, turnip, celery and potato and the sliced carrot. Cook for 4 minutes, stirring from time to time.

3 Add the lentils, bouquet garni, seasoning and enough water to cover. Bring to the boil and simmer for 1 hour or until the lentils are tender.

4 Ladle the soup into warm bowls and serve garnished with flat leaf parsley.

Energy 359kcal/1500kJ; Protein 24.5g; Carbohydrate 23.5g, of which sugars 4.6g; Fat 19.2g, of which saturates 7.1g; Cholesterol 60mg; Calcium 42mg; Fibre 2.8g; Sodium 1759mg.

GALICIAN BROTH

THIS DELICIOUS MAIN-MEAL SOUP IS VERY SIMILAR TO THE WARMING, CHUNKY MEAT AND POTATO BROTHS OF COOLER CLIMATES.

SERVES 4

INGREDIENTS

450g/1lb piece gammon (smoked or cured ham)
2 bay leaves
2 onions, sliced
1.5 litres/2½ pints/6¼ cups cold water
10ml/2 tsp paprika
675g/1½lb potatoes, cut into large chunks
225g/8oz spring greens (collards)
400g/14oz can haricot (navy) or cannellini beans, drained
salt and ground black pepper

1 Soak the gammon overnight in cold water.

2 Next day, drain the gammon and put it in a large pan with the bay leaves and onions. Pour the water on top.

3 Bring to the boil, then reduce the heat and simmer for about 1½ hours until the meat is tender. Keep an eye on the pan to make sure it doesn't boil over.

4 Drain the meat, reserving the cooking liquid, and leave to cool slightly. Discard the skin and any excess fat from the meat then cut into small chunks. Return to the pan with the cooking liquid, paprika and potatoes. Cover and simmer gently for 20 minutes.

5 Cut away the cores from the greens. Roll up the leaves and cut into thin shreds. Add to the pan with the beans and simmer for about 10 minutes. Season with salt and freshly ground black pepper to taste, ladle into warmed soup bowls and serve piping hot.

COOK'S TIP
Bacon knuckles can be used instead of the gammon. The bones will give the juices a delicious flavour.

Energy 419kcal/1763kJ; Protein 32.1g; Carbohydrate 52.7g, of which sugars 11.5g; Fat 10.3g, of which saturates 3.2g; Cholesterol 26mg; Calcium 226mg; Fibre 10.9g; Sodium 1412mg.

IRISH COUNTRY SOUP

TRADITIONALLY, BUTTERED CHUNKS OF BROWN BREAD, OR IRISH SODA BREAD, WOULD BE SERVED WITH THIS HEARTY ONE-POT MEAL WHICH IS BASED ON THE CLASSIC IRISH STEW.

SERVES 4

INGREDIENTS
    15ml/1 tbsp vegetable oil
    675g/1½lb boneless lamb chump
      chops, trimmed and cut into
      small cubes
    2 small onions, quartered
    2 leeks, thickly sliced
    1 litre/1¾ pints/4 cups water
    2 large potatoes, cut into chunks
    2 carrots, thickly sliced
    sprig of fresh thyme, plus extra
      to garnish
    15g/½oz/1 tbsp butter
    30ml/2 tbsp chopped fresh parsley
    salt and ground black pepper
    brown or Irish soda bread, to serve

VARIATION
The vegetables can be varied according to the season. Swede (rutabaga), turnip, celeriac and even cabbage could be added in place of some of those listed.

1 Heat the oil in a large pan, add the lamb in batches and fry, turning occasionally, until well browned all over. Use a slotted spoon to remove the lamb from the pan and set aside.

2 When all the lamb has been browned, add the onions to the pan and cook for 4–5 minutes, until the onions are browned. Return the meat to the pan and add the leeks. Pour in the water, then bring to the boil. Reduce the heat, then cover and simmer for about 1 hour.

3 Add the potatoes, carrots and fresh thyme, and cook for 40 minutes, until the lamb is tender. Remove from the heat and leave to stand for 5 minutes, then skim off the fat.

4 Pour off the stock into a clean pan and whisk the butter into it. Stir in the parsley and season well, then pour the liquid back over the soup ingredients.

5 Ladle the soup into warmed bowls and garnish with sprigs of fresh thyme.

Energy 453kcal/1893kJ; Protein 36.5g; Carbohydrate 20.5g, of which sugars 6.2g; Fat 25.6g, of which saturates 11.3g; Cholesterol 136mg; Calcium 53mg; Fibre 3.7g; Sodium 185mg.

MOROCCAN HARIRA

THIS IS A HEARTY MAIN-COURSE MEAT AND VEGETABLE SOUP, EATEN DURING THE MONTH OF RAMADAN, WHEN THE MUSLIM POPULATION FASTS BETWEEN SUNRISE AND SUNSET.

SERVES 4

INGREDIENTS
  450g/1lb well-flavoured tomatoes
  225g/8oz lamb, cut into pieces
  2.5ml/½ tsp ground turmeric
  2.5ml/½ tsp ground cinnamon
  25g/1oz/2 tbsp butter
  60ml/4 tbsp chopped fresh
    coriander (cilantro)
  30ml/2 tbsp chopped fresh
    parsley
  1 onion, chopped
  50g/2oz/¼ cup split red lentils
  75g/3oz/½ cup dried chickpeas,
    soaked overnight in cold water
  600ml/1 pint/2½ cups water
  4 baby (pearl) onions or shallots
  25g/1oz/¼ cup fine noodles
  salt and ground black pepper
  fresh coriander, lemon slices
    and ground cinnamon, to garnish

COOK'S TIPS
• Most of the vitamins in fruits and vegetables are just under the skin. So, if you wish to improve the nutritional content, or simply save some time, the skins of the tomatoes can be left on.
• For maximum cinnamon flavour, grind a broken cinnamon stick in a spice grinder or a coffee grinder kept especially for spices.

1 Plunge the tomatoes into boiling water for 30 seconds, then refresh in cold water. Peel off the skins. Cut into quarters and remove the seeds. Chop the flesh roughly.

2 Put the pieces of lamb, ground turmeric, cinnamon, butter, fresh coriander, parsley and onion into a large pan, and cook over a medium heat, stirring, for 5 minutes.

3 Add the chopped tomatoes and continue to cook for 10 minutes, stirring the mixture frequently.

4 Rinse the lentils under running water and drain them well. Stir them into the contents of the pan, with the drained chickpeas and the measured water. Season with salt and pepper. Bring to the boil, lower the heat, cover, and simmer gently for 1½ hours.

5 Add the onions or shallots. Cook for 25 minutes. Add the noodles and cook for 5 minutes more. Spoon into bowls and garnish with the coriander, lemon slices and cinnamon.

Energy 294kcal/1234kJ; Protein 19.7g; Carbohydrate 25.2g, of which sugars 4.9g; Fat 13.5g, of which saturates 6.6g; Cholesterol 58mg; Calcium 55mg; Fibre 4g; Sodium 119mg.

SCOTCH BROTH

SUSTAINING AND WARMING, SCOTCH BROTH IS CUSTOM-MADE FOR THE CHILLY SCOTTISH WEATHER, AND MAKES A DELICIOUS WINTER SOUP ANYWHERE. TRADITIONALLY, A LARGE POT OF IT IS MADE AND THIS IS DIPPED INTO THROUGHOUT THE NEXT FEW DAYS, THE FLAVOUR IMPROVING ALL THE TIME.

SERVES 6–8

INGREDIENTS
    1kg/2¼lb lean neck (US shoulder
      or breast) of lamb, cut into large,
      even-size chunks
    1.75 litres/3 pints/7½ cups cold
      water
    1 large onion, chopped
    50g/2oz/¼ cup pearl barley
    bouquet garni
    1 large carrot, chopped
    1 turnip, chopped
    3 leeks, chopped
    1 small white cabbage, finely
      shredded
    salt and ground black pepper
    chopped fresh parsley, to garnish

1 Put the lamb and water in a large pan over a medium heat and gently bring to the boil. Skim off the scum that rises to the top with a spoon.

2 Add the onion, pearl barley and bouquet garni, and stir in thoroughly.

3 Bring the soup back to the boil, then reduce the heat, partly cover the pan and simmer gently for a further 1 hour. Make sure that it does not boil dry.

4 Add the remaining vegetables to the pan and season with salt and ground black pepper. Bring to the boil, partly cover again and simmer for about 35 minutes, until the vegetables are tender.

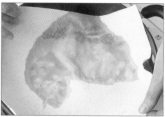

5 Remove the surplus fat from the top of the soup with a sheet of kitchen paper. Serve the soup hot, garnished with chopped parsley, and accompanied by chunks of fresh bread.

Energy 387kcal/1619kJ; Protein 36.2g; Carbohydrate 17.7g, of which sugars 9.1g; Fat 19.5g, of which saturates 8.8g; Cholesterol 127mg; Calcium 86mg; Fibre 4.3g; Sodium 157mg.

CLAM AND PASTA SOUP

THIS SOUP IS A VARIATION OF THE TRADITIONAL PASTA DISH, SPAGHETTI ALLE VONGOLE, *USING STORE-CUPBOARD INGREDIENTS. SERVE IT WITH HOT FOCACCIA OR CIABATTA FOR AN INFORMAL SUPPER WITH FRIENDS.*

SERVES 4

INGREDIENTS

  30ml/2 tbsp olive oil
  1 large onion, finely chopped
  2 garlic cloves, crushed
  400g/14oz can chopped tomatoes
  15ml/1 tbsp sun-dried tomato paste
  5ml/1 tsp granulated sugar
  5ml/1 tsp dried mixed herbs
  about 750ml/1¼ pints/3 cups fish
    or vegetable stock
  150ml/¼ pint/⅔ cup red wine
  50g/2oz/½ cup small pasta shapes
  150g/5oz jar or can clams in
    natural juice
  30ml/2 tbsp finely chopped fresh flat
    leaf parsley, plus a few whole leaves
    to garnish
  salt and ground black pepper

1 Heat the oil in a large pan. Add the garlic, tomatoes, tomato paste, sugar, herbs, stock and wine, with salt and pepper to taste. Bring to the boil. Lower the heat, half-cover the pan and simmer for 10 minutes. Cook the onion gently for 5 minutes until softened.

2 Add the pasta and simmer, uncovered, for about 10 minutes or until *al dente.* Stir occasionally to prevent the pasta shapes sticking together.

COOK'S TIP
Use whichever small pasta shapes you have in the store cupboard (pantry), or spaghetti broken into small pieces.

3 Add the clams and their juice to the soup and heat through for 3–4 minutes, adding more stock if required. Do not allow it to boil, or the clams will become tough. Remove from the heat, stir in the chopped parsley and adjust the seasoning. Serve hot, sprinkled with coarsely ground black pepper and parsley leaves.

Energy 196kcal/821kJ; Protein 9.3g; Carbohydrate 20.2g, of which sugars 8.9g; Fat 6.5g, of which saturates 1g; Cholesterol 25mg; Calcium 67mg; Fibre 2.6g; Sodium 466mg.

SQUASH, BACON AND SWISS CHEESE SOUP

THIS IS A LIGHTLY SPICED SQUASH SOUP, ENRICHED WITH PLENTY OF CREAMY MELTING CHEESE. SERVE IT WITH CRUSTY BREAD FOR LUNCH OR SUPPER.

SERVES 4

INGREDIENTS

900g/2lb butternut squash
225g/8oz smoked lean back bacon
15ml/1 tbsp oil
225g/8oz onions, roughly chopped
2 garlic cloves, crushed
10ml/2 tsp ground cumin
15ml/1 tbsp ground coriander
275g/10oz potatoes, cut into small
   chunks
900ml/1½ pints/3¾ cups vegetable
   stock
10ml/2 tsp cornflour (cornstarch)
30ml/2 tbsp crème fraîche
Tabasco sauce, to taste
salt and freshly ground black pepper
175g/6oz/1½ cups Gruyère cheese,
   grated, to serve
crusty bread, to serve

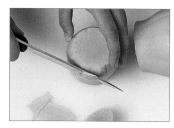

1 Cut the squash into large pieces. Using a sharp knife, carefully remove the skin, wasting as little of the flesh as possible.

2 Scoop out and discard the seeds. Chop the squash into small chunks. Remove all the fat from the bacon and roughly chop it into small pieces.

3 Heat the oil in a large pan and cook the onions and garlic for 3 minutes, or until beginning to soften.

4 Add the bacon and cook for about 3 minutes. Stir in the spices and cook on a low heat for a further minute.

COOK'S TIPS
• Pumpkin can be used in place of butternut squash and is equally delicious.
• The soup will have a superior flavour if you make your own vegetable stock (see page 30).

5 Add the chopped squash, potatoes and stock. Bring to the boil and simmer for 15 minutes, or until the squash and potatoes are tender.

6 Blend the cornflour with 30ml/2 tbsp water and add to the soup with the crème fraîche. Bring to the boil and simmer, uncovered, for 3 minutes. Adjust the seasoning and add Tabasco sauce to taste.

7 Ladle the soup into bowls and sprinkle the cheese on top. Serve with crusty bread to scoop up the melted cheese.

Energy 438kcal/1823kJ; Protein 24g; Carbohydrate 23g, of which sugars 8.1g; Fat 27.4g, of which saturates 15.3g; Cholesterol 81mg; Calcium 414mg; Fibre 3.7g; Sodium 1195mg.

LAMB, BEAN AND PUMPKIN SOUP

THIS IS A HEARTY SOUP TO WARM THE COCKLES OF THE HEART IN EVEN THE CHILLIEST WEATHER.
THE CARAWAY SEEDS AND CHILLI ADD A SPICY FLAVOUR.

SERVES 4

INGREDIENTS

115g/4oz/⅔ cup split black-eyed
  beans (peas), soaked for 1–2 hours
  or overnight
675g/1½lb neck (US shoulder or
  breast) of lamb, cut into medium-
  size chunks
5ml/1 tsp chopped fresh thyme or
  2.5ml/½ tsp dried thyme
2 bay leaves
1.2 litres/2 pints/5 cups stock
  or water
1 onion, sliced
225g/8oz pumpkin, diced
2 black cardamom pods
7.5ml/1½ tsp ground turmeric
15ml/1 tbsp chopped fresh coriander
  (cilantro)
2.5ml/½ tsp caraway seeds
1 fresh green chilli, seeded
  and chopped
2 green bananas
1 carrot
salt and ground black pepper

1 Drain the black-eyed beans, place
them in a pan and cover with fresh
cold water.

2 Bring the beans to the boil, boil
rapidly for 10 minutes and then reduce
the heat and simmer, covered, for about
40–50 minutes until tender, adding
more water if necessary. Remove the
pan from the heat and set aside to cool.

COOK'S TIP
Wear rubber gloves to protect your hands
when preparing the green chilli.

3 Meanwhile, put the lamb in a large
pan, add the thyme, bay leaves and
stock or water and bring to the boil.
Cover and simmer over a moderate heat
for 1 hour until tender.

4 Add the onion, pumpkin, cardamoms,
turmeric, coriander, caraway, chilli and
seasoning and stir.

5 Bring back to a simmer and cook,
uncovered, for 15 minutes, stirring
occasionally, until the pumpkin is tender.

6 When the beans are cool, spoon into
a blender or food processor with their
liquid and blend to a smooth purée.

7 Peel the bananas and cut into
medium slices. Cut the carrot into thin
slices. Stir into the soup with the bean
purée and cook for 10–12 minutes,
until the carrot is tender. Adjust the
seasoning and serve immediately.

Energy 469kcal/1971kJ; Protein 41g; Carbohydrate 34g, of which sugars 19.6g; Fat 19.7g, of which saturates 9g; Cholesterol 128mg; Calcium 72mg; Fibre 6.6g; Sodium 156mg.

LAMB AND LENTIL SOUP

*LAMB AND LENTILS GO TOGETHER SO WELL, THEY ALMOST SEEM TO HAVE BEEN MADE FOR ONE
ANOTHER. THIS IS A GREAT DISH TO SERVE FOR A WINTER LUNCH.*

SERVES 4

INGREDIENTS

About 1.5 litres/2½ pints/6¼ cups
   water or stock
900g/2lb neck (US shoulder or
   breast) of lamb, cut into chops
½ onion, chopped
1 garlic clove, crushed
1 bay leaf
1 clove
2 sprigs fresh thyme
225g/8oz potatoes, cut into
   2.5cm/1in pieces
175g/6oz/¾ cup red lentils
salt and ground black pepper
chopped fresh parsley

2 Add the potato and lentils to the pan
and season with a little salt and plenty
of black pepper. Pour the remaining
stock or water to come just above
surface of the meat and vegetables –
add more if the soup becomes too thick.

3 Cover and allow to simmer for 25
minutes or until the lentils are cooked
and well blended into the soup.

4 Check the seasoning and adjust as
necessary. Stir in the parsley and serve.

1 Put about 1.2 litres/2 pints/5 cups of
the stock or water and the meat in a
large pan with the onion, garlic, bay
leaf, clove and sprigs of thyme. Bring
to the boil and simmer for about 1 hour
until the lamb is tender.

COOK'S TIP
Red lentils do not need soaking before
they are cooked; simply pick them over
and remove any pieces of grit and debris,
then rinse well.

Energy 587kcal/2465kJ; Protein 55.7g; Carbohydrate 34.9g, of which sugars 2.6g; Fat 26g, of which saturates 11.9g; Cholesterol 171mg; Calcium 48mg; Fibre 2.9g; Sodium 216mg.

CHUNKY BEAN AND VEGETABLE SOUP

A SUBSTANTIAL SOUP, NOT UNLIKE MINESTRONE, USING A SELECTION OF VEGETABLES, WITH CANNELLINI BEANS FOR EXTRA PROTEIN AND FIBRE. SERVE WITH A HUNK OF WHOLEGRAIN BREAD.

SERVES 4

INGREDIENTS
30ml/2 tbsp olive oil
2 celery sticks, chopped
2 leeks, sliced
3 carrots, sliced
2 garlic cloves, crushed
400g/14oz can chopped tomatoes with basil
1.2 litres/2 pints/5 cups vegetable stock
400g/14oz can cannellini beans (or mixed pulses), drained
15ml/1 tbsp pesto sauce
salt and ground black pepper
Parmesan cheese shavings, to serve

1 Heat the olive oil in a large pan. Add the celery, leeks, carrots and garlic and cook for about 5 minutes until softened.

2 Stir in the tomatoes and stock. Bring to the boil, then cover and cook gently for 15 minutes.

3 Stir in the beans and pesto, with salt and pepper to taste. Heat through for a further 5 minutes.

4 Serve in warmed bowls, sprinkled with shavings of Parmesan cheese.

COOK'S TIP
Extra vegetables can be added to the soup to make it even more substantial. For example, add some thinly sliced courgettes (zucchini) or finely shredded cabbage for the last 5 minutes of the cooking time. Or, stir in some small whole-wheat pasta shapes, if you like. Add them at the same time as the tomatoes, as they will take 10–15 minutes to cook.

Energy 204kcal/857kJ; Protein 10.6g; Carbohydrate 23.6g, of which sugars 8.8g; Fat 8.1g, of which saturates 1.9g; Cholesterol 4mg; Calcium 150mg; Fibre 9.3g; Sodium 451mg.

CARIBBEAN VEGETABLE SOUP

THIS VEGETABLE SOUP FROM THE CARIBBEAN IS REFRESHING AND FILLING, AND A GOOD CHOICE FOR A MAIN LUNCH DISH.

SERVES 4

INGREDIENTS

25g/1oz/2 tbsp butter or margarine
1 onion, chopped
1 garlic clove, crushed
2 carrots, sliced
1.5 litres/2½ pints/6¼ cups
  vegetable stock
2 bay leaves
2 sprigs fresh thyme
1 celery stick, finely chopped
2 green bananas, peeled and cut into
  4 pieces
175g/6oz white yam or eddoe, peeled
  and cubed
25g/1oz/2 tbsp red lentils
1 christophene, peeled and chopped
25g/1oz/2 tbsp macaroni (optional)
salt and ground black pepper
chopped spring onions (scallions)

1 Melt the butter or margarine and fry the onion, garlic and carrots for a few minutes, stirring occasionally, until beginning to soften. Add the stock, bay leaves and thyme and bring to the boil.

COOK'S TIP
Use other root vegetables or potatoes if yam or *eddoes* are not available. Add more stock if you want a thinner soup.

2 Add the celery, green bananas, white yam or eddoe, lentils, christophene and macaroni, if using. Season with salt and ground black pepper and simmer for 25 minutes or until all the vegetables are cooked.

3 Spoon the soup into warmed bowls and serve garnished with chopped spring onions.

Energy 214kcal/903kJ; Protein 3.8g; Carbohydrate 39g, of which sugars 21.4g; Fat 5.9g, of which saturates 3.4g; Cholesterol 13mg; Calcium 55mg; Fibre 3.6g; Sodium 61mg.

BEEF AND HERB SOUP WITH YOGURT

THIS CLASSIC IRANIAN SOUP, AASHE MASTE, IS A MEAL IN ITSELF AND IS A POPULAR COLD-WEATHER DISH. SERVE IT WITH WARMED NAAN BREAD.

SERVES 4

INGREDIENTS

2 large onions
30ml/2 tbsp oil
15ml/1 tbsp ground turmeric
90g/3½ oz/scant ½ cup yellow
  split peas
1.2 litres/2 pints/5 cups water
225g/8oz minced (ground) beef
200g/7oz/1 cup rice
45ml/3 tbsp each chopped fresh
  parsley, coriander (cilantro) and chives
15g/½oz/1 tbsp butter
1 large garlic clove, finely chopped
60ml/4 tbsp chopped fresh mint
2 or 3 saffron strands dissolved in
  15ml/1 tbsp boiling water (optional)
salt and ground black pepper
natural (plain) yogurt and naan
  bread, to serve
fresh mint, to garnish

1 Chop one of the onions. Heat the oil in a pan and fry the chopped onion until golden brown. Add the turmeric, split peas and water, bring to the boil, reduce the heat and simmer for 20 minutes.

2 Grate the other onion into a bowl, add the minced beef and seasoning and mix well. Form the mixture into small balls about the size of walnuts. Carefully add to the pan and simmer for 10 minutes.

3 Add the rice, parsley, coriander and chives. Simmer for 30 minutes until the rice is tender, stirring frequently.

4 Melt the butter in a small pan and fry the garlic. Stir in the mint and sprinkle over the soup with the saffron, if using.

5 Spoon the soup into warmed serving dishes. Garnish with mint and serve with yogurt and warm naan bread.

Energy 497kcal/2074kJ; Protein 21.9g; Carbohydrate 61g, of which sugars 6.6g; Fat 18.7g, of which saturates 6.6g; Cholesterol 42mg; Calcium 87mg; Fibre 3.4g; Sodium 85mg.

VEGETABLE BROTH WITH MINCED BEEF

THIS IS A VERITABLE CORNUCOPIA OF FLAVOURS, COMBINING TO PRODUCE A RICH AND SATISFYING BROTH THAT IS PERFECT FOR LUNCH OR SUPPER.

SERVES 6

INGREDIENTS

30ml/2 tbsp groundnut (peanut) oil
115g/4oz finely minced (ground) beef
1 large onion, grated or finely chopped
1 garlic clove, crushed
1 or 2 fresh chillies, seeded and chopped
1cm/½in cube terasi, prepared
3 macadamia nuts or 6 almonds, finely ground
1 carrot, finely grated
5ml/1 tsp soft brown sugar
1 litre/1¾ pints/4 cups chicken stock
50g/2oz dried shrimps, soaked in warm water for 10 minutes
225g/8oz spinach, finely shredded
8 baby corn cobs, sliced, or 200g/7oz canned corn kernels
1 large tomato, chopped
juice of ½ lemon
salt

3 Pour in the stock and bring the mixture gently to the boil.

4 Reduce the heat to a simmer, and then add the soaked shrimps, together with their soaking liquid. Simmer for about 10 minutes.

5 A few minutes before serving, add the spinach, corn, tomato and lemon juice. Simmer for 1–2 minutes, to heat through. Do not overcook at this stage because this will spoil both the appearance and the taste of the end result. Ladle into warmed bowls and serve immediately.

1 Heat the oil in a pan. Add the beef, onion and garlic and cook, stirring, until the meat changes colour.

2 Add the chillies, terasi, macadamia nuts or almonds, carrot, sugar and salt to taste.

COOK'S TIP
To make this broth very hot and spicy, add the seeds from the chillies.

Energy 187kcal/780kJ; Protein 11.7g; Carbohydrate 12g, of which sugars 6.1g; Fat 10.6g, of which saturates 2.2g; Cholesterol 54mg; Calcium 183mg; Fibre 2.1g; Sodium 524mg.

MULLIGATAWNY SOUP

MULLIGATAWNY (WHICH LITERALLY MEANS 'PEPPER WATER') WAS INTRODUCED INTO ENGLAND IN THE LATE 18TH CENTURY BY MEMBERS OF THE COLONIAL SERVICES RETURNING HOME FROM INDIA.

SERVES 4

INGREDIENTS

50g/2oz/4 tbsp butter or 60ml/4 tbsp oil
2 large chicken joints (about
  350g/12oz each)
1 onion, chopped
1 carrot, chopped
1 small turnip, chopped
about 15ml/1 tbsp curry powder,
  to taste
4 cloves
6 black peppercorns, lightly crushed
50g/2oz/¼ cup lentils
900ml/1½ pints/3¾ cups chicken
  stock
40g/1½oz/¼ cup sultanas (golden
  raisins)
salt and ground black pepper

1 Melt the butter or heat the oil in a large pan, then brown the chicken over a brisk heat. Transfer the chicken to a plate and set aside.

2 Add the onion, carrot and turnip to the pan and cook, stirring occasionally, until lightly coloured.

3 Stir in the curry powder, cloves and crushed peppercorns and cook for 1–2 minutes, then add the lentils.

4 Pour the stock into the pan, bring to the boil, then add the sultanas, the chicken and any juices from the plate. Cover the pan and simmer gently for about 1¼ hours.

5 Remove the chicken from the pan and discard the skin and bones. Chop the flesh, return to the soup and reheat. Check the seasoning before serving the soup piping hot.

COOK'S TIP
Choose red split lentils for the best colour, although either green or brown lentils could also be used.

Energy 347kcal/1447kJ; Protein 28.7g; Carbohydrate 16g, of which sugars 9.6g; Fat 19.1g, of which saturates 8.9g; Cholesterol 142mg; Calcium 54mg; Fibre 2.1g; Sodium 160mg.

SMOKED TURKEY AND LENTIL SOUP

LENTILS SEEM TO ENHANCE THE FLAVOUR OF SMOKED TURKEY, AND COMBINED WITH FOUR TASTY
VEGETABLES THEY MAKE A FINE MEAL-IN-A-POT.

SERVES 4

INGREDIENTS
    25g/1oz/2 tbsp butter
    1 large carrot, chopped
    1 onion, chopped
    1 leek, white part only, chopped
    1 celery stick, chopped
    115g/4oz/1½ cups mushrooms,
      chopped
    50ml/2fl oz/¼ cup dry white wine
    1.2 litres/2 pints/5 cups chicken
      stock
    10ml/2 tsp dried thyme
    1 bay leaf
    115g/4oz/½ cup green lentils
    75g/3oz smoked turkey meat, diced
    salt and ground black pepper

1 Melt the butter in a large pan. Add the carrot, onion, leek, celery and mushrooms. Cook for 3–5 minutes until golden.

2 Stir in the wine and chicken stock. Bring to the boil and skim off any foam that rises to the surface. Add the thyme and bay leaf. Lower the heat, cover and simmer gently for 30 minutes.

3 Add the lentils and continue cooking, covered, for a further 30–40 minutes until they are just tender. Stir the soup occasionally.

4 Add the turkey and season to taste with salt and pepper. Cook until just heated through. Ladle into warmed bowls and serve hot.

Energy 201kcal/844kJ; Protein 15g; Carbohydrate 20.4g, of which sugars 4.1g; Fat 6.3g, of which saturates 3.5g; Cholesterol 27mg; Calcium 39mg; Fibre 3.4g; Sodium 73mg.

PROVENÇAL FISH SOUP WITH PASTA

THIS COLOURFUL SOUP HAS ALL THE FLAVOURS OF THE MEDITERRANEAN. SERVE IT AS A MAIN COURSE FOR A DELICIOUSLY FILLING LUNCH.

SERVES 4

INGREDIENTS
    30ml/2 tbsp olive oil
    1 onion, sliced
    1 garlic clove, crushed
    1 leek, sliced
    1 litre/1¾ pints/4 cups water
    225g/8oz canned chopped plum
      tomatoes
    a pinch of Mediterranean herbs
    1.5ml/¼ tsp saffron strands
      (optional)
    115g/4oz small pasta
    about 8 live mussels in the shell
    450g/1lb white fish, filleted
      and skinned
    salt and ground black pepper
For the rouille
    2 garlic cloves, crushed
    1 canned pimiento, drained
      and chopped
    15ml/1 tbsp fresh white breadcrumbs
    60ml/4 tbsp mayonnaise
    toasted French bread, to serve

1 Heat the oil in a large pan and add the onion, garlic and leek. Cover and cook gently for about 5 minutes, stirring occasionally, until the vegetables are softened.

2 Add the water, tomatoes, herbs, saffron, if using, and pasta. Season with salt and pepper and continue cooking for a further 15–20 minutes.

COOK'S TIP
Any type of white fish, such as cod, haddock, plaice or monkfish, can be used for this dish.

3 Scrub the mussels and pull off the 'beards'. Discard any that do not close when sharply tapped.

4 Cut the fish into bite-size chunks and add to the soup, placing the mussels on top. Simmer for 5–10 minutes until the mussels open and the fish is cooked. Discard any unopened mussels.

5 To make the rouille, pound together the garlic, canned pimiento and breadcrumbs in a pestle and mortar (or in a blender or food processor). Stir in the mayonnaise and season well.

6 Spread the toasted French bread with the rouille. Ladle the soup into warmed bowls and serve with the French bread.

Energy 386kcal/1618kJ; Protein 27g; Carbohydrate 28.9g, of which sugars 4.8g; Fat 18.8g, of which saturates 2.8g; Cholesterol 67mg; Calcium 45mg; Fibre 2.7g; Sodium 195mg.

PRAWN CREOLE

RAW PRAWNS ARE COMBINED WITH CHOPPED FRESH VEGETABLES AND CAYENNE PEPPER TO MAKE THIS TASTY SOUP. SERVED WITH BOILED RICE IT MAKES A FILLING MEAL.

SERVES 4

INGREDIENTS

675g/1½lb raw prawns (shrimp) in
  the shell, with heads, if available
475ml/16fl oz/2 cups water
45ml/3 tbsp olive or vegetable oil
175g/6oz/1½ cups onions, very finely
  chopped
75g/3oz/½ cup celery, very finely
  chopped
75g/3oz/½ cup green (bell) pepper,
  very finely chopped
25g/1oz/½ cup chopped fresh parsley
1 garlic clove, crushed
15ml/1 tbsp Worcestershire sauce
1.5ml/¼ tsp cayenne pepper
120ml/4fl oz/½ cup dry white wine
50g/2oz/1 cup chopped peeled
  plum tomatoes
5ml/1 tsp salt
1 bay leaf
5ml/1 tsp sugar
fresh parsley, to garnish

1 Peel and devein the prawns, reserving the heads and shells. Set aside in a covered bowl in the refrigerator.

2 Put the prawn heads and shells in a pan with the water. Bring to the boil and simmer for 15 minutes. Strain and reserve 350ml/12fl oz/1½ cups of stock.

3 Heat the oil in a heavy pan. Add the onions and cook over a low heat for 8–10 minutes until softened. Add the celery and green pepper and cook for 5 minutes further. Stir in the parsley, garlic, Worcestershire sauce and cayenne. Cook for another 5 minutes.

4 Increase the heat to medium. Stir in the wine and simmer for 3–4 minutes.

5 Add the tomatoes, reserved prawn stock, salt, bay leaf and sugar and bring to the boil. Stir well, then reduce the heat to low and simmer for about 30 minutes until the tomatoes have fallen apart and the sauce has reduced slightly. Remove from the heat and leave to cool slightly.

6 Discard the bay leaf. Pour the sauce into a food processor or blender and purée until quite smooth. Taste and adjust the seasoning as necessary.

7 Return the tomato sauce to the pan and bring to the boil. Add the prawns and simmer for 4–5 minutes until they turn pink. Ladle into individual soup bowls and garnish with fresh parsley.

Energy 250kcal/1044kJ; Protein 30.8g; Carbohydrate 5.6g, of which sugars 4.5g; Fat 9.6g, of which saturates 1.2g; Cholesterol 329mg; Calcium 170mg; Fibre 1.6g; Sodium 830mg.

GREEN HERB GUMBO

TRADITIONALLY SERVED AT THE END OF LENT, THIS IS A JOYFUL, SWEETLY SPICED AND REVITALIZING DISH, EVEN IF YOU HAVEN'T BEEN FASTING.

SERVES 6–8

INGREDIENTS

350g/12oz piece raw smoked gammon (smoked or cured ham)
30ml/2 tbsp lard or cooking oil
1 large Spanish (Bermuda) onion, roughly chopped
2 or 3 garlic cloves, crushed
5ml/1 tsp dried oregano
5ml/1 tsp dried thyme
2 bay leaves
2 cloves
2 celery sticks, finely sliced
1 green (bell) pepper, seeded and chopped
½ medium green cabbage, stalked and finely shredded
2 litres/3½ pints/9 cups light stock or water
200g/7oz spring greens (collards) or kale, finely shredded
200g/7oz Chinese mustard cabbage, finely shredded
200g/7oz spinach, shredded
1 bunch of watercress, shredded
6 spring onions (scallions), finely shredded
25g/1oz/½ cup chopped fresh parsley
2.5ml/½ tsp ground allspice
¼ nutmeg, grated
a pinch of cayenne pepper
salt and ground black pepper
warm French or garlic bread, to serve

1 Dice the gammon quite small, keeping any fat and rind in one separate piece. Put the fat with the lard or oil in a deep pan and heat through until it sizzles. Stir in the diced ham, onion, garlic, oregano and thyme and cook over a medium heat for 5 minutes, stirring occasionally.

2 Add the bay leaves, cloves, celery and green pepper and stir over a medium heat for 2–3 minutes, then add the cabbage and stock or water. Bring to the boil and simmer for 5 minutes.

3 Add the spring greens or kale and mustard cabbage, boil for a further 2 minutes, then add the spinach, watercress and spring onions. Return to the boil, then lower the heat and simmer for 1 minute. Add the parsley, allspice and nutmeg, salt, black pepper and cayenne to taste.

4 Remove the piece of ham fat and, if you can find them, the cloves. Ladle into individual soup bowls and serve immediately, with warm French bread or garlic bread.

Energy 138kcal/573kJ; Protein 10.7g; Carbohydrate 8.8g, of which sugars 7.8g; Fat 6.8g, of which saturates 1.5g; Cholesterol 10mg; Calcium 129mg; Fibre 3.6g; Sodium 440mg.

CHUNKY CHICKEN SOUP

THIS THICK CHICKEN AND VEGETABLE SOUP IS GARNISHED WITH GARLIC-FLAVOURED FRIED CROÛTONS. SERVE IT FOR AN INFORMAL LUNCH OR SUPPER.

SERVES 4

INGREDIENTS
  4 skinless, boneless chicken thighs
  15g/½oz/1 tbsp butter
  2 small leeks, finely sliced
  25g/1oz/2 tbsp long grain rice
  900ml/1½ pints/3¾ cups chicken
    stock
  15ml/1 tbsp chopped mixed fresh
    parsley and mint
  salt and ground black pepper
For the garlic croûtons
  30ml/2 tbsp olive oil
  1 garlic clove, crushed
  4 slices bread, cut into cubes

1 Cut the chicken into 1cm/½in cubes. Melt the butter in a pan, add the leeks and cook until tender. Add the rice and chicken and cook for 2 minutes.

2 Add the stock, then cover the pan and simmer gently for 15–20 minutes until tender.

COOK'S TIP
The croûtons can be made from plain or flavoured bread, but it's best if the bread is a few days old rather than fresh.

3 To make the garlic croûtons, heat the oil in a large frying pan. Add the crushed garlic clove and bread cubes and cook until the bread is golden brown, stirring all the time to prevent burning. Drain on kitchen paper and sprinkle with a pinch of salt.

4 Add the chopped parsley and mint to the soup. Taste and adjust the seasoning.

5 Ladle the soup into warmed bowls and serve piping hot, garnished with the garlic croûtons.

Energy 276kcal/1158kJ; Protein 27.4g; Carbohydrate 18.8g, of which sugars 1.8g; Fat 10.4g, of which saturates 3.1g; Cholesterol 78mg; Calcium 46mg; Fibre 1.5g; Sodium 214mg.

BEEF BROTH WITH CASSAVA

THIS 'BIG' SOUP IS ALMOST LIKE A STEW. THE ADDITION OF WINE IS NOT TRADITIONAL, BUT IT
ENHANCES THE RICHNESS OF THE BROTH.

SERVES 4

INGREDIENTS
    450g/1lb stewing beef, cubed
    1.2 litres/2 pints/5 cups beef stock
    300ml/½ pint/1¼ cups white wine
    15ml/1 tbsp soft brown sugar
    1 onion, finely chopped
    1 bay leaf
    1 bouquet garni
    1 sprig fresh thyme
    15ml/1 tbsp tomato purée (paste)
    1 large carrot, sliced
    275g/10oz cassava or yam, cubed
    50g/2oz spinach, chopped
    a little hot pepper sauce, to taste
    salt and ground black pepper

1 Put the beef, stock, wine, sugar, onion, bay leaf, bouquet garni, thyme and tomato purée in a large pan, bring to the boil and then cover and simmer for about 1¼ hours, until the beef is tender.

2 Add the carrot, cassava or yam, spinach, a few drops of hot pepper sauce, salt and pepper, and simmer for a further 15 minutes until both the meat and vegetables are tender. Ladle into warmed bowls and serve.

Energy 308kcal/1295kJ; Protein 27.4g; Carbohydrate 26.7g, of which sugars 7.4g; Fat 10.9g, of which saturates 4.4g; Cholesterol 65mg; Calcium 49mg; Fibre 1.9g; Sodium 105mg.

CORN CHOWDER WITH CONCHIGLIETTE

CORN KERNELS COMBINE WITH SMOKED TURKEY AND PASTA TO MAKE THIS SATISFYING AND FILLING ONE-POT MEAL, PERFECT FOR A HUNGRY FAMILY OR FOR GUESTS.

SERVES 6–8

INGREDIENTS

1 small green (bell) pepper
450g/1lb potatoes, diced
350g/12oz/2 cups canned or
  frozen corn kernels
1 onion, chopped
1 celery stick, chopped
1 bouquet garni
600ml/1 pint/2½ cups chicken stock
300ml/½ pint/1¼ cups skimmed
  milk
50g/2oz conchigliette
oil, for frying
150g/5oz smoked turkey rashers
  (strips), diced
salt and ground black pepper
bread sticks, to serve

3 Add the milk and salt and pepper. Process half of the soup in a food processor or blender and return to the pan with the pasta. Simmer for 10 minutes or until the pasta is *al dente*.

4 Heat the oil in a non-stick frying pan and fry the turkey rashers quickly for 2–3 minutes. Stir into the soup. Ladle the soup into warmed bowls and serve hot with bread sticks.

1 Seed the green pepper and cut into dice. Cover with boiling water and leave to stand for 2 minutes. Drain and rinse.

2 Put the potatoes into a pan with the corn, onion, celery, diced pepper, bouquet garni and stock. Bring to the boil, cover and simmer for 20 minutes.

Energy 169kcal/716kJ; Protein 8.4g; Carbohydrate 29.1g, of which sugars 8.7g; Fat 2.9g, of which saturates 1.1g; Cholesterol 6mg; Calcium 59mg; Fibre 1.9g; Sodium 495mg.

BOUILLABAISSE

PERHAPS THE MOST FAMOUS OF ALL MEDITERRANEAN FISH SOUPS, THIS RECIPE, ORIGINATING FROM MARSEILLES IN THE SOUTH OF FRANCE, IS A RICH AND COLOURFUL MIXTURE OF FISH AND SHELLFISH, FLAVOURED WITH TOMATOES, SAFFRON AND ORANGE.

SERVES 6

INGREDIENTS

1.5kg/3–3½lb mixed fish and
   225g/8oz well-flavoured tomatoes
a pinch of saffron strands
90ml/6 tbsp olive oil
1 onion, sliced
1 leek, sliced
1 celery stick, sliced
2 garlic cloves, crushed
1 bouquet garni
1 strip orange rind
2.5ml/½ tsp fennel seeds
15ml/1 tbsp tomato purée (paste)
10ml/2 tsp Pernod
salt and ground black pepper
6 slices French bread and 45ml/3 tbsp
   chopped fresh parsley, to serve

1 Remove the heads, tails and fins from the fish and set the fish aside. Put the trimmings in a large pan with 1.2 litres/2 pints/5 cups water. Bring to the boil and simmer for 15 minutes. Strain and reserve the liquid.

2 Scald the tomatoes, then drain and refresh in cold water. Peel them and chop roughly.

3 Cut the fish into large chunks. Leave the shellfish in their shells.

4 Soak the saffron in 15–30ml/1–2 tbsp hot water.

5 Heat the oil in a large pan, add the onion, leek and celery and cook until softened. Add the garlic, bouquet garni, orange rind, fennel seeds and chopped tomatoes. Stir in the saffron and soaking liquid and the reserved fish stock. Season, then bring to the boil and simmer for 30–40 minutes.

6 Add the shellfish and boil for about 6 minutes. Add the fish and cook for 6–8 minutes more, until it flakes easily.

7 Using a slotted spoon, transfer the fish to a warmed serving platter. Keep the liquid boiling, to allow the oil to emulsify with the broth. Add the tomato purée and Pernod, then check the seasoning.

8 Ladle the soup into warm bowls, sprinkle with chopped parsley and serve with French bread.

COOK'S TIPS
• Choose fish such as red mullet, John Dory, monkfish, red snapper and whiting, and large raw prawns and clams.
• Saffron comes from the orange and red stigmas of a type of crocus, which must be harvested by hand and are extremely expensive. Its flavour is unique and cannot be replaced by any other spice. It is an essential ingredient in traditional bouillabaisse and should not be omitted.

ITALIAN ROCKET AND POTATO SOUP

THIS FILLING AND HEARTY SOUP IS BASED ON A TRADITIONAL ITALIAN PEASANT RECIPE. IF ROCKET IS UNAVAILABLE, WATERCRESS OR BABY SPINACH LEAVES MAKE AN EQUALLY DELICIOUS ALTERNATIVE.

SERVES 4

INGREDIENTS
  900g/2lb new potatoes
  900ml/1½ pints/3¾ cups well-
    flavoured vegetable stock
  1 medium carrot
  115g/4oz rocket
  2.5ml/½ tsp cayenne pepper
  ½ loaf stale ciabatta bread, torn into
    chunks
  4 garlic cloves, thinly sliced
  60ml/4 tbsp olive oil
  salt and ground black pepper

1 Dice the potatoes. Place them in a pan with the stock and a little salt. Bring to the boil and simmer for 10 minutes.

2 Finely dice the carrot and add to the potatoes and stock, then tear the rocket leaves and drop them into the pan. Stir to mix the ingredients. Simmer for a further 15 minutes, until the vegetables are tender.

3 Add the cayenne pepper, plus salt and black pepper to taste, then add the chunks of bread. Remove the pan from the heat, cover and leave to stand for about 10 minutes.

4 Meanwhile, heat the olive oil in a frying pan and sauté the garlic until golden brown.

5 Pour the soup into bowls, add a little sautéed garlic to each bowl and serve.

Energy 336kcal/1413kJ; Protein 7.3g; Carbohydrate 50.7g, of which sugars 5.1g; Fat 12.9g, of which saturates 2g; Cholesterol 0mg; Calcium 96mg; Fibre 3.7g; Sodium 203mg.

MEATBALL AND PASTA SOUP

THIS DELICIOUS SOUP, WHICH COMES FROM SUNNY SICILY, IS ALSO SUBSTANTIAL ENOUGH FOR A HEARTY SUPPER, WHATEVER THE WEATHER.

SERVES FOUR

INGREDIENTS

    2 x 300g/11oz cans condensed beef
      consommé
    90g/3½oz/¾ cup very thin pasta,
      such as fidelini or spaghettini
    chopped fresh flat leaf parsley, to
      garnish
    grated Parmesan cheese, to serve
For the meatballs
    1 very thick slice white bread, crusts
      removed
    30ml/2 tbsp milk
    225g/8oz/1 cup minced (ground) beef
    1 garlic clove, crushed
    30ml/2 tbsp grated Parmesan cheese
    30–45ml/2–3 tbsp fresh flat leaf
      parsley leaves, coarsely chopped
    1 egg
    a generous pinch of freshly grated
      nutmeg
    salt and ground black pepper

1 Make the meatballs. Break the bread into a small bowl, add the milk and set aside to soak. Meanwhile, put the minced beef, garlic, Parmesan, parsley and egg in another large bowl. Grate the nutmeg liberally over the top and add salt and pepper to taste.

2 Squeeze the bread with your hands to remove as much milk as possible, then add the bread to the meatball mixture and mix everything together well with your hands.

3 Wash your hands, rinse them under the cold tap, then form the mixture into tiny balls about the size of marbles.

4 Pour both cans of consommé into a large pan, add water as directed on the labels, then add an extra can of water. Season to taste, bring to the boil and add the meatballs.

5 Break the pasta into small pieces and add it to the soup. Bring to the boil, stirring gently. Simmer, stirring frequently, for 7–8 minutes or according to the instructions on the packet, until the pasta is *al dente*. Taste and adjust the seasoning, if necessary.

6 Serve hot in warmed bowls, garnished with chopped parsley and freshly grated Parmesan cheese.

COOK'S TIP
When shaping the meatballs, dust the work surface and your fingers lightly with flour to prevent the meat sticking.

Energy 276kcal/1158kJ; Protein 19.9g; Carbohydrate 20.5g, of which sugars 1.4g; Fat 14g, of which saturates 6.1g; Cholesterol 89mg; Calcium 133mg; Fibre 1g; Sodium 731mg.

PLANTAIN AND CORN SOUP

HERE THE SWEETNESS OF THE CORN AND PLANTAINS IS OFFSET BY A LITTLE CHILLI TO CREATE AN UNUSUAL SOUP.

SERVES 4

INGREDIENTS

    25g/1oz/2 tbsp butter or margarine
    1 onion, finely chopped
    1 garlic clove, crushed
    275g/10oz yellow plantains, peeled
      and sliced
    1 large tomato, peeled and roughly
      chopped
    175g/6oz/1 cup corn kernels
    5ml/1 tsp dried tarragon,
      crushed
    900ml/1½ pints/3¾ cups vegetable
      or chicken stock
    1 fresh green chilli, seeded
      and chopped
    a pinch of freshly grated nutmeg
    salt and ground black pepper

1 Melt the butter or margarine in a pan over a moderate heat, add the onion and garlic and fry for a few minutes until the onion is soft.

2 Add the plantains, tomato and corn kernels, and cook for a further 5 minutes.

3 Add the tarragon, stock, green chilli and salt and freshly ground black pepper, then simmer for 10 minutes or until the plantain is tender.

4 Stir in the grated nutmeg. Ladle the soup into warmed bowls and serve immediately, piping hot.

GROUNDNUT SOUP

GROUNDNUTS (OR PEANUTS) ARE WIDELY USED IN SAUCES IN AFRICAN COOKING – HERE THEY MAKE A WONDERFULLY RICH SOUP FLAVOURED WITH GINGER AND CHILLI. WHITE YAM AND OKRA COMPLETE THE AFRICAN EXPERIENCE.

SERVES 4

INGREDIENTS

    45ml/3 tbsp groundnut (peanut)
      paste
    1.5 litres/2½ pints/6¼ cups stock
      or water
    30ml/2 tbsp tomato purée (paste)
    1 onion, chopped
    2 slices fresh root ginger
    1.5ml/¼ tsp dried thyme
    1 bay leaf
    chilli powder
    225g/8oz white yam, diced
    10 small okras, trimmed (optional)
    salt

COOK'S TIP
Groundnut paste should be available in health food stores, but if it is unobtainable you could use peanut butter instead.

1 Place the groundnut paste in a bowl, add 300ml/½ pint/1¼ cups of the stock or water and the tomato purée. Using a wooden spoon, blend together to make a smooth paste.

2 Spoon the nut mixture into a pan and add the onion, ginger, thyme, bay leaf, chilli powder, salt to taste and the remaining stock.

3 Heat gently until simmering, then cook for 1 hour, whisking from time to time to prevent the nut mixture sticking to the base of the pan.

4 Add the white yam, cook for a further 10 minutes, and then add the okra, if using, and simmer until both vegetables are tender.

5 Ladle into warmed bowls and serve immediately, piping hot.

Top: Energy 190kcal/803kJ; Protein 2.4g; Carbohydrate 33.8g, of which sugars 9.8g; Fat 6g, of which saturates 3.4g; Cholesterol 13mg; Calcium 15mg; Fibre 2g; Sodium 162mg.
Bottom: Energy 144kcal/604kJ; Protein 4g; Carbohydrate 19.6g, of which sugars 3.1g; Fat 6.1g, of which saturates 1.5g; Cholesterol 0mg; Calcium 19mg; Fibre 1.8g; Sodium 59mg.

SOUPS FOR ENTERTAINING

Soups can be made in advance and reheated, which makes them the ideal appetizer when entertaining. This section contains luxurious and creative recipes for elegant dinner parties. Impress your friends with Oyster Soup, Winter Melon Soup with Tiger Lilies, or Mediterranean Seafood Soup with Saffron Rouille. Adding a little liqueur or spirits makes a soup really special. Try Iced Tomato and Vodka Soup, or Chilled Vegetable Soup with Pastis.

SHERRIED ONION AND ALMOND SOUP
WITH SAFFRON

THE SPANISH COMBINATION OF ONIONS, SHERRY AND SAFFRON GIVES THIS PALE YELLOW SOUP
A BEGUILING FLAVOUR THAT IS PERFECT AS THE OPENING COURSE OF A SPECIAL MEAL.

2 Add the saffron strands and cook, uncovered, for 3–4 minutes, then add the ground almonds and cook, stirring constantly, for another 2–3 minutes. Pour in the stock and sherry and stir in 5ml/1 tsp salt. Season with plenty of black pepper. Bring to the boil, then lower the heat and simmer gently for about 10 minutes.

SERVES 4

INGREDIENTS
40g/1½oz/3 tbsp butter
2 large yellow onions, thinly sliced
1 small garlic clove, finely chopped
good pinch of saffron strands (about
  12 strands)
50g/2oz blanched almonds, toasted
  and finely ground
750ml/1¼ pints/3 cups good chicken
  or vegetable stock
45ml/3 tbsp dry sherry
salt and ground black pepper
30ml/2 tbsp flaked or slivered
  almonds, toasted and chopped,
  and fresh parsley, to garnish

1 Melt the butter in a heavy pan over a low heat. Add the onions and garlic, stirring to coat them thoroughly in the butter, and then cover the pan and cook very gently, stirring frequently, for 15–20 minutes, until the onions are a soft texture and golden yellow in colour.

VARIATION
This soup is also delicious served chilled. Use olive oil rather than butter and add a little more chicken or vegetable stock to make a slightly thinner soup, then leave to cool and chill for at least 4 hours. Just before serving, taste for seasoning. Float 1–2 ice cubes in each bowl.

3 Process the soup in a blender or food processor until smooth, then return it to the rinsed pan. Reheat slowly, stirring occasionally, but do not allow the soup to boil. Taste for seasoning, adding more salt and pepper if required.

4 Ladle the soup into heated bowls, garnish with the toasted flaked or slivered almonds and a little parsley, and serve immediately.

Energy 255kcal/1054kJ; Protein 5.8g; Carbohydrate 11.5g, of which sugars 8.1g; Fat 19.6g, of which saturates 6.1g; Cholesterol 21mg; Calcium 82mg; Fibre 3.2g; Sodium 68mg.

VERMOUTH SOUP WITH SEARED SCALLOPS, ROCKET OIL AND CAVIAR

SEARED SCALLOPS FORM AN ELEGANT TOWER IN THE CENTRE OF THIS CRÈME DE LA CRÈME OF FINE SOUPS. THE CAVIAR GARNISH LOOKS — AND TASTES — SUPERB.

SERVES 4

INGREDIENTS
    25g/1oz/2 tbsp butter
    5 shallots, sliced
    300ml/½ pint/1¼ cups dry
      white wine
    300ml/½ pint/1¼ cups vermouth
    900ml/1½ pints/3¾ cups fish stock
    300ml/½ pint/1¼ cups double
      (heavy) cream
    300ml/½ pint/1¼ cups single
      (light) cream
    15ml/1 tbsp olive oil
    12 large scallops
    salt and ground black pepper
    15ml/1 tbsp caviar and chopped
      chives, to garnish
For the rocket oil
    115g/4oz rocket (arugula) leaves
    120ml/4fl oz/½ cup olive oil

1 Prepare the rocket oil first. Process the rocket leaves and olive oil in a food processor or blender for 1–2 minutes to give a green paste. Line a small bowl with a piece of muslin (cheesecloth) and scrape the paste into it. Gather up the muslin and squeeze it well to extract the green, rocket-flavoured oil from the paste. Set aside.

2 Melt the butter in a large pan. Add the shallots and cook over a gentle heat for 8–10 minutes, until soft but not browned. Add the wine and vermouth and boil for 8–10 minutes, until the liquid is reduced to about a quarter of the volume.

3 Add the stock and bring back to the boil. Boil until reduced by half. Pour in the double and single creams, and return to the boil. Reduce the heat and simmer gently for 12–15 minutes, until just thick enough to coat the back of a spoon.

4 Strain through a fine sieve (strainer) into the rinsed pan, and set aside.

5 Heat a ridged griddle or frying pan. Brush the scallops with oil, add them to the pan and sear for 1–2 minutes on each side, until just cooked, when they will be white and tender.

6 Reheat the soup gently, then check and adjust the seasoning to taste.

7 Arrange three scallops, one on top of the other, in the centre of each of four warmed, shallow soup plates. Ladle the hot soup around the scallops and top them with a little of the caviar. Drizzle some rocket oil over the surface of the soup, then sprinkle with chopped chives.

TORTILLA TOMATO SOUP

THERE ARE SEVERAL TORTILLA SOUPS. THIS ONE IS AN AGUADA – OR LIQUID – VERSION, AND IS INTENDED FOR SERVING AS AN APPETIZER OR LIGHT MEAL. IT IS VERY EASY AND QUICK TO PREPARE, OR MAKE IT IN ADVANCE AND FRY THE TORTILLA STRIPS AS IT REHEATS. THE CRISP TORTILLA PIECES ADD INTEREST AND GIVE THE SOUP AN UNUSUAL TEXTURE.

SERVES 4

INGREDIENTS
4 corn tortillas
15ml/1 tbsp vegetable oil, plus extra
   for frying
1 small onion, chopped
2 garlic cloves, crushed
350g/12oz ripe plum tomatoes
400g/14oz can plum tomatoes, drained
1 litre/1¾ pints/4 cups chicken stock
small bunch of fresh coriander (cilantro)
50g/2oz/½ cup grated mild Cheddar
   cheese
salt and ground black pepper

1 Using a sharp knife, cut each tortilla into four or five strips, each measuring about 2cm/¾in wide. Pour vegetable oil to a depth of 2cm/¾in into a frying pan. Heat until a small piece of tortilla, added to the oil, floats on the top and bubbles at the edges.

2 Add a few tortilla strips to the hot oil and fry until crisp and golden brown.

3 Remove the tortilla chips with a slotted spoon and drain on kitchen paper. Cook the remaining tortilla strips in the same way.

4 Heat the 15ml/1 tbsp vegetable oil in a large pan. Add the onion and garlic and cook over a medium heat for 2–3 minutes, until the onion is soft and translucent. Do not let the garlic turn brown or it will give the soup a bitter taste.

5 Skin the fresh tomatoes by plunging them into boiling water for 30 seconds, refreshing them in cold water, draining them and then peeling off the skins with a sharp knife.

6 Chop the fresh and canned tomatoes and add them to the onion mixture. Pour in the chicken stock. Bring to the boil, then lower the heat and simmer for 10 minutes, until the liquid has reduced slightly. Stir the mixture occasionally.

7 Roughly chop or tear the coriander into pieces. Add it to the soup and season with salt and ground black pepper to taste.

8 Place a few of the crisp tortilla pieces in each of four large heated soup bowls. Ladle the soup on top. Sprinkle each portion with some of the grated mild Cheddar cheese and serve immediately.

COOK'S TIP
An easy way to chop fresh herbs is to put them in a mug and snip with a pair of scissors. Hold the scissors vertically with one hand on each handle and work the blades back and forth until the herbs are finely and evenly chopped. If you are using woody herbs, such as rosemary or thyme, remember to strip the leaves from the stalks before putting them in the mug. They are then ready to be chopped.

Energy 270kcal/1135kJ; Protein 8.3g; Carbohydrate 36.9g, of which sugars 7.2g; Fat 10.7g, of which saturates 3.6g; Cholesterol 12mg; Calcium 164mg; Fibre 3.3g; Sodium 248mg.

ICED TOMATO AND VODKA SOUP

THIS FRESH-FLAVOURED SOUP PACKS A PUNCH LIKE A FROZEN BLOODY MARY. IT IS DELICIOUS SERVED AS AN IMPRESSIVE FIRST COURSE FOR A SUMMER'S DINNER PARTY WITH SUN-DRIED TOMATO BREAD.

SERVES 4

INGREDIENTS

450g/1lb ripe, well-flavoured
   tomatoes, halved or
   roughly chopped
600ml/1 pint/2½ cups jellied beef
   stock or consommé
1 small red onion, halved
2 celery sticks, cut into large pieces
1 garlic clove, roughly chopped
15ml/1 tbsp tomato purée (paste)
10ml/2 tsp lemon juice
10ml/2 tsp Worcestershire sauce
a handful of small fresh basil leaves
30ml/2 tbsp vodka
salt and ground black pepper
crushed ice, 4 small celery sticks and
   sun-dried tomato bread, to serve

1 Put the halved or chopped tomatoes, jellied stock or consommé, onion and celery in a blender or food processor. Add the garlic, then spoon in the tomato purée. Pulse until all the vegetables are finely chopped, then process to a smooth paste.

2 Press the mixture through a sieve (strainer) into a large bowl and stir in the lemon juice, Worcestershire sauce, basil leaves and vodka.

3 Add salt and pepper to taste. Cover and chill. Serve the soup with a little crushed ice and place a celery stick in each bowl.

COOK'S TIPS
• Canned beef consommé is ideal for this recipe, but vegetable stock, for vegetarians, will work well too.
• If you or your guests are fond of celery, you can stand more celery sticks in a jug (pitcher) of iced water on the table for people to help themselves. The celery sticks can be used as additional edible stirrers and taste delicious after being dipped into the soup.
• Making your own sun-dried tomato bread is easy and is bound to impress your guests. If you don't have time, however, look out for tomato-flavoured ciabatta or focaccia.

Energy 46kcal/194kJ; Protein 1.3g; Carbohydrate 5.5g, of which sugars 5.2g; Fat 0.4g, of which saturates 0.1g; Cholesterol 0mg; Calcium 22mg; Fibre 1.6g; Sodium 44mg.

TOMATO AND PEACH JUS WITH PRAWNS

AMERICAN-STYLE SOUPS, MADE FROM THE CLEAR JUICES EXTRACTED FROM VEGETABLES OR FRUITS AND REFERRED TO AS "WATER" SOUPS BY CHEFS, PROVIDE THE INSPIRATION FOR THIS RECIPE.

SERVES 6

INGREDIENTS
    1.5kg/3–3½lb ripe peaches
    1.2kg/2½lb beef tomatoes
    30ml/2 tbsp white wine vinegar
    1 lemon grass stalk, crushed
      and chopped
    2.5cm/1in fresh root ginger, grated
    1 bay leaf
    150ml/¼ pint/⅔ cup water
    18 tiger prawns (shrimp), shelled
      with tails on and deveined
    olive oil, for brushing
    salt and ground black pepper
    fresh coriander (cilantro) leaves and
      2 vine-ripened tomatoes, peeled,
      seeded and diced, to garnish

1 Peel the tomatoes and peaches and cut into chunks. Put into a food processor and purée them. Stir in the vinegar and seasoning.

2 Line a large bowl with muslin (cheesecloth). Pour the purée into the bowl, gather up the ends of the muslin and tie tightly. Suspend over the bowl and leave at room temperature for 3 hours or until about 1.2 litres/2 pints/ 5 cups juice have drained through.

3 Meanwhile, put the lemon grass, ginger and bay leaf into a pan with the water, and simmer for 5–6 minutes. Set aside to cool.

4 When the mixture is cool, strain into the tomato and peach juice and chill in the refrigerator for at least 4 hours.

5 Using a sharp knife, slit the prawns down their curved sides, cutting about three-quarters of the way through and keeping their tails intact. Open the prawns out flat.

6 Heat a griddle or frying pan and brush with a little oil. Sear the prawns for 1–2 minutes on each side, until tender and slightly charred. Pat dry on kitchen paper to remove any remaining oil. Cool, but do not chill.

7 When ready to serve, ladle the soup into bowls and place three prawns in each portion.

8 Add some torn coriander leaves and diced tomato to each bowl, to garnish.

Energy 188kcal/797kJ; Protein 12.7g; Carbohydrate 25.2g, of which sugars 25.2g; Fat 4.8g, of which saturates 0.8g; Cholesterol 98mg; Calcium 71mg; Fibre 5.8g; Sodium 116mg.

CORN AND CRAB BISQUE

THIS IS A LOUISIANA CLASSIC, WHICH IS CERTAINLY LUXURIOUS ENOUGH FOR A DINNER PARTY AND IS THEREFORE WELL WORTH THE EXTRA TIME REQUIRED TO PREPARE THE FRESH CRAB. THE CRAB SHELLS, TOGETHER WITH THE CORN COBS, FROM WHICH THE KERNELS ARE STRIPPED, MAKE A FINE-FLAVOURED STOCK. SERVE THE SOUP WITH HOT FRENCH BREAD OR GRISSINI BREADSTICKS.

SERVES 8

INGREDIENTS
    4 large corn cobs
    2 bay leaves
    1 cooked crab (about 1kg/2¼lb)
    25g/1oz/2 tbsp butter
    30ml/2 tbsp plain (all-purpose) flour
    300ml/½ pints/1¼ cups whipping
      cream
    6 spring onions (scallions), shredded
    a pinch of cayenne pepper
    salt and ground black and white
      pepper
    hot French bread or grissini
      breadsticks, to serve

1 Pull away the husks and silk from the cobs of corn and strip off the kernels.

2 Keep the kernels on one side and put the stripped cobs into a deep pan or flameproof casserole with 3 litres/5 pints/12½ cups cold water, the bay leaves and 10ml/2 tsp salt. Bring to the boil and leave to simmer while you prepare the crab.

3 Pull away the two flaps between the big claws of the crab, stand it on its 'nose', where the flaps were, and bang down firmly with the heel of your hand on the rounded end.

4 Separate the crab from its top shell, keeping the shell.

5 Push out the crab's mouth and its abdominal sac immediately below the mouth, and discard.

6 Pull away the feathery gills around the central chamber and discard them. Scrape out all the semi-liquid brown meat from the shell and set aside.

COOK'S TIP
It is vital to stir constantly to darken the roux without burning. Should black specks appear at any stage of cooking, discard the roux and start again.

7 Using a rolling pin, crack the claws in as many places as necessary to extract all the white meat. Pick out the white meat from the fragile cavities in the central body of the crab. Set aside all the crab meat, brown and white.

8 Put the spidery legs, back shell and all the other pieces of shell into the pan with the corn cobs. Simmer for a further 15 minutes, then strain the stock into a clean pan and boil hard to reduce to 2 litres/3½ pints/9 cups.

9 Meanwhile, melt the butter in a small pan and sprinkle in the flour. Stir constantly over a low heat until the roux is the colour of rich cream.

10 Off the heat, slowly stir in 250ml/ 8fl oz/1 cup of the stock. Return to the heat and stir until it thickens, then stir this thickened mixture into the pan of strained stock.

11 Add the corn kernels, return to the boil and simmer for 5 minutes.

12 Add the crab meat, cream and spring onions and season with cayenne, salt and pepper (preferably a mixture of black and white). Return to the boil and simmer for a further 2 minutes.

13 Ladle the soup into warmed bowls and serve with hot French bread or grissini breadsticks.

Energy 273kcal/1136kJ; Protein 7.7g; Carbohydrate 17.5g, of which sugars 6.1g; Fat 19.6g, of which saturates 11.3g; Cholesterol 60mg; Calcium 40mg; Fibre 0.9g; Sodium 255mg.

LEMON AND PUMPKIN MOULES MARINIÈRE

BASED ON THE CLASSIC FRENCH SHELLFISH DISH, THIS MUSSEL SOUP IS THICKENED WITH FRESH PUMPKIN AND FLAVOURED WITH DILL AND LEMON. THIS IS A VERY ELEGANT AND IMPRESSIVE SOUP, IDEAL FOR SERVING AT A SPECIAL DINNER PARTY.

SERVES 4

INGREDIENTS

1kg/2¼lb fresh mussels
300ml/½ pint/1¼ cups dry
  white wine
1 large lemon
1 bay leaf
15ml/1 tbsp olive oil
1 onion, chopped
1 garlic clove, crushed
675g/1½lb pumpkin or squash
900ml/1½ pints/3¾ cups
  vegetable stock
30ml/2 tbsp chopped fresh dill
salt and ground black pepper
lemon wedges, to serve

1 Scrub the mussels in cold water and pull away the dark hairy beards protruding from the shells. Discard any open mussels that do not shut when tapped sharply, and put the rest into a large pan. Pour in the white wine.

2 Pare large pieces of rind from the lemon and squeeze the juice, then add both to the mussels with the bay leaf. Cover and bring to the boil, then cook for 4–5 minutes, shaking the pan, until all the mussels have opened.

3 Drain the mussels in a colander over a large bowl. Reserve the cooking liquid and the mussels.

4 Remove and discard the lemon rind and the bay leaf, and any mussels that have not opened.

5 When the mussels are cool enough to handle, set aside a few in their shells for the garnish. Remove the remaining mussels from their shells. Strain the reserved cooking liquid through a sieve (strainer) lined with muslin (cheesecloth) to remove any sand or grit.

6 Heat the oil in a large, clean pan. Add the onion and garlic and cook for 4–5 minutes, until softened.

7 Peel the pumpkin, remove the seeds and pith and roughly chop into chunks. Add the pumpkin flesh and the strained mussel cooking liquid to the pan. Bring to the boil and simmer, uncovered, for 5–6 minutes.

8 Pour in the vegetable stock and cook for a further 25–30 minutes, until the pumpkin has almost disintegrated.

9 Cool the soup slightly, then pour into a food processor or blender and process until smooth.

10 Return the soup to the rinsed pan and season well. Stir in the chopped dill and the shelled mussels, then bring just to the boil.

11 Ladle the soup into warmed soup plates and garnish with the reserved mussels in their shells. Serve lemon wedges with the soup.

Energy 161kcal/678kJ; Protein 14.3g; Carbohydrate 4.2g, of which sugars 3.3g; Fat 4.6g, of which saturates 0.8g; Cholesterol 30mg; Calcium 203mg; Fibre 1.7g; Sodium 161mg.

.

CLAM AND BASIL SOUP

SUBTLY SWEET AND SPICY, THIS SOUP IS AN IDEAL APPETIZER FOR SERVING AS PART OF A CELEBRATION DINNER. TO MAKE THE SOUP REALLY SPECIAL, BUY A JAR OF CLAMS IN THEIR SHELLS FROM AN ITALIAN DELICATESSEN, AND STIR SOME INTO THE SOUP BEFORE SERVING.

SERVES 4–6

INGREDIENTS
30ml/2 tbsp olive oil
1 medium onion, finely chopped
leaves from 1 fresh or dried sprig of
  thyme, chopped or crumbled
2 garlic cloves, crushed
5 or 6 fresh basil leaves, plus extra
  to garnish
1.5–2.5ml/¼–½ tsp crushed red
  chillies, to taste
1 litre/1¾ pints/4 cups fish stock
350ml/12fl oz/1½ cups passata
  (bottled strained tomatoes)
5ml/1 tsp granulated sugar
90g/3½oz/scant 1 cup frozen peas
65g/2½oz/⅔ cup small pasta shapes,
  such as chifferini, rigatoni or penne
225g/8oz frozen shelled clams
salt and ground black pepper

1 Heat the oil in a large pan, add the onion and cook gently for about 5 minutes until softened but not coloured.

2 Add the thyme, then stir in the garlic, basil leaves and chillies.

3 Add the stock, passata and sugar to the pan, with salt and pepper to taste. Bring to the boil, then lower the heat and simmer for 15 minutes, stirring from time to time to prevent sticking.

4 Add the frozen peas and cook for a further 5 minutes.

5 Add the pasta to the stock mixture and bring to the boil, stirring. Lower the heat and simmer for about 5 minutes or according to the packet instructions, stirring frequently, until the pasta is *al dente*.

6 Turn the heat down to low, add the frozen clams and heat through for 2–3 minutes. Taste and adjust the seasoning. Serve hot in warmed bowls, garnished with basil leaves.

COOK'S TIPS
• Frozen shelled clams are available at delicatessens, good fishmongers and supermarkets. If you can't get them, use bottled or canned clams in brine (not vinegar).
• To make the fish stock, ask your fishmonger for heads, bones and trimmings from white fish. Lobster or crab shell pieces may also be used. Boil the trimmings with chopped onion, celery, carrot, herbs and a little white wine.

Energy 123kcal/518kJ; Protein 8.9g; Carbohydrate 13g, of which sugars 3g; Fat 4.3g, of which saturates 0.7g; Cholesterol 25mg; Calcium 42mg; Fibre 1.5g; Sodium 585mg.

PEAR <u>AND</u> ROQUEFORT SOUP
<u>WITH</u> CARAMELIZED PEARS

*LIKE MOST FRUIT-BASED SOUPS, THIS IS SERVED IN SMALL PORTIONS. IT MAKES AN UNUSUAL AND
SEASONAL APPETIZER FOR AN AUTUMN DINNER PARTY.*

3 Cool the soup slightly and purée it in a food processor until smooth, then pass it through a fine sieve (strainer). Return the soup to the pan.

4 To make the caramelized pears, melt the butter in a frying pan and add the pears. Cook for 8–10 minutes, turning occasionally, until golden.

5 Reheat the soup gently, then ladle into small, shallow bowls and add a few caramelized pear wedges to each portion. Garnish with tiny sprigs of watercress and serve immediately.

VARIATION
Any blue cheese with a strong flavour could be used in place of Roquefort, for example Stilton or Gorgonzola.

SERVES 4

INGREDIENTS
   30ml/2 tbsp sunflower oil
   1 onion, chopped
   3 pears, peeled, cored and
      chopped into 1cm/½in chunks
   400ml/14fl oz/1⅔ cups
      vegetable stock
   2.5ml/½ tsp paprika
   juice of ½ lemon
   175g/6oz Roquefort cheese
   salt and ground black pepper
   watercress sprigs, to garnish
For the caramelized pears
   50g/2oz/¼ cup butter
   2 pears, halved, cored and cut
      into wedges

1 Heat the oil in a pan. Add the onion and cook for 4–5 minutes until soft.

2 Add the pears and stock. Bring to the boil and cook for 8–10 minutes, until the pears are soft. Stir in the paprika, lemon juice, cheese and seasoning.

Energy 381kcal/1579kJ; Protein 10.1g; Carbohydrate 21.8g, of which sugars 20.9g; Fat 28.7g, of which saturates 15.6g; Cholesterol 59mg; Calcium 246mg; Fibre 4.7g; Sodium 616mg.

MEDITERRANEAN SEAFOOD SOUP WITH SAFFRON ROUILLE

VARY THE FISH CONTENT OF THIS SOUP ACCORDING TO THE FRESHEST AVAILABLE, BUT CHOOSE FIRM VARIETIES THAT WILL NOT FLAKE AND FALL APART EASILY DURING COOKING.

SERVES 4

INGREDIENTS
450g/1lb fresh clams, scrubbed
120ml/4fl oz/½ cup white wine
15ml/1 tbsp olive oil
4 garlic cloves, crushed
5ml/1 tsp fennel seeds
pinch of dried chilli flakes
1 fennel bulb, cored and sliced
1 red (bell) pepper, seeded
   and sliced
8 plum tomatoes, halved
1 onion, cut into thin wedges
225g/8oz small waxy potatoes, sliced
1 bay leaf
1 fresh thyme sprig
600ml/1 pint/2½ cups fish stock
1 mini French stick
225g/8oz monkfish fillet, sliced
350g/12oz red mullet or snapper,
   scaled, filleted and cut into strips
45ml/3 tbsp Pernod
salt and ground black pepper
fennel fronds, to garnish
For the rouille
   a few saffron strands
   150ml/¼ pint/⅔ cup mayonnaise
   a dash of Tabasco sauce

1 Discard any open clams that do not shut when tapped sharply. Place the rest in a large pan with the wine. Cover and cook over a high heat for 4 minutes, until the shells have opened.

COOK'S TIP
Always use clams and other shellfish within one day of purchase.

2 Drain the clams, strain their cooking liquid and set it aside. Discard any unopened shells and reserve 8 clams in their shells. Remove the remaining clams from their shells and set aside.

3 Heat the oil in a pan. Add the garlic, fennel seeds and chilli flakes and cook for about 2 minutes, until softened.

4 Add the fennel, pepper, tomatoes, onion and cooking liquid. Cover and cook for 10 minutes, stirring occasionally.

5 Stir in the potatoes, bay leaf and thyme, then pour in the fish stock. Cover and cook for 15–20 minutes, until the vegetables are tender.

6 Meanwhile, make the saffron rouille. Pound the saffron strands to a powder in a mortar, then beat it into the mayonnaise with the Tabasco sauce. Cut the French stick into eight thin slices and toast them on both sides. Set aside.

7 Add the monkfish, red mullet and Pernod to the soup and cook for 3–4 minutes, until tender. Add all the clams (with and without shells) and heat through for 30 seconds. Remove the bay leaf and thyme sprigs, and season the soup well. Spoon the rouille on to the toasts. Ladle the soup into bowls, garnish each bowl with a frond of fennel and serve with the toasts.

Energy 728kcal/3048kJ; Protein 50.2g; Carbohydrate 40g, of which sugars 10.9g; Fat 37.1g, of which saturates 5.4g; Cholesterol 111mg; Calcium 238mg; Fibre 4.7g; Sodium 1940mg.

SPANISH SEAFOOD SOUP

*THIS HEARTY SOUP CONTAINS ALL THE COLOURS AND FLAVOURS OF THE MEDITERRANEAN. IT IS
SUBSTANTIAL ENOUGH TO SERVE AS A MAIN COURSE, BUT CAN ALSO BE DILUTED WITH A LITTLE
WHITE WINE AND WATER TO MAKE AN ELEGANT APPETIZER FOR SIX.*

SERVES 4

INGREDIENTS

675g/1½lb raw prawns (shrimp),
  in the shell
900ml/1½ pints/3¾ cups cold water
1 onion, chopped
1 celery stick, chopped
1 bay leaf
45ml/3 tbsp olive oil
2 slices stale bread, crusts removed
1 small onion, finely chopped
1 large garlic clove, chopped
2 large tomatoes, halved
½ large green (bell) pepper,
  finely chopped
500g/1¼lb cockles (small clams)
  or mussels, cleaned
juice of 1 lemon
45ml/3 tbsp chopped fresh parsley
5ml/1 tsp paprika
salt and ground black pepper

COOK'S TIP

Good fish and shellfish dishes are
normally based on proper fish stock
(including the juices saved from opening
mussels). This is equivalent to the French
court bouillon, and takes 30 minutes'
simmering. The method used here is one
of the quickest, because the prawn heads
come off neatly, and the rest of the shells
are simply added as they are removed.

1 Pull the heads off the prawns and
put them in a pan with the cold water.
Add the onion, celery and bay leaf and
simmer for 20–25 minutes.

2 Peel the prawns, adding the shells to
the stock as you go along.

3 Heat the oil in a wide, deep
flameproof casserole and fry the bread
slices quickly, then reserve them. Fry
the onion until it is soft, adding the
garlic towards the end.

4 Scoop the seeds out of the tomatoes
and discard. Chop the flesh and add
to the casserole with the green pepper.
Fry briefly, stirring occasionally.

5 Strain the stock into the casserole and
bring to the boil. Check over the cockles
or mussels, discarding any that are
open or damaged.

6 Add half the cockles or mussels to
the stock. When open, use a slotted
spoon to transfer some of them out
on to a plate. Remove the mussels or
cockles from the shells and discard
the shells. (You should end up having
discarded about half of the shells.)
Meanwhile, repeat the process to cook
the remaining cockles or mussels.

7 Return the cockles or mussels to
the soup and add the prawns. Add the
bread, torn into little pieces, and the
lemon juice and chopped parsley.

8 Season to taste with paprika, salt and
pepper and stir gently to dissolve the
bread. Serve immediately in soup bowls,
providing a plate for the empty shells.

Energy 234kcal/978kJ; Protein 23.3g; Carbohydrate 11.3g, of which sugars 4.5g; Fat 10.9g, of which saturates 1.7g; Cholesterol 67mg; Calcium 216mg; Fibre 2g; Sodium 1193mg.

WILD MUSHROOM SOUP
WITH SOFT POLENTA

THIS RICH SOUP, SERVED WITH SOFT PARMESAN-ENRICHED POLENTA, PROVIDES PLENTY OF SCOPE FOR INDIVIDUAL VARIATIONS, DEPENDING ON YOUR CHOICE OF WILD MUSHROOMS.

SERVES 6

INGREDIENTS

20g/¾oz/scant ½ cup dried
  porcini mushrooms
175ml/6fl oz/¾ cup hot water
50g/2oz/¼ cup butter
1 large red onion, chopped
3 garlic cloves, chopped
115g/4oz/1¾ cups mixed wild
  mushrooms, trimmed
120ml/4fl oz/½ cup light red wine
1.2 litres/2 pints/5 cups
  vegetable stock
2.5ml/½ tsp wholegrain mustard
salt and ground black pepper
chopped fresh parsley, to garnish
For the polenta
750ml/1¼ pints/3 cups milk
175g/6oz/1 cup quick-cook polenta
50g/2oz/¼ cup butter
50g/2oz/⅔ cup freshly grated
  Parmesan cheese, plus extra to serve

1 Put the dried porcini in a bowl and pour over the hot water. Leave them to soak for about 30 minutes. Drain, then strain the liquid through a fine sieve (strainer); reserve both the liquid and the mushrooms.

2 Melt the butter in a large pan. Add the onion and garlic and cook for 4–5 minutes, until softened. Add the mixed wild mushrooms and cook for a further 3–4 minutes.

3 Add the dried mushrooms and strain in the soaking liquid through a sieve lined with muslin (cheesecloth) or a coffee filter. Pour in the wine and stock, and cook for 15 minutes or until the liquid has reduced by half. Remove from the heat and cool slightly.

4 Ladle half the soup into a food processor or blender and process until almost smooth. Pour the processed soup back into the soup remaining in the pan and set aside.

5 To make the polenta, bring the milk to the boil and pour in the polenta in a steady stream, stirring continuously. Cook for about 5 minutes, or until the polenta begins to come away from the side of the pan. Beat in the butter, then stir in the Parmesan.

6 Return the soup to the heat and bring just to the boil. Stir in the wholegrain mustard and season well.

7 Divide the polenta among six bowls and ladle the soup around it. Sprinkle over the grated Parmesan and the chopped parsley. Serve immediately.

COOK'S TIP

Many large supermarkets now sell a range of wild and cultivated mushrooms, both fresh and dried. If you can't find any, then substitute a mixture of well-flavoured cultivated varieties such as shiitake and chestnut.

SAIGON PORK AND PRAWN SOUP WITH RICE STICKS

THIS VIETNAMESE SOUP RELIES ON A RICHLY FLAVOURED STOCK. WITHOUT IT THE TASTE WOULD BE BLAND AND INSIPID. IT IS A SPECIALITY OF SAIGON, NOW HO CHI MINH CITY.

SERVES 4

INGREDIENTS

225g/8oz pork fillet (tenderloin)
225g/8oz dried rice sticks
   (vermicelli), soaked in lukewarm
   water for 20 minutes
20 prawns (shrimp), shelled and
   deveined
115g/4oz/½ cup beansprouts
2 spring onions (scallions), finely
   sliced
2 green or red Thai chillies, seeded
   and finely sliced
1 garlic clove, finely sliced
1 bunch each coriander (cilantro) and
   basil, stalks removed, leaves roughly
   chopped
1 lime, cut into quarters, and *nuoc
   cham*, to serve
For the stock
   25g/1oz dried squid
   675g/1½lb pork ribs
   1 onion, peeled and quartered
   225g/8oz carrots, peeled and cut into
      chunks
   15ml/1 tbsp *nuoc mam*
   15ml/1 tbsp soy sauce
   6 black peppercorns
   salt

1 To make the stock, soak the dried squid in water for 30 minutes, rinse and drain. Put the ribs in a large pan and cover with 2.5 litres/4½ pints/10 cups water. Bring to the boil, skim off any fat, and add the dried squid with the remaining stock ingredients. Cover the pan and simmer for 1 hour, then skim off any foam or fat and continue to simmer, uncovered, for 1½ hours.

2 Strain the stock and check the seasoning, adding a little more if necessary. You should have roughly 2 litres/3½ pints/8 cups.

COOK'S TIP
If you cannot find dried squid, you can use dried shrimp instead.

3 Pour the stock into a wok or deep pan and bring to the boil. Reduce the heat, add the pork fillet and simmer for 25 minutes. Lift the pork out of the stock, place it on a board and cut it into thin slices. Meanwhile, keep the stock simmering gently over a low heat.

4 Bring a pan of water to the boil. Drain the rice sticks and add to the water. Cook for about 5 minutes, or until tender, separating them with chopsticks if they stick together. Drain the rice sticks and divide them among four warm bowls.

5 Drop the prawns into the simmering stock for 1 minute. Lift them out with a slotted spoon and layer them with the slices of pork on top of the rice sticks. Ladle the hot stock over them and sprinkle with beansprouts, spring onions, chillies, garlic and herbs. Serve each bowl of soup with a wedge of lime to squeeze over it and *nuoc cham* to splash on top.

Energy 346kcal/1449kJ; Protein 27.6g; Carbohydrate 51.3g, of which sugars 6.1g; Fat 3.3g, of which saturates 0.9g; Cholesterol 133mg; Calcium 106mg; Fibre 2.7g; Sodium 159mg.

OYSTER SOUP

OYSTERS MAKE A DELICIOUS SOUP THAT IS REALLY LUXURIOUS. SERVE IT AS AN APPETIZER FOR A SPECIAL DINNER PARTY OR CELEBRATION MEAL.

2 Heat the mixture over medium heat until small bubbles appear around the edge of the pan, being careful not to allow it to boil. Reduce the heat to low and add the oysters.

3 Cook, stirring occasionally, until the oysters plump up and their edges begin to curl. Add the paprika and season the soup to taste.

4 Meanwhile, warm six soup plates or bowls. Cut the butter into 6 pieces and put one piece in each bowl.

SERVES 6

INGREDIENTS
475ml/16fl oz/2 cups milk
475ml/16fl oz/2 cups single (light) cream
1.2 litres/2 pints/5 cups shucked oysters, with their liquor reserved
a pinch of paprika
25g/1oz/2 tbsp butter
salt and freshly ground black pepper
15ml/1 tbsp chopped fresh parsley, to garnish

1 Combine the milk, single cream and oyster liquor in a heavy pan.

Energy 385kcal/1609kJ; Protein 26.5g; Carbohydrate 17.6g, of which sugars 12.2g; Fat 22.6g, of which saturates 13.8g; Cholesterol 174mg; Calcium 430mg; Fibre 0g; Sodium 1112mg.

ASPARAGUS SOUP WITH CRAB

A BEAUTIFUL GREEN SOUP WITH THE PURE TASTE OF FRESH ASPARAGUS. THE CRAB IS ADDED AT THE LAST MOMENT AS A LUXURIOUS GARNISH.

SERVES 6–8

INGREDIENTS
1.5kg/3–3½ lb fresh asparagus
25g/1oz/2 tbsp butter
1.5 litres/2½ pints/6¼ cups
  chicken stock
30ml/2 tbsp cornflour (cornstarch)
30–45ml/2–3 tbsp cold water
120ml/4fl oz/½ cup whipping cream
salt and ground black pepper
175–200g/6–7oz white crab meat, to
  garnish

1 Trim the woody ends from the bottom of the asparagus spears and cut the spears into 2.5cm/1in pieces.

3 Add the stock and bring to the boil, skimming off any foam that rises to the surface. Simmer over medium heat for 3–5 minutes until the asparagus is tender, yet crisp. Reserve 12–16 of the asparagus tips for the garnish.

4 Season the soup, cover and continue cooking for 15–20 minutes until the asparagus is very tender.

5 Purée the soup in a blender or food processor and pass the mixture through the fine blade of a food mill back into the pan. Return the soup to the boil over a medium-high heat. Blend the cornflour with the water and whisk into the boiling soup to thicken, then stir in the cream. Adjust the seasoning.

6 To serve, ladle the soup into warmed bowls and top each with a spoonful of the crab meat and a few of the reserved asparagus tips.

2 Melt the butter in a heavy pan or flameproof casserole over medium-high heat. Add the asparagus and cook for 5–6 minutes, stirring frequently, until it is bright green but not browned.

Energy 157kcal/652kJ; Protein 9.7g; Carbohydrate 7.6g, of which sugars 4g; Fat 9.9g, of which saturates 5.6g; Cholesterol 38mg; Calcium 87mg; Fibre 3.2g; Sodium 147mg.

SEAFOOD WONTON SOUP

THIS IS A VARIATION OF THE POPULAR WONTON SOUP THAT IS TRADITIONALLY PREPARED USING PORK. IN CHINA IT WOULD BE SERVED AS A SNACK, OR DIM SUM, RATHER THAN AS AN APPETIZER TO A MEAL.

SERVES 4

INGREDIENTS

50g/2oz raw tiger prawns (shrimp)
50g/2oz queen scallops
75g/3oz skinless cod fillet, roughly
  chopped
15ml/1 tbsp finely chopped fresh
  chives
5ml/1 tsp dry sherry
1 small egg white
2.5ml/½ tsp sesame oil
1.5ml/¼ tsp salt
large pinch of ground white pepper
20 wonton wrappers
2 romaine lettuce leaves, shredded
900ml/1½ pints/3¾ cups fish stock
fresh coriander (cilantro) leaves and
  garlic chives, to garnish

3 Place the cod in a food processor and process until a paste is formed. Scrape into a bowl and stir in the prawns, scallops, chives, sherry, sesame oil, salt and pepper.

4 Lightly beat the egg white and add to the seafood filling. Mix well, cover and leave in a cool place to marinate for 20 minutes.

6 Bring a large pan of water to the boil. Drop in the wontons. When the water returns to the boil, lower the heat and simmer gently for 5 minutes or until the wontons float to the surface. Drain the wontons and divide them among four heated soup bowls.

7 Add a portion of lettuce to each bowl. Bring the fish stock to the boil. Ladle it on top of the lettuce and garnish each portion with coriander leaves and garlic chives. Serve immediately.

1 Peel and devein the prawns. Rinse, dry on kitchen paper and cut into pieces.

2 Rinse and dry the scallops. Chop into pieces the same size as the prawns.

COOK'S TIP
The filled wonton wrappers can be made ahead, then frozen for several weeks and cooked straight from the freezer.

5 Make the wontons. Place 5ml/1 tsp of the seafood filling in the centre of a wonton wrapper, then bring the corners together to meet at the top. Twist them together to enclose the filling. Fill the remaining wonton wrappers in the same way. Tie with a fresh chive if you like.

Energy 92kcal/388kJ; Protein 10.7g; Carbohydrate 10.8g, of which sugars 0.9g; Fat 0.7g, of which saturates 0.2g; Cholesterol 39mg; Calcium 44mg; Fibre 0.7g; Sodium 74mg.

RED PEPPER SOUP WITH LIME

THE BEAUTIFUL, RICH RED COLOUR OF THIS SOUP MAKES IT AN ATTRACTIVE APPETIZER OR LIGHT LUNCH. FOR A SPECIAL DINNER, TOAST SOME TINY CROÚTONS AND SPRINKLE THEM INTO THE SOUP.

SERVES 4–6

INGREDIENTS

1 large onion, chopped
4 red (bell) peppers, seeded
   and chopped
5ml/1 tsp olive oil
1 garlic clove, crushed
1 small fresh red chilli, sliced
45ml/3 tbsp tomato purée (paste)
900ml/1½ pints/3¾ cups chicken
   stock
finely grated rind and juice of 1 lime
salt and ground black pepper
shreds of lime rind, to garnish

1 Cook the onion and peppers gently in the oil in a covered pan for about 5 minutes, shaking the pan occasionally, until just softened.

2 Stir in the garlic, chilli and tomato purée. Add half the stock, then bring to the boil. Cover and simmer gently for about 10 minutes.

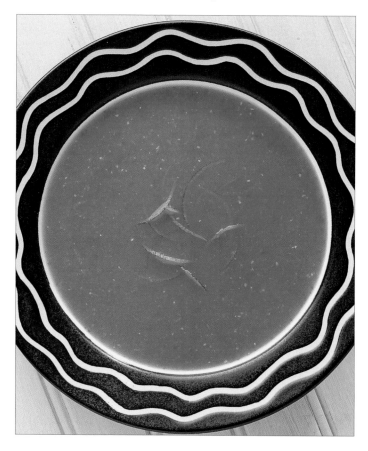

3 Cool slightly, then purée in a food processor or blender. Return to the pan and add the remaining stock, the lime rind and juice, and salt and pepper.

4 Bring the soup back to the boil, then serve immediately, with a few strips of lime rind sprinkled into each bowl.

Energy 66kcal/274kJ; Protein 2.2g; Carbohydrate 12.5g, of which sugars 11g; Fat 1.1g, of which saturates 0.2g; Cholesterol 0mg; Calcium 25mg; Fibre 2.8g; Sodium 24mg.

RED ONION AND BEETROOT SOUP

THIS ATTRACTIVE, RUBY-RED SOUP, WITH ITS CONTRASTING SWIRL OF YOGURT, WILL LOOK STUNNING AT ANY DINNER PARTY.

SERVES 4–6

INGREDIENTS

15ml/1 tbsp olive oil
350g/12oz red onions, sliced
2 garlic cloves, crushed
275g/10oz cooked beetroot, cut
   into sticks
1.2 litres/2 pints/5 cups vegetable
   stock or water
50g/2oz/1 cup cooked soup pasta
30ml/2 tbsp raspberry vinegar
salt and ground black pepper
natural (plain) yogurt or fromage
   blanc and chopped fresh chives,
   to garnish

1 Heat the olive oil in a large pan or flameproof casserole and add the onions and garlic.

COOK'S TIP
Substitute cooked barley for the pasta to give extra nuttiness to the flavour.

2 Cook gently for about 20 minutes or until the onion is soft and tender, stirring occasionally to prevent it sticking to the base of the pan.

3 Add the beetroot, stock or water, cooked pasta and vinegar and heat through. Season and garnish with swirls of yogurt or fromage blanc and chives.

Energy 87kcal/366kJ; Protein 2.8g; Carbohydrate 15.1g, of which sugars 7.6g; Fat 2.2g, of which saturates 0.3g; Cholesterol 0mg; Calcium 30mg; Fibre 1.9g; Sodium 53mg.

SPICED CREAMED PARSNIP SOUP WITH SHERRY

PARSNIPS ARE A NATURALLY SWEET VEGETABLE AND THE MODERN ADDITION OF CURRY POWDER
COMPLEMENTS THIS PERFECTLY, WHILE SHERRY LIFTS THE SOUP INTO THE DINNER-PARTY REALM.

2 Cut the parsnips into even-size pieces, add to the pan and coat with butter. Stir in the curry powder.

3 Pour in the sherry and cover with a *cartouche* (see Cook's Tip) and a lid. Cook over a low heat for 10 minutes or until the parsnips are softened, making sure they do not colour.

4 Add the stock and season to taste. Bring to the boil then simmer for about 15 minutes or until the parsnips are soft. Remove from the heat.

5 Allow to cool for a while then purée in a blender or food processor.

6 When ready to serve, reheat the soup and check the seasoning. Ladle into warmed soup bowls and add a swirl of natural yogurt.

COOK'S TIPS
• A *cartouche* is a circle of greaseproof (waxed) paper that helps to keep in the moisture, so the vegetables cook in their own juices along with the sherry.
• Avoid buying large parsnips, which can be rather woody and lacking in flavour.

SERVES 4

INGREDIENTS
115g/4oz/½ cup butter
2 onions, sliced
1kg/2¼lb parsnips, peeled
10ml/2 tsp curry powder
30ml/2 tbsp medium sherry
1.2 litres/2 pints/5 cups chicken or
   vegetable stock
salt and ground black pepper
natural (plain) yogurt, to serve

1 Melt the butter in a pan, add the onion and sweat gently without allowing it to colour.

Energy 437kcal/1820kJ; Protein 5.9g; Carbohydrate 39.5g, of which sugars 20.2g; Fat 28.7g, of which saturates 16.8g; Cholesterol 67mg; Calcium 134mg; Fibre 12.9g; Sodium 218mg.

STAR-GAZER VEGETABLE SOUP

IF YOU HAVE THE TIME, IT IS WORTH MAKING YOUR OWN STOCK — EITHER VEGETABLE OR, IF YOU PREFER, CHICKEN OR FISH — FOR THIS RECIPE.

SERVES 4

INGREDIENTS

1 yellow (bell) pepper
2 large courgettes (zucchini)
2 large carrots
1 kohlrabi
900ml/1½ pints/3¾ cups well-
flavoured vegetable stock
50g/2oz rice vermicelli
salt and ground black pepper

3 Place the vegetables and stock in a large pan and simmer for 10 minutes, until the vegetables are tender. Season to taste with salt and pepper.

4 Meanwhile, place the vermicelli in a bowl, cover with boiling water and set aside for 4 minutes. Drain, then divide among four warmed soup bowls. Ladle over the soup and serve.

1 Cut the pepper into quarters, removing the seeds and core. Cut the courgettes and carrots lengthways into 5mm/¼in slices and slice the kohlrabi into 5mm/¼in rounds.

2 Using tiny pastry (cookie) cutters, stamp out shapes from the vegetables or use a very sharp knife to cut the sliced vegetables into stars and other decorative shapes.

COOK'S TIP
Sauté the leftover vegetable pieces in a little oil and mix with cooked brown rice to make a tasty risotto.

Energy 96kcal/399kJ; Protein 3.4g; Carbohydrate 19.1g, of which sugars 8.9g; Fat 0.8g, of which saturates 0.2g; Cholesterol 0mg; Calcium 58mg; Fibre 3.1g; Sodium 20mg.

PUMPKIN SOUP WITH ANIS

LIQUORICE-FLAVOURED ANIS ADDS A TOUCH OF EXCITEMENT TO THIS WINTER SOUP. HOT BREAD MAKES AN IDEAL ACCOMPANIMENT.

SERVES 4

INGREDIENTS

675g/1½lb pumpkin
30ml/2 tbsp olive oil
2 large onions, sliced
1 garlic clove, crushed
2 fresh red chillies, seeded
  and chopped
5ml/1 tsp curry paste
750ml/1¼ pints/3 cups vegetable or
  chicken stock
15ml/1 tbsp anis
salt and ground black pepper
150ml/¼ pint/⅔ cup single (light)
  cream, to serve

COOK'S TIP

Use hollowed-out small squashes or pumpkins as individual soup bowls.

1 Peel the pumpkin, remove the seeds and chop the flesh roughly.

2 Heat the oil in a large pan and fry the onions until golden. Stir in the garlic, chillies and curry paste. Cook for 1 minute, then add the chopped pumpkin and cook for 5 minutes more. Pour over the stock and season.

3 Bring to the boil, lower the heat, cover and simmer for about 25 minutes.

4 Process until smooth in a blender or food processor, then return to the clean pan. Add the anis and reheat. Taste and season if necessary. Serve the soup in individual heated bowls, adding a spoonful of cream to each portion.

Energy 188kcal/780kJ; Protein 3.6g; Carbohydrate 12.5g, of which sugars 9.3g; Fat 13.2g, of which saturates 5.5g; Cholesterol 21mg; Calcium 107mg; Fibre 3.1g; Sodium 14mg.

FRENCH ONION SOUP WITH COGNAC

COGNAC ADDS A DELICIOUS KICK TO THIS TIME-HONOURED, CLASSIC FRENCH SOUP AND MAKES IT SPECIAL ENOUGH TO SERVE AT A DINNER PARTY.

SERVES 4

INGREDIENTS
    30ml/2 tbsp olive oil
    25g/1oz/2 tbsp butter
    3 onions (about 450g/1lb total
      weight), sliced
    5ml/1 tsp soft light brown sugar
    2 garlic cloves, crushed
    1.2 litres/2 pints/5 cups vegetable or
      chicken stock
    60ml/4 tbsp cognac
    4 slices French bread
    15ml/1 tbsp Dijon mustard
    115g/4oz/1 cup Gruyère cheese,
      grated
    salt and ground black pepper

COOK'S TIP
Don't rush the browning of the onions.
Their sweetness emerges through long,
gentle cooking.

1 Heat the oil and butter in a heavy pan
and cook the onions very gently for
about 30 minutes until they are very
soft. Sprinkle the brown sugar and
garlic over and cook until the onions
are golden brown.

2 Stir in the stock and cognac, with salt
and pepper to taste. Bring to the boil,
then lower the heat and simmer for
about 30 minutes.

3 Just before serving, toast the bread
under a hot grill (broiler) on one side
only. Turn the slices over, spread them
with the mustard and cover with the
grated cheese. Grill (broil) until all the
cheese has melted and is golden.

4 Ladle the soup into warmed bowls
and float the toasted bread on top.
Serve immediately.

Energy 395kcal/1646kJ; Protein 12.3g; Carbohydrate 31.4g, of which sugars 7.5g; Fat 21g, of which saturates 10.4g; Cholesterol 41mg; Calcium 290mg; Fibre 2.5g; Sodium 496mg.

CHILLED VEGETABLE SOUP WITH PASTIS

FENNEL, STAR ANISE AND PASTIS GIVE A DELICATE ANISEED FLAVOUR TO THIS SOPHISTICATED SOUP, WHICH IS IDEAL AS AN APPETIZER FOR A DINNER PARTY.

2 With a slotted spoon, remove the star anise, then process the vegetables until smooth in a blender or food processor and place in a clean pan.

3 Stir in the single cream, bring to the boil, taste and and adjust the seasoning if necessary.

4 Strain into a bowl, cover and leave until cold.

5 To serve, stir in the pastis, pour into bowls, add a swirl of double cream or crème fraîche and garnish with chives.

COOK'S TIP
To chill the soup quickly, stir in a spoonful of crushed ice.

SERVES 6

INGREDIENTS
    175g/6oz leek, finely sliced
    225g/8oz fennel, finely sliced
    1 potato, diced
    3 star anise, tied in a piece of muslin
    (cheesecloth)
    300ml/½ pint/1¼ cups single (light)
    cream
    10ml/2 tsp pastis
    90ml/6 tbsp double (heavy) cream or
    crème fraîche
    salt and ground black pepper
    chives, finely chopped, to garnish

1 Pour 900ml/1½ pints/3¾ cups boiling water into a pan, add the sliced leek and fennel, the diced potato and the star anise, and season to taste with salt and pepper. Bring to the boil and simmer for 25 minutes.

Energy 219kcal/909kJ; Protein 3.3g; Carbohydrate 8.9g, of which sugars 3.1g; Fat 17.9g, of which saturates 11.2g; Cholesterol 48mg; Calcium 70mg; Fibre 1.9g; Sodium 27mg.

WINTER MELON SOUP WITH TIGER LILIES

THIS SIMPLE SOUP USES TWO TRADITIONAL SOUTH-EAST ASIAN INGREDIENTS — WINTER MELON TO ABSORB THE FLAVOURS AND TIGER LILIES TO LIFT THE BROTH WITH A FLORAL SCENT.

SERVES 4

INGREDIENTS

350g/12oz winter melon
25g/1oz tiger lilies, soaked in hot
  water for 20 minutes
salt and ground black pepper
1 small bunch each coriander
  (cilantro) and mint, stalks removed,
  leaves chopped, to serve

For the stock

25g/1oz dried shrimp, soaked in
  water for 15 minutes
500g/1¼lb pork ribs
1 onion, peeled and quartered
175g/6oz carrots, peeled and cut
  into chunks
15ml/1 tbsp *nuoc mam*
15ml/1 tbsp soy sauce
4 black peppercorns

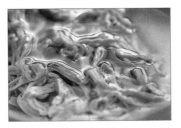 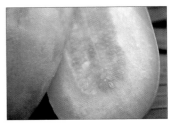

1 To make the stock, drain and rinse the dried shrimp. Put the pork ribs in a large pan and cover with 2 litres/3½ pints/8 cups water. Bring to the boil, skim off any fat, and add the dried shrimp and the remaining stock ingredients. Cover and simmer for 1½ hours, then skim off any foam or fat. Continue simmering, uncovered, for a further 30 minutes. Strain and check the seasoning. You should have about 1.5 litres/2¼ pints/6¼ cups.

2 Halve the winter melon lengthways and remove the seeds and inner membrane. Finely slice the flesh into half-moons. Squeeze the soaked tiger lilies dry and tie them in a knot.

3 Bring the stock to the boil in a deep pan or wok. Reduce the heat and add the winter melon and tiger lilies. Simmer for 15–20 minutes. Season to taste, sprinkle the coriander and mint over the top, and serve immediately.

Energy 57kcal/241kJ; Protein 4.4g; Carbohydrate 9.6g, of which sugars 9g; Fat 0.4g, of which saturates 0.1g; Cholesterol 32mg; Calcium 101mg; Fibre 1.6g; Sodium 309mg.

INDEX